THE ROUTLEDGE HANDBOOK OF FRANZ BRENTANO AND THE BRENTANO SCHOOL

Both through his own work and that of his students, Franz Clemens Brentano (1838–1917) had an often underappreciated influence on the course of twentieth- and twenty-first-century philosophy. *The Routledge Handbook of Franz Brentano and the Brentano School* offers full coverage of Brentano's philosophy and his influence. It contains 38 brand-new essays from an international team of experts that offer a comprehensive view of Brentano's central research areas—philosophy of mind, metaphysics, and value theory—as well as of the principal figures shaped by Brentano's school of thought. A general introduction serves as an overview of Brentano and the contents of the volume, and three separate bibliographies point students and researchers on to further avenues of inquiry.

Systematic and detailed, this volume provides readers with a valuable reference to Brentano's work and to his lasting importance.

"A well-conceived and timely introduction to the work of an influential but much under-appreciated philosopher whose writings repay study and deserve a much wider audience. For anyone curious about Brentano and the significance of his philosophical contributions, this is the place to start."
—*John Heil, Washington University in St. Louis*

"This Handbook is among the most significant contributions to the history of contemporary philosophy of the last decades. It offers the first comprehensive survey of Brentanian contributions to early analytical philosophy and philosophical psychology, documenting the sophistication, breadth and historical significance of their theories. Through conscientious editorial choices, Uriah Kriegel aptly shows that the issues that were central to Brentano and his students go far beyond intentionality and continue to drive philosophical research. As such, the Handbook affords a superb occasion to re-examine the philosophical canon. It is an indispensable resource for teachers and researchers, and one that does not come one day too soon."
—*Sandra Lapointe, McMaster University*

"This collection by the foremost Brentano scholars of today is far from a mere summary of standard views. It brings new light into all corners of Brentano's philosophy. It illuminates his profound influence on generations of his brilliant students and grandstudents. Above all, it incorporates the latest thinking and textual evidence to provide a wealth of new insights into the many facets of this fascinating, challenging and many-sided philosopher."
—*Peter Simons, Trinity College Dublin*

Uriah Kriegel is a Research Director at the Jean Nicod Institute in Paris. He has published more than 80 research articles, including many on Brentano. His monographs include *Subjective Consciousness: A Self-Representational Theory* (2009), *The Sources of Intentionality* (2011), *The Varieties of Consciousness* (2015), and *Mind and Reality in Brentano's Philosophical System* (2017).

ROUTLEDGE HANDBOOKS IN PHILOSOPHY

Routledge Handbooks in Philosophy are state-of-the-art surveys of emerging, newly refreshed, and important fields in philosophy, providing accessible yet thorough assessments of key problems, themes, thinkers, and recent developments in research.

All chapters for each volume are specially commissioned, and written by leading scholars in the field. Carefully edited and organized, *Routledge Handbooks in Philosophy* provide indispensable reference tools for students and researchers seeking a comprehensive overview of new and exciting topics in philosophy. They are also valuable teaching resources as accompaniments to textbooks, anthologies, and research-orientated publications.

Recently published:

The Routledge Handbook of Embodied Cognition
Edited by Lawrence Shapiro

The Routledge Handbook of Philosophy of Well-Being
Edited by Guy Fletcher

The Routledge Handbook of Philosophy of Imagination
Edited by Amy Kind

The Routledge Handbook of the Stoic Tradition
Edited by John Sellars

The Routledge Handbook of Philosophy of Information
Edited by Luciano Floridi

The Routledge Handbook of the Philosophy of Biodiversity
Edited by Justin Garson, Anya Plutynski, and Sahotra Sarkar

The Routledge Handbook of Philosophy of the Social Mind
Edited by Julian Kiverstein

The Routledge Handbook of Philosophy of Empathy
Edited by Heidi Maibom

The Routledge Handbook of Epistemic Contextualism
Edited by Jonathan Jenkins Ichikawa

The Routledge Handbook of Epistemic Injustice
Edited by Ian James Kidd, José Medina and Gaile Pohlhaus

The Routledge Handbook of Philosophy of Pain
Edited by Jennifer Corns

The Routledge Handbook of Brentano and the Brentano School
Edited by Uriah Kriegel

The Routledge Handbook of Metaethics
Edited by Tristram McPherson and David Plunkett

The Routledge Handbook of Philosophy of Memory
Edited by Sven Bernecker and Kourken Michaelian

The Routledge Handbook of Evolution and Philosophy
Edited by Richard Joyce

The Routledge Handbook of Mechanisms and Mechanical Philosophy
Edited by Stuart Glennan and Phyllis Illari

THE ROUTLEDGE HANDBOOK OF FRANZ BRENTANO AND THE BRENTANO SCHOOL

Edited by
Uriah Kriegel

NEW YORK AND LONDON

First published 2017
by Routledge
711 Third Avenue, New York, NY 1001

and by Routledge
2 Park Square, Milton Park, Abingdon, Oxon OX14 4RN

Routledge is an imprint of the Taylor & Francis Group, an Informa business

© 2017 Taylor & Francis

The right of Uriah Kriegel to be identified as the author of the editorial material, and of the authors for their individual chapters, has been asserted in accordance with sections 77 and 78 of the Copyright, Designs and Patents Act 1988.

All rights reserved. No part of this book may be reprinted or reproduced or utilised in any form or by any electronic, mechanical, or other means, now known or hereafter invented, including photocopying and recording, or in any information storage or retrieval system, without permission in writing from the publishers.

Trademark notice: Product or corporate names may be trademarks or registered trademarks, and are used only for identification and explanation without intent to infringe.

Library of Congress Cataloguing in Publication Data
Names: Kriegel, Uriah, editor.
Title: The Routledge handbook of Franz Brentano and the
Brentano school / ed. Uriah Kriegel.
Description: New York : Routledge, 2017. |
Series: Routledge handbooks in philosophy | Includes bibliographical references and index.
Identifiers: LCCN 2016040045 | ISBN 9781138023444 (hardback)
Subjects: LCSH: Brentano, Franz, 1838-1917. | Brentano, Franz, 1838-1917–Influence. | Philosophy, Austrian–19th century. | Philosophy, Austrian–20th century.
Classification: LCC B3212.Z7 .R68 2017 | DDC 193–dc23
LC record available at https://lccn.loc.gov/2016040045

ISBN: 978-1-138-02344-4 (hbk)
ISBN: 978-1-315-77646-0 (ebk)

Typeset in Minion Pro and Frutiger
by Deanta Global Publishing Services, Chennai, India

Printed and bound in Great Britain by
TJ International Ltd, Padstow, Cornwall

Contents

Introduction   1
Uriah Kriegel

PART I: BRENTANO'S PHILOSOPHY

1. Franz Brentano: Life and Work   15
   Thomas Binder
2. Brentano's Philosophical Program   21
   Uriah Kriegel

1.1: MIND

3. Brentano's Project of Descriptive Psychology   35
   Denis Seron
4. Brentano on Intentionality   41
   Tim Crane
5. Brentano on Consciousness   49
   Mark Textor
6. Brentano on the Unity of Consciousness   61
   Barry Dainton
7. Brentano on Time-Consciousness   75
   Guillaume Fréchette
8. Brentano on Sensations and Sensory Qualities   87
   Olivier Massin

9. Brentano's Classification of Mental Phenomena 97
   Uriah Kriegel

10. Brentano on Judgment 103
    Uriah Kriegel

11. Brentano on Emotion and the Will 110
    Michelle Montague

12. Brentano on Self-Knowledge 124
    Gianfranco Soldati

1.2: METAPHYSICS

13. Brentano's Reism 133
    Werner Sauer

14. Brentano on the Soul 144
    Susan Krantz Gabriel

15. Brentano on Time and Space 150
    Wojciech Żełaniec

16. Brentano on Properties and Relations 156
    Hamid Taieb

17. Brentano on Truth 163
    Johannes L. Brandl

18. Brentano on Appearance and Reality 169
    Denis Seron

19. Brentano on Negation and Nonexistence 178
    Alessandro Salice

1.3: VALUE

20. Brentano's Metaethics 187
    Jonas Olson

21. Brentano's Normative Ethics 196
    Lynn Pasquerella

22. Brentano on Beauty and Aesthetics 202
    Wolfgang Huemer

23. Brentano on Genius and Fantasy 210
    Ion Tănăsescu

24. Brentano's Philosophy of Religion 216
    Richard Schaefer

PART II: THE BRENTANO SCHOOL

25. The Rise of the Brentano School — 225
    Arnaud Dewalque
26. The Unity of the Brentano School — 236
    Arnaud Dewalque

2.1: BRENTANO'S STUDENTS

27. Marty and Brentano — 251
    Laurent Cesalli and Kevin Mulligan
28. Stumpf and Brentano — 264
    Denis Fisette
29. Meinong and Brentano — 272
    Johann Christian Marek
30. Ehrenfels and Brentano — 283
    Maria E. Reicher
31. Husserl and Brentano — 293
    Dermot Moran
32. Twardowski and Brentano — 305
    Arianna Betti

2.2: STUDENTS' STUDENTS AND FURTHER INFLUENCES

33. The Prague School — 313
    Hynek Janoušek and Robin Rollinger
34. Bergman and Brentano — 323
    Guillaume Fréchette
35. Brentano and the Lvov-Warsaw School — 334
    Arianna Betti
36. The Innsbruck School — 341
    Wilhelm Baumgartner
37. Brentano, Stout and Moore — 349
    Maria van der Schaar
38. Chisholm and Brentano — 358
    Dale Jacquette

Notes on Contributors — 365
Brentano Bibliography — 368
Brentano Bibliography—Archival Material — 371
References — 372
Index — 395

Introduction

Uriah Kriegel

In analytic philosophy, Franz Brentano is known almost exclusively for reintroducing the notion of intentionality into modern philosophy. In continental philosophy, he is known mostly for being Husserl's teacher. In truth, however, Brentano was a highly sophisticated thinker with contributions across all areas of philosophy. As this book attempts to show, Brentano's thought is historically rich and yet bears striking relevance to many current-day debates—and the ambit of his influence, sometimes overt but often subterranean, is striking. His style of discussion and argumentation are thoroughly analytic, and his overarching project is fundamentally phenomenological; as such, he stands at the root of both major twentieth-century philosophical movements.

The book comprises five sections divided into two parts—a long first part about Brentano himself and a shorter second one about his "school." The first part has three sections, dedicated to Brentano's philosophy of mind (Chapters 3–12), his metaphysics (Chapters 13–19), and his value theory (Chapters 20–24). The book's second part has two sections, dedicated to Brentano's most prominent immediate students (Chapters 27–32) and to his further influences (Chapters 33–38). Each part also includes two introductory chapters, one historically accentuated (Chapters 1, 25) and one more systematic (Chapters 2, 26). Below, I describe the central thrust of each of the book's 38 chapters.

1 BRENTANO'S PHILOSOPHY

The book opens with a historical introduction to Brentano's life and work by Thomas Binder (Chapter 1). It is well known within the circles of Brentano scholarship that Brentano was an ordained priest who left the priesthood in the early 1870s over the introduction of the dogma of papal infallibility. But as Binder describes it, Brentano's life was in fact a lengthy process of ever-growing estrangement from Catholicism and indeed from religious faith as such, both pressed on him from an early age by his deeply pious mother. Binder also paints a portrait of a man deeply engaged socially, politically, culturally, and religiously in his nonprofessional life.

This biographical portrait is followed by a systematic presentation of Brentano's overarching philosophical program, as I understand it (Chapter 2). Brentano's thought was always in flux—always progressing, revising, updating—but certain stable patterns can be detected virtually throughout Brentano's career. In particular, I claim that Brentano had a program for a grand philosophical system in the classical sense of a unified account of the true, the good, and the beautiful. The program is to cast the *true* as that about which it is correct or fitting to have a positive judgment, the *good* as that toward which it is correct or fitting to have a positive emotion, and the *beautiful* as that with which it is correct or fitting to be delighted. In this approach, the notions of truth, goodness, and beauty are analyzed in terms of different kinds of mental activity; hence the inordinate place of the philosophy of mind in Brentano's thought.

1.1 Brentano's Philosophy of Mind

Brentano does not use the expression "philosophy of mind," of course. Rather, he develops his own framework for the philosophical study of the mind—what he calls "descriptive psychology" (Chapter 3). As Denis Seron shows, Brentano's conception of a scientifically rigorous discipline was thoroughly empiricist, requiring foundations in perceptual encounter with the relevant phenomena. In the case of psychological phenomena, this is a kind of "inner perception" that enables certain kinds of introspective appraisal of the phenomena. However, a regimented scientific inquiry also separates (i) the task of *causally explaining* the occurrence of these phenomena from (ii) the (logically prior) task of *describing* the phenomena in need of explanation. Brentano calls the explanatory project "genetic psychology" and the other, more foundational project "descriptive psychology." Seron traces the main steps of descriptive-psychological inquiry: initial inner-perceptual encounter with the phenomena, then analysis of what is given to inner perception, and finally inductive inference from there to natural laws.

For Brentano, the two most basic deliverances of descriptive psychology concern (i) the demarcation of mental phenomena and (ii) their "fundamental classification."[1] In his chapter on Brentano's notion of intentionality (Chapter 4), Tim Crane emphasizes the role the notion plays in addressing both issues. Brentano in fact identifies a number of features he claims to be common and peculiar to mental phenomena. But he also claims that the most important of those is intentionality, and it is by reference to kinds or modes of intentionality that he proposes to classify mental phenomena at the most fundamental level. Crane then presents the later developments of Brentano's conception of intentionality, in particular the move away from the idea that intentionality involves a relation to an object that may or may not exist and its replacement with the claim that intentionality is merely "relation-like" (*etwas Relativliches*).

One of the most interesting aspects of Brentano's philosophy of mind is his claim that every mental act in fact exhibits *two* kinds of intentionality: it has a *primary* intentionality directed at a worldly object, but it also has a *secondary* intentionality directed at itself. This "secondary intentionality" is the heart of Brentano's theory of consciousness, as Mark Textor shows in the following chapter (Chapter 5). But according to Textor, traditional scholarly interpretations of Brentano have misunderstood Brentano's main *reason* to hold that conscious experiences are always intentionally self-directed. His real argument, claims Textor, is that conscious experiences are things we are aware of, but unless we were aware of them in virtue of their being self-directed, their intentional object would have to be presented *twice* in every conscious experience: once *qua* direct object of the experience itself and once again *qua* indirect object of our awareness of that experience. Yet there is no sign of such duplication of the intentional object in our stream of consciousness. Therefore, conscious experiences must involve a self-directed secondary intentionality.

In Brentano's full account of consciousness, we find substantive theories of a variety of related phenomena, including the unity of consciousness, the nature of time-consciousness, and the intentional character of sensory experience. Barry Dainton argues that Brentano's considered position on the unity of consciousness is that a subject's overall conscious experience at a time is a complex whose constituents are mere *divisives*, that is, parts that can be distinguished in thought but cannot be separated in reality (Chapter 6). As an example of such parts, Brentano mentions the different spatial parts of a fundamental physical particle: *qua* fundamental, it admits of no partition, and yet we can distinguish spatial parts in it. The crucial feature of such inseparable parts ("divisives") is that they are incapable of assuming independent existence. According to Dainton's Brentano, this is exactly the model for what happens with the parts of a subject's overall conscious experience at a time.

The unity of consciousness Brentano (and Dainton) address is unity *at a time*. But consciousness involves also the experience of the *passage* of time. Understanding this aspect of conscious experience has been a real challenge for Brentano. Indeed, according to Guillaume Fréchette, Brentano held (at different times in his career) no fewer than five different accounts of this phenomenon (Chapter 7). Brentano's final view, on which he settled in the last two years of his life, according to Fréchette, is that what makes a certain experience the experience of pastness or futureness is a certain modality of *in obliquo* presentation. If I think to myself that my friend hopes to move to Hawaii, my thought presents both my friend and Hawaii. But according to Brentano, it presents them in two importantly different ways: it presents my friend *in recto* and Hawaii *in obliquo*. By the same token, when I experience a part of the melody just past, I am aware of it precisely as having occurred *just before the present part* of the melody (the part I am experiencing *as now*), and this means—on this view—that I am aware of the present moment *in recto* and of the just-past moment *in obliquo*.

The case of sensory consciousness becomes especially interesting within Brentano's philosophy of mind. A traditionally dominant view is that sensations are nonintentional and contrast in that way with intellectual or cognitive activity. But for Brentano, all mental phenomena are intentional, so he must also provide an intentionalist account of sensations. According to Olivier Massin (Chapter 8), Brentano does so by claiming that a sensation is always directed at a proprietary secondary-quality-at-a-place and then showing that sensations (i) *individuate* by these intentional objects of theirs and (ii) have their experiential *intensity* in virtue of a corresponding intensity in these objects. This applies, for Brentano, not only to *perceptual* sensations but also to *algedonic* sensations of pain and pleasure, which are directed at *sui generis* algedonic qualities (at locations).

Recall that the second main mandate of descriptive psychology is to provide a "fundamental classification" of mental phenomena. Here, *fundamental* means something like the following. Mental phenomena can be taxonomized according to their natural similarities and dissimilarities at various levels of abstraction. How should they be taxonomized at the *highest* level of abstraction (one that still recognizes *some* dissimilarities)? According to Brentano, at that highest level, mental phenomena should be divided into three kinds: presentations, judgments, and "phenomena of love and hate." The grounds for this particular taxonomy, I try to show (Chapter 9), is that there are three basic kinds, or *modes*, of intentionality: judgments present their intentional objects under the guise of the true, in some sense, while phenomena of love and hate present their objects under the guise of the good; presentations, meanwhile, present their objects in a more neutral fashion—under no substantive guise. Or perhaps more accurately, that is the case with *mere* presentations. For according to Brentano, every phenomenon of the other two categories presupposes and is grounded in some presentation.

The following two chapters are dedicated to judgment and the phenomena of love and hate. Brentano's theory of judgment is, in my opinion, one of the most creative theories in the history of philosophy (Chapter 10). Bucking an essentially exceptionless tendency in the history of Western philosophy, Brentano argues that judgment does not involve predication and does not have propositional content. Instead, judgment is an "objectual," nonpropositional attitude akin to loving one's child and fearing a cackle of hyenas (as opposed to loving *that* one's child is cute or fearing *that* the hyenas will maul one). The argument for this goes through two extraordinary claims. The first is that all judgments are at bottom existential—they commit to the existence or nonexistence of something, nothing more. (For example, the judgment that all Greeks are mortal is just a judgment that there are no immortal Greeks.) The second is that an existential judgment's commitment to the existence or nonexistence of something does not come from its content but from its intentional mode. (The negative judgment about immortal Greeks does not present immortal Greeks as nonexistent, but rather presents-as-nonexistent immortal Greeks; that which is presented is thus exhausted by immortal Greeks.) I try to show how these claims lead to Brentano's nonpropositional theory of judgment.

Brentano's account of "phenomena of love and hate" is taken up in Michelle Montague's chapter on will and emotion in Brentano (Chapter 11). For the relevant category covers for Brentano a range of mental phenomena, from pleasure and pain through pride and anger to desire and decision. As Montague shows, one reason Brentano thinks there is nonetheless internal unity in this category is that one can construct "series" of mental states that exhibit a certain continuity between any two links but lead from one end of the spectrum to the other. And the other reason is that all these states present their intentional objects under the guise of the good (or bad). Thus, both (positive) emotions and desires inherently evaluate their objects positively. This in turn provides Brentano with an important claim in moral epistemology, namely, that our knowledge of value is based ultimately on experienced contrasts between different states of this category—a topic that will come up again in the book's third section (on Brentano's theory of value).

To close this first section of the book, Gianfranco Soldati looks into Brentano's theory of self-knowledge (Chapter 12). For Soldati, the theory can be captured through the combination of three theses. The first is that inner perception provides each of us with a kind of knowledge of his or her conscious experiences that is unavailable to anybody else. The second is that this knowledge of one's experiences qualifies as knowledge of *oneself* as subject (and not just as knowledge of a state or act of one). And the third thesis is that the subject of which one thereby has this kind of knowledge is a mental substance underlying all her experiences.

1.2 Brentano's Metaphysics

The most important thesis in Brentano's metaphysics is one that, according to most interpreters, he reached only later in his life: reism. This is the thesis that there are only "things," where this appears to rule in only concrete particulars and rule out propositions, (merely) intentional objects, states of affairs, universals, abstract objects, and so on. Importantly, for Brentano, this does not mean that all entities are individual substances—he recognizes also individual *accidents*, though ones that turn out to be concrete particulars as well. In his chapter on Brentano's reism, Werner Sauer locates Brentano's conversion to this extremely parsimonious outlook sometime between January and October 1903 (Chapter 13). Much of Sauer's chapter is dedicated to meticulous reconstruction and careful evaluation of what in the secondary literature has come to be thought of as the master argument for reism (though see Kriegel 2015). The centerpiece of this argument is the claim that it is impossible to even contemplate, or represent to oneself, anything other than "things" in the relevant sense. Sauer's verdict is that the argument as it stands does not work, but that a certain modification casting accidents as tropes or abstract particulars (rather than concrete particulars) might.

Brentano's ontology is thus a *monocategorial* ontology, insofar as it recognizes only one category of being: things. Yet Brentano allows that there are two categorically distinct *kinds* of things: physical and mental. Indeed, he is a substance dualist who posits mental substances (and their accidents) irreducible to physical substances (and their accidents). These mental substances are moreover immortal and are thus souls in the traditional philosophical sense. Susan Krantz Gabriel reconstructs Brentano's theory of the soul as it emerges from two posthumous collections of essays (Chapter 14). The first is a metaphysically oriented collection from the last years of Brentano's life (Brentano 1933/1981a), the second a theologically oriented collection based on lecture notes from the core years of Brentano's teaching career (Brentano 1929a/1987b). In the former, the soul is cast as the paradigmatic substance, insofar as it is the only substance we have direct (inner-)perceptual encounter with. In the latter, an argument is offered for the immateriality of the mental substance: inner perception reveals a spiritual or immaterial aspect of the mental substance, but if that substance had also a material component, claims Brentano, this would undermine the unity of consciousness.

Wojciech Żełaniec presents Brentano's metaphysics of time and space (Chapter 15), topics that were dear to Brentano's heart in the final decade of his life. They open on issues such as the nature of the continuum and the foundations of topology, where Brentano made crucial contributions (see Zimmerman 1996). As Żełaniec notes, for Brentano, the fundamental metaphysical questions raised by time and space concern the status of temporal and spatial determinations of substance, the determinations in virtue of which certain temporal and spatial truths can be uttered about substances.

Such "determinations" are what properties and relations become within a reist framework. Hamid Taieb dedicates a chapter to this area of Brentano's metaphysics (Chapter 16). As he shows, Brentano treats properties as special *parts* of a thing—*metaphysical* parts (in the case of particularized properties, such as Socrates' wisdom) or *logical* parts (for universal properties, such as wisdom as such). Only the former are "real," for Brentano, in the sense of being causally efficacious. Taieb brings out in particular the sophistication of Brentano's ontology of relations, where distinctions are drawn between relations, relational properties, and objects *qua* bearing relational properties—"relatives." The latter are all that will survive in Brentano's ontology after his reistic turn.

The question of the nature of truth in Brentano is a notoriously difficult one, with traditional interpretations attributing to Brentano the rather implausible "epistemic view" that *p* is true iff we judge that *p* with self-evidence or at least would do so if we could judge on whether *p* with self-evidence. However, Johannes Brandl argues for a much more nuanced interpretation, according to which Brentano was in effect an early deflationary theorist of truth (Chapter 17). According to Brandl, the epistemic story linking truth to self-evidence is only a story about the *acquisition* of the concept of truth. Regarding the nature of truth itself, there is a sense in which we cannot "get underneath" truth by finding something more fundamental in which it is grounded. Accordingly, only a deflationary characterization in terms of the truth schema is available.

What this means, though, is that Brentano's theory of truth will not illuminate his conception of the relationship between appearance and reality. This is the topic of the following chapter, by Denis Seron (Chapter 18). Seron argues that Brentano's theory of appearances is one and the same as his theory of intentionality—appearances are the intentional objects of conscious experiences, and the intentional objects of conscious experiences are appearances. Brentano's notion of intentional inexistence is just the notion of an object *appearing in* a conscious experience.

The final chapter in this section on Brentano's metaphysics is Alessandro Salice's on negation and nonexistence—two delicate issues in Brentano's work (Chapter 19). Recall that according to Brentano's theory of judgment, all judgments are existential, and their existential commitment comes from the judgment's attitude rather than its content. This applies also to negative existentials: the act of judging that Pegasus does not exist is just the act of rejecting Pegasus (where "rejecting" means representing-as-nonexistent). Salice points out that this treatment of negation becomes problematic for such statements as "some man is not learned," which must be paraphrased "a non-learned man exists," in which we find negation inside the *content* of the judgment (namely, in denying the man's learnedness). Salice shows that this leads Brentano to his "doctrine of double judgment," according to which sentences such as "a non-learned man exists" actually express *two* judgments: a first-order judgment that accepts (represents-as-existent) a man and a second-order judgment that rejects (represents-as-nonexistent) the accepted man's learnedness. Brentano uses this device to address a number of difficult cases for his theory of judgment, but, as Salice argues, these quickly become increasingly complicated and inelegant.

1.3 Brentano's Value Theory

One of the areas of Brentano's thought that have the greatest resonance in contemporary philosophy is his metaethics. One way to think of the organizing question of metaethics is as follows: when we say that something is good, what exactly are we doing? And one of the "hottest" answers in contemporary metaethics is that to say that something is good is to say that it is fitting to have a pro attitude toward it. In these discussions, Brentano is often cited as a precursor, perhaps the first precursor. According to Brentano, to say that something is good is to say that it is correct to love it. But his notions of love and correctness are such that the view is essentially the same as those of contemporary fitting-attitude theorists. In his chapter on Brentano's metaethics (Chapter 20), Jonas Olson further positions Brentano within our contemporary metaethical landscape, showing how Brentano incorporates elements of both rationalism and sentimentalism, both cognitivism and expressivism, and both motivational internalism and externalism—while being thoroughly realist and naturalist.

The following chapter, by Lynn Pasquerella, is dedicated to Brentano's first-order normative ethics (Chapter 21). Brentano's ethics is a sort of pluralist consequentialism, where things are instrumentally good when their consequences are intrinsically good, and there are a handful of different intrinsic goods. Brentano does not offer a definitive list of intrinsic goods, but he is very much definitive about knowledge, pleasure, mental activity, and correct love belonging on that list. Note that the last element listed is normatively characterized. To that extent, claims Pasquerella, Brentano anticipated the kind of "justicized consequentialism" defended more recently by the likes of Fred Feldman.

Moving from moral to aesthetic value, Wolfgang Huemer discusses in some detail Brentano's program for aesthetics with solid scientific foundations (Chapter 22). The framework is similar to the one we find in Brentano's metaethics, except that for Brentano to say that something is beautiful is to say that it is correct to be delighted with that thing. Accordingly, the study of the nature of delight, and of the laws governing correct delight, is effectively the study of beauty—but founded on scientific psychology rather than on subjective speculation.

As Huemer noted, Brentano was less interested in pursuing aesthetic questions himself than in setting up the framework within which they could be pursued. Two areas of the aesthetics of his day in which Brentano did dabble, mostly in the second half of the 1880s and the first half of the 1890s, are the question of artistic genius and the role in art of fantasy and imagination. These are the topics of the next chapter, by Ion Tănăsescu (Chapter 23). On the question of genius, Brentano argued that the so-called artistic (or scientific) genius is not qualitatively or categorically distinct from the average person—the difference is merely quantitative (a difference of degree, not of kind). The genius does not engage in mental processes unfamiliar to the average person but rather exhibits a higher capacity to engage in the same old processes. The artistic genius, for example, exhibits greater sensitivity to beauty. For Brentano, artworks divide into two kinds, depending on the mental faculties used in their production: some works involve merely imitation of nature and are thus based entirely on perception and memory, while others depend in part on the artist's creativity and imagination. To clarify the nature of the latter, Brentano goes on to develop a sophisticated analysis of the nature of imaginative presentations, which Tănăsescu reconstructs carefully.

The final chapter of this book's first part, by Richard Schaefer, concerns Brentano's philosophy of religion (Chapter 24). Brentano is an ardent defender of rational theology, and to that extent subordinates theology to philosophy. As Schaefer notes, Brentano thinks that in the history of religion appeal to "revelation" is for the most part indirect acceptance of what someone else claims about God. And he dismisses religious dogmas as a device for treating as certain that for which there is no warranted certainty. It is ultimately on the grounds of sound rational arguments that the existence, nature, and expectations of God can be asserted. Brentano offers four arguments for the existence of God, but the one he relies on most heavily is a variant on the teleological argument that appeals centrally to probability theory.

2 THE AMBIT OF BRENTANO'S THOUGHT

The book's greater part is dedicated to the specifics of Brentano's own thought. But one cannot fully appreciate Brentano's significance without a proper acquaintance with the work of his followers within the so-called Brentano School. This is what the book's second, shorter part is dedicated to. It opens with a pair of chapters by Arnaud Dewalque, the first tracing the historical emergence of the Brentano School (Chapter 25) and the second attempting to identify the philosophical core that unifies the commitments of members of the school (Chapter 26). Dewalque claims that Brentano and his immediate students, notably Stumpf and Marty, started using the expression "Brentano School" from about 1873. A diagram at the end of Chapter 25 provides a useful depiction of the school's main members. For Dewalque, what unifies the school intellectually is first of all Brentano's particular version of metaphilosophical naturalism. Naturalism here is the notion that philosophy is continuous with the sciences. Indeed, according to Brentano, it is *itself* a science or a collection of sciences. Brentano's particular version holds that the science all philosophy depends upon is descriptive psychology, so that, ultimately, inner perception of mental phenomena provides an empirical foundation for the philosophical sciences. It is this conception of philosophy and how it should be done, claims Dewalque, that underlies and unifies all the research activity conducted under the heading of the Brentano School.

To impose a measure of structure on this part of the book, I have divided it into two parts. The first concerns Brentano's own students; the second, his students' students and further influences. The distinction is not entirely straightforward, as starting in 1880 Brentano lost his right to formally supervise doctoral students (after losing his professorship in Vienna), and several philosophers who had studied with him there ended up either finishing their studies with one of Brentano's students (typically Stumpf, Marty, or Meinong) or having a *pro forma* supervisor other than Brentano. Thus we have several figures who can be considered either among Brentano's own students or among his students' students; this includes Husserl, Ehrenfels, Arleth, and Höfler. In some cases, we have included special chapters for the relevant thinker *qua* direct Brentano student (e.g., Husserl, Ehrenfels); in others (e.g., Arleth, Höfler), we have included lengthy discussions within chapters dedicated to the centers of Brentanian orthodoxy in Prague and Innsbruck.

2.1 Brentano's Own Students

This part of the book is organized almost chronologically but opens with a chapter about Anton Marty, who was Brentano's *second* student but his most dedicated follower. Indeed, as we will see below, he may have done more than Brentano himself to further Brentano's legacy. Laurent Cesalli and Kevin Mulligan divide their discussion of the philosophical relationship between the two (Chapter 27) into (i) philosophy of mind and

(ii) philosophy of language. Regarding (i), Marty diverged from Brentano in rejecting the objectual theory of judgment and holding that judgments are directed at states of affairs, and also in rejecting a fitting-attitude theory of value in favor of reversing the explanatory order, that is, explaining the fittingness of attitudes in terms of value rather than the other way round. But Marty is best known for his contributions in (ii), where he developed a classification of linguistic acts patterned after Brentano's classification of mental acts as well as an early version of intention-based semantics.

Carl Stumpf was Brentano's very first student. As Denis Fisette tells it (Chapter 28), they met during Brentano's habilitation defense, when Brentano was only 28 and Stumpf just 18. Stumpf inherited from Brentano a penchant for classification, which he pursued vigorously to classify the sciences as a whole and the branches of psychology in particular. The classification of the latter is driven largely by Stumpf's notion of mental function and the variety of mental functions he distinguishes within his own descriptive psychology. According to Stumpf, philosophy is the ultimate science, whose proprietary scope is topic-neutral phenomena that appear in all sciences alike (hence both in the natural sciences and the "human sciences"—what in the English-speaking world are called, tellingly, simply "the humanities"). In Stumpf's work, we thus find a mixture of independence and acceptance of Brentano's framework. Their personal relationship was apparently somewhat tumultuous, marred by a number of disputes both personal and intellectual (reconstructed in some detail by Fisette!).

The student of Brentano's best known to analytic philosophers is probably Alexius Meinong, thanks mostly to his theory of intentional relations to nonexistent objects. But as Johann Marek shows (Chapter 29), many other parts of Meinong's thought address questions set within Brentano's agenda. This includes notably two areas: first, the classification of mental phenomena, where Meinong (i) rejects Brentano's assimilation of feeling and will and (ii) posits a *sui generis* category of "assumptions" or "suppositions" in between presentations and judgments; second, the self-evident character of inner consciousness, where Meinong posits a second-class kind of self-evidence that is "conjectural" rather than demonstrative.

Christian von Ehrenfels studied with Brentano from 1880 to 1883 and then finished his studies with Meinong. Maria Reicher describes an "opalescent figure" interested in an astonishing range of topics, but whose main philosophical contributions were in descriptive psychology and value theory (Chapter 30). In an 1890 paper, he defines the notion of a "Gestalt quality" as a quality that wholes have not in virtue of the character of their individual parts, but in virtue of the *interrelations among* their parts—a notion that was of course to enjoy remarkable uptake. Another interesting contribution in this area is Ehrenfels' reductive analysis of desire in terms of a combination of presentations and emotions. The notion of desire then plays a central role in Ehrenfels' value theory, as he essentially identifies intrinsic value with that which enhances desire-satisfaction, thus adopting a monistic consequentialism in contradistinction to Brentano's pluralistic variety.

Brentano's best-known student is of course Edmund Husserl, whose oeuvre had an unparalleled influence on twentieth-century philosophy on the European continent. Husserl came to Vienna to study with Brentano from 1884 to 1886 and finished his studies in Halle with Stumpf, and he claimed he would never have been a philosopher if it had not been for Brentano. It would be only a slight caricature to summarize Husserl's mature phenomenological program as nothing but Brentanian descriptive psychology with a transcendental-idealist twist. Although the transcendental twist Husserl's thought acquired circa 1905 distanced Husserl from Brentano considerably, as Dermot Moran shows (Chapter 31) the two maintained a mostly warm relationship until Brentano's death. And yet, claims Moran, a closer examination shows that Husserl was critical of central aspects of Brentano's program more or less right from the start.

Brentano's last major student was Kazimierz Twardowski, who actually did his doctoral work with Brentano, though submitting it formally (in 1891) with Brentano's Viennese colleague Robert Zimmerman. Arianna Betti presents a systematic list of areas where Twardowski adopted Brentanian positions and areas where he diverged from Brentanian doctrine (Chapter 32). In the former category, we find the notion of descriptive psychology as first philosophy (along with the primacy of descriptive psychology over explanatory/genetic psychology and the inner-perception-cum-analysis methodology for descriptive psychology), as well as the fitting-attitude framework in value theory. Contrary to Brentano, however, Twardowski welcomed nonexistent objects in his theory of intentionality, claims Betti, and his theory of judgment diverged in central respects from Brentano's.

2.2 The Further Influences of Brentano's Thought

Anton Marty set up in Prague a veritable Brentanian orthodoxy—what would come to be known as the "Prague School of Brentano." If Marty and Stumpf (who was professor in Prague early on too) represent the first generation of Prague Brentanists, the second generation consists of Marty's many students, including Hugo Bergman, Emil Arleth, Josef Eisenmayer, Oskar Engländer, Franz Hillebrand, Alfred Kastil, Oskar Kraus, and Emil Utitz. Kraus then became himself professor at Prague and "raised" a third generation of Brentanians in Georg Katkov, Walter Engel, and Eberhard Rogge. Much of these thinkers' work, discussed by Hynek Janoušek and Robin Rollinger (Chapter 33), pursued Brentano's reistic project with some sophistication, attempting to provide workable nominalist paraphrases in difficult cases. The Prague School of Brentano was a vibrant, half-century-long philosophical tradition. One of Marty's students (who even studied with Brentano himself for a year) was Tomáš Masaryk, who was later to become Czechoslovakia's first president—and who endowed the Brentano Society in Prague and the Brentano Archives. Rather tragically, this entire philosophical tradition was swept away after the Nazi invasion of 1939 and the war's communist aftermath. Thus, Georg Katkov, probably the most talented of the third-generation Prague Brentanists, could not find employment as a philosopher after the war and became a historian back in Russia.

The most tragic figure of the Brentano School, though, was probably Hugo Bergman, the "godfather" of Israeli philosophy. As Guillaume Fréchette notes (Chapter 34), as a Jewish academic, Bergman had very few career options at the time; the school's other prominent Jews, Husserl and Utitz, had converted to Protestantism in time to pursue their career. Bergman was not only fully committed to his Judaism, however—he was an ardent and active Zionist. The consequences of this, in terms of Bergman's treatment by Brentano and Marty, are recounted in Fréchette's chapter. Despite remarkable early contributions to the philosophy of physics and Brentano's descriptive psychology, Bergman was forced to work as a librarian until he moved in 1920 to Palestine (then under British mandate), where in 1935 he became the first Rector of the Hebrew University in Jerusalem and taught the founding generation of Israeli philosophers. At this point in his career, he had moved away from Brentanian orthodoxy and became more of a neo-Kantian, developing broadly Kantian theories in epistemology and metaphysics, philosophy of mind, and philosophy of mathematics and conducting seminal studies in the history of Jewish logic and philosophy.

The farthest-flung outpost of the Brentano School consisted of Twardowski's Polish students, first in Lvov (now Lviv, in the Ukraine) and then in Warsaw. Twardowski's best-known students are the logicians Jan Łukasiewicz and Stanisław Leśniewski, but his more Brentanian students are Tadeusz Czeżowski, Władysław Witwicki, and Tadeusz Kotarbiński. As Betti shows (Chapter 35), however, these thinkers show relatively little *doctrinal* continuity with Brentano (and indeed Twardowski). The main influence of Brentano's thought here is metaphilosophical, in particular the notion of descriptive psychology as first philosophy and the systematic and analytic style of philosophizing. In this respect, the Lvov-Warsaw School provides support for Dewalque's diagnosis (Chapter 26) of what the Brentano School's philosophical unity consists in.

It is in Innsbruck that the doctrinal bond with Brentano was strongest, as a result of a number of Marty students successively taking up professorships there. Indeed, Wilhelm Baumgartner describes the "Innsbruck School" as a "Brentanian franchise" (Chapter 36). Baumgartner discusses in order the main philosophical contributions (and their Brentanian core) of the four most prominent Innsbruck Brentanists: Franz Hillebrand, Emil Arleth, Alfred Kastil, and Franziska Mayer-Hillebrand. The last two have played a major role in publishing materials from Brentano's *Nachlass* (literary estate) and Mayer-Hillebrand published on Brentano until the 1960s (see, e.g., Mayer-Hillebrand 1963b). With her death in 1978, 122 years after Brentano's habilitation, comes to an end the chain of direct teacher–student links starting in Brentano and going through his students and students' students working within the Brentanian framework.

However, not all philosophical influence is mediated by personal links of the sort. Thus, Maria van der Schaar brings out Brentano's (largely unrecognized) influence on the inception of analytic philosophy in England (Chapter 37). The familiar narrative designates two Cambridge contemporaries, G. E. Moore and Bertrand Russell, as the key figures in this development. What the two have in common is their 1894 tutor, George Stout. Stout published in 1896 a book titled *Analytic Psychology* (Stout 1896), which follows in its organization, and discusses at length themes from, Brentano's *Psychology from an Empirical Standpoint*. According to van der Schaar, both Moore and Russell read *Analytic Psychology* carefully, and Moore's work in particular engages with Brentano extensively, not only within moral philosophy but also as concerns the theories of judgment, knowledge, and part–whole relations.

Brentano's tentacles reached even the United States. In 1937, Hugo Bergman delivered a lecture on Brentano's naturalistic metaphilosophy at the Harvard Philosophical Society. In Anglo-American philosophy, such naturalistic metaphilosophy is associated primarily with Quine (see especially Quine 1951). Since Quine was already lecturing at Harvard from 1934, one could speculate about his presence at Bergman's lecture and any role it might have played in the development of naturalism. In any case, a year after Bergman's lecture, Roderick Chisholm started his doctoral studies at Harvard. There, he was first exposed to Brentano's thought in a seminar with Edwin Boring. In the book's final chapter, Dale Jacquette reconstructs Brentano's influence on Chisholm (Chapter 38). Apparently,

Chisholm was later drawn to Brentano's work on intentionality, after reading Russell's *Analysis of Mind*, and started reading Brentano himself. He would eventually publish a long series of articles and a pair of books on various facets of Brentano's philosophy, most focally Brentano's notion of intentionality and his fitting-attitude theory of intrinsic value. Several of Chisholm's students wrote their PhD dissertation either specifically on Brentano (Susan Krantz Gabriel, Linda McAlister, Lynn Pasquerella) or at least centrally addressing Brentanian ideas (Dale Jacquette, Matthias Steup, Dean Zimmerman).

CONCLUSION

It is useful to close this book with chapters on Brentano's impact on Anglo-American philosophy, where his footprints involved no personal links. For although the School of Brentano narrowly construed (that is, in terms of a chain of personal teacher–student links) is no more, the Brentanian framework writ large can still be thought of as a live philosophical program, deserving serious consideration and indeed earnest pursuit. It is in this spirit that Brentano's various philosophical theories have been covered here—his project of descriptive psychology and its pride of place in his metaphilosohical outlook; his theories of intentionality, consciousness, self-consciousness, the unity of consciousness, and time-consciousness; his taxonomy of mental phenomena and his theories of judgment, will, and emotion; his reistic metaphysics and his treatment of substances (including mental), properties, relations, space, and time; his conception of truth, reality, and existence; as well as his theories of moral, aesthetic, and religious value. In many of these areas, I hope the chapters that follow make clear that Brentano's extraordinarily original ideas hold considerable philosophical potential for us today.[2]

NOTES

1. Brentano's magnum opus, *Psychology from an Empirical Standpoint* (Brentano 1874), divides into two "books." The first concerns methodological and foundational issues with the project of descriptive psychology (though Brentano does not use that expression back then). The second concerns the pursuit of these two basic questions of descriptive psychology. In a way, Chapters 1–4 of Book II address the first question (demarcation), while Chapters 5–8 address the second (classification).
2. My editorial work for this book was supported by the French National Research Agency's grants ANR-11-0001-02 PSL* and ANR-10-LABX-0087. I am grateful to all the authors who contributed to the volume, and who showed great commitment and flexibility in harnessing their erudition and competence to the common task of putting together as comprehensive a presentation as possible of Brentano's philosophy and its significance.

I
Brentano's Philosophy

1

Franz Brentano: Life and Work

Thomas Binder

"Descending from a devout Catholic family I was led to dedicate myself to the priesthood; but later on I broke up with the Church. Only the desire to serve the noblest interests had directed me in the choice of a profession. But the subsequent transformation of my convictions made me realize that the path pursued so far could not possibly lead to its destination" (Brentano 1922: xv). This might be—in his own words—the shortest version of a biography of Franz Brentano, but it undoubtedly hits the central point: Brentano's changing and problematic relationship to Catholicism and to religious faith in general overshadowed his entire career. A more detailed approach to his biography will improve our understanding of this fact.[1]

Franz Brentano was born on January 16, 1838, in Marienberg near Boppard on the Rhine, but shortly afterwards the family moved to Aschaffenburg, where Franz was raised. The roots of the Brentano family were in Italy, at the shores of Lake Como. Brentano's closer family circle was part of the so-called Frankfurt branch, which produced successful merchants as well as famous intellectuals (Brentano's uncle and aunt, Clemens Brentano and Bettina von Armin, were two of the most important representatives of German Romanticism; his younger brother, Lujo, became a famous economist and was one of the *Kathedersozialisten*). Brentano's father, Christian (1784–1851), was a businessman and author and his mother, Emilie (1810–1882), a tutor and translator of devotional literature; both parents were strongly engaged in the Catholic movement. As Alfred Kastil (see Chapter 36) wrote later with a dramatic touch, Brentano grew up under the spell of the Catholic worldview.

After private schooling and one year in the Lyceum at Aschaffenburg, Brentano studied philosophy, mathematics, history, and theology in Munich, Würzburg, Berlin, and Münster. His most influential philosophical teachers were Friedrich Adolf Trendelenburg in Berlin, who was a leading Aristotle expert; and Franz Clemens in Münster, a fervid representative of Neothomism. In 1862, Brentano submitted his doctoral dissertation *On the Several Senses of Being in Aristotle* at the University of

Tübingen (Brentano 1862). Almost at the same time, Brentano finally decided to become a priest. However, the above cited formulation "I was led to dedicate myself to priesthood" supports the conclusion that his mother and her spiritual advisers were involved in this decision. Many years later, moreover, Brentano told Oskar Kraus (see Chapter 36) that religious doubts had dated back to his early university years. But for the time being, Brentano managed to silence his scruples and joined the Catholic seminary at Würzburg. On August 8, 1864, Brentano was ordained a Catholic priest by Bishop Stahl of Würzburg.

Remarkably enough, after ordination, the bishop permitted Brentano to resume philosophical studies. As a result, Brentano presented his *Habilitationsschrift* on *The Psychology of Aristotle* to the University of Würzburg (Brentano 1867). Brentano's public "apology" of his 25 Habilitation Theses (among them the famous fourth thesis that the method of philosophy is none other than that of natural science) on July 7, 1866, was such an overwhelming success that the young Carl Stumpf decided spontaneously to give up law studies and to study philosophy instead (see Chapter 28).

Brentano's accomplishments in the following years were amazing: in 1867, he started with a lecture course on history of philosophy, and a year later he had a course on metaphysics, adding lectures on logic and psychology from 1871 onward. Although Brentano was very popular with the students, he still was only a "private lecturer" (*Privatdozent*).[2] An application for the post of an "extraordinary professor" in 1870 was rejected by the faculty because its more liberal members had reservations regarding a Catholic priest dominating the chair of philosophy (the only holder of the chair, Franz Hofmann, a student of Franz von Baader, was no longer actively teaching due to health problems, which did not prevent him from plotting against Brentano).

At that time, Brentano was still a Catholic priest on the surface, but almost nobody knew that his views had already changed dramatically. First, his philosophical views changed. Supposedly in 1868 he read the French translation of John Stuart Mill's monograph on Auguste Comte's positivist philosophy. Brentano was so impressed with Mill's outline that he gave a lecture course on Comte in the following year and published an article in which he himself confessed to "positive philosophy." (In addition, this article is of special interest because it shows the first signs of Brentano's distancing from Aristotle.) It may well be that the preoccupation with the antidogmatism of French and British Empiricism had consequences for one the most crucial episodes in his life.

In 1869, Bishop Wilhelm Emmanuel von Ketteler engaged Brentano to write a memorandum against the dogma of papal infallibility (which was promulgated in the following year at the first Vatican Council of July 1870). It is little known that Brentano wrote two memoranda. The first argued only against the appropriateness of declaring papal infallibility. Because it failed, Brentano wrote a second one, this time attacking several dogmas of the Catholic Church directly and demonstrating their inconsistency (see Freudenberger 1979 for a detailed description). Stumpf witnessed Brentano's definite break with religious faith at Easter 1870, describing it as a painful struggle. There is a certain irony in the fact that Brentano eventually became extraordinary professor of philosophy in Würzburg in May 1872 (primarily due to the intervention of Hermann Lotze), when Brentano was no longer able to give the appearance of being a ultramontanist Catholic priest: in March 1873, he resigned from his professorship, and in April he withdrew from the priesthood.[3]

Brentano's position after the resignation was quite difficult because most of the universities in Protestant Germany were barred for him. A conversion to Protestantism (as his brother Lujo suggested) was not an option for Brentano. He (unsuccessfully) applied for a post in Giessen, but it was the University of Vienna that raised his hopes: in the capital of the Habsburg monarchy, a chair of philosophy had turned vacant (its former holder was the Herbartian Franz Karl Lott) and therefore the faculty was looking for a philosopher especially qualified in psychology. Brentano postponed other projects and began immediately to work on what should eventually become his philosophical masterpiece: the *Psychology from an Empirical Standpoint*. Old family connections to Vienna, an emphatic recommendation by Lotze, and Karl von Stremayr, the liberal minister of cultural affairs, made it possible to overcome the influence of the Catholic clergy and the doubts of the deeply religious Emperor Franz Josef I: on January 18, 1874, Brentano was finally appointed full ("ordinary") professor of philosophy at the University of Vienna.[4] In April, he gave his acclaimed inaugural lecture on *Die Gründe der Entmutigung auf philosophischem Gebiete*. In May, the first volume of his *Psychology* was published. In the preface, Brentano announced a second volume, which he never delivered for reasons still discussed controversially today.[5]

In Vienna, Brentano continued his successful teaching career. The number of his students was increasing steadily, not least because of the lecture course on ethics he had to give for the law students (a topic that Brentano had not yet addressed in Würzburg). Among his early students in Vienna were such remarkable personalities as Thomas G. Masaryk (later president of Czechoslovakia), Alexius Meinong (see Chapter 29), and Sigmund Freud (see Merlan 1945). In his early Viennese years, Brentano was successful not only in university matters but also in the refined society of Vienna's bourgeoisie, especially in their Jewish circles; he was in fashion, as he puts it himself in a letter to Marty. Nevertheless, most of these social relationships did not satisfy his demands for friendship.

Sometime around 1878, Brentano decided to delete the last remaining marks of priesthood and to get married. In September 1880 (shortly before he had left the Church officially), he married Ida von Lieben, the sister of Richard von Lieben, an economist and a colleague of Brentano's at the University of Vienna. At that point, though, Brentano was no longer member of the faculty. This was due to the fact that, concerning former priests in the conservative Habsburg monarchy, the Civil Code adopts the regulations of Church law—and Church law denied marriage to all ordained priests, even if they have resigned from the priesthood (priesthood is a *character indelebilis*, which means that under no circumstances it can be canceled). So Brentano had been forced to renounce his Austrian citizenship in order to marry and turned Saxon instead, which automatically resulted in the loss of his full professorship. Only a few days later, he returned to Vienna and resumed his lectures as a *Privatdozent*. This new status was hardly appropriate for Brentano, as he was not entitled to supervise any doctoral theses or to participate in hiring decisions. With the unanimous support of the faculty members, Brentano tried several times to regain his former position but in vain; times had changed and turned more conservative than in his first Viennese years.

Between 1874 and 1894, Brentano was very reluctant to publish his thoughts. There was no major publication, only a small number of short lectures on various topics (aesthetics, ethics, historiography) resulting from occasional events. It should be mentioned nevertheless that even among these writings one can find a classic: In *The Origin of the Knowledge of Right and Wrong* Brentano presented for the first time what he thought was a totally new foundation of ethics and value theory (See Chapter 20); it was also his first book to be translated into English, in 1902. Also as a private lecturer Brentano was still extraordinarily successful. In a letter to Hermann Schell, he mentioned proudly that he had more students than Robert Zimmermann, a Herbartian who held the only chair of philosophy in Vienna at this time. And Brentano's students obviously were more gifted: Edmund Husserl, Kazimirz Twardowski, Alois Höfler, and Christian von Ehrenfels (among others) joined the ranks of what nowadays is well known as the "Brentano School" (see Chapter 25). There is another aspect of Brentano's teaching that is noteworthy. Brentano was not only a charismatic teacher, he was also strongly interested in personal contact with his students; Stumpf (1919) tells of long philosophical strolls in Würzburg, and in Vienna, Brentano often invited his students to his apartment to continue the discussions that had started during his lectures and seminars. It is highly probable that the Philosophical Society at the University of Vienna initially emerged from these private discussions; the society was founded in 1888 and Brentano gave the inaugural address, *On the Method of Historical Research in Philosophy*.

In the same year, Brentano's son, Johannes Christian Michael, was born (later called by his friends only Giovanni or "Gio"). In 1887, Brentano had acquired a large old house in Schönbühel near Melk in Lower Austria, because it had reminded him of his parent's house in Aschaffenburg; it was to become his summer residence until the outbreak of World War I. But Brentano's domestic happiness was not destined to last: within a few days of visiting a hospital in March 1894, his wife Ida died unexpectedly. After a further humiliating rejection of an attempt to regain his professorship (by the polish minister Madeyski, who was especially under the spell of the Catholic Church),[6] Brentano finally decided to leave Vienna. In a series of articles published in the Viennese newspaper *Die neue freie Presse*, entitled *Meine letzten Wünsche für Österreich* (my last wishes for Austria), Brentano attacked sharply the ingratitude of the Austrian government, for which he had educated so many students without any payment of salary; in these articles, it is also the first time that Brentano officially labels his psychological doctrine as "descriptive psychology or psychognosy" (see Chapter 3).

After leaving Vienna in April 1895, Brentano stayed for several months in Lausanne, where he rejected a professorship and met Alexander Herzen. In 1896, he decided to settle down in Florence and became an Italian citizen. In the following year, Brentano married Emilie Rueprecht, a young woman he had met at Aggsbach near Schönbühel. From then on, for almost two decades, Brentano's life followed more or less the same pattern: in summer and autumn he lived with his son and his wife at Schönbühel; during the rest of the year, they stayed at Florence. Public appearances became sparse: in 1896, Brentano attended an international psychological congress in Munich (organized by Stumpf) and in 1905 he took part in another psychological meeting in Rome. Around 1900 Brentano's eyesight began to deteriorate. A glaucoma operation in 1903 was only partly successful, so that Brentano depended more and more on the assistance of his wife and alternating secretaries, to whom he dictated his inexhaustible thoughts; nevertheless, he was able to write short manuscripts and letters at least until 1912 or 1913. All these problems could not prevent Brentano from intense scientific work; in 1907, he published *Untersuchungen zur Sinnespsychologie*, a collection of shorter articles dealing with perceptual psychology;

and 1911 was an especially prolific year: he presented not only *The Classification of Mental Phenomena* but also two monographs on Aristotle (Brentano 1911a, b, c).[7]

Disgusted with Italy's entry into the war, in May 1915 Brentano moved to Zurich, where his son, Gio, was a physics teacher at the ETH (or Swiss Federal Institute of Technology). Even in Zurich, Brentano continued to work restlessly: a manuscript on the teachings of Jesus was finished (Brentano 1922) and his last dictation on "Anschauung und abstrakte Vorstellung" (intuition and abstract presentation) was taken down on March 9, 1917. Brentano died a week later, on March 17, 1917. He was buried at the cemetery of Sihlfeld near Zurich but was later moved to the family grave at Aschaffenburg.

As it turned out in the months after Brentano's death, he had left not only a huge number of philosophical manuscripts (far exceeding what he had published in his lifetime), but also poetry and an extensive correspondence with colleagues, friends, and family members. Shortly before his death, Brentano had authorized Oskar Kraus and Alfred Kastil (both students of Marty in Prague; Kraus was professor of philosophy there, Kastil in Innsbruck) to prepare an edition of his *Nachlass* (literary estate). At first, Kraus and Kastil collected the documents that were dispersed in Zurich, Florence, and Schönbühel and transferred most of them to Innsbruck, where Kastil established a first Brentano archive and began to produce copies of the manuscripts. There is little known about this archive but much more about the second; with the financial support of Tomas G. Masaryk (who was a student of Brentano in Vienna and from 1918 to 1935 president of the Republic of Czechoslovakia), Kraus managed in 1932 to set up the Brentano archive in Prague. Due to an agreement with Gio Brentano, the archive held all of the precious original manuscripts, and typists began to produce transcriptions in a large style. But unfortunately the archive worked only for a few years; the imminent danger of war in September 1938 made it necessary to transfer the manuscripts to England and place them in the custody of their legal owner, who still was Brentano's son. When the Nazi troops marched into Prague in March 1939, Kraus himself was arrested immediately. Six weeks later, he was released and emigrated to England, which entailed the end of the Brentano archive in its original form. In 1950, Brentano's *Nachlass* was transferred from England to the United States, where Gio was teaching radiation physics at the Northwestern University (see Binder 2013 for a detailed history of the *Nachlass*).

In the years from 1922 to 1939, Kraus and Kastil managed to publish eight major works and numerous shorter articles from the *Nachlass* (most notably Brentano 1925, 1928, 1929a, and 1933). It is beyond any doubt that their efforts were meritorious and prevented Brentano's philosophy from passing into oblivion. It is also true that some of Brentano's manuscripts—especially his large lectures—are extremely difficult to edit. So Kraus and Kastil tried to transform the manuscripts into readable texts, but very often they followed editorial criteria that are hardly acceptable from a contemporary point of view. In the preface to *On the Existence of God*, Kastil summarizes his editorial methods. These involve 1) putting together different texts by Brentano (even different types of text such as dictations and letters) to produce a new text, which is strictly speaking no longer a text by Brentano himself; and 2) trying to present only the "mature" views of Brentano, which means that all obsolete arguments were omitted or corrected in terms of Brentano's late philosophy. Kraus was less permissive in rearranging Brentano's texts, but usually his introductions contain fierce attacks on disloyal students of Brentano. This prompted Husserl—who was among them—to reply to Kraus as early as 1928: "Brentano is a timeless figure—which of course does not mean waved aside once and for all—so the edition should also be guided by a certain timelessness" (see Kraus 1928: xlviii). Later editions of Brentano's work (e.g., by Rolf George or Klaus Hedwig) were more careful but cannot compensate for what is the most needed instrument for all future research on Brentano: a critical edition of his complete works.

NOTES

1. Biographical literature on Brentano in English is very sparse (even *The Cambridge Companion to Brentano* offers only a short chronological table). The most comprehensive portrait is perhaps contained in Albertazzi (2006), but it is not always reliable (as is most of the biographical literature on Brentano). In German, the situation is not much better. The best portrait of Brentano to date, both as a man and a philosopher, is still Carl Stumpf's obituary (Stumpf 1919).
2. Besides Stumpf, the most prominent of Brentano's students in Würzburg were Anton Marty, Georg von Hertling, and Hermann Schell.
3. The name "ultramontanist" was polemically applied to all people—laymen and clergymen alike—who supported the superiority of the pope over the general council.
4. One can find different dates for the appointment in the literature. I rely here on a letter of Brentano to Carl Stumpf (see Brentano 1989: 124).
5. Kraus' reissue of the *Psychology* in three volumes (1924, 1925, and 1928) does not correspond to Brentano's original plans. In particular, the third volume edited from the *Nachlass* is not a work by Brentano but a scheme by Kraus himself. We shall address the editorial issues in more detail below.
6. The scene is described in detail in Brentano 1895b: 13–6.
7. Brentano (1911c) presents an overall view of Aristotle's philosophy, while Brentano (1911b) tries to speak his last word in a decade-long debate with Eduard Zeller about the origin of the human soul.

2

Brentano's Philosophical Program

Uriah Kriegel

Franz Brentano was not a systematic writer, but he was very much a systematic *thinker*. Through his manuscripts, lecture notes, letters, dictations, and occasional published writings, one can discern a systematic, unified approach to the true, the good, and the beautiful. My goal here is to articulate explicitly this approach, and the philosophical program it reflects. The exercise requires going over big stretches of terrain with some efficiency; I will go just as deep into Brentano's approaches to the true, the good, and the beautiful as is required to make explicit their structural unity.

The basic idea behind Brentano's program is that there are three distinctive types of mental act that proprietarily target the true, the good, and the beautiful. To understand the true, the good, and the beautiful, we must obtain a clear grasp (i) of the distinctive mental acts targeting them and (ii) of success in such targeting. According to Brentano, the true is that which it is correct, or fitting, or appropriate to believe; the good is that which it is correct/fitting to love or like or approve of; and the beautiful is that with which it is correct/fitting to be delighted.[1] The next three sections develop and (do the minimum to) motivate each of these claims.

1 THE TRUE AS THAT WHICH IT IS FITTING TO BELIEVE

Many things can be said to be true—notably sentences, utterances, and thoughts. However, for Brentano, truth attaches originally only to judgments; other things can be said to be true only derivatively, insofar as they are suitably related to true judgments (Brentano 1966b: 6).

There are many divisions among judgments, but the most fundamental is this: some judgments are positive and some are negative. Positive judgments are judgments that, by their nature, are committed to the truth of what is judged; negative judgments are ones committed to the falsity of what is judged (Brentano 1973a: 223). When one person believes that the sun rotates around the earth and another disbelieves that the sun rotates around the earth, both are making a judgment about the same thing: whether the sun rotates around the earth. But one is making a positive judgment, committing to the truth of < the sun rotates around the earth >, while the other makes a negative judgment, committing to the falsity of < the sun rotates around the earth >.

Belief is committed to the truth of what is believed, then, whereas disbelief is committed to the falsity of what is disbelieved. In both cases, we can ask whether the commitment is built into the *content* of the judgment or the *attitude*. This is not Brentano's terminology; Brentano would put this by asking whether the commitment is an aspect of the intentional *object* or of the *mode* of intentionality. But the point is the same: either belief's commitment to truth is part of what is represented by the belief, or it is an aspect of the way belief represents what it does. Brentano's view is clearly the latter: truth-commitment is an *attitudinal* feature of belief (Brentano 1973a: 201). This makes sense, of course: we typically believe *that the sun rotates around the earth*, not that *it is true* that the sun rotates around the earth. The commitment to the proposition that the sun rotates around the earth is built into the very act of believing, not into what is believed. We may put this (though Brentano does not) by saying that for any given proposition p, believing that p is not a mental act that represents p as true, but rather a mental act that represents-as-true p. More generally:

> What constitutes the distinctive feature of judgment ... can[not] be a difference in content.... [T]he distinctive feature of judgment [is rather] a particular kind of *relation* to the [intentional] object.
> (Brentano 1973a: 222; my italics)

In our terminology: representing-as-true is the essential property of belief, while representing-as-false is the essential property of disbelief.

From this perspective, the answer to the question "what is truth?" is simply: the kind of thing targeted by belief (rather than disbelief or other types of mental act). More precisely, to say of any given sentence "p" or proposition p that it is true is just to say that the right attitude to take toward p is that of believing it (Brentano 1966b: 122). The correct or fitting attitude to take toward p, of all attitudes in our psychological repertoire, is belief—that attitude which, by its very nature, represents-as-true.

The idea that the true is that which it is fitting to represent-as-true might seem circular. And indeed it would be if the only way to understand the notion of representing-as-true is compositionally, by understanding the meaning of "representing" and "true." But this is not what Brentano thinks. For Brentano, there is only one way to grasp the distinctive, essential property of belief. It is to encounter in introspection, or rather in inner perception,[2] mental acts of believing, disbelieving, contemplating, and so on; and to pay attention to the felt difference between them. Through such comparison and contrast, one can zero in on the distinctive property of belief. For Brentano, the true is that toward which it is fitting to have the kind of mental act that exhibits this distinctive property encountered in inner perception. Accordingly, a person who has never experienced an inner-perceived belief, disbelief, and so on would be unable to grasp the nature of truth: "our definition would convey nothing to one who lacked the necessary intuition" (Brentano 1966b: 25).[3]

So far, I have conducted the discussion as though Brentano, along with virtually every other philosopher, takes judgment to be a propositional attitude. But one of the most fascinating parts of Brentano's philosophy is his nonpropositional theory of judgment as an *objectual* attitude. This theory allows Brentano to turn his account of truth into an account of *existence*. This move is based on two central ideas.

The first is that all beliefs are existential (Brentano 1973a: 218). We do not believe that the weather is nice but rather that *there is* nice weather. We do not believe that all dogs are cute but rather that *there is no* uncute dog. Every belief report, claims Brentano, can be paraphrased perfectly into an existential-belief report. Accordingly, the truth-commitment of beliefs boils down to existence-commitment: all our beliefs and disbeliefs commit to the existence or nonexistence of something.

The second idea is that this existence-commitment is, again, an aspect of the belief's attitude rather than content. Our beliefs do not represent things as existent but rather represent-as-existent things. To that extent, belief reports are better formulated not in terms of "belief that" but in terms of "belief in." We do not believe *that there is nice weather* but rather *believe in* nice weather. We do not believe *that there is no uncute dog* but rather *disbelieve in* an uncute dog. Observe, now, that belief-in is an objectual (and not propositional) attitude: what is believed-in is nice weather, not the existence of nice weather; what is disbelieved-in is uncute dogs, not the existence of uncute dogs. As Brentano puts it,

> the being of A need not be produced in order for the judgment "A is" to be … correct; all that is needed is A.
>
> (1966b: 85)

In a slogan: the truthmakers of existentials are not existences but existents.

What motivates this attitudinal account of existence-commitment is the (highly plausible) traditional idea that existence is not an attribute (Brentano 1973a: 229). If existence is not an attribute, (true) existentials cannot be understood as attributing existence to something (if things do not *have* such an attribute, any judgment which attributed it to them would be erroneous). How, then, can a *true* judgment involve commitment to the existence of that which it is about? The answer is that the judgment must not represent its object as existing but instead represent-as-existing its object. That is, existence-commitment must be an aspect of the judgment's attitude, not its content.[4]

Brentano's reasoning may be summarized in two steps. First: all (dis)belief reports can be paraphrased into existential-(dis)belief reports; all existential-(dis)belief reports can be paraphrased into (dis)belief-in reports; therefore, all (dis)belief reports can be paraphrased into (dis)belief-in reports. The fact that A-statements are paraphraseable into B-statements does not in itself guarantee that the latter capture the real structure of what those statements are about. A substantive argument is needed for taking the B-statements to be more faithful to how things are. This is provided by the second part of Brentano's reasoning: the truth of (dis)belief-in reports does not require there to be an existence attribute, whereas the truth of existential (dis)belief-that reports does; there are good reasons to reject an existence attribute, but no good reasons to think there are no true existential judgments; therefore, there are good reasons to take (dis)belief-in reports to capture the real structure of judgments.[5]

The upshot is that Brentano's fitting-belief account of the true effectively becomes a fitting-belief-in account of the existent. To say that a duck exists, for example, is just to say that the right or correct attitude to take toward a duck is that of believing in it. (By the same token, to say that there are no dragons is to say that the correct attitude to take toward a dragon is that of disbelieving in it.) Brentano writes:

> If "the existent," in its strict sense, is a name, it cannot be said to name anything directly. It comes to the same thing as "something (*etwas*) which is the object of a correct affirmative judgment" or "something which is correctly accepted or affirmed."
> (Brentano 1969: 68)

Since for Brentano all beliefs are existential, he sometimes runs his correct-attitude accounts of truth and existence together: "We call something true when the affirmation relating to it is correct/fitting" (1969: 18).

Here too, Brentano maintains that our only grip on the crucial property of representing-as-existent derives from inner perception of beliefs-in. We only truly grasp the notion of existence when we understand it as that toward which it is fitting to have a mental act with the kind of distinctive attitudinal property we encounter in comparing and contrasting beliefs-in and other mental acts in our psychological repertoire (Brentano 1973a: 210).

Crucially, the same holds of the correctness or fittingness of our (dis)beliefs-in. Actually, for Brentano, we may be able to analyze correctness in terms of self-evidence (*Evidenz*); but the notion of self-evidence itself is primitive and can only be grasped in inner perception through the same sort of contrastive exercise:

> The correct method is one that we use in many other cases where we are concerned with a *simple* mark or characteristic. We will have to solve the problem by considering a multiplicity of judgments which are self-evident and then *comparing and contrasting* (*vergleichend gegenüber stellen*) them with other judgments which lack this distinguishing characteristic.
> (Brentano 1966b: 125; my italics)

Thus both the distinctive property of belief-in and the property of fittingness are to be grasped originally in inner perception. Once we do, and given certain theoretical positions, we can appreciate the nature of existence and truth.

2 THE GOOD AS THAT TO WHICH A PRO ATTITUDE IS FITTING

Just as judgments embody commitment to the existence or nonexistence of what they are about, Brentano maintains that there are mental acts that embody commitment to the goodness or badness of what they are about. He uses the terms "love" and "hate" to denote those mental acts but uses them widely to cover any favorable or unfavorable mental act, such as loving a certain wine (Brentano 1973a: 199) or hating the weather. Indeed, he argues that under the headings of "love" and "hate," so understood, fall all pain and pleasure, all emotions as such, and all acts of the will (Brentano 1973a: 236–7). Essentially, his "love" and "hate" are what we refer to in contemporary philosophy of mind as *pro attitudes* and *con attitudes*. Pro attitudes embody commitment to the goodness of their intentional objects, con attitudes commitment to the badness of theirs. Thus, liking ice cream involves mental commitment to the goodness of ice cream, while disliking rain involves mental commitment to the badness of rain.[6]

As with judgment and existence, Brentano construes the goodness-commitment of pro attitudes as an *attitudinal* property. We may put this by saying that approving of world peace is not a matter of representing world peace as good but a matter of representing-as-good world peace. The goodness is not a part of *what* is represented but a modification of the representing itself. What is approved of—the content of the approval—is just world peace. The commitment to goodness comes in only at the level of attitude. And indeed, excluding goodness from the content of a pro attitude is as intuitive as excluding truth from the content of belief: one desires ice cream, not the goodness of ice cream, or that the ice cream be good.

A more theoretical motivation for the attitudinal account of goodness-commitment parallels the motivation for an attitudinal account of existence-commitment—namely, the notion that there is no worldly goodness that inheres in the things themselves. Brentano dismisses the notion of goodness as an intrinsic attribute of ice cream, for instance, in a 1909 letter to Kraus:

> What you seek to gain here with your belief in the existence (*Bestehen*) of goodness with which the emotions are found to correspond (*in einer adäquatio gefunden*) is incomprehensible to me.
> (Brentano 1966a: 207; see also Chisholm 1986: 51–2)

Given that there is no such intrinsic property as goodness, if approving of world peace were a matter of attributing that property to world peace, it would be a misattribution and thus a misrepresentation. Since approving of world peace is quite appropriate, though, the mental commitment to world peace's goodness must be an aspect of the *attitude* of approval.

Accordingly, when we say that peace is good, we are not attributing anything to peace. In a sense, we are not (in the first instance) really characterizing peace. What we are characterizing is, in the first instance, the attitude it would be fitting to take *toward* peace. We are saying that, of all the attitudes in our psychological repertoire, a *pro* attitude would be the right attitude to take toward peace. In that respect, peace is a suitable or appropriate object of a pro attitude; it is the kind of thing it would be correct to like, desire, or approve of (see Chapter 20). In sum:

> everything that can be thought about belongs in one of two classes—either the class of things for which love [pro attitude] is appropriate, or the class of things for which hate [con attitude] is appropriate. Whatever falls into the first class we call good, and whatever falls into the second we call bad.
> (Brentano 1966b: 21–2; see also 1969: 18 and even 1973a: 247)

Our only grasp on the good, then, is as that to which a pro attitude—a mental act that by its nature represents-as-good—would be fitting.[7]

Since goodness is not an attribute of external items, we cannot acquire the concept of the good by outer-perceptual encounter with items that exhibit or fail to exhibit it. Rather, our competence to engage in goodness talk and thought is ultimately based on inner-perceptual grasp of the fittingness or correctness of our own pro and con attitudes:

> When we ourselves experience such a love (a love with the character of correctness [*als richtig charakterisierte*]) we notice not only that its object is loved and loveable, and that its privation or contrary hated and hateable, but also that the one is love-*worthy* and the other hate-*worthy*, and therefore that the one is good and the other bad.
>
> (Brentano 1969: 22; my italics)

Further: not only is our grasp of the distinctive and essential property of a pro attitude derived from direct inner-perceptual encounter, so is our grasp of the fittingness that sometimes characterizes a mental act with that property. (More accurately, just as a judgment's correctness can be understood in terms of self-evidence, which itself can only be grasped through direct acquaintance in inner perception, so there is a practical "analogue of self-evidence in the domain of judgment" (1969: 22) in terms of which an attitude's fittingness can be understood; but this practical self-evidence itself can only be grasped directly in inner perception.)

It is easy to see the symmetry between Brentano's approaches to the true and the good. The characterization of pro attitudes as embodying mental commitment to goodness, the attitudinal take on goodness-commitment, the fitting pro attitude account of goodness, and the inner-perceptual grasp of both the relevant attitudinal property and its fittingness echo parallel views in Brentano's account of truth and existence. Brentano himself emphasizes this symmetry:

> In calling an object good we are not giving it a material (*sachliches*) predicate, as we do when we call something red or round or warm or thinking. In this respect the expressions good and bad are like the expressions existent and nonexistent. In using the latter, we do not intend to add yet another determining characteristic of the thing in question; we wish rather to say that whoever acknowledges [believes in] a certain thing and rejects [disbelieves in] another makes a true judgment. And when we call certain objects good and others bad we are merely saying that whoever loves [has a pro attitude toward] the former and hates [has a con attitude toward] the latter has taken the right stand. The source of these concepts is inner perception, for it is only in inner perception that we comprehend ourselves as loving or hating something.
>
> (1973b: 90; see also Brentano 1969: 73–5,
> as well as manuscripts Ms 107c 231 and
> Ms 107c 236, quoted in Seron 2008)

This passage includes in an extraordinarily compressed way virtually all the elements making up Brentano's accounts of the true and the good.

It is worth noting that Brentano does recognize that the phenomena force certain disanalogies between the two cases. First, the fittingness of judgments and that of pro/con attitudes is not exactly the same feature (Brentano 1969: 144). More interestingly, the good comes in degrees, whereas the true does not. Accordingly, while the theory of the true requires no account of "the truer," the theory of the good does require an account of *the better*. Brentano's account is in terms of fitting *preference*: to say that *a* is better than *b* is to say that it would be fitting or correct to prefer *a* to *b* (Brentano 1969: 26, 1973b: 92). Despite such differences, it is easy to appreciate that Brentano's fundamental philosophical approach to the true and the good is structurally extremely similar.

3 THE BEAUTIFUL: DELIGHT AND AESTHETIC VALUE

Brentano's psychology divides mental acts into three fundamental categories (Chapter 9). We have already encountered judgments (affirmative or negative) and attitudes (pro or con). According to Brentano, both of these presuppose a third, more basic type of act consisting merely in the entertaining, or contemplation, or presentation (*Vorstellung*) of an object—without committing to either its existence/nonexistence or its goodness/badness (Brentano 1973a: 198). This may suggest that just as existence and goodness are tied to judgment and attitude (respectively), so beauty is tied to presentation or contemplation. After all, it is plausible to say that a beautiful thing is worthy of contemplation in more or less the same sense in which a good thing is worthy of approval and a real thing is worthy of acceptance.

This might suggest the following account of the beautiful: to say that something is beautiful is to say that it would be fitting to contemplate it. However, this "clean" account is frustrated by the fact that while acceptance and approval carry existence- and goodness-commitment (respectively), contemplation does not by itself carry *beauty-commitment*: I am not mentally committing to the beauty of a book on my desk merely by contemplating it. In addition, there is no *standard of fittingness* for presentation (Brentano 1973a: 223), but there would have to be one if we were to appeal to fitting contemplation in accounting for beauty. Finally, while judgment and attitude come in positive and negative varieties, contemplation does not (1973a: 222), so the opposition between the beautiful and the ugly could not be captured through the fittingness of two opposing types of contemplation.

Something else must be added to contemplation, then, to capture beauty-commitment. What? Brentano notes a peculiar feature of the experience of encounter with the beautiful: it always entrains a measure of joy or pleasure. If one manages to contemplate El Greco's *Saint Martin and the Beggar* joylessly, one cannot be said to experience it as beautiful. "Only when a presentation is in itself good and joyful (*erfreulich*) we call its primary object beautiful" (Brentano 1959: 123). Thus the account of the beautiful requires positing a special mental act composed of both contemplation and joy—a kind of joyful contemplation. In some places, Brentano calls this mental act "delight" (*Wohlgefallen*). Delight, rather than mere contemplation, is the kind of mental act that embodies commitment to the beauty of that which it is about. It is also the kind of mental act for which there is a standard of correctness and one for which a contrary is available in the form of dejected or wretched contemplation (we might call this *dismay*).

Note well: the joy component of delight is a pro attitude, so delight is a compound state with a presentation component and a pro-attitude component. More specifically, to be delighted with x is to be in a state which is directed contemplation-wise at x and enjoyment-wise at the contemplation-of-x. By the same token, to be dismayed with

x is to be in a state which is directed contemplation-wise at x and dejection-wise at the contemplation-of-x.

With this in place, Brentano can offer a "fitting delight" account of beauty analogous to his accounts of truth and value:

> The concept of beauty [has to do with] a delight with the character of correctness (*als richtig charakteriesiertes*) being elicited in us.
>
> (1959: 17)

To say that something is beautiful, then, is to say that it would be fitting to be delighted by it. That means it would be fitting to contemplate it while taking joy in the contemplating—both the contemplating and the enjoyment must be fitting. Meanwhile, the ugly is that which is a fitting object of dismay. Note that since delight and dismay involve the fittingness of a pro or con attitude, the fittingness of delight or dismay is ultimately a species of fitting (pro or con) attitude. This captures nicely, within Brentano's framework, the fact that aesthetic value is a species of value.

The motivation for, and consequences of, this account are broadly the same as those associated with the fitting belief-in and fitting pro-attitude accounts of truth and value. To start, Brentano rejects the existence of a worldly attribute of beauty, exhibited by some items and not others, just as he rejects the attributes of truth and goodness:

> But it may well happen that a word which has the grammatical form of a noun or adjective actually denotes nothing at all.… For example: … "good" and "evil," as well as "truth" and "falsehood" and the like. Strictly speaking, there is no concept (*Begriff*) of the good, *or of the beautiful*, or of the true.
>
> (Brentano 1966b: 71; my italics)

The last sentence in this passage is surely an infelicitous overstatement (of the sort one is liable to find in an unpublished fragment). Brentano does accept, after all, the existence of the *concepts* of truth and goodness (ultimately acquired, as we have seen, through inner perception). His view is rather that there are no such *attributes* as truth, goodness, and apparently beauty. Presumably, though, just as Brentano embraced existents and goods as worldly things in spite of rejecting existence and goodness as worldly attributes, so he embraces *beauties* despite rejecting beauty.

As before, this leads to a construal of beauty-commitment as an attitudinal rather than a content feature of delight. It is an aspect of *how* delight represents, not of *what* it represents. To experience aesthetic delight with an orchid is not to represent the orchid as beautiful but to represent-as-beautiful the orchid. The content of the delight is simply the orchid. The commitment to the orchid's beauty comes in at the level of attitude. It does not appear in the delight's content. This makes sense: we delight at the orchid, not at its beauty; the orchid's beauty is just the *reason* why we delight in the orchid.

Since there is no attribute of beauty that some worldly items exhibit and others do not, presumably we do not acquire the concept of the beautiful through outer-perceptual interaction with external-world beauties. Instead, we grasp the notion of beauty through inner-perceptual interaction with our delights' distinctive property of representing-as-beautiful and with its characteristic fittingness. We have no other handle on the beautiful.

The parallelism with Brentano's accounts of the true and the good is evident: beauty is accounted for in terms of the fittingness of a specific kind of attitude. At the same time, there are disanalogies here too. First, unlike the attitudes relevant to the true and the good, that relevant to the beautiful is not primitive but compound; it is therefore to be understood not through direct acquaintance but through analysis into its components. Secondly, there appears to be no *sui generis* fittingness special to delight: its fittingness reduces to the fittingness of second-order enjoyment.

4 BRENTANO'S PROGRAM

In what is quite possibly the most scholarly English-language overview of Brentano's philosophy, Liliana Albertazzi writes that "It is the general opinion that Brentano's theories do not constitute a system" (Albertazzi 2006: 295). As a sociological remark, this may be unobjectionable.[8] But as the foregoing discussion suggests, Brentano's philosophical thought is, in reality, extraordinarily systematic. If the goal of a philosophical "grand system" in the style of seventeenth- and eighteenth-century philosophy is to provide a unified, structurally symmetric account of the true, the good, and the beautiful, then Brentano clearly had at least a *program* for such a system. Indeed, his may well be the last grand system of Western philosophy. For a variety of reasons, twentieth-century philosophy has taken a distance from systematic thinking in this sense. Brentano, whose system reached a certain resting point circa 1915, seems to be the last philosopher to have offered a system in the sense of a structurally unified account of the true, the good, and the beautiful. One suspects it is primarily the unsystematic character of Brentano's *writings* that has encouraged the otherwise implausible notion that there is no systematicity in his philosophical *thinking*. Arguably, however, in his mind Brentano was continuously refining and chiseling away at a unified grand system, a system that harmonized and stabilized the bits and pieces in his messy literary estate.

The superstructure of Brentano's program is quite straightforward. We grasp the nature of the true, the good, and the beautiful by grasping (i) the distinctive or essential feature of three types of mental act—affirmative judgment, pro attitude, and delight—and (ii) the standard of fittingness or correctness for each. Thus, six notions are essential to Brentano's system: affirmative judgment, judgment-fittingness, pro attitude, attitude-fittingness, delight, and delight-fittingness. However, since delight is analyzable in terms of (first-order) contemplation and (second-order) pro attitude, and its fittingness is but the fittingness of pro attitudes, Brentano's account of the true, the good, and the beautiful requires only *five* basic and unanalyzable notions: affirmative judgment, pro attitude, contemplation, judgment-fittingness, and attitude-fittingness. These five notions receive no informative philosophical account in Brentano's system. They are treated as primitives. As such, we do not grasp *their* nature by appreciating some philosophical theory. We can only grasp their nature *directly*—through acquaintance in inner perception (against the background of the right contrast). At the end of an 1889 lecture on truth, Brentano says:

> We have been concerned with a definition, i.e., with the elucidation of a concept ... Many believe that such elucidation always requires some general determination

> [i.e., definition by *genus et differentia*], and they forget that the ultimate and most effective means of elucidation must always consist in appeal to the individual's intuition ... What would be the use of trying to elucidate the concepts of red and blue if I could not present one with something red or with something blue?
>
> (Brentano 1966b: 24–5)

In our case, we appreciate the nature of belief-in by inner-perceiving mental acts that *are* beliefs-in alongside ones that are not; we understand what judgment-fittingness is, ultimately, by inner-perceiving judgments that are self-evident alongside judgments that are not; we appreciate the nature of a pro attitude by inner-perceiving mental acts that *are* pro attitudes alongside ones that are not; and so on. In each case, some contrast brings into sharper inner-perceptual relief the feature whose nature we are trying to grasp. We grasp that nature simply *as* that which is present in the one case and absent in the other. There is no fuller, more articulated, more informative, more theoretical account to be had.

It is a central feature of Brentano's program, then, that the ultimate basis for our grasp of the nature of the true, the good, and the beautiful is inner perception of our mental acts and their fittingness. This explains psychology's pride of place in Brentano's system:

> We see that ... the triad of ideals, the beautiful, the true, and the good, can well be defined in terms of the system of mental faculties. Indeed, this is the only way in which it becomes fully intelligible.
>
> (Brentano 1973a: 263)

Insofar as the study of the true, the good, and the beautiful is grounded in the study of the mind, philosophy of mind (or Brentano's "descriptive psychology") assumes the role of *first philosophy*. The status of philosophy of mind as first philosophy will remain a unifying theme of the Brentano School. In fact, since for Brentano, all mental life is conscious, his philosophy of mind is at bottom a philosophy of consciousness. In Brentano's thought, then, we find a rare instance of a philosophical system based ultimately on the philosophy of consciousness.

Despite this *methodological* primacy of philosophy of consciousness, Brentano's picture of the world is thoroughly realist. Brentano's world contains just so many individual objects, and nothing more (see Chapter 13). When we say of any of the concrete particulars inhabiting Brentano's world that it exists, or is good, or is beautiful, we are just saying that it would be fitting to believe in it, have a pro attitude toward it, or delight in it (respectively). It is in this way that the notions of the true/real, the good, and the beautiful make their entry into our worldview. This entry does not entrain, however, a transcendental mind that does the accepting, approving, and delighting. Rather, among the individual objects inhabiting this austere world are individual minds, including believing-minds, approving-minds, and delighted-minds, and indeed even some correctly-believing-minds, rightly-approving-minds, and fittingly-delighted-minds! It is because (and only because) each of us has on occasion *been* a correctly-believing-mind, rightly-approving-mind, and fittingly-delighted-mind, and has *inner-perceived* himself or herself to be such a mind, that each of us is able to experience the world in terms of truth, goodness, and beauty.

CONCLUSION: THE THREE LEGS OF THE BRENTANIAN STOOL

As noted, Brentano's classification of mental acts divides them into three basic categories: presentation, judgment, and (pro or con) attitude. All three are species of a single more generic phenomenon, namely intentionality:

> Nothing distinguishes mental phenomena from physical phenomena more than the fact that something is immanent [that is, intentionally inexistent] as an object in them. For this reason it is easy to understand that the fundamental differences in the way something [in]exists in them as an object constitute the principal class differences among mental phenomena.
>
> (Brentano 1973a: 197)

The three categories correspond to three different modes of intentionality, or three different modifications of the basic intentional relation. These are the modes of representing-as-existent/nonexistent for judgment, representing-as-good/bad for attitudes, and a kind of neutral mere-representing for presentation. These are obviously different, but they are all modifications of the same underlying phenomenon of intentionality. As noted, the natures of both intentionality and the fittingness of different intentional modifications can ultimately be grasped only through inner perception. Together, intentionality, fittingness, and inner perception can be seen as the three legs of the Brentanian stool; they are the central concepts in his system. It is through their interrelations, modifications, and interrelations of modifications that we obtain philosophical illumination of the true, the good, and the beautiful.[9]

NOTES

1. The term Brentano prefers in this context is *Richtig*, most naturally translated as "correct" or "fitting." But in one place he offers a number of synonyms—*konvenient, passend,* and *entsprechend* (Brentano 1969: 74)—which are more or less interchangeably translatable as "appropriate," "suitable," "fitting," and "adequate."
2. Brentano draws a sharp distinction between introspection and inner perception, and hangs his epistemic hopes only on the latter. On the difference between the two, see Chapter 3.
3. Plausibly, it is precisely because the only way to grasp the essential property of belief is by direct inner-perceptual encounter that Brentano does not characterize this property as "representing-as-true." But the expression is useful for bringing out that the characteristic commitment of belief is an aspect of its attitude, not its content. Nonetheless, we must treat this expression with care and keep in mind that it is hyphenated for a reason: "true" is intended as a merely morphological, and *not* syntactic, part of "representing-as-true" (just as "apple" is a merely morphological part of "pineapple").
4. In more Brentanian terminology: it is not an aspect of the *object* of consciousness but of the *mode* of consciousness (1973a: 201).
5. Brentano also has other arguments to plug into the second part of the reasoning. For example, he thinks that (dis)belief-in reports are more parsimonious than (dis)belief-that reports, since they concern only concrete objects and not propositions (see Brentano 1966b: 84). Here I focus on one particular argument Brentano employs, because it is one that recurs in the domains of the good and the beautiful.
6. Such commitment need not be all-things-considered commitment; it can be just prima facie commitment. In fact, it appears to be the crucial difference between emotion and will, for Brentano, that the former's value-commitment is prima facie and the latter's is all-things-considered (1969: 150). Both, however, qualify as pro/con attitudes.

7. This, at least, is Brentano's view of *intrinsic* goodness; *instrumental* goodness may be understood in terms of its relation to intrinsic goodness (Brentano 1969 §16).
8. There are clearly exceptions to this rule, though (see Gabriel 2013).
9. This work was supported by the French National Research Agency's grants ANR-11-0001-02 PSL* and ANR-10-LABX-0087. For comments on a previous draft, I am grateful to Johannes Brandl, Géraldine Carranante, Arnaud Dewalque, Guillaume Fréchette, Anna Giustina, and especially Lylian Paquet.

1.1
Mind

3

Brentano's Project of Descriptive Psychology

Denis Seron

Brentano's most famous work, *Psychology from an Empirical Standpoint*, published in 1874, was primarily concerned with epistemology. Its central aim was to present new foundations for scientific—that is, empirical—psychology. As such, Brentano's project in the *Psychology* cannot be dissociated from the broader context of the birth and development of empirical psychology around the mid-nineteenth century by philosophers such as Lotze (1852), Hamilton (1859), Fechner (1860), Wundt (1874), and the British associationists.

For Brentano, an "empirical" science is a "purely phenomenal science" *(ausschliesslich phänomenale Wissenschaft)* (Brentano 1874: 20/1973a: 14)—a science whose objects are not substances but phenomena. Empirical natural science should not be viewed as the science of physical substances, namely of bodies, but as the "science of physical phenomena." Likewise, empirical psychology is not the science of mental substances, namely souls, but the "science of mental phenomena" (Brentano 1874: 13, 16/1973a: 9, 11). The idea is that science in general can, and should, dispense with the metaphysical assumption that there *are* substances that underlie the phenomena we witness. Thus, as indicated in the title of an 1888–9 lecture course, descriptive psychology is best seen as a "descriptive phenomenology" (Brentano 1982: 129/1995b: 137).[1]

Applied to psychology, Brentano's empiricist claim is that psychological knowledge refers to phenomena and only to phenomena. Put otherwise: it must have its source in perceptual experience. However, the descriptive psychologist is not concerned (at least primarily) with any phenomena whatsoever; her objects are specifically mental phenomena, namely objects of inner perception. In consequence, "inner perception of our own mental phenomena," that is, consciousness, "is the primary source of the experiences essential to psychological investigations" (Brentano 1874: 48/1973a: 34; see also Brentano 1874: 40–41/1973a: 29).

We should not be misled, however, into regarding Brentano's program of descriptive psychology merely as a reaction against physiological psychology in the style of Fechner and Wundt. In his lectures of 1887–8, he considers both descriptive and physiological psychology to be branches of psychology in general (Brentano 1982: 1ff., 10ff., 154ff./1995b: 3ff., 13ff., 163ff.). The former is a purely psychological science aimed at classifying mental phenomena into types and analyzing them into their elements and structural relations (compatibility, separability, etc.). The latter, which Brentano also terms "genetic psychology," deals with the development over time and causal conditions of inner life—which requires reference to physiological processes. But although the Brentanian program leaves room for genetic psychology, descriptive psychology can be seen, to some extent, as a foundation for it: descriptive psychology is independent of genetic psychology and provides conceptual distinctions that are presupposed by genetic psychology (Brentano 1982: 156/1995b: 165). This stands to reason: the purpose of genetic psychology is to offer a causal explanation of mental phenomena, but before we can achieve this, we must know what the phenomena are that need explanation; it is the purpose of descriptive psychology to *describe* mental phenomena, the phenomena genetic psychology is to explain. The distinction between descriptive and genetic psychology, which is central to Brentano's epistemology of psychology, will be detailed in §4.

Another point of importance is that, despite his radical empiricism, Brentano held the laws of descriptive psychology to be a priori laws. As will be explained in §4, Brentano saw no contradiction between his empiricism and the idea of a psychological a priori. This is certainly one of the most interesting and fruitful aspects of Brentano's descriptive psychology in the context of recent epistemological debates.[2]

1 INTROSPECTION

Like most of his contemporaries, including a number of experimental psychologists, Brentano thought that the method of psychology must involve introspection, that is, self-observation of one's own inner life. Mental phenomena, like physical phenomena, can be objects of observation and knowledge. But on the other hand, Brentano draws a sharp distinction between introspection and consciousness or inner perception (Feest 2014: 699–700). To observe oneself seeing a coffee mug is not merely to consciously see the mug; it requires an attentional shift from the seen mug to the seeing itself, that is, from the "primary object" of the act to its "secondary object" (Brentano 1874: 176ff./1973a: 126ff.).

That being so, couldn't self-observation, at least in some cases, be a new inner perception, numerically distinct from mere consciousness? Brentano thought otherwise. Introspection, he claims, is possible only in the mode of memory (Brentano 1874: 48ff./1973a: 34ff.). It does not present one's mental acts as present, as inner perception does, but as past mental acts. Brentano's example is well known: you cannot both feel angry and reflect on your anger at the same time, simply because reflection alters your anger or even may cause you to cease to feel angry (Brentano 1874: 41/1973a: 30). At the moment when you have an introspective representation of your own mental act, your mental act no longer exists. Thus, psychological observation must be different from inner perception. What the psychologist innerly perceives when she introspects her mental act *A* is not *A* but her act of remembering *A*.

One important consequence of this is that psychological knowledge, unlike inner perception (Brentano 1874: 128/1973a: 91), is subject to self-deception, doubt, and uncertainty (Brentano 1874: 49-50/1973a: 35). It would be absurd to doubt the existence of your feeling angry at the very moment you feel angry. But you can certainly be wrong in attributing to yourself a past feeling. Furthermore, psychological knowledge is also made fallible by the fact that obviously it must also deal with other subjects' experiences, to which the psychologist has no immediate access. Brentano thus attaches major significance to studying the mental life of children, members of non-Western civilizations ("primitives"), born-blinds, nonhuman animals, mental patients, great personalities, and the like—mental life that is normally cognoscible only through outer observation of verbal reports, bodily responses, voluntary or involuntary behavior, and so on.

To sum up: outer observation and inner observation through memory are "sources" of psychological knowledge. However, the former presupposes the latter, which in turn presupposes inner perception: attributing a feeling of anger to another person means attributing to her a feeling similar to the anger you previously felt and now remember. Therefore, "inner perception constitutes the ultimate and indispensable precondition of the other two sources of knowledge" (Brentano 1874: 61/1973a: 43).

2 ANALYSIS

The method of Brentano's descriptive psychology is a combination of introspection and analysis. First, the object of psychology is the flow of consciousness, thus something that is experienced in the first person. Secondly, Brentano adheres to a compositional view of mental life. On this view, the flow of consciousness is a whole composed of often separable parts. The descriptive psychologist's task is to analyze the whole into its separable parts, the most basic of which are supposed to correspond to primitive concepts. On the one hand, the descriptive psychologist analyzes experiences into their elements; on the other hand, she classifies them under basic concepts. For example, your aesthetic experience of a piece of music is a compound of an auditory presentation and a feeling of pleasure.

Brentano's intentionality thesis—"is a mental phenomenon" is necessarily equivalent to "is intentional"—may be construed in terms of such analysis or decomposition (Brentano 1982). The idea is that, however far one pushes psychological analysis, the elements obtained must necessarily be what Brentano calls "intentional acts." To put it otherwise: the most basic separable parts of the mental flow are not mere sensory data, as associationists and other psychologists of the time claimed. Rather, they must be mental phenomena with an intentional object appearing in them.

For this reason, Brentano's position is best seen as a phenomenological dualism in the vein of William Hamilton (Dewalque and Seron 2015): every phenomenon is necessarily such that it appears within something else or that something else appears in it. This view was largely polemical at the time the *Psychology* was published. Many psychologists of the period—including Wundt, whose famous *Principles of Physiological Psychology* came out the same year—conceived of representations as compounds of (nonrepresentational) sensations, and sensations monistically as the ultimate elements of mental life.

Thus understood, the intentionality thesis entails both that the intentional object is a part of the act, something that appears "within" it, and that it is not separable from the act. Therefore, it must be an *inseparable* part of the act, with the consequence that it is not an "element" in the proper sense of the term (Brentano 1982: 157/1995b: 166) and that the mereological relation "appears in" is not a relation of composition properly speaking. The intentional object is not a real part as is the partial act of hearing *Peter and the Wolf* within the complex act of feeling pleasure when hearing *Peter and the Wolf*, but an abstract or "distinctional" part obtained by purely conceptual means (Brentano 1982: 13-14/1995b: 16; see also Antonelli 2000: 109–10, Dewalque 2013). More on this in §4.

3 INDUCTION

Brentano's plea for an empirical psychology was one aspect of his conviction that the method of psychology should be modeled on the method of natural science (Brentano 1874: 102/1973a: 71; see also Haller 1989, Ierna 2014): where natural science is ultimately based on *external* perception, empirical psychology is ultimately based on *inner* perception, and both target phenomena rather than underlying substances. Another key aspect was the idea that the psychologist's task was to set out the laws that govern mental phenomena, and that this required using the inductive method of natural science (Brentano 1874: 66, 102ff./1973a: 47, 70ff.). The most general psychological laws, he claims, are won by "psychological induction." At a second stage, special laws are derived deductively from the higher laws and then tested "by direct induction from experience."

In the *Psychology*, however, Brentano holds that there is at least one major difference between physical and psychological laws. Although the highest laws of psychology are laws "of a very comprehensive universality" (Brentano 1874: 102/1973a: 71), Brentano disagrees with Herbart and Fechner that they are "exact" or a priori laws such as those found in mathematics. Insofar as psychological knowledge is grounded in memory, and as long as mental intensity cannot be measured accurately enough, psychological laws are to be understood as mere "empirical laws," fraught with inaccuracy and uncertainty (Brentano 1874: 102/1973a: 70). That is, they are inductive laws rather than exceptionless laws. (It is worth noting that, for Brentano, this did not preclude the use of mathematics, especially statistics, in empirical psychology [Brentano 1874: 102/1973a: 70]. To Wundt, who argued that mental phenomena were mathematizable and therefore lend themselves to exact knowledge, Brentano replied that everything knowable is countable and hence mathematizable, and that it would be absurd to infer from this that all knowledge is exact [Brentano 1874: 94–95/1973a: 65–66].)

Brentano also suggests that, beside ordinary induction, the psychologist may in some cases use the "historical" or "inverse deductive method" elaborated by John Stuart Mill (Brentano 1874: 104/1973a: 72; see also Mill 1843: 585ff.). On this method, instead of trying to confirm general laws through direct induction, one starts with direct induction and then explains the special laws obtained by appeal to more general laws. This is, then, a kind of inference to the best explanation.

4 A PRIORI PSYCHOLOGICAL LAWS?

It is important to note that the only psychological laws considered in the *Psychology* were "laws of the succession of mental phenomena" (Brentano 1874: 66, 91–92, etc./1973a: 47,

63, etc.), that is, the kind of laws that Brentano would later call "genetic laws." It was only in the late 1880s, after Brentano had introduced the distinction between descriptive and genetic psychology, that he began to investigate the nature and epistemological status of psychological laws that are not genetic. This led him to step back and explore the possibility of a psychological a priori. Thus, in the lectures of 1887–8, he presents descriptive psychology as an exact science, as opposed to genetic psychology, which "will presumably have to renounce forever any claim to exactness" (Brentano 1982: 1–5/1995b: 3–7).

Suppose you see a rectangle of which one half is blue and the other is yellow. The chromatic contrast between the two surfaces can be causally explained, say, by the presence of different types of cones in the retina. This explanation can be expressed as an inductive law that associates something physical (the presence of different types of cones) with something mental (the chromatic contrast between the two half rectangles). Such laws, in Brentano's view, pertain to genetic psychology. However, it is plausible to think that something more is required. For the explanandum—the chromatic contrast as a purely mental fact—is somehow presupposed. The genetic psychologist would not investigate the blue–yellow contrast if she had no previous evidence that blue contrasts with yellow. Now, we know that blue contrasts with yellow not by observing the structure of the retina but simply by experiencing the contrast. For Brentano, it is precisely one of the descriptive psychologist's tasks to identify and clarify the mental facts to be then explained genetically. As Brentano's student Carl Stumpf summarizes, "supply is always on the side of phenomenology, and demand on the side of physiology" (Stumpf 1907c: 32).

The descriptive psychologist, like the genetic psychologist, enunciates laws. For example: every judgment is either positive or negative, every feeling requires a presentation, blue is a different color from yellow, green is composed of blue and yellow, and so on. However, both kinds of laws appear to be very different in their epistemological character. The descriptive psychologist's laws are presumably exceptionless. She does not claim, for example, that green is *in most cases*, or *until shown otherwise*, composed of blue and yellow (Brentano 1982: 3–4/1995b: 5–6). Rather, it is a priori self-evident that this is so *in all possible cases*.

The question that immediately arises is how to make the idea of a psychological a priori compatible with empiricism at all. According to Brentano, answering this question requires making clear what a concept actually is, and this requires dispelling many confusions generated by Kant's conception of a priori knowledge.

Fundamental to Brentano's position on this point is his rejection of Kant's synthetic a priori (Brentano 1925, 1956). All a priori knowledge, he claims, consists in analytic judgments and hence in judgments about concepts. This must apply to descriptive psychology as well. Psychological laws such as "there can exist no judgment that is neither positive nor negative" require no more than analyzing concepts, for example that of judgment; they are about relations of *conceptual* inseparability or incompatibility.

At first glance, Brentano's view seems very paradoxical and hardly tenable. On this view, for example, Helmholtz's law of harmonics is an analytic judgment, as are logical and mathematical laws (Brentano 1925: 10). No observation is needed to know that all musical sounds produce harmonics at the octave; it is enough to analyze the concept of sound, namely to "make it distinct in reference to intrinsic features without which it would not be the same concept" (*ibid.*). According to Brentano, this view seems paradoxical only because it is usually assumed, following Kant, that being a priori involves not deriving from an experiential source (or deriving from a nonexperiential source).

On the one hand, it seems obvious that Helmholtz's law—in one sense or another—is empirical. On the other hand, Brentano contends it is a priori and thus merely conceptual. Brentano's claim, however, is that this Kantian understanding of the a priori is misleading and should be abandoned.

In fact, he argues, the laws of descriptive psychology are, without contradiction, both empirical and analytic. His argument is twofold. First, all our concepts are empirical, that is, "either taken immediately from experience *(Anschauung)* or combined out of marks that are taken from experience" (Brentano 1976: 3/1988: 1). Even logical concepts—including Kant's "pure concepts of the understanding"—are actually psychological concepts derived by abstraction from inner experience. Secondly, and more importantly, concepts are mental phenomena; they are *thought* and thus *experienced*. Far from involving turning away from experience, conceptual analysis must consist in making distinct phenomena that are given in inner experience. For example, although (inner) perception is needed in order to *acquire* the concept of judgment, once the concept has been acquired, it is enough to analyze it to realize that all judgments must be either positive or negative.

For this reason, Brentano holds that the core of descriptive psychology's method must be "intuition" in the sense of direct acquaintance or *insight* (*Einsicht*). Inner experience gives us acquaintance with conceptual representations and hence with apodictic relations of inseparability or incompatibility, which are to be distinguished through conceptual analysis. We take it as a priori self-evident—even if indistinctly—that green with no hue of yellow is impossible, that no judgment that is neither positive nor negative can possibly be experienced, and so on.

What is important here is that the a priori laws of descriptive psychology, like those of logic and mathematics, are neither about nonexperiential entities nor obtained from nonexperiential sources. They are a priori judgments about the data of inner experience, and they are won through analysis of inner experience. Thus, Brentano's view of descriptive psychology's laws as a priori is fully consistent with his empiricist rejection of pure concepts and "a priori evidence" (Brentano 1982: 74/1995b: 76; cf. Brentano 1925: 26, 40).[3]

NOTES

1. This terminology goes back to William Hamilton (1859: 85–6, 88, 91), who uses the term "empirical (or descriptive) psychology" as synonymous with "phenomenology of the mind." The term "phenomenal psychology" (*phänomenale Psychologie*) is also used in Brentano (1874: 105/1973a: 72). The term "psychognosy," which Brentano used in place of "descriptive psychology" from 1891 until his death, can be traced back to 1880–81 (Brentano 1982: 1/1995b: 3; Albertazzi 2006: 119).
2. The question of whether "intuition" and a priori knowledge are compatible with empiricism plays a central role in the current epistemological debate. See Bealer 1992, BonJour 1998, Boghossian and Peacocke 2000.
3. I am grateful to Uriah Kriegel for his many helpful comments on earlier versions of this chapter.

4

Brentano on Intentionality

Tim Crane

Brentano's account of what he called *intentionale Inexistenz*—what we now call intentionality—is without question one of the most important parts of his philosophy and one of the most influential ideas in late 19th-century philosophy. Here I will explain how this idea figures in Brentano's central text, *Psychology from an Empirical Standpoint* (Brentano 1995a). I will then briefly explain how Brentano's ideas about intentionality evolved after the first publication of this work in 1874 and how they were then misinterpreted by some influential analytic philosophers.

The *Psychology* is in no sense a finished work, and the text that was translated into English in 1973 has a somewhat complex history and structure. Brentano originally planned a six-volume work. The first two volumes, published together in 1874, form the bulk of what has been passed down to Anglophone readers in the 1973/1995 edition (Brentano 1995a). These are Book One, "Psychology as a Science", and Book Two, "Mental Phenomena in General." Three further volumes were planned on each of the fundamental categories of mental phenomena—presentation, judgement, and the phenomena of love and hate (see Chapter 9)—and the work was to be concluded by a final volume on the immortality of the soul and the mind–body relation. But these last four volumes were never published, though the third exists in draft form.

In 1911, part of Book Two was published under the title *Von der Klassifikation der psychischen Phänomene* ("On the Classification of Mental Phenomena") along with a substantial appendix, in which Brentano developed some of his ideas and indicated some changes of mind. After Brentano's death in 1917, his follower Oskar Kraus produced a second edition of the *Psychology*, published in 1924, which included the appendix from the 1911 book plus some further supplementary essays from Brentano's unpublished writings. The English edition published by Routledge and Kegan Paul in 1973 was the work of three translators: Linda L. McAlister, Antos C. Rancurello, and D. B. Terrell, with McAlister in charge. The translation was based on Kraus's 1924 edition and so included not only the appendix and supplementary essays but also Kraus's footnotes, which attempt to explain Brentano's ideas. These are marked in the English text by numbers, whereas Brentano's footnotes are indicated by asterisks and other footnote symbols. Kraus's footnotes are of some historical interest, but they are not always entirely accurate in their exposition of Brentano's views and so must be approached with care. The supplementary material in the appendices, however, contains many philosophical insights and provides a valuable guide to the ways in which Brentano's thought developed after 1874.

But we must begin with the core of Brentano's thinking: the conception of intentionality in his 1874 work. What was Brentano's overall picture of the mind, and what was the role of the concept of intentionality in this picture? One central aim of the *Psychology* was to establish psychology as a science distinct from philosophy on the one hand and physiology on the other. Psychology is a science whose data come from experience and introspection—hence this is psychology from an *empirical* standpoint.

It's important to recognize the difference between this use of 'empirical' and the contemporary conception of psychology as an empirical science. From today's intellectual perspective, to say that psychology is an empirical science implies that it uses the kinds of methods (e.g., quantitative or statistical methods) which are characteristic of the other natural sciences. From that perspective, Brentano's introspective psychology is no more empirical than William James's. (I ignore here the distinction Brentano makes between descriptive and genetic psychology; see Chapter 3.) But Brentano's use of the word 'empirical' is supposed to indicate that psychology must be based on experience: "experience alone is my teacher," as he says in the foreword to the *Psychology*. From his reflections on experience, Brentano aimed to outline the distinction between psychology and other sciences.

Brentano believed that to make this distinction, there must be a criterion which distinguishes its subject matter from the subject matter of physical science. In Book One of the *Psychology*, Brentano had defined psychology as the "science of mental phenomena," opposing the etymologically more precise definition of it as the "science of the soul." To understand what Brentano meant by his definition, we have to understand 'phenomena' and 'mental'.

In the tradition in which Brentano is writing, 'phenomenon' means *appearance*. Broadly speaking, phenomena or appearances are typically contrasted, in various ways, with *reality*. In the most famous version of this contrast, Kant contrasted phenomena with *noumena*, or "things in themselves." Brentano was an Aristotelian rather than a Kantian, but the emphasis on science's relationship to phenomena rather than things in themselves is nonetheless central to his philosophy. Throughout the first chapter of the *Psychology*, Brentano clearly distinguishes between "that which really and truly exists" and appearances or phenomena. He did think there is an underlying reality behind the phenomena, but this cannot be what he calls an "object of science." Science can only study phenomena. Before we examine what makes a phenomenon mental, we should say something about this use of the terms 'phenomenon' and 'science'.

These two terms should really be understood together. As we have seen, Brentano believed that natural science does not uncover the real nature of things. In particular, physics is not the science of bodies, because even if we can be said to encounter the properties of bodies, "we never encounter that something of which these things are properties" (1995a: 11). All that science can ever discover are the appearances of things: these are the "physical phenomena" like "light, sound, heat, spatial location and locomotion."

As Brentano puts it, "what are physical phenomena if not the colours, sounds, heat and cold, etc., which manifest themselves in our sensations?" (1995a: 69).

Science studies phenomena; that is all that science can do—even if there is an underlying reality behind the phenomena. The differences between sciences reduce to the differences between the phenomena studied by the sciences. The distinction between psychology and physics therefore reduces to the distinction between mental and physical phenomena. It is crucial for understanding Brentano's *Psychology* that this distinction is a distinction among the "data of consciousness" (1995a: 77) and not among entities as we would conceive them in a realist metaphysics. Brentano talks approvingly of Lange's idea of "psychology without a soul" (1995a: 11). What he means here is that psychology can proceed while being indifferent on the question of whether there is a soul: for "whether or not there are souls, there are mental phenomena" (1995a: 18).

Phenomena or appearances are, in a certain way, mind-dependent. However, to say that all phenomena are mind-dependent does not mean that all phenomena are mental. So what, then, are mental phenomena? Brentano's answer to this question is the source of his famous doctrine that "intentional inexistence" is the distinguishing mark of mental phenomena. In the most famous passage in the book, he writes:

> Every mental phenomenon is characterised by what the Scholastics of the Middle Ages called the intentional (or mental) inexistence of an object, and what we might call, though not wholly unambiguously, reference to a content, direction toward an object (which is not to be understood here as meaning a thing) or immanent objectivity. Every mental phenomenon includes something as an object within itself, although they do not all do so in the same way. In presentation, something is presented, in judgement something is affirmed or denied, in love loved, in hate hated, in desire desired, and so on.
>
> (Brentano 1995a: 88)

This complex passage has given rise to much philosophical discussion; here we can start by identifying the key elements of Brentano's terminology. The "object" of a mental phenomenon is what it is directed on. "Intentional inexistence" does not have anything to do with the possible or actual nonexistence of the object of a mental act; rather, it means that the object "exists in" the mental phenomenon itself. Brentano's introduction of the terminology of intentional inexistence does not appeal to, and nor does it presuppose, any distinction between existent and nonexistent objects of thought. That is not the issue.

Since there has been much confusion about this terminology, it is worth dwelling a little on the difference between Brentano's assumptions and the typical assumptions of today's analytic philosophy. These days, the problem of intentionality is introduced against the background of a "commonsense" realism that assumes a realm of ordinary objects that exist independently of our minds, that relations hold between such objects, and that science studies these objects. I have already stressed that this is not Brentano's starting point. As Barry Smith has nicely put it, "one will find no coherent interpretation of Brentano's principle of intentionality so long as one remains within the framework of our usual, commonsensical notions of both the mind and its objects" (1994a: 40). In particular, Brentano's original 1874 doctrine of intentional inexistence has nothing to do with the problem of how we can think about things that do not exist. Although his account of intentionality would certainly yield an account of thought about, say, Pegasus, this is only because it is an account of thought *in general*, and not because Pegasus was what was motivating the account.

The other terms he uses, "relation to a content" and "immanent objectivity," are verbal alternatives to "intentional inexistence." Content and object are the same thing for Brentano, and the "objectivity" of mental phenomena is just a matter of them having an object. The object is immanent in the sense that it is "in" the mental act itself, as an Aristotelian form is immanent in a substance, unlike "transcendent" Platonic forms, which belong outside of the world of experience.

As Smith comments, the thesis that "every mental phenomenon includes something as object within itself" is "to be taken literally—against the grain of a seemingly unshakeable tendency to twist Brentano's words at this point" (Smith 1994a: 40). So, taken literally, the intentional inexistence of an object really does mean its existence *in* the mental act itself. The phenomena on which a mental act is directed may be physical or mental. In the former case, a mental act has as its object something like a sound or a shape or a colour. In the latter case, a mental act would have as its object another mental act. For example, one may think about the mental act of *hearing* a sound. But whether physical or mental, the objects of acts are still phenomena and hence, it is important to emphasize, fundamentally mind-dependent. Brentano was not, therefore, proposing an account of how we think about mind-independent "external" objects. This is because, according to his methodological phenomenalism, the phenomena, which are the only objects for science, are not "external" objects. Physical phenomena have underlying causes, but these underlying causes are not the objects of science. (More later on the notion of "methodological phenomenalism.")

The background to Brentano's view is partly Aristotelian, as Brentano indicates in a well-known footnote (1995a: 88). Aristotle had talked in *De Anima* about how in perception, the perceiving organ takes on the "form" of the perceived object: in seeing something blue, the eye takes on blueness without taking on the matter of blueness. Brentano, like Aquinas, wanted to follow Aristotle in at least this respect: the proper objects of thought and perception—what it is that we are thinking of, and what makes thought possible at all—are actually *immanent* in the act of thinking and do not transcend the mental act. In this respect, objects of thought may be compared to universals on an Aristotelian conception of them, according to which they are immanent in the particulars which instantiate them and do not transcend those particulars.

In his illustration of his doctrine of intentional inexistence in the famous quotation, Brentano uses these examples: in presentation, something is presented; in judgement, something is judged; and in love, something is loved. These examples correspond to Brentano's division of mental phenomena into three fundamental classes (1995a: Book Two, Chapter VI). These are the classes of (1) presentations, (2) judgement, and (3) phenomena of love and hate (which for Brentano includes desire). This classification is original to Brentano, as he himself observes, and a few remarks are necessary in order to elucidate Brentano's conception of the mind.

The word that is normally translated here as "presentation" is *Vorstellung*, a word with a rich philosophical history and many connotations. English translations of Kant typically render it as "representation." The standard translation of Gottlob Frege's famous paper "The Thought" translates *Vorstellung* as "idea" (Frege 1920). Frege distinguished there between thoughts (*Gedanken*), which are objective, mind-independent bearers of truth and falsehood, and ideas, which are subjective and mind-dependent and do not serve as the locus of objective truth. 'Idea' is sometimes used by Brentano's translators; but it is not always a good term for what he meant, since (like 'thought') the English word is more naturally used for what a subjective state is directed on (its content or object), rather than the state itself. Ideas in the ordinary sense can be discussed impersonally—in an encyclopaedia or dictionary, for example—whereas a *Vorstellung* is meant to be something particular to an individual at a given time. As Brentano puts it: "by 'presentation' we do not mean that which is presented, but rather the presenting of it" (1995a: 79).

Presentation, for Brentano, is the fundamental way of being conscious of an object: all other mental phenomena involve presentations, and therefore all mental phenomena are conscious. Judgement, the second fundamental class of mental phenomena, always involves presentation of an object, but this is distinct from the conscious act of judging itself. When one judges X, X is before one's mind in two ways: as the object of the presentation, and as the object of judgement. Brentano's conception of judgement, however, is very different from the conception of many 20th-century philosophers. Those philosophers who take their lead from Frege, G. E. Moore or Bertrand Russell, for example, treat judgement as a relation to a proposition: the kind of thing expressible in a sentence, assessable as true or false. Brentano's theory does not contain propositions and took all judgement to involve affirming or denying the existence of something (see Chapter 10). To judge that it is raining, for example, is to affirm (or better, acknowledge) the existence of rain.

The third main category of mental phenomena, which Brentano calls "the phenomena of love and hate," incorporates not just emotions but also acts of will and desire. These phenomena also involve presentation, as every mental phenomenon does, but they also involve some kind of motivational or affective attitude to the object of the presentation. Much of Book Two of the *Psychology* is concerned with articulating the distinction between the three kinds of mental phenomena (see Mulligan 2004 for a useful discussion).

Two other features of presentation are worth noting here. First, a presentation may be inner or outer. An inner presentation may be a feeling or an awareness of some mental act; the objects of inner perception are thinking, feeling, and willing. The objects of outer presentation or perception are warmth, colour, sound, and so on (i.e., physical phenomena). A distinctive feature of his view is that every mental act is also directed on itself (although in what Brentano called a "secondary" sense) as well as on its primary object. Second, in the 1874 book, Brentano held that every mental activity involves an emotional or affective element, but he later came to abandon this view and to hold instead that some sensations have no such element. He makes clear this change of mind in the 1911 edition of selections from the *Psychology* (1995a: 276).

The picture of Brentano's 1874 views that I have sketched here is in some ways foreign to contemporary discussions of intentionality, which, as noted above, tend to assume a commonsense realism about the material world, often accompanied by a physicalist conception of the findings of science. But placed in wider context, the views should not be so strange. For Brentano's conception of science has a lot in common with the kind of phenomenalism which was common in 19th-century philosophy of science, which survived into the 20th century in logical positivism and which has echoes in W. V. Quine's claim that the purpose of science is to explain and predict the course of experience. At the beginning of the *Psychology*, Brentano mentions Mill approvingly as "one of the most important advocates of psychology as a purely phenomenalistic science" (1995a: 14), and he expressed sympathy with Ernst Mach's phenomenalism on a number of occasions (cf. Smith 1994a: 41, n.8).

Brentano was not a phenomenalist, because phenomenalism holds that the world is constructed from phenomena (e.g., sense-data). Yet as we saw, Brentano did believe that there is a world that transcends the phenomena; physical phenomena are "signs of something real, which, through its causal activity, produces presentations of them" (1995a: 19). This is what distinguishes Brentano from phenomenalism proper: he believes that there is something beyond the phenomena, although we can never know it through science. As far as science is concerned, though, phenomenalism might as well be true. Peter Simons has helpfully labelled Brentano's view *methodological phenomenalism* (1995: xvii).

By the time the 1911 book came out, Brentano had changed his mind on a number of important issues. In the preface to this 1911 edition, describing the ways in which his views had evolved, Brentano wrote that "one of the most important innovations is that I am no longer of the opinion that mental relation can have something other than a thing as its object" (1995a: xxvi). This is Brentano's "reism," the idea that only concrete particular things are the objects of thought (see Chapter 13). This was a departure from the view expressed in the 1874 version, which allowed things belonging to many different ontological categories to be objects of thought.

Another way in which his view changed was in his rejection of the idea that all mental activity involves a genuine relation to an object. In the supplementary remarks published in the 1911 book, he writes:

> What is characteristic of every mental activity is, as I believe I have shown, the reference to something as an object. In this respect, every mental activity seems to be something relational.... If I take something relative from among the broad class of comparative relations, something larger or smaller for example, then, if the larger thing exists, the smaller one must exist too. If one house is larger than another house, the other house must also exist and have a size.... It is entirely different with mental reference. If someone thinks of something, the one who is thinking must certainly exist, but the object of his thinking need not exist at all.... For this reason, one could doubt whether we are really dealing with something relational here, and not, rather, with something somewhat similar to something relational in a certain respect, which might therefore be called "quasi-relational."
>
> (1995a: 272)

This is a clear departure from the relational conception of intentionality advanced in 1874 and shows similarities with the realist conception of intentionality and intentional objects famously defended by Edmund Husserl in his *Logical Investigations* (1901/1970). Husserl had argued there that although we might say that the nonexistent intentional object of a mental act (e.g., the god Jupiter) has "mental inexistence" in the act, the truth of the matter is that this "immanent, mental object" is not "really immanent or mental. But it also does not exist extramentally, it does not exist at all" (Husserl 1901/1970: V, §11). The object of thought, existent or not, transcends the mental act. And the mental act is not essentially constituted by the relation to the object. For Husserl, as for Brentano after 1911, the mental act cannot be relational but only "quasi-relational" (*Relativliches*).

So what are these nonexistent objects of thought? Later in the supplementary remarks, Brentano writes that

> all mental references refer to things. In many cases, the things to which we refer do not exist. But we are accustomed to saying that they then have being as objects. This is a loose use of the verb "to be" which we permit with impunity for the sake of convenience, just as we allow ourselves to speak of the sun "rising" and "setting."
> (1995a: 291)

Brentano does not allow himself to follow his student Alexius Meinong (1910) and his "theory of objects," which aimed to investigate intentional objects regardless of their existence. Talk of there "being" such objects Brentano saw as a kind of loose talk; all it really means is that a thinker is representing something (1995a: 291).

Brentano's influence on the phenomenological school founded by Husserl is well known. It took a little longer for his ideas to be introduced into analytic philosophy. This can largely be credited to Roderick Chisholm, who was unusual among mainstream American philosophers of the time in having an active interest in phenomenology and published various things in the 1950s that took inspiration from Brentano (see Chapter 38). Chisholm's work, though valuable in itself, has led to a number of persistent misunderstandings of Brentano in the analytic tradition. His famous paper "Sentences about Believing" (Chisholm 1955–6), for example, attempted to reformulate Brentano's criterion as a way of distinguishing between sentences describing mental phenomena and sentences describing physical phenomena, and of demonstrating the irreducibility of the mental to the physical, and hence the falsity of physicalism.

The criteria Chisholm came up with were in fact criteria for nonextensional linguistic contexts, usually known as *intensional* contexts: the failure of truth-functionality, the failure of substitution of co-referring terms to preserve truth-value, and the failure of existential generalisation. (On the relation between intentionality and intensional contexts, see Crane 2001, Chapter 1, and Searle 1983, Chapter 1.) But Brentano's distinction was not a distinction between linguistic contexts, and the idea that the mark of mental phenomena may be captured in this way is totally foreign to the project of his *Psychology*. Moreover, Brentano did not use his criterion to refute physicalism. Nonetheless, analytic philosophers persisted for a few decades in associating Brentano's ideas with Chisholm's, which only obstructed the proper understanding of Brentano.

A striking example of this can be found in W. V. Quine's *Word and Object* (1960). In a famous and influential discussion of intension and meaning, Quine makes two claims about Brentano. The first is that "the Scholastic word 'intentional' was revived by Brentano in connection with the verbs of propositional attitude and related verbs … —'hunt,' 'want' etc." The second is that "there remains a thesis of Brentano's, illuminatingly developed of late by Chisholm, that … there is no breaking out of the intentional vocabulary by explaining its members in other terms" (Quine 1960: 219). As should be obvious from what I have said so far, both these claims are false. First, Brentano did not revive the Scholastic word 'intentional' to describe propositional attitude verbs, since as we saw, Brentano did not believe in propositional attitudes in anything like the 20th-century sense. (Curiously, the example of "hunt" is from Quine's own work (1956), not from Brentano's; and nor could it be since hunting is not a mental phenomenon.) Second,

Brentano's thesis of the irreducibility of the intentional was not a claim about whether one can break out of the intentional vocabulary. It was not a claim about vocabulary at all; it was a claim about the categorial distinction between mental and physical phenomena. The natural conclusion to draw from this is that Quine had never read Brentano but took the description of his views wholesale from Chisholm.

Quine's main concern was not, of course, the interpretation of Brentano but the theory of meaning. However, *Word and Object* was an influential book, and inevitably the misunderstandings embodied in these casual remarks spread like diseases. To take just one example: in a famous paper, "Mental Events," Donald Davidson proposed a "test of the mental" according to which the mental's distinguishing feature is that "it exhibits what Brentano called intentionality." He explains this by saying that "we may call those verbs mental that express propositional attitudes like believing, intending, desiring, hoping, knowing, perceiving, noticing, remembering, and so on" (Davidson 1980: 211). Here again we find mixed up with a real thesis of Brentano's—that intentionality is the mark of the mental—the idea that intentional verbs are those that express propositional attitudes. Brentano's thesis was about phenomena, not about verbs. And none of the mental phenomena in Brentano's three categories—presentation, judgement, and emotion—are propositional attitudes. Indeed, the notion of a propositional attitude itself was only introduced into philosophy some 30 years after Brentano's *Psychology* was first published, in a 1904 paper by Bertrand Russell ("belief is a certain attitude towards propositions, which is called knowledge when they are true, error when they are false" [Russell 1904: 523]). Neither the term 'propositional attitude' nor the concept were current when Brentano wrote his *Psychology*; Davidson's association of the idea with Brentano is as anachronistic as it is incorrect.

The problem here is not simply a failure in scholarship. It has also led to a misconception of the subject matter itself. The association of the idea of intentionality with the logical properties of certain verbs took years to break. In recent years, rather than simply relying on Chisholm, Quine and Davidson, analytic philosophers have been reading Brentano's actual texts for themselves, and finding inspiration in them for new developments in the study of intentionality and consciousness. There is reason to be optimistic that a better understanding of Brentano's idea of intentionality is now emerging from this work.[1]

NOTE

1. Thanks to Uriah Kriegel for very helpful comments and to Dan Brigham for discussion of the "propositional attitudes." This paper was written with the help of a grant from the John Templeton Foundation, New Directions in the Study of the Mind.

5

Brentano on Consciousness

Mark Textor

Consider a perceptual activity such as seeing a colour, hearing a tone, tasting a flavour. How are these activities related to one's awareness of them? I will use Brentano's struggle with this question to guide the reader through the development of his view on consciousness. My starting point will be Brentano's book *Die Psychologie des Aristoteles* (Brentano 1867), in which he developed an inner sense view of consciousness (§§1–2). Brentano's early view is underexplored in the literature but is crucial for understanding the development of his thought on the matter. In his major work *Psychologie vom Empirischen Standpunkt* (1874), he rejected the existence of an inner sense: the exercises of our five senses yield awareness of the world (or at least of intentional objects) as well as awareness of these perceptions. This same-level view of consciousness has been explored and developed by contemporary philosophers of mind. I will discuss the arguments that moved Brentano to change his mind, outline the view, and, finally, respond to Husserl's influential criticism of Brentano's view (§§3–5).

1 BRENTANO ON THE SENSE OF SENSATION

Let's start with the question that Brentano (inspired by Aristotle) wanted to answer. Imagine, for instance, that you see a green leaf in good light. If the question is raised what colour the leaf is, your perception puts you in a position to answer this question knowledgably. Furthermore, you do not need to do anything further to be in a position to answer the further question "How do you know this?" Seeing the green leaf provides perceptual knowledge of the colour and knowledge of the ongoing seeing itself. We would be astonished if someone—looking at a green leaf—said, "The leaf is green, but now let me find out how I know this." Locke aimed to capture this observation as follows:

> [It is] impossible for any one to perceive, without perceiving, that he does perceive. When we see, hear, smell, taste, feel, meditate, or will anything, we know that we do so.
>
> (Locke 1690, II, xxvii, 9)

If we take Locke by his word, he tried to articulate the observation about perception in terms of perceiving-that:

(PP1) Necessarily, if S perceives x, then S perceives *that S perceives x*.

Now, one perceives that p if, and only if, one judges that p on the strength of one's perceiving. For instance, to use one of Dretske's examples, I can see that the tank is half-empty without the tank itself looking some way to me: I just need to see the gasometer. All I need to do is to acquire the knowledge that the tank is half-empty by seeing. Locke's (PP1) is therefore a controversial philosophical thesis that goes beyond the observation we started from. *Prima facie*, one wants to credit some subjects with the ability to perceive something even though they are not able to *judge* that they themselves are perceiving.

(PP2) is not subject to this difficulty:

(PP2) Necessarily, if S perceives x, then S perceives S's perceiving of x.

However, what is it to *perceive* one's perceiving? Consider your seeing a green leaf again. The colour looks a particular way to you; your seeing green doesn't. Hence, if one perceives one's seeing at all, it must be perceived by a different sense than sight. In his early work *Die Psychologie des Aristoteles*, Brentano developed this argument in detail:

> Because we sense (*empfinden*) that we see and hear, the question arises whether we perceive this [that we see and hear] with sight and hearing, or with another sense. If we perceive by means of sight itself that we see, we must see that we see, for the activity (*Tätigkeit*) of this sense is seeing, and the seeing as seeing should therefore belong either to the distinctive object of sight or to one of the common objects of sight.
>
> (Brentano 1867: 85–6; my translation)

Brentano talked here about perceiving *that one sees*. But the point under consideration does not arise for perceiving *that* one perceives. He was not sensitive to the distinction between perceiving an object and perceiving-that. But we can reformulate his thought in a charitable way as follows:

Extra-Sense Argument

(P1) We perceive seeing when we see.
(P2) Either we perceive seeing by sight or by another sense.
(P3) The distinctive object of sight is colour; by means of sight, one can also perceive shape and size together with colour.

(P4) Seeing is not coloured, nor has it form or size that can be seen together with colour.
(C1) Hence, we don't perceive seeing by sight.
(C2) Hence, we perceive seeing by another sense.
(P5) Seeing is not a distinctive object of any of the other four senses.
(C3) Therefore, we don't perceive seeing by any of the five known senses.
(C4) Hence, we perceive seeing by an extra sense.

Brentano's extra-sense argument relied on an Aristotelian principle for the individuation of senses (see Sorabji 1971: 60ff). A sense is a power of perception (*Empfindungsvermögen*) (1867: 82). Different powers of perception are exercised in different acts of perception, and acts of perception are distinguished in terms of their objects, namely properties of perceptible objects. Sight is the power to perceive colours, taste the power to perceive flavours, hearing the power to perceive sounds, and so on. The well-known problem with this proposal is that we can see a shape as well as feel it. In order to distinguish senses in line with our intuitive way of counting senses, we need at least to invoke how the object perceived is given to us: sight is the power to perceive shapes together with colours by the way they look, touch is the power to perceive shapes by the way they feel when touched, and so on.

If we accept the Aristotelian criterion for counting and individuating senses, the inner sense has a distinctive object. What is it? Sensation, answered Brentano. The sense under consideration is the sense of *sensation* (*Sinn der Sensation*). He wrote about this sense:

> Just as the colours are the distinctive object of sight, its distinctive objects are solely sensations. But by perceiving that we see the white and taste the sweet, and distinguish these sensations, it makes simultaneously the analogous difference between the white and the sweet known to us [kennen lernen].
> (Brentano 1867: 93; my translation)

What are sensations (*Empfindungen*)? "Sensation" seems here to be nothing but a catch-all for perceptions of different senses. According to the last quote, the sense of sensation is the sense by means of which we perceive that we see, taste, and so on; that is, the sense of sensation provides us with propositional knowledge. If this were correct, it would be difficult to see how this sense could also make the difference between white and sweet known to us. For in order to know the difference between white and sweet, I must actually see white and taste sweet; propositional knowledge about seeing and tasting is insufficient. This speaks in favour of strengthening passages in which Brentano speaks of the sense of sensations as a sense by means of which we perceive sensations (See, for instance, Brentano 1867: 95).

How does the sense of sensation make not only the difference between the *perceptions* of white and sweet but also the difference between the *properties* white and sweet known to us? Brentano held that the perceptions of, for instance, colours, stand in relations to each other that are similar to the relations that obtain between the colours perceived. Because of these analogies, distinguishing between the perceptions of white and sweet is also distinguishing between the white and the sweet (Brentano 1867: 93). This has some independent plausibility. Consider experiential recall. If I can episodically recall *seeing* red and *seeing* blue, I can, *ceteris paribus*, also recall how the *red* and *blue* looked to me and can distinguish between them.

However, Brentano still owes us an informative answer to the question as to how this is possible. Aristotle said that when an object looks green to one, one's seeing itself is "in a way coloured." In his theory of the sense of sensation, Brentano will have had this remark in mind. Caston (2002: 790–1) spells Aristotle's remark out by proposing that when something looks green to me, my seeing is green in the following extended sense: it has a particular what-it-is-likeness property that can only be exhaustively described by mentioning green. Possessing a particular what-it is-likeness property (phenomenal character) does not make my seeing green visible or look a certain way, but its phenomenal character distinguishes it from other perceptions. If the sense of sensation distinguishes between perceptions in terms of their phenomenal character, we have the beginning of a story how the sense of sensation can make us aware of relations between the properties perceived. If I am, for example, aware of seeing blue and seeing red, I am aware of the phenomenal character of these acts and thereby aware of the difference between red and blue things in terms of how they look. This idea needs further development and, as far as I know, Brentano did not provide any. However, Brentano's discussion of the sense of sensation introduced an important philosophical theme: awareness of perceiving an object and awareness of the object perceived are connected. In *Die Psychologie des Aristoteles*, awareness of perceiving makes distinctions between objects perceived known. In *Psychologie vom empirischen Standpunkt*, an even tighter connection will emerge.

2 THE SENSE OF SENSATION = THE COMMON SENSE

The assumption of a sense of sensation seems *ad hoc* if there is no independent motivation. Brentano argued that we have independent reason to assume that there is a common sense. The sense of sensation, as it turns out, is the same sense as the common sense. Since we have independent reason to accept a common sense, we have an independent reason to believe in the sense of sensation (Brentano 1867: 87f.).

What is the common sense? The common sense is the sense by means of which we make comparisons "across" different, more specific senses. The example of the comparison between the white and the sweet was already used in the previous section. Let us flesh it out a bit. Imagine you drink a White Russian and you try to fully appreciate all aspects of the drink. You can *perceive* the difference between the white colour and the sweetness of the White Russian. But the difference between white and sweet is perceived neither by sight nor by taste. Aquinas used observations of this kind to connect inner and common sense:

> [N]either sight nor taste can discern white from sweet: because what discerns between two things must know both. Wherefore the discerning judgement must be assigned to the common sense; to which, as to a common term, all apprehensions of the senses must be referred: and by which, again, all the intentions of the senses are perceived; as when someone sees that he sees.
> (Aquinas 1265ff, 78, 4, ad.2)

The inner sense perceives that we see the white as well as that we taste the sweet. If the inner sense knows the perceptions *and* their objects, it can serve as the common sense by means of which one can compares qualities across sense modalities.

Brentano (1867: 87) developed this idea. Consider his sense of sensation. The inner sense has simultaneously access to perceivings that are exercises of different senses such as seeing a colour and tasting a flavour. It can distinguish between them and thereby come to know relations between their objects. Hence we get:

> Sense of sensations = the power to perceive simultaneously perceivings in virtue of their phenomenal character = power to come to know relations between the qualities that are the objects of the perceived perceptions = common sense.

Hence, if there is a sense of sensation, it does what the common sense is supposed to do. Therefore, evidence for the existence of the common sense is evidence for the existence of the sense of sensation.

Joint and multidimensional perception is a real phenomenon. But does it require a new sense? Why can't the joint perception of white and sweet be the simultaneous exercise of sight and taste? If the senses collaborate, no further distinct sense is needed. Aristotle himself seems to leave this possibility open:

> Therefore discrimination between white and sweet cannot be effected by two agencies which remain separate: both the qualities discriminated must be present to something that is one and single.
> (*De Anima*, 426b1, 9–18; Hamlyn's translation)

The "one and single" thing need not be a sense. Just as different rivers may supply the same lake, different senses may work as a team to produce joint consciousness of their respective objects.

Brentano argued that the common sense is a faculty that is distinct from the five senses. He rejects the "sense collaboration" thesis:

> [C]an we perhaps perceive the distinction between white and sweet by means of simultaneous sensations of two different senses? Certainly not. This is as little possible as it is possible for two different people to be able to recognise the difference between two objects if each of them senses one of those objects.
> (Brentano 1867: 87; my translation)

Brentano's analogy between different senses and different people does not support his conclusion. Different people may work together to achieve a common aim: I read the map, you steer and together we manoeuvre the car to the right destination. Why should different senses not also jointly contribute to one state of awareness? Brentano is missing a premise. Tye expresses the missing premise as follows:

> If loudness is experientially "trapped" in one sense and yellowness in another, how can the two be experienced together?
> (Tye 2007: 289)

Talk of being "experientially trapped" is suggestive but hard to spell out in a satisfactory manner.

I conclude that Brentano has not made a good case for the assumption of a distinct common sense and, in turn, for a sense of sensation. This speaks in favour of his later view. For, as we will now see, he will go on and deny the existence of the sense of sensation.

3 BRENTANO AGAINST THE INNER SENSE VIEW

According to Brentano, Aristotle wavered on the question of whether we perceive perceiving by means of a further sense or not. Sometimes Aristotle seems to say NO, sometimes YES. In his *Die Psychologie des Aristoteles*, Brentano tried to work out the positive answer with his sense of sensation view. Seven years later in *Psychologie vom empirischen Standpunkt*, Brentano retracted this proposal. Looking back, he wrote:

> It seems that [Aristotle's] general theory of mental faculties can be more easily reconciled with this sort of view [that there is a sense of sensation]. It is for this reason that in my *Psychologie des Aristoteles* I went along with the majority of his commentators and ascribed it to him. However, since the passage of *De Anima*, III, 2, speaks so clearly against it, and since it is highly unlikely that there is a contradiction among his different statements on this point, I adhere now to the conception presented here in the text.
>
> (Brentano 1874: 185-6fn/1995: 102fn)

Brentano provided several considerations that strengthen the case against the sense of sensation theory and that indirectly make it implausible to attribute it to Aristotle.

Consider hearing and seeing a band play. Here the scene seen and sounds heard are, as one might intuitively put it, in the foreground: *they* are seen and heard together. The mental acts are not primary, qualities like colour are; we perceive them, and we do so not in virtue of relations they bear to our perceptions. However, in the theory of *Die Psychologie des Aristoteles*, the joint perception of qualities was described as a product of the sense of sensation. By means of it, we were supposed to perceive simultaneously seeing and hearing. We would thereby also apprehend relations between the perceived qualities. Now Brentano thinks that his former common sense/sense of sensation view singled out the wrong objects as primary. In joint perception, sounds and etc. are perceived, *not* our perceptions of them.

In *Psychologie*, Brentano gave pride of place to Aristotelian arguments that speak *against* the inner sense theory.[1] He referred his readers to Aristotle's *De Anima* book 3.2, where Aristotle seems to reject the assumption of an inner sense:

> Since we perceive that we see and hear, it must either be by sight that one perceives that one sees or by another [sense]. But in that case there will be the same [sense] for sight and the colour which is the subject for sight. So either there will be two [senses] for the same thing or [the sense] will be the one for itself.
>
> Again if the sense concerned with sight were indeed different from sight, either there will be an infinite regress or there will be some [sense] which is concerned with itself, so that we had best admit this of the first in the series.
>
> ($425^b 12$–17; Hamlyn's translation)

Aristotle suggested here two arguments against the inner sense theory: the infinite regress argument and the duplication argument.

David Woodruff Smith and others take Brentano to use the infinite regress argument to argue for his view:

> Reviving an ancient argument, Brentano reasoned that the secondary presentation cannot be a second presentation, a reflection or judgement upon the primary presentation. For that would lead to an infinite regress […].
>
> (Smith 1986: 149)

A presentation P1 is supposed to be conscious if and only if there is a "secondary presentation" P2: a presentation directed upon P1. If the secondary presentation is a "second," distinct presentation, a vicious infinite regress threatens. No such regress threatens if P1 presents, among other things, itself.

I am doubtful, however, whether this is Brentano's argument. He expected his reader to be initially inclined to take any mental act to be conscious:

> Only when one calculates for him that there must a threefold consciousness, like three boxes, one inside the other (*dreifach ineinandergeschachteltes*), and that besides the first idea and the idea of the idea he must also have an idea of the idea of the idea, will he become wavering.
>
> (Brentano 1874: 182/1995a: 100; my translation)

The regress threat is an obstacle that needs to be removed to clear the way for accepting the view that every mental act is conscious; but it is not used by Brentano in an argument in favor of his positive view.

Brentano's argument for his new view, I submit, is a development of Aristotle's duplication argument (Brentano 1874: 176–9/1995a: 97–8). Anton Marty, a devoted follower, expounded Brentano's argument in an accessible way:

> We hear some note, we have therefore a presentation of a note and are conscious of this presentation. How are these two presentations related to each other? Are these two different mental acts? If this were the case, one would have to present the note twice. For it belongs indirectly to the presentation of the note. But inner experience shows without doubt that we present the tone only once. From this follows that the presentation of the tone and the presentation of the presentation of the tone are not two, but one act. The first presentation coalesces in the second and is so intimately connected with it that it contributes to its being. Only one mental phenomenon, only one act of presenting is there, but in virtue of one [act] two things come about.
>
> (Marty 2011: 28; my translation)

In schematic form, the argument is this:

Brentano's Duplication Argument

(P1) Assume for reductio that S's perceiving S perceiving x is distinct from S's perceiving x.

(P2) S's perceiving S perceiving x is directly of S's perceiving x as well as indirectly of x.
(C1) Hence, when S perceives S's perceiving x, x is presented twice: once in S's perceiving S perceiving x, and a second time in S's perceiving x.
(P3) There is no double presentation of x when S perceives S's perceiving x.
(C2) Hence, S's perceiving S perceiving x is the same act S's perceiving x.

(P1) is set up for refutation. Brentano, like Aristotle before him, took (P3) to be phenomenologically plausible. When we are aware of perceiving an object, the object is not given to us "twice." The crucial premise of Brentano's argument is (P2). Is it better justified and more plausible than (P1)? Brentano thought so: when we are aware of hearing a tone, it

> seems evident (*einleuchtend*) that the tone is not only contained as presented in the hearing but also contained in the simultaneous presentation of the hearing.
> (Brentano 1874: 171/1995a: 94; my translation)

In *Psychologie*, Brentano left it at that. But (P2) is in need of further argument and clarification. For Brentano's opponents hold that awareness provides us *only* with access to mental acts and not *also* with access to their objects. Further argument is needed.

How can S's perceiving S perceiving x be the same act as S's perceiving x? When we, for example, distinguish between S's awareness of hearing the note F and S's hearing F, we make a conceptual distinction:

> The presentation of the tone and the presentation of the presentation of the tone form one single mental phenomenon, it is only by considering it in its relation to two different objects, one of which is a physical phenomenon and the other a mental phenomenon, that we divide it conceptually into two presentations.
> (Brentano 1874: 179/1995a: 98)

Let us work through Brentano's example of hearing a tone to get a grip on his positive view. "Hearing tone F" and "awareness of hearing tone F" express different concepts of the same act. The act has two objects: the tone and itself.[2] Each concept conceptualises the act with respect to one these objects: namely as awareness of the note (hearing) and as awareness of itself (awareness of hearing). The concepts are not concepts of two distinct acts that are parts of one complex act. For otherwise the note F were presented twice: once in the subact hearing tone F and then again in the subact awareness of hearing tone F.

If the act is atomic, how can it answer to different concepts? Compare the geometrical point a: it has no spatial parts, yet it may be *the left neighbour of point b* and *the right neighbour of point c*. In a similar way, conscious hearing of F is atomic yet related to different objects, and therefore it can be conceptualised in different ways.

How can an *atomic* act have more than one object? Compare the plural demonstrative 'these'. It is syntactically simple, yet in the right context of utterance, it refers to some things and not just one. If plural reference without syntactic complexity is possible, why not plural intentionality without mental complexity?

In conclusion, Brentano arrived at a distinctive version of what is now termed the *same-order view* of consciousness. Levine (2006, 190) distinguishes within same-order views between two- and one-vehicle views. According to the first kind of view, conscious mental acts are complex and have a part that presents the complex; according to the second kind of view, one act has two propositional contents, one of them directed on the mental act. For the reasons given above, Brentano's same-order view is neither a two- nor a one-vehicle view.

Brentano took his conclusion also to show that no vicious infinite regress ensues if all mental acts are conscious (see Brentano 1874: 182/1995a: 99–100). If perceiving x is the same act as awareness of perceiving x, no distinct further mental act is required to make perceiving x conscious. However, in the German-speaking literature on consciousness, it is a standard complaint that Brentano's view gives rise to a "revenge regress" because the awareness of perceiving must present itself *as a presentation of itself*.[3] Whether Brentano must accept this characterization of awareness is controversial.

4 IS ALL CONSCIOUSNESS CONSCIOUS?

Brentano's conceptual division view was intended by him as a contribution to the metaphysics of mind (Brentano 1874: 198–9/1995a: 109). We want our metaphysics of mind to be in harmony with what awareness reveals to us about the mind. Brentano's view is progress in this respect. If awareness of hearing and hearing are only conceptually different, then one cannot be aware of hearing without hearing actually going on. But what about the other direction? Is every mental act conscious in the sense of it being an object of a mental act, namely itself? Brentano's answer was a clear YES.[4] He wrote, for instance, in a letter to Stumpf (8.5.1871):

> No presentation (*Vorstellung*) without knowledge of the presentation [...] and no thinking without any emotion. Yesterday I found this acknowledged most determinately by a number of writers, among them Hamilton and Lotze. The feeling belongs to the act as a most intimate accessory (*aczessorium*) in the same way as the cognition (*Erkenntnis*).
> (Brentano and Stumpf 2014: 49; my translation)

In *Psychologie*, Brentano argued that every mental phenomenon presents itself, acknowledges itself and emotionally evaluates itself. Later, he came to abandon the claim that all mental phenomena involve an emotion toward themselves (Brentano 1911a).

How does one decide whether all mental acts are conscious or not? Brentano took the burden of proof to lie with philosophers who hold that there are unconscious mental acts. Why should one accept this view? Because, some argued, the assumption that all mental acts are conscious leads to a vicious infinite regress. We have seen in Section 3 how Brentano proposed to disarm this objection. In *Psychologie*, Brentano responded also to arguments to the effect that the assumption of unconscious mental acts pulls its weight in psychological explanation and is therefore empirically plausible (see Brentano 1874, II, Chap. 2, § 4–6.) These arguments often have the following form: the best explanation of the occurrence of or the properties of a mental phenomenon posits an unconscious mental phenomenon. Hence, there are unconscious mental acts. In response, Brentano argued that the explanation proposed is not the best one. There are equally good explanations that don't posit unconscious perceptions.

According to Brentano, a number of additional and unwarranted assumptions lead to the conclusion that there are unconscious mental acts. For example, if one takes (a) consciousness to consist in judgement and (b) judgement to consist in predication, one will reject the view that every mental act is conscious. How could the sensations and pains of a baby on this view be conscious? Brentano's response is to reject (b) on independent grounds (see Chapter 10) and keep (a) (Brentano 1874: 200/1995a: 141). Likewise, if one takes consciousness to require attention, one will also find the thesis that every mental act is conscious hard to believe. Brentano's response is to disentangle consciousness and attention:[5]

> If one takes into account that being co-given in consciousness [*mit ins Bewusstsein fallen*] is different from being specifically noticed, and from being comprehended with clarity which allows a correct determination and description, then the illusion that some psychical activity can be devoid of the secondary psychical relation disappears completely and with ease.
> (Brentano 1982: 23/2002: 25–6. I have changed the translation.)

5 HUSSERL AGAINST BRENTANO: THE OBJECTIFICATION OBJECTION

Brentano held that every mental act is consciousness of something and of itself. *Prima facie*, the act presents itself in the same way as it presents an object distinct from itself. Husserl, the founder of phenomenology, argued that Brentano was wrong about this. When I am aware of a note, it is given to me *as an object*; when I am aware of my hearing the note, it is not given to me *as an object* (see Zahavi 2004 §iv). Let us first explain and motivate the objection and then see whether it meets its target.

For Brentano, mental acts are directed toward objects. Husserl used the picture of directing something to a goal to bring out what, in his view, Brentano had missed. Mental acts are not only directed on objects; they aim for something and they can be fulfilled (Husserl 1913a: 379). For example, we desire food, and the desire is satisfied when we have eaten and we are aware of this fact. Object perception is a further example. When I perceive the house in perceiving its front, I am aware that further perceptions of it are available: I can see the house *better*; I can see *more* of it. In order to see the house better, I must have a sense of tracking it through different perceptions in which it may appear differently. For Husserl, we *experience* identity of object through changes of appearance:

> We experience "consciousness of identity," that is, the presumption that one apprehends identity.
> (Husserl 1913a: 382; my translation)

It seems to us that we perceive *one and the same object* through changes of appearances because in perceiving an object we have expectations (in a broad sense) about how it will appear differently when we perceive it from different standpoints and in different conditions.

Husserl explains "appearing as *an object*" with respect to object perception:

> The sensations and similarly the acts that "apprehend" or "apperceive" them are here *experienced*, but they *appear not as objects* (*erscheinen nicht gegenständlich*); they are *not* seen, heard, or *perceived* by means of any "sense." In contrast, *objects* appear, are perceived, but they are *not experienced*. Obviously we exclude here the case of adequate perception.
>
> (Husserl 1913a: 385; my translation)

Something appears to us as an object, argued Husserl, if and only if we experience it as the same in changing appearances and expect such changes when perceiving it. This makes good intuitive sense if we take an object to be a mind-independent particular. According to Husserl, perception is not only of such particulars, but in perception they seem to us also to be mind-independent particulars. For example, it seems to us that there is more to such objects than their current appearance. Husserl held that this is not the case for the appearances themselves and the mental acts that "interpret" them. There are no changing appearances through which we are aware of the same expectation, judgement, sensation or feeling.

Husserl hit on an important distinction between those perceptions in which something is given to us as an object and other forms of awareness in which we are directed upon something without it being given to us as an object. He argued further that mental acts as well as physical objects can be given to us as objects when we reflect on them (1913b: 240–2). But crucially, only mental acts can be *experienced*, that is, not presented to us as objects. We experience mental acts when we are conscious of them and then they are not given *as objects*.

Whether Husserl's criticism is plausible depends on the plausibility of his assumptions. For instance, are there nonintentional sensations, as Husserl claimed? Clearly, Brentano didn't think so (Chapter 4). Whether Husserl's criticism hits its target depends on whether his understanding of Brentano's talk of consciousness as perceptual awareness of *objects* is right. Husserl takes Brentano to commit himself to the view that we are not only aware of a hearing but also aware of it *as an object* in the sense explained above. However, Brentano seemed to appreciate the difference between perception in which something appears as an object and awareness that is not "objectifying," although he framed it in a different terminology. In *Psychologie*, he wrote:

> It is a peculiar feature of inner perception that it can never become inner observation. Objects which one, as one puts it, perceives outwardly can be observed; one focuses one's attention completely on them in order to apprehend them accurately (*genau*). *But with objects of inner perception this is absolutely impossible.* [...] It is only while our attention is turned toward a different object that we are able to perceive, incidentally, the mental processes which are directed toward that object.
>
> (Brentano 1874: 41/1995a: 22; my translation and emphasis)

If we are aware of a mental act, we are not aware of it as an object (in Husserl's sense). For instance, hearing and tone are given together, but only the tone can be observed; it "appears as an object" that we can explore further and seems to us to be the same in different appearances. Brentano did not articulate this distinction fully, but nothing he said seems to me incompatible with Husserl's claim that in awareness, mental acts do not appear as objects when we don't reflect on them. Brentano's theory of consciousness may be incomplete, but nothing stands in the way of completing it.[6]

NOTES

1. For discussions of Brentano's *Psychologie* view of consciousness, see Brandl 2013, Kriegel 2003, and Thomasson 2000.
2. The tone is the primary object of the act, but the act has also an intentional correlate—the tone heard—that exists whenever the acts exists. See Brentano 1982:21/2002: 23–4.
3. See Frank 2012 and the references given there. See also Zahavi 2006, sect. 2, and the response by Williford 2006.
4. For discussion, see Kriegel 2013.
5. See Textor 2015 for a reconstruction of Brentano's view of attention.
6. I am grateful to Jessica Leech, Maik Niemeck, Bruno Leclercq, and Uriah Kriegel for criticism, comments and suggestions.

6

Brentano on the Unity of Consciousness

Barry Dainton

Over the course of an average day, the character and contents of our streams of consciousness vary a good deal, depending on where we are and what we are doing. We all know what it's like to spend a minute or so standing in our bathrooms brushing our teeth. The kind of experiences we have then are very different—in all sorts of obvious ways—from those we have when we are taking a shower (or lying in a bath, or swimming in the sea), or walking along a busy city street while listening to music through headphones (or along a mountain trail in silence), or sitting quietly reading a book, alone with our thoughts. But although the contents of our consciousness vary enormously, in one respect they are always the same: at any moment during our waking hours, everything we are experiencing is *unified*. Our bodily sensations are not experienced separately from our visual and auditory experiences or our conscious thoughts, mental images, and emotional feelings. From moment to moment, all the different forms of experience we are enjoying occur together as parts or aspects of a single unified conscious state.

This pervasive unity is such a familiar feature of consciousness that we may rarely pause to reflect on it, but it is a crucially important feature. If it were absent, the overall character of our experience would be radically—unimaginably—different. No sooner is the importance of the unity of consciousness recognised than questions arise. How is this mode of unity best characterized? How does it compare to other forms of unity, such as those to be found in the atoms in a brick, or the cells in our bodies? What explanation can we give of it? Is *any* sort of explanation of it possible? Is it in fact a mistake to think there is a special sort of unity to be found in consciousness, as Hume claimed?

Cartesian dualism generates quick and easy answers to many of these questions. According to Descartes, our consciousness resides in a metaphysically simple immaterial substance, and it is the essential nature of this substance to sustain unified states and streams of consciousness. Since particular experiences are modes (or properties) of immaterial substances, it makes no sense—within the Cartesian framework at least—to suppose that any experience could exist apart from the particular substance within which it occurs. By virtue of being simple, such substances lack parts, and there is no question of them dividing into two (or more) in the manner of an apple or an amoeba. Evidently, if all this is the case, the unity of consciousness is a necessary and inviolable feature of our mental lives: our experiences cannot ever be anything but fully unified, and there is no possibility of this unity breaking down, or dividing (or merging).

When Brentano addressed the unity of consciousness in Book II, Part IV of *Psychology from an Empirical Viewpoint* (Brentano 1874/1973a), these quick and definitive answers were not available to him. Humean doubts held little attraction: Brentano was firmly convinced that consciousness does possess a distinctive and deep form of unity. But committed as he was to F. A. Lange's project of "psychology without a soul", he was determined to remain methodologically agnostic on the issue of whether immaterial souls exist (but see Chapter 14). He was thus obliged to conduct his investigations without starting from the assumption that our experiences are modes of immaterial substances. However, he also found himself drawn to the view that the relationship between our unified conscious states and their constituent parts was not altogether different from the Cartesian stance on that relationship. As we shall see, whether he had adequate reasons for adopting this position is one of the more intriguing—and difficult—aspects of his writings on this topic.

1 EXPERIENCING CO-EXISTENCE: BRENTANO'S BASIC ACCOUNT

Several of the most distinctive features of Brentano's position on the unity of consciousness are in display in the following passages:

> Our investigations lead to the following conclusion: the totality of our mental life, as complex as it may be, always forms a real unity. This is the well-known fact of the *unity of consciousness* which is generally regarded as one of the most important tenets of psychology.... The unity of consciousness, as we know with evidence through inner perception, consists in the fact that all mental phenomena which occur within us simultaneously such as seeing and hearing, thinking, judging and reasoning, loving and hating, desiring and shunning, etc., no matter how different they may be, all belong to one unitary reality only if they are inwardly perceived as existing together. They constitute phenomenal parts of a mental phenomenon, the elements of which are neither distinct things nor parts of distinct things but belong to a real unity. This is the necessary condition for the unity of consciousness, and no further conditions are required.
>
> (Brentano 1973a: 126)

Since Brentano denied the existence of mental states or processes that are nonconscious, when he refers here to the *totality of our mental life*, he is talking about the totality of our conscious *experiences* at a particular time—let us refer to these as "total" or "maximal" experiences. In suggesting that our total experiences are "real unities", he is making an ontological claim: the kind of unity to be found in our total experiences is such that they are more akin to bricks, bullets, or organisms than they are to clouds, heaps of beans or collections of coins—more on this shortly. In this passage, he also tells us what is responsible for conscious unity: mental phenomena belong to a single unified consciousness by virtue of being *experienced as existing together*. This relationship of experienced togetherness is necessary for the unity of consciousness—experiences that aren't so related are not experientially unified—and since nothing further could conceivably be required, it is also sufficient.

Brentano talks of "inwardly perceiving" mental phenomena existing together. In the chapters of the *Psychology* immediately preceding his discussion of phenomenal unity (Chapters 2–3 of Book II), he expounds and defends his distinctive doctrine that mental items are conscious if, and only if, they are accompanied by an "inner perception" or "inner consciousness" (see Chapter 5). Like many others, Brentano believed that we don't just have experience—of pain, say—but we are also *aware* that we are having them, and that the presence of this awareness or knowledge is one of the essential or defining features of conscious states. One way of developing this doctrine is by positing a special form of higher-order act of awareness, one that is capable of apprehending what we see, hear, feel and think. Although initially attracted to this solution (see Brentano 1867: 93), he later found it problematic and argued against it. His mature view was that inner perception is not a separate act that exists in addition to first-order phenomenal contents but is rather an intrinsic feature of phenomenal contents themselves.[1] Inner perception is *so* intimately related to the contents it apprehends that it apprehends them infallibly, or so Brentano held. If he is right about this, then it is also clearly the case that when our phenomenal contents coexist in unified ensembles, this unity will register in our inner perceptions.

From a purely phenomenological standpoint, Brentano's account has a good deal of prima facie plausibility. At any given time, what we see *is* experienced together with what we hear, what we hear is experienced with our bodily sensations, our conscious thoughts, and so on. When phenomenal contents are related in this manner, the relationship—again at a purely phenomenological level—appears to be direct and unmediated. For example, when the sound of a passing car is experienced together with a pain in the foot, all that I am aware of is the sound and the pain-sensation coexisting in my consciousness; I am not aware of any kind of link or connecting phenomenal glue binding them together. Brentano himself makes this point in his *Descriptive Psychology* when finding fault with Hume's "bundle" account of phenomenal unity: "A 'bundle', strictly speaking, requires a rope or wire or something else binding it together. In the case of human consciousness it is out of the question that there is something of this sort, or even just something analogous to it" (Brentano 1995b: 14).

2 ELABORATIONS AND CLARIFICATIONS: UNITY, FISSION AND FUSION

Brentano tells us that "The doctrine of the unity of consciousness as outlined here has a more modest content than that which has often been assigned to it … and it has shown itself to be safe from every objection" (1973a: 169). As he goes on to elaborate and clarify his position, it becomes clearer what he took "modest" to mean. First, Brentano was notably undogmatic on the relationship between the unity of consciousness and other forms of unity. Second, his own stance was not subject to the same metaphysical constraints as views such as Descartes', which confine consciousness to simple indivisible substances.

By way of an illustration of the first point, Brentano makes it clear that he sees no obstacle to a single physical system (or organism) hosting a multiplicity of unified conscious states at the same time—that is, states whose constituents are *not* phenomenally unified with one another. This would arise, for example, if he were to become victim of demonic possession, and another spirit came to occupy his own body: "There would be no real unity between the consciousness of this spirit and my own consciousness ... I would not directly apprehend its mental phenomena in inner perception along with my own" (1973a: 164).

In a slightly less fanciful vein, he suggests that corals may well provide another case. Individual coral polyps—taken by Brentano to be "little animals"—might well each have their own discrete consciousnesses, but when polyps form into colonies, they also develop organic unity, sharing nutrients through complex systems of gastrovacular canals. Here, too, we have an example of a single organic unity sustaining a (large) multiplicity of distinct centres of unified consciousness.[2]

Is it possible that the organisms in a colony of corals possess a communal consciousness that is unified in a *partial* less-than-absolute manner? Brentano draws the line here and dismisses the proposal: "I see no reasons which compel us to assume this something-in-between which is so full of contradictions" (1973a: 173).[3] It is true that the constituents of a colony are often found to be acting in a synchronized way, but this is because they are all subject to the same external influences. But all this is true of the large numbers of human beings that can be found in large cities or nations: they too sometimes act in synchronized ways, without the separateness of their consciousnesses being in any way impugned or diminished.

By way of an illustration of the second point—and in a notable and intriguing anticipation of contemporary debates in personal identity—Brentano raises the issues posed by fission and fusion.

He draws our attention to Lange's observation in his *History of Materialism* (Lange 1865) that there are organisms—some species of protozoa for instance—that reproduce by undergoing binary fission. There are others—such as the appropriately named parasitic flatworm *diplozoon paradoxum*—which reproduce by first fusing with others of their species to produce a single organism. Should we conclude that organisms of this sort cannot be conscious, on the grounds that the unity of consciousness is simply incompatible with fission and fusion? Anyone who locates conscious unity in simple and indivisible substances is obliged to reject the possibility of streams of consciousness dividing or merging. Brentano finds himself under no such obligation and is happy to accept the possibility of a consciousness undergoing fission or fusion. The unity of consciousness, he claims, "does not require either the simplicity or the indivisibility of consciousness" (1973a: 132).

What we should conclude from such cases, Brentano suggests, is that consciousness may be grounded (or have "quantitative parts") in physical systems that are spatially extended; it is only because of this that the division of an organism or its brain can bring about the branching of a consciousness—and similarly, *mutatis mutandis*, for fusion. Brentano concedes that it can seem odd to think that our unified conscious states could be grounded in physical systems that are complex and spatially extended (in the manner of our bodies and brains). Certainly introspection (or inner perception) does not reveal this to be the case. But there is a difference between (a) failing to prove that X obtains, and (b) proving that X does not obtain. Inner perception provides us with (a) but not (b).

This open-mindedness influences Brentano's interpretation of a further intriguing puzzle case. When ordinary earthworms are cut into pieces, the resulting sections often remain alive and capable of voluntary movement. Aristotle held that in such cases, when a worm's body is cut into pieces, the same happens to its soul. In which case the "unitary consciousness of the dissected animal … must have been in some sense spatially extended." (1973a: 166) Others take the view that in such cases, there are several different souls in the worm's body prior to its dissection. Brentano does not take a stand on which of these interpretations is correct, but does not rule either out. If consciousness is spatially distributed, then it is at least possible that a worm's originally unified consciousness undergoes (multiple) fission when its body is divided into several pieces.

3 EXPERIENTIAL WHOLES AND THEIR PARTS: THE DIVISIVES HYPOTHESIS

We have seen that Brentano regards total experiences—the complexes that comprise everything we are experiencing at a given time—to consist of "real unities". We also saw that he regarded entities of this sort to be ontologically distinguished, at least with respect to entities that are *not* real unities. Since Brentano introduces the distinctions between different kinds of entity and different kinds of unity in the opening section of "On the Unity of Consciousness". we might expect them to play a significant role in the subsequent discussion. And indeed they do—but they are also the source of a good deal of difficulties.

Brentano pronounces that "It is impossible for something to be one real thing and a multiplicity of real things at the same time" (1973a: 156).[4] He contrasts "real things" with "collectives", which are composed of a number of real things. Examples of collectives are "herds of animal" or "the plant world". Although we often give *names* to entities of this sort, we should not let this mislead us into thinking that they are genuine things, for they are not.

> A city, indeed each house in a city, each room in the house, the floor of each room, which is composed of many boards, are also examples of collectives. Perhaps the boards themselves are collectives composed of many elements, whether points, or indivisible atoms.… One thing, however, is certain: without some real unities there would be no multiplicities, without things there would be no collectives.
>
> (ibid.)

Although some collectives (in Brentano's sense) *are* what we would ordinarily call collections, many ordinary material objects are also collectives. Indeed, so far as material objects are concerned, it looks as though Brentano holds that the only things that are *not* collectives are the elementary particles.

He goes on to make an important clarification. Although a genuine (or real) thing can never be a multiplicity of things (or a collective), this does not mean that "no multiplicity can be discerned within it" (1973a: 157). A real thing can contain a multiplicity of *elements* or *parts*, even if it cannot be composed of other real things. Collectives can also contain parts—for example, the individual animals that make up a herd, or the individual people who inhabit a city—but the kind of part Brentano is now concerned with is different. The parts in question are not individual things, and they are not capable of existing independently of the wholes they find themselves in, even if the fact that we often name them might lead us to think otherwise. To mark the difference, he calls these dependent parts or aspects *divisives*. If we suppose that elementary physical particles are indivisible but also possess a finite (if very small) size, then the top and bottom halves of a particular atom will count as divisives, as will its shape and colour (assuming it has one). The halves of an atom cannot be separated in reality but they can *in thought*, and that is sufficient to make them divisives.

With these distinctions in play, Brentano is in a position to formulate the issue he wants to address in a more precise way. In the case of our complex total experiences—the rich and varied states that most of us enjoy most of the time—are they collectives that are composed of separable parts? Or are the so-called parts of such total experiences merely divisives that are incapable of independent existence?

Brentano has already made some progress in addressing this question. When defending and elaborating his inner perception doctrine in earlier chapters of the *Psychology*, he focused on the example of a very simple experience: the hearing of a single sound. After establishing that the presentation is necessarily (if it is conscious at all) accompanied by an inner perception, he went on to ask whether or not the presentation and inner perception were distinct and separable phenomena or indivisibly bound together. He argues that the latter is the case, concluding:

> inner experience seems to prove undeniably that the presentation of the sound is connected with the presentation of the presentation of the sound in such a peculiarly intimate way that its being contributes inwardly to the being of the other.
> This suggests that there is a peculiar interweaving of the object of the inner presentation and the presentation itself, and that both belong to one and the same act.
> (1973a: 127)[5]

In the case of a single simple experience, the presentation and its inner perception are *so* intimately related that they are merely divisives of real unity. We are not dealing here with two independent phenomena at all but rather two distinguishable features of a single entity; these features are not separable in reality, only in thought—or so Brentano argues. The question that has yet to be addressed is whether what holds of *simple* experiences of this kind also applies to far more *complex* states of consciousness.

A natural first thought is that this is bound to be the case. Why should complex states differ from simpler ones with regard to such a fundamental feature? And in fact, this is the conclusion Brentano is eventually led to: he *does* reach the conclusion that the constituents of complex total experiences are divisives that are incapable of enjoying an independent existence. However, the route to this conclusion is by no means a direct or straightforward one, and—as Brentano is honest enough to concede, remarking "This hypothesis has its difficulties"—there are substantial obstacles to be overcome.

4 TWO DIFFICULTIES

The first difficulty mentioned by Brentano is a direct consequence of the fact that we have now moved on from unrealistically simplified examples and are dealing with complex, multifaceted states of consciousness. A total experience consisting of a single auditory sensation, of (say) a particular pitch, timbre and volume, is an all-or-nothing affair: it either exists or it doesn't; if it does exist, it is experienced—together with its accompanying inner perception. As soon as we consider more complex compound total experiences, matters are very different. To bring this out, let's look at a simple example. Suppose at a given time t, you are enjoying a total experience consisting of an auditory sensation A (a C-tone), a bodily experience B (a twinge of pain in your ankle), and a visual experience V (a clear blue sky). We can represent this thus:

$T(t) = (A + B + V)$

If the clearly distinguishable elements within a total experience are divisives, rather than ordinary separable parts, it is impossible for A, B or V to exist independently of one another. But on the face of it, this does not seem impossible at all. It seems perfectly possible, for example, that the pain in your ankle disappeared just prior to t, resulting in this less complex total experience:

$T(t)^* = (A + V)$

It seems equally possible that the pain in your ankle could have become a good deal more severe a few seconds earlier (you foolishly banged it into a table while walking across the room). Using "B^*" to refer to this more severe bodily pain, the result is a different total experience at t:

$T(t)^{**} = (A + B^* + V)$

A moment's reflection suggests that these variations are only a fraction of the possible ones. Instead of seeing an entirely empty clear blue sky, let's suppose that at t you saw a bird flying across the sky. Would the character of your auditory or bodily experiences have been different as a result? It seems plausible to think that they would not. Why should they? Similarly, if the sound you hear at t were a fraction louder, would your pain or visual experiences have been any different? Again, it seems not. Here is Brentano making the point:

> If our simultaneous mental acts were never anything but divisives of one and the same unitary thing, how could they be independent of one another? Yet this is the case; they do not appear to be connected with one another either when they come into being or when they cease to be. Either seeing or hearing can take place without the other one, and, if they do occur at the same time, the one can stop while the other continues. In this case of complexity, the mental acts are mutually independent.
>
> (1973a: 157–8)

The diversity of ordinary human consciousness makes for a second difficulty. If total experiences are ontologically basic entities, it seems natural to suppose that their states and properties will all be related to them in the same sort of way. This is certainly the case for Descartes' immaterial soul-substances. On this view, all forms of consciousness have exactly the same status: they are simply modes of these substances. Brentano suggests the position he has been led to adopt rules out this kind of simplicity:

> With seeing and hearing there is nothing like the reciprocal interrelationship that we find among the three aspects of inner consciousness, where each one has each of the others as its object. If seeing and hearing, like the three forms of inner consciousness, were part of the same real unity, then we should expect to find differences in the intimacy of the connection to be impossible. For it is obvious that nothing can be more of a unity than that which is really one by nature. Consequently it appears that the totality of a complex mental state must be thought of as a collective.
> (1973a: 158)

Inner consciousness, at least as construed by Brentano at this stage of his career, always comprises three inseparable components: presentation (the current intentional object of our mental act), judgement (a more or less explicit acknowledgement of this presentation) and feeling (positive or negative to some degree). These three elements within total experiences are *absolutely* inseparable and necessarily present. As we have just seen, it is quite different with other forms of consciousness. During many periods of our waking hours, we may be enjoying visual and auditory experience simultaneously, but this is not always the case: there are also periods when we experience only silence. There are times when we are exercising our memories and replaying episodes of our earlier lives, but there are other occasions when we are not.

Quite generally, our capacities for different kinds of sensory experience and intellectual activity (broadly construed) are capable of being exercised independently. Yet it is quite different with the three components of inner perception. Does it really make sense to suppose that this diversity could exist within total experiences if the latter are ontologically basic entities? Is it compatible with these independent forms of experience being divisives (rather than ordinary parts) of total experiences?

5 BRENTANO'S RESPONSES

Having drawn attention to these obstacles to holding that *all* rather than just some forms of experience have the status of divisives, Brentano goes on to argue that they are not compelling.

In connection with the second line of argument, Brentano registers this counterobjection:

> The relation of real identity is necessarily always the same wherever it is actually present; it does not matter whether it is a thing, a collective or a divisive, or what it is that is called identical with itself. Nothing is more identical with itself than anything else. But this is not true of the relation between the parts which belong to a real unity.
> (1973a: 162)

To illustrate that a metaphysically simple entity can contain ingredients that are related in different ways, Brentano considers the case of physical atoms. Let us suppose, as previously, that these are indivisible but finite in size—we can think of them as tiny spheres. If we conjure up an atom of this kind in our imaginations (or draw one on paper), it is easy enough to introduce a flat plane through the centre point that exactly divides the atom into two halves. Since the atom does not have separable parts, the resulting half-spheres cannot exist as separate entities; they are divisives that will belong to the atom for as long as it exists. But other features of the atom are *not* permanent. An atom that is in motion needn't always be in motion; it can be brought to a stop or given a different state of motion.[6] We can thus see that "when we are dealing with parts which belong to one and the same reality, we can *conceive* of them to be connected with one another in many ways and with greater or lesser intimacy" (1973a: 162).

What of the first problem that Brentano raised? Seeing and hearing can take place independently of one another, and if on an occasion they *do* occur simultaneously, it's possible for one to stop but the other to continue. Brentano argues that the difficulty here is more apparent than real:

> That which is really identical cannot undergo any separation, since this would mean something being separated from itself. But that which belongs as a distinct part, along with others, may cease to be, while the other parts continue, without there being any contradiction.
>
> (1973a: 163)

The plausibility of this can again be illustrated by considering an atom and its properties. Consider a particular atom that, at a certain time, has two properties F and G, where F is the capacity to repel atoms with property X and G is the capacity to repel atoms with property Y. Could the same atom, at a later time, possess F but not G, or G but not F? It seems perfectly both conceivable and possible. Consequently, Brentano suggests, we have an explanation for why hearing and seeing can be both independent of one another yet deliver experiences that are nonetheless divisives of total experiences.

This is fine as far as it goes, but we are not yet out of the woods. Brentano has explained how it is possible for different experience-producing capacities to operate independently of one another and to contribute to different total experiences over time. But what of the counterfactual scenarios we considered earlier? Consider again the total experience consisting of an auditory, bodily, and visual experience occurring at t:

$$T(t) = (A + B + V)$$

It seems perfectly conceivable that instead of continuing on until t, the bodily experience in question—a pain sensation—should have ceased a few seconds earlier. If so, then at t the relevant subject would have had a less complex total experience with this character:

$$T(t)^* = (A + V)$$

As we also saw, instead of fading away, the pain might have worsened by the time t occurs, resulting in yet a different total experience:

$$T(t)^{**} = (A + B^* + V)$$

These cases present Brentano with a problem. The three total experiences in question—T(t), T(t)* and T(t)**—clearly have different experiential characters and constituents. Let us assume, as is standardly done, that experiences are individuated by their precise phenomenal character (how they seem), their time of occurrence, and their subject. It follows at once that T(t), T(t)* and T(t)** are three numerically distinct experiences; they have the same subject and time of occurrence, but their phenomenal characters are very different. Hence the problem. If A, B and V are divisives, they are essentially dependent on the total experience in which they occur, namely T(t). But A also exists in a different and distinct total experience T(t)*, and V exists (along with A) in another total experience T(t)**. If A and V are divisives, it should only be possible for them to exist in T(t); but it seems that it is perfectly possible for them to exist in different total experiences. Since the same applies quite generally, to all parts of all total experiences, Brentano's thesis that experiential parts are *not* parts, but mere divisives, incapable of existing outwith their actual wholes, is thus seriously threatened.

Brentano can respond by arguing that the problem is entirely a product of a misrepresentation of the envisaged scenarios, and so not really a problem at all. Focusing on the second example, if we take seriously the thesis that experiences such as A and V are divisives, then since T(t) and T(t)* are different total experiences, it is a blatant error to assume that A and V *could* exist anywhere but T(t). Hence a proper representation of T(t)* would be along these lines:

$$T(t)^* = (A^* + V^*)$$

Here, A^* and V^* are experiences (or experiential features) that resemble A and V qualitatively but are numerically distinct divisives. The same applies *mutatis mutandis* in the case of T(t)**.

6 INNER PERCEPTION AND THE VINDICATION OF HOLISM

In a recent article on conscious unity, Giustina (forthcoming) argues that Brentano's position is in some ways superior to a position she calls *Priority Unity monism*. According to the latter,

> All the conscious states a subject S has at t are unified in virtue of S's having only one basic conscious experience at t. The different conscious states S has at t are non-basic experiential parts of the overall experience.
> (Giustina forthcoming: 7–8)

As Giustina characterizes the situation, Brentano and the Priority monist both hold that there is a relation of ontological priority between total experiences and their parts. But the Priority monist's position is confronted by a serious difficulty: the priority of experiential wholes with regard to their parts is simply left unexplained.[7] But it is otherwise with Brentano's position: the "priority relation between the overall experience and the experiential parts holds *in virtue of the latter's being distinctional parts of the former*. Thus Brentanian monism provides priority with a backing explanation, and does not incur the difficulty met by Priority monism" (forthcoming: 17).

It is certainly the case that Brentano's position would be superior to the Priority monist's if he really had provided the explanation that Giustina claims. But is this the case? A "distinctional part" is simply another term for divisive. Given the way Brentano defines divisives, it certainly makes no sense to suppose they cannot exist independently of their wholes, and in this sense the wholes have priority over their parts. If experiential parts truly *are* divisives, then total experiences have ontological priority. The question that needs answering is whether Brentano was *correct* to include experiential parts in the divisive category. What reasons did he provide? Are these reasons adequate?

When arguing against the thesis that experiential parts are akin to the parts of ordinary physical things (and hence collectives), we find Brentano drawing our attention to the intimate and distinctive way in which experiences within a single total experience are related to one another. As he rightly points out, these experiential parts have a togetherness, a distinctive unity, that the experiences in total experiences had by different subjects utterly lack.

> We do compare colours which we see with sounds which we hear; indeed this happens every time we recognize that they are different phenomena. How would this presentation of their difference be possible if the presentations of colour and sound belong to a different reality?... [Supposing that the presentations *do not* belong to the same reality] would be like saying that, of course, neither a blind man nor a deaf man could compare colours with sounds, but if one sees and the other hears, the two together can recognize the relationship. And why does this seem so absurd? Because the cognition which compares them is a real objective unity, but when we combine the acts of the blind man and the deaf man, we always get a mere collective and never a unitary real thing.
>
> (1973a: 159)

Although Brentano makes his point well, in fact considerations of this kind only take us so far. A question remains unanswered, for a critic could argue thus: "Yes, it's true that there exists a distinctive relationship among the parts of total experiences, but why think that this relationship, or the resulting wholes, are composed of parts that cannot exist in isolation, or in different wholes, or amid different sets of parts?"

Although Brentano does not directly address this question in *Psychology from an Empirical Standpoint*, a response can nonetheless be derived from the basic structure of consciousness, as construed by Brentano, and other claims he does explicitly make. To keep things simple, let's again focus on a simple schematic example, a total experience that consists of an auditory and a bodily sensation, which we can represent thus:

$T(t) = (A + B)$

Here as previously, the "+" sign indicates the relationship of experienced co-existence that Brentano takes to be constitutive of the unity of consciousness. Recall precisely what he says about this relationship:

> The unity of consciousness, as we know with evidence through inner perception, consists in the fact that all mental phenomena which occur within us simultaneously

such as seeing and hearing, thinking, judging and reasoning, loving and hating, desiring and shunning, etc., no matter how different they may be, all belong to one unitary reality only if they are inwardly perceived as existing together.

(1973a: 163–4)

The unity of consciousness, for Brentano, doesn't just consist in presentations being experienced together; it also includes an *inner perception* of the presentations being related in this way. We can represent this more complex state of affairs thus:

$T(t) = [(A + B) \S \underline{(A \S B)}]$

Here the underlined $\underline{(A \S B)}$ stands for the relevant inner perception, and the "§" indicates the fact that the presentation and inner perception, along with the different elements constituting the inner perception, are bound together by the particularly strong bond that Brentano associates with the contents and objects of inner perceptions.

As we also saw earlier, Brentano held that there is an "interweaving" of inner perceptions with their objects:

> the presentation of the sound is connected with the presentation of the presentation of the sound in such a peculiarly intimate way that its being contributes inwardly to the being of the other.
>
> (1973a: 127)

When an inner perception and a presentation contribute inwardly to each other's being, what precisely is going on? It's not entirely clear, but we can make some reasonable surmises. We are concerned here with *experiences*, and the "being" of an experience largely consists—presumably—in its phenomenal character. When Brentano says that inner perceptions and their presentations contribute *inwardly* to each other's being, he might well mean that the fusion of these two aspects of consciousness is of such a deep and intimate kind that the phenomenal character of each is influenced by the phenomenal character of the other.

Phenomenal interdependence can, in principle, come in different forms, but one variety is of particular interest in this context. Returning to our example, $T(t)$ has two ingredients, a presentation $P = (A + B)$ and an inner perception $IP = (A + B)$. Let's suppose that the phenomenal interdependence that exists between them is such that a maximally complete and accurate description of the phenomenal character of each will necessarily include reference to the precise phenomenal character of the other. If so, then a characterization of the phenomenal character of presentations A and B will be of this form:

A in $T(t)$: an auditory sensation of character X, experienced as co-existing with an inner perception with character $(A + B)$

B in $T(t)$: a bodily sensation of character Y, experienced as co-existing with an inner perception with character $(A + B)$

The consequences of this are significant: it results in a powerful and pervasive holism. To see why, consider a counterfactual scenario in which presentation A exists in a different total experience T(t)*: rather than being experienced with presentation B, it is experienced with visual presentation V. It is legitimate to consider such a possibility because we are currently *not* assuming that presentations are divisives, and so by definition incapable of existing in different wholes. Let's focus on presentation A. If we attempt a full description of its phenomenal character, the result will be along these lines:

A in T(t)*:   an auditory sensation of character X, experienced as co-existing with an inner perception with character (A + V)

In our original total experience T(t), the phenomenal character of the A-presentation reflects the fact that this presentation is experienced as co-existing with an inner perception (A + B). This aspect of A's character cannot possibly be carried over to the new total experience T(t)*. Why? According to Brentano, inner perceptions perfectly and incorrigibly reflect the character of their objects. Since in T(t)* the A-presentation is experienced together with a V-presentation, not a B-presentation, the inner perception associated with this total experience has to be of the form (A + V). Moreover, we are currently working on the assumption that inner perceptions "contribute inwardly to the being" of their presentations by influencing their phenomenal character in a manner that reflects their own character. The A-type presentation in our hypothetical T(t)* will therefore necessarily reflect that fact that is experienced as co-existing with an inner perception possessing the character (A + V) and *not* (A + B). The hypothesis that the auditory sensation that exists in T(t) is numerically the same presentation as the auditory sensation that exists in T(t)* is thus revealed to be incoherent: the latter has a different overall phenomenal character than the former, and the identity of token experiences essentially depends (in part) on their phenomenal character.

Confronted with this argument, a sceptic with regard to phenomenal holism might be tempted to respond along these lines. Perhaps it is impossible for a particular presentation to exist in a total experience whose overall phenomenal character is different in the manner of T(t) and T(t)*, where the latter contains a presentation not found in the former. But what about cases of this sort:

T(t) = [(A + B) § (A § B)]
T(t)* = [(A + B*) § (A § B*)]

Here we are to suppose that T(t) is the total experience a subject S actually has at t, and T(t)* is a total experience that same subject *could* have had at t. Both of the presentations in each of T(t) and T(t)* have exactly the same kind of phenomenal character: A is of type X and B is of type Y. There is nonetheless a significant difference between T(t) and T(t)*: B and B* are numerically distinct instances of a Y-type presentation. T(t) and T(t)* are thus numerically distinct total experiences.

Since A is to be found in both of them, Brentano's claim that all presentations are divisives has been shown to be false.

Once again a swift response is available to the Brentanian. For the sake of the argument, let us grant that a total experience comprising [A + B] would be a distinct total experience from one consisting of [A + B*], if B and B* really were numerically distinct tokens of the same type of experience. The objection still fails and for a simple reason. For two token presentations to be numerically identical, they must have the same phenomenal character, the same subject, and the same time of occurrence. Since in the envisaged case, B and B^* have the same subject and also precisely the same phenomenal characters and times of occurrence, it is simply incoherent to suppose they could be anything other than numerically identical. The envisaged $T(t)^*$ is therefore *not* a numerically distinct total experience, and so the objection fails.

Since analogous considerations rule out *any* element of any total experience existing in a total experience of a different type, Brentano's claim that all presentations are divisives of total experiences looks to be vindicated. Needless to say, since this consequence rests both on Brentano's doctrine of inner perception, and the particularly intimate relation that exists between inner perceptions and their objects, it will not be available to those who find these doctrines implausible.

NOTES

1. "In the same mental act in which the sound is present to our minds we simultaneously apprehend the mental act itself. What is more, we apprehend it in accordance with its dual nature insofar as it has the sound as content within it, and insofar as it has itself as content as the same time" (1874: 127).
2. Brentano's willingness to countenance the possibility that simple forms of consciousness might be found in very primitive life-forms is one of the more striking features of the "unity" chapter of the *Psychology* and may well be a consequence of an Aristotelian influence. Given the recent surge of interest in panpsychism over the past decade or so, it is less idiosyncratic than it might otherwise have been.
3. Brentano does not expand on what these contradictions are, but he may have had in mind the sorts of problems with the "compounding of consciousness" with which William James (1909) grappled and which remain a problem for panpsychists.
4. As so often, he traces this doctrine back to Aristotle.
5. I use here Mark Textor's translation of this important passage—see Textor 2006, §4.
6. Anyone who doesn't like motion—Brentano's own example—because they have doubts as to whether motion is truly an intrinsic property can think instead of atoms that vary their charge (or some other attractive or repulsive force) over time. There is nothing incoherent in the idea of this kind of change, even if most actual particles don't vary their properties in this manner.
7. This issue aside, it is not obvious that Guistina's Priority monist has provided a viable account of the unity of consciousness. If a *partially* unified consciousness is possible, of the kind that some argue split-brain patients possess, then what is arguably a "single experience" is not necessarily fully unified (see Lockwood 1989).

7

Brentano on Time-Consciousness

Guillaume Fréchette

1 THE RECEPTION OF BRENTANO'S ACCOUNT

For many years, the importance and significance of Brentano's conception of time-consciousness in contemporary philosophy was closely tied with Husserl's adaptation of this conception in his own lectures on time-consciousness. These lectures, which Husserl held in Göttingen in 1904–05, were edited in the 1920s by the brilliant phenomenologist Edith Stein and are the source of many of the central ideas of transcendental phenomenology. In April 1926, Stein's work was then taken over by Martin Heidegger, a young careerist who, after spending some years as Husserl's assistant in Freiburg, took over many of Husserl's ideas and published a volume on being and time that would convince Husserl to choose him as his successor.[1] Soon enough, and thanks to the publication of Husserl's lectures, "Brentano's conception of time-consciousness" became the heading of a supposedly surpassed and defective theory, which was to be replaced subsequently by transcendental phenomenology and its heirs in Freiburg and later in France.[2]

This brief and quite tragic history of the reception of Brentano's conception of time-consciousness has meanwhile been rectified to some extent by a number of works that offer a less biased picture of Brentano's *various* conceptions of time-consciousness.[3] The picture remains incomplete, however, without a consideration of the motivations behind the different conceptions advocated by Brentano. By taking Brentano's metaphysical views into account as his background motivation, it is possible to draw a comprehensive picture of the different conceptions he defended and to get around the uneasy division of his works into early and "mature" views, which has often been taken as a starting point for assessing the importance of reism (see Chapter 13) at the expense of the rest of his works.[4] While such divisions may be historically justified, they tend to hide the forest behind the trees. For this reason, I will first start with a description of the forest (§§2–3) and will finish with a classification of the trees (§4).

2 THE BACKGROUND MOTIVATION

Brentano's first (and last) answer to the question "What is there?" was the following: there are substances, which are also called *things* or *beings*.[5] In his early 1867 lectures on metaphysics from the Würzburg period (henceforth *Metaphysics*),[6] a substance and its accidents are taken to be only *metaphysically* separable. A thing, like the cup of coffee on my desk, is a being (*Seiendes*) that is fully determined by the relation holding between the underlying substance and the totality of its accidents. It is called a *substance* to mark a distinction from its metaphysical parts, but "the substance together with its accidents is *one single* being (*Seiendes*) ... it constitutes with them a unitary whole (*einheitliches Ganzes*)" (*Metaphysics*, p. 31793, §195).[7] "The metaphysical parts are posited as particular things only through a fiction of the mind" (*Metaphysics*, p. 31972, §478).

There are different sorts of accidents: Brentano considers spatial and temporal accidents of substance as absolute accidents, which means that a substance, properly speaking, cannot lose spatial or temporal properties. It is always at a place and at a time.

Now if location and duration are accidents, what about the *species* of these accidents, namely time and space? Brentano considers both time and space to be continua (see Chapter 15). Here too, he follows Aristotle in conceiving of continuity as an attribute applying to the quantity of substance. The water in the glass on my desk has a certain spatial quantity (it occupies some place in the glass), and this spatial quantity is a continuum. In Brentano's view, continua are not composed of discrete atoms and as such are *potentially* infinitely divisible. In that sense, the divisions of a continuum, the boundaries, only exist *potentially*, since the existence of the parts of the continuum depends on the existence of the continuum as a whole.[8]

The case of time is dealt with analogously to space in the *Metaphysics*. As in the case of spatial boundaries (e.g., a point on a line), Brentano rejects the idea that temporal boundaries have any kind of reality. They rather are to be called fictions *cum fundamentum in rei*. Taking such fictions seriously would lead to a vicious regress: admitting boundaries as realities would call for further boundaries to mark the separation between boundaries as realities, and so on. Boundaries are simply metaphysical parts of the whole of which they are the boundaries.

In the *Metaphysics*, Brentano considers time and space to be two different kinds of continua: space is a perfect continuum or reality (*fertige Wirklichkeit*), since all parts of the spatial extension are real. Time is often characterized as an imperfect continuum (*unfertige Wirklichkeit*), in which only the now-point of a given duration is real. Therefore, in the strict sense of "real," Brentano is a presentist with regard to time but still sees time as an unreal continuum.

3 TWO OPTIONS ON TIME-CONSCIOUSNESS

With this metaphysical setting in place, we are now in a position to give an account of our perception of time. If time is a continuum of which only the now-point is real, then trivially, any object purportedly extending over time (e.g. a melody, Socrates) is perceivable as such only from the perspective of its now-point. And since the perception of duration is by definition the perception of something with temporal extension, there can't be a perception of time in a strict analogical sense to spatial perception. In seeing time as a continuum only in a special sense (as an "imperfect continuum"), Brentano is bound to say that temporal objects like melodies are continua, though imperfect ones. Not only are they different from the sum of the single tones, but, strictly speaking, they are *irrealia*. Since a perception is always accompanied by consciousness of this perception for Brentano, and since consciousness in general (and time-consciousness in particular) is itself part of the general structure of the world—as an accident or metaphysical part of the soul—time-consciousness (with its bearer) must be a temporal continuum in the same relevant (nonreal, or "imperfect") sense, which is to say real only at the now-point. In other words, if time is a continuum in the relevant sense, then there must be a time-consciousness that is (with its bearer) a temporal continuum in the same relevant, "imperfect" sense for the concept of time-consciousness to be intelligible at all.

This reflection seems to be at the origin of a fundamental assumption of Brentano's conception of the mind, namely that consciousness, both in its synchronic and diachronic forms, is characterized by unity. In its synchronic form, it is the unity of the act with the content or the unity of different acts and contents at a time; in its diachronic form, it is the unity of different acts and contents through time. Applied to the latter case, the assumption of unity could be formulated as follows:

> Unity of Time-Consciousness (UTC): our experience of succession is a unitary phenomenon and not a succession of experiences.

Following UTC, but also taking into consideration the point mentioned above, namely that consciousness is real only at its now-point, a retentional conception of time-consciousness recommends itself. Brentano has two main options at his disposal when it comes to accounting for UTC:

1. The properties of temporal consciousness are grounded in the perceived properties of time itself;
2. The perceived properties of time are grounded in the properties of temporal consciousness.

Following (1), the nonreal continuity of the time-continuum itself (in its relevant sense) is what *makes* our time-consciousness seem to be the perception of something that is temporally extended. Therefore, temporal properties are special properties of objects in the time continuum. Time-consciousness is unextended, and the unity of our experience of succession comes from the nonreal continuity of the time-continuum itself. Following (2), the relevant sense of nonreal continuity describes a special temporal property of our acts, often called *original association* (in the sense of innate associative link), which allows some of them to "reach back" in the direction of the past or to anticipate something to come. Under this description, the unity of our experience of succession comes from the original association.

These two options are analogous to the options at Brentano's disposal concerning intentionality and the nature of intentional objects:[9]

1. The *special way of being* contained in mental phenomena is what makes these phenomena intentional.

2. The *special kind of directedness* or reference of mental phenomena is what *makes* them intentional.

In the case of both time-consciousness and intentionality, type-1 solutions involve the treatment of nonreal continuity as a "being in the sense of the true," which is the sense of being involved for instance in true attributions to *entia irrealia*:[10] in this case, both *realia* and *irrealia* are beings, although in different senses. Type-2 solutions allow only for real continua and attribute the relevant sense of nonreal continuity to a feature of the perception of continuity.

Finally, it is important to note that type-1 and type-2 conceptions are not necessarily exclusive: one might want to say that temporal properties are special properties of objects in the time continuum and that these play an important role in our perception of change, without necessarily excluding the fact that our perception has built-in retentional and anticipative features that *also* play a role in our perception of time. In most of the numerous versions of his theory of time-consciousness, Brentano adopts this alternative.

4 FIVE VARIATIONS

From this perspective, it seems that Brentano's whole philosophical development between 1862 and 1917 evolves around the relation between these two main conceptions of reality (or to put it in Brentano's words, of continuity) and around different possible combinations of the two. As far as time-consciousness is concerned, this is at least partly confirmed by the autobiographical reconstruction of the evolution sketched by Brentano in his directives on how to lecture on time-consciousness, sent to Marty in 1895:

> My opinion is that it would be best for you to: (a) develop the old view, (b) point out the objections to it, in particular the objection that heterogeneous elements are supposed to form a continuum. Also, that there would be less difference between a non-thing and a thing than there would be between two non-things; indeed there would be infinitesimally little difference between them! Then, (c) you could speak about the earlier view I once entertained, independently of Mill, but in agreement with him, and show why it had to appear untenable (according to it, time was not a continuum at all). Then (d) how, in spite of this, I revived it, but with considerable modifications. (e) The way for the revival was paved by the view, at which I arrived quite independently of these considerations, that every sensation is bound up with an apprehension of that which is sensed. (Irrevocably; this does not even cease to apply with the knowledge that the phenomenon is not real. Comparisons with higher and lower desires. This holds true also of proteraesthesis).
>
> (Kraus 1930: 7/1976: 228)

Following Brentano's personal reconstruction, it seems that his conception of time consciousness between 1867 and 1895 is composed of three basic theories:

1. The "earlier" view (c): continuum of modes of judgment (1867–1868)
2. The "old" view (a): continuum of modified objects (1869–1893)
3. The "new" view (d, e): continuum of modes of judgment (1893–1905)

After 1905, Brentano defended two further views:

4. The penultimate view: continuum of modes of presentations (1905–1915)
5. The last view: continuum of oblique modes of presentations (1915–1917)

4.1 View 1: The "Earlier" View (1867)

The "earlier" view, according to which time-consciousness is a matter of the *attitude or mode of the act of judgment*, is exclusively a type-2 account. In the *Metaphysics*, the view is developed in the context of a discussion of truth as correspondence. Brentano rejects the idea that truth is *adaequatio rei et intellectus* on the grounds that one may express true judgments that are not about a reality, but he still believes that truth is a kind of correspondence, though in a "very improper sense." In his view, a judgment is true "when it acknowledges (*zustimmt*) a presentation which corresponds to the thing, or when it rejects (*verwirft*) a presentation which doesn't correspond to it" (*Metaphysics*, p. 31951, §395). According to him, true judgments expressed by tensed sentences, such as "Napoleon existed 200 years ago," are also true for the same reason, but with the following proviso: "if time were a perfect reality like space etc., a reality *would* correspond to the presentation" (*Metaphysics*, p. 31952, §398). This conditional formulation is what Brentano calls "a different mode of acknowledgment (*Zustimmung*)" (ibid.) and doesn't involve any type-1 consideration. It technically offers a type-2 explanation, since judgments are acts of the mind, but it is also complemented by a basic account of what will later (around 1872) be labeled the "original association," and which explicitly accounts for UTC: following Aquinas' view that "the multitude itself of intelligible species causes a certain vicissitude of intelligible operations, according as one operation succeeds another,"[11] Brentano adds:

> Our presenting presents succession simultaneously, but [it presents it] as being successive. "Being presented simultaneously" and "being presented as simultaneous" are to be distinguished. Our sensory presentation has a temporal depth (*zeitliche Tiefe*), so to speak. Without this wonderful device, through which the teleology of the soul shows itself on a par with the teleology of nature, we wouldn't have any presentation of movement, melody, etc. and [we wouldn't have] any presentation of time at all. As a further consequence, we wouldn't have any memory.
> (*Metaphysics*, p. 31804, §257)

In short, the "earlier" view sees time-consciousness as constituted by a modality of our judgings and as supported by the temporal depth of our presentings without recourse to any type-1 explanation.[12] The rejection of such an explanation is particularly clear in the *Metaphysics* when Brentano discusses the reistic paraphrase strategy to which he will revert almost 40 years later, although with a restriction concerning tensed sentences:

> [I]n the case of "a dog is thought-of," I cannot say … "a thought-of-dog is," but I can say "a thinker-of-a-dog is." Is such a paraphrase (*Übersetzung*) also possible for past things? It does not seem so, for if I say "a *n-times-later-thing* is," this relation is an *ens rationis*.
> (*Metaphysics*, p. 31952, §398)

In other words, judgments expressed in tensed sentences, in contrast with all other judgments seemingly about *entia rationis*, cannot even be paraphrased in a sentence directly about a substance and indirectly about an *ens rationis*. This distinction will be cast later in terms of *modo recto/modo obliquo* (see next section).

4.2 View 2: The "Old" View (1869–1893)

The "old" view stipulates that time-consciousness is a matter of the *content* of the mental act; I hear past sounds *as past-things*: the ontological modification of the content (type-1) is paired with what Brentano calls the original association (type-2), according to which there are no pure sensations in reality, but these are always coupled with phantasy, which gives us the impression that we hear the "past sound" or that we hear a melody. In 1873, Brentano used the following picture to illustrate this conception:[13]

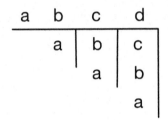

Figure 7.1

In this schema, the horizontal line *a, b, c, d* represents a series of sounds on the time-continuum. The vertical lines represent time-consciousness; while hearing the tone *b*, the tone *a* is part of the content *b* in a modified way, that is, through retention, a process for which Brentano also uses the expression "original association."

It is important to stress that the contents in retention (*a, a b, a b c* on the vertical lines) are *not* proper sound contents: already in the logic lectures of 1869–70 and 1870–71, Brentano describes these contents as sounds "*in obliquo*," abandoning the exception made in the "earlier" view (1) about the applicability of the *in recto/in obliquo* distinction for the objects of judgments expressed by tensed sentences.[14] According to the "old" view (2), past sounds, like painted fish, are not *real* sounds or fish; rather, they are sounds in a modified way, and their status in the presentations of the contents *b, c, d* of the vertical line is the status of a part in a modified way. In the 1869–70 and 1870–71 logic lectures, Brentano did not add any further element to this type-1 explanation, probably because his first concern there was to revise the solution proposed in 1867 for the truth of judgments about the past. It is in the *Psychology* lectures of 1872–73 that he supplements view (2) with a type-2 explanation in addition to the type-1 explanation in order to account for the psychological process underlying the presentation of contents *in obliquo*. The basic idea behind the concept of "original association"—as discussed in the *Psychology* lectures of 1872–73—is that of a "persistence (*Fortbestand*) of the presentations through a continual modification of their temporal determination" (Brentano Ps 62, p. 54007).[15] When hearing a sequence of tones *a*, *b*, and *c*, my presentation of *a* "persists" through time (notably "through" the further presentations of *b* and *c*) thanks to an original (i.e., innate) association of each presentation of the "now" point with past and future presentations.

According to Brentano, original association as a psychological process is genetically determined by the central and fundamental law of genetic psychology, namely the law of habit (*Gesetz der Gewohnheit*): "once a mental phenomenon occurs, the occurrence of the same or of a similar phenomenon in the same or similar conditions is thereby prepared" (ibid., p. 54001).[16] In other words, the occurrence of a mental phenomenon "leaves a dispositional trace" (see Brentano 1874: 86; Ps 53, p. 53071). The "original" association, therefore, is the process that links successive presentations on the basis of their dispositional trace.

On the level of type-1 explanation, we have said that the contents of the vertical lines—the lines bound together by original association—are parts of the presentations on the horizontal line *only in a modified way*. On the level of type-2 explanation, this means that we only have the dispositional trace of the presentations, not the presentations themselves; and since they are not presentations, judgments, or acts of love and hate, they also are not conscious.[17]

A last important feature of view (2) is the possibility of inner proteraesthesis, which is the original association proper to inner consciousness. Besides the fact that my hearing of *c* also contains *a* and *b* as tones in a modified way, a similar phenomenon would occur in inner consciousness: since all mental acts are conscious, my consciousness of hearing *c*, which accompanies the hearing, would also reach back to my consciousness of hearing *a* and *b*. Proteraesthesis of *a* and *b* in the presentation of *c* and inner proteraesthesis of the consciousness of hearing *a* and *b* in the consciousness of hearing *c* would be "inseparable from one another and so, from the standpoint of real separability, they are not different parts ... [I]t seems to be so e.g. in the tones of a melody" (Brentano, EL 74, p. 12850a). The time-consciousness schema offered by Brentano in one of his lectures looks like this:

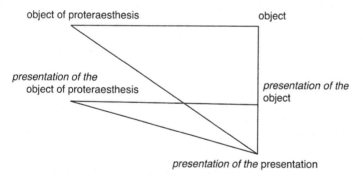

Figure 7.2

Italicized expressions designate the inner proteraesthesis (formed by the lower triangle), while nonitalicized expressions designate the proteraesthesis (formed by the upper triangle).[18] The idea of inner proteraesthesis is discussed in particular in the lectures on descriptive psychology of 1890–91, as an option on view (2), but a mention in Stumpf (1919: 136/1976: 38) indicates that it was taken into account as early as 1872.[19] Its objective seems to be the following: where proteraesthesis explains the unity of temporal perception (how the contents *a, b, c,* and *d* are united in consciousness at a time), inner proteraesthesis aims to explain how we experience this unity as such (and not as a succession of sounds). A few years later, Brentano explicitly rejected this idea (see for instance Brentano 1976: 109ff.),[20] but at least three central ideas developed by his students—Meinong's theory of the self-evidence of memory (Meinong 1886), his higher-order objects given in inner perception (Meinong 1899), and Ehrenfels' Gestalt qualities (Ehrenfels 1890)—are based on the idea of inner proteraesthesis.

4.3 View 3: The "New" View (1893–1905)

The "new" view is considered an expansion of (c), and according to it the intuition of time is the intuition of a special mode of judgment.[21] Here, the modification is not a modification of the content, as in (c), but of the attitude of acknowledgment in judgments. The result is that time-consciousness is considered a limited continuum of acknowledgments of the same object (Kraus 1930: 20/1976: 237). The new view is mentioned in a letter from Brentano to Marty from November 23rd, 1893. As Marty puts it, "with the blind belief encountered in external intuition and with the evident kind in inner intuition there is connected a continuum of judgments which judge the intuited content to be more and more past and temporally removed" (Kraus 1976: 227) (type-2).

The "new" view is structurally analogous to the "old" view (2), with the exception that the continuum on the vertical lines is a continuum of modes of acknowledgment rather than a continuum of modified objects. The intuition behind the view is that sensory presentations (e.g., of sounds) and proteraestheses of these presentations are always bound up with a blind belief in the existence of the presented objects. An important consequence of this view is that when hearing c now, the continuum in the proteraesthesis (on the vertical line c, b, a) is a continuum of modes of judgments about the same object (the sound c). Curiously enough, the "new" view (3) is very similar to the view presented in Husserl 1928, a view that Husserl presented precisely as an improvement of Brentano's "old" view (2)![22]

4.4 View 4: The Temporal Modalities of Presentation View (1905–1915)

The "new" view was defended between 1893 and 1905. Between 1903 and 1905, Brentano became doubtful of his earlier classification of acts. In a short research manuscript from 1903 (Brentano 1987c), reflecting upon his conception of sensations, he came to the conclusion that "what we usually consider a presenting which is free from any judicative character, is in fact a judgment" (Brentano 1987c: 28). In other words, even the most basic presentations have the same kind of modalities that we find in judgments.[23] In a letter to Marty from 1905, he accepts the consequences of this view for his conception of time-consciousness:

> I must say that when I return from Aristotle to myself and I characterize the presentation as a particular fundamental class, I do acknowledge in this class (1) the temporal modes as modes of presenting, and (2) attributions (analogous to the reconstruction through phantasy). The expression "presenting" is not bad. It would be better however to say "thinking."
> (Brentano 1966: 122–3).

This conclusion about the consequences of his new conception of the class of presentations is sometimes seen as marking a fourth view, according to which temporal modalities are already present at the level of presentations (type-2).

However, since presentations are thought to involve acknowledgment after 1903, view (4) should only be considered a specification of view (3): according to this specification, temporal modalities are not *only* modes of acknowledgment but *also* modes of presentation. The case of temporal desires, emotions, and wills illustrates this well: I can wish that something should have happened or that it will happen, "without forming the least judgment as to whether the wish can or cannot be fulfilled" (Brentano 1976: 23/1988: 12).

4.5 View 5: The Final View (1915–1917)

Finally, a fifth and final view could be isolated from Brentano's late manuscripts on time, according to which temporal modalities such as past or future are not modes of presentation in general but aspects specifically of the *oblique mode* of presentation, while the presentation of the present is *in recto*. This view is formulated in a dictation from 1915, which was edited by Kraus in 1925:

> It seems certain that we can never think of anything without thinking of something as present, that is to say, however, as on a boundary line which exists as the connecting point of an otherwise non-existent continuum or as providing its beginning or its end. So along with the idea of the present, we also get those of the past and future *in modo obliquo* as that the boundary of which is formed by the present.
>
> (Brentano 1973a: 326)

This last view (5) comes back to the point discussed in the earlier view (1) and, in some way, closes the loop from views (1) to (5). First, view (5), like view (1), is based on modes of judgments and rejects *irrealia* and with them any kind of special temporal properties of objects. The basic explanation is therefore in both cases a type-2 explanation. However, view (5) differs importantly from view (1) in two respects: it *also* allows for temporal modes of presentations but, more importantly, the late Brentano changed his mind on the inapplicability of the *in recto/in obliquo* distinction to the objects of judgments expressed by tensed sentences. In the case of "Napoleon existed 200 years ago," the paraphrase should be read as "There is a thing that is 200 years later than Napoleon," in which Napoleon's past existence is acknowledged *in modo obliquo*, and this on the basis of the acknowledgment of this thing (i.e., a thinker of Napoleon) *in modo recto*. In the case of the hearing of a series of sounds, the main difference from the interpretation of the schema proposed in view (2) is that the presentation contents on the vertical lines are not determined by their special ontological features but by their relations to a sound heard as present:

When hearing c now, I perceive:

i. The tone itself, c;
ii. Something that stands apart from it as earlier (b) and
iii. Something that stands apart from it as later (d).

When I now hear d, c is no longer present, but something standing apart from c as later is perceived as such. In other words, I cannot hear d now (as part of the tone series, in *modo recto*) without presenting (in *modo obliquo*) something standing apart from *c* as later.[24] On this view (5), the psychological process of original association is given a pure type-2 explanation, without imposing upon it a type-1 explanation, as was the case in view (2).

5 CLOSING THE LOOP

The five views discussed seem to suggest that the development of Brentano's conception of time-consciousness directly depends on what seems to him to be the best metaphysical account of time itself. Views (1) and (2) consider time to be some kind of continuum and were abandoned precisely for this reason: in the late 1860s and early 1870s, Brentano rejected the idea of a "continuum in an improper or imperfect sense" (view 1); and in the early 1890s, he rejected the idea of a "continuum of real and unreal moments" (view 2). This rejection of a conception of time as a special kind of continuum also called for the rejection of all type-1 solutions to the problem of time-consciousness.[25] Views (3) to (5) may be seen as a succession of attempts to offer a type-2 solution that would match his conception of the fundamental classes of mental phenomena. In some sense, view (5) might be seen as a purified version of view (1): it preserves the gist without some of the difficult assumptions and adds a few sophisticated devices that were developed over the years on the grounds of Brentano's investigations into the possibility and limitations of a type-1 account (view (2) and its immediate critique, view (3)).[26]

NOTES

1. After succeeding Husserl in his position at Freiburg, Heidegger published Husserl's lectures, mostly using Stein's editorial work, as Husserl 1928.
2. In 1930, Brentano's faithful disciple Oskar Kraus reacted to the publication of Husserl 1928 by publishing a short but insightful *précis* of Brentano's conceptions of time-consciousness (Kraus 1930). The 1976 English translation of Kraus 1930 made Brentano's conception of time-consciousness available to a wider audience. Besides Ryle 1976, however, few philosophers became aware of this translation. On the French reception of Brentano's conception of time-consciousness, see for instance Gilson 1955: 154–8, Derrida 1973: 64, Derrida 1990: 114/2003: 58, and Ricoeur 1988: 36, 38, 272.
3. See for instance Chisholm 1981, Albertazzi 1990/91, Chrudzimski 1998/99 and 2005 (see also Chrudzimski 2004: 157–64, 200-1, 204–7), Huemer 2002/03, Fugali 2004, Borsato 2009, Volpi 1989, De Warren 2009: 50–87. On Brentano's accounts in connection with Broad, see Dainton 2000 and elsewhere.
4. From the 1920s onward, Kraus, Kastil, and Mayer-Hillebrand played a major role in orienting the scholarship on Brentano almost exclusively around reism and in presenting it as a break with the earlier works. See especially Brentano 1930/1966b, 1954, 1959, 1966a, on both the editorial and ideological aspects.
5. The late Brentano has a particular view of the relation between substance and accident, the latter being then conceived of as a whole, while the former is considered as a part of the latter. Therefore, "accidents" should be added as part of the last answer, insofar as they are constituted by substances (their parts).
6. The *Metaphysics* is still unpublished. M96 from Brentano's *Nachlass* at Harvard is the main document of the first 1867 lectures. When quoting this document, I refer to the draft edition of Baumgartner *et al.* (Brentano forthcoming–1). All translations of these quotes and of other quotes from works that are still unavailable in English or unpublished are my own.
7. Here and elsewhere, all quotations from original manuscripts and from German editions are my translations.
8. See Aristotle, *Physics*, V, 3. Brentano agrees with Aristotle's answer to Zeno's paradox. See *Metaphysics*, p. 31774 (§123). The account of boundaries in the *Metaphysics* will be developed further in the late manuscripts on time, space, and continuum, published in Brentano (1976/1989).

9. I discuss this alternative since it may also be found in the *Psychology from an Empirical Standpoint* in Fréchette (2013).
10. Brentano discusses this distinction between being in the sense of the true and being in the sense of the categories in many places in his works: it has a central place not only in Brentano (1975a)[1862] (esp. 1975a, 25f.; 1862, p. 37f) but also in the *Metaphysics* and in many later texts published in Brentano (1966b) [1930]. For a detailed discussion of being in the sense of the true in Brentano and Aristotle, see Sauer (2013).
11. Aquinas, *Summa Theologica*, I, *Quaestio* 85, reply to the objection 1 (transl. by the fathers of the English Dominican Province). Brentano refers to this passage in the *Metaphysics*, p. 31804, §257.
12. Chrudzimski (2005: 49) suggests a different reading of what I call view (1), interpreting *Metaphysics*, p. 31952, §398 as a first step toward a type-1 solution. I doubt that the reduction of true judgments about the past to conditional judgments and the restricted conception of truth as correspondence would speak for such an interpretation.
13. This schema is reproduced in Stumpf (1919), 136; 1976, 38. To my knowledge, we don't find this schema in any of Brentano's manuscripts.
14. See Brentano, *Logic lectures* (1869/70), p. 24902 (classified as Marty, Br 7/1).
15. More fully: "The original associations. A case which belongs here (phantasy) and probably the only case belonging here is the persistence of presentations under a continual modification of their temporal determination. Proof that we have here a case of association and in particular of original association. The more specific laws of this association still haven't been studied. But it is certain that the associated presentation is less intense than the one to which it is associated. This explains the decrease of intensity which comes together with the temporal distance and proximity of the time length. A further consequence is that the associated temporal segment is sometimes longer, sometimes shorter. The length of the associated temporal segment is sometimes quite significant: discourse, melody. Some other conditions might also be at play here."
16. Since Brentano (1874) contains only the first book and the first part of the second book of the six-book project of *Psychology from an Empirical Standpoint*, the part of the second book dealing with the law of habit remained unpublished. An advanced draft of the chapter can be found in Brentano, Ps 53, p. 53070ff. Stumpf (1919: 135/1976: 37) says that this formula is the "most correct and most comprehensive" in Brentano's psychology.
17. What I call here view (2) is view (3) in Chrudzimski 2005. Chrudzimski's addition of a further view is due in part to his interpretation of view (1) as a combination of type-1 and type-2 explanation but in part also to his inexact dating (1890/91) of the quotes given in Chrudzimski 2005: 47–8. These actually stem from the logic lectures of 1869/70, which suggests, against most interpretations, that Brentano's acceptance of *entia irrealia* would have already begun in 1869 in Würzburg and not in the 1880s in Vienna.
18. Interestingly, we find the exact same passages of text and the exact same schema in one version of Marty's lectures on descriptive psychology (Marty, IIIg č 46, p. 10).
19. The new edition of the lectures on descriptive psychology held by Brentano between 1887 and 1891 in Brentano forthcoming-2 will include these parts, which were left out of the short edition in Brentano 1982/1995. Huemer (2002/03) notes the mention in Stumpf 1919.
20. Chisholm (1981: 12ff) overstates Brentano's point in Brentano 1976 in stipulating that the denial of inner proteraesthesis is essential to his theory of time-consciousness.
21. At first glance, it might seem that view (3) comes back to view (1), considering time-consciousness as a continuum of modes of judgment. However, the similarity is superficial: judgments in view (1) are considered as predications, and the continuum holds merely on the basis of conditional formulations of tensed sentences. The predicative conception of judgments will be abandoned in the early 1870s. The continuum of modes of judgments involved in view (3) is simply a continuum of blind and evident judgings.
22. Where Brentano speaks of modes of acknowledgment, Husserl speaks of modifications of consciousness (*Bewußtseinsmodifikationen*). For a parallel between Husserl 1928 and Brentano's "new" view (3), see Kraus 1930: 18ff.
23. This view is presented in the following way: "While I here unite presentation with judgment, I expressly emphasize that I withdraw nothing from what I have said in my earlier discussions of the fundamental classes of mental relations in opposition to the dominant view on the nature of judgment. I found myself obliged to correct my view not on the nature of judgment, but on the nature of presentation, a view which was too much influenced by the Tradition" (Brentano 1987c: 30).

24. Brentano explains this in the following way: "The presentation of the tone *in modo obliquo* will always include within itself something as present by way of a relation of later to earlier" (Brentano 1976: 157/1988: 94).
25. A similar phenomenon occurring at about the same time is observable with regard to Brentano's rejection of type-1 solutions for his conception of intentionality.
26. Many thanks to Wilhelm Baumgartner, Johannes Brandl, Arkadiusz Chrudzimski, Marcello Oreste Fiocco, and Uriah Kriegel for helpful comments. This paper has been written as part of the project "Franz Brentano's Descriptive Psychology" funded by the Austrian Science Fund, project number P-27215.

8

Brentano on Sensations and Sensory Qualities

Olivier Massin

The term "sensation" (*Empfindung*) famously displays an act/object ambiguity. It might be used to refer

1. To our sensing of something: a sensory act (e.g. a hearing);
2. To what we sense: a sensory object (e.g. a sound);
3. To some mental episode of ours having no object distinct from itself. Pain is sometimes said to be such a "subjectively subjective" mental episode, some sensing which is its own sensa.[1]

In his relentless prowl for act/object conflations, Brentano systematically uses "sensation" in the first sense, to denote only sensory acts—hearings, smellings, seeings, and so on. Each sensation bears on something distinct from itself, which Brentano calls its sensory *object* or *content*. There is no "subjectively subjective" mental episode for Brentano: no sensation, not even pain, is purely self-reflexive, in the sense of referring to itself only. Sensations are all intentional and therefore mental.

While sensations are mental phenomena, their objects are physical phenomena (in Brentano's idiosyncratic sense, which does *not* entail that physical objects exist in reality, apart from being apprehended by sensations; see Chapter 18). As a result, the superficially similar expressions "a sensation of sound" and "a sensation of hearing" have fundamentally different structures: in "a sensation of sound" the "of" is intentional (as in "the seeing of a tree"; "the remembering of a concert"); but in "a sensation of hearing", the "of" is specificatory (as in a "piece of cake"; "a textbook of psychology").

Brentano discusses sensations and sensory qualities abundantly; such discussions are found in his psychological as well as in his metaphysical works, in his earlier as well as later works (1907, 1981a, 1981b, 1988, 1995a, 1995b, 2009). This is due to the fact, first, that he takes sensations and sensory qualities to be *fundamental* mental and physical phenomena (as we shall see), and second, that although he denies the reality of sensory qualities and objects, he amply uses them as paradigmatic examples through which to introduce his metaphysical views.

Sensations have two kinds of features. Some, such as their intentional mode or their temporal features, cannot be explained away by looking at their object. Others, such as their intensity or the difference between senses, are features that sensations inherit from their objects.

Accordingly, this chapter has three sections. The first introduces Brentano's view of *sensations* by presenting the intentional features of sensations irreducible to features of the sensory objects. The second presents Brentano's view of *sensory objects*—which include *sensory qualities*—and the features of sensations that such objects allow to explain, such as their intensity. The third section presents Brentano's approach to *sensory pleasures and pains*, which combines both appeals to specific modes of reference and to specific sensory qualities.

1 SENSATIONS

Sensations are mental acts that are intentionally directed at sensory objects. Brentano calls such objects "concrete", but these are not concrete objects such as lemons, persons, or mountains. Sensory objects are rather colour spots, sounds, smells, and so on. These constitute the *primary* objects of sensations. Thus seeing, hearing, and so on are sensations intentionally directed toward colour spots, localised sounds, and so on as their primary objects.

Sensations are also their own *secondary* objects, in conformity with Brentano's doctrine that mental acts essentially have two objects: an object distinct from themselves (the primary object) and themselves (the secondary object) (see Chapter 5). Together with the presentation of a colour spot, we have the presentation of that presentation (1995a: 127–8; 1995b: 25; 1981b: 41).

Sensations are, furthermore, *fundamental* mental acts (1995b: 91) by contrast to *superposed* acts, which depend on fundamental acts. Thus the presentation of the general concept of colour presupposes some sensory presentation of a concrete instance thereof, and is thus superposed. But that latter is not grounded in any other presentation, and is thus fundamental.

Sensations are, third, the *only* fundamental acts, and all general presentations are superposed on them (1995b: 149). This constitutes a substantive empiricist strand in Brentano's thought (see Chrudzimski 2001a: 71ff).

How do sensations refer to their objects? Brentano distinguishes three modes of intentional reference: (i) presentation, (ii) acceptance and rejection, (iii) love and hate (see Chapter 9). Sensations are not sheer presentations of their object: seeing a red dot does involve a presentation of the red dot, but is not exhausted by such a presentation. It also involves a "blind assertoric accepting" of the red dot, in the sense that one accepts it, judges it real. This primitive belief in the primary object is an inseparable part of the sensation, by contrast to a merely superposed act that would merely be caused by it, as is the presentation of the general concept of colour (1995b: 92–4, 168; see §2.1 below on inseparable parts).

Although Brentano speaks of judgement as being intrinsic to sensations (such as hearing sounds), it is worth stressing that he is by no means committed to some form of conceptualist approach to sensations. His idea is that within a sensation, the sensory object is not merely presented but also accepted, in the sense that its existence is taken for granted; it is not that sensory contents are conceptualised in any way (1995a: 209; 1995b: 104).

Whether sensations also essentially involve the love and hate of their primary and secondary objects is an issue on which Brentano changed his mind, which we shall address in §3.

On top of these questions pertaining to the psychological status of sensations, Brentano addresses the following questions:

1. How are sensations *individuated*?
2. How should we understand the *intensity* of sensations?
3. Which sensation belongs to which *sense*; what are the different senses?

Contrary to the questions pertaining to the psychological status of sensations, these further questions are answered by looking at the *objects* of sensation. Thus:

1. The question of the individuation of sensations is answered by providing an account of the individuation of sensory objects;
2. The question of the intensity of sensations is answered through Brentano's account of the intensity of sensory qualities;
3. The question of the number of senses is answered by classifying sensory qualities into homogeneous kinds.

Let us therefore turn to the question of sensory objects and qualities so as to present these various answers.

2 SENSORY QUALITIES

2.1 Sensory Objects: Qualities and Places

Sensations bear on objects, such as blue spots, which Brentano describes as "physical" and "concrete" objects. This terminology may be misleading: for Brentano, objects of sensations have no actual existence, but only an intentional one—they exist only within the mind (1995a: 10, 19, 88n1, 92; 1995b: 10, 17; 1981a: 208). Sensory objects are *determinate* and *individual*. Contrary to the objects of abstract, intellectual or "noetic" consciousness, they do not have any indeterminate or general features (1995b: 152).

Sensory objects are complex: they are made of different parts. These parts are of two sorts:

- The first are *separable* parts, such as, typically, *spatial* parts: the upper half of a blue spot might be removed while its lower half remains intact.
- The second are *inseparable* parts: these are, to begin with, the *extension* and the *quality* (e.g., colour) of a coloured dot, which Brentano calls respectively its spatial and qualitative "determinations". Inseparable parts cannot be *actually* separated from the whole

they compose; we can only get at them through an act of distinction. Brentano therefore calls these inseparable parts "distinctional" [*distinktionelle*] parts (1995b: 16).[2]

All sensory objects therefore have qualitative and spatial determinations. Brentano here agrees with the "nativists", who, contrary to "empiricists", maintain that all sensations have, on top of their qualitative determination, also spatial determination (this way of drawing the nativist/empiricist distinction comes from Helmholtz). His views on the relation between these two determinations have, however, evolved.

In his *Descriptive Psychology* (1995b), Brentano thought that the spatial and qualitative determinations were nearly on a par. He describes them as "mutually pervading parts", and equates them to mutually dependent distinctional parts of sensory objects (1995b: 19); likewise in his *Theory of Categories* (1981a), he claims that "determination of place and the determination of quality are so closely associated with each other that each is individuated by the other" (1981a: 72). To this mutual dependency between qualitative and spatial determinations corresponds a mutual dependency between the mental acts directed at them: "If, for example, in the case of seeing, colour, and spatial determination pervade one another in the object, then we must accordingly distinguish in it the seeing of place [*das Ortsehen*] and the seeing of colour [*das Farbsehen*] as two mutually pervading parts" (1995b: 104; see also 1995b: 152–3).

Yet already at the time, Brentano ascribes some priority to spatial determinations over qualitative ones. For while he denies that one and the same sensory object can change its sensory location, he maintains that one and the same stationary sensory object can change its colour. Qualities do not survive changes of locations, but locations survive changes of qualities (1995b: 19)—all locations need is *some* quality filling them. While colours are inseparable from the individual location they fill, locations only require some colour, *whatever it is*, to fill them. In other terms, visual qualities are *individually* dependent on visual locations, but visual locations are only *generically* dependent on visual qualities.

Why does Brentano deny that red spots can move? In what sense is the colour of a blue spot inseparable from its location? This is a consequence of the view he came to explicitly adopt around 1889, according to which locations[3] *individuate* sensory objects: "The principle of individuation for sensory qualities must consist in some sort of spatial category" (2009: 132, my translation; see also 1995b: 19, 63). Motion, in the strict sense, implies that what moves remains numerically the same across places. But since locations individuate sensory objects, that is, since the numeric identity of a sensory object is given by its location, motion is impossible. What we get instead is this: a first sensory object, say, blueness-here, which ceases to exist just when another object, blueness-there, begins to exist (1995b: 19).

A corollary of this view is that sensory qualities are individually dependent on (inseparable from) the place they fill. Brentano thus notices that in the case of two exactly similar blue spots, there are not only two individual places—the ones occupied by the spots—but also "two individually different qualities" (1995b: 19), making Brentano an upholder of what contemporary metaphysicians call "tropes".

That primacy of place over qualities became stronger after 1896, when Brentano ended up accepting the existence of "empty phenomenal locations", that is, of phenomenal—although unnoticeable—places not filled with any qualities (2009: 134; see also 1981b: 50; 1995b: 169; 1995a: 216; 1988: 152). While qualities are dependent on locations,

locations are no longer dependent—even only generically—on the qualities filling them. The exception is visual places, sight being the only sense in which no empty phenomenal locations are to be found (see next subsection on intensity).

"Unqualified places" also became central to Brentano's late theory of perception in a second respect. Brentano held in 1917 that all localised sensory qualities are perceived as being at certain distance in a certain direction from an unqualified point of reference (1995a: 311-4), corresponding to what we would naturally call a point of view (which is, however, the same for all senses). That unique and empty point *from* which sensory objects are perceived is perceived *in modo recto*. These sensory objects—localised sensory qualities—cannot be perceived *in modo recto* but only derivatively, *in modo obliquo*, on the basis of the direct perception of that empty spatial point of reference.

That evolution of Brentano's thought toward a hypostatizing of places within the realm of sensory objects is paralleled by a similar evolution in his metaphysics.[4] Thus, from 1915 (see 1981a: 208-11; 1988: 150-5), Brentano argues that space is the only physical substance, that accidents attach to part of that unitary substance, that such spatial parts—i.e., places—can be empty ("the portion of the substance between these accidents are themselves free of accidents", 1981a: 209), and that motion of substance is thereby impossible—all we have is a succession of accidents at different places (see Kriegel 2016).[5]

2.2 Intensity and Multiple Qualities: Brentano's Chessboard

Although Brentano abandoned his early view that all mental phenomena have intensity (1995a: 286), he never gave up the view that all *sensations* have intensity. His view is that the intensity of a sensation consists in the intensity on the sensory quality toward which it is directed (1995a: 120). How, then, should we understand the intensity of sensory qualities?

Before addressing this question, it is worth raising another one, which will receive a very similar answer. Compound qualities are sensory qualities, such as purple, orange, or chords, that are phenomenal compounds of simple qualities. Brentano argues that compound qualities are real—in the sense that there is a genuine phenomenal difference between simple and compound qualities (2009: 91-160). Besides, he wants to maintain that compound qualities do not violate the impenetrability of sensory qualities of a same kind: a purple dot is composed of red and blue, yet red and blue can never fill the very same place at the very same time. How can the existence of compound qualities be reconciled with the impenetrability of qualities of a same kind?

Brentano's answer to these two questions—intensity and compound qualities—relies on the assumption that our sensory field is made up of small pixels, much like a chessboard, which are each filled by a sensory quality or left empty. Crucially, these chessboard "squares" are individually too small to be perceived. They can only be collectively perceived. But such a perception is doomed to be *indistinct*: since we cannot perceive the squares individually, we cannot perceive the details of their distribution within the chessboard. Suppose half of the squares of such a chessboard are red. Looking at it, we cannot see where exactly the different red squares are; we are only presented with there being some redness in that whole area. (The original presentation of this chessboard account is in 2009: 132-4; the proposal is then appealed to in various places: 1988: 8, 147, 152; 1981a: 67-70; 1981b: 50-1; 1995a: 275-8; 1995b: 50).

The intensity of sensory qualities is then explained in the following way: a sensory quality is more intense the more imperceptibly small pixels of the field it fills. The more empty parts there are, the lower the intensity of a perceived quality. Intensity of sensory qualities, in other words, is equated with the spatial density of such qualities (1981b: 51, 54). That account of the intensity of sensations has an immediate consequence for the disputed question of the relation between intensive and extensive magnitudes. The latter, contrary to the former, have parts. Thus, while a small extensive magnitude is a part of the larger, a small intensive magnitude is never a part of a large one (1981b: 50). Thanks to his "chessboard account" of intensity, Brentano is in a position to reject intensive magnitudes (1907: 176–87) and to claim that the intensity of sensation is in fact extensive (see Seron 2012).

Brentano notes that the existence of phenomenally empty pixels is nonetheless impossible in the case of sight (while it is possible in the case of other senses), since the absence of colour corresponds to a phenomenally positive colour: black (by contrast, small locations of the auditory field may contain no sound, for silence, by contrast to black, is not a positive quality—silence is not a sound). According to Brentano, this particularity of vision turns out to support his theory of intensity. Brentano, in effect, agrees with Hering (1878) that sight is the only sense where no differences in intensity can be found (2009: 134–5; 1988: 152).

The chessboard account also allows Brentano to reconcile the reality of compound qualities with the impenetrability of sensory qualities of a same kind. Purple is equated to a chessboard of alternately blue and red squares. Although no small square is both red and blue, in accordance with the impenetrability of sensory qualities, the indistinct perception of the whole chessboard presents us with red and blue participating in the purple whole, in accordance with the reality of compound colours.

2.3 The Classification of the Senses and of Sensory Qualities

What, finally, distinguishes the different senses and how many senses are there? Brentano's most detailed treatment of this question is to be found in his text "On the number of senses" (1907: 157–63). Brentano rejects the views that senses should be individuated thanks to differences of organs, or thanks to differences in modes of intentional reference (all senses having an assertoric mode of reference). Following Aristotle, he argues that the difference between senses consists in the differences between the kinds of sensory qualities on which they bear. Since space or bodily motions are not sensory qualities, there is no sense of space and no sense of the position of the body (the sensations of pressure through which we maintain our equilibrium belong to the same sense as the sensation of pressure on our skin; 1907: 157–63; 1981b: 46).

The key question becomes how to group sensory qualities together. Here Brentano takes his lead from Helmholtz, who argues that two sensory qualities belong to a same kind if and only if gradual transitions from the one to the other are possible.[6] While Brentano first considered such a solution as unproblematic (1995a: 150), he later worries that Helmholtz's criterion is not secure enough as it stands (1907: 158). His worry stems from the existence of compound qualities, which Brentano granted, as we saw. To travel from blue to red, one passes through purple, which is a compound colour—a mixture of blue and red. Now, given the possibility of compound qualities, one may also, apparently, start from blue, pass through a mixture of blue and, say, hot, so as to arrive at pure hot.

The dilemma is then the following:

- Either it is possible to "travel" from one simple sensory quality to another via some compound qualities, and one is led to the conclusion that there is only *one* sense (for it is always possible to mix qualities of different kinds—e.g., red and hot);
- Or one forbids transit through compound qualities, and one is led to the view that the sense of blue is distinct from the sense of red, for one can no longer travel from red to blue.

We get either only one sense, or too many. Brentano's solution to this worry is to accept that compound qualities are necessary to mediate between simple qualities, but to deny that red and hot, by contrast to red and blue, can compose a compound quality. Why can't red and hot be mixed together? Brentano believes that all kinds of sensory qualities can be said to be "light and dark" in some sense: thus there are light and dark colours, but also light and dark tones (high and low), light and dark tastes (sweet and bitter), light and dark temperatures (cold and warm). However, qualities of different kinds are said to be light and dark only in an *analogous* sense (1981b: 47; see also 1995b: 122; 1907: 162-3, 215n17); only qualities that are light and dark in the same sense can be mixed, and hence are qualities of a same kind. Colours and sounds alternately filling imperceptibly small pixels will never give rise to a medium degree of clarity, because they are light and dark only in an *analogous* sense. Hence Helmholtz's criterion of continuous transition is reliable, as long as only genuine compound qualities—compounds of qualities of a same kind of clarity—are allowed to mediate between simple qualities. The different kinds of sensory qualities therefore boil down to the different kinds of light and dark: "We determine the number of senses according to the number of genera of light and dark" (1995b: 122).

This idea, that sensory qualities are grouped together thanks to their kind of clarity, led Brentano to the astonishing view that sensory qualities are of only *three* kinds: colours, sounds, and the qualities of the third sense, which he calls the "*Spürsinn*", which includes temperatures, pressures, tastes, smells, but also algedonic qualities (i.e., the qualities presented by pleasure and pain), as we shall now see. As a consequence, Brentano thinks that there are only three senses: sight, hearing, and the "*Spürsinn*". While the group of quality proper to the *Spürsinn* may sound heterogeneous, Brentano maintains that they are all light and dark in the same sense, one of his main arguments being that sensations of temperature and pressure, or sensations of temperature and taste, commonly influence each other (1995b: 47-8; 1907: 160-3).

3 SENSORY PLEASURES AND PAINS

3.1 Pleasures and Pains as Affective Sensations

Brentano takes sensory pleasure [*sinnliche Lust*] and sensory pain [*sinnliche Schmerz*] to be opposites and stresses that neither of them is a sensory quality: both are intentional acts. Brentano thus strongly opposes Stumpf, who held such affective sensations [*Gefühlsempfidungen*] to be sensory qualities (see Brentano 2009:176-90 for Brentano's objection to Stumpf's views).

How do sensory pleasures and pains refer to their object? For Brentano, sensory pains and pleasures are *affective* acts, together with "longing, feeling, hoping, fearing, anger" (1981b: 59; see Chapter 11). One might have thought that, in the same way that sensory qualities are presented, they might be loved or enjoyed: that we could refer to them affectively. But Brentano rejects this. What we enjoy in sensory pleasures and pains are not the localised sensory qualities but the sensations directed toward them: "where I hear a harmonious sound, the pleasure which I feel is not actually pleasure in the sound but pleasure in the hearing" (1995a: 90; see also 1995a: 144; 1981b: 14). This clearly does not mean that sensory pleasures are second-order acts whose primary objects would be sensations: the pleasure is rather the sensation itself, which on top of presenting its primary object (the localised sensory quality) and presenting itself also *affectively* refers to itself (but *not* to its primary object). Thus among the three modes of reference involved in sensations, only presentation and judgement are directed at the secondary object (the sensations) *and* at the primary object (the sensory quality). Love and hate are only directed at the secondary object.

We can still *say*, however, that sensory pleasures have sensory qualities as objects. But when we do, we must keep in mind that this is true only in the sense that we take pleasure in the sensations that present these sensory qualities. In Brentano's terminology, we take pleasure in the sensation *in modo recto* and in the sensory quality only *in modo obliquo* (1981b: 59; see Chisholm 1987; Mulligan 2004; Massin 2013 for discussions).

Which sensations can be sensory pleasures? Brentano changed his view on this matter. He first thought that *all* sensations are accompanied by some pleasant or unpleasant sensory feeling. No sensations are neutral, and hence, no sensory quality can be sensed indifferently. At best, some sensation "involves a mixture of pleasant and unpleasant feeling" (1995a: 151). Brentano later came to accept neutral sensations (1995a: 276; 1995b: 92, 168; 1981b: 48) and, consequently, to considerably restrict the class of sensory pleasures. According to this later view, all sensations of sight and hearing, as well as some (not all) sensations of the *Spürsinn* (1981b: 48), are held to be essentially neutral. Only a subclass of the sensations of the *Spürsinn* are genuine sensory pleasures and pains. When we speak of the pleasure of hearing, of seeing, or of tactual perception, what happens in fact is that our visual, auditory, or tactile sensations are accompanied by co-sensations (*Mitempfindungen*) that are bodily pleasures and pains (2009: 84, 171).

3.2 Algedonic Qualities

On such bodily pleasures and pains, Brentano never changed his mind: already in 1874, at the time he was accepting other sensory pleasures (visual, auditory, tactile, etc.), Brentano considered these bodily pleasures and pains to have a special status.[7] What are the objects of these paradigmatic sensory pleasures and pains? They are directed at a *sui generis* class of sensory qualities, which fill space in the very same way as colours, sounds, and other sensory qualities, and which are distinct from sounds, colours, pressures, temperatures, tastes, and smells (1995a: 82–3; 1973: 113; 1981b: 13, 46). Some instances of these are the quality corresponding to the sensation of being cut, burned, or tickled (1995a: 82–3) or "stuck with a needle" (1981b: 46). Let us call such sensory qualities "algedonic qualities". Brentano is clear that such qualities constitute a specific subclass of sensory qualities. In his late view, algedonic qualities are included within the third sense, the *Spürsinn*.

Among the qualities of the third sense, and in fact among all sensory qualities, algedonic qualities are the only ones whose sensations are necessarily affective: warmth or pressure, by contrast, are objects of neutral sensations (1981b: 48).

Bodily pleasures and pains are of special importance to Brentano for, as he repeatedly notes, they constitute the most pressing objection to his view that all mental phenomena are intentional, an objection he attributes to Hamilton (see note 1 above). Brentano's answer to this objection is straightforward: even in the case of bodily pains, one should distinguish the pain, which is a sensation, from the algedonic quality that the pain presents. But Brentano does not only want to *answer* the objection from bodily pain; he also takes great care explaining its intuitive appeal. How is it that we tend to conflate the pain-presentations with the pain-qualities, while we are not in the least tempted to conflate the pleasure taken in a sound with the sound toward which it is—obliquely—directed? Brentano advances two answers.

The first is that we typically have only one name for the affective acts and for the algedonic qualities. This is so, for instance, in the case of "pain" (1995a: 84; 1981b: 118). Such equivocations are "one of the main obstacles in recognizing distinctions" (1995a: 84).

The second explanation is more complex (it appears first in 1995a: 83–4 and is reformulated in 1995a: 145 and 1981b: 14). It starts from the observation that bodily pleasures and pains are typically co-sensations, sensations that accompany other sensations (auditory, visual, tactile, etc.). For instance, when we have some bodily pleasure or pain (say, a tickle), we have not only the presentation of the corresponding algedonic quality (some tickling quality) but also the presentation of some other quality (say, some slight pressure). We are then presented, primarily, with two physical localised sensory qualities (an algedonic tickling quality, and a pressure extent), and, secondarily, with two mental sensations referring to them (a bodily pleasure and a neutral tactile sensation).

Now, Brentano notices: "when several sensory phenomena appear at the same time, they are not infrequently regarded as *one*" (1995a: 43). This leads us to conflate the algedonic qualities with the other qualities with which they are associated. In our example, we tend to conflate the tickling quality with the pressure quality. Besides, on the mental side, we tend to retain only the sensation whose affective self-reference is stronger, namely the one that is directed at the algedonic qualities. As a result, although we have two sensations directed at two corresponding qualities, we end up believing that we have only one affective sensation (of tickling) directed at one sensory quality (of slight pressure). Suppose now, Brentano pursues, that the sensation of pressure ceases. In such a case, we are led to believe that we have an affective sensation of tickling to which corresponds no object. We are thus naturally led to fail to notice the distinction between pains or tickles and their objects.

CONCLUSION

Wrapping up, Brentano's account of sensations and sensory qualities contains the seeds not only of the key aspects of his general theory of intentionality—the distinctions between acts and objects, between primary and secondary objects, between three modes of intentional reference, the theory of indistinct perception—but also of central strands of his metaphysics—the primacy of place, the concept of inseparable/distinctional part, and the principle of impenetrability, not to mention his account of the spatial continuum (1988: 8, 147).

That Brentano's metaphysics was influenced by his account of sensory qualities may be found surprising: after all, Brentano insists that such qualities are not real (see §2.1). Let us, to conclude, try to dissolve that air of paradox. Brentano's antirealism about sensory qualities is moderate in the following respect. Contrary to "a subjectively subjective sensation" (see n. 1), "a colour which is not presented" (1995: 93), Brentano urges, is not contradictory. He thus strongly criticizes Bain's view that unseen colours would be self-contradictory (1995a: 92–4). Realism about sensory qualities is, for Brentano, not logically defective but only inconsistent with empirical science. This is what allows him to "fictitiously" treat sensory qualities as real (1995b: 17). Still, what licenses the move from descriptions of such fictitious objects to metaphysical conclusions? Brentano's tacit assumption here is that the *formal* distinctions drawn about such fictitious objects—for example, between numerical difference and numerical identity; between separable and distinctional parts; between spatial and qualitative determinations; between generic and specific determinations—generalize to mind-independent reality. Under that hypothesis, although our sensory contents "do not exist outside of us" (1995a: 10), their minute description provides an entry point to reality.

NOTES

1. The expression "subjectively subjective" comes from Hamilton (1882, vol. 2: 432, 463), who uses it to describe feelings of pain and pleasure. Brentano often quotes this expression (1995a: 89, 91, 144, 244; 1981b: 59), which he takes to capture the main alternative to his thesis that all mental episodes are intentional, but which he also deems to be "self-contradictory".
2. For a detailed presentation of Brentano's theory of parts, see Mulligan and Smith (1985).
3. By which Brentano means absolute rather than relative locations (1981b: 50). He stresses, besides, that local determinations are homogeneous accross all senses—visual and auditory locations are not of different kinds, *pace* Berkeley (1981b: 54–5).
4. See Kastil notes 134 and 230 in Brentano (1981a) and Smith (1987, 1989).
5. See Smith (1989) and Schultess (1999) for presentations of this late view of Brentano, which anticipates in several respects the view of supersubstantivalism discussed in contemporary metaphysics (see esp. Schaffer 2009).
6. Such a view were to be endorsed by Carnap (1967), Goodman (1977), or Clark (1993).
7. Brentano lacks a clear terminology to refer to these—he sometimes speaks of "the pleasure of the so-called sense of feeling [*Gefühlssinnes*]" (1995a: 145).

9

Brentano's Classification of Mental Phenomena

Uriah Kriegel

In Chapter 3 of Book I of *Psychology from an Empirical Standpoint*, Brentano articulates what he takes to be the four most basic and central tasks of psychology. One of them is to discover the "fundamental classification" of mental phenomena. Brentano attends to this task in Chapters 5–9 of Book II of the *Psychology*, reprinted (with appendices) in 1911 as a standalone book (Brentano 1911a). The classification is further developed in an essay entitled "A Survey of So-Called Sensory and Noetic Objects of Inner Perception," published posthumously in Brentano 1928/1981b, as well as in a 1907 dictation entitled "Loving and Hating," reprinted in Brentano 1969.

1 THE FUNDAMENTAL CLASSIFICATION

To produce a classification, or taxonomy, of phenomena in some domain is to order them by genus–species relations. Thus, it is part of zoological taxonomy that the dog is a species of mammal. A *full* zoological classification organizes *all* zoological phenomena (animals) into a comprehensive scheme of genus–species relations. Likewise, a full classification of mental phenomena would organize them into such a genus–species scheme. According to Brentano, such a scheme is not merely pragmatic, but must correctly capture natural homogeneity and heterogeneity relations in the phenomena themselves (Brentano 1973a: 177).

The genus–species relation is relative: the dog is a species relative to the mammal, but a genus relative to the beagle. Likewise, visual perception is a genus relative to color perception, but a species relative to perception. The highest mental genus is mentality as such. Just below it are mental phenomena, which are species of only one mental genus, namely mentality as such. These are what Brentano refers to as the "fundamental classes" of mental phenomena. Accordingly, the task of producing the fundamental classification of mental phenomena is that of identifying those mental phenomena that are species of only one mental genus.

According to Brentano, there are three such classes: presentation (*Vorstellung*), judgment (*Urteil*), and "interest" (*Interesse*) or "emotion" (*Gemütsbewegungen*) (Brentano 1973a: 198). Although Brentano considers presentation the most basic of the three, insofar as the other two are grounded in it (1973a: 80, 198), my exposition will proceed in a different order.

The fundamental class Brentano calls "judgment" covers any mental state that presents what it does as true or false (veridical or falsidical, accurate or inaccurate, and so on):

> By "judgment" we mean, in accordance with common philosophical usage, acceptance (as true) or rejection (as false).
> (Brentano 1973a: 198).

Importantly, this includes not only the products of conceptual thought, such as belief, but also perceptual experience. A visual experience of a yellow lemon has veridicality conditions in the same sense belief has truth conditions. Both are in the business of *getting things right*. Accordingly, Brentano writes that "all perceptions are judgments, whether they are instances of knowledge of just mistaken affirmations" (Brentano 1973a: 209). What characterizes judgment is this kind of *truth-directedness* (see Chapter 10).

This contrasts with Brentano's second fundamental class, whose essential feature is not truth-directedness but *goodness*-directedness:

> Just as every judgment takes an object to be true or false, in an analogous way every phenomenon which belongs to this class takes an object to be good or bad.
> (Brentano 1973a: 199; see also 1973a: 239)

This category covers a large group of phenomena, including emotion, affect, the will, and pain/pleasure. For this reason, Brentano has no satisfactory name for this class, and calls it alternately interest, emotion, or (often) "phenomena of love and hate." What unifies these phenomena is the fact that they present what they do as good or bad. Wanting a beer presents beer as good, but so does taking pleasure in the beer, wishing for beer, liking beer, and so on (see Chapter 11).

Brentano's other fundamental class is presentation.[1] This is supposed to be an intentional state that in itself presents what it does neither as true or false nor as good or bad but in an entirely neutral manner. Its most general characterization is thus this: "We speak of a presentation whenever something appears to us" (Brentano 1973a: 198). This is the sense in which presentation grounds judgment and interest: every state of judgment or interest is also a presentation, but not every presentation is either a judgment or an interest. This means that some mental phenomena are *mere* presentations. When you contemplate or entertain something, it appears to you neither as true/false nor as good/bad; it just appears to you.

Brentano's three fundamental classes, then, are three modes of presenting something: "neutral" presenting (presentation), presenting as true/false (judgment), and presenting as good/bad (interest). All mental phenomena belong to one of these classes, and each class is a species of only one mental genus, mentality as such.

We might be tempted to "translate" this into modern jargon through the notion of *direction of fit*.[2] The idea would be that judgment has a mind-to-world ("thetic") direction of fit, interest a world-to-mind ("telic") direction of fit, and presentation a null direction of fit. This is plausible, but only if we construe direction of fit in terms of modes of presenting. In current philosophy of mind, direction of fit is often glossed in terms of functional role: the mind-to-world direction amounts to *inferential* role, the world-to-mind direction to *motivational* role. This kind of functional classification is rejected by Brentano as extensionally inadequate. For it fails to classify wish as a form of interest:

> Kant defined the faculty of desire as "the capacity of one's ideas to bring the objects of those ideas into existence." … This is why we find in Kant that curious claim that any wish, even if it were recognized to be impossible, for example the wish to have wings, is an aspiration to attain what is wished for and includes the idea of our desire's causal efficacy. This is a desperate attempt to bring the boundary line that the one set of considerations requires into harmony with the other one.
>
> (Brentano 1973a: 259)

It is possible to wish for what is unachievable (immortality, say), which means that wish is not characterized by a motivational functional role—and yet it is a state of interest, precisely because it presents what it does *as good*. Thus if we want to use the modern notion of direction of fit to elucidate Brentano's trichotomy, we must not construe direction of fit functionally but in terms of presentational modes.

2 BRENTANO'S ARGUMENT FOR HIS FUNDAMENTAL CLASSIFICATION

Presumably, there is more than one fundamental classification of mental phenomena both exhaustive and exclusive. What makes Brentano's specific one better than others?

Brentano's argument for his fundamental classification focuses on the role of presentational mode in capturing the deep homogeneity and heterogeneity relations among mental phenomena:

> Nothing distinguishes mental phenomena from physical phenomena more than the fact that something is [intentionally] immanent as an object in them. For this reason it is easy to understand that the fundamental differences in the way something exists in them as an object constitute the principal class differences among mental phenomena.
>
> (1973a: 197)

Since intentionality is the deep mark of the mental (see Chapter 4)—the definitive property of mentality as such—different *kinds* of intentionality should distinguish different kinds of mentality. Compare: if a vehicle is a machine that gets you from A to B, then different *kinds* of vehicle are distinguished by the different *ways* they get you from A to B (flying, floating, wheeling, etc.).

In other words, Brentano adopts mode of intentional directedness as his principle of *classification* because intentional directedness is his principle of *demarcation*. Once adopted, this principle of classification delivers his classification:

> It is clear that all modes of [intentional] relation to an object fall into three classes: presentation, judgment, and emotion. The second and third modes always presuppose the first.
> (Brentano 1981b: 42)

As we saw, presentation is characterized by the neutral mode, judgment by the present-as-true/false mode, and emotion or interest by the present-as-good/bad mode.

Brentano's argument is this, then: (1) the correct principle for classifying mental phenomena is by mode of intentionality; (2) the three fundamental modes of intentionality are presentation (neutral presenting), judgment (presenting as true or false), and interest (presenting as good or bad); therefore, (3) the three fundamental classes of mental phenomena are presentation, judgment, and interest. The argument is clearly valid. What supports Premise 1 is (i) the claim that intentionality demarcates the mental and (ii) the idea that the principle of classification should derive from the principle of demarcation. What supports Premise 2 is Brentano's careful analysis, in the *Psychology*, of the relation between (i) presentation and judgment (Chapter 7) and (ii) feeling and will (Chapter 8).

3 THE NON-FUNDAMENTAL CLASSIFICATION

The fundamental classification of mental phenomena divides them into species of only one mental genus, mentality as such. But the resulting fundamental classes have their own species, which have their own species, and so on. A full taxonomy of mental phenomena would thus require some non-fundamental classifying too.

In the *Psychology*, Brentano goes very little beyond the fundamental classification. He divides judgment and interest into a positive and a negative variety: judgment into acceptance (*Anerkennung*) and rejection (*Verwerfung*), interest into love (*Liebe*) and hate (*Hasse*)—while denying that a similar distinction applies to presentation. Recall that judgment is characterized by presenting what it does as true or false. It is clear from this that the two main species of judgment are (i) mental acts that present what they do as true and (ii) mental acts that present what they do as false. The former Brentano calls "acceptance," the latter "rejection."[3] In the same way, interest divides into two species: (i) love, which presents what it does as good, and (ii) hate, which presents what it does as bad.[4]

Later in his career, Brentano distinguished two kinds of acceptance and rejection: "assertoric" and "apodictic." Assertoric acceptance presents what it does as *contingently* true, while apodictic acceptance presents what it does as *necessarily* true (Brentano 1981b: 42). Importantly, these are still differences in mode of presenting, not in what is presented. In modern parlance, they are difference in attitude rather than content. Thus, an apodictic judgment that $2 + 2 = 4$ has $2 + 2 = 4$ as content; the commitment to the *necessary* truth of this content is part of the judgment's attitude.[5]

As we saw, the domain of interest is analogous to that of judgment in dividing into positive and negative: love presents what it does as good, hate as bad. There is, however, an important disanalogy between the domains of interest and judgment: we can present things as *better* or *worse*, but not as truer or falser. Accordingly, Brentano posits a third *sui generis* species of interest on a par with love and hate: preference (Brentano 1969: 26, 143). To prefer *x* over *y* is to present *x* as better than *y* in the same sense in which to love *x* is to present *x* as good. For all three, there is a further distinction analogous to the assertoric/apodictic distinction. Consider the difference between loving ice cream, on the one hand, and loving happiness, on the other. There is a sense in which the latter love derives from the very nature of what is presented, whereas the former love is contingent. Likewise for hating eating licorice versus hating being tortured, or preferring happiness over being tortured versus preferring ice cream over licorice (Brentano 1981b: 42–3).[6]

As for presentation, unlike judgment and interest it does not come in positive and negative varieties. Nor is there an assertoric/apodictic-like distinction in this case. However, there is an important difference in mode that characterizes presentation. This is the distinction between a direct mode (*modus recto*) and an oblique mode (*modus oblique*) of presenting things. When you think that your friend wants a vacation, your thought presents your friend *directly*, but it also presents a vacation *obliquely*. Interestingly, according to Brentano, temporal orientation is based on this modal distinction: when you think that Mandela has already died, what your thought comes down to is that Mandela's death predates the occurrence of that very thought, which means that the thought presents itself *directly* and Mandela's death *obliquely* (Brentano 1981b: 36). Objects presented obliquely in this way need not exist for judgments based on the relevant presentation to be true; by contrast, objects presented directly must exist if any judgment based on those presentations is to be true.

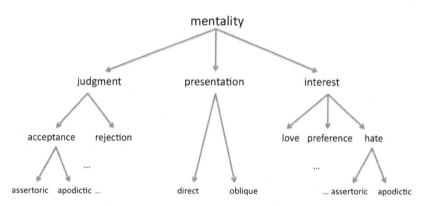

Figure 9.1 Brentano's Classification of Mental Phenomena.

The result is the following classification (Figure 9.1), both fundamental and not, of mental phenomena:
This may well be a *complete* classification as far as *modes* of intentionality go. Further classifications are possible but only by *contents*.[7] Some of these, however, are quite important. For example, the distinction between the sensory and the intellectual is, for Brentano, a difference in the objects presented: some presentations are directed at sensi-

bles and some at intelligibles (1981b: 44).[8] One may further divide sensory presentations according to the types of sensibles they present. Somewhat oddly, Brentano does not do so according to the five/six senses but argues instead that there are three main classes of sensibles: colors, sounds, and the rest (1981b: 48; see Chapter 8).

CONCLUSION: THE PLACE OF THE CLASSIFICATION IN BRENTANO'S PHILOSOPHY

The fundamental classification of mental phenomena is a centerpiece of Brentano's philosophy of mind. The original, six-book plan for the *Psychology* involved a Book III on presentation, a Book IV on judgment, and a Book V on interest (see Rollinger 2012 for details). But it also serves a foundational role in Brentano's wider philosophical program: his metaphysics is based in part on the theory of judgment, his metaethics in part on his theory of interest, and his aesthetics in part on his theories of presentation and interest (see Chapter 2).[9]

NOTES

1. Brentano's "*Vorstellung*" is variously translated as presentation, representation, idea, thought, and contemplation. Here I go with "presentation."
2. For more on the notion of direction of fit, see Searle 1983.
3. It is significant that for Brentano these constitute two categorically different kinds. On this view, to disbelieve that p is not just to believe that $\sim p$. Nor is it to fail to believe that p. Rather, it is a *sui generis* attitude irreducible to belief's presence or absence, an attitude that employs its own proprietary mode of intentional directedness. In this respect, disbelief parallels displeasure: being displeased that p is nothing like being pleased that $\sim p$.
4. Clearly, the terms "love" and "hate" are used in a wide sense here. I love my wife, but I also love ice cream. It is the second, less demanding sense of "love" that Brentano has in mind (1973a: 199).
5. Likewise, an apodictic judgment that $2 + 2 \neq 5$ presents as necessarily false that $2 + 2 \neq 5$.
6. There is also the important distinction between intrinsic and instrumental varieties of interests (Brentano 1969: 144). We love happiness for its own sake but dental health for the sake of something else. It is unclear to me, however, whether Brentano takes this distinction to pertain to the mode of presentation (attitude) or to the object presented (content).
7. At one point in the *Psychology*, Brentano tells us that there must exist modal differences between subclasses of interest (Brentano 1973a: 250), but without telling us what they are. By contrast, Brentano does suggest, for example, some content differences between pain/pleasure and will (1973a: 249) and what appear to be content differences between will and (at least some) emotions (Brentano 1969: 150).
8. This is in the first instance a distinction between kinds of presentation. But it resurfaces in judgments based on these presentations: judgments that accept or reject sensibles are perceptions, ones that accept or reject intelligibles are judgments in the more traditional, conceptual sense.
9. This work was supported by ANR-10-IDEX-0001-02 PSL* and ANR-10-LABX-0087 IEC. I am grateful to Arnaud Dewalque for useful conversations and comments on a previous draft.

10

Brentano on Judgment

Uriah Kriegel

"Judgment" is Brentano's term for any mental state liable to be true or false. This includes not only the products of conceptual thought, such as belief, but also perceptual experiences, such as seeing that the window was left open. "Every perception counts as a judgment," writes Brentano (1874: II, 50/1973a: 209). Accordingly, his theory of judgment is not exactly a theory of the same phenomenon we today call "judgment" but of a larger class of phenomena, one (perhaps the main) species of which is what we call "judgment". Even if we keep this in mind, though, the profound heterodoxy of Brentano's theory of judgment is still striking.

Brentano develops this heterodox theory in some detail already in the *Psychology from Empirical Standpoint* (Brentano 1874/1973a). But he continued to work out its details, and various aspects of it, until his death.[1] Many of the relevant articles, notes, and fragments of relevance were collected by Oskar Kraus in 1930 and published under the title *Truth and Evidence* (Brentano 1930/1966b). Kraus prefaces this volume with an elaborate reconstruction, of dubious plausibility, according to which Brentano's accounts of judgment and truth have gone through four distinct stages. In reality, there is a unified underlying conviction underwriting Brentano's work both on judgment and on truth (see Chapter 17 on the latter). Here I present this unified core of this highly original theory of judgment, which can be captured in terms of three main theses. The first is that, contrary to appearances, all judgments are *existential* judgments (§1). The second is that the existential force of judgment is indeed a *force*, or *mode*, or *attitude*— it does not come from the judgment's *content* (§2). The third is that judgment is not a propositional attitude but an "objectual" attitude (§3).

1 ALL JUDGMENTS ARE EXISTENTIAL

The most fundamental thesis in Brentano's theory is that every judgment is in the business of affirming or denying the existence of something. The judgments that there are zebras and that there are no dragons are thus paradigmatic instances. It is natural to think that not all judgments are of this sort—some are in the business of not only affirming or denying the existence of something but also of saying what something is like, what properties it has. Thus, the judgment that all zebras are striped predicates stripedness of zebras, thereby committing not only to the existence of zebras but also to their character. Brentano, however, insists that the psychological reality of judgments is very different from this. Judging that all zebras are striped, for example, is in reality an existential judgment as well—it is the judgment *that there is no non-striped zebra*.

To show that this generalizes, Brentano systematically goes over the four types of categorical statements in Aristotle's logic and shows that they are all reducible or "traceable back" (*rückführbar*) to existential statements (Brentano 1874: II, 56–7/1973a: 213–4; see also Brentano 1956: 121):

(A) < All zebras are striped > traces back to < There is not a non-striped zebra >.
(E) < No zebras are striped > traces back to < There is not a striped zebra >.
(I) < Some zebras are striped > traces back to < There is a striped zebra >.
(O) < Some zebras are not striped > traces back to < There is a non-striped zebra >.

These are the only four types of *categorical* statements in Aristotle's logic. In addition, however, Aristotle recognizes *hypothetical* judgments. Brentano offers an existential "account" or "tracing back" of those as well. He writes:

> The statement (*Satz*) "If a man behaves badly, he harms himself" is a hypothetical statement. As far as its meaning is concerned, it is like the categorical statement "All badly-behaving men harm themselves." And this, in turn, has no other meaning than that of the existential statement "A badly-behaving man who does not harm himself does not exist," or to use a more felicitous expression, "There is no badly-behaving man who does not harm himself."
> (Brentano 1874: II, 59–60/1973a: 218)

The proposed treatment of hypotheticals is this:

(H) < If a clown does not wear a pointy hat, then he is not funny > is traceable back to < There is not a non-pointy-hat-wearing funny clown >.

Brentano concludes:

> The traceability-back (*Rückführbarkeit*) of categorical statements, indeed the traceability-back of all statements which express a judgment, to existential judgments is therefore indubitable.
> (Brentano 1874: II, 60/1973a: 218)

More cautiously, Brentano should have concluded that all statements used *in Aristotelian logic* turn out to be disguised existentials. He does not consider other kinds of statements in any notable detail.

What does this "traceability-back" prove? For Brentano, it shows that nonexistential judgments are *dispensable*—positing them plays no explanatory role. Yet, it involves considerable ontological cost. In a 1906 letter to his student Anton Marty, he writes:

> every assertion affirming your *entia rationis* [notably, propositions] has its equivalent in an assertion having only *realia* [i.e., concrete individual objects] as objects … Not only are your judgments equivalent to judgments about concrete objects (*reale Gegenstände*), the latter are always available [for paraphrasing the former]. Hence the *entia rationis* are entirely unnecessary/superfluous (*unnütz*) and contrary to the economy of nature.
> (Brentano 1930: 93/1966b: 84; see also Brentano 1956 §17)

The argument evidently proceeds in two steps. The first is to show, as we have just seen, that every indicative statement that expresses a judgment can be paraphrased into an existential. The second step is to argue that significant ontological economies are enabled by the paraphrase. Two such seem close to Brentano's heart. First, if some judgments are predicative, then their contents are propositional, which means that there *are* propositions. Secondly, what such predicative would seem to be *about* are states of affairs, which means that there *are* states of affairs as well. In contrast, Brentano seems to claim, existential judgments do not require a propositional content, and what they are about can be individual objects.

What motivates this last claim is Brentano's notion that existential judgments are not about existential states of affairs, and thus do not have existential propositions as their contents, but are simply about the entities whose existence they affirm. Brentano makes the point clearly in the already quoted 1906 letter to Marty:

> [T]he being of A need not be produced in order for the judgment "A is" to be … correct; all that is needed is A.
> (Brentano 1930: 95/1966b: 85)

The existential is about the *existent itself*, and not *the fact of the object's existence*, that makes true the relevant existential. If this is true, then indeed we have here a remarkable result: all judgments are existential, and existentials are about individual existents, not existence-facts.

What is the reason to take the existent itself, rather than the fact of its existence, to make true the existential judgment? Brentano offers an argument from infinite regress (1930: 95–6/1966b: 85–6; see also Bergmann 1946: 84 and Brentano 1930: 122/1966b: 108). Suppose for *reductio* that belief in my dog Julius is made true not by Julius but by Julius' existence. Then in addition to Julius, we must add to our ontology the state of affairs of Julius existing. That is, we must commit to the existence of this state of affairs. To commit to this state of affairs' existence is to judge that the state of affairs of Julius existing *exists*. But then what makes *this* judgment true? If it is the state of affairs of *the existence of* the state of affairs of Julius existing, then we are off on a regress. The simplest way to avoid the regress is to recognize Julius himself as the making true the judgment that he exists.

2 THE EXISTENTIAL FORCE OF JUDGMENT

If the existence of Julius does not show up in the content of the existential judgment that affirms Julius' existence, then in what sense is the relevant judgment an *existential* judgment at all? The answer is that the judgment's existence-affirmation must be built into its *intentional mode* (since it does not figure in its intentional content and has nowhere else it could be "put").

The idea here is that existential judgments are existence-affirming, but not existence-ascribing. Their existence-affirmation is an aspect of the judgment *attitude* rather than *content*. Brentano writes:

> The most natural expression is "A is," not "A is existent," where "existent" appears as a predicate ... [Such an existential statement] means rather "If anyone should think of A in a positive way, his thought is fitting (*entsprechend*)."
> (Brentano 1930: 79/1966b: 69)

On this view, mental commitment to the existence of X is not an aspect of *what* the judgment represents but of *how* it does the representing. We may put this by saying that an existential judgment's commitment to the existence of X is not a matter of representing X as existent, but a matter of representing-as-existent X. Thus, to judge that some zebras are striped is to perform a mental act that represents-as-existent striped zebras, that is, represents striped zebras in an existence-affirming *manner*.

As for *negative* existential judgments, such as that no zebra can fly backwards, Brentano's view is that these represent-as-*non*existent their intentional objects, in this case a backward-flying zebra. This means that for Brentano, there is a categorical difference between negative and positive judgments—the former cannot be reduced to the latter. Whereas we are now inclined to think that there is only one judgment-mode, and that negative judgment regarding *p* just amounts to judging that ~*p*, Brentano's view is that there are two primitive and mutually irreducible judgment-modes—the positive-judgment mode and the negative-judgment mode. We might put this by saying that Brentano posits *disbelief* as a fundamental doxastic state on a par with *belief*.

Brentano appears to have three arguments for the "attitudinal" or "modal" account of (positive) judgments' existence-affirmation. The more explicit (and weakest) argument appears, to my knowledge, only in Brentano's lecture notes from his logic courses in Vienna at 1878–9 and 1884–5 (Brentano 1956 §15). Those who maintain that existence-affirmation is an aspect of content, says Brentano, must have the following picture in mind. When you judge that the pope is wise, you put together the concept of pope and the concept of wisdom. If so, then likewise, when you judge that the pope exists, you put together the concept of pope and the concept of existence. But note, says Brentano, that you cannot judge that the pope is wise without acknowledging (*annerkenen*) the pope, that is, representing-as-existent the pope. By the same token, you cannot judge that the pope *exists* without acknowledging the pope. But now, it would seem that acknowledging the pope is not only necessary but also *sufficient* for judging that the pope exists—there is nothing in the latter not already in the former. Since the commitment to the pope's existence is already built into this attitude of acknowledging, there is no point in replicating that commitment within the act's content. All there is to judging that *X* exists, then, is acknowledging *X*, that is, taking a certain distinctive *attitude* toward *X*.

Brentano's second argument for building existence-affirmation into the judgment-mode can be found in the *Psychology*. The basic idea is that acts of judging and acts of mere representing (i.e., contemplating or entertaining) can have the same content (Brentano 1874: II, 44–5/1973a: 205). Yet the judging commits the subject to the reality of what is judged, while the mere representing does not commit to the existence of the represented. Therefore, the existence-commitment exhibited by the former but not the latter cannot come from the content, which *ex hypothesi* is shared. It must come from some other difference between judging and presenting. The best candidate, says Brentano (1874: II, 64–5/1973a: 221–2), is an attitudinal or modal difference: the judging represents the judged in a *way* that the mere presenting does not represent the presented.

A further argument close to the surface in the *Psychology* builds on the Kantian claim that "existence is not a property," which Brentano cites approvingly:

> In his critique of the ontological argument for the existence of God, Kant made the pertinent remark that in an existential statement, i.e. in a statement of the form "A exists," existence "is not a real predicate, i.e. a concept of something that can be superposed (*hinzukommen*) on the concept of a thing." "It is," he said, "only the positing of a thing or of certain determinations, as existing in themselves."
> (Brentano 1874: II, 53/1973a: 211)

If there is no such thing as a property of existence, any attribution of existence to something would be attribution of a property that nothing has. That is, it would perforce be a *mis*attribution. But in fact, not all existential beliefs are *false*: it is true, for example, that there are ducks. So it must be possible for us to affirm the existence of ducks without quite attributing the property of existence, which they do not have. The only way to makes sense of *that* is to suppose that to affirm the existence of ducks is just to adopt a certain attitude toward ducks.

3 JUDGMENT IS NOT A PROPOSITIONAL ATTITUDE

If the commitment to something's existence or nonexistence shows up in judgments' attitude rather than content, then the content itself must be exhausted by the individual item whose existence is affirmed or denied. If a judgment that a three-legged dog exists simply represents-as-existent a three-legged dog, then *what* is represented is just a certain kind of individual object: a three-legged dog. On this view, then, judgment turns out to be an *objectual* rather than *propositional* attitude (Chisholm 1976a).

It has sometimes been held, at least in analytic philosophy of mind, that all attitudes are propositional. But the psychological reality of mental life suggests many objectual attitudes. Typically, one loves *one's child*, not (just) *that* she or he is one's child. One is afraid of *dogs*, not (just) *that* the dog might bite one. Brentano's theory of judgment models judgment on the case of love and fear: judgments are always directed at some sort of individual object, and simply represent-as-existent/nonexistent that object. In fact, for Brentano, *all* mental states are objectual in this way—this is why he writes that "All mental references refer to things" (1973a: 291). (Here, "thing" is used to refer to an individual object or concrete particular, and "mental reference" is another term for intentionality.)

It might seem strange to posit a *doxastic* attitude directed at objects rather than propositions. Love and fear are *emotional* attitudes. Perhaps emotional attitudes can be objectual, but are not doxastic attitudes paradigmatically propositional? Clearly, Brentano does not think so. But in fact, we do recognize doxastic objectual attitudes in our folk psychology. Consider such statements as "Jimmy believes in Santa Claus." Belief-in is clearly a doxastic objectual attitude: the content of Jimmy's state is exhausted by some individual object, Santa Claus, the commitment to whose existence comes in at the level of attitude, through the attitude of believing-in. Now, *philosophers* may wish to paraphrase this into "Jimmy believes that Santa Claus exists," so that belief is always construed as propositional. But for Brentano, this paraphrase gets things backwards. Talk of objectual belief-in is actually more faithful to the psychological reality of judgment than talk of propositional belief-that. In a way, we can see it as the whole of Brentano's theory of judgment that positive judgment is just belief-in and negative judgment is just disbelief-in (Textor 2007, Kriegel forthcoming).

In fact, since belief-in talk is talk of an ostensibly objectual rather than propositional doxastic state, the Brentanian should offer the *opposite* paraphrase, paraphrasing belief-that reports into belief-in reports. Consider again the four types of categorical proposition in Aristotle's logic, and the four corresponding types of categorical belief. The Brentanian should offer the following paraphrases for reports of such beliefs:

(A) S believes that all zebras are striped ⇔ S disbelieves in a non-striped zebra
(E) S believes that no zebras are striped ⇔ S disbelieves in a striped zebra
(I) S believes that some zebras are striped ⇔ S believes in a striped zebra
(O) S believes that some zebras are not striped ⇔ S believes in a non-striped zebra

As for hypothetical-belief reports, they admit of the following Brentanian paraphrase:

(H) S believes that if a clown does not wear a pointy hat, then he is not funny ⇔ S disbelieves in a non-pointy-hat-wearing funny clown

Here, "⇔" just means "can be paraphrased into." The arrow is bidirectional because paraphraseability is a symmetric relation: if "p" is a good paraphrase of "q," then "q" is an equally good paraphrase of "p." As we have seen, Brentano has substantive arguments for using this bilateral paraphraseability specifically to underwrite a uniform account of judgment as an objectual (dis)belief-in.

An immediate concern with this nonpropositional take on judgment is its implication for our understanding of reasoning and the viability of standard logic for modeling it. Certainly propositional logic must go out the window, but so does predicate logic, since in Brentano's picture there is no element of predication in existential judgments (and all judgments are existential!). Brentano was actually acutely aware of this problem and tried to address it in some of his logic lectures, notes for which were posthumously published in *The Theory of Correct Judgment* (Brentano 1956). One of Brentano's and Marty's students, Franz Hillebrand (see Chapter 36), developed Brentano's logic in some detail in his habilitation (Hillebrand 1891). The idea for both is to just reformulate the known laws of valid inference within a nonpropositional framework. Consider a straightforward instance of *modus ponens*: if the window is open, the room gets cold; the window is open; therefore, the room gets cold. In Brentano and Hillebrand's reform of syllogistics, this becomes: there is no open window without a cold-getting room; there is an open window; therefore, there is a cold-getting room. Formally, the idea is to replace the familiar

$$\frac{p \to q \qquad p}{q}$$

with something like

$$\frac{-a^-b \qquad +a}{+b}$$

Here + is an existence-indicator, − is a nonexistence-indicator, and a^-b means "a without b." The rule thus reads: there is not a without b; there is a; therefore, there is b. This rule for valid inference is either to be deduced from more basic rules or is to be added as a basic rule in its own right. The program is to put in place all the rules we accept as valid, using a uniform formalism, and then prove consistency and completeness. Although this program has not to my knowledge been fully carried out yet, see Terrell 1976 and Simons 1984, 1987 for important contributions.

CONCLUSION

Brentano's theory of judgment is so heterodox that it has never made any notable inroads outside the most entrenched centers of Brentanian philosophy, in Vienna, Prague, and Innsbruck. Certainly within analytic philosophy, it was doomed by its nonpropositional take on judgment, which greatly limits the possibility for informative linguistic representation of judgments and their content. Yet even if we concede that propositional structure is much more powerful for purposes in modeling in public language, the *psychological reality* of judgment need not be so accommodating to our purposes. Brentano's arguments that the psychological reality of judgment reveals an objectual existence-affirming attitude must be contended with. As the above brief discussion suggests, these are by no means frivolous.[2]

NOTES

1. It is possible to maintain that late in life Brentano had a change of heart and allowed that some judgments have a predicative structure (see Hillebrand 1891: 95–102).
2. This work was supported by the French National Research Agency's grants ANR-11-0001-02 PSL* and ANR-10-LABX-0087. For comments on a draft of this paper, I am grateful to Hynek Janousek.

11

Brentano on Emotion and the Will

Michelle Montague

Franz Brentano's theory of emotion is tightly bound up with many of his other central claims, in such a way that one has to work out how it relates to these other claims if one is to understand its distinctive character. There are two main axes of investigation. The first results from the fact that Brentano introduces his theory of emotion as part of his overall theory of mind, which consists of a number of closely interconnected theses concerning the nature of mental phenomena, the nature of consciousness, and the classification of mental phenomena into fundamental kinds (Brentano 1874/1973a). The second derives from the fact that his theory of emotion also forms the foundation of his epistemology of objective value, which he elaborates in a framework constituted by an epistemic theory of truth and an extended analogy he draws between emotions and judgments (Brentano 1889/1969). I will consider both of these axes in what follows.

1 TWO CENTRAL CLAIMS ABOUT EMOTIONS

Brentano classifies mental phenomena into three fundamental kinds: presentation, judgment, and emotion (see Chapter 9). This classification is not in itself surprising; philosophers such as Descartes (1641/1985) offered the same tripartite distinction. What is surprising, at least initially, is the kinds of mental phenomena Brentano includes under the heading of *emotion*. In addition to uncontroversial examples such as joy, anger, and sadness, he classifies desires, wishes, decisions, and volitions as emotions. He holds, in short, that

[1] "feeling and will [are] united into a single fundamental class."[1]

[1] is most thoroughly defended in Book Two, Chapter VIII, of *Psychology From an Empirical Standpoint* (Brentano 1874/1973a), and I will summarize what I take to be the

two main arguments for it that Brentano gives in this chapter. I will call them "the nature of desire" argument and "the transition" argument.

Brentano's second main claim, as remarked, is that

[2] Emotions can provide us with knowledge of objective value.

[2] is most thoroughly defended in *The Origin of Our Knowledge of Right and Wrong* (Brentano 1889/1969). Since the defense is based on an extended analogy between emotion and judgment, I will need to introduce central aspects of Brentano's theory of judgment—namely his epistemic theory of truth and the role "self-evident" judgments play in this theory—in order to expound it.

My main task is simply to explicate Brentano's theory of emotion, but I will also briefly consider how his theory relates to some of the main themes in the contemporary debate about emotion. Of particular interest are Brentano's claim that emotions are essentially intentional phenomena and his claim that emotions are essentially evaluative phenomena. Both have gained widespread acceptance in contemporary theories of emotion.

2 EMOTIONS ARE INTENTIONAL PHENOMENA

One of Brentano's main goals in the *Psychology* was to demarcate the field of psychology in a way that showed it to be a distinctive and unified discipline. The first thing to do, on his view, was to identify psychology's proprietary subject matter: mental phenomena. In order to do this, Brentano thought, one had to come up with a single condition that was diagnostic of being a mental phenomenon—a single necessary and sufficient condition of qualifying for the status of mental phenomenon. Brentano's proposed diagnostic condition is well known: *intentionality*, or "direction toward an object" (see Chapter 4). In fact, Brentano himself never used the term "intentionality," but his characterization of mental phenomena in terms of "object-directedness" is still the standard gloss on intentionality in twenty-first-century philosophy of mind.

It is essential to note that in using the phrase "direction toward an object" in his original characterization of intentionality, Brentano does not mean objects like tables and chairs. This is clear from his qualification that "object" does not mean "thing." A *thing* [*Reales*] is a concrete entity; tables and chairs qualify as things. In the 1874 publication of the *Psychology*, Brentano was only concerned with "phenomena" in the original sense of the word, that is, appearances, entities that are rightly considered mental in our contemporary sense. Brentano distinguishes between physical phenomena (appearances)—color, sound, and light—and mental phenomena (appearances)—judging, feeling, and thinking—and he maintains that both kinds of phenomena (all of which, again, count as mental phenomena in *our* sense of "mental") can be the objects of further mental phenomena. It is therefore clear that Brentano is using "object" in a very specific way.[2]

According to Brentano, emotions display the fundamental mark of being mental (in his sense); they have intentionality, object-directedness: "There is no hoping unless something is hoped for, no striving unless something is striven for; one cannot be pleased unless there is something one is pleased about" (Brentano 1969: 14).

This view is clearly in line with "cognitivist" theories of emotion of the kind that are popular today.[3] There are many different types of cognitivist theories, but all accept the central Brentanian claim about the intentionality of emotions and are for this reason regularly contrasted with what is known as the "James-Lange" theory of emotion, according to which emotions are nonintentional feelings, which are caused by and track certain physiological conditions.[4]

Brentano's main consideration in favor of the intentionality of emotions seems to be the simple phenomenological observation that emotions appear to be object-directed. More recent arguments for contemporary cognitivist theories involve the claim that the "feeling" theory doesn't have the resources to distinguish between emotions that are distinct but seem to involve the same feeling or to account for the fact that emotions seem capable of being justified.[5]

3 MENTAL PHENOMENA ARE DIVIDED INTO THREE FUNDAMENTAL CLASSES: PRESENTATION, JUDGMENT, AND EMOTION

All mental phenomena share the distinguishing feature of being object-directed, according to Brentano, and may be subdivided into three fundamental classes—presentation, judgment, and love/hate (emotion)—by reference to how they "mentally relate" or "mentally refer" to objects (see Chapter 9). All the finer distinctions we might make between mental acts—for example, desiring, wondering, deciding, entertaining, expecting, hoping, fearing, and so on—fall under one of these three fundamental classes.[6]

By "presentation," Brentano does not mean what is presented, but the act of presentation. An act of presentation is required for anything to appear in consciousness at all. To be presented with something is precisely to have something appear to one in consciousness. Acts of presentation, therefore, form the foundation of every judgment and emotion. Just as judgments require antecedent presentations of objects, the loving or hating of an object also requires that the object be presented in a presentation. Brentano (1969: 16) then goes on to explicate loving and hating in terms of "inclination or disinclination, being pleased or displeased"—what we may call *pro-attitudes* and *anti-attitudes*. Very generally, pro-attitudes (love, joy, and worship) take an object to be good, while anti-attitudes (anger, fear, and sadness) take an object to be bad. In discussing the class of emotions, Brentano (1973a: 199) says: "Just as every judgment takes an object to be true or false, in an analogous way every phenomenon which belongs to this class takes an object to be good or bad."

Brentano's claim that emotions are intrinsically evaluative phenomena has gained wide acceptance in contemporary theories of emotion, although there is still a lot of disagreement about what exactly the claim amounts to. Solomon (1976) and Nussbaum (2001), for example, claim that emotions are evaluative *judgments*, while other contemporary philosophers claim that emotions are evaluative *perceptions*. Part of what distinguishes Brentano's theory from both of these contemporary views is that he holds that emotions are *sui generis* intentional phenomena that cannot be reduced to either judgments or perceptions.[7]

4 EMOTIONS AND THE WILL ARE UNITED INTO A SINGLE FUNDAMENTAL CLASS

So far I have highlighted two aspects of Brentano's theory of emotion: [a] emotions are *sui generis* intentional phenomena; and [b] emotions are essentially evaluative phenomena.

I turn now to what initially seems a more puzzling aspect of Brentano's theory of emotion—the fact that he categorizes desires, wishes, decisions, and volitions or acts of the will as emotions. Categorizing these mental phenomena as emotions certainly departs from our ordinary understanding of what they are. We do not naturally call a desire for a cup of coffee an emotion, nor a decision to go on vacation.

Brentano is well aware of this *prima facie* oddity and comments on his widening of the use of the term "emotion":

> the term "emotion" is usually understood to mean only affects which are connected with noticeable physical agitation. Everybody would call anger, anxiety and passionate desire emotions; but in the general way in which we use the word, it also applies to all wishes, decisions and intentions.
>
> (1973a: 153)

> emotions in the widest sense of this term ... include, not only the simplest forms of inclination and disinclination which may arise from the mere *thought* of an object, but also the joy or sorrow that is grounded in the *beliefs* that we have ... [All emotion] involves an intentional relation of love or hate, or (as we may also put it) inclination of disinclination, being pleased or being displeased. This relation is in the simplest forms of inclination and disinclination, in victorious joy and despairing sorrow, in hope and fear, and in every act of the will.
>
> (1969: 10)

Noting this terminological extension, one may still wonder whether a desire to go to the grocery store and a feeling of sorrow about a friend's death have enough in common to warrant grouping them into the same fundamental class. So let me now turn to Brentano's two arguments for this claim—"the nature of desire" argument and "the transition" argument.

4.1 "The Nature of Desire" Argument

In what follows, I'll present a reconstruction of "the nature of desire" argument in deductively valid form, but before doing so, I'll begin with a very general and uncontroversial characterization of desire. This general characterization will allow us to mark off the way in which Brentano distinguishes between different kinds of desire.

Desires are mental phenomena that are directed at objects we want or are directed at ways we want the world to be. Note that this initial characterization of desire includes no reference to action. It seems plausible that some of my desires are not related to action in any way, for example my desire that it rain or my desire that God exist. It also seems possible that there could be creatures that are permanently and constitutionally incapable of any sort of intentional action although they have certain preferences and desires.[8]

We can now begin the reconstruction of Brentano's argument with a substantive claim about the nature of desire. With Aristotle, Brentano takes it that any desire must ultimately involve a desire for what is good or apparently good.[9] He quotes Aristotle's understanding of desire approvingly: "The object of desire is either the good or the apparent good" (*On the Soul*, III. 10).[10] This gives us the first premise:

[i] Desire is constitutively an experiencing, or a taking, of something as good.

Brentano also accepts the claim that

[ii] If a mental phenomenon takes an object as good or bad, then it is an emotion. (If x is an experiencing of something as good or bad, then x is an emotion.)

Therefore,

[iii] Desire is an emotion.[11]

The final premise is that

[iv] Wishes, decisions, intentions, and all acts of the will are desires or expressions of desires.

Clearly, wishes involve wanting something: I wish for world peace, the end of hunger, and happiness for everyone. Decisions and intentions are taken to be expressions of desires. A decision is an expression of a desire that is usually the result of deliberation. After thinking about where to go on vacation, after weighing all of the pros and cons of various destinations, I've decided to go to Brazil—that's where I want to go. A decision in this sense should be distinguished from a judgment that may be the result of deliberation. After viewing all of the facts about capital punishment, I've decided (concluded, judged) that it is morally impermissible. An intention is an expression of a desire that typically relates to some future course of action—for example, "I intend to go to the party" or "I have no intention of going." The question "Did you really intend to do that?" makes explicit the connection we make between intentions and desires.

Unlike the initial maximally general characterization of desire I started with, decisions, intentions, volitions or "acts of will" are special kinds of desire that are essentially related to action. Brentano offers the following definition:

> Every volition or striving in the strict sense refers to an action. It is not simply a desire for something to happen but a desire for something to happen as a result of the desire itself. An act of will is impossible for someone who does not yet know, or at least suspect, that certain phenomena of love and desire directly or indirectly bring about the loved object.
>
> (1973a: 200)[12]

Anscombe (1978: 148), in her discussion of Brentano's theory of emotion, confirms the definition of will as essentially connected to action. To will something is (a) to make a decision; or (b) to have an intention; or (c) to try to do something; or (d) to act voluntarily.

With this brief explication of [iv], we can see that it and [iii] entail:

[v] Wishes, decision, intentions, and all acts of the will are emotions.[13]

We now have Brentano's unification of emotion and the will: since all desires take objects to be good (in some way) and, given Brentano's understanding of emotions, all desires are emotions. And since all acts of will are a kind of desire, then all acts of the will are emotions.

This argument involves many controversial steps, but here I'll only consider a pressing objection to [ii]. It seems intuitively possible that a creature that lacked all emotion could still make decisions to act, and so, in the present terms, take objects to be good or bad. Consider the fictional character Commander Data in Star Trek. Data is a robot with artificial intelligence who lacks all emotion but seems to perform many actions based on his decisions to act.

Brentano never considers this objection, but one can imagine the following kind of response. Although Data can "act" in some sense—he can move his body in ways that we would call "action" if we were to move our bodies in similar ways in similar circumstances—he can't really *will* anything in the relevant sense. That is, he can't really *endorse* anything, including his own actions. What does it take to truly will or endorse something? Genuine endorsement of something essentially involves taking it as good, but Data can't really take an object as good because any such "taking" necessarily requires having emotions. This is a controversial claim and requires further argumentation. Brentano does in fact argue for it in the course of expounding his epistemology of value, which I'll turn to in §5.

4.2 "The Transition" Argument

The second argument Brentano offers for classifying desires as emotions is a response to an obvious objection to this classification. According to the objection, there seems to be a conspicuous gap, phenomenologically speaking, between feeling an emotion and an act of will. For example, my feeling sad about being far away from my husband doesn't seem to be related in any phenomenologically obvious way to an act of will to get on a plane to visit him. These two mental phenomena just don't seem to "feel" similar in any way. Brentano argues that, despite appearances, there is in fact a seamless phenomenological transition from one to the other:

> To be quite truthful, I, at least, do not know where the boundary between the two classes is really supposed to lie. There are other phenomena which have an intermediate position between feelings of pleasure and pain, and what is usually called willing or striving. The distance between the two extremes may appear great, but if you take the intermediate states into consideration, if you always compare the phenomena which are adjacent to one another, there is no gap to be found in the entire sequence—the transitions take place very gradually.
>
> Consider the following series, for example: sadness—yearning for the absent good—hope that it will be ours—the desire to bring it about—the courage to make the attempt—the decision to act. The one extreme is a feeling, the other an act of will; and they may seem to be quite remote from one another. But if we attend to the intermediate members and compare only the adjacent ones, we find the closest connections and almost imperceptible transitions throughout.
>
> (1973a: 183–4)

… it may at least be true that sadness at being deprived of something is related to the desire to possess it in the same way that the denial of an object is related to the affirmation of its non-existence. But is there not already a germ of the striving lying unnoticed in the yearning, which germinates when one hopes, and blooms when one thinks of possibly doing something oneself, when one wishes to act and then has the courage to do so, until finally the desire overcomes both the aversion to any sacrifice involved and the wish to reflect any longer, and it ripens into a decision?

(1973a: 184)

This kind of transition argument may seem compelling for an act of the will that is intimately connected with a strong emotion, such as sadness over the absence of a loved one. But what about a decision to go to the grocery store? Although I may admit that this act needs to be done and that there is an essential good involved in going to the grocery store, does it really bear any relation, phenomenologically speaking, to a pro-attitude such as joy or delight? This example is related to the difficulty raised by the example of the character Data, and it seems that Brentano could respond in a similar fashion. Even in the most mundane of desires, in order to genuinely endorse the goods to which they are related, we must have a phenomenological feeling associated with the good, even if it is only the weakest of pro-tinges.

5 THE FOUNDATION OF BRENTANO'S EPISTEMOLOGY OF VALUE: OPPOSING MENTAL RELATIONS GIVE RISE TO THE POSSIBILITY OF CORRECTNESS AND INCORRECTNESS

I now turn to Brentano's epistemology of value. To begin, it is worth making two preliminary points. First, Brentano is concerned with objective value, about whose reality he has no doubt. At the beginning of *The Origin of Our Knowledge of Right and Wrong*, he says:

Is there a moral law that is natural in the sense of being universally and incontestably valid—valid for men at all places and all times, indeed valid for any being that thinks and feels—and are we capable of knowing that there is such a law? ... My own answer is emphatically affirmative.

(1969: 6)

Second, although Brentano is concerned with objective value, he does not take this to mean that objects or states of affairs have objective value *properties* like "good" and "bad." According to Brentano, the terms "good," "bad," and "better" are syncategorematic. That is, when they are used in sentences where they seem to be predicates, they aren't really predicating goodness and badness of anything. Rather, a sentence like "insight is good" expresses a truth about *the experience of loving insight correctly*. "Good" is not a term that refers to a property and so in this sense is not independently meaningful; it is an expression such that when it occurs in the context of a sentence, it contributes to the meaning of that sentence. It functions in a way similar to the way in which definite descriptions function in Russell's theory of descriptions. According to Russell's theory, "The *F*" in the sentence "The *F* is *G*" is not an independently meaningful expression; rather, it only contributes to the meaning of the sentence as a whole.[14]

An epistemology of value aims to provide an explanation of how we can come to know what value and disvalue are. This task is more difficult if one takes value to be objective, as Brentano does. Brentano's epistemology of value is based on an extended treatment of an analogy he draws between judgments and emotions. He begins by noting that both kinds of mental phenomena intrinsically involve the possibility of taking opposing relations to an object. Judgments can either affirm or deny an object, and emotions can either love or hate an object. The kind of opposition exhibited by judgments and emotions gives rise to the possibility of their being either correct or incorrect. But opposition in and of itself doesn't give rise to the possibility of correctness or incorrectness; neither does merely presenting or thinking of opposing things. One can see this by considering oppositions such as black and white, up and down, negative and positive charge, and thinking of such oppositions. It is only when mental relations can take opposing stands on the same object that we get the possibility of correctness or incorrectness.

It is worth quoting Brentano at length here. In discussing presentation, judgment and love/hate (i.e., emotion), he says:

> Comparison of these three classes of phenomena reveals that the last two exhibit a certain analogy that is not shared by the first. The last two but not the first involve an opposition of intentional relation. In the case of judgement there is the opposition between affirmation or acceptance, on the one hand, and denial or rejection, on the other. In the case of the emotions there is the opposition between love and hate or, as we may also put it, the opposition between inclination and disinclination, between being pleased and being displeased. But in the case of mere presentation—in the mere having of an idea—there is no such opposition. Of course, I may think of things which are opposites—for example, black and white—but there are not opposite ways of thinking of these things. There are two opposing ways of judging about a black thing and two opposing ways of feeling about it, but there are not two opposing ways of merely thinking about it.
>
> This fact has an important consequence. Psychological acts that belong to the first class cannot be said to be either correct or incorrect. But in the case of the acts that belong to the second class, one of the two opposing modes of relation—affirmation and denial—is correct and the other is incorrect, as logic has taught since ancient times. Naturally, the same thing is true of the third class. Of the two opposing types of feeling—loving and hating, inclination and disinclination, being pleased and being displeased—in every instance one of them is correct and the other incorrect.
>
> (1969: 10–11)

The possibility of correctness and incorrectness in the category of judgment allows us to ask: what does truth consist in, and what is the origin of our concept of truth? Similarly, the possibility of correctness and incorrectness in the category of emotion allows us to ask: what does goodness consist in, and what is the origin of our concept of goodness? And now Brentano gives his answer. Just as

> We call a thing *true* when the affirmation relating to it is correct, [so too] we call a thing *good* when the love relating to it is correct. In the broadest sense of the term,

the good is that which is worthy of love, that which can be loved with a love that is correct.

(1969: 11)

To articulate the proposed analogy between judgment and emotion further, it will be helpful to say something about Brentano's views on the relationship between judgment and truth. These views are most explicitly laid out in *The True and the Evident* (Brentano 1930/1966b), a book that consists of some of Brentano's unpublished writings, mainly taken from his notebooks for his lectures and letters from the years 1889–1916. Although in his early work Brentano accepted the correspondence theory of truth—the idea that truth consists in a correspondence between our judgments and reality—he later came to reject it. In a letter to Oscar Kraus on March 21, 1916, Brentano states his central objection:

> What does it mean to say of a judgment or of an emotive attitude [*Gemütsbeziehung*] that it is correct? You say that this question has not been answered. And, according to you, we cannot see that such correctness obtains unless we have knowledge of an *adaequatio rei et intellectus* and of an *adaequatio rei et amoris*. But to me nothing could be easier than to show than this last is false. If it is necessary to have knowledge of an *adaequatio rei et intellectus*, then we would find ourselves in an absurd *regressus in infinitum*. For how is one to know that there is a correspondence between the intellect and reality without first having knowledge both of the intellect and reality?
>
> (Quoted by Chisholm 1976b: 163)

In lieu of the correspondence theory, Brentano offers an epistemic characterization of truth. It is empiricist in the sense that, according to Brentano, any "concept ... has its origin in certain intuitive presentations" (1969: 13). This means that all of our concepts must be based in experience. For Brentano, the experiential element that gives us our fundamental insight into what truth consists in, and so anchors our concept of truth, is the experience of an immediately self-evident and infallible judgment. If a judgment is immediately self-evident, it constitutes certain knowledge, and no reason can override it. So our concept of truth, our concept of a correct judgment, is based on our experiences of self-evident judgments.[15]

Following Chisholm 1986, it may be helpful to distinguish between a "loose" and "strict" sense of *correct*. All self-evident judgments are correct in a "strict" sense. However, not all of our true judgments are self-evident judgments, and sometimes Brentano refers to non-self-evident true judgments as "blind judgments." Blind judgments can either be true or false, and when they are true, they are true because they are in agreement with self-evident judgments.[16] True but blind judgments are therefore correct in a "loose" sense.

For human beings, there are two kinds of self-evident judgments. [i] First, there are judgments of inner perception; these are affirmative judgments about our current conscious mental acts. According to Brentano, all conscious experiences constitutively involve a self-evident affirmation (nonpropositional judgment) of their own existence. Since the very existence of a conscious experience is partly constituted by an affirmation of its existence, one cannot possibly doubt its existence. That is, one cannot simultaneously affirm and doubt a conscious experience's existence. [ii] Second, there are apodictic judgments that arise from negative judgments about what cannot exist and are the source of a priori knowledge. For example, in making a self-evident judgment to the effect that all squares are rectangles, one thinks of a square that is not rectangular and one rejects it "apodictically." Apodictic judgments are caused or motivated in a special way. The judgment is immediately caused by the judger's contemplation of the content of the judgment: "if this kind of motivation is not present, the judgment is said to be assertoric" (Brentano 1956: 128–9). In making the judgment that all squares are rectangles, we consider a square-that-is-not-a-rectangle. Our consideration of a square-that-is-not-a-rectangle causes (motivates) us to reject it, and we perceive this causation (or motivation). This apodictic rejection is the source of our a priori knowledge that all squares are rectangles and so is a generalization from a single instance. That is, in rejecting this instance, we see that any instance of such a square-that-is-not-a-rectangle must be rejected.

It is one thing to have experiences of self-evident judgments, but how exactly do we acquire the concept of a correct (true) judgment from them? According to Brentano, "concepts are made manifest to us [when] we consider a multiplicity of things each of which exemplifies the concept and we direct our attention upon what these things have in common."[17] To begin to notice the commonalities between self-evident judgments, we can first compare self-evident judgments to blind judgments or judgments that contradict self-evident judgments, and by doing this we notice that self-evident judgments are different from these other kinds of judgments. Brentano describes this comparative process as follows:

> The fact that we affirm something does not mean that it is true, for we often judge quite blindly. Many of the prejudices that we acquired in our infancy may take on the appearance of indubitable principles. And all men have by nature an impulse to trust certain other judgements that are equally blind—for example, those judgements that are based upon so-called external perception and those that are based upon memories of the recent past. What is affirmed in this way may often be true, but it is just as likely to be false. For these judgements involve nothing that *manifests correctness*. But they may be contrasted with certain other judgements which are "insightful" or "evident." The law of contradiction is one example. Other examples are provided by so-called inner perception, which tells me that I am now having such-and-such sound or colour sensations, or that I am now thinking or willing this or that. What, then, is the essential distinction between these lower and higher forms of judgement? Is it a distinction with respect to degree of conviction or is it something else? It does not pertain to degree of conviction. Many of those blind, instinctive assumptions that arise out of habit are completely uninfected by doubt. Some of them are so firmly rooted that we cannot get rid of them even after we have seen that they have no logical justification. But they are formed under the influence of obscure impulses; they do not have the clarity that is characteristic of the higher form of judgement. If one were to ask, "Why do you really believe that?", it would be impossible to find any rational grounds. Now if one were to raise the same question in connection with a judgement that is immediately evident, here, too, it would be impossible to refer to any grounds. But in this case the clarity of the judgement is such as to enable us to see that the question has no point; indeed, the question would be completely ridiculous. Everyone experiences the difference between

these two classes of judgement. As in the case of every other concept, the ultimate explication consists only in a reference to this experience.

(1969: 20, my emphasis)

By comparing a self-evident judgment with a blind (or non-self-evident) judgment or with a judgment that contradicts a self-evident judgment, one can notice an *experiential* difference. This experiential difference, namely the experience of the self-evident that accompanies a self-evident judgment, allows one to acquire the concept SELF-EVIDENT (or, as it has been called here, *strict* correctness), and once one has this concept, whenever one makes a self-evident judgment, one can know that one is making an evident judgment because one is able to identify its experiential marker.

With this in place, we may turn to the case of the emotions. Based on the opposing relations emotions can take to the same object, we have the idea that emotions can be correct, and with this idea, according to Brentano, we have found the source of our concepts of good and bad:

> And now we have found what we have been looking for. We have arrived at the source of our concepts of the good and the bad, along with that of our concepts of the true and the false. We call a thing *true* when the affirmation relating to it is correct. We call a thing *good* when the love relating to it is correct. In the broadest sense of the term, the good is that which is worthy of love, that which can be loved with a love that is correct.
>
> (1969: 18)

By identifying the source of the concept GOOD, we now say what the good consists in—a thing is good when the love relating to it is correct (see Chapter 20). (Recall, Brentano uses "love" widely to essentially mean any pro attitude.)

But how do we *know* that a thing is good? How do I know when I'm correctly loving something? People love different things; what one person loves, another hates. Brentano records this point in the following passage:

> Should we say that whatever is loved or is capable of being loved is something that is worthy of love and therefore good? Obviously this would not be right, and it is almost impossible to comprehend how it could be that some have fallen in to such an error. One person loves what another hates. And, in accordance with a well-known psychological law already touched upon in this lecture, it often happens as a result of habit that what is at first desired merely as a means to something else comes to be desired for itself alone. Thus the miser is reduced to heaping up riches irrationally and even to sacrificing himself in order to acquire them. And so we may say that the fact that a thing is loved is no indication that it is worthy of being loved—just as we may say that the fact that something is affirmed or accepted is no indication that it is true.
>
> (1969: 18–19)

Mere love is not enough for something to be good, nor is it enough to know the good, and so Brentano argues that there is an analogue of the experience of self-evident judgment in the sphere of emotions. In a self-evident judgment, the evidence of that judgment is experienced. In the case of a correct emotion (in the strict sense), the emotion is *experienced* as being correct. According to Brentano, therefore, we have two ways of experiencing correctness—experiencing the self-evidence of a judgment and experiencing the correctness of an emotion. (Brentano only uses the term 'self-evident' with respect to judgments.)

From experiences of correct emotion, we can then acquire the concept CORRECT EMOTION. Brentano offers the following examples of emotions that manifest themselves as being correct:

- Love of insight
- Love for joy (that is not *Schadenfreude*)
- Love of correct love

Emotions experienced as being correct are not feelings of compulsion. But how are we to distinguish a feeling of correctness from a feeling of compulsion? Compulsion has nothing to do with correctness. According to Brentano, one only has to consider one's own compulsions. I have a feeling of compulsion to smoke cigarettes, but this is utterly unlike what it feels like to love insight. Acquiring the concept of correct emotion is anchored in comparing correct emotions with emotions that lack this experiential correctness. Brentano offers the following example:

> Imagine now another species quite different from ourselves; not only do its members have preferences with respect to sense qualities which are quite different from ours; unlike us, they also despise insight and love error for its own sake. So far as the feelings about sense qualities are concerned, we might say that these things are a matter of taste, and "De gustibus non est disputandum." But this is not what we would say of the love of error and the hatred of insight. We would say that such love and hatred are basically perverse and that the members of the species in question hate what is indubitably and intrinsically good and love what is indubitably and intrinsically bad. Why do we answer differently in the two cases when the feeling of compulsion is equally strong? The answer is simple. In the former case the feeling of compulsion is merely instinctive. But in the latter case the natural feeling of pleasure is a higher love that is experienced as being correct. When we ourselves experience such a love we notice not only that its object is loved and capable of being loved, and that its privation or contrary hated and capable of being hated, but also that the one is worthy of love and the other worthy of hate, and therefore that the one is good and the other bad.
>
> (1969: 22)

> Our knowledge of what is truly and indubitably good arises from the type of experience we have been discussing, where a love is experienced as being correct.
>
> (1969: 24)

Once I acquire the concept of correct emotion through this comparative process, I can know the good, according to Brentano, because I can identify when I am experiencing an emotion that manifests correctness. I know insight is good, because I experience my love of insight as correct and I recognize the correctness, which is part of this experience.[18]

Even after Brentano's careful elaboration of what goodness consists in, and how we know goodness, one may still feel like asking, *why* is my love of insight correct? What is the connection between insight and correct love? Recall that Brentano cannot appeal to objective value properties, and so he cannot say something to the effect that correct love tracks objective value properties. Chisholm (1986: 52) offers an answer to this question in terms of the idea of requirement: "To say that a pro attitude is *fitting* or *appropriate* to an object A, is to say that the contemplation of A requires a pro attitude to A." Insight requires me to love it, not because it possesses the property of goodness, but because of what it is. Similarly, justice requires me to love it, not because it possesses the property of goodness, but because of what it is. The appeal to the idea of requirement is clearly not a full or satisfactory answer. For one may now ask: what is it exactly about justice that requires me to love it? A full answer to this question is beyond the scope of this chapter, but the idea that there is something about the nature of justice that requires one to love it is a provocative and compelling suggestion.

In conclusion: Brentano's theory of emotion is a rich and important contribution to his overall theory of mind. I have considered two of its central claims: [1] "feeling and will [are] united into a single fundamental class"—the class of emotions; [2] emotions can provide us with knowledge of objective value. These claims are related in a number of ways, but I'd like to end by calling attention to one in particular. One of Brentano's arguments for the unification of emotion and the will relied on the claim that one can take objects as good or bad only if one experiences emotions. He does indeed provide an argument for this claim in articulating his epistemology of value. To really *know* value and disvalue, to really know what value and disvalue are, one must experience emotions as correct. To return to the example of Data, although he can say what is of value and disvalue, and know *what* is of value and disvalue, he cannot really *know* value and disvalue at all: he cannot really know what value and disvalue *are*. Data is like someone who is blind from birth who can say that something is red when told that it is a ripe tomato, and indeed can know that it is red but not know what red is.[19]

NOTES

1. This is the title of chapter VIII of Book Two of *Psychology from an Empirical Standpoint* (Brentano 1874/1973a).
2. In the republication of Book II of the *Psychology* in 1911, there is a notable change in Brentano's views on intentionality. In the foreword, he says (xxvi/xxiii): "One of the most important innovations is that I am no longer of the opinion that the mental relation can have something other than a thing [*Reales*] as its object." For Brentano, *reales* is a particular, concrete thing, whereas an *irreales* is a universal, a species, a state of affairs or a value.
3. See, for example, Deigh 1994, de Sousa 1987, Gordon 1987, Greenspan 1988, Lyons 1980, Oakley, Nussbaum 2001, Solomon 1976.
4. See, for example, James 1884, Lange 1887. For a contemporary version of this kind of view, see Prinz 2004.
5. See, for example, Oakley 1992 and de Sousa 1987 for a general discussion of these objections.
6. Brentano is not claiming that we can't make fine distinctions between all of these different kinds of mental phenomena; it's just that most of these distinctions do not mark off mental phenomena into *fundamental* classes.

7. For an overview of perceptual theories of emotions, see Deonna and Teroni 2012. Brentano explicitly disavows a perceptual theory of emotion (1973a: 241): "I do not believe that anyone will understand me to mean that phenomena belonging to this class are cognitive acts by which we perceive the goodness or badness, value or disvalue of certain objects. Still, in order to make such an interpretation absolutely impossible, I explicitly note that this would be a complete misunderstanding of my real meaning. In the first place, that would mean that I viewed these phenomena as judgments; but in fact I separate them off as a separate class. Secondly, it would mean that I would be assuming quite generally that this class of phenomena presupposes presentations of good and bad, value and disvalue. This is so far from being the case, that instead I shall show that such presentations can stem only from inner perception of these phenomena."
8. I have in mind Strawson's "Weather Watchers," creatures that have beliefs and desires about the weather although they are constitutionally incapable of any sort of intentional action and don't even possess the concept of intentional action. "The fundamental and only essential element in desire is *just*: wanting (or liking) something. It is wanting some thing, or wanting something to be the case. And being in this state does not necessarily involve being disposed to act or behave in any way" (Strawson 1994: 266).
9. There are many theories of desire, which I don't have the space to address here. For example, there are action-based theories, pleasure-based theories, and attention-based theories. I only wish to emphasize here that Brentano understands the nature of desire in terms of goodness.
10. For contemporary advocates of this view see, for example, Stampe 1986, Oddie 2005.
11. Note that Brentano is claiming that all desires are emotions, not that all emotions are desires.
12. Thus, the Weather Watchers cannot will anything.
13. To my knowledge, Brentano never discusses the possibility of weakness of the will, and so it is unclear how his theory would account for this apparent phenomenon.
14. Russell 1905a. See Stephen Neale 1990 for an excellent discussion of Russell's theory of descriptions.
15. Brentano's conception of an "evident judgment" clearly has a rationalist flavor and shares a great deal with Descartes' theory of clear and distinct ideas.
16. What exactly is involved in a blind judgment being in agreement with an evident judgment is a difficult issue, which I don't have the space to address here. See, for example, Parsons 2004.
17. A letter to Kraus, cited in Chisholm (1976): 163.
18. It is worth mentioning that Brentano also recognizes certain important disanalogies between judgment and emotion, which I don't have the space to deal with here. I'll briefly mention three: [i] in the sphere of emotion, there is the phenomenon of indifference such that "not correct" when understood as indifference neither implies correct nor incorrect; [ii] there is the phenomenon of preference in emotion but not in judgment; and [iii] conjunctions of true and false work differently from conjunctions of goodness and badness.
19. Thanks to Uriah Kriegel for his comments on a previous draft.

12

Brentano on Self-Knowledge

Gianfranco Soldati

Self-knowledge is first-personal knowledge about oneself, that is, knowledge about oneself that is typically expressed by usage of the first-person pronoun. It is sometimes distinguished from self-awareness, self-consciousness and the feeling of self (Gertler 2011: 1–2). These terminological distinctions are not always used consistently, in part because similar terms have different meanings in various languages.[1] Brentano occasionally talks about *Selbstbewusstsein* (self-knowledge) and *Selbsterkenntnis* (cognition of self), but more often he uses *inneres Bewusstsein* (inner consciousness) and *innere Wahrnehmung* (inner perception) to speak about one's awareness of one's own mental acts. He thinks that every mental act "includes within it a consciousness of itself" (Brentano 1973a: 153), which is both an inner perception and a "cognition of the act" (1973a: 154). In other places, he speaks of *Selbstbewusstsein* as "knowledge about the substance which has that knowledge as a property" (1933: 153*; see also 1928: 6; 1981a: 116).[2] Thus Brentano discusses both inner perception and self-knowledge. The two are related but not identical, and this article explains what they mean and how they are related in Brentano's philosophy.

What follows starts with an overview of four central philosophical questions connected to self-knowledge and a brief description of two traditions that have influenced the debate about self-knowledge. This sets the background against which Brentano's position will be presented and evaluated. Brentano's conception of self-knowledge will then be presented, situated with respect to the four questions and the historical background, and evaluated. It will appear that inner perception plays a central role in Brentano's conception of self-knowledge.

Four questions stand at the core of philosophical theories of self-knowledge. There is first a question about the nature of *de se* knowledge, first-personal knowledge about oneself. What is the feature in virtue of which such knowledge is distinguished from third-personal knowledge about oneself? A second question concerns the asymmetry between first-personal and third-personal knowledge about one's own conscious states and experiences. I normally know what I think, feel and desire in a way you don't.

What is distinctive of the first-personal access to one's own conscious life, and what features characterize such knowledge? There is further a question about the metaphysical import of self-knowledge. What exactly is this self of which we have knowledge *de se*, and which has properties we access in a way that is not open from the third-person perspective? Is it a material object, a body like many others, or some other sort of entity? There is, finally, a whole set of rather fundamental questions about the relation between self-knowledge and rational self-determination. When I seem to wonder what I believe, or what I desire, do I not in fact wonder what I *should* believe, or what I should desire, given the circumstances in which I find myself? To know what I should believe and desire is not to find something out about me. It is rather a way of making up my mind.

Two traditions have dominated the debate about self-knowledge in Western philosophy. The first, which has its modern roots in Descartes, has concentrated on knowledge about one's conscious life. The second, which moves from Kant, has insisted on the nature of knowledge *de se*, knowledge about oneself *as a subject*. Descartes is famous for the idea that knowledge about our own thinking is indubitable and infallible (Descartes 1641/1985). From there, he moved to the conclusion that the self cannot be a material object, that it must be a mental substance. Kant thought that genuine *de se* knowledge is not simply knowledge about one's conscious life; it must also be knowledge about the subject *qua* subject. Since he believed, however, that we can only know ourselves as objects, he concluded that although we experience ourselves as subjects when we think, we never really know ourselves as such (Kant 1998: B157ff.). Brentano's notion of inner perception speaks to the Cartesian tradition (it is perception of one's *conscious acts*), while his notion of self-knowledge speaks to the Kantian tradition (it is knowledge of one*self*). Both Descartes and Kant thought that self-knowledge plays a pivotal role in our understanding of human knowledge. But one finds in both the Cartesian and the Kantian traditions philosophers who rejected such a role. Hume, for instance, who would not accept Descartes' conclusion about the ontology of the self, was persuaded that there is no knowledge about the self in addition to knowledge about one's individual experiences (Hume 1740/1978: I.iv.6). Wittgenstein maintained that knowledge about oneself as a subject really boils down to identification-free knowledge about oneself (Wittgenstein 1958: 66–67; see also Shoemaker 1968 and Evans 1982).

At the beginning of his *Psychology*, Brentano suggests that psychology is best defined as concerned with mental phenomena, and not with the soul, because according to some "there is no such thing as a soul" (1973a: 8). Their argument is that in inner perception "we encounter appearances of thinking, feeling and willing," but "we do not notice anything of which they are properties. Such a thing," they conclude, "is a fiction" (*ibid.**; see also 1982: 10). If the soul, as bearer of mental properties, is a fiction, then one might expect that the self, understood as a subject rather than as a bundle of those experiences, is just as spurious. And if there is no special self to know, then one might wonder what self-knowledge could possibly be over and above knowledge of one's own mental acts. Although Brentano does not endorse this line of thought, he adopts a conception of psychology compatible with it in order to preserve theoretical neutrality at the outset (see Chapter 3).

In a later text, nonetheless, Brentano stipulates that "self-knowledge (*Selbstbewusstsein*) is knowledge about the substance which has that knowledge as a property" (1981a: 116). He states that "one and the same mental substance must underlie all mental activities" and that "this substance, insofar as it has consciousness of itself, is what we call our self or I" (*ibid.*: 121*). He argues that the self is given in inner perception with "immediate evidence" (*ibid.*). He airs the Cartesian rhyme that the self is given "as a mental substance" (*ibid.*: 120), a "thinking soul" (1925: 162), but rejects the idea that it appears unextended (1981a: 192). He concedes that a person feeling a pain may "not distinguish the substance, which here feels pain, from the accident by means of which the substance appears to him" (1981a: 117; 1925: 162). The thinking substance, however, can be "brought to awareness as a result of the frequent change of its accidents.... One then grasps this substance as that which permanently underlies this change and which gives unity to its manifold character" (*ibid.*). Animals may never reach the capacity to make such a distinction (*ibid.*). We humans are entitled to the belief that in inner perception we access one and the same self, because "nothing can be perceived with immediate evidence, which is not identical to the perceiver" (Brentano 1928: 98). Even so, nothing one knows about one's own self by inner perception suffices to individuate oneself as opposed to somebody else: "we can imagine without contradiction that another being has the very same determination as the being that we perceive" (1928: 82; 1981a: 121). Brentano is finally aware of the fact that the kind of self-knowledge he is dealing with is supposed to be "self-knowledge *per se*", which he distinguishes from "self-knowledge *per accidens*" (Brentano 1981a*: 123–124), that is, knowledge about oneself in the third person.

Brentano's conception of self-knowledge explicitly addresses three of the four questions about the nature of self-knowledge mentioned above. There is first the metaphysical claim that the self is a mental substance, the unifying and unique bearer of mental activities. There is second the contention that there is a special, first-personal route to this kind of knowledge that is provided by inner perception, which is exclusively first-personal infallible knowledge of one's own experiences. And there is finally the explicit assumption that knowledge obtained through inner perception qualifies for self-knowledge *de se*. The general view is that one has *de se* knowledge about oneself in so far as one knows oneself as the bearer of one's own experiences on the basis of a special kind of access, called *inner perception*. So the view is that inner perception is a route to *de se* self-knowledge by virtue of some of its epistemic features. By attributing a special role to inner perception, Brentano stands firmly in the Cartesian tradition. By recognising the need to explain the nature of knowledge *de se*, he acknowledges a requirement that characterises the Kantian tradition. Brentano did not explicitly discuss the relation between self-knowledge and self-determination. Some interpretations make room for considerations that are relevant in this respect. I shall briefly mention them at the end.

Let us then discuss the three central claims of Brentano's theory of self-knowledge. I shall start with some remarks about the ontology of the self. I shall then concentrate on Brentano's theory of inner perception. I shall present the theory and assess its potential in answering questions concerning the *de se* character of self-knowledge. Some interpretations will be mentioned at the end in order to indicate possible enhancements.

Issues related to the ontology of the self are part of a general account of Brentano's ontology. A few remarks will have to suffice. At the time of his *Psychology* (1874), Brentano takes the self to be a unified whole. It is not a mere collective, as Hume thought, but it *is* complex, insofar as simultaneous psychic acts are "divisives", that is, parts of a whole that cannot exist by themselves (see Chapter 6). Brentano later thinks that the self must be simple, since two persons don't exchange their identities just by changing "all their sensations, judgements, and emotions" (1981a: 118).

Inner perception is supposed to provide access to the self, an access that qualifies for self-knowledge *de se*. We need to rehearse Brentano's doctrine of inner perception in order to evaluate this contention (for more, see Chapter 5). Five ideas stand at the core of Brentano's doctrine. First, "every mental act has a double object, a primary and a secondary object" (1973a: 153). The primary object of an act of hearing, for instance, is a sound; the secondary object is the act itself (1973a: 128). Inner perception is the awareness of the secondary object. There are not two acts involved. The act and its inner perception "form a single mental phenomenon" (1973a: 98, 100, 107); they stand in a relation of "fusion" (1973a: 100, 107). Second, inner perception involves a judgement. This consists in the "simple affirmation (*Anerkennung*) of the mental phenomenon" (1973a: 110). When I imagine Zeus, I represent the Greek god and affirm, or rather acknowledge, my act of imagining it. Third, the judgement of inner perception constitutes unmotivated, immediately self-evident, indubitable, and infallible knowledge of the act itself (1973a: 26, 70, 97, 107, 111). It is immediate and unmotivated because having the act suffices for knowing it: there is no need for any further justification, nor for a reason to believe that I have it. It is infallible and indubitable because the judgement is a constitutive part of the act itself. Further, inner perception, which is constitutive of each act, has to be distinguished from inner observation, which involves an additional act, as when one remembers one's past experiences. Inner observation involves attention, noticing and focussing; inner perception does not. Indeed, at one point, Brentano states that "we can *never* focus our attention upon the object of inner perception" (1973a: 22). Fifth, and relatedly, inner perception is confused (1973a: 216), in the sense that we do not distinguish all the elements we innerperceive in a single episode, and it may lead to mistakes concerning its content (1928: 16, 20). This doesn't prevent it from being self-evident and infallible. The fact that one has a false belief concerning the content of one's inner perception does not show that inner perception *itself* is deceptive (*ibid.*).

In what sense does inner perception deliver self-knowledge, and what kind of selfknowledge do we obtain from it? In a first, rather immediate sense, inner perception delivers self-knowledge, or rather reflexive knowledge, by virtue of the fact that each mental act represents itself, in addition to some external object. Three features characterize this kind of reflexivity. First, it is compatible with a Humean metaphysics of the self. No subject is needed to whom the experience would be given as her own in addition to a bundle of self-referential experiences. Second, it is insufficient for an account of selfknowledge of a more substantial self, as the one Brentano came to accept later in his career. If the self is a substance, and experiences are its attributes, then the self does not come to know itself simply by virtue of the fact that its experiences refer to themselves. Even if, as a matter of fact, all the experiences belong to one and the same enduring substance, the fact that each experience represents itself does not entitle the subject to attribute the experience to herself. Third, this kind of reflexive knowledge does not qualify as self-knowledge *de se*. For an act to represent itself, it is not required that it does so in "the first person". First-personal representations need to be reflexive, but not all reflexive representations are first-personal.

Brentano did not share Hume's conception of the self, and he intended his account to meet the *de se* requirement. That is, he intended it as an account of self-knowledge as conceived in the Kantian tradition, not just as conceived in the Cartesian tradition. What further resources, in addition to the reflexivity of the act, can one find in Brentano's doctrine of inner perception in order to meet these ambitions? Brentano's claim that "nothing can be perceived with immediate evidence, which is not identical to the perceiver" (Brentano 1928: 98) could be meant to address the second remark made above. The argument might be this: (1) each act represents itself, so its content provides not only (indirect) justification for the existence of the object it is about but also (immediate) justification for its own existence; (2) inner perception is immediately self-evident; (3) somebody else's experiences cannot be given with immediate self-evidence; therefore, (4) a subject is entitled to attribute the experience to herself.

This argument has its drawbacks. First, the entitlement ought to be external in the sense that it cannot plausibly require the subject to entertain the second and third premises, which articulate sophisticated intellectual insights. It is not clear that such an external entitlement corresponds to the kind of self-knowledge Brentano had in mind. Second, and for related reasons, the entitlement does not suffice for *de se* knowledge. Although I obtain an immediate justification for believing that there is an experience simply by having it, and although this justification can be immediate only if the experience is indeed mine, this alone does not suffice for me to be justified in believing that *I* have the experience. It should further appear to me that the experience is mine. Third, the argument depends on the acceptance of the idea that experiences are immediately self-evident. Philosophers worried about avoiding the myth of the given often find the idea of immediate justification awkward, especially if it is associated, as in Brentano's case, with infallibility. An account of self-knowledge should preferably not depend on the acceptance of this form of immediate justification.

Brentano's doctrine has inspired many philosophers interested in consciousness and self-knowledge. Ever since the publication of Brentano's views, influential philosophers have dealt with it with more or less critical purposes (e.g. Husserl 1901). More recently, a number of authors have suggested various modifications, some of which could be used to handle the difficulties mentioned above. Thomasson has suggested that inner perception should not be considered a transitive form of "awareness of" but rather as a case of a mental state "having a phenomenological character" (Thomasson 2000: 204). This conception would make the infallibility claim needless, since inner perception would not involve any representation that could possibly misrepresent anything (Thomasson 2000: 206). Kriegel agrees that inner perception is not "representation of": he suggests instead that we should read it as meaning representation *to*. "When I consciously think of the Sydney Opera House, I am in an internal state," he submits, "that instantiates two representation relations: it bears a representation-of relation to the Opera House and a representation-to relation to me" (Kriegel 2013: 25). This appears to satisfy the *de se* requirement. Brandl has provided textual evidence in favour of the claim that the distinction between inner perception and inner observation is about degrees of distinctness: "when this degree is high, we can focus on our experiences as primary objects, when it is low, we can only be aware of them as secondary objects" (Brandl 2013: 62). This line of reasoning could be used in order to consider inner perception as a state that finds in articulated self-knowledge its proper expression. When you judge that you are experiencing something, you don't inform me about what you found out about yourself, but you explicitly articulate, and make up your mind about, the way the world seems to you. This could be the beginning of a conception concerning the relation between self-knowledge and self-determination that is inspired by Brentano's theory of inner consciousness.

NOTES

1. In German, *Selbstbewusstsein* (literally: self-consciousness) is often used as a general term, covering *Selbstgefühl* (feeling of self), *Selbstwahrnehmung* (self-awareness), *Selbsterkenntnis* (cognition of oneself) and *Selbstwissen* (self-knowledge). Note: the verb *wissen* requires a that-clause in German, whereas *kennen* does not. On some occasions, *kennen* can be translated by "being acquainted with," but in most cases one can safely use the verb "to know". For Brentano's "classical" notion of knowledge, see Brentano 1925: 159.
2. The asterisk indicates that I have translated or modified the translation.

1.2
Metaphysics

13

Brentano's Reism

Werner Sauer

On January 7, 1903, Brentano wrote to Anton Marty that by now he thought it to be "impossible that factuality (*Tatsächlichkeit*) should belong to an *irreale* except in dependence on something real" as "concomitantly" occurring (Brentano 1966a: 106). For instance, when someone is thinking of a *reale* or thing (*Ding*) *A*, say the sun or a centaur, there exists concomitantly to the *A*-thinker (who is a thing) also an *irreale*, namely, a thought-of thing (*Gedankending*) which is the thought-of *A* (Brentano 1930: 31, 48). Thus, when writing this letter, Brentano still held the view that the realm of beings comprises besides *entia realia* or things also *entia irrealia*.[1] But then on September 10, 1903, he tells Marty that now he "is making a new attempt to understand all *entia rationis* [i.e., *irrealia*] as fictions, viz., to deny that they are" (1966a: 108). So it was during the time between these two letters that there occurred what has been dubbed the "reistic turn" in Brentano's ontological thinking.

In the following, we will, first, give a rough outline of the scope of the *entia realia*; second, what we may call Brentano's master argument for reism will be discussed; and third, we will attempt to sketch a way out Brentano might have taken in the face of the difficulties inherent in his brand of reism.

1 THINGS

According to Brentanian reism, "everything which in the authentic sense (*eigentlich*) is, was, or will be, is, was, or will be a *reale*" (Brentano 1966a: 347).[2] It is, moreover, even "impossible to think anything but things" (1966a: 384). The notion of a thing, or *reale*—sometimes also called *Wesen*, essential being (see Brentano 1933: 53)—is thus the absolutely first and most universal ontological notion. Its role in the reistic framework is comparable to that of *ens* as the notion *quod primo intellectus concipit quasi notissimum* in Aquinas,[3] as Brentano himself points out.[4] Echoing Aquinas, he says that

the concept of the *reale* is of all concepts the most simple and most universal one. As the most simple concept it does not allow any elucidation. But neither does it require any: on the contrary, it is at once perfectly clear to anyone who understands the name.
(1966a: 347)

Things are concrete individuals existing independently of someone thinking something,[5] as well as collectives and parts of such concrete individuals. Examples of things are

a man, an animal, a physical body, a mind, a four-dimensional topoid, a people ... an atom, half of an atom, the 1000th part of an atom, [a boundary,] a judger (*ein Urteilender*), a willer (*ein Wollender*), a judger-and-willer, a judger and a willer. Every true collective of things is a thing and every true part of a thing is a thing.
(1966a: 385; "a boundary" is inserted from the list of examples on p. 380)

In terms of the basic division of things into substances and accidents,[6] which Brentano inherited from Aristotle, these examples are either substances or accidents: the judger and the willer are simply accidents, the judger-and-willer (i.e., a mind simultaneously both judging and willing) is a "multiple accident" (Brentano 1933: 11). The thesis of reism, then, is tantamount to saying that "a being in the authentic sense," that is, a thing, "is not only every substance, every multiplicity of substances, and every part of a substance, but also every accident" (*ibid.*).[7] This does not tell us whether a collective of substances again is a substance, but in another place he explicitly says that also "a plurality of bodies taken together, or a plurality of minds, or a mind taken together with a body belong under this concept" (1933: 145f.), namely of substance.

As admitting only things, i.e., concrete individuals, the ontology of reism is a very parsimonious one.[8] Earlier, Brentano had countenanced a great variety of *entia irrealia*, some of which—namely the collectives, the parts, and the boundaries of things[9]—then did fall on the side of the *realia*. This is not the place to give a detailed survey of the *irrealia* (of which we have previously met the *Gedankendinge*) and of the strategies the reistic Brentano employs to eliminate them. In general, he treats them as mere "entia linguae, as fictions that are due to a misunderstood multiplication of linguistic expressions" (1966a: 174).[10] Expressions allegedly referring to *irrealia* are names only in the grammatical but not in the "logical" or "psychological" sense, that is, not autosemantic but only synsemantic expressions (just like conjunctions or prepositions). Their role in our language, properly understood, is only as abbreviating devices that we hardly can avoid given how natural language is, such that completely dispensing with them would amount to no less than having "to refrain from using this language altogether, and to invent an entirely new and most unwieldy language" (Brentano 1924a: 275).

But nevertheless we ought to make special mention of the kind of *irrealia* that are *abstract entities* allegedly introduced by abstract pseudo-names, since their rejection is crucial to the entire reistic programme. These are rejected because they would lead to abstract and even universal parts of concrete individuals, for example, to roundness as part of a sphere. But such a "partition of the concrete into two parts one of which would equate to the abstract ... is absolutely impossible" (Brentano 1933: 7). Their alleged names are to be paraphrased away by means of "as such" locutions, for example, "colour" will give way to "a coloured thing as such (*Farbiges als solches*)," or "Seeing is not hearing" to "A seer as such (*ein Sehender als solcher*) is not a hearer," and the like.[11]

2 THE MASTER ARGUMENT FOR REISM

As the concept of the *reale* or thing is his supreme all-encompassing ontological notion, such that "an accident is a thing in the same sense as a substance" (1933: 28), in the division of ontologies into unicategorial and pluricategorial ones, Brentano belongs in the camp of the unicategorialists, espousing the thesis that the term 'being' is univocal; whoever denies this, he tells Oskar Kraus, not without a touch of self-aggrandizement, "has Aristotle on his side, but the truth against him."[12]

Although Brentano's account of substance and accident as such is not our topic, we must take notice of his construal of the substance–accident relationship as far as it is pertinent to the question of the feasibility of his reism *in toto*. Now, Brentano's doctrine is that while a substance like a mind or soul thinks, the accident is the thinking-mind, which is a whole containing the substance (the mind or soul in this case) as a one-sidedly separable proper part, but without having another proper part:

> Among the essential beings (*Wesen*) [i.e., things] that show parts, some are such that the whole is not composed of a plurality of parts; it rather appears as an enrichment of one part, but not by addition of a second part. An example for this is offered by a thinking soul. It ceases to be thinking and yet remains the same soul, but when it becomes thinking again no second thing is added to the essential being which is the soul.
>
> (Brentano 1933: 53)

Thus Brentano rejects for the part–whole relation which is the substance–accident relation what Peter Simons has called the principle of weak supplementation, stating that if x is a proper part of y, then there exists another proper part z of y such that z is disjoint from x. Simons holds that this principle is "analytically contained in the concept of part" in that it "serves to distinguish part/whole relations from other irreflexive and transitive relations such as being larger than" (Simons 1988: 56f.).[13] Indisputable as this appears to be, we nevertheless would be forced to abandon the principle in the case of Brentano's substance–accident relation if what we have called his master argument for reism is indeed that flawless and irresistible piece of reasoning Brentano himself believes it to be.

A full exposition of this argument,[14] which Brentano repeats more or less extensively on many occasions, is in the letter to Kraus of October 31, 1914, in which Brentano says that he can

> in a very simple and strict way prove that nothing but things can be objects of our representing and hence of our thinking in general. The proof is based on this that the concept of representing is unitary (*einheitlich*) such that the name ["representing"] is univocal, not equivocal. But in this concept is included that every representing is representing something, and thus, if this "something" itself would not be unequivocal neither the name "representing" could be unequivocal. If this

is certain, then it is impossible that by this something now a thing and then an *irreale* can be understood. For there is no concept which could be common both to a *reale* and an *irreale*. In my opinion … this proof is absolutely decisive.
(Brentano 1930: 106 = 1966a: 249)

Now let us set out step by step this master argument of Brentano's according to which we cannot even think what would be an *ens irreale*:

(1) The concept of representing is unitary, which is to say that "representing" is univocal.
(2) To represent is to represent something.
(3) If the "something" of "representing something" were not univocal, then "representing" too would not be univocal.
(4) Hence the "something" of "representing something" is univocal, and that means that it stands for one single concept[15] applying to whatever can be an object of representing.
(5) There is no concept applying both to *realia* and *irrealia*, that is, there cannot be one single *summum genus* comprising both *realia* and *irrealia*.
(6) Thus *realia*-words (e.g., "horse") and *irrealia*-words (e.g., "thought-of-horse" or "horsehood") cannot both be substitutes for the "something" of "representing something"; in other words, we cannot represent both *realia* and *irrealia*.

A trivial premise not explicitly stated is

(7) We can represent *realia*.

From (7) and (6) the conclusion follows that

(8) *We cannot even represent, or think in general, entia irrealia.*

Of the multitude of comments this argument has prompted, we will have to confine ourselves to two recent ones.

Jan Woleński (2012, sec.1) considers the argument successful at the most to the extent that "if 'something' refers to the objects *a* and *b*, both belong to the same ontological category," such that it is at best only "an argument for a unicategorial ontology," but not an argument for reism. He thus queries premise (5), and it is a good question indeed what makes Brentano that sure of its truth. For even within Brentano's own framework, there is something that might be put to use against (5), namely, what he holds concerning the relation of the concept *coloured thing* to the various colour concepts such as *red*. Brentano says that "we can distinguish in the concept red (*Rot*) the concept coloured thing (*Farbiges*), but we cannot conceive that which distinguishes the red things (*das Rote*) from other kinds of coloured things (*Farbigem*) in separation from the concept coloured thing" (Brentano 1933: 151f.). This is so because the concept *red* as a whole is the differentia marking off the red things from the blue things and so on, such that "the differentia red thing (*Rotes*) includes conceptually the concept coloured thing (*Farbiges*)" (1933: 53). Brentano uses this as an analogy that should support his abandonment of the supplementation principle in the case of the substance–accident relation, but it could be applied much more directly, and much more plausibly, against (5): the analogy would be positing *entity* (say) as the highest concept and postulating "that the concept *entity* differentiates itself into the concepts *thing* and *non-thing*, but not by way of addition of a differentiating concept which would not include the concept *entity*, *thing* and *non-thing* themselves being these differentiae"; and this would at once lead to replacing (7) with

(7*) We can represent both *realia* and *irrealia*,

with (1) to (4) remaining untouched. Indeed, the pre-reistic Brentano was possibly thinking along these lines, as can be gathered from his 1889 lecture "*Über den Begriff der Wahrheit.*" There he says that

> the range of the domain over which judging can extend ... is utterly unlimited. The matter [of judging] can be chosen completely at random. Certainly, it is always "something" that is judged. But what does this "something" mean? It is a word that could be applied equally to God and the world, to any thing and non-thing (*Unding*) ... Here there is initially no question at all of a being in the sense of the *reale*, the thingly, the essential (*im Sinne des Realen, Dinglichen, Wesenhaften*).
> (Brentano 1930: 24–5)

Here Brentano posits, presumably on the basis of (7*) *plus* (1)–(4), "something" as the highest concept-word, to which both "thing" and "non-thing" are subordinated, and thus what Woleński calls a unicategorial ontology that, however, is not restricted to reism. In other words, just as in his reistic phase, Brentano appears earlier to have championed the univocality thesis. The difference is only that the pre-reistic Brentano did believe in the generic unity of *realia* and *irrealia* but the reistic Brentano did not, and consequently he did away with the *irreale* as an object of representation.

A much more negative assessment of the master argument than Woleński's has been put forth by Simons, who finds it even "extraordinarily bad" (Simons 2006: 90). According to Simons, the fatal defects of the argument are two. First, it ignores the distinction between "think that" and "think of." Secondly, it overlooks the transcategorial nature of the pronoun "something" as being merely "a catch-word which connotes no category whatsoever," such that "even if 'think of something' is univocal ... it does not follow that everything that can be thought of falls into a single category" (*ibid.*). But neither objection can be accepted. As for the first, even leaving aside Brentano's reduction of "think that" to "think of" in his "nonpropositional theory of judgment" (see Chapter 10), as Chisholm (1982: 17) has called it, the master argument turns on representing, the basic kind of thinking, and representing is of course straightforwardly of the "think of" kind. Thus the "think that"/"think of" distinction tells us nothing against it. The second objection depicts the situation as if Brentano did fail to notice the transcategorial nature of "something." But this is not true, as his letter to Kraus—who apparently did actually think that the master argument relied on the supposition that "something" already by itself is unicategorial (i.e., synonymous with "thing")—of March 9, 1915, shows:

> You ascribe to me the opinion that "something" could mean only *realia*. Not at all! "Something" is not a substantive or an adjective, but a pronoun which could

relate as proxy as well to substantives or adjectives that do not signify things. My contention only was that it could not stand … as a proxy both for things and non-things without becoming equivocal.

(Brentano 1966a: 283)

It is plain, then, that Brentano did not commit the mistake of taking the univocality of "something" for granted.

Earlier, the discussion of the master argument focussed on the question of whether or not *realia* and *irrealia* can constitute a common genus, that is, on premise (5). But let us now, motivated by the Simons criticism, change the perspective by concentrating on premise (3), which inevitably gives rise to this question: given that "representing something" is univocal, does it follow that therefore its "something" must also be univocal?

The answer would be affirmative if a substitute of this "something" would signify a differentia of representing something. But of course, this is not the case, since otherwise a (coloured thing)-representing would itself have to be coloured.[16] Now this is plain, and yet it would seem that the construal of the "something"-substitutes as signifying differentiae of representing something would be the only way in which (3) could be ascertained beyond doubt.

The "something" of "representing something" indicates the intentional object, and in his pre-reistic phase, Brentano accounted for it in terms of its being a part "that is extractable" from the whole of the representing act "by a modifying distinction" (Brentano 1982: 25). Put the other way around, "representing—" is a modifying context, or a modifier, for whatever may be inserted in the gap. And thus, there arises the question of *why attaching the modifier "representing—" to "something" should, if this "something" is equivocal, render also the entire expression "representing something" equivocal*. There seems to be no answer to this question in Brentano, which is to say that premise (3) of the master argument remains without solid foundation. We may put the point also in terms of the distinction between representing something *modo recto* and *modo obliquo*, which since at least 1906 was Brentano's tool for handling the difference between representings and their objects.[17] If I represent an *A*-representing, I represent the *A*-representing *modo recto* and *A* itself *modo obliquo*, the difference being that accepting the *A*-representing does not include accepting A as well. And then, only couched in another mode of speaking, there arises the very same question as before, namely, if "representing something" is univocal, does it follow that when I represent a representing-something in *modo recto*, whatever I thereby represent in *modo obliquo* must be unicategorial such that the "something" of "representing something" will also be univocal?

Thus, we have come back to Simons' contention that if "think of something" is univocal, it does not follow that its "something" too must be univocal but without resting the case from the outset on the transcategorial nature of "something."

Let us finally look at the issue from a very different point of view. As noted above, Brentano takes the "something" of "representing something" as a concept-word. We of course look at it rather as a (bound) variable; indeed, in his statement quoted in the fifth paragraph of this chapter, Brentano himself speaks as if he were viewing it thus, but of course he cannot really do so, as the notion of a variable is alien to his conception of logic. Now, in conformity with its transcategorial nature, the pronoun "something" performs the roles of logically heterogeneous variables:

(a) He killed something – individual or nominal variable, $(\exists x)$(he killed x),
(b) He is something – predicate variable, $(\exists \phi)$(he is a ϕer).

But now, what about

(c) He represents something – ?

An assimilation of (c) to (a) or to (b) is out of the question: in the case of (a), because from his representing something it does not follow that there is something that he represents; in the case of (b), already for the syntactical reason that in (c) "something" is attached to a main verb but in (b) only to the copula. Therefore, the linguistic conformity of (c) with (a) and (b) is logically spurious, that is, the "something" of (c) must be a type of variable different from both the others. Thus there remains to view it as a variable the substitutes of which are adverbial phrases expressing ways in which representings are how they are.[18] That is, the "something" of (c) is to be read as

'somehow' or 'somewise' (generalized from 'piecewise' etc.),

of which these two would be substitutes:

'horse-wise', 'horsehood-wise',

to take two cases one of which is a *reale*-word and the other an *irreale*-word adverbialized by '-wise'. Thus (c) turns into

(*c) He represents some-wise,

with these two substitutions

(*c^1) He represents horse-wise,

(*c^2) He represents horsehood-wise.

For Brentano's master argument, it is essential that the "something" of "represent something" be a concept-word. However, it has shown that it has to give way to the adverbial variable "somewise." But in Brentano's own view, adverbs are only synsemantic expressions (see 1924b: 229): thus it is unclear why, for the reason that this variable takes both *reale*- and *irreale*-words adverbialized by "-wise" as substitutes, the whole expression "represent somewise" should become equivocal.

To sum up, Brentano's master argument is by no means firm enough to provide an unshakeable foundation for his reism, a reism that would force us into denying even the supplementation principle for the substance–accident relation.

3 AN ARISTOTELIAN IMPROVEMENT?

Let us in concluding speculate on how Brentano's reistic ontology could be reconstrued with the least divergences but consistently with the supplementation principle for the substance–accident relation.

The most promising path would seem to be a reconstruction in terms of a theory of (individual) property instances, or *tropes*. According to this, if something, for instance a block of ice, is cold, then there exists an individual that is its coldness (Bigelow 1998: 237f.). Such a theory was adumbrated already by Aristotle in *Categories*, chapter 2. There he distinguishes, among the beings (τῶν ὄντων), the accident from the substance, the former being what is *in* an underlying subject (ἐν ὑποκειμένῳ), that is, "what is in something, but not as a part, and cannot exist in separation from what it is in" (1a24–25). Among the accidents, he again distinguishes those that are predicable from those that are not predicable, his examples for the latter being τὸ τὶ λευκόν, this individual white, and ἡ τὶς γραμματική, this individual knowledge-of-grammar, which are, just like ὁ τὶς ἄνθρωπος and ὁ τὶς ἵππος, the individual substances *this man* and *this horse*, ἄτομα καὶ ἓν ἀριθμῷ, "in-dividua and one in number" (1b6–7). On this conception of an individual accident (which is introduced by Aristotle only to disappear again even in the *Categories* themselves), the whole of the white horse consists of two different individual entities: the horse, which is one-sidedly separable from the relevant whole; and this white, which is inseparable from it, as it depends for its existence on standing in the relation of being-*in* to the horse.[19] In tune with Brentano's verbiage, the whole made up of this horse and this white which is *in* this horse could still be called the accident containing the horse as one-sidedly separable part; this white by itself, the inseparable part, could then perhaps be called the *principium accidentis*.

The substance–accident ontology based thereon would then be, perhaps with "categorial entity" as a convenient covering label:

categorial entities,
dividing into
– substances: entities that are not *in* another entity,
– accidental principles: entities that are *in* another entity, and
– accidents: entities that are wholes consisting of an accidental principle and another entity *in* which the accidental principle is.

Brentano was of course acquainted with the *Cat.* chap. 2 conception of individual accidents. Criticizing unnamed thinkers for positing "odd intermediates (*Mitteldinge*) between the absurd universals and the real individuals" (Brentano 1933: 60), he says that some of them

> do not fabricate special [intermediate] things for all universals but limit such fictitious divisions to the case of the accidents. Where an accident includes a substance as a part, they do as if to this substantial part there would be added within the whole another purely accidental part which would be as free from the substance as a substance does not include anything accidental. This second part would then be a thing as well, to which then—in contrast to the concrete name that would be assigned to the substance together with the accident—an abstract name would apply, for instance, thinking, willing (*Denken, Wollen*) as opposed to thinking thing, willing thing (*Denkendes, Wollendes*).
>
> (Brentano 1933: 61)

Brentano raises two objections against the *Cat.* chap. 2 individual accidents, which we have called accidental principles. The one stated in the quote is that they would be referred to by abstract names, which would relegate them into the ontological waste bin of the *entia irrealia*. The other objection he has given right before that passage, namely, that such an entity "would not include that by which it is individualized" (*ibid.*).

As for the first objection, we note first that without the master argument, it is without force anyway. But secondly, it may well be suspected that in raising it, Brentano got entangled in a linguistic snare, as using an abstract term for referring to that individual which is *in* the horse (such that it is a white horse) can be considered a mere *modus significandi* serving to make something the subject of discourse which is not an authentic (i.e., independently existing) subject. Consider the word 'white' in

"This white[1] is that by which this horse is white[2]."

Although as "white[1]" it is used as an abstract term, it refers in this use to the very same item, only individualized by this horse as against that rabbit and made a subject of discourse, to which it refers as "white[2]," where it is a concrete term. That is, from the use of the adjective as an abstract term, by itself, nothing follows concerning the ontological nature of that which is signified in this way. Hence, it might, perhaps, even be claimed that an ontology of accidental principles, substances, and accidents as just outlined would actually be unicategorial in Brentano's own sense.

Concerning the other objection, it is, despite Kastil's explanation of it (see Brentano 1933: 315f. note 6), difficult to see what it could establish; after all, classes might be absurd pseudoentities, but if so then certainly not because they are "individuated" by something different from themselves, namely, their elements.

To conclude, then, it seems that reconstructing Brentano's substance–accident theory in terms of a sort of trope theory would perhaps have been a viable way out from the impasse of abandoning the supplementation principle, and viable especially because it would perhaps preserve at least his main objective of subsuming both substances and accidents under one single ontological category; whether there would be further ontological categories to be added may be left open.[20]

NOTES

1. Albeit in a restricted way, since before he had acknowledged also *irrealia* that are entirely independent of *realia*: see Brentano 1930: 26.
2. The words "in the authentic sense" have been inserted from p. 384.
3. *Qaest. disp. de Veritate* qu.1 art.1 co.
4. In his letter to Oskar Kraus of January 9, 1915 (Brentano 1966a: 272). He refers to the "Summa theologica," presumably with *S. Th* IaIIae qu.94 art.2 co in mind. Cf. also the letter to Kraus of November 8, 1914 (1966a: 251).
5. This proviso is to exclude the thought-of-things (*Gedankendinge*) from the realm of the *realia*.
6. "I say that the substance contrasts with the accident. The name 'substance' applies to a thing insofar it is not an accident" (1930: 146), which makes the distinction explicitly exclusive.
7. The occurrence of the word 'being', '*Seiendes*', in the quote, taken from a 1914 dictation, prompts an explanatory remark. Brentano distinguishes two senses of the word. In the way it is used here in the quote, "being" does not imply existing; in the other use, "being" is simply "existing"; in the way it is used in the quote, Brentano says in another 1914 dictation, "the name 'being' is synonymous with 'thing'. This is its authentic meaning (*eigentliche Bedeutung*), but besides that the word has also several other meanings," of which the first is this one: "We distinguish among the things we think those that are from those that are not. This is another sense of 'being' ('*Seiend*'). Here it does not enunciate the most universal concept thing, but no concept at all. You may very well apply to the city of Nineveh the name thing, but one who knows that the city is not, will not say that it is a being in the sense that I am considering now

... Used in this sense, the word 'a being' is, properly speaking, not a name" (Brentano 1933: 58f.), that is, not an autosemantic word signifying a concept, because it expresses only a judger's correct acceptance of something. (In drawing this distinction, even the Brentano of 1914 is still following in the steps of Aquinas, who is accustomed to say, usually with reference to Aristotle, that *ens dupliciter dicitur,* as in chap. 1 of his early treatise *De Ente et Essentia* already; in one way, *ens* is everything about which a true affirmation can be formed, that is, *ens* in this sense is what exists, whereas in the other way *ens* is only what falls into the categories, that is, what has an *essentia*. Thus Brentano's drawing this distinction is not as gratuitous as it *prima facie* might appear but follows a grand tradition.) It is important to pay heed to Brentano's distinguishing between these two senses of "being", since otherwise one could be wondering how we ever could reject correctly beings, as we do in rejecting for instance centaurs, or a round square.

8. In more familiar terms, it is a certain brand of nominalism (see Kriegel 2015); but since Brentano himself rejects nominalism as *he* understands it (see, e.g., Brentano 1930: 75, 1928: 111f., these texts covering the time from 1901 to 1915), we will refrain from using the term for his reism in order to avoid verbal inconveniences.

9. See "*Über den Begriff der Wahrheit*" (Brentano 1930: 23): "Just as our true affirmative judgings sometimes refer to *one* thing, at another time they refer to a collective of things, and again to a part or to a boundary of a thing—nothing but objects that are themselves not things."

10. Letter to Marty of September 2, 1906. What follows till the next note, Brentano says again and again; see, just for instance, Brentano 1911a: 162f., 1930: 81, 90, 1933: 7.

11. See the letter to Marty of March 1, 1906 (Brentano 1966a: 148) and the letter to Kraus of July 11, 1916 (1966a: 315). The abstract entities had already been dismissed in 1901; see the excerpt from a letter to Marty from March 1901 in Brentano 1930: 73-5.

12. Letter to Kraus of July 5, 1916 (Brentano 1966a: 311). Of course, Brentano is dismissing the Stagirite's claims that "being is spoken of in many ways" (*Metaphysics* Z.1 1028a10), "for being is not a genus" (*Posterior Analytics* II.7 92b14), such that the categories of being "are neither dissolved into one another nor into some one thing" (*Metaphysics* Δ.29 1024b15–16).

13. Perhaps a better example than the larger-than relation, because it brings in one-sided separability, would be the following mirroring arrangement: Socrates, his image in a mirror A, and the image of the A-image in a mirror B. The image relation in which the B-image stands to the A-image, and the A-image to Socrates, is irreflexive and transitive, and it shares with the accident–subject relation the property of one-sided separability, since the mirroring of the A-image in mirror B may be interrupted such that the B-image ceases to be without the A-image too ceasing to be, and again the A-image ceases to be when Socrates, the ultimate base of the whole mirroring arrangement, walks away, for instance. Thus its structure is exactly like that of the accident–substance relation in Brentano, the B-image comparing to a judger, the A-image to the representer underlying the judger, and Socrates to the mind underlying the representer and hence the judger too. But it would be nonsense to say that Socrates is a one-sidedly separable *part* of the A-image and the A-image of the B-image.

14. Of which the first traces can be found in Marty's letter to Brentano of September 18, 1904: "You say ... that we only can think *realia*" (Brentano 1966a: 111). And Brentano responded with a clarification: "When I said that we can think only *realia*, this of course was meant to say nothing else than this: we can think only what would be a *reale* if it existed" (1966a: 114).

15. That he takes the pronoun "something" to be a concept-word, Brentano says on various occasions (see Brentano (1924c: 214; 1933: 18, 43; 1966a: 272).

16. Or as Brentano himself in one place puts the salient point, "if colour were the differentia that separates seeing from other species of sensing ... then seeing ... itself would have to be coloured, which is not true" (Brentano 1982: 26). This statement of the pre-reistic Brentano is of course not affected by the reistic turn.

17. See "*Vom Objekt*" of February 1906, where on the last page Brentano (1966a: 340) briefly presents the distinction. The *locus classicus* for it is perhaps Brentano 1911a: 134, where Brentano uses it to account for the mental (or intentional) relation as a *Relativliches*: "If I think a flower lover, then the flower lover is the object which I think in recto, but the flowers are what I think in obliquo."

18. While the variables occurring in (a) and (b) are familiar, the idea of adverbial variables might appear somewhat odd. It was in particular Prior who drew attention to the occurrence of such variables, or

quantifiers, in colloquial language: "We form colloquial quantifiers, both nominal and non-nominal, from the words which introduce questions—the nominal 'whoever' from 'who', and the non-nominal 'however', 'somehow', 'wherever', and 'somewhere' from 'how' and 'where'. No grammarian would seriously regard 'somewhere' as anything but an adverb; 'somewhere', in 'I met him somewhere', functions as the adverbial phrase 'in Paris' does in 'I met him in Paris'.... Similarly, no grammarian would count 'somehow' as anything but an adverb, functioning in 'I hurt him somehow' exactly as the adverbial phrase 'by treading on his toe' does in 'I hurt him by treading on his toe'" (Prior 1971: 37).

19. This is called by Smith (1994a: 66) the A-conception of one-sided separability of a part (as against the B-conception, which is that of the reistic Brentano).
20. I am grateful for the many suggestions made by Uriah Kriegel, which in most cases I did accept.

14

Brentano on the Soul

Susan Krantz Gabriel

Especially in his later work, Brentano articulated a clear metaphysical theory of the soul. The best sources for his mature view on this topic are to be found in his *Theory of Categories* (Brentano 1981a) and *On the Existence of God* (Brentano 1987b). Also useful are passages in some of his other works: *Psychology from an Empirical Standpoint, Sensory and Noetic Consciousness, Descriptive Psychology,* and *The Psychology of Aristotle.* In *Psychology from an Empirical Standpoint*, Brentano connects Aristotle's treatise *On the Soul* with late 19th- and early 20th-century psychology and natural science, often avoiding the term 'soul' (*die Seele*) as being an antiquated and easily misunderstood expression, in keeping with scientific usage that persists today when discussing the human subject of experience (Brentano 1973a: 4–11).[1] In the later works, however, Brentano specifically addresses the existence and nature of the soul, taking up perennial philosophical questions in a traditional manner but aiming to bring these issues into contemporary philosophical discussion.

In what follows, I shall focus only on Brentano's view concerning the soul as it is to be found in *The Theory of Categories* and *On the Existence of God*.[2] In order to be oriented toward Brentano's discussions, it is important to know that he lived and worked at a time when materialistic theories of human mental phenomena prevailed in Continental Europe. Brentano decisively rejected materialism and also disagreed with what he called Aristotle's "semi-materialistic" view of the soul; rather, he considered the soul to be a substance in its own right. For Aristotle (and for Thomas Aquinas who followed him in this), the soul is the "form" of the body. Thus the complete substance is the ensouled body as a whole (although Aristotle did allow that the intellectual soul is in some sense immaterial, and Aquinas granted it a kind of independent existence). The soul acting as form of the body lends unity to the individual or substance, which is a human being. The fact that the body takes on and loses matter steadily all the time, due to metabolic processes, does not mean that the individual differs over time; presumably the persistent form guarantees that it is the same individual or substance. For Brentano, this is not possible. One way to capture the difference between the two thinkers is to say that Aristotle was not a mereological essentialist while Brentano was. In other words, for Brentano, at least in his mature thinking, the parts are essential to the whole and therefore any change in parts results in the constitution of an entirely distinct individual. Ultimately, this means that in order to persist through time, an individual substance such as the human soul must have no parts at all.

1 THE VIEW FROM *THE THEORY OF CATEGORIES*

In *The Theory of Categories*, Part Two, Section II, a dictation from the years 1912–13, and Part Three, Section III, a dictation from 1916, Brentano explains his concept of substance in terms of "one-sided separability"[3] and illustrates the concept in a way somewhat reminiscent of Descartes' "thinking thing." He suggests:

> Suppose an atom were capable of thinking: then the thinking atom would be a whole which, if the atom ceased to think, would be reduced to one of its parts. But one could not at all say that its thinking could be preserved if the atom ceased to exist. Just as the concept red contains as red the concept of color, so the thinking thing would contain as thinking thing the nature of the atom. If another atom were to think the same thing, it would differ from the first not only *qua* atom but also *qua* thinking thing; as a thinking thing it would be individuated by the individuality of the atom.
>
> (1981a: 115)

By "atom," Brentano means here not the physicists' atom, but a *mereological* atom, that is, any entity that has no parts. This imaginary atom is one-sidedly separable from its accidents, which are thinking things,[4] because it is a substance; that is, it is an ultimate subject that cannot have a further subject, and this is the defining feature of substance *qua* substance (1981a: 192). Brentano quickly concedes: "Now perhaps it is incorrect to ascribe mental activity to an atom, but there is a non-spatial substance within ourselves.…This part is called the soul [*Seele*]" (1981a: 116). It would not be inappropriate to conclude from this that the soul is, for Brentano, the prime example of a substance, and its nature the prime example of what it means to be a substance (1981a: 193).

Part of the reason why the soul has this kind of metaphysical priority for Brentano is that we find ourselves to be clearly aware of it. The soul provides what is called "the unity of consciousness." As Brentano says, "We see that one and the same mental substance must underlie all the psychical activities that fall within our inner perception. And this substance, to the extent it has an awareness of itself, is that which we call our self or our ego (*Ich*)" (1981a: 121). Note that he does not claim that we have full or complete self-awareness—the psychological impossibility of which is sometimes raised against the Cartesian view—but only that "to the extent it has awareness of itself" the self or ego is aware of being a mental substance. He continues:

> I have said that our self appears to us as a mental substance. I now add that it appears to us as a pure mental substance. It does not appear, say, as a substance which is mental with respect to one part and which is corporeal, and thus extended

in three dimensions, with respect to another part. I emphasize this expressly, for the contrary has been asserted by important philosophers—for example, by Aristotle in ancient times and by many present-day thinkers who have been influenced by his opinion.

(1981a: 121–2)

Brentano appeals to the direct evidence of inner perception in claiming that the self or soul is a purely mental substance. Aristotle's view, by contrast, appeals to the perception we have of "the individual man or ox," a unified being with physical parts that act together as one individual. The Aristotelian concept of substance is thus quite different from Brentano's, even though both consider substance to be an ultimate subject that cannot have a further subject. An example of a primary substance in Aristotle's view would be, for instance, an organism, that is, an organized body such that its proper matter takes the form common to its species. Thus in Aristotle we see both matter and form referred to as "substance" (*ousia*), separately and together.[5] The several senses of "substance" in Aristotle do not survive Brentano's analysis because Brentano takes the evidence of inner perception so seriously. Inner perception shows us an individual, that is, a non-divisible entity that can be the subject of different thoughts at once and over time while yet retaining its identity.

For Brentano, the individual soul retains its identity over time and while entertaining a variety of perceptions and thoughts because, in a sense, it participates in those perceptions and thoughts. We could say, it has perceptions and thoughts as "accidents," or properties. Here we encounter another peculiarity of Brentano's thinking because he regards those accidents not as properties that merely *subsist* and need to be instantiated in order to *exist* but rather as existing individuals in their own right (see Chapter 13). Each mental accident has a substance (the soul) as a proper part (1981a: 122). Accidents can thus *have* parts, but a substance in the strict sense cannot have parts; as an ultimate subject, it can *be* a part but it cannot *have* parts.[6] Further, mental accidents can come into existence and cease to exist while their subject, the soul, continues to exist.

It follows that the soul is of necessity entirely an immaterial substance and its continuity over time is an aspect of the "unity of consciousness" (1981a: 123). This unity of consciousness, peculiar to the soul, evident to each of us via inner perception, is essential to explaining the fact that we can both have a variety of perceptions and thoughts at once and also have differing perceptions and thoughts over time. If the soul were a material, physical entity, or necessarily bound to such an entity, then none of this would be possible. It would be as though different perceptions and thoughts were mapped onto a spatially extended field, each area or point of which would have a different function and no area or point of which would perceive the whole. Similarly, the meaning of a complete sentence requires an understanding of the whole; if several different people in different places were each assigned one word of the sentence without any knowledge of the others, then none of them would comprehend the whole sentence as such.

2 THE VIEW FROM *ON THE EXISTENCE OF GOD*

The lectures on the existence of God, delivered by Brentano in the years 1868 to 1891 in Würzburg and Vienna, were compiled and edited by Alfred Kastil from the notes Brentano himself had used. These notes are in many cases quite complete, but the notes for the section entitled "The Psychological Proof" were sparse and not fully detailed by Brentano. Thus Kastil filled them out in accordance with Brentano's mature thinking on the relevant topics. I rely on Kastil's version in what follows, but I think justifiably so, given that he consulted other students of Brentano and is generally regarded as having been faithful to Brentano's thought (see Kastil's introduction to the German edition, 1929, xiii–xvi).

Brentano offered four proofs of God's existence:[7] a teleological proof, a proof from contingency, a proof from motion, and a psychological proof. By far the most extensive of these is the teleological proof, a salient feature of which is Brentano's careful attention to developments in the natural science of his day (1987b: 155–259). Likewise, in the psychological proof, scientific discoveries play a crucial role (1987b: 290–301). I shall not address the question of God's existence here but shall rather confine my remarks to what the psychological proof tells us about Brentano's view of the soul.

Brentano begins by affirming that the subject of our experience *appears* to us to be spiritual and thus unextended (i.e., non-spatial). He then raises the question of whether this *must* be the case, since "inner perception lacks completeness and full determinacy" (1987b: 290). Unlike Descartes, who considered our concept of the "thinking thing" to be clear and distinct, Brentano holds that what *appears* to us in inner perception requires examination in order to determine whether it is *real*, even though the fact that it appears to be real is necessarily evident, that is, indubitable. In order to carry out this examination, he discusses what he calls the "semi-materialism" of Plato and Aristotle, according to which at least our sensory functions are embodied, that is, they have a corporeal subject, e.g., the eye, the ear (1987b: 294). He then rejects this view on the grounds that a "partially spiritual, partially corporeal soul" is incompatible with the unity of consciousness, something we experience with evidence as being necessarily real (1987b: 295). Were it not for the unity of consciousness, there could never be any complexity in our inner experience, but clearly there is such complexity, even in simple cases like hearing something and simultaneously seeing something. Unity of consciousness is a fact that shows the semimaterialistic theory to be false. Thus for Brentano, in keeping with the central line of argument on this topic from the *Theory of Categories*, the unity of consciousness is a fundamental truth from which the immateriality of the soul is inferred.

Already in Brentano's day, however, studies of the brain tended to show that the seat of consciousness is in a physical organ, thus, "people today are generally convinced that if thought actually has a bodily organ for its subject, this could be nothing else but the cerebrum" (1987b: 296). Further, "Anatomically it is established that two hemispheres may be distinguished in it, which correspond to one another in such a way that neither has more claim than the other to be regarded as the subject of thought" (*ibid.*). This poses an insurmountable problem, though, because a single complete thought would have to be supposed to attach identically to every part of both hemispheres if both hemispheres are equally the seat of thought. Yet, two spatial objects cannot have the necessary uniformity. In order to get around this problem, physiologists had developed the idea of different functions for different areas of the brain, and even suggested that "each separate idea has a separate neuron in the brain as its subject" (1987b: 297). Again, however, "all of this is utterly absurd in light of the conclusions based on the unity of consciousness" (*ibid.*).

Still, Brentano does not reject discoveries concerning the physiology of the brain. Rather he takes the view that the different areas of the brain *serve* our mental activity, although they do not *constitute* our mental activity. The distinction is important. As he puts it, "our soul stands in a direct causal relation with each of these different parts [of the brain] equally" (1987b: 298). In this way, the complexity of mental activity can be accounted for together with the unity of consciousness because the soul, being an immaterial entity without parts, is not forced, as a corporeal entity is, to delegate different functions to different parts of it.

Further consideration of the immateriality of the soul reveals that it is required for the emotive phenomena of regret and shame as well as confidence and proper pride. The body, including the brain, undergoes steady changes due to metabolism and thus is not strictly speaking identical with itself over time. But each of us regards our self or soul as identical over time, something that can only be said of an immaterial entity. Moreover, perceptions, ideas, and knowledge are not inherited from our parents as our physical characteristics are. It follows either that the subject of our thoughts has existed forever, or else that it has been created in an immaterial way at a particular time. But if it had pre-existed this life, there should be some evidence of that, as we find that earlier experiences generally have an effect on later ones. So Brentano, somewhat in harmony on this point with Aristotle, considers that "it is to be regarded as a law that a soul always and necessarily comes to be as soon as an organism is ripe for undertaking interaction with it" (1987b: 300). Not that the human soul is a byproduct or emergent property of the sufficiently developed human body, but rather that the sufficiently developed human body becomes capable of receiving its separately created soul. From this point it is easy to see how Brentano turns to the question of God's existence.

3 CONCLUSION: THE SIGNIFICANCE OF BRENTANO'S VIEW OF THE SOUL

As I mentioned in the introductory paragraph, the soul is not normally considered a topic for scientific or philosophical discussion today. Conversations on topics as disparate as abortion and animal rights typically relegate soul-talk to the realm of religious belief, something considered to be a matter for personal opinion, not for logical or experiential analysis. By contrast, although he was surely quite aware of this modern tendency, Brentano insisted that an understanding of the soul is essential to an understanding of who we are as human beings. It seems to me that despite the difficulties we face in articulating a clear understanding of human thought and experience, there is something appealing and important about the integrity of the soul as understood by Brentano. As in other cases where we deal with something transcendent—and Brentano did hold that our individuality is transcendent for us, that is, it is not fully disclosed to us by inner perception (1987b: 290)—there is much to be gained by showing what the soul is *not*. Negative theology is a similar endeavor, that is, an approach to God that proceeds by detailing what God is not, not confined in space, not an idol, not subject to human control, and so on. Likewise, a negative psychology in the spirit of Brentano can show us that our soul is not a bodily organ, not identical either with the whole body or with the brain, not reducible to physical conditions, not subject to the laws of physical bodies, not in fact a material entity at all; and yet it is something, and something real.

As is well known, philosophies today often involve the attempt to explain thought and experience in terms of language use or of physical processes. Even the self can be explained away as a projection of the various parts of the brain and thus in effect a fictitious entity. These reductive analyses certainly can be illuminating in various ways regarding language and physiology, but they run the risk of carrying Ockham's Razor to extremes. Yes, we should not multiply entities *beyond* necessity. But it is not necessarily clear that we can explain human thought and experience without recourse to an immaterial soul, and even William of Ockham would admit that his soul exists.

Most recent research on the topic of the soul is confined to the area of history of philosophy. Thus there is a wealth of literature on the soul as discussed by Plato, Aristotle, Thomas Aquinas, Descartes, Leibniz, and so on. But these works typically do not consider the existence and nature of the soul to be a vital topic today. A notable exception is Stewart Goetz and Charles Taliaferro, *A Brief History of the Soul*, which, going beyond the apparent scope of its title, takes seriously questions about the human soul, discussing these questions in the metaphysical spirit of Brentano and Chisholm.

In sum, Brentano in his mature theory of the soul outlines a rejection of materialistic theories in all their various forms. At the same time, he also rejects the so-called hylomorphic (matter and form) theory of the Aristotelians. Rather, somewhat like the Socrates of Plato's *Phaedo*, Brentano insists on the integrity and independence of the human soul, regarding it as a cause rather than a mere effect and resisting efforts to reduce the soul to something less. It is true that difficulties remain. For instance, what is this one-sidedly separable part, this soul, without its accidents, its perceptions and thoughts?[8] How do we explain its nature if it appears to be a "bare particular"? Perhaps answers to these questions could be pursued by an explication of the phenomena of memory and recognition together with a theory of potentiality. In any event, some knowledge of what the soul is *not* constitutes a step forward.[9]

NOTES

1. He calls attention to Albert Lange's expression "psychology without a soul" and rejects the materialistic outlook behind it.
2. Two articles by Barry Smith are enlightening concerning Brentano's earlier view of the soul, as evidenced in *Psychology from an Empirical Standpoint* and *Descriptive Psychology*: Smith 1988 and 1992–3. On the later view, however, the soul is a one-sidedly separable proper part of any presentation, judgment, or emotive phenomenon; it can be said to *be* a part, but it cannot be said to *have* parts.
3. This captivating idea should be understood initially by contrast with the far more familiar "bilateral separability" to which physical (i.e., three-dimensionally extended) things are susceptible and which always leaves a part or parts as a remainder. In cases of one-sided separability, there is no remainder.
4. For reasons that will become clear shortly, Brentano's later view is that psychic accidents (or properties) are, in fact, individual things; so it would not be correct to say that the imaginary atom's accidents are thoughts. Rather, such accidents would be thinkers.
5. See Aristotle, *Metaphysics*, Book Zeta, chs. 10–11.
6. In this I follow Chisholm 1978.
7. Since Kant, philosophers in general have largely thought that the proofs "do not work," but Brentano was well aware of that, and disagreed (1987b: 51–147). It is true that his proofs do not lead to an evident conclusion in the technical sense. But when Brentano argues that God's nonexistence is "infinitely improbable" or "infinitely many times infinitely improbable" (1987b: 252), he's offering a substitute for the technical sense of evidence and is aware of doing so. This is a consequence of his reliance on the so-called empirical proofs rather than proofs a priori, such as the ontological argument.
8. I am indebted to the late Professor Vincent Tomas of Brown University for his unrelenting pursuit of such questions, and for pointing out that I couldn't answer them.
9. My thanks to Uriah Kriegel for editorial changes and helpful suggestions on an earlier draft.

15

Brentano on Time and Space

Wojciech Żełaniec

Brentano's mature teachings on time and space, expounded in his dictations from 1914 onward (Brentano 1976/1988; Brentano 1994b), are closely connected with his work on the (perceived, intuited) continuum ("complete dense linearly ordered set" or a "Dedekind complete set", in contemporary terminology) and the concomitant theory of boundaries (*Grenze*).[1] It is meant as no competition to Einstein's, despite Brentano's occasional remarks on "Einstein's error" (Brentano 1988b: 22); it cannot be sensibly taken as meant to be a contribution to either physics or mathematics (Körner and Chisholm 1988: xxii). It will not tell us anything along the lines of "spacetime is a smooth Lorentzian manifold." In fact, Brentano would not accept the idea of "spacetime," which he misconstrued as the idea that time is a fourth dimension of space,[2] a

> [f]iction [that will reveal itself as harmless in a number of respects]. Lagrange ... found it admissible that mechanics should treat time as a fourth dimension of space. [T]here must obtain a precise relation of magnitude between intervals of time and the lengths of lines [so] that ... the present is at precisely one meter's distance from a certain point in the past.
> (Brentano 1988b: 175)

It is, much rather, a purely philosophical theory.

A true, albeit unorthodox Aristotelian, Brentano asks not "What is time?" or "What is space?," but rather "What are the temporal and spatial characteristics of substances?," the characteristics thanks to which these substances can be talked of as temporal and spatial. And his answer starts thus:

> Above all [they are] something real.
> (Brentano 1988b: 175)

This means, first of all, that Brentano rejects the notion that time and space are purely phenomenal (Brentano 1988b: 163), or that they are "additions of the mind" of whatever sort.[3] In particular, with a characteristically polemical reference to Kant—the "philosopher, [who,] as is well known, places great difficulties in the way of understanding" (Brentano 1988b: 59)—Brentano rejects in rather harsh words his doctrine that "[i]f things appear to us as temporal, then this temporal character is due to our subjectivity alone" and thus that time is a "form of inner sense" (1988b: 63).[4] Can something analogous be said of space, given that Brentano spills so much ink on the difference between space and time (1988: 12ff., though see also 1988b: 23)? It seems so.

Let's first turn to time: it is a continuum (a particular instance of "the continuous") but a one-dimensional one, as the boundaries of its parts have no temporal extension (Brentano 1988b: 10).[5] Without going into Brentano's theory of the continuum (see Bell 2005: 202–8, 326, 328, Libardi 1996: 61–4, Albertazzi 2006: 233–67, Ierna 2012: 368–96), let it suffice to say that the continuum for Brentano is the referent of a "concept [that] is gained not through any intricate process of combination but rather in immediate fashion through simple abstraction from our intuition" (Brentano 1988b: 7), and this is because "every single one of our intuitions—both those of outer perception as also their accompaniments in inner perception, and therefore also those of memory—bring to appearance what is continuous" (1988b: 6), spatially, spatially-qualitatively (1988b: 21), or temporally (1988b: 12). As for the concept of a boundary, Brentano does not refer to Peano's then little-known definition of the concept (Peano 1887: 152–60). But Brentano's concept, clearly a primitive and not explicitly definable in his theory, is for most practical purposes similar enough to the mathematical one (see Poli 2012: 369–428). In particular, the concept was meant to help solve a traditional philosophical problem:

> If a thing begins to move, is there a last moment of its being at rest or a first moment of its being in motion? There cannot be both, for if there were, then there would be a time between the two moments, and at that time the thing could be said neither to be at rest nor to be in motion.
>
> (Körner and Chisholm 1988: xvi)

Brentano's solution is that there are both, in the sense that there is just one moment, which at the same time is the last moment of rest and the first moment of motion. And this, in substance, is what the real numbers afford us, with their complete linear order: for a given real number, a, there is both the greatest real number amongst those less than or equal to a, and the least element amongst those greater than or equal to it, namely a. This was precisely what the Dedekind cuts, rejected by Brentano (1988b: 42), were meant to achieve (and did achieve, at least for the mathematicians). Technically speaking, however, Brentano denies that that moment is truly *one*: with reference to Galileo (Brentano 1988b: 41), he notes that

> a boundary, even when itself continuous, can never exist except as belonging to something continuous of more dimensions (indeed receives its fully determinate and exactly specific character only through the manner of this belongingness), it is, considered for itself, nothing other than a *universal*, to which—as to other universals—more than one thing can correspond. And the geometer's

> proposition that only one straight line is conceivable between two points, is *strictly speaking false* if one conceives the matter in terms of lines of incomplete plerosis (πλήρωσις) whose pleroses, even though they coincide with one another, relate to different sides.
>
> (Brentano 1988b: 12; italics mine)[6]

So, strictly speaking, the last moment of rest and the first moment of motion are different moments that coincide. The moment dividing (or conjoining) Tim's bicycle ride on September 14, 2012 AD from his immediately preceding not-yet-riding is, strictly speaking, a universal, with two instantiations: the end of the rest (incomplete plerosis in the direction of the past) and the beginning of the ride (incomplete plerosis in the direction of the future). These two moments *coincide*, but they are differentiated by the direction in which they function as boundaries. "Coincidence" is, then, a crucial primitive term of Brentano's theory of boundaries.[7] However, although boundaries can coincide in the way just described, they are still "nothing in themselves," which Dedekind and Poincaré, Brentano thinks, overlooked in their constructions of the continuum (Brentano 1988b: 40), carelessly assuming that the real numbers are already there, as if prefabricated and independent of the continuum they were meant to go into the construction of (1988b: 10). And, as observed above, "a boundary ... can never exist except as belonging to something continuous of more dimensions (indeed receives its fully determinate and exactly specific character only through the manner of this belongingness)" (1988b: 12).

Given all this, the temporal is just an instant or a moment, a fleeting nondimensional boundary between the past and the future (Körner and Chisholm 1988: xvi). It does not have an extension—obviously, Brentano would not believe in the specious present (see Brentano 1988b: 137). We see or feel movement or hear melodies, he claims (Brentano 1988b: 71), not because they are given as present to our senses, and still less because we see the movement's subsequent phases or hear the melody's subsequent notes one by one and then, remembering what we have seen or heard, assemble the perceived and the remembered. Rather, we perceive such things because they are given in a special kind of retrograde sensation, which Brentano calls "proteraesthesis" (*Proterästhesis*) precisely as past (Brentano 1988b: 87–93; see Chapter 7).[8] More technically,

> the determinations of present, past and future are relative, more particularly comparative, determinations of the [subject] ... in relation to that of which he ... senses. In the case of the present this is a matter of agreement, of sameness in regard to time. In the case of past and future it is a matter of differences in regard to time, in both cases of differences of something that is in relation to something that is not. It is, in the two cases, a matter of differences in opposite senses, in that what is is characterised in the one as later, in the other as earlier. If one now accepts the ... [subject] who is, as later than something or as earlier than something, then here ... there will be besides what is presented and accepted *in recto* also something presented and accepted in *obliquo*. [That is:] if something is presented and accepted as past or future, then it is presented and accepted *in obliquo* as a result of the acceptance *in recto* of something which stands to it in the comparative relation of the earlier or of the later.
>
> (Brentano 1988b: 107)

Strangely enough, for all symmetry between the past and the future, perceivable even in the above quotation, Brentano recognizes no (what could be called) *hysteraesthesis* (sensation or presentation of things imminently future as such), which, however, seems to be common experience. For instance, in a well-known symphony, the beginning of the second movement can often be literally sensed as imminently future (to-be) after the ending of the first. Kastil seems to be denying this when he says:

> The boundary character of a temporal reveals itself, in the case of primary objects of sensation in such a way that a fragment of the past is always co-presented *in obliquo*, i.e. in a continuum of temporal *modi obliqui*, from which the *modus rectus* is at a distance in just one direction, namely as later, whereas his boundary contact with the future is given at best generally, because no ever so tiny glimpse of the future can be sensed.
>
> (Kastil 1951: 169; my translation)[9]

After his 1904 "turning away from non-realia" (Brentano 1966a; see Chapter 13), only the present *is*, to Brentano, while the past *has been* (and is no longer), though it has a certain historical factuality that the future lacks (Brentano 1988b: 12). The future will be but is not yet (1988b: 114, 116). Even God lives in an ever-changing "now" (1988b: 77, 85). Things "proceed in time" from one moment to another (1988b: 12), constituting the temporal continuum, which exists only "according to a mere boundary" (*einer bloßen Grenze nach*) (1988b: 16), that is, as the ever-fleeting "now." They do not belong to a larger-dimension continuum (against the repudiated idea of a space-time) as a boundary (1988b: 10). In other words, this ever-fleeting "now" belongs "as boundary to a temporal continuum that begins with it or ends with it or endures through it" and is such that it "exists actually entirely and uniquely in this boundary" (1988b: 167). This is the view currently known as "presentism": "Being and being present amount to one and the same" (Brentano 1988b: 179).

Strictly speaking, each thing constitutes its own temporal continuum (1988b: 20) and in this sense "has its own time." This gives rise to the Einstein-reminiscent problem of simultaneity: in what sense can different events, accidents of different substances, be considered simultaneous? Brentano rejects, with the notion of time as a big "container," the idea that things can be simultaneous in the sense of taking place at *one* time, but not in the sense of *equal* times (1988b: 83), i.e. the same *qua* temporal determinations. So "for example all things existing in the instant of the birth of Christ would have a common specific determination as things to be found within this instant. And similarly those falling in the same instant one century later" (1988b: 80).

The chief difference between time and space consists in that the spatially continuous exists at once, with all of its parts (Brentano 1988b: 15f., 42), at the (specifically, though not numerically) same time. For this reason, welding together time and space into one four-dimensional "space" will not work,[10] because "in regard to time, nothing that *is* can stand apart from anything else that *is*" (1988b: 174), while in regard to space, the same is false. Time and space are different continua (1988b: 176), the continuum of the spatial being that of the corporeal (*ibid.*). However, not everything is corporeal, as there are mental substances that can exist "perfectly well … without spatial extension and position and without in any way belonging to something spatially extended," while "nothing [not even God] could exist except as belonging to something temporally extended that proceeds in one dimension"; so what is temporal coincides with the category of "things as such" (1988b: 176).

Spatial and temporal characteristics, being real, are "absolutely determined, specified and individuated in reality" (Brentano 1988b: 175f.), yet to us they are "capable of being thought intuitively and conceptually only with relative specifications" (1988b: 176)—"relative," ultimately, not just in the purely "modal" but, too, in the "material" (contentual) sense, that is, not just distinguished with a peculiar mode of presentation, such as "past" or "distant," but furnished with positive (but relative) characteristics, such as "before my birth" or "in front of the oven" (1988b: 135f.). Absolute determinations, by contrast, are beyond our cognitive reach (1988b: 129–37, 167f.): we are all in the situation of one who knows "that one man is twice as rich as another [but] nothing ... as to the absolute magnitudes of the fortunes of either" (1988b: 136). But such magnitudes exist, and so do, Brentano thinks, the absolute "wheres" and "whens" of things. However, just like our selves (1988b: 75), they are given to us only as to their most general concept (1988b: 89, 101, 152–3, 176), that is, as "(somewhere in) space" and "(somewhere in) time."

But the (absolutely) spatial and temporal is, for Brentano, not just individuated and individuating but also—unlike for Aristotle—substantial (Brentano 1988b: 150–5, 175f.; Brentano 1981a: 84, 89, 114f., 122, 158, 175–95).[11] Being substantial—we need not go into the details of Brentano's concept of substance (see Chapter 13)—is here construed as being the ultimate subject, similar, despite the familiar differences (see Smith 1987), to Aristotle's *Categories* 1. The criterion of substantiality of x is, by contrast, "whether the ... thing [that has x] could still be the same thing if it [did not have x]" (Brentano 1988b: 151). The answer is obviously "no" for space, extension, and time. A colored point is an accident of a localized point, and any "something" whatever is—we have seen—an accident of a temporal "something" (1988b: 176). On the other hand, this would suggest that local change (movement) is substantial change, but presumably the—relative—attributes that change through movement are all accidental.[12] More importantly, perhaps, Brentano notes that what blocks our way to the appreciation of temporal and spatial characteristics as substantial is the belief that what is substantial must be "important," "interesting," rich in epistemologically significant consequences, heuristically "profit-yielding" (1988b: 151, 155). Brentano's insists that it need not—the soul, the substance of thinking, is less interesting than its thoughts, which are, *pace* Descartes, accidental (1988b: 150, 155).

Tantalizing are Brentano's speculations on further—beside time and space—series of substantial determinations, and the consequences of their existence or not for the issue of the impenetrability of material bodies (Brentano 1988b: 151–4). One cannot help wondering how Brentano would have reacted to Black's (1952) famous two-sphere thought-experiment. But this would be the subject matter of a different essay.

NOTES

1. Brentano's work on the topic is not mentioned in Callender (2011), nor Jacquette (2004). In Bardon and Dyke (2015: 391f.) Brentano's theory of time perception does receive a treatment. Albertazzi (2014) examines time and space *perception*.
2. The correct idea is, speaking very roughly, that space and time are, on a par, dimensions of a so-called manifold, a kind of topological space that is not a "space" in the physical sense.

3. Kavanaugh makes Brentano out to be perhaps somewhat more Kant-friendly than he really was (Kavanaugh 2008: 44).
4. On a possible source of this error, as Brentano saw it, see Brentano 1988b: 157 n.1). Kastil suggests that Brentano might have shared this error in a certain sense not very much time before formulating his final views (Brentano 1988b: 195 n. 149).
5. Brentano's concept of a dimension is reasonably close to the topological "small inductive" dimension (Czyż 1994: 261). Brentano distinguishes explicitly one-, two-, and three-dimensional continua (Brentano 1988b: 10), defining "one-dimensional [as having] no other boundaries than such as are not themselves continuous" (*ibid.*). Time "is a continuum of one dimension, since its boundaries, as also the boundaries of its parts, themselves possess no temporal extension. We call them moments or instants of time" (*ibid.*).
6. Plerosis is one of the most fundamental concepts of the Brentanian theory of boundaries (Körner and Chisholm 1988: xviif.), roughly meaning: the number of directions in which the given boundary functions as such.
7. See Brentano 1988b: 5, 7, 16, 167. And "if an existing thing persists [through time], then this happens through a continuously reiterated renewal" (Brentano 1988b: 113). Brentano's conception of coincidence has inspired certain contemporary ontologists (e.g., Baumann, Loebe and Herre 2014: 10ff.).
8. Strictly speaking, proteraesthesis is also a kind of memory, albeit a rather atypical one; at least, Brentano is prepared to speak of it under the heading of "memory" (Brentano 1988b: 71–83).
9. This is one of the disanalogies between time and space Brentano likes to stress: "the relation of before and after may certainly bear a number of analogies to that of spatial distance, it is … not identical therewith…. The spatial point is a boundary for something spatial in many conceivable spatial directions, perhaps even in all, but it is never a boundary in either of the two temporal directions, and the converse holds of the temporal point" (Brentano 1988b: 174f.).
10. Unless, perhaps, we construe space as a secondary continuum (see note 3) "filling" time, a kind of "space snapshot" (hypersurface) or a continuum thereof (Brentano 1988b: 28f.).
11. The topics of substantiality and individuality are most intimately connected in Brentano (see Żełaniec 1996, 1997, 2013).
12. This is suggested by Brentano's critique of Descartes, who "sets the essence of mind in thinking without accepting change of thought as change of substance" (Brentano 1988b: 150).

16

Brentano on Properties and Relations

Hamid Taieb

Brentano wrote his doctoral dissertation on Aristotle's ontology (Brentano 1862/1975a). However, the books and articles that Brentano published during his lifetime do not contain much information about his own theory of properties and relations. His main texts on this topic can be found in the posthumous volumes *The True and the Evident* (Brentano 1930/1966b), *The Theory of Categories* (1933/1981a), and *The Renunciation of the Unreal* (1966a), which mainly contain documents from after his reistic turn of 1904 (see Chapter 13). The manuscripts "About the Theory of Categories" (Brentano 1992–3), "On Substance" (1993), and "Abstraction and Relation" (2013a/c), all from approximately 1900, are Brentano's most important published pre-reistic texts on properties and relations. Some information is also present in Brentano's logic lectures, given from 1869–1870 until 1877 in Würzburg and Vienna (Brentano, EL 80).[1] Much information on the young Brentano's theory of properties and relations can be found in the metaphysics lectures given in Würzburg from 1867 onward (ms. M 96), but these lectures are unpublished.

In this chapter, I will focus on Brentano's theory of properties and relations as established during his mature period, from *Psychology from an Empirical Standpoint* (Brentano 1874) until his death in 1917, and indicate the most important changes that his reistic turn entailed for his theory of properties and relations.[2] First, I discuss the ontological features common to properties and relations (§1); then I deal with relations in particular (§2).

1 ONTOLOGICAL FEATURES COMMON TO PROPERTIES AND RELATIONS

Abstract names, for Brentano, designate either "metaphysical parts" or "logical parts" (Brentano EL 80: 86). "Metaphysical parts" are particular properties and relations, either essential or accidental, of a given concrete particular or "metaphysical whole." "Logical parts" are the "general marks" composing the definition, or "logical whole," of an individual of a given genus. Thus, "redness" can either designate the particular redness of a given red thing or the species 'redness' composing the definition of this particular redness; the former is a metaphysical part, the latter a logical part.[3]

Metaphysical wholes and parts, or concrete and abstract particulars, are correlatives: a red thing is red through redness, and redness is the redness of a red thing (Brentano 2013a/c: 473-4/439-40). Both concrete and abstract particulars exist. However, they do not have the same ontological status. Concrete particulars are "real," whereas abstract particulars are "unreal" (not to be confused with "nonexistent") (Brentano 2013a/c: 472/438). The distinction between *realia*—real beings, also called "subsistent" (*wesenhaft*)—and *irrealia*—unreal beings, also called "nonsubsistent" (*unwesenhaft*)—is based on causality:

> There is being that begins without itself being caused, [but the beginning of which] is simply due to the fact that something else is caused. Likewise it ceases to be without itself undergoing a destructive influence or being deprived of a sustaining influence. It begins, persists, and ceases to be *en parergo*, so to speak. [...] Such being we call "non subsistent". Something subsistent, by contrast, is that which as such can and does causally bring something about, and which as such cannot begin without being causally brought about and cannot as such cease to be without as such undergoing a [destructive] influence or removal of a sustaining influence.
> (Brentano 2013a/c: 466-7/432-3, translation slightly modified)

Thus, concrete particulars are causally efficacious and sensible and have a proper generation and corruption, whereas abstract particulars, as Chrudzimski says, are not, as such, "integrated into the causal network of the world." Yet both concrete and abstract particulars exist (see Chrudzimski 2004: 138-41 for a detailed analysis of these passages from Brentano 2013a).

According to Chrudzimski and Smith, Brentano is a trope theorist, that is, he only admits abstract particulars as properties in his ontology, not abstract universals. In other words, of the two kinds of part that abstract names designate, "metaphysical" and "logical," only the first would find a place in Brentano's ontology (Chrudzimski 2004, Chrudzimski and Smith 2004). It is true that Brentano is not a friend of universals. He rejects both "Platonic" or "transcendent" and "Aristotelian" or "immanent" universals: the world of Ideas "leads to a thousand absurdities," and "in the things, there is nothing universal" (Brentano EL 80: 34 and 1930/1966b: 74/43).[4] Thus, certainly the only *abstracta* that Brentano *wants to admit* in his ontology are abstract particulars. However, as I shall show, in view of some specific texts, one could have worries about Brentano's theory of individuation and think that some of his properties and relations are disguised universals.[5]

Contemporary philosophers hold that tropes must be simple, that is, that their qualitative and individuating features should not be ontologically distinct from each other. Indeed, if tropes were entities with two distinct "ontological grounds," providing them with quality and individuality respectively, they would become complex entities constituted by a universal and a "substrate" or individuator: the individuator would be extrinsic to the quality, which, thus, would be a universal; and the particular would be the complex entity made of the universal and the individuator (Maurin 2002: 11-21; see also Campbell 1990: 56-7). As Moreland (2001: 59) writes:

The trope view must assay a basic trope as a simple in order to avoid assigning the individuating and qualitative roles to non-identical constituents in the quality-instance, for this is what realists do (e.g. red$_1$ has an individuator, say, a bare particular expressed by 1, the universal redness, and a tie of predication).

For example, someone who thinks that tropes are individuated through their "spatiotemporal position" does not mean "that place and the quality present at that place are distinct beings, one the particularizer and the other a universal, but that 'quality-at-a-place' is itself a single, particular, reality" (Campbell 1981: 483; see also Moreland 2001: 54, Maurin 2002: 18).

What does Brentano say? According to him, accidents are individuated by the substance of the concrete particular of which they are the parts (Brentano 1992–3: 263, 267–8, 1993: 30–4). For physical accidents, this substance is the body, and for psychic accidents, it is the self:

> Specifically similar acts are individually distinct when they are mine or someone else's. The individualizer is the subject.
> (Brentano 1993: 33; my translation)

Thus, Brentano's particular accidents have ontologically distinct qualitative and individuating grounds. What about bodies and selves?

Regarding the body, it is a combination of a series of abstract qualitative properties and an abstract spatial localization property (see Brentano 1992–3: 259–64, 1993: 30, 34 and Chrudzimski 2004: 145–6). The body's qualitative properties and its spatial localization property mutually individuate each other. More precisely: two things "of such quality" are individuated by their simultaneous differences of localization, whereas two things successively "at such a place" are individuated by their qualitative differences (Brentano 1993: 259–61, 2013a/c: 471–2/437–8; see also the later Brentano 1911c: 59 n. 1). Again, there is a distinction between the properties of the body and their individuators, which are also properties. Yet this distinction is probably only conceptual. Indeed, according to Brentano, although the colour and the spatial localization of a given spot in the perceptual field fall under distinct "genera" or concepts, they "penetrate one another" ontologically (Brentano 1982/1995b: 14–20/17–22). Generalizing this idea, one could say that, for Brentano, the body's qualitative properties and its spatial localization are only conceptually distinct; that is, that bodies are constituted by simple "qualities-at-a-place," or simple "qualified-spatial-localizations."

Regarding the self, Brentano, in his *Psychology*, says that it is a "unified whole" constituted by mental acts, which are abstract entities (Brentano 1874/1973a: bk. II Ch. 4 and Mulligan 2004: 86–8). Later, he affirms that the self is a "part" of consciousness, more precisely a "metaphysical part," that is, apparently an abstract entity (Brentano 1992–3: 267). The self seems to be simple (i.e., without ontologically distinct qualitative and individuation grounds) and primitively individuated (see Brentano 1993: 35, and Chapter 14; on primitive individuation of tropes, see Maurin 2014).

Thus, the body's properties and the self, for Brentano, seem to be genuine tropes, whereas his particular accidents have ontologically distinct qualitative and individuation grounds and resemble complex entities constituted by a universal and an individuator. Apparently, Brentano and his pupils saw the problem. During his reistic period, Brentano says that one would be wrong to think that

> many individual things correspond [to a general concept], but such that they are parts of another individual thing and receive their individuation from outside through their connection with this thing and its other parts.
> (Brentano 1933/1981a: 60–1/52–3, unfaithful to ms. M 70, n°30837; translation modified on the basis of the manuscript[6])

And Kastil adds that such extrinsically individuated parts are "a special kind of intermediate thing falling between the absurd universal things and the real individual things."[7]

After his reistic turn, Brentano rejects the existence of all *abstracta*: only things exist, i.e. concrete particulars. Redness as such, i.e. as abstract, does not exist but is a mere "fiction"; only something red exists (Brentano 1933/1981a: 6–7/17). Concrete particulars are either substances or accidents. Accidents are not abstract parts but concrete wholes with a substance as a part (Brentano 1933/1981a: 11/19). They are individuated by their substances. Bodies are no longer substances but qualitative accidents, individuated by the spatiotemporally localized, individual substance that they contain. Souls are concrete, individual substances (see notably Brentano 1933/1981a: 246–8/177–8 and Kastil 1933/1981: 363–4 n. 1/253–4 n. 297).[8] What about individuation of accidents? As wholes, Brentano's accidents are no longer individuated "extrinsically" but intrinsically, since their individuator, the substance, is a part of them. However, they still have ontologically distinct qualitative and individuation grounds: a nonsubstantial, qualitative portion[9] and an individuating substance. Thus, one could wonder whether these qualitative portions as such are individual.[10]

2 ONTOLOGICAL FEATURES PROPER TO RELATIONS

Brentano, before his reistic turn, distinguishes between relations, *relata*, and relatives. Relations are (allegedly) abstract particulars, e.g. this fatherhood and this sonship. *Relata* are particular bearers of relations, e.g., Sophroniscus and Socrates. Relatives are concrete particulars constituted by a relation and a *relatum*, e.g., this father and this son.

It has been argued that Brentano's relations are monadic properties, since they depend on Aristotle's theory of relations or "*pros ti*," which would be monadic properties (Chrudzimski 2001b: 194, Sauer 2006: 22). However, it is not clear that this is true in Aristotle, since, at least in the standard cases, the existence of a relative entails the existence of a correlative: if a relation exists, then its own *relatum*, a converse relation, and the *relatum* of the converse relation exist (see Aristotle, *Categories* VII, 6b28–8a12 and Hood 2004: 96). For example, the existence of A's property of being larger than B implies not only the existence of A but also the existence of B's property of being smaller than A and, of course, the existence of B. Moreover, for Brentano, the logical form of relations seems not to be $x(Ry)$, where (Ry) would be a monadic predicate, but something closer to the polyadic Russellian logical form xRy:[11]

When I predicate "larger than A" of something, I do not predicate A of it, but I relate it to A.

(Brentano 1966a: 205; my translation)

Besides, one finds clear affirmation of the polyadic dimension of relational properties in Brentano's pre-reistic texts:

[Relative determinations] depend, for their individual subsistence, on the one of the absolute [determinations] (certainly also on the [subsistence] of another thing than the one to which they are ascribed), but the latter do not inversely [depend on the former].

(Brentano 1992–3: 258–9; my translation, and my additions, except for "subsistence")

Thus, A's property of being larger than B depends on B's existence, but A's size, which is the absolute property underlying A's being larger than B, does not. In brief, a relation, contrarily to an absolute property, is polyadic.

For Brentano, before reism, relatives are ontologically and conceptually dependent on one another. A relation can only exist and be thought with its own *relatum*, a converse relation, and the *relatum* of the converse relation (Brentano 2013a/c: 435–6/469–70). Thus, unlike philosophers who consider converse relations to be a matter of mere "linguistic presentation" (Massin 2009: 580, Williamson 1985; see also Fine 2000), Brentano takes them seriously both conceptually and ontologically.

Following a medieval distinction, Brentano considers some relations to be real (*relationes reales*), whereas others are unreal (*relationes rationis*).[12] A relation is real when its corresponding relative begins or ceases to exist by having itself been "causally brought about" or having itself undergone "a [destructive] influence or removal of a sustaining influence"; a relation is unreal when its corresponding relative comes into existence or goes out of existence because something else has been generated or destroyed (Brentano 2013a/c: 466–7/432–3). For example, regarding what Brentano counts as "relations of comparison", 'something larger' or 'something smaller' come into existence or go out of existence not by themselves undergoing a causal influence but because their size or the size of their correlative has changed. Thus, both relations are unreal. Interestingly, some relations are real while their converse relations are unreal. An example is the relations of causing and of being caused: 'something caused' obviously begins to exist by undergoing a causal effect itself, which is clearly not the case for 'something causing'. When an active thing brings about 'something caused', for example, when the sun heats a stone, it becomes 'something causing' *en passant*. Thus, the effect is *really* related to the cause, but not the cause to the effect. Regarding the intentional relation, the thinking-thing is a real relative, whereas the thought-thing is an unreal relative. Indeed, the thought-thing is generated when the mental act is generated and disappears when the mental act disappears (Brentano 2013a/c: 470–1/436–7, 1982/1995b: 21/23–4). There is a major difference between these three examples of correlations: unreal relatives of comparison and unreal causal relatives have a real *relatum* as a part (two things with size for the relations of being larger and smaller, an active thing for the relation of the cause to the effect); in the case of the intentional correlation, the unreal correlate has an unreal *relatum* as a part, i.e. the thought-thing, as an "immanent object," depends on the act with respect to all its parts (see Chapter 4).

After his reistic turn, Brentano will abandon *irrealia* and, thus, unreal relatives. As a consequence, his correlations will be ontologically impoverished. In some cases, there is just one relative left, but with a *relatum* in front of it. Consider causality: there is an effect left, i.e. a real relative containing a real *relatum*, and an active thing, i.e. a real *relatum* (Brentano 1976/1988b: 125–6/75). In other cases, there is only one relative left. Consider intentionality: there is just the thinking subject left, a real relative containing a real *relatum*, and nothing in front of it. Brentano will nevertheless remain a "realist" about relatives: while relatives of comparison (e.g., the larger-than thing) ontologically "coincide" with an underlying absolute thing (e.g., the thing with a certain size), this does not hold for other relatives, e.g., intentional or causal ones, which are ontologically irreducible (Brentano 1933/1981a: 258–9/184–5, 1966a: 310–11).

How can a thing be a relative if it has no correlative? Initially, Brentano held that relatives without a term (i.e., without even a *relatum* in front of them) are merely "conceptually" relative. The direct (or "*in recto*") presentation of a thinking subject entails the concomitant indirect (or "*in obliquo*") presentation of the object toward which the subject is directed. Yet, from an ontological point of view, the thinking subject is not a relative proper, but something "relative-like" (Brentano 1911a/1973a: Appendix I). However, Brentano changes his mind on this point around 1915–6 and argues that "isolated" relatives are genuine relatives: the thinking subject is genuinely relative also when its object does not exist, or even is impossible; the "aftereffect" is genuinely relative even when its cause has disappeared (Brentano 1933/1981a: 237–8/171; see Gilson 1955: 138–54, Sauer 2006: 21–4, Taieb 2015). Thus, in nonreistic, abstract terms, Brentano admits in his ontology what Grossmann (1969: 31–2) calls "abnormal relations," that is, relations without an existent term. Certainly this is an abnormal thesis, and Brentano's death in 1917 unfortunately deprived it of an extensive justification.[13]

NOTES

1. For the dating of these lectures, see Rollinger 2011.
2. I will briefly outline the young Brentano's theory of properties and relations in the footnotes. For the recognition of three periods in Brentano's ontology, namely "conceptualism" (1862–1874), "ontology of intentionality" (1874–1904), and "reism" (1904–1917), see Chrudzimski 2004, Chrudzimski and Smith 2004.
3. The most detailed discussion of the notions of metaphysical and logical parts is found not in Brentano EL 80 but in Brentano's Würzburgian metaphysics lectures, presented in Baumgartner and Simons 1992–3: 60–2, Chrudzimski 2004: 95–110, Chrudzimski and Smith 2004: 202–4, and Baumgartner 2013: 232–6, which I follow here.
4. For the distinction between "Platonic" and "Aristotelian" universals, see Armstrong 1978. One might wonder whether "Aristotelian realism" was actually defended by Aristotle. At any rate, Brentano was not attributing immanent realism to Aristotle, but to William of Champeaux, a philosopher of the 12th century (see notably Brentano 1966a: 317). On immanent realism in the history of philosophy, see Erismann 2011.
5. Chrudzimski 2004: 140 n. 133 evokes such an hypothesis on the basis of Brentano 2013 a/c: 472/438, but finally rejects it and maintains that Brentano's properties and relations are tropes. In my opinion, the "disguised universals" hypothesis emerges from, and is confirmed by, Brentano 1992–3 and 1993.

6. As I learned from Guillaume Fréchette (directly) and Robin Rollinger (indirectly), Kastil took some liberties in editing Brentano 1933. Indeed, the passage that I quote here is not faithful to the manuscript, which I follow.
7. This remark, in Brentano 1933/1981a: 60–1/52–3, is probably Kastil's own, since it is missing in the manuscript (ms. M 70, n°30837).
8. Since Brentano, in his Würzburgian metaphysics lectures, rejects the existence of *abstracta*, considering them simply "fictions," his early position resembles his reistic theory (see Chrudzimski 2004, Baumgartner 2013: 236, Kriegel 2015: 153 n. 1).
9. Brentano strangely affirms that an accident is a whole having no other "part" than its substance. This said, it is clear that (in one sense or another) "something more" than the substance constitutes the accident. It is this "something more" that I call "qualitative portion".
10. See also Simons 1988: 53–4 about the "lack of individuality" of Brentano's reistic accidents, as well as Chrudzimski 2004: 188.
11. On Russell's criticism of the logical form of "monadistic" relational predicates like (Ry), see Russell 1903: §214.
12. On the medieval distinction between "real relations" and "relations of reason", see Henninger 1989.
13. I am grateful to Uriah Kriegel for his comments and suggestions on an earlier version of this text, and I thank Nicole Osborne for having checked my English.

17

Brentano on Truth

Johannes L. Brandl

How to understand Brentano's account of truth is a question of some controversy. A number of different views have been put forward as positions that Brentano held at some stage in his career. The received view has it that the early Brentano subscribed to a form of correspondence theory which he later rejected in favor of a definition of truth in terms of correct judging, where the correctness of a judgement is defined in terms of the notion of self-evidence (see Kraus 1966, Szrednicki 1965, Stegmüller 1969, Kamitz 1983, Chrudzimski 2001a). This fundamental shift in Brentano's view is regarded as a change from an ontological to a "gnoseological," i.e. epistemic, theory of truth (see Kastil 1934). Brentano's mature view is sometimes said to resemble a neo-Kantian conception of truth or related views (see Kraus 1966, van der Schaar 1999, 2003); it has been compared with a coherence theory of truth (see Krantz 1990/91); and it is regarded as embracing a form of alethic antirealism that places a substantial epistemic constraint on the concept of truth (see Künne 2003). More recently, Charles Parsons suggested that the early Brentano may also be regarded as a precursor of a deflationist theory of truth (see Parsons 2004). Following up on this proposal, the received view has been challenged by a new interpretation that ascribes to Brentano a deflationist position that he held throughout his career in combination with the view that truth pertains primarily to self-evident judgement (see Brandl 2017).

Section 1 first summarizes the received view and then indicates two problems raised by this interpretation. Section 2 explains in which sense Brentano may have been a deflationist and how this interpretation avoids the problems of the received view.

1 THE RECEIVED VIEW ON BRENTANO'S ACCOUNT OF TRUTH

In 1930, Oskar Kraus first published, under the title *Wahrheit und Evidenz (The True and the Evident*, 1966), a collection of writings by Brentano on truth. In the introduction to this collection, Kraus presents a narrative that he followed in organising the volume: Part I of his collection is supposed to represent Brentano's early view as it is expressed most clearly in a lecture, "On the concept of truth", that Brentano delivered to the Vienna Philosophical Society in 1889. This view Brentano is said to have held until about 1901–2. In part II Kraus presents documents from what he describes as a transitional period during which Brentano came to reject the correspondence theory and moved toward his later doctrine that only real things exist and form the proper objects of our thoughts ("reism"; see Chapter 13). At this time, Brentano presumably also discovered the importance of self-evident judgements for our understanding of the concept of truth. Part III in Kraus's collection finally documents what Kraus calls Brentano's mature view, according to which our concept of truth is grounded in the experience of self-evident judgements.

Kraus, and many scholars after him, have done much to flesh out this narrative with further details. One important point concerns Brentano's criticism of the correspondence theory in its classical form. According to Brentano, the theory is built on the mistaken premise that all judgements have a subject–predicate form. Thus it is presumed that a judgement of the form "S is P" is true if, and only if, a relation of instantiation holds between the object and the property denoted by the terms S and P respectively. Brentano challenges this view by pointing out that it does not apply to simple judgements of the form "S exists", because the predicate *exist* does not denote a property. Brentano goes even further in suggesting that all judgements can be represented as having nonpropositional content: they are judgements that either accept or reject the existence of an object (see Chapter 10). While this undermines the classical correspondence theory, which focuses on correspondence between propositions and facts, it still leaves open the possibility of a nontraditional correspondence theory, where the correspondence is between judgements and entities other than facts.

This has led advocates of the received view to propose that Brentano experimented with various ontological innovations to revise and improve the correspondence theory. In the case of a positive judgement, they take him to consider nonreal objects ("*irrealia*") as potential objects corresponding with true judgements. For instance, the judgement "There was a king" is about a real king that may no longer exist, but the judgement nevertheless corresponds with something, namely with a propositional entity that is not a real thing for Brentano. Entities like the existence of a former king are sometimes called "states of affairs". In the case of negative judgements, similar moves may be considered. The judgement "There are no unicorns", despite being a judgement about something nonexisting, may be said to correspond with the state of affairs that no unicorns exist. Equally, the statement "No object can be both round and square" may be said to correspond with the impossibility of round squares or with the necessary state of affairs that a figure instantiating both properties does not exist (see Chrudzimski 2001a: 60).

Turning now to Brentano's mature conception of truth, the received view holds that Brentano arrived at this view because of his scruples to inflate ontology too much in order to meet the demands of the correspondence theory. The idea that truth pertains primarily to self-evident judgements seemed to offer him an alternative. But it required the solution of another problem, since self-evidence is found only in judgements that are infallible or at least beyond any reasonable doubt. According to Brentano, there are two areas in which we can judge with self-evidence: when we make judgements the denial of which would lead to an obvious contradiction, or when we form judgements on the basis of inner perception. An example of a self-evident judgement of the first kind would be the judgement that every cause has an effect or that two is not identical with one. These are axioms that are beyond any reasonable doubt and therefore self-evident. The same holds, according to Brentano, when we judge about the existence of a current sensation or consider whether every judgement presupposes the presentation of an object. Provided that inner perception clearly shows us what we are judging in these cases, we cannot doubt that what it shows us exists, and therefore these judgements are also self-evident (see Brentano 1966b: 123–34).

Now the problem is that judgements may be true without being self-evident, or as Brentano says, despite being "blind" judgements (1966b: 110). This is why Brentano suggests, according to the received view, that a definition of truth involves two parts: it defines truth first for self-evident judgements and secondly for those judgements that are not self-evident. In an undated manuscript that the editors presume not to have been written before 1914, Brentano says:

> "a true judgement" means originally as much as a self-evident judgement. In the secondary sense also, a non-self-evident judgement is called true, if it corresponds in all other respects with a self-evident one.
> (transl. in Szrednicki 1965: 135)[1]

There are two respects in which a blind judgement must agree with a self-evident one to be true: the judgement must have the same object and it must have the same quality, which means that it must be a positive judgement if the self-evident judgement is positive, or a negative judgement if the self-evident judgement is negative. What is not required in this explication is a correspondence relation between a true judgement and some thing in reality. Such a relation does not obtain in those cases when a self-evident judgement denies the existence of an object. In the quotation above, Brentano still speaks of a form of correspondence, but this is a relation between two judgements, namely a blind judgement and a self-evident one. As Brentano makes clear in other passages, this relation is not a normal one, since the requirement merely says that a true judgement agrees with how a subject *would* judge if she were to make the same judgement with self-evidence (see 1966b: 122).

Given the texts collected by Kraus, the narrative of Brentano's changing views on truth may seem completely convincing. Doubts about this interpretation arise, however, when one considers the costs of this interpretation. The received view seems to be uncharitable to Brentano in several respects.

First, it downgrades the importance of his earlier writings on truth. This includes not only the Vienna lecture of 1889 but also his Würzburg lectures on metaphysics, where Brentano already exposes his main points in a chapter entitled "Vom *On Hos Alethes*" (On Being in the Sense of Truth, MS 96: 104–13).

Secondly, the received view is uncharitable to Brentano because it assumes that he overlooked the obvious problems that ensue from allowing nonreal things to appear in a correspondence relation with true judgements. Suppose that a subject correctly judges that there are no humans with three legs but falsely judges that there are no tables with three legs either. Both judgements may have as "correlates", as Brentano puts it, a nonreal thing (or rather pseudo-thing): the nonexistence of three-legged humans and the nonexistence of three-legged tables. These objects may be said to correlate with the two judgements like "being left to" correlates with "being right to" or "cause" correlates with "effect". But if such correlates can be introduced for every judgement, then one cannot explain the difference between a true and a false judgement by saying that the former, but not the latter, corresponds with a nonreal thing (see Brandl 2017).

Thirdly, as several commentators have noted, Brentano's mature view that truth pertains primarily to self-evident judgements raises some serious problems when considered as a definition of truth (see Stegmüller 1969, Kamitz 1983, Künne 2003). Perhaps the most severe problem is that such a definition becomes circular unless one is willing to give up a very basic realist intuition. Suppose we ask how a subject would respond to a question "*p*?" when the answer is not known to us, and suppose we add that we are assuming that this person will know the answer on the basis of a self-evident judgement. If we have no independent reason to believe that the person we ask possesses such knowledge, we must find out ourselves what the answer to our question is. How else should we know how someone would judge in this case, whether or not she does so with self-evidence? This consideration strongly suggests that the question "Is *p* true?" is more basic than the question "What would a person's self-evident judgement be in this matter?" But if the question "Is *p* true?" is the basic one here, then a definition of truth that includes the clause "how a subject would judge with self-evidence" becomes circular.

The circularity is unavoidable given our realist intuitions. From this perspective, a judgement is not true *because* it would agree with a self-evident judgement, but conversely: it would agree with a self-evident judgement because it is true. A definition of truth in terms of self-evidence therefore seems to be warranted only if one gives up this realist view and conceives of the agreement between true and self-evident judgements as that which makes a true judgement true. Such a view might be congenial to advocates of some version of idealism. That Brentano subscribed to a view with such implications is hard to believe.

2 THE NEW INTERPRETATION

Charles Parsons was the first to note that Brentano's early writings on truth do not necessarily support the view that the received interpretation ascribes to him. While Brentano talks in his 1889 lecture as if his goal was a mere revision of the correspondence theory, what he actually proposed at the end of this lecture was a much bolder idea. He makes clear that in explicating the concept of truth, we can do completely without the notion of "correspondence" or any of its cognates, like "harmonizing with reality" or "fitting with reality". This is what his final conclusion reveals:

> Following Aristotle's statement ... we can say: a judgement is true if it asserts of some object that is, *that* the object is, or if it asserts of some object that is not, *that* the object is not – and a judgement is false if it contradicts that which is, or that which is not.
>
> (Brentano 1966b: 21) [2]

This statement is not only reminiscent of similar claims in Aristotle, it also anticipates the equivalence principles that deflationists currently use in explicating the meaning of the predicate "true", for instance the principle used in Horwich's minimalist theory of truth:

(E) The proposition that *p* is true if and only if *p*.

According to Horwich, it is the "underived acceptance of the equivalence schema" that constitutes the meaning of the truth-predicate (Horwich 2010: 27). The principle that Brentano derives from Aristotle differs from schema (E) in using object-variables instead of propositional variables. It therefore accords nicely with Brentano's claim that in making a judgement, we are not accepting a proposition as true, but we are accepting objects as existing or rejecting them as nonexisting. A slightly more perspicuous formulation of the principle makes this transparent:

(B) A judgement of the form "*X* exists", "*X* does not exist", "No *X* exists", or "No non-*X* exists" is true, respectively, if and only if an *X* exists, an *X* does not exist, a non-*X* exists, or a non-*X* does not exist.

Another important difference between this principle and principle (E) concerns the limited generality of (B). As it stands, it is not a principle about *all* judgements but only about those of a particular form. Brentano believed, however, that he had a method for overcoming this restriction. His plan was to show that all judgements either have existential form or can be explained as combinations of such judgements (see Brandl 2014; also Chapter 10). If one grants Brentano that this is possible—and this is of course a large concession—principle (B) may be considered as equally powerful as principle (E).

Parsons restricts his claim that Brentano was a precursor of contemporary deflationism to Brentano's early period. He agrees in this with the received view that in his later years, Brentano held a theory of truth that must count as robust, since it defines truth in epistemic terms. But in this respect, too, an alternative interpretation is available.

Brentano mentions already in his 1889 lecture that defining a concept (either implicitly or explicitly) is not the only way one can explicate it. As a concept empiricist, he believes that we could not understand a concept if we had not appropriate experiences on which our understanding is grounded: "The ultimate and most effective means of elucidation", Brentano says, "must consist in an appeal to the individual's intuition, from which all our general criteria are derived" (1966b: 24–5).

There is then no need to ascribe to Brentano a new definition of truth when he refers to self-evident judgements as the primary bearers of truth. His concept empiricism suffices to explain what Brentano has here in mind, namely an argument that leads him to reject Kant's epistemology. Kant's conception of synthetic a priori judgements is closely related to his doctrine that some of our concepts are pure concepts of reason. Space and time are two primary examples of concepts that are not derived from experience, according to Kant. Brentano rejects this claim as unfounded and offers instead an empiricist explication of space and time. In a nutshell, Brentano says that these concepts are constructed on the basis of spatial and temporal experiences. We have experiences of things in our vicinity and experiences of past, present and future. We also notice a structure in these experiences. Once such structure is apparent, we can go on to construct on this basis the concept of a three-dimensional infinite space, or the concept of a temporal continuum that forms another dimension in multidimensional space–time (see Brentano 1925: 26f.).

Following the same line, we can see how Brentano applies concept empiricism to the concept of truth. He starts from experiences of self-evident judgements that provide us with a basis for constructing this concept. Self-evidence here is not a subjective feeling of certainty, or a compulsion to judge this way or that way, as Brentano emphasizes. Therefore, he is confident that a notion of truth based on such experiences can pass as an objective notion.

This interpretation overcomes the problems facing the received view of Brentano's account of truth. As a deflationist, Brentano has no need to appeal to nonreal (pseudo-) things as the terms of a correspondence relation. When Brentano introduced nonreal things, he did this in the context of his theory of intentionality, where he considered nonreal things as playing the role of mere objects of thought (see Chapter 4). From this, one should not conclude that he gave these objects also an important role to play in his account of truth. Equally, the difficulty with explicating truth in terms of self-evident judging disappears. That the experience of self-evidence is indispensable for acquiring the concept of truth, as Brentano claims, does not imply that it is also indispensable to the nature or essence of truth. The deflationist principle (B) makes this clear, since it contains neither the concept of *correspondence* nor the concept of *self-evidence*. The question therefore remains whether Brentano ever moved beyond his early deflationist position. The following passage from a manuscript dated March 1915 provides evidence that he elaborated the same idea only further:

> Can we find some other interpretation for "*adaequatio*" which might make the thesis [*veritas est adaequatio rei et intellectus*] more acceptable? My answer would be that the thesis tells us no more nor less than this: Anyone who judges that a certain thing exists, or that it does not exist, or that it is possible, or impossible, or that it is thought of by someone, or that it is believed, or loved, or hated, or that it has existed, or will exist, *judges truly* provided that the thing in question does exist, or does not exist, or is possible, or is impossible, or is thought of, etc.
>
> (Brentano 1966b: 122)

NOTES

1. The manuscript, entitled "*Kurzer Abriß einer allgemeinen Erkenntnislehre*", was published in an earlier collection of Brentano's epistemological writings (Brentano 1925) and therefore not included in Kraus's collection of 1930. It is translated and published with related material not included in Kraus's collection in the appendix of Szrednicki 1965. The translation in Szrednicki 1965 has been amended by replacing "evident" by "self-evident".
2. I corrected the English translation to make it fit the German original: "*wahr sei ein Urteil dann, wenn es von etwas, was ist, behaupte, dass es sei; und von etwas, was nicht ist, leugne, dass es sei*". Chisholm unfortunately translates "*leugnen, dass ist*" as "asserting that is not," thereby mislocating the negation in the content and not in the quality of the judgement.

18

Brentano on Appearance and Reality

Denis Seron

Empiricism is one of the most distinctive features of Brentano's work as a whole (see Chapter 3). "Experience alone is my teacher," he declared on the opening page of his *Psychology from an Empirical Standpoint* (Brentano 1874: 1/1973a: xxvii). In very general terms, this suggests that his philosophy gives some priority to appearances over objective reality, to the first-person over the third-person perspective. My suggestion in what follows is that Brentano's aim in the *Psychology* was basically to consolidate his empiricism through a theory of appearance, and that this theory of appearance is identical with his theory of intentionality. I will here discuss two aspects of this view. First, I will argue that Brentano offers an empirical or phenomenological definition of intentionality. Secondly, my claim will be that his theory of intentionality is basically an epistemological theory.

1 EMPIRICISM

Brentano's empiricism has two distinct components. The first is the view that all knowledge, including psychological knowledge, is based on experience; the second is the view that all concepts derive from experience. Brentano's theory of intentionality is an empirical theory insofar as it fulfills both conditions. Let us examine this point in a little more detail.

Regarding the first view, it is important to note that Brentano, already in the *Psychology*, endorses a very strong version of empiricism. What he opposes is not only the speculative rationalism of Hegel and Schelling; he also challenges the Locke-style view that science provides indirect knowledge of substances through their appearances (Brentano 1874: 28/1973a: 19; Brentano 1907: 5ff.; Brentano 1986: 121–2; see also Haller 1989, Potrč 1997). Maybe, he argues, physical phenomena are really caused by things existing in the outside world. However, this does not entail that there holds between them a relation of similarity in virtue of which phenomenological knowledge provides (indirect) objective knowledge. Even accepting that such a relation exists at the level of "spatial phenomena, shapes, and sizes," the same can certainly not be said of many other phenomena that are also studied in physics, for example "the phenomena of light, sound, heat, spatial location and locomotion" (1874: 28/1973a: 19). Knowing physical phenomena does not involve (indirectly) knowing bodies presumed to cause them. Physical phenomena are not such that there really exist bodies that appear in or through them. Rather, if there exist any such bodies (physical substances) in the external world, they simply don't appear at all: "That which truly exists does not come to appearance, and that which appears does not truly exist" (1874: 28/1973a: 19). In short: all knowledge has as its objects—all scientific theories actually refer to—phenomena and only phenomena. For this reason, some commentators have suggested that Brentano's position in his *Psychology* is a form of phenomenalism, namely an epistemological or methodological phenomenalism (Tolman 1987, Pacherie 1993: 13, Simons 1995, Crane 2006, Seron 2014).

The implications of this are straightforward. As is well known, intentionality is used in the *Psychology* to define psychology (see Chapter 4). In opposition to other philosophers and psychologists of the time—especially Wundt, the positivists, and the neo-Kantians—Brentano thought that the sciences differ from one another not primarily by their *methods* but by their *objects*, and that defining psychology consequently involves defining the mental. Since science in general must refer to phenomena and only phenomena, the question is, what is a mental phenomenon? "Our aim," says Brentano, "is to clarify the meaning of the two terms 'physical phenomenon' and 'mental phenomenon', removing all misunderstanding and confusion concerning them" (1874: 111/1973a: 78). Within the flux of what we experience, some phenomena we are aware of have distinctive features that suffice to qualify them as "mental." According to Brentano, intentional directedness is such a feature: necessarily, every mental phenomenon is representational and vice versa (1874: 124–5/1973a: 88–9).

Let us now turn to the second view: all concepts derive from experience (Brentano 1929b: 139). According to Brentano, this can be understood in two different ways (Brentano 1976: 3/1988b: 1). In a first sense, an empirical concept is a primitive concept directly abstracted from experience. In a second sense, a concept is said to be empirical insofar as it is defined in terms of primitive concepts thus conceived. For example, the concept of a "four-dimensional topoid" is certainly not taken directly from experience, but it is empirical insofar as it is a combination of, say, the concepts "four," "spatial coordinate," and "shape," which are directly taken from experience.

For the sake of convenience, we may call concepts of the first kind "observational" and concepts of the second kind "theoretical." My contention is that, for Brentano, intentionality falls into the second category. In other words, intentionality is not an observational concept but a compound of observational concepts, hence a concept that is to be defined through observational concepts. Brentano never used the word "intentionality", nor did he use the word "intentional" in the sense of "intentionally directed toward something." He used instead the term "relation to a content" (1874: 124/1973a: 88). Thus, my aim in the following pages is to show that both "relation" and "content" here are to be taken as observational concepts.

2 INTENTIONALITY EMPIRICALLY DEFINED

Now with this in mind, Brentano's reasoning in the *Psychology* is simply as follows. First, psychology is defined as the "science of mental phenomena," with the consequence that defining what psychology is requires defining what a mental phenomenon is. Secondly, according to Brentano's intentionality thesis—necessarily, all mental phenomena are representational and vice versa—mental phenomena are to be defined in terms of intentionality. Thirdly and finally, intentionality is not a primitive term and still needs to be defined. As a result, the ultimate goal is to define intentionality, namely to define it using concepts that are directly abstracted from experience.

For Brentano, as for most empiricist philosophers of his time, defining is not merely clarifying what a word means and how it should be used, but also, and more importantly, indicating what it actually refers to. The relation of equivalence between the *definiendum* and the *definiens* means that the actual objects of the concept to be defined must be those objects which the defining concepts directly refer to. And since intentionality is an empirical concept, these objects must be experiential data. In this sense, the definition required must be a *phenomenological* definition of intentionality (hereafter PDI). As I will try to show, such a definition is the core of Brentano's theory of intentionality in the 1874 *Psychology*.

Since psychology is the science of mental phenomena, and mental phenomena are essentially representational, it is to be expected that most of the psychologist's judgments will be expressible by sentences with intentional verbs. Accordingly, the question of what the objects of psychology are is equivalent to the question of what sentences of the form "R represents A" refer to. For example, a psychologist affirms that a subject imagines Peter Pan. The question is, what are the objects of this judgment? What does the sentence refer to? When you accept it as true that the subject imagines Peter Pan, are you committed to the existence of Peter Pan? Or to the existence of the subject? Or to neither (or both)?

In a sense, this is a question of "deep grammar." Another way to express the same idea is to say that intentional sentences may be referentially misleading and need to be rephrased. Defining what an intentional fact is requires rephrasing sentences of the form "R represents A" in such a way as to make apparent the objects actually referred to. Debates about Brentano's theory of intentionality are of course rife (see Chapter 4). Here is what I believe to be Brentano's rephrasing of "R represents A" and hence his definition of intentionality:

(PDI) For all x, x is a representation of A iff x appears and x (really) exists and A does not (really) exist and A appears in x.[1]

Put more simply: something is an intentional act and hence a mental phenomenon if, and only if, it (really) exists and something else that does not (really) exist appears in it. In other words, "x and A appear" is synonymous with "x and A are phenomena" or "x and A are phenomenally conscious" (in the intransitive sense of the term) or "x and A are subjectively experienced." More precisely: x is a mental phenomenon, A is a physical or mental phenomenon.

The overall idea behind (PDI) is fairly intuitive. It is that appearing does not involve existing. Many things appear in your mind, and among them some exist, some do not. When you imagine Peter Pan, what appears to you, what you experience, is both Peter

Pan and your imagining Peter Pan. Peter Pan does not need to exist for you to imagine Peter Pan—it is a "mere appearance." But you imagining Peter Pan must exist, otherwise you would not imagine Peter Pan.

All the conditions on the right-hand side of the biconditional can easily be found in the 1874 edition of the *Psychology* (Brentano 1874: 14, 114, 124–32/1973a: 10, 81, 88–94).[2] The most important point for our purposes is that the *definiens* is only about phenomena and their phenomenal properties. The primitive terms are "appears", "exists", and "appears in", which are observational concepts in the sense indicated above.

Several things should be noted here.

First, (PDI) is obviously false if inner perception is a form of representation. For in this case, A should be the mental act itself and hence be identical with x, with the consequence that x should be said to exist and not exist at the same time. For reasons I cannot go into here, I think that inner perception is not a form of representation in the contemporary sense of the word, that is, a mental act that has a "content." In my view, what corresponds to inner perception in (PDI) is the verb "appears".[3]

Second, the condition "A does not exist" clearly serves as a criterion for marking off the intentional content A from other parts of the mental act x that are not represented by x. For example, both the represented thunder and the auditory perception of it are parts of the act of feeling scared when hearing thunder. But they differ from each other by the fact that the former, unlike the latter, does not need to exist for the whole act to exist.

Third, the conjunction "A does not exist and A appears in x" corresponds to what Brentano—ambiguously—calls "intentional in-existence" (*intentionale Inexistenz*). That the intentional object "intentionally in-exists" means that it is merely "intentional" in the late-medieval sense of the term, namely a mere appearance in the mind. It is thus noteworthy that Brentano uses the term "intentional existence" interchangeably with "phenomenal existence" (1874: 129/1973a: 92).

Fourth and finally, the condition "A appears in x" turns out to be central for understanding what intentionality means for Brentano. Intentionality is not a metaphysical relation between mind and world; it is better seen as a pheno-mereological relation in virtue of which some phenomena appear in our mind as having a *content*, that is, as containing in themselves another phenomenon which does not exist. Both kinds of phenomena are, strictly speaking, appearances *in the mind*, and thus the relation between them is, as Brentano says, a purely "mental relation" (Brentano 1911a: 133ff./1973a: 271ff.). That is why Brentano claims that psychology is also concerned with physical phenomena, as far as they are conceived as *contents*—as psychological features—of mental phenomena (Brentano 1874: 140/1973a: 100). Nonetheless, mental phenomena—phenomena that include within them other phenomena that do not exist—are the proprietary subject matter of psychology.

"All phenomena," claims Brentano, "are to be called 'inner' because they all belong to one reality, be it as constituents or as correlates" (Brentano 1982: 129/1995b: 137). In Brentano's view, a phenomenon is something that occurs in one's mind in such a way that one is acquainted with it through perception. Since all objects of perception are phenomena, it follows from this that all perception, even so-called outer perception, is in some sense "inner" (Brentano 1874: 128/1973a: 91; Brentano 1982: 129/1995b: 137). Accordingly, "the objects of the so-called external perception … demonstrably do not exist outside of us. In contrast to that which really and truly exists, they are mere phenomena" (1874: 14/1973a: 10).

3 A PHENOMENOLOGICAL APPROACH TO THE PROBLEM OF INTENTIONALITY

The main benefit of this approach, in my view, is that it offers an intuitive solution to the so-called "problem of intentionality", or at least to some version of it. Roughly, the problem of intentionality arises from the fact that some representations seem to represent both something and nothing. On the one hand, your representation of Peter Pan is about something, namely Peter Pan rather than Robin Hood. On the other hand, Peter Pan does not exist and so there is nothing your representation is about. The problem clearly resides in the relational character of intentional verbs, namely in the fact that they grammatically require an object and, at the same time, are often used to express intentional states that have no object. Crane (2001: 23; cf. Kriegel 2007: 307–8) analyzes the problem using the following three propositions:

(PI1) For all x, if x represents A, then x stands in a relation to A.
(PI2) For all x, if x stands in a relation to A, then A exists.
(PI3) There exists an x such that x represents A and A does not exist.

The conjunction of (PI1) and (PI2) implies that

(PI4) For all x, if x represents A, then A exists.

The problem lies in the fact that each of the three propositions (PI1–3) seems true individually, but that the conjunction of (PI4) and (PI3) is necessarily false.

The Brentanian strategy for solving the problem of intentionality becomes apparent if, as prescribed in (PDI), we substitute each occurrence of "x represents A" with the equivalent sentence "x appears and x exists and A does not exist and A appears in x." We then obtain the following propositions:

(PI1*) For all x, if x appears and x exists and A does not exist and A appears in x, then x stands in a relation to A.
(PI2) For all x, if x stands in a relation to A, then A exists.
(PI3*) There exists an x such that x appears and x exists and A appears in x and A does not exist.

There are at least two things worth noting here. First, (PI1*) is a tautology, since "appears in" denotes a relation. Second, the conjunction of (PI1*) and (PI2*), at least at first glance, implies a contradiction, namely:

(PI4*) For all x, if x appears and x exists and A does not exist and A appears in x, then A exists.

Since the problem of intentionality lies in the apparent inconsistency of (PI1–3), one may be tempted to conclude that Brentano's phenomenological approach leaves it unsolved. However, I think there is a flaw in this line of reasoning. My suggestion is that the phrase "appears in" actually introduces something fundamentally new, which requires us to approach the problem in quite a different way.

The key point is that, although "appears in" certainly denotes a relation, that relation is not of the usual kind. Suppose you hallucinate a ghost in armor standing in the doorway. The ghost appears to you as do the doorway and the armor. Moreover, it is true that he *appears in* the doorway and *in* armor. However, "the ghost is in the doorway" and "the ghost is in armor" do not imply that the ghost or his armor exist. In consequence, (PI2) is false: some relations are such that some or even all of their relata do not exist, and this is the case with "appears in." In some sense, both relata are required for the ghost and the doorway to stand in the relation "appears in." But this simply means that both relata must *appear* (not exist) for the relation to *appear*. (PI2) is certainly true of real relations, but it is not true of purely phenomenal relations: "appears in" is not a relation such that, if x stands in it to y, then y exists.

Most importantly, this is not just a stipulation required in order to accommodate the fact that some representations have no object. Rather, this is just how we use appearance words in ordinary language. In this respect, Brentano's phenomenological approach to the intentionality problem may be considered more intuitive than the approach using intentional verbs (Seron, forthcoming).

Brentano conceives of intentionality as a "relation to a content" (1874: 124/1973a: 88). However, this "mental relation," although similar to real relations, is not a genuine relation, and one could even doubt whether it is really fit to be called a relation.[4] The reason for this, Brentano argues, is that the mental relation can obtain even if one of its relata does not exist:

> If someone thinks of something, the one who is thinking must certainly exist, but the object of his thinking need not exist at all.... The only thing which is required by mental reference is the person thinking. The terminus of the so-called relation does not need to exist in reality at all.
> (Brentano 1911a: 134/1973a: 272)

It is clear that, once intentionality is construed as involving no real relation, that is, no relation such that it cannot obtain unless all its relata exist, the so-called "problem of intentionality" ceases to be a problem at all. Indeed, the conjunction of (PI1) and (PI2) no longer implies (PI4). From the fact that intentionality is a *phenomenal* relation and all *real* relations are such that their existence necessarily entails that of all their relata, it does not follow that intentionality is such that its existence necessarily entails that of all its relata. As a result, the conjunction of (PI1) and (PI2) is consistent with (PI3). The phenomenological approach to intentionality makes this solution more intuitive insofar as it makes more intuitive the view that some relations can obtain in the absence of one or more of their relata.

4 BRENTANO'S THEORY OF INTENTIONALITY AS AN EPISTEMOLOGICAL THEORY

The condition "A appears (in x) and does not exist"—intentional in-existence—has to do with what philosophers call "representational opacity." Just as "S has a representation of A" does not entail that there exists something that is represented by S and is identical to A, so "A appears" does not entail that there exists something that appears and is identical to *A*. But what is important here is that, once phenomenologically construed, intentional in-existence is no more a puzzling logical feature of intentional verbs but is normally allowed by the grammar of appearance words.

To some extent, the above suggests an adverbial theory of intentionality (Moran 1996). The claim that intentionality is not a real relation may be taken to mean that "represents *A*" is not a relational but a one-place predicate. To put it otherwise: the belief that you have a representation of *A* commits you only to the existence of your representation with its psychological properties, and being about *A* is just one of these properties. However, Brentano's view actually involves something more.

According to (PDI), a mental act consists in a combination of two phenomena, of which one exists and the other does not. A mental act is basically this: a mental phenomenon appears in such a way that something else, its "content" or "primary object," appears in it. As we have just seen, this content is, ontologically speaking, nothing more than the act's property of being about this or that. As Husserl claims in the *Logical Investigations*, the intentional content exists in the act in the same way as the red exists in the red stripe (Husserl 1984: 105–6/2001: 230; Husserl 1979: 157).

A highly paradoxical consequence of this is that judgments are not made true by the primary object they are about. The psychologist talks about her past mental states. The physicist talks about colors, shapes, temperatures. None of these things really exist; they are mere appearances. Yet some physical or psychological theories are really true. So what makes them true if they are about mere appearances? Mere appearances do not exist and thus cannot make anything true!

Assuming that scientific theories refer not to external reality, but only to appearances in the mind, how is it possible for them to be true? The challenge is twofold. As a phenomenalist, Brentano must deny, for example, that the natural scientist's judgment that some owls are brown is made true by physical substances to which it should correspond. As a "science of physical phenomena," physics has no other objects than (physical) appearances in the mind. However, unlike other phenomenalists, Brentano does not consider such judgments to be illusory or physical knowledge as such to be impossible: it *is* true—in the sense of what Brentano sometimes calls "phenomenal truth" (Brentano 1933: 169)—that some owls are brown. So what makes them true? Brentano's view is that the judgment's truthmaker is neither its primary object nor any extraphenomenal substance. All that we have is its secondary object, namely the mental act the natural scientist presently experiences.

Accordingly, there is a sense in which Brentano's theory of intentionality is an epistemological theory, in the sense that its purpose is to establish the validity of the empirical sciences, that is, of sciences whose objects are only mere phenomena. Brentano tries to demonstrate that a science can yield truths even if its objects are mere phenomena. And his solution is as follows: the natural scientist can say true things about physical phenomena, but she ought to know that she actually refers only to present mental phenomena, for example to her remembering of the owl. The upshot of this is that

> If we investigate what it means to say the color is not known as actually existing, but as phenomenally existing, it becomes clear that in the final analysis I do not know that a color exists, but that I have a presentation of the color, that I see it … Hence it follows that we do not really recognize that which is known as the

"object", what we recognize is only the mentally active being who has it as his object ... It is certain that neither we nor any other being who grasps something with direct evidence as a fact can have anything but himself as the object of his knowledge.

(Brentano 1928: 4–6/1981b: 5–6)

This view may be regarded as a variant of the "thesis of the relativity of knowledge" (defended, among others, by Lotze and Hamilton).[5] "The truth of physical phenomena," Brentano claims in the 1874 *Psychology*, "is only a relative truth" (1874: 28/1973a: 19). The owls that the knowledge that some owls are brown is about are no more than "correlates" that appear in the mental act.

As Brentano put it in the late 1880s, the owls are presented "in an oblique mode" (*in modo obliquo*) as brown.[6] The oblique mode corresponds to intentional aboutness, while the real reference, the existing object that is presented in a direct mode (*in modo recto*), is the present mental act. The empirical scientist's judgments rest upon oblique presentations. The idea is that, although owls are mere appearances, they can be truly ascribed objective properties through a nonreferential use of language (cf. Parsons 2004: 179–80). Again, this nonreferential use is in line with our ordinary use of appearance words. We obviously can, in virtue of the grammar of appearance words, say true things about appearances that do not exist, for example "The ghost appears to me in armor."

Importantly, this should apply to psychology as well. For the method of empirical psychology is inner observation through memory, and memory is a variety of oblique presentation (Brentano 1928: 38ff.; Dewalque 2014: 68–9). Affirming or knowing that you felt angry a moment ago involves accepting as existent not your past feeling—which indeed no longer exists—but your present memory of having felt angry. Your anger is what your judgment is about, not the object it actually refers to. Psychology, like natural science, pertains to oblique knowledge.[7]

NOTES

1. The condition "*A* doesn't exist" on the right-hand side of the formula forbids us to quantify over *A*. This impossibility is due to the fact that, as I will argue further on, Brentano plausibly offers an adverbial account of intentionality, construing "represents *A*" as a one-place predicate.
2. For further details, see Seron 2014, 2015. This line of interpretation is very close to that of Potrč 2013.
3. It is true that Brentano conceives of inner perception as a form of "presentation" (*Vorstellung*), namely as a "presentation of a presentation" (1874: 179/1973a: 127). The word, however, should not be understood in the contemporary sense of a full intentional state, but rather in the sense of the appearance of something in the mind. Dermot Moran rightly points out that "Brentano uses the term 'presentation' much as Locke and Hume used the term 'idea'" (Moran 2000a: 45). This is clearly reflected in the following quotes: "As we use the verb 'to present', 'to be presented' means the same as 'to appear'" (Brentano 1874: 114/1973a: 81); "We speak of a presentation whenever something appears to us" (Brentano 1911a: 34/1973a: 198). The view proposed here does not rule out the possibility for the mental act to be represented in the contemporary sense of the word. A mental act can have a mental act as its intentional content. In this case, however, Brentano's view is that the act being represented must be numerically different from the act that represents it. The represented act is a *past* act—an act that no longer exists really and whose only "existence" is its appearing in one's mind. Of course, (PDI) is not self-contradictory when applied to self-representation thus conceived, namely as a representation of a numerically distinct representation.

4. Katalin Farkas (2013) has proposed to construe intentionality as an "apparent directedness." I think this is exactly what Brentano had in view when he characterized intentionality as a "mental relation." Brentano's use of the term "relation," however, is rather ambiguous. He sometimes regards intentionality as a special kind of relation (Brentano 1928: 42/1981b: 31; Brentano 1933: 167ff.) and sometimes as something that is not really a relation at all but an appearance of a relation (Brentano 1911a: 133ff./1973a: 271ff.).
5. Cf. Hamilton 1859: 96–7: "All human knowledge, consequently … all human philosophy, is only of the relative or phenomenal. In this proposition, the term 'relative' is opposed to the term 'absolute'; and, therefore, in saying that we know only the relative, I virtually assert that we know nothing absolute—nothing existing absolutely; that is, in and for itself, and without relation to us and our faculties.… It is only in its qualities, only in its effects, in its relative or phenomenal existence, that <the object> is cognizable or conceivable." The terms "correlate" and "phenomenal existence" commonly used by Brentano are clearly Hamiltonian.
6. Brentano (EL 80) explains the relation between relativity and obliqueness as follows: "Something that is designated in a relative manner is something that is determined in relation to something else. Relative names are names in which, besides the named object, another object is named *in obliquo*." See also Brentano 1874: 134ff./1973a: 272ff., Brentano 1933: 169, 174, De Libera 2011.
7. I am indebted to Uriah Kriegel for very insightful comments on an earlier draft of this paper.

19

Brentano on Negation and Nonexistence

Alessandro Salice

Franz Brentano's considerations about negation and nonexistence are developed mainly in connection with his investigations into the theory of judgment and metaphysics. Metaphysics in particular can arguably be said to represent one of the most persistent interests in Brentano's thought, accompanying the maturing of his entire philosophy from his 1862 dissertation *On the Manifold Sense of Being in Aristotle* (Brentano 1862/1975a) to the posthumously published manuscripts collected under the title *Theory of Categories* (Brentano 1933/1981a). Some of his most interesting insights about negation and nonexistence are secured in *Psychology from an Empirical Standpoint* against the background of his existential and nonpredicative theory of judgments (see Chapter 10). As §1 below explains, Brentano's theory can be qualified as nonpredicative, since it does not regard predication (or the subject–predicate form) as an essential trait of judgments: *individual things* (*Dinge*) are held by him to be the intentional objects of judgments. Initially, Brentano considered that *all* judgments with apparent subject–predicate structure could be traced back to *simple* existential judgments (of the form "A exists" or "A does not exist," cf. Brentano 1995a: 169). Over the course of the years, however, he revised his theory by introducing the notion of "double judgments." As shown in §2, this revision is motivated by further considerations regarding the role of negation in judgments. This entry places Brentano's insights about negation and nonexistence in the context of this development.

From a historical angle, it should be stressed that Brentano's view about negation has been embraced by only a few members of the so-called Brentano School (see Hillebrand 1891: 28, Twardowski 2016; cf. Albertazzi *et al.* 1996). His ideas were also rejected on the basis of a more general disagreement about the intentional object of judgment. In particular, Edmund Husserl, Anton Marty, and Alexius Meinong, among others, dismissed Brentano's nonpredicative theory of judgment, claiming that the judgmental act is directed toward an irreducibly propositional kind of object. Although the different terminology with which this object is referred to—"state of affairs (*Sachverhalt*)," "content of judgment (*Urteilsinhalt*)," "objective (*Objektiv*)," and so on—reflects important divergences within the above authors' theories of judgment, these authors generally agree on the idea that the propositional object of judgment can be either positive or *negative* (cf. Meinong 1983: 37f, Marty 1908: 294).[1] For a period of time, Brentano seems to have endorsed the view that the act of judgment is directed toward a propositional object (Brentano 1930: 26f), in which negation would also have to be located (cf. Fréchette 2014). However, he eventually dismisses this idea (Brentano 1930: 89–118, Kriegel 2015) for reasons to be addressed below.

1 THE EXISTENTIAL THEORY OF JUDGMENT AND NEGATIVE EXISTENTIALS

In the *Psychology*, Brentano argues for the classification (inspired by Descartes, cf. Brentano 1969: 15) of all mental acts into three kinds: presentations, judgments, and emotions or love and hate phenomena (see Chapter 9). Presentations are the most fundamental acts in the sense that they are always presupposed by judgments and emotions. This explains why Brentano refers to the latter acts as "superposed acts" (Brentano 1995b: 90). For instance, if a subject judges that this particular rose is red, then the judgmental act can be said to be "superposed" on a presentation of the red rose, in the sense that the former act could not exist without the latter. Similarly, if a subject likes something, then a presentation of that thing underlies that act of liking.

Insofar as judgments are always superposed on presentations, every judgment is directed toward the same object as its underlying presentation ("nothing is an object of judgment which is not an object of presentation," Brentano 1995a: 156). If so, the difference between judgments and presentations cannot be accounted for in terms of a difference in their objects (and the same holds for emotions). What rather distinguishes these mental phenomena is the very kind of intentional relation in which their subject is involved; in particular, all superposed acts come either in a positive or in a negative form. For instance, in emotions, one is directed toward an object with inclination or disinclination (love or hate, pleasure or displeasure). Similarly, judgments are characterized by the fact that the subject, when judging, adopts either a positive or a negative stance, either belief or disbelief, about the object. To have a belief about the object is to accept (*anerkennen*) the object, while to have a disbelief is to reject (*verwerfen*) it. No analogous opposition is observable in presentations (Brentano 1969: 17). Accordingly, Brentano's theory of judgment could be qualified as "idiogenetic," as it relies on the idea that judgment is a distinct, irreducible kind of mental act.[2]

As noted, the difference between judgments and presentations cannot be explained by a difference in their respective objects. But the identification of (dis)belief as the essential mark of judgment allows Brentano to dismiss other attempts to distinguish these two kinds of act. Most importantly, he resists an influential theory held by, among others, John Stuart Mill (Mill 1843: 116–7), according to which judgments are combinations of two presentations by means of the copula. On this view, the copula expresses the connection or synthesis between the presentation of the object or substance (linguistically represented by the subject of the sentence) and the presentation of the property or accident (represented by the predicate of the sentence). One argument that Brentano adduces against this view is that not all judgments show a subject–predicate form. For instance (cf. Brentano 1956: 99), no subject figures in the sentence

(1) it rains

and in the existential sentence

(2) the planet Jupiter exists

the grammatical predicate "is existent" does not point to an accident or to an attribute (*Merkmal*) of the object, but rather expresses the positive quality (the act of acceptance) of the judgmental act (cf. Brentano 1995a: 161). Brentano's idea is that the singular term "the planet Jupiter" expresses a presentation and that, on top of this first act, a second act occurs, namely, a (positive) judgment that points at the same object as the underlying presentation (namely, the planet Jupiter) and whose occurrence is linguistically signaled by the merely grammatical predicate "is existent."[3]

This analysis is conducive to the idea that, in negative existentials such as

(3) Pegasus does not exist

the grammatical predicate, again, is not about an accident that the object at issue lacks but rather expresses the *negative quality of disbelief*. That is, it expresses that the object is *rejected* by the subject. Two consequences can be drawn from this.

First, since the concept of negation coincides with the concept of refusal, negation can only occur in judgments and not in presentations, for presentations do not come in a positive or negative form (more on this in §2).

The second consequence is that, if the existential predicate ("is existent") is the expression of a belief, then this suggests that it is not a true predicate—it does not refer to any part or property or accident of the object. Brentano fleshes out this descriptive-psychological observation by developing a mereological argument: when one accepts a whole (e.g., a substance together with an accident), one accepts all of its parts; but when one rejects a whole, one *does not* reject all of its parts. For instance, if one accepts the learned Socrates (i.e., a whole composed of the substance Socrates and the accident being learned), then one also accepts Socrates; but if one rejects the learned Socrates, this does not imply rejecting Socrates. If existence were a true predicate (just as "being learned" is, insofar as it is about an accident of Socrates), then by denying the existing Socrates, one would not deny Socrates—but this is obviously absurd. Hence, existence cannot be considered a true predicate (cf. Brentano 1995a: 162). According to this view, it can be argued that a *positive* existential is made true by the object referred to by the judgment, and a *negative* existential is true if there is no object to which the judgment refers—or, to put this differently, if the world is such that no such object is included in it (for a problem with this idea, cf. van der Schaar 1997: 314f).

This leaves open the question of how one should understand the intentionality of judgment (an issue about which Brentano seems to have changed his mind over the years). Some commentators argue that, at least during a certain period of time (stretching from 1874 up to the turn of the twentieth century), Brentano interpreted intentionality as a genuine dyadic relation (cf. Chisholm 1967, Chrudzimsky 2004, Smith 1994a). If that were the case, Brentano's approach to negative existentials could be employed to defend the claim that the intentional object of judgment is a *sui generis* mental object (sometimes called "immanent object"): a positive judgment would be true if the immanent object of the judgment were to correspond to the transcendent object (and false otherwise), while a negative judgment would be true if there were no transcendent object corresponding to the immanent object (and false otherwise). Others, however, contend that Brentano always conceived of the intentional relation in Aristotelian terms, namely, as a *monadic* predicate (cf. Antonelli 2012, Sauer 2006). On this view, the truth or falsity of a judgment would still depend on the existence of its transcendent object, but there would be no need for introducing further entities mediating between the act and the transcendent object.

Since all judgments either accept or reject the object of a presentation, and since the existential predicates "is existent" and "is nonexistent" express belief and disbelief (respectively), it seems legitimate to infer that all judgments can be paraphrased into existential judgments (see Chapter 10). For instance, "some man is sick" would be paraphrased into "a sick man *exists*," "some man is not learned" into "a non-learned man *exists*," "all men are mortal" into "an immortal man *does not exist*," and "no stone is living" into "a living stone *does not exist*" (Brentano 1995a: 165f).

Brentano's paraphrase of the particular negative judgments (e.g., "some man is not learned") and of the universal positive judgments (e.g., "all men are mortal"), however, is problematic. For it seems to directly conflict with one main assumption of the theory, namely, that the place of negation is only in the judgmental *act*. The paraphrases at issue conflict with this assumption because, in them, negation already applies to the singular term, which Brentano takes to be the linguistic expression of a presentation. The notion of double judgment, to which we turn next, is able to block this potentially pernicious outcome of the theory.

2 NEGATIVE PREDICATES AND DOUBLE JUDGMENTS

The notion of double judgment might be seen as an extension of the existential theory of judgment.[4] In addition to what are now considered merely simple (or "thetic") judgments, such as those expressed in (2) and (3) above, Brentano gives an account of the four kinds of categorical judgment in terms of several judgments compounded together. For instance, based on the idea of double judgment, Brentano now analyzes a particular positive judgment, such as "some man is sick," in terms of *two* judgments: a first judgment, by means of which a man is accepted; and a second one, which ascribes (*zusprechen*) the accident, being-sick, to the man. Another way to put this is that, once the subject is accepted, its connection (*Verbindung*) with the accident is accepted as well (Brentano 1995a: 230). Linguistically, the judgment "some man is sick" would thus be equivalent to the complex judgment "there is a man and this man is sick."

Once the idea of double judgment is introduced, the problematic term-negation in particular negative judgments, such as "some man is not learned," can easily be dealt with. Here, Brentano argues that a first judgment accepts the subject, and a second judgment denies (*absprechen*) the accident of being-learned. In other words, once the subject is accepted, the connection with the accident is *rejected*—with the necessary *addendum* that, as we saw in §1, since the rejection of a whole is not the rejection of all of its parts, the subject of the judgment is still accepted: there *is* a man to whom the accident of being learned is denied. The judgment "some man is not learned" could hence be paraphrased into "there is a man and there is not this learned man."

Things get more complex when it comes to universal judgments. In the case of universal negative judgments, such as "there is no living stone," Brentano's analysis takes a different direction. He now suggests that the adequate psychological analysis would be that person A, who makes the judgment, (i) is presenting some person B as judging that there is a living stone, and (ii) is judging that B is judging incorrectly (Brentano 1995a: 232). Brentano does not provide the reader with any reading of the judgment "there is no living stone," but a possible paraphrase could be "no one exists who correctly judges 'there are living stones'" (cf. Brandl 2014). An analogous strategy is applied to universal positive judgments, such as "all men are mortal." Here, Brentano again reverts to the idea that this judgment amounts to the judgment that there is no one who correctly judges that there are immortal men.

Actually, one might wonder whether one can ever gain introspective evidence of such psychological processes when uttering those judgments. Brentano himself signals awareness of the psychological complexity of his analysis when he writes: "[t]hese are the *somewhat complicated results* of a psychological analysis of the four logical forms of categorical statements" (cf. Brentano 1995a: 232, my emphasis). But he is also aware that such psychological complexity enables ontological simplicity. If one leaves out of consideration the intricacies related to the notion of purely mental objects and to the role that these objects might have played for this theory of intentionality, the ontological apparatus on which Brentano's theory of judgment relies neatly reduces to individual things together with their accidents, for no other kinds of entity—and, in particular, no propositional objects—appear to be required by the theory (see Chapter 13). Having propositional objects in his ontological *repertoire* would have allowed Brentano to develop simpler psychological analyses of the judgmental act, but would also have pushed him into problems that he eventually might have considered more pressing than pure psychological complexity.

There are several problems that Brentano voices against the ideas of propositions, contents of judgment, and states of affairs (cf. especially 1930: 91ff). One is particularly interesting for our purposes, as it specifically concerns the idea of *negative* states of affairs. The problem can be summarized as follows. As seen in §1, Brentano claims that every time one *accepts* a thing, one accepts all of its parts. For instance, if one accepts a sparrow, then one accepts a bird ("bird" being a logical part of the sparrow) and one accepts a beak (the beak being a physical part of the sparrow). All these further acceptances are implicit in the acceptance of a sparrow, but for the judgment to be self-evident, all these acceptances have to be explicit (cf. 1930: 102). Note that this implies that things have only a *finite* number of parts. Brentano then invites his reader to assume that it is possible to accept the *nonbeing of a sparrow*. If that were the case, then such a judgment would be evident only if all the parts of its object are explicitly accepted. But, upon closer consideration, such a judgment can never be self-evident because, if there were negative states of affairs, then they would have infinite parts: the nonbeing of a sparrow would also be the nonbeing of a young sparrow, of an old sparrow, of a sick sparrow, of a healthy sparrow, etc. (cf. 1930: 99). This, according to Brentano, is absurd and should encourage us to dismiss the idea of (negative) states of affairs.

3 CONCLUSION: NEGATION IN BRENTANO'S PHILOSOPHY

The crucial role that negation plays in Brentano's philosophy can be assessed against the background of his theory of judgment and of his metaphysics. Negation is important for the former theory because it is one aspect that essentially qualifies the act of judgment in respect to other acts (and especially in respect to presentations): only judgments can be negative. However, and in contrast to many of his pupils, Brentano does not draw any specific metaphysical consequence from this psychological consideration. He maintains that a judgment is negative just because it is a refusal (or a disbelief) of an individual thing, and he resists any attempt to cash out the concept of a negative judgment by introducing metaphysical notions (like that of negative states of affairs) that he holds to be problematic.

NOTES

1. Things are more nuanced when it comes to Husserl (cf. Husserl 2009). Within the Göttingen circle of phenomenology, Adolf Reinach most prominently argued for the idea of negative states of affairs (cf. Reinach 1911/1982).
2. The term "idiogenetic" was coined by Hillebrand and literally means "of an autonomous genus" (Hillebrand 1891: 26).
3. By "merely grammatical predicate," I mean a linguistic expression whose syntactic role is that of a predicate but which does not have a property or accident as semantic value.
4. The doctrine of double judgment was first introduced, briefly, in a short essay of 1883 entitled "Miklosich on Subjectless Propositions" (Brentano 1969: 98–108).

1.3 Value

20

Brentano's Metaethics

Jonas Olson

Brentano's main metaethical writings are two: *The Origin of Our Knowledge of Right and Wrong*, which is based on an 1889 lecture before the Vienna Law Society (Brentano 1889/1969), and *The Foundation and Construction of Ethics*, based on Brentano's lectures on practical philosophy from 1876–94 (Brentano 1952/1973b).

Early on in *Origin*, Brentano presents his metaethical stance succinctly:

> Is there such a thing as a moral truth taught by nature itself and independent of ecclesiastical, political, and every other kind of social authority? Is there a moral law that is natural in the sense of being universally and incontestably valid—valid for men at all places and all times, indeed valid for any being that thinks and feels—and are we capable of knowing that there is such a law? ... My own answer is emphatically affirmative.
>
> (1969: 6)

Brentano's metaethical stance thus appears thoroughly realist and objectivist. However, his theory has several features that one does not expect to find in a theory that holds that moral truths are objective and universal. Most notably, Brentano holds that moral judgements conceptually presuppose emotions, and that emotions are a precondition for moral knowledge. He denies that there is a separate realm of values and norms, independent of the emotive attitudes of love and hate, and he also denies that evaluative properties and facts are among the contents of acts of valuing.

These features of Brentano's view all tie in with notorious difficulties for realist objectivist views in metaethics, chief among which are accounting for (i) the nature of moral truths and how we come to know them, and (ii) moral judgements' connection to attitudes that motivate action. This chapter explains Brentano's metaethical theory and how it purports to deal with such difficulties. §1 considers Brentano's account of moral judgement, moral truth, and moral knowledge. §2 considers Brentano's metaethics from the perspective of the modern metaethical debate.

1 BRENTANO ON MORAL JUDGEMENT, MORAL TRUTH, AND MORAL KNOWLEDGE

1.1 Three Kinds of Intentional Acts

In order to understand Brentano's views about moral judgements and in particular the way in which they presuppose emotions, we first need to consider briefly a pivotal ingredient in Brentano's philosophy, namely the threefold classification of intentional acts (see Chapter 9).[1]

First, there are what Brentano calls "*Vorstellungen*," often translated in English as "ideas" or "presentations," such as my thought of the fiords in New Zealand. Second, there are judgements ("*Urteile*"). Every judgement presupposes a presentation in that the content of the presentation is what the judgement is about. But the judgement is an additional intentional relation that consists either in an act of affirmation ("*Anerkennen*") or rejection ("*Verwerfung*") of what is presented (see Chapter 10). Third, there are emotions or conative attitudes ("*Gemütsbewegungen*"). The most fundamental are love and hate.[2] Like judgements, emotions also presuppose presentations in that they are directed at the contents of presentations (see Chapter 11).

1.2 Valuing and Valuing Correctly

Brentano's ethics is teleological. He thinks of ethics as the practical discipline that studies the "highest end" and the means of attaining it (1973b: 7, 79, 121–2): it is *right* to choose, or strive for, the best option or end of those available, and it is *wrong* not to do so (see Chapter 21). Consequently, evaluative judgements, and in particular judgements about intrinsic goodness, badness, and indifference, are central to moral judgement and moral theorising. So what is it to judge something valuable? In order to understand this, we need to start with *valuing*. To value something positively is to love it, and to value something negatively is to hate it. To value something intrinsically is to love it or hate it for its own sake or as an end. Clearly, however, some things that are valued are not valuable. To see the difference between what is valued and what is valuable we need to consider the Brentanian notion of *correctness* (*Richtigkeit*).

Unlike presentations, judgements and emotions can be correct or incorrect. For a thing to be positively valuable is for it to be such that loving it is *correct*; for a thing to be negatively valuable is for it to be such that hating it is *correct* (1969: 18). If it is correct to love (hate) a thing, it is incorrect to hate (love) that thing. For a thing to be indifferent is for it to be such that neither love nor hate is the correct response to it. For a thing to be better than another is for it to be such that preferring it to the other thing is correct (1969: 26).[3] For example, to say that pleasure is intrinsically good is to say that it is correct to love pleasure as an end; to say that pain is intrinsically bad is to say that it is correct to hate pain as an end; to say that pleasure is intrinsically better than pain is to say that it is correct to prefer as an end pleasure to pain. To say that the number 2 is indifferent is to say that it is correct neither to love nor to hate the number 2.

To value something is not yet to judge that thing valuable, and judging a thing valuable is distinct from valuing it. Valuing belongs in the third category of basic kinds of intentional acts—that of emotions—and emotions are not judgements. Still, Brentano holds that evaluative judgements presuppose emotions in that evaluative judgements are primarily judgements *about* emotions. For example, to judge that pleasure is intrinsically good is to judge that loving pleasure as an end is correct. Brentano holds that emotions are a precondition for moral and evaluative knowledge in that in loving something, for example, pleasure, and experiencing that love as correct, I immediately see that pleasure is the kind of thing that can be loved with a love that is correct, and so I can reject loving pleasure with a love that is not correct.

All of this raises a host of questions. For example, how can my experience of loving pleasure with a love that is correct reveal to me a moral truth (that pleasure is among the highest ends) and thereby provide me with moral knowledge? And most fundamentally, what is it for an emotion to be correct?

1.3 Correct Emotions

Brentano explains correctness in emotions by analogy with correctness in judgements. For a judgement to be correct is for it to concord with a judgement made by someone who judges with self-evidence (*Evidenz*). Self-evident judgements are guaranteed to be correct, and they are based either on "inner perception" or on presentations of objects that are rejected apodictically (1966b: 130; 1969: 19–20). An example of an evident judgement of the former kind is my judgement that I now have a visual experience of blue. It may or may not be true that my visual experience of blue corresponds to something in nonmental reality, but when I have the experience of sensing blue, I can go on immediately to affirm with self-evidence that I am now sensing blue. An example of an evident judgement of the second kind is the judgement that three is equal to two plus one. Here we consider the presentation of a combination of three with two plus one "by means of a negative copula" (1969: 112), and we reject this combination apodictically. That is, we deny apodictically that $3 \neq 2 + 1$. By reflecting on this judgement, Brentano says, we obtain the concept of impossibility (in this case we reject apodictically that three is not equal to two plus one, and by reflecting on this judgement we conclude that it is impossible that three is not equal to two plus one) (1969: 112).

Judgements that are based on self-evidence in either of these two ways are *experienced as correct* (*als richtig charakterisierten*). It is important to see that this is not a matter of an experience of a high degree of conviction (1969: 20). Many judgements are held with great confidence, although they are neither evident nor correct. How, then, can I come to recognise an experience of correctness? Brentano holds that the experience of correctness becomes manifest when I compare a self-evident judgement with a contrary judgement (e.g., affirmation versus rejection of my present visual experience of blue or rejection versus affirmation of $3 \neq 2 + 1$). I then see that the judgements differ in a crucial respect: the original judgement is experienced as being correct, while the contrary judgement is not (1969: 20; Chisholm 1986: 49–50). Once I have grasped the experiential feature of correctness through this kind of comparative manoeuvre, I am able to recognise it in other judgements too.

I shall not here consider whether Brentano is right that there is an experiential feature of correctness in our judgements and that we can become aware of it by comparing different kinds of judgements. Let us note instead that truth, according to Brentano, reduces to correctness: a true judgement is simply a correct judgement. As we have seen, all evident judgements are correct, but not all correct judgements are evident. Judgements that are not evident are blind judgements. Blind judgements can still be correct; they are so if they concord with judgements that would be made by someone whose judgements are based on self-evidence. As with judgements in general, so with moral and evaluative judgements: For example, for the judgement that knowledge is intrinsically good to be true is for the judgement that it is correct to love knowledge for its own sake to be correct.

At this point, one may feel that we are still in the dark about what a correct emotion is. We have been told that for a judgement to be correct is for it to concord with an evident judgement, but there seems to be no such thing as a "self-evident emotion," so the analogy between correct judgement and correct emotion may seem to fail. However, Brentano insists that there is an analogue of self-evidence in the emotional domain (1969: 22), for just as some judgements are experienced as correct, some emotions are experienced as correct. Just as correctness of judgements can become experientially manifest by comparing these judgements to conflicting judgements (i.e., judgements that are not correct), correctness of emotions can become experientially manifest by comparing conflicting emotions. For example, when we love for its own sake an experience of pleasure or a piece of knowledge, we may compare this love with an imagined attitude of hating for its own sake that experience of pleasure or that piece of knowledge. We then see that the love has something that the hatred lacks: the love is experienced as correct and the imagined hatred is not.

Just like correctness of judgements, correctness of emotions is thus an experiential feature with a distinctive phenomenology, such that "we know it when we have it." And just as in the case of judgements, we can come to know that we have it by comparing experiences of correct emotions to experiences of emotions that are not correct. Ultimately, then, it seems that we have to rest content with the conclusion that correctness of judgements and emotions is not susceptible to analysis or constitutive explanation; in order to understand what correctness is, one has to experience it.

1.4 Moral Knowledge

But how do I go from love of a particular experience of pleasure or particular piece of knowledge to love of pleasure or knowledge quite generally, that is, to love of other instances of the same kind? That is, how do I go from valuing (for its own sake) a particular experience of pleasure or a particular piece of knowledge to valuing (for their own sake) other instances of pleasure or knowledge? The answer is that in loving for its own sake an experience of pleasure or a piece of knowledge, I consider and love it *as such*. On the basis of loving for its own sake a particular experience of pleasure or a particular piece of knowledge, I can universalise my love, so that it takes as its object pleasure or knowledge quite generally. If I experience as correct my loving for its own sake a particular experience of pleasure or a particular piece of knowledge, what I experience as correct is loving for its own sake a particular experience of pleasure or piece of knowledge *as such*. On that basis, I can realise immediately that anything relevantly similar, that is, any other relevantly similar experience of pleasure or relevantly similar piece of knowledge, is such that loving it for its own sake is correct.[4] Via this kind of universalisation manoeuvre,

I can come to experience as correct loving for its own sake pleasure or knowledge quite generally (see, e.g., Brentano 1969: 111–13).

This is meant to be analogous to the way in which I can go from the judgement about a thing to a universal judgement about a class of things, for example, from the rejection of a round square to the rejection of all round squares. When I reject round squares, I consider *as such* a square that is round, and this presentation causes me to reject all round squares. I perceive the causal link between the presentation of a round square and my rejection of round squares, the latter of which I experience as correct. This apodictic judgement constitutes my a priori insight that there are no round squares.[5] Similarly, when I judge that every experience of pleasure is good, I start by considering a particular experience of pleasure, which is such that it is not correct to love it as such. This presentation causes me to reject *experiences of pleasure that are not correct to love as such* (i.e., insofar as they are experiences of pleasure). I perceive the causal link between the presentation of *an experience of pleasure that is not correct to love as such* and my rejection of *experiences of pleasure that are not correct to love insofar as they are experiences of pleasure*.[6] This constitutes my insight that the nature of pleasure is such that any experience of pleasure, insofar as it is an experience of pleasure, is correct to love (for its own sake).

Knowledge about what one ought to do depends ultimately on knowledge about what is good,[7] which, as we have seen, relies on insights into what can be correctly loved for its own sake. Since there is a plurality of (kinds of) things that are such that they can be loved with a love that is correct, knowledge about what to do also relies on insights about what (kinds of) things can be correctly preferred to other (kinds of) things. This is because, as noted in §1.2 above, Brentano's normative ethics is teleological, holding that we ought always to bring about the best available outcome. To that extent, Brentano takes the good to be prior to the (morally) right. But it is important to bear in mind that one distinctive feature of his view is that the correct is conceptually prior to the good.

This last feature makes Brentano's view immune to the so-called "wrong kind of reason problem," which has prompted extensive discussions in connection with recent attempts to reduce the evaluative to the normative (see Rabinowicz and Ronnow-Rasmussen 2004). The leading idea behind such attempts is that for a thing to be good is for it to be such that there are reasons to respond to it with a favourable attitude (Scanlon 1998). This idea has considerable intuitive appeal, but a major difficulty is that it is easy to imagine situations in which there are reasons to favour a thing although the thing in question is not good. Consider a powerful and evil demon who threatens to punish us with severe pain unless we favour him for his own sake. Intuitively, there is in such a dire circumstance reason to favour the demon for his own sake, but it is not at all intuitive that the demon is thereby good.

Brentano's view is not vulnerable to this problem since on his view, for a thing to be good is not for it to be such that there is reason to favour it but to be such that loving it is (would be) correct. It may well be that there is conclusive reason to love the evil demon for his own sake, that is, it may well be that we ought to love him for his own sake, because doing so shields us from severe pain. For Brentano, this means that loving the love of the demon for his own sake would be correct, because loving him for his own sake would prevent something that is correct to hate for its own sake (in this case, experiences of severe pain). However, loving the demon for his own sake cannot be correct.[8]

It is a natural complaint that Brentano's account sheds no light, as it merely replaces one presumed primitive (value) with another (correctness). But note first that if Brentano is right that we have an "inner" access to an experiential feature of correctness of emotions, independently of our intuitive judgements about value, his account of value in terms of correct emotions does shed light after all. This is admittedly a very big "if," however. Note, secondly, that regardless of whether Brentano's view of correctness as an experiential feature with a distinctive phenomenology is defensible, his account establishes in a neat way a necessary connection between values and correct emotion.

2 BRENTANO'S METAETHICS AND MODERN METAETHICS

We saw in the beginning of this article that while Brentano's metaethical stance is avowedly realist and objectivist, it has some features that readers familiar with modern metaethical debates would not expect to find in views based on such a stance. In this section, we shall explore further how Brentano's view is best categorised and understood using distinctions and taxonomy of modern metaethics.

2.1 Rationalism or Sentimentalism?

The first part of Brentano's *The Foundation and Construction of Ethics* is a critical survey of what other philosophers before him, in particular British and German rationalists and sentimentalists of the eighteenth and nineteenth centuries, said about how we acquire moral knowledge. The rationalists maintained that moral knowledge is attainable on purely rational grounds. Samuel Clarke and Richard Price, for example, argued that by means of rational reflection alone we can come to know necessary moral truths. Brentano rejected synthetic a priori principles in ethics and elsewhere (1973b: 73), and he found a lot to agree with in Hume's sentimentalist account and in his critique of rationalist views like Clarke's and Price's. Brentano took Hume's own position to be that moral judgements are feelings, but he complained that Hume's arguments did not in fact support that conclusion. What they supported was something weaker, namely that feelings are necessary preconditions for moral judgements (1973b: 50).

According to Brentano, Hume overlooked the phenomenon of *correct* feelings. If I experience the love of an object as correct, I can affirm immediately, on that basis, that the love of the object is correct. In such a case, the judgement is a "*cognition*" (*Erkenntnis*), that is, a correct judgement (1973b: 68). My judgement that my feeling of love or hate is correct might of course be incorrect, in which case it is not a cognition. In sum, Brentano's view incorporates both rationalist and sentimentalist elements. We have seen that feelings are a precondition for moral judgements and that moral judgements are judgements about the correctness of feelings. We saw in §1.4 how my love or hate of a particular object can be universalised, by focusing on the object *as such*, to other particular objects of that kind.

2.2 Cognitivism or Non-Cognitivism?

Brentano's metaethical theory concerns first and foremost the psychology of valuing and of moral judgement. As we have seen, Brentano is clearly a cognitivist about evaluative and moral judgement; such judgements are judgements about the correctness of feelings, and judgements are cognitive acts. There is, however, one aspect of his position that seems congenial to contemporary expressivism. This has to do with expressivist treatments of disagreement. When two people disagree about whether, say, knowledge is good, standard cognitivist accounts explain what is going on in terms of the two people taking the same kind of cognitive attitude—belief—to different propositions—*that knowledge is good* and *that knowledge is not good*, respectively. Expressivists cannot do that. They have to say instead something to the effect that the persons' utterances of "knowledge is good" and "knowledge is not good" express different attitudes to the same object, and that this amounts to disagreement.

This is structurally similar to how Brentano thinks of disagreement. Recall that the judgement that there are pink rats consists in an affirmation of pink rats, while the judgement that there are no pink rats consists in a rejection of pink rats. Similarly, to judge that knowledge is good is to affirm correct love of knowledge, and to judge that knowledge is not good is to reject correct love of knowledge. These cases amount to disagreement because simultaneous affirmation and rejection of the same thing are inconsistent, that is, they cannot both be correct. As expressivist Allan Gibbard puts it, "Fregeans" start out with negation and explain disagreement in terms of believing the negation of what the other person believes. "Non-Fregeans," like Brentano and many contemporary expressivists, start out instead with different kinds of mental attitudes that are inconsistent with one another, in terms of which they explain disagreement (Gibbard 2012: 273–4).[9]

2.3 Realism or Anti-Realism?

What counts as realism is a notoriously disputed issue, but we saw at the outset that Brentano's metaethical stance seems thoroughly realist in that he takes moral truth to be "universally and incontestably valid" and independent of human conventions. We have seen, however, that on Brentano's view, facts about what is valuable, right, wrong, etc., are not independent of our attitudes, for to be valuable, right, wrong, etc., reduce to being something that can be correctly loved or correctly hated. One might worry that this dependence of evaluative and moral facts on our attitudes is in tension with realism. But this worry can be put to rest. For recall that evaluative and moral facts are dependent on, indeed reducible to, *correct* attitudes, and not simply to our actual attitudes or to attitudes we would have under nonnormatively specifiable ideal circumstances.[10] Brentano's account is thus not a version of a standard response-dependence account. Brentano does hold that it is correct to love attitudes that are correct (e.g., love of knowledge and hatred of pain), but that is a substantive evaluative claim and not an analysis or what it is for an attitude to be correct.[11]

It is also noteworthy that Brentano holds that the property of goodness is not part of the content of acts of valuing. For example, to value knowledge positively is simply to love knowledge. And the object of such love is simply knowledge considered as such. One might think that this is in tension with a thoroughgoing realism, but it is not clear why it should be. According to Brentano, for an object to be good (bad) is for it to be such that it can be loved (hated) with a love (hatred) that is correct, and this merely commits him to the view that goodness and badness are not conceptually primitive. It is not clear why that should affect the account's claim to being a thoroughgoing version of realism.

2.4 Naturalism or Non-Naturalism?

As we have seen, it is a distinctive feature of Brentano's account that *correctness* of attitudes is the primitive normative notion, in terms of which goodness, rightness, wrongness, ought, etc., are analysed. Since correctness is a primitive notion, it cannot be analysed in other terms, but that leaves open the question of whether it is a natural or a non-natural property. It is well known that G. E. Moore found much to favour in Brentano's philosophy,[12] and Brentano's views seem akin to the kind of foundationalist intuitionism that is traditionally associated with non-naturalism.

It is difficult to draw a clear-cut distinction between natural and non-natural properties, but the distinction is still very much in use, and it is therefore worth investigating where Brentano's position fits in. According to one influential proposal, which stems from Moore, natural properties are all and only the kinds of properties that form the subject matter of the natural sciences, including psychology (Moore 1903b: 92).[13] On this view, correctness seems to be natural property. For recall that we have said that correctness is an experiential feature of judgements and emotions. As such, it seems to be a kind of property that belongs to the subject matter of psychology. According to another influential view, related to Moore's, non-natural properties are causally inert and epistemically accessible to us only via a priori reflection. But this is not the case with Brentanian correctness. For again, the correctness of a judgement or emotion can be experienced as a feature of judgements and emotions, and such experiences can cause apodictic judgements. Correctness is epistemically accessible to us only in experiences of judgements and emotions and not via mere a priori reflection.

2.5 Internalism or Externalism?

On Brentano's view, there seems to be a necessary connection between valuing something and being motivated, for to value something is to love or hate it, and love and hatred seem clearly to be motivationally efficacious attitudes. But what about the connection between judgements that something is good or bad and motivation? Here Brentano's view is more nuanced than to simply affirm or deny that there is a necessary connection between evaluative judgements and motivation. My judgement that something is good may be based on my love of that (kind of) thing and my experiencing that love as correct. It is only in such cases that I can be said to possess knowledge that the thing in question is good. However, it is also possible to judge that something is good, i.e., such that it can be loved with a love that is correct, on other bases, e.g., testimony. In such cases, my judgement may or may not be correct, but it is not experienced as correct. As we saw in §1.3 above, such a judgement is blind and does not amount to knowledge. We can thus say that Brentano's position is a qualified version of internalism, according to which there is a necessary connection between knowing that something is good and being motivated to pursue it.[14]

NOTES

1. The ontology of intentional objects is a notoriously difficult issue on which Brentano's views changed over time. However, the issue has no immediate bearing on the discussion of Brentano's metaethics pursued in this chapter. Suffice it to say here that Brentano at no point accepted a Fregean view according to which the

content of intentional acts are abstract propositions. Brentano rather thought of the content of intentional acts as things and their properties, and in his reistic period, toward the end of his life, simply as things. For a general discussion of Brentano's ontological views, see Chrudzimski and Smith (2004).
2. The terms 'love' and 'hate' should be interpreted broadly. R. M. Chisholm suggests that 'pro-emotion' and 'anti-emotion' may be less misleading terms (Chisholm 1986: 18). For Brentano's own account of love and hate, see, for example, 1969: 142–60.
3. Brentano conceives of preferences not as choice dispositions but as emotions with a phenomenological nature. He says that to prefer A to B is to love A more than B (or to hate B more than A) (1969: 143), but he also says that 'more' does not signify greater intensity of love or hate (1969: 26). Brentano seems to think of preference as an emotive phenomenon of comparative acts of loving or hating (e.g., loving A more than B), as opposed to simple acts of loving or hating (e.g., loving A) (1969: 143).
4. Here one might of course wonder what exactly is meant by "relevantly similar." Is an experience of sadistic pleasure relevantly similar to an experience of nonsadistic pleasure? What about an undeserved experience of pleasure and a deserved experience of pleasure? What about pieces of trivial knowledge (such as the number of hairs on my head) and pieces of nontrivial knowledge (such as whether there is extraterrestrial life)? Different possibilities are open here, but Brentano's view was that any experience of pleasure (or piece of knowledge) is good *insofar as* it is pleasure (or knowledge). For example, sadistic pleasure (pleasure in the bad) is good, that is, correct to love insofar as it is pleasure; but bad, that is, correct to hate insofar as it is pleasure in the bad. See, for example, Brentano 1973b: 196.
5. As we saw above, Brentano also held that reflection on apodictic judgements is the basis of our modal judgements. See Chisholm (1986: 42–5, 49–51) for a helpful discussion.
6. The italics are meant to forestall scope ambiguities.
7. According to Brentano, "[e]thics must first determine which ends are rightly to be striven for as the highest ones" (1973b: 79), and "[o]nly the end that exceeds all others in value can be the correct ultimate end, i.e., it must be the best, but only in so far as it is attainable" (1973b: 122).
8. See Danielsson and Olson (2007) for discussion.
9. Whether this is a good explanation of disagreement is a matter of debate in contemporary metaethics. Mark Schroeder argues that in explaining disagreement in this way, expressivists help themselves to everything that needs to be explained (Schroeder 2008: ch. 3). Gibbard (2012: appendix 2) responds to Schroeder.
10. According to Brentano, "there is no guarantee that every good thing will arouse in us an emotion that is experienced as being correct" (Brentano 1969: 24).
11. See Danielsson and Olson 2007: 518–20.
12. See Moore's review of *The Origin of Our Knowledge of Right and Wrong* (Moore 1903a).
13. The implicit suggestion is that all other kinds of properties are nonnatural. This is unsatisfactory, since it implies that supernatural properties are also nonnatural, and that does not sit well with Moore's own views.
14. An earlier version of this chapter was presented at a seminar at Stockholm University. I thank the participants, in particular Per Algander, Krister Bykvist, Per Martin-Löf, and Frans Svensson, for very useful discussions. I am also very grateful to the editor of this volume for his helpful suggestions. Work for this chapter was supported by a generous grant from *Riksbankens Jubileumsfond* (Grant no. 1432305).

21

Brentano's Normative Ethics

Lynn Pasquerella

Brentano's theory of value, derived from his philosophical psychology, is a theory of intrinsic value, that is, of what is good or bad in and of itself, not merely as a means to an end. Though Brentano's attention to theoretical ethics took precedence over his practical ethics, the fundamentals of a system of practical or normative ethics are outlined in both *The Origin of Our Knowledge of Right and Wrong* (Brentano 1889/1969) and *The Foundation and Construction of Ethics* (Brentano 1952/1973b). In these works, the one supreme imperative upon which all others depend, referred to by Brentano as the "principle of the summation of good," is that one should further the good in as wide a sphere as possible.

For Brentano, the sphere of the highest practical good includes:

> [T]he whole area that is affected by our rational activities insofar as anything good can be brought about within it. Thus one must consider not only oneself, but also one's family, the city, the state, every living thing upon earth, and one must consider not only the immediate present but also the distant future. All this follows from the principle of the summation of good. To further the good throughout this great whole so far as possible—this is clearly the correct end in life (*der richtige Lebenszweck*), and all our actions should be centered around it.
>
> (Brentano 1969: 32)

When choosing the best among the ends attainable, however, Brentano advises that the likelihood of success must be considered alongside the best end. Thus,

> [W]e must take account of the respective probabilities. If A is three times better than B, but B has ten times more chances of being realized than does A, then the man of practical wisdom will prefer to strive after B. For if such a course were always pursued

under such circumstances and if there were a sufficient number of cases, then, given the law of large numbers, the greater good would be realized on the whole.

(Brentano 1969: 13)

Brentano's principle of the summation of good positions him as a utilitarian. Indeed, much of Brentano's normative ethics is derived from the philosophy of J. S. Mill. Like Mill, Brentano holds that an act is right if, and only if, it produces maximum intrinsic value. Yet, whereas Mill's utilitarianism proffers pleasure or happiness as the one ultimate good, Brentano sides with G. E. Moore in rejecting all forms of hedonistic utilitarianism. Instead, Brentano's pluralistic utilitarianism is much closer to that of Moore, who posits friendship and beauty, together with pleasure, as intrinsic goods. Among the intrinsic goods Brentano countenances are pleasure, happiness, love, knowledge, justice, beauty, and the exercise of virtue. Their opposites—displeasure, unhappiness, hatred, ignorance, ugliness, injustice, and the exercise of vice—are intrinsic evils (for fuller discussion see esp. Brentano 1973b Pt 2; also Kraus 1914).

Beyond recognizing a multiplicity of goods, there is another way Brentano departs from hedonistic utilitarianism—namely in his assertion that not *all* experiences of pleasure are intrinsically good and not *all* experiences of displeasure are intrinsically bad. According to Brentano, there is an inextricable link between the quality of states of pleasure and displeasure and the intrinsic value of their intentional objects, such that the quality of an emotion is a function of the intrinsic value of its intentional object. One pleasure is better than another if the intentional object of one is better than the intentional object of another. Conversely, one displeasure will be better than another if the intentional object of one is worse than the intentional object of the other. Thus, my taking pleasure in another's deserved happiness will be qualitatively better than my taking pleasure in someone's undeserved pain.

Nevertheless, it is important to note that what renders pleasure in the bad a worse emotion than pleasure in the good are not the intentional objects themselves, since my pleasure in someone's happiness or pain does not entail the actual existence of the other's happiness or pain. Rather, pleasure in the bad is itself bad because it is an incorrect emotion (see Chapter 11, 20). Unlike Bentham, who regards all instances of pleasure as good, Brentano maintains,

> Pleasure in the bad, insofar as it is pleasure, is something that is good, but insofar as it is at the same time an incorrect emotion, it is something that is bad. It is not purely bad, but it is predominantly bad. While in doing so we are not just abhorring (*verabscheuen*) the bad; rather we are exercising an act of preference (*Bevorzugung*). We prefer being free of what is bad in this situation to being in possession of what is good. Here we have an act of preference which is seen to be correct and which justifies our avoidance of pleasure in the bad. We say to ourselves: Better that there be no pleasure at all than pleasure in the bad.
>
> (Brentano 1969: 90–1)

Pleasure in the bad is a mixed evil, then, involving an incorrect emotion that contains pleasure as a good part. In contrast, displeasure in the bad is a mixed good, where the emotion is correct, which is good, but contains displeasure, which in itself is bad, as part of the good whole.

In his notes on the lecture from *The Origin of Our Knowledge of Right and Wrong*, Brentano contends that pleasure in the bad and displeasure in the bad count as "two unique cases of preferability," and he regards his failure to consider these earlier to be a lacuna in his ethics (Brentano 1969: 91). His subsequent treatment of these cases lends support to Moore's concept of "organic unities" in which "the value ... of a whole bears no regular proportion to the sum of the value of its parts" and "the value of a whole must not be assumed to be the same as the sum of the value of the parts" (Moore 1903b: 27–8).

Though Brentano never explicitly acknowledges Moore's principle, Chisholm has attempted to demonstrate the consistency between Moore's notion and Brentano's position on pleasure and displeasure in the bad. Chisholm characterizes these instances of preferability by appeal to the notion of "defeasability," arguing that the intrinsic goodness of pleasure is such that in certain instances it is defeated by the wider state of affairs entailing it. Similarly, displeasure is intrinsically bad, and yet at times its badness is defeated by the wider whole of which it is a part. Pleasure in the bad and displeasure in the bad are examples of this phenomenon and are wholes whose value is not proportionate to the value of the sum of their parts (Chisholm 1986: 91–2).

For Brentano, it is the will, which is a product of free and rational deliberation, that has a moral character in the strict sense, with actions being moral in the derivative sense of following from the will. The morality of willing is determined by its efficacy in promoting the supreme practical good (Brentano 1973b: 286). Still, Brentano does not call for a constant consideration of every possible choice that might result in the highest practical good. Instead, he refers to a type of habituation whereby the highest practical good is sought incrementally as part of a broad plan, relying on past experience (Brentano 1973b: 284–5). In this, Brentano anticipates current-day virtue utilitarianism (Driver 2004).

Additionally, Brentano draws a distinction between objective and subjective morality applied to willing and acting alike, allowing that one may strive for the good and fall short. An act of will is *subjectively moral* iff the agent forms the intention to perform an act with the belief that the act will produce the greatest good. The same act of will is *objectively good* iff what is willed would actually lead to the greatest good if performed. In this way, a given act of will may be objectively but not subjectively moral, or alternatively, subjectively but not objectively moral. An act is objectively moral iff it leads to the highest practical good, independently of the agent's motives or intentions. In contrast, behavior is subjectively moral only when it arises from an act of will that is good (Brentano 1973b: 286).

Just as Brentano joins Mill in maintaining that constant contemplation of how to bring about the highest good is not required since it would diminish utility, he sides with Mill in arguing that utilitarianism does not require the performance of what might be considered supererogatory acts. In speaking against a moral obligation to always bring about the highest practical good, both Brentano and Mill separate what is morally right from what is morally obligatory. However, Brentano balks at Mill's suggestion that individuals are obligated merely to do as much as the average person in society:

> We ... agree when it is said that duty consists of what is common in human behavior, but unlike Mill we have in mind not the great mass of people, but the best among them. Duty is what the average among the best men will do; whatever goes beyond this is supererogatory, and hence merely advisable.
>
> (Brentano 1973b: 297)

Brentano's proposal follows from the fact that while he fears that requiring individuals to live up to standards of saintliness will ultimately thwart the highest practical good, he recognizes that Mill's average person might be morally evil, entailing standards that are not nearly high enough.

In elucidating the nature of moral obligations within society, Brentano delineates duties of justice and duties of love, with the former having moral priority over the latter. Whereas duties of love consist of promoting the supreme practical good, duties of justice require restraint with respect to others' autonomous choices. Justice is defined as "the arrangement of matters that allows the individual to promote the supreme practical good, the general best, freely and without interference" (Brentano 1973b: 326). Brentano believes it impossible to inflict injustice on oneself, the dead, someone who consents to what is being done, or upon God, whose domain is unalterable. Nevertheless, Brentano warns that

> It is a grave error to assume that whatever falls within the boundaries of my rights is thereby simply left at the disposal of my egoism. Even within this sphere, I am merely the manager of the realm of power that has been entrusted to me, and ... I ought to employ it in the service of the supreme practical good.
> (Brentano 1973b: 326)

Despite attempts by Brentano and other pluralistic utilitarians to build justice into their normative ethical systems, proposed counterexamples based on principles of justice and fairness have been commonplace in attacking utilitarianism. One of the most notable critiques of classical utilitarianism is mounted by Rawls, who argues that utilitarianism "does not take seriously the distinction between persons" (Rawls 1971: 26). There are a number of famous examples intended to illustrate this point, involving the sacrifice of an innocent person, or otherwise unjust treatment of an individual, for the sake of the good of the whole. For instance, Ross (1930) asks us to imagine a scenario in which an agent has the choice of giving 1000 units of value to a very good man or 1001 units of value to a very bad one. Ross contends that any ethical system that would make it morally obligatory to give value to the bad man is mistaken, and he is convinced that classical utilitarianism implies this consequence. If utilitarianism requires ignoring the facts regarding an individuals' character or past behavior by mandating that we ought to behave in a way that maximizes value, as Ross's example seems to demonstrate, then utilitarianism is counterintuitive.

Similarly, the case of the dilemma posed for a sheriff in a small Southern town (Carritt 1947) suggests that framing and executing an innocent person might in some instances be morally obligatory under utilitarianism. In one version, there have been a series of brutal rapes and murders that have terrorized townspeople in a close-knit community. As the sheriff responsible for their safety, you are concerned that there have been threats of rioting if the perpetrator is not apprehended. By happenstance, you discover the culprit red-handed, but when you confront him, he drops dead from a heart attack. The killer is a prominent member of the community whom no one would readily believe capable of committing such heinous crimes. Since you know that these grievous acts will not continue, facing the likelihood that riots will ensue if you bring forward evidence of the real killer, you decide to plant the evidence next to the body of an indigent, dying drug addict who has always been the primary suspect in the minds of the residents. This man has such a poor quality of life, and the residents would receive such enormous pleasure by removing him from society, that utilitarianism seems to warrant killing the innocent.

In response to contemporary debates regarding the adequacy of utilitarian responses to such objections, there has been a renewed interest in the normative ethical principles set forth by Brentano. For instance, Fred Feldman has argued that Ross's and similar proposed counterexamples fail to refute consequentialism and instead point to defects in the axiologies associated with it, that is, in what they take to have final or intrinsic value. Following Brentano, Feldman defends an axiology sensitive to both justice and injustice, incorporating the idea that the value of pleasure or pain may depend on whether it is justly or unjustly experienced (Feldman 1997: 160).

When this new axiology is applied, a justicized consequentialism ensues, allowing that greater value might arise from the amount of justice in a certain set of circumstances. Feldman defends the perspective raised by Brentano in his 1907 essay "Loving and Hating" (Brentano 1969 Appendix IX) that the value of pleasure and pain may vary depending on whether it is justly or unjustly experienced. The result, Feldman contends, enables consequentialist normative theories to deal more successfully with challenges concerning justice.

Feldman's axiology is based on the premise that justice is done when people receive goods and evils according to what is deserved. He cites Brentano's suggestion that facts about desert affect the value for the world of goods and evils:

> We may distinguish between realizing what is good in general, a good in the whole world-order, and realizing a good in a particular individual. If at the Last Judgment a greater amount of bliss were given to a person who actually deserved it less, then he would have a greater amount of good than he otherwise would have, but the good in the universe, considered as a whole, would be less.
>
> (Brentano 1969: 149)

Drawing upon Brentano's distinction, Feldman's axiology posits the intrinsic value of an episode of pleasure or pain as a function of receipt and desert—the amount of pleasure or pain the recipient receives and the amount of pleasure or pain the recipient deserves in a given episode (Feldman 1997: 163). Pleasure is intrinsically good, but is better if deserved and worse if undeserved. Building upon Chisholm's development of Brentano's theory of value, Feldman insists that positive desert enhances the intrinsic goodness of pleasure. In this way, normative ethics is grounded in the information provided by axiology as the basis for prescriptions of right action.

Feldman further maintains that Brentano offers an approach for dealing with Derek Parfit's "Repugnant Conclusion":

> For any possible population of at least ten billion people, all with a very high quality of life, there must be some much larger imaginable population whose existence, if other things are equal, would be better even though its members have lives that are barely worth living.
>
> (Parfit 1984: 388)

Parfit rejects the idea that the latter world is better than the former. Feldman points to a Brentanian solution, noting that justicism implies that the world is made worse when people do not receive what they deserve, thereby avoiding the repugnant conclusion (Feldman 1997: 197–8).

While some contemporary critics, such as Simon Wigley (2012: 479), have objected to Feldman's efforts by asserting that consequentialist theories cannot legitimately ascribe intrinsic value to complex states of affairs involving deontic constraints such as desert and justice, Feldman contests these claims, noting similar constraints with respect to Mill's axiology based on higher and lower pleasures. Whether or not one accepts justicized consequentialism as necessarily adhering to deontologic considerations, it should be clear that Brentano's normative ethics still has much to offer when grappling with the most fundamental questions of normative ethics.

22

Brentano on Beauty and Aesthetics

Wolfgang Huemer

In his entire *oeuvre*, Brentano defended a scientific conception of philosophy and advocated the adoption of a rigorous, scientific method. Given this background, it might come as a surprise that in his reflections on aesthetics, he firmly rejected the classic definition of aesthetics as the *science of beauty*. This must not be read as an expression of disinterest in—or a dismissal of—aesthetics, though. It is rather an expression of Brentano's view concerning the position of aesthetics in his overall system. He conceived it—on a par with logic and ethics—not as a theoretical science but as a practical discipline that was rooted in psychology: aesthetics, Brentano suggests, is not constituted by a set of intrinsically related propositions; it rather serves the practical purpose of instructing those who want to experience the beautiful with correct taste or to create works of art. The task of aesthetics is, in other words, to formulate a set of rules or instructions that teach us how to correctly experience beauty, not only how to come to prefer the more over the less beautiful but also how to create beauty and how to produce works of art that have the power to bring about aesthetic pleasure in the beholder.

1 BRENTANO'S WRITINGS ON AESTHETICS

Brentano hardly published on aesthetics during his lifetime. Apart from occasional remarks that mainly treat the position of aesthetics in his overall philosophical system, he published only two short texts that discuss specific aesthetic problems, both of which are based on manuscripts for invited lectures that were intended for a broad audience.[1] In 1959, Franziska Mayer-Hillebrand edited a collection of Brentano's writings on aesthetics in a volume with the telling title *Grundzüge der Ästhetik* [*Outline of Aeshtetics*] (Brentano 1959). It contains—next to the two aforementioned texts—Brentano's lecture notes for the course on *Ausgewählte Fragen aus Psychologie und Ästhetik* ["*Selected questions from psychology and aesthetics*"] that he taught at least two times in the mid-1880s at the University of Vienna, as well as short drafts on beauty, on value-presentations, on the classification of the arts, and on music. It seems that Mayer-Hillebrand was mainly interested in making Brentano's texts on aesthetics accessible to a broader audience in compact form, which unfortunately had a strong influence on the editorial criteria that were adopted. Instead of presenting a critical edition, Mayer-Hillebrand took the liberty of cutting, revising, and emending the text. With this, she hoped to make the text less fragmentary and to better convey what she thought were Brentano's intentions when writing the texts. Alas, she did not think it necessary to trace the textual changes or to make them recognizable as such.[2]

A closer look at Brentano's writings on aesthetics unveils that he was not primarily interested in developing a systematic or even comprehensive aesthetic theory but rather in providing the theoretical foundations on which future work in the field could rest. This impression is confirmed by Edmund Husserl's comments on Brentano's lectures on aesthetics, which he attended in 1885–86. Husserl describes the course as most stimulating because, unlike other courses by Brentano with which he was familiar—he mentions the courses on practical philosophy, logic, and metaphysics—they did not create the impression that Brentano aimed to present final truths and theories but rather to show the problems in the flow of investigation (cf. Husserl 1919).[3] This suggests that Brentano did not have an elaborate aesthetic theory to present but was rather interested in reflecting on the relations between psychology and aesthetics (as the title of the lectures suggests) and likely to invite young researchers to take up his foundational work as the basis on which to erect their own aesthetic theories.

2 AESTHETICS AND PSYCHOLOGY

Brentano, as is well known, maintained that there was a close tie between psychology and all other philosophical disciplines. In a series of articles that appeared in the newspaper *Neue freie Presse* shortly before Brentano left Austria in 1895, in which Brentano summarized his philosophical position and achievements, he states that it was on the basis of psychological results that he could reform elementary logic and grant a deeper insight into the principles of moral knowledge. "And similarly," he continues, "one could most easily prove for aesthetics and every other discipline of philosophy that separated from psychology it would have to wither like a branch that was detached from the trunk" (Brentano 1895b: 39; my translation[4]). This strong bias toward psychology did show some influence on the choice of topics that Brentano discussed in aesthetics: he mainly focused on the nature and structure of aesthetic experience, while questions concerning the definition of art, the nature of artworks, the ontological status of aesthetic value, the role of interpretation, and so on are hardly considered.

At the beginning of his lectures on aesthetics, Brentano recalls that psychology is a theoretical science that consists of "a set of truths that are internally related to each other" (Brentano 1959: 3, my translation[5]) and has a clearly defined and homogeneous subject matter. Logic, ethics, and aesthetics, on the other hand, are, according to Brentano, practical disciplines that contain truths that are held together by a goal that is external to their fields of studies. While logic is supposed to teach us to judge and infer correctly and ethics to choose and act correctly, the truths or principles of aesthetics ought to instruct the beholder to correctly experience beauty and the artists to produce works that have the power to arouse pleasant aesthetic experiences. In Brentano's words, aesthetics

> is the practical discipline that teaches us to experience the beautiful and the not-beautiful with correct taste, to prefer what is more beautiful over what is less beautiful, and that provides instructions for creating it [the beautiful] and for making it suggestive and significant for everyone.
>
> (Brentano 1959: 5; my translation[6])

This definition not only underlines the primacy of aesthetic experience, it also states that we can experience with *correct taste*, which might raise the question of the standards of correctness: what is it that determines whether we experience an object with correct taste as beautiful or not? For Brentano, these standards do not depend on some form of correspondence between experience and an independent reality; they are rather determined by aspects related to the experience itself. To better understand how, we need to see where Brentano situates aesthetics in his overall system of psychology.

3 THE PLACE OF AESTHETICS IN PSYCHOLOGY

Brentano, as is well known, makes a basic distinction between three kinds of mental phenomena, that is, between kinds of ways in which we can be directed toward the intentional object: presentations, judgments, and phenomena of love or hate, that is, phenomena in which we take an emotional stance toward an object (see Chapter 9). Moreover, he shares the view that this distinction is mirrored in the subdivision of areas of philosophical research, arguing that the

> triad of the *Beautiful*, the *True*, and the *Good* ... [is] related to three aspects of our mental life; not, however, to knowledge, feeling, and will [as Kant has suggested], but to the triad that *we* have distinguished in the three basic classes of mental phenomena.
>
> (Brentano 1995a: 261)

The first of these three classes is the most basic and constitutes a foundation for the other two, as all mental phenomena are presentations or based on presentations (cf. Brentano, 1995a: 80). Judgments and emotions, on the other hand, consist in taking an affirmative or negative stance toward an object. Moreover, each of these stances can be correct or incorrect: both positive and negative judgments can be true or false; positive and negative emotions can be fitting or not. In the case of presentations, on the other hand, we do not take a positive or a negative stance toward an object, nor can we speak of correctness. All presentations do have, however, an intrinsic value:

> Every presenting, taken by itself, is a good and recognizable as such because an emotion that can be characterized as correct can be directed towards it. There is no doubt that anyone who had to choose between a state of unconsciousness and the having of some presentation whatsoever, would welcome even the poorest

one rather than envying lifeless objects. Every presentation appears of value as it constitutes an enrichment of life.

(Brentano 1959: 144; my translation[7])

Thus, while judgments and emotions consist in correctly or incorrectly taking a positive or a negative stance, the value of a presentation is always positive, but comes in degrees: presentations cannot be said to be correct or incorrect, but some presentations are of higher value than others. For example, presentations of mental phenomena are more valuable than presentations of physical phenomena (Brentano 1973b: 136).

But, one might ask, if all presentations are valuable, how can we distinguish between presentations that are of high aesthetic value from those that have a negative aesthetic value, that is, presentations of objects that are disgusting, repellent, or simply ugly? Can we have (valuable) presentations of objects that have no aesthetic value whatsoever? And, finally, how can we determine whether the respective objects have been experienced with "correct taste"?

In order to address these questions, it is important to note that Brentano distinguishes between the value a presentation has *per se* and the particular aesthetic value it might have. The latter comes into play only if a specific presentation brings about a correct positive emotion; when, in other words, the presentation arouses a pleasure in us. This second mental phenomenon, the emotion or pleasure, is intentionally directed toward the presentation and so allows us to grasp the latter's value. Moreover, the emotion aroused is (like all emotions) correct or incorrect:

> The point is not merely that a presentation is valuable, but that its value is grasped in an actually experienced pleasure that is manifested as being correct.
>
> (Brentano 1959: 32; my translation[8])

Thus, Brentano does not want to reduce aesthetic value or beauty to the mere occurrence of a presentation; not every object toward which we are directed in a presentation is aesthetically valuable or beautiful. It is so only if it becomes the intentional object of a presentation the value of which is so intense that it arouses correct positive emotion:

> But it was not my intention to identify the concept beauty with that of value of the presentation. Not only beautiful presentations please correctly. Beauty is the narrower concept. We tend to call beautiful only those presentations that are of such immense value that they justify a particularly high degree of pleasure. It does not suffice, however, that they merit a high degree of pleasure, in order to be beautiful they must be given to us in such a way that this pleasure is actually aroused.
>
> (Brentano 1959: 152; my translation[9])

An object is ugly, on the other hand, if the presentation in which we are directed toward it arouses a correct negative emotion, a form of displeasure (cf. Brentano 1959: 147f).

This conception of beauty underlines the strong psychologistic tendencies of Brentano's aesthetics that have already emerged in his definition of the discipline. The only phenomena that are relevant for aesthetics are psychological phenomena. Works of art are considered aesthetically valuable or beautiful only insofar as they are suitable to become objects of presentations that are intense enough to arouse pleasure in the beholder. Like secondary qualities, the aesthetic value is not an intrinsic property of the object but rather depends on the way we experience it. We tend to attribute beauty to the objects of experience, but strictly speaking, the experienced objects are neither beautiful nor ugly:

> When we call a girl beautiful, the term is used in a figurative sense. It is similar when we call objects that are outside of us green, red, warm, cold, sweet, bitter. All these expressions refer initially to what appears, and are then also transferred to that which possibly evokes in us this appearance by having an impact on us.
>
> (Brentano 1959: 123; my translation[10])

Although he explains the notion of beauty on the basis of the notion of experience, Brentano does not advocate a subjectivist aesthetics. Since the pleasure that is aroused by a presentation in which we are directed toward an artwork must be a correct emotion, it is impossible that one person correctly experiences the work as beautiful while another person correctly experiences it as ugly. Cases of divergence in aesthetic experience merely show that at least one of the two persons involved does not experience the object correctly;[11] she has not, in other words, developed correct taste. And, as we have seen above, Brentano considers aesthetics as the discipline that should teach us to experience with correct taste.

4 BRENTANO'S EMPIRICAL APPROACH: AESTHETICS "FROM BELOW"

In order to achieve this task, aesthetics will not primarily be involved in the formulation of abstract principles, that is, principles that could be arrived at by a priori reasoning and from which judgments concerning the correct taste are to be deduced. Brentano holds that aesthetics should rather be based on an exact description of the relevant phenomena: concrete aesthetic experiences that we know from inner perception. By trying to systematically have experiences of this kind, one can cultivate and refine one's taste. Moreover, based on their respective experience, aestheticians can come to formulate rules or instructions that guide both the aesthetic experience of beholders and the aesthetic production of artists. In order to characterize this empirical approach to aesthetics, Brentano borrows a slogan from Fechner and suggests that aesthetics was to be done "from below."

In concrete terms, this means that aesthetics should start out with the observation of "perfectly beautiful works (*vollkommen schönen Werke*)" (Brentano 1959: 23). Brentano does not explain how we could identify perfectly beautiful works, nor does he seem to think that this is a question that needs to be discussed. The choice of the examples he mentions, however, testifies to his confidence that the works generally considered to constitute the canon are among them.

Our descriptions of aesthetic experiences are based on inner perception and so have a high degree of evidence. When formulating them, we should aim at distinguishing the aspects of the work that are aesthetically valuable *per se* and which, in combination with the others, increase the overall beauty of the work. Brentano nonetheless insists, however, that our main focus should not be that of discerning potential "atomic elements of beauty," of which different aesthetic experiences could be composed, but should remain focused on the mental phenomena, the concrete aesthetic experiences, as a whole. With this, Brentano distances himself from Fechner's attempt to identify basic elements of beauty, that is, basic facts that are nearly insignificant in themselves but can add up, when combined in the right way with other elements, to the experience of real beauty. Brentano discusses in detail why the idea of there being a "pleasant rectangle" or a particularly pleasant color is untenable: not only does he think it impossible to individuate these elementary, minimal units of beauty, he also considers this strategy of explaining and predicting the experience of beauty by analyzing how it is composed by basic elements misguided. He writes:

> whether or not and, if so, to what degree something will be beautiful cannot be deduced on the basis of elementary pleasures that are grounded in experience and that are combined in a specific way, it must rather be tested by direct experience.
> (Brentano 1959: 23; my translation[12])

Brentano's conception of an aesthetics "from below" is thus based on the same method as his empirical method in psychology: it is a descriptive approach that rests on inner perception (see Chapter 3). Whenever we experience a truly beautiful work of art, we not only have an aesthetic experience but also are aware of this experience through inner perception. In this way, every

> truly beautiful work is a kind of scientific discovery.... But new beauty can hardly be unveiled by exact deduction, but always by inner experience, once the respective presentation was actually formed.
> (Brentano 1959: 24; my translation[13])

The concrete experiences allow us to formulate rules and instructions that aim not only to improve the way we experience beauty, but are also guidelines for artists to create works of high aesthetic value. With this, Brentano places himself in the tradition of rule-aesthetics that puts more emphasis on the acquisition of certain artistic techniques than on the stroke of genius (see Chapter 23 on genius). He admits that there might be artists who are so talented that they can create beauty without knowing or consciously applying these rules, but even they can profit from the instructions—especially because they can help them to acquire dispositions that can improve their artistic production.

In his reflections on the relevant rules, Brentano merely explains what role they should play in aesthetics. He does not make any attempt, however, to formulate a concrete rule or instruction, nor does he try to describe a technique to be adopted in artistic production; the few examples he mentions have more the status of commonplaces than that of detailed descriptions of artistic techniques. This underlines once more how Brentano understood his contributions to aesthetics: his main interest was to lay the theoretical foundations for the discipline and to unveil its relation to psychology—likely in the hope that students or future aestheticians would take up the lead and elaborate a comprehensive aesthetic theory on this foundation.

5 THE IMPACT OF BRENTANO'S AESTHETICS

Brentano's hope has not come true, however. The fact that most of his writings on aesthetics were published more than 40 years after his death (with questionable editorial criteria) made it very difficult for a larger philosophical community to get access to Brentano's contributions. Moreover, none of his direct students took up his lead to develop a more articulate aesthetic theory. And even though we can note that some of his reflections are echoed in the aesthetics of the so-called Graz school and in the phenomenological movement, we find hardly any direct acknowledgments of Brentano's influence in these traditions—and in the few places where he is mentioned, the reference is typically to his achievements in psychology, not to his reflections on aesthetics.[14]

The situation could improve to some degree if Brentano's writings on aesthetics were made available to a broader audience in a critical edition, which would allow us not only to gain a better understanding of the development of empirical approaches to aesthetics in the 19th century but also, first and foremost, to get a better insight into the systematicity of Brentano's approach to philosophy and psychology, an approach that aimed at a comprehensive picture that brings together all philosophical disciplines in a systematic unity but at the same time knows to avoid the pitfalls of the system-philosophies of German idealism.

NOTES

1. "Das Genie" ["The Genius"] was presented at the chamber of the *Association of Engineers and Architects in Vienna*; "Das Schlechte als Gegenstand dichterischer Darstellung" ["Evil as object of poetic representation"] was presented at the *Society of the Friends of Literature in Vienna*. Both texts have been published in 1892 by Dunker and Humblot in Leipzig (Brentano 1892a and 1982b).
2. The editor even felt free to make changes to texts that had been published in Brentano's lifetime, in particular to "Das Genie," where the text was changed in order to remove all references to the fact that it was originally presented as a lecture—none of these changes is documented, though (cf. Brentano 1959: 236, n.1). In her introduction to the volume, Mayer-Hillebrand acknowledges that the editorial work "was connected to certain difficulties and responsible decisions (mit gewissen Schwierigkeiten und verantwortungsvollen Entscheidungen verbunden)" (Brentano 1959: xiv). She does not explain, however, why these decisions were not documented explicitly in the editor's notes. In the few notes that do not contain interpretations of Brentano's views, the editor only indicates where text had been cut—with approximate information on the quantity, that is, how many pages of the manuscript were omitted.
3. Husserl's fascination is also documented in the fact that he refers in warm terms to this lecture course in several places of his work (cf. Bernet *et al.* 1993: 142).
4. "Auf Grund neuer psychologischer Ergebnisse schmeichle ich mir, die elementare Logik reformiert und in die Prinzipien ethischer Erkenntnis einen tieferen Einblick gewährt zu haben. Und ähnlich ließe sich für die Aesthetik und jede andere Disziplin der Philosophie aufs leichteste nachweisen, daß sie, losgetrennt von der Psychologie, wie ein vom Stamme losgetrennter Zweig verdorren müßte."
5. "... eine Gruppe von Wahrheiten, die innerlich verwandt sind."
6. "... sie ist jene praktische Disziplin, welche uns lehrt, mit richtigem Geschmack Schönes und Unschönes zu empfinden, das Schönere vor dem minder Schönen zu bevorzugen, und uns Anweisungen gibt, um es hervorzubringen und für die Gesamtheit eindrucksvoll und wirksam zu machen."
7. "Jedes Vorstellen ist aber, an und für sich betrachtet, ein Gut und als solches erkennbar, weil sich eine als richtig charakterisierte Gemütstätigkeit darauf richten kann. Ohne Frage würde jedermann, wenn er zwischen dem Zustande der Bewußtlosigkeit und dem Besitz irgendwelcher Vorstellungen zu wählen hätte, auch die ärmlichste begrüßen und die leblosen Dinge nicht beneiden. Jede Vorstellung erscheint als eine Bereicherung des Lebens von Wert."

8. "Es kommt nicht bloß darauf an, daß eine Vorstellung wertvoll ist, sondern daß ihr Wert in einer als richtig charakterisierten, wirklich erlebten Freude erfasst wird."
9. "Aber es war durchaus nicht meine Absicht, die Begriffe Schönheit und Wert der Vorstellung zu identifizieren. Nicht nur schöne Vorstellungen gefallen mit Recht. Schönheit ist der engere Begriff. Schön pflegen wir nur eine Vorstellung von so erheblichem Werte zu nennen, daß sie ein besonders hohes Maß von Wohlgefallen rechtfertigen. Es genügt aber nicht, daß sie ein hohes Wohlgefallen verdienen, sie müssen, um schön zu sien, uns in solcher Weise dargeboten werden, daß dieses Wohlgefallen auch tatsächlich erweckt wird."
10. "Wenn wir ein Mädchen schön nennen, so wird der Name in übertragenem Sinne gebraucht. Es ist ähnlich, wie wenn wir Körper, die außer uns sind, grün, rot, warm, kalt, süß, bitter nennen. Alle diese Ausdrücke bezeichnen zunächst das, was erscheint, werden dann auch auf solches übertragen, was unter Umständen auf uns einwirkend diese Erscheinung hervorruft."
11. It would be inappropriate here to talk of disagreements in aesthetic judgments as, for Brentano, we can speak of judgments of taste only in a metaphorical way: "Taste is not a judgment, but a feeling" ["Der Geschmack ist kein Urteil, sondern ein Gefühl"] (Brentano, 1959: 31).
12. "Daß und wie sehr etwas schön sein werde, läßt sich nicht auf Grund von elementaren Wohlgefälligkeiten deduzieren, die durch Erfahrung begründet sind und die in eine gewisse Verbindung gesetzt werden, sondern muß durch direkte Erfahrung erprobt werden."
13. "Jedes wahrhaft schöne Werk ist eine Art wissenschaftlicher Entdeckung.… Aber kaum wird eine neue Schönheit durch exakte Deduktion aufgedeckt, sondern immer in direkter Erfahrung, nachdem die betreffende Vorstellung sich wirklich gebildet hat."
14. For a discussion of Brentano's place in the history of psychologial approaches to aesthetics cf. Allesch (1987); for the relations between Brentano's and Fechner's aesthetics, Allesch (1989); for a discussion of Brentano's aesthetics in its relation to that of other Austrian philosophers, cf. Huemer (2009); for Brentano's relation Husserl, cf. Huemer (2004).

23

Brentano on Genius and Fantasy

Ion Tănăsescu

Franz Brentano addressed the genius issue in a presentation held in Vienna for the Association of Engineers and Architects and published in 1892 as the pamphlet *Das Genie* (*The Genius*). The text was later reprinted in *Grundzüge der Ästhetik* (Brentano 1959). The genius issue is also addressed occasionally in *Psychology from an Empirical Standpoint* and is involved in Brentano's view on aesthetics as practical discipline in his 1885–6 course "*Ausgewählte Fragen aus Psychologie und Ästhetik*" (Selected Questions from Psychology and Aesthetics), also published (in an abbreviated and amended version) in *Grundzüge der Ästhetik*. I shall present Brentano's views on genius from his 1892 paper, using the other mentioned texts to complete some less clear aspects of *The Genius*. I will also address the issue of fantasy presentation in the 1885–6 course and its relevance to Brentano's analysis on genius.

The main task of *The Genius* is to clarify the nature of the activity of the creative genius, whether scientist or artist. In his analysis, Brentano starts from the usual characterization of the word: a genius is an unusual, uncommon talent. From his standpoint, the work of a creative genius raises two issues: (1) whether there is a gradual difference or an essential one between the activity of a genius and the activity of a common creator; and (2) whether this activity is or is not an unconscious activity, a result of "inspiration" (perhaps divine), leaving no room for rational activity (Brentano 1959: 88–9).[1] Brentano's view of genius is a combination of the following two theses: first, that the difference between genius and common creativity is gradual rather than essential, a difference of degree rather than a difference of kind; secondly, that the activity of genius is conscious rather than unconscious.

In *The Genius*, this second issue is addressed partly in terms of a traditional opposition between common artist and genius with respect to their conforming to rules. Common artists are working by the rules, are inspired by their predecessors, and do not hesitate to resort to means of rational reflection in order to overcome the difficulties faced in the process of artistic labor. In contrast, artists of genius create unconsciously, with no respect to rules or to rational thinking. Aeschylus, Euripides, Plato, Aristotle, Ovid, Jean Paul, Goethe, and Kant are only some of the artists and philosophers who maintained this view on the creative genius's work (1959: 93–6). At first glance, Brentano's view in the 1885-6 course seems to differ: Brentano claims that rules do play a role in the activity of the creative genius (1959: 10-12). However, Brentano's course does not deal with the issue of the nature of the creative activity but with the issue of rules that *maintain and enhance* the creative "inner tendencies," including the "ingenious ability" of artists. Establishing these rules is important to Brentano because it is meant to justify his view of aesthetics as a practical discipline. According to Brentano, one of the main tasks of aesthetics is to provide guidance on how beauty is produced, and how it is acting upon the sensitivity of the contemplator. In this respect, Brentano believes that rules are important for the genius, not in the sense that the genius creates by following rules, however, but in the sense that his innate aesthetic sensitivity is shaped by studying the works of his forerunners and by internalizing the rules according to which they were created (1959: 6–14).

The thesis of the unconscious work of the creative genius clearly contradicts one of the basic theses of Brentano's psychology, namely the idea that *there are no unconscious mental phenomena*. In his empirical psychology, Brentano examines no less than four arguments for the existence of unconscious mental phenomena, only to reject them in favor of the thesis that mental life consists exclusively of conscious phenomena (Brentano 1995a: 105–26). For Brentano, a conscious act is directed primarily toward its object, and secondarily *toward itself*: I see a red spot on the horizon, and at the same time *I am aware of seeing it* (see Chapter 5). Thus, the thesis of the unconscious work of the creative genius actually implies that there are unconscious mental acts, acts characterized by directedness toward a primary object but lacking directedness toward themselves.

From this perspective, Brentano's first thesis about creative genius can be formulated as follows: between the activity of a genius and that of a common artist there is no essential difference but only a gradual one. For an essential difference between the two would open the possibility of a narrow group of people, the geniuses, who, unlike ordinary people, would appear as supermen privileged by the fact that, during the process of creation, they have access to a mental life consisting of unconscious mental acts (Brentano 1959: 97, 119). Such a view would compromise the conscious character of all mental life, something Brentano could not accept. In his discussion of the idea that some mental phenomena can be defined as a result of the action of some other unconscious mental phenomena, Brentano refers only occasionally to geniuses (Brentano 1995a: 106). However, what he says here anticipates clearly enough the view presented in *The Genius*. He claims that the genius issue should not be invoked by the defenders of unconscious mental phenomena, because geniuses are rare, and their analysis cannot be considered scientifically well grounded. In any case, the work of brilliant scientists such as Newton, for example, cannot be conceived as a result of unconscious thinking. Moreover, even the genius artists confess that the distinction between them and common artists is not essential but gradual. From this perspective, one could say that *The Genius* complements the analysis in the *Psychology*, because in *The Genius* Brentano *demonstrates* that even the creative activity of geniuses does not involve unconscious mental phenomena. In the *Psychology*, the thesis was only stated but not argued for.

Throughout *The Genius,* Brentano argues for the gradualness thesis starting from cases of genius scientists such as Newton. Unlike common scientists, they have the ability for assiduous and abiding reflection on the topics they are concerned with and for combining ideas at a higher level than the usual. These features support the gradualness thesis. Against this background, Brentano refers to the fact that in the *Critique of Judgment* Kant explicitly argues for the same view (without specifying, however, that Kant does not use the word "genius" with reference to scientists but limits its use to the realm of art). With respect to *artists* of genius, however, Kant maintained a thesis opposite to Brentano's: that the distinction between their work and that of common artists is not gradual but essential (Kant 2000: 187–8, Brentano 1959: 90–3; see also Brentano 1987a: 303).

Brentano defines the goal of his research in opposition to the Kantian view:

> In any case, in the realm of art it is worth trying to conceive genius work so that it could be comprehended on the ground of general psychological laws, and that the difference between it and the work of a common artist would be only a gradual, and not an essential one. Only this can be considered an actual explanation in the spirit of natural science (*Naturerklärung*), a reduction of the particular case to the general laws.
>
> (Brentano 1959: 97–8; my translation)

Unlike Dilthey, who claimed that the methodology used by the human sciences to explain their object has to be different from that of the natural sciences (Dilthey 1991: 56–72, 78–9), Brentano believes that both sets of sciences should be guided by the same methodological rule: the reduction of the individual case, in this case the creation of the genius artist, to the general laws, psychological ones in this case, to which it subordinates.

To argue for his gradualness thesis in the realm of art, Brentano assumes Aristotle's theory of art as mimesis and distinguishes between two categories of artwork, depending on the mental faculties involved in their creation: works of art created directly from nature, based on memory and perception; and works of art produced by the artist's creative fantasy (Brentano 1959: 98–9).

With respect to the first category, artists of genius are characterized by a particular sensitivity to what is aesthetically valuable. This sensitivity allows them to easily accomplish what Brentano calls aesthetical abstraction: to grasp in a glance the typical, the aesthetically significant in what is observed. The result of this apprehension is then safely and spontaneously transposed into an artwork that reveals the implicit beauty, unnoticed by a common regard, from what is observed. Although Brentano acknowledges that the spontaneity and the ease with which geniuses produce their works could be seen as a result of inspiration or of unconscious thinking, he insists that the differences between the activities of the two types of artist can be conceived as gradual. His main argument is: the particular *sensitivity* of the creative genius for what is aesthetically significant is not essentially different from that of the common artist but merely a superior development of the common artistic sensitivity (1959: 102–8).

Unlike artworks created by nature, where the artist extracts and gives expression to the aesthetic beauty inherent in nature, artworks produced by creative fantasy are a fundamentally different thing. Here, we are no longer dealing with a pre-existing natural beauty to which the artist gives aesthetic expression, but beauty is produced by the creative imagination of the artist. Things are happening here "as if a superior hand would leave a gift to fall in the artist's lap." Kant, emphasizes Brentano, had in mind exactly this when claiming that the word "genius" refers to "the genius of the artist who attends him, allowing him, by its divine power ... to achieve perfection" (1959: 107; my translation; see also Kant 2000: 187). Brentano explains this form of artistic creation as well by resorting to the particular sensitivity of genius for what is aesthetically valuable. This sensitivity is manifested through the genius's creative fantasy, which constantly develops and produces artistic images in a fully accomplished aesthetic way (Brentano 1959: 107–14). The explanation in the spirit of natural science mentioned above—which aimed at reducing the individual, unique case of brilliant creation to general psychological laws—takes into account the fact that creative fantasy produces its artistic images following the laws of a fundamental class of psychological phenomena, namely, that of presentations (1959: 111–15). In other words, for Brentano, the activity of the creative fantasy constitutes only a particular case of application of general psychological laws.

Brentano's solution is a democratic one: both geniuses and common talents have the same kinds of skill, though not at the same development level, and their creative activity is subject to the same general psychological laws. There is no unconscious creation or thought special to genius. The distinction between the two categories of artists is thus overstated by assuming an essential difference where, in fact, there is only a gradual difference (Brentano 1959: 119).

In *The Genius*, Brentano provides a general characterization of the creative fantasy presentation that can be reduced to the intuitive, aesthetically accomplished character of its content. Since the fantasy presentation is addressed extensively in the lectures of 1885–6, it has been considered that this analysis was intended to clarify more precisely the fantasy presentation of the creative genius. This is one of the reasons why Mayer-Hillebrand put these two texts together in the first section of *Grundzüge der Ästhetik*. Experts have not questioned this assumption. At the same time, when not avoiding the issue, they deplored the lack of clarity of the expression "fantasy presentation" in those lectures, where Brentano speaks not of intuitive presentations of fantasy but of improper unintuitive presentations of it, conceived as *concepts with intuitive core* (Brentano 1959: vii, 83; Haller 1994, Allesch 1989). Preliminarily, it is worth noticing that the text of the lectures was not intended for publication, as *The Genius* was, and that Brentano has never held the course again. For this reason, his analysis does not have the character of a fully developed solution, but that of a well-articulated hypothesis designed from the outset to explain certain subclasses of psychological phenomena. Accordingly, both the editor and the exegetics have started from a false premise—that the role of Brentano's 1885–6 analysis was to explain the presentation of creative fantasy, whereas, as Brentano explicitly claims, its role was to clarify the nature of fantasy presentation as an ordinary psychological phenomenon in relation to sensory presentation (Brentano 1959: 43–5).

Brentano's fundamental idea is that both the common and the philosophical conceptions (Aristotle, Aquinas, Descartes) have misconstrued the nature of this presentation, for they conceived it based on the model of sensory presentation, that is, as a presentation in the proper sense, an intuitive presentation. In reality, he argues, most cases of fantasy presentations are not intuitive but improper unintuitive presentations, or *concepts with intuitive core* (i.e., concepts obtained from intuitions). On the one hand, by their abstract character, they resemble surrogate presentations, for example the presentations "God" or "unlimited," whose object cannot be directly viewed (1959: 166–7). On the other hand, Brentano consistently emphasizes their intuitive character, their similarity to sensory presentations, requiring them to satisfy two conditions: that their improperly presented object could be intuitively presented; and that they could be obtained based on an intuitive presentation of the object—the improper fantasy presentation "red square" can be both illustrated by and obtained from the sensory intuition of a red square.

The fact that the goal of Brentano's analysis is not aesthetic but *psychological* is clearly shown by the phenomena he attempts to explain. He is not concerned with artistic creation but with the presentation of others' mental phenomena, of physical phenomena, and of our own mental phenomena as past or future phenomena. When we refer to such phenomena, we cannot present them intuitively and directly, as happens with our own mental phenomena experienced in inner consciousness. Instead, we present them through concepts gained from the direct experience of phenomena similar to those presented. In order to present a certain mental phenomenon, for example someone's toothache, I do not need to experience now that phenomenon, but only to have once lived such phenomena and to have acquired their concept based on those experiences. In this respect, Brentano argues:

> It is impossible to present foreign individuality in a proper sense. That is possible only via ... our own mental phenomena. We speak of fantasy presentation when talking to someone, when looking at someone else's gestures or contemplating artworks ... The intuitive core of our mental phenomena, similar to foreign mental phenomena, is then subject to a certain conceptual abstraction and determination.
> (Brentano 1959: 83; my translation)

This passage emphasizes the role of improper fantasy presentation in normal mental life and in the reception of artwork, but not in artistic creation. In fact, Brentano refers only once to the aesthetic importance of this issue, when arguing that a presentation satisfies mostly the conditions of fantasy presentation as it becomes so close to intuitive presentation as to cause "certain aesthetic experiences" similar to those caused by intuitive presentations. The idea is not further developed in the course, but is based on other texts we can assume that these experiences consist of associated images and pleasant emotional states caused by concepts with intuitive core (1959: 160, 219).[2]

With respect to Brentano's analysis on fantasy presentation in his published works, the analysis of the 1885–6 lectures is an exception, for Brentano never analyzed fantasy presentation as a concept with intuitive core but usually approached it as intuitive (Brentano 1995a: 80, 1995b: 107). At the same time, the 1885–6 lectures were attended by Husserl and constituted the direct starting point of Husserl's analysis in "Phantasy and Image Consciousness," the third part of his lectures "Principal Parts of the Phenomenology and Theory of Knowledge" (WS 1904/5). Unlike contemporary exegesis, Husserl knew exactly what presentations with intuitive core were for Brentano. He did not pursue, however, the path of Brentano's analysis, but approached fantasy presentation at an intuitive level (Husserl 2005: 1–115).

It must be said that Brentano's thesis of the gradual difference between genius and common artist does not constitute an original standpoint in the history of the issue. However, his argument for the view is original, namely through his empirical psychology. In this way, his statements on the nature of the work of brilliant artists become relevant to the program of his empirical psychology, since they appear as a development of the arguments in the *Psychology* against the existence of unconscious mental phenomena. In any case, the genius issue constitutes an episodic topic of his thought addressed by him only in the 1892 paper, one that Brentano did not resume afterwards. Unlike his research devoted to psychology or foundation of ethics, this theme was not inherited nor developed by any of his students.[3]

NOTES

1. References in this chapter will be to the 1988 edition from Meiner.
2. Although Brentano does not use the last phrase in a paper on art classification published posthumously, however, the fact that he considers there poetry as "the most spiritual" of arts (for it operates with words as *signs evoking concepts*) indicates a possible aesthetic utilisation of concepts with intuitive core. Given the fragmented and disparate character of his analysis, this path is a mere suggestion (Brentano 1959: 211, 217–9; on these issues see extensively Tănăsescu 2011).
3. This work was supported by a grant of the Romanian National Authority for Scientific Research, CNCS-UEFISCDI, project number PN-II-ID-PCE-2011-3-0661. I thank Oana Vasilescu for his translation of my paper.

24

Brentano's Philosophy of Religion

Richard Schaefer

Though only a handful of essays devoted to religion appeared in his lifetime, Franz Brentano spent his life thinking about religion, the nature of God, and the immortality of the soul. At the very beginning of his academic career in 1866, Brentano defended 25 habilitation theses in which he tackled the issue of the right relationship between philosophy and theology (Brentano 1866). He also gave a lecture on Schelling that, among other things, stressed how idealism was insufficient as a means to grasp the doctrine of the trinity. In a review of Auguste Comte in 1869, he suggested that the famed positivist offered keen insight into the need for an empirical and rigorously scientific approach to knowledge, and that this insight was relevant to the renewal of Catholic theology in spite of Comte's rejection of religion (Brentano 1869). In 1873, Brentano defended Christianity's record of scientific achievement against atheist attacks (Brentano 1873). On two occasions, Brentano developed a critical stance vis-à-vis Aristotle's ideas about God and creationism (Brentano 1882, 1911b). He also discussed religion constantly in his voluminous correspondence. Perhaps the most important letters include his now published correspondence with Hermann Schell, which takes up the vexed question of the potential for reform in the Catholic Church (Hasenfuss 1978).

However, Brentano's major statements in the philosophy of religion all appeared after his death. In *Die Lehre Jesu in ihre bleibende Bedeutung*, Brentano defended Jesus as an unrivalled exemplar of how to live a moral life in the eyes of God (Brentano 1922). In *Vom Dasein Gottes*, Brentano evaluated the various arguments for and against God's existence and advanced an argument for God based on probability (Brentano 1929a). And finally, in *Religion und Philosophie*, a collection of various unpublished essays and fragments composed over the course of his lifetime, Brentano addressed a range of issues including God, the soul, primitive religions, modernism, theodicy, and, as always, the relationship between religion and philosophy (Brentano 1954).

Though it is certainly true that Brentano was a systematic thinker, the unsystematic character of his writings complicates any clear picture of the overall trajectory of his thoughts on religion (see Chapter 2). Thomas Binder has written an extensive account of the complex fate of Brentano's *Nachlass* that need not be repeated here. Nevertheless, it bears stressing that the preference for organizing Brentano's work according to categories such as logic, religion, epistemology, and so on makes it difficult to assess the more complex evolution of Brentano's ideas (Binder 2013: 383). Moreover, Alfred Kastil's decision to "complete" Brentano's thoughts where unfinished in his editing of *Vom Dasein Gottes* obligates us to be especially mindful when reading that text. The same caution should be extended to Brentano's *Religion und Philosophie*, given the fact that it was initially edited by Kastil before being completed by Franziska Mayer-Hillebrand. These problems notwithstanding, Brentano's writing on religion shows him to have been a determined theist, who used natural theology to mount a campaign against skepticism, defend a cautious optimism, and integrate arguments for God's existence with some of the latest findings in the empirical sciences. Though we may never have a definitive account of his philosophy of religion, Susan Gabriel is right to point out that "questions in natural theology often lie behind and sometimes even motivate Brentano's inquiries in other areas of philosophy" (Gabriel 2013: 248). Anyone working on Brentano therefore would do well to become familiar with the major outlines of his religious thought.

1 THE RELATIONSHIP BETWEEN PHILOSOPHY AND RELIGION

For Brentano, "religion" is not something that can be strictly defined, but is a term that serves to identify a type of thought and activity. Religion is not static but has undergone significant mutation over the course of history, and Brentano holds that monotheism represents religion in its fullest development. Though all religions share an ability to satisfy certain practical human desires for consolation, and so on, monotheistic religions are marked by their ability to stimulate deeper theoretical questions. Though religion falls short of the purely theoretical interest that he considered the hallmark of scientific philosophy, it gives people "belief in the existence of an infinitely perfect and superior being, enlightenment about the order of things, and with it, solace and hope for the mind, and increased power for the will" (Brentano 1954: 28). Of the monotheistic religions, Brentano held that Christianity's ethics, adaptability, and vision of a personal God comes closest to the theoretical interest of scientific philosophy.[1] Of course, making Christianity the paradigm case of religion was prevalent among scholars throughout the west in the nineteenth and early twentieth centuries (Smith 1991, Bell 2006). Defining religion according to distinctly Christian presuppositions of "belief" versus "practice" was part of an invidious distinction between real (developed) religion and its primitive counterparts, whose roots lay in European imperialism but also in the intra-Christian conflict between Protestants and Catholics over the relative importance of faith and works. What concerns Brentano, however, is less a desire to dismiss what is primitive and more his respect for the distinct way that Christianity has of satisfying theoretical urges that are, if not exactly, then well-nigh philosophical. Indeed, Brentano called religion a powerful surrogate for philosophical knowledge, by which he did not mean that religion distracts from true knowledge but rather that it was an imperfect form of knowledge. Religion raises the right questions but is too mired in dogma and revelation to satisfy the rigorous demands of philosophy (Brentano 1954).

According to Brentano, revelation consists in God's activity in awakening cognition in a person. Brentano pulls no punches, however, when he states that what historical religions generally mean by revelation consists to a very great extent in trusting what someone else says about God revealing himself. Even in those instances when a person claims to witness a miracle directly, and thus interprets this as God revealing something to that person directly, Brentano counters that there is generally no way to verify that the so-called miracle is in fact from God. Brentano also points out that religions themselves generally apply a strict standard when it comes to revelation, one that holds that no revelation may be counted as such if it contradicts earlier revelation. And yet, this criterion presumes certain ideas about reason and consistency that cannot themselves be credited to prior revelations.

But Brentano reserves his sharpest criticism for *dogmas* deriving from revelation, arguing that they exact too heavy a price on the believer. Dogma requires the believer to behave as though he or she is certain, even when the dogma in question entails manifest uncertainty. Uncertainty, in turn, is then offset by measures designed to reinforce belief. These measures include promises, threats, and practices that habituate believers into accepting dogma. They also include supplemental ideas regarding the infusion of divine grace whose purpose is to strengthen the believer precisely in view of the burden of being asked to accept what is so difficult. This process becomes particularly odious when the believer is not merely unsure, but has grounds for thinking that the dogma is incorrect. In such instances, the believer is frequently expected to be obedient in spite of his or her reasoned objections. This is all the more complicated for those who sincerely want to believe, and even go so far as to forgo their reasoned objections in the name of an abiding desire to fulfill the dictates of religion.

(As Brentano himself knew only too well, this situation can be painful in the extreme. Brentano was an ardent Catholic early in his life, studied theology as well as philosophy, and became a priest in 1864. However, he left the priesthood in 1873 after finding he could no longer support certain key doctrines, and left the Church altogether in 1880. The break with Catholicism strained his relationship with family and former friends, but at no point did it degenerate into thoughtless hostility toward the Church. This is all the more remarkable given the fact that he suffered significant professional disadvantages because of having been ordained.[2] For Brentano, the resolution of inner religious conflict was not to be sought in attacks on religious institutions. Instead, he advised that "those who value healthy reason will be able to find peace and be a friend to truth by giving witness to his consciousness" [Brentano 1954: 52]. In the end, demanding that one continue to believe under these circumstances is "too unreasonable and unworthy to consider it something God would ask of us" [*ibid*].)

2 THE EXISTENCE OF GOD

Brentano's pointed critique of revealed religion sets the stage for his strong commitment to natural theology: to showing one can have knowledge of God that is based on careful consideration of consciousness and empirical reality. His point of departure consists in being attentive to the necessity of all mental and physical things.[3] Brentano argues that all things that are, are necessary, though some are "directly necessary" while others are "indirectly necessary" (Brentano 1987b: 315). Accidental things, by definition, would have equally accidental beginnings and ends, and would be just as likely to appear as to disappear at any moment. This contradicts experience and what it means to "exist," since things do not simply appear and disappear in this way. By the same token, all things that exist, if they did so accidentally, would be as likely to occupy any part of space as any other. Since, however, there is much more space that is unoccupied than occupied, and since the possibility of all space being occupied is absurd, Brentano concludes that all things that exist do so necessarily. At the same time, however, those things that exist in time and space do so indirectly. Precisely because bodies must have a location and can in principle occupy any location in space, where they actually are is not directly necessary but due to something else. The same is true of what Brentano calls our "psychological life": in our mental life, we are aware of how certain premises lead to conclusions and how certain motives lead to choices. Like perception, which depends on physical causes, mental life depends on immaterial causes. But like physical phenomena, these cannot be infinite. Thus for Brentano, "since an actually infinite multiplicity of things is as impossible in the immaterial as in the material realm, it is apparent that also in this case direct necessity must be denied" (Brentano 1987b: 313). There must therefore be "something outside of our direct experience which, in opposition to the things of experience, is directly necessary," something "vastly different from all that we experience … because it can produce something out of nothing" (ibid.). That directly necessary being is God.

Brentano's natural theology is grounded in his particular commitment to empirical psychology, or what Liliana Albertazzi has described as "immanent realism." This refers to his "attempt to conciliate the presence of an often irreducible transcendent foundation of perception with its immanent and equally irreducible categorization by the intentional acts" (Albertazzi 2006: 128). Brentano's ideas about God derive from paying careful attention to the perception of mental and physical phenomena and what these tell us about the insufficiency of a purely materialist explanation of consciousness and, by extension, the universe. To explain the particular character of the universe, Brentano points to the existence of a directly necessary being that is the cause of all things. Such a being must be wholly transcendent. It must also be creative, since it is capable of producing something out of nothing. And it must be changing. Contrary to Aristotle, Brentano holds that a changing world could not be caused by something changeless. A wholly transcendent, directly necessary being, must be itself subject to change, since "if it knows that something does not exist but will exist, then it knows later that it is and still later that it was" (Brentano 1987b: 317). Above all, according to Brentano, the directly necessary being must be an intelligence, for: 1) the indirect necessity of an order to things in physical space tells us that a directly necessary and intelligent being created it; 2) such a being could not act blindly, lest it also be subject to random appearance and disappearance in space ordering, and thus be physical (which contradicts its transcendence); 3) the ability to understand creation as an order enables us to see that it is a being in harmony with its creation; and 4) it is impossible to deny (contra Hume) that the universe is itself evidence of an intelligent creator. Though one might object that a complex natural order is often produced blindly out of a previous one (e.g., a lion from a lion), Brentano counters that this explanation does not resolve the question of a first cause. Brentano also rejects Darwinism and the idea that the universe is governed by chance, arguing that "Darwinian explanation is applicable neither to the growth of new organs and their development up until they are first useful, nor to the perfecting of organs which are already developed" (Brentano 1987b: 320).

Brentano thus makes an *a posteriori* argument for the existence of God, and rejects all a priori arguments for the existence of God, including all versions of the ontological argument. These fail because, in seeking to argue that God exists based on the inherent necessity of existence in the very concept *God*, they overestimate the power of human thought. For Brentano, only God is capable of formulating a concept adequate to his reality. In contrast to this, and any other kind of deductive reasoning, Brentano stresses that his arguments are physical proofs, resting on the empirical evidence of psychology and of the created world. He insists that order is eminently observable in nature and points to facts in the natural world to bolster his claim that there is a creative intelligence at work in the universe. Citing James Maxwell's observations, for example, Brentano comments on the fact that all atoms appear "cast from the same mold," and that this fact seems essential for their ability to combine in so many ways (Brentano 1987b: 325). Brentano claims, furthermore, that his notion of a directly necessary being with creative intelligence does not depend on finite probability, that is to say, on a finite number of possible outcomes that, in principle, could be observed and verified. Precisely because the being in question must decide over an infinite range of possible outcomes, and the issue at hand "is not a momentary instance, but an eternal directly necessary truth," its direct necessity warrants attributing to it infinite probability (Brentano 1987b: 322). Brentano cites the fact that this being actually prefers those things that exist over the infinite set of possible things that do not as physical evidence for its existence. Of course, it also raises the important question of why such a being chooses this world, with all of its evident flaws, pain, and suffering. Brentano's answer—his theodicy—reflects much of what he says all along, namely: that it must be better that those things which do exist, exist rather than not exist, and one must be hopeful that, in the aggregate, a world that unfolds in time tends toward becoming better and contains more good than bad.

3 BRENTANO'S RELEVANCE TO CONTEMPORARY RELIGIOUS STUDIES

The significance of Brentano's religious thought extends beyond philosophy, and his ideas intersect with a number of recent developments in the broader field of religious studies. His unremitting focus on the nature of God as the proper object of serious philosophy reinforces David Bentley Hart's important *The Experience of God: Being, Consciousness, Bliss*, which protests against the impulse to oversimplify ideas about God (Hart 2013). Brentano's stress on psychology also complements Ann Taves's *Religious Experience Reconsidered* and its insistence on the need to move away from a fixed conception of religious experience (Taves 2009). Though Brentano rejects Darwinian conclusions about a random universe, his commitment to ideas about God-as-changing might possibly be taken up in conjunction with Robert Bellah's important attempt to view religion from an evolutionary perspective in *Religion in Human Evolution* (Bellah 2011). Likewise, his view of a God-as-changing might be interrogated from the perspective of kenotic theology, which stresses God's self-emptying in creation, an idea that has important implications for questions of evil and theodicy. One might also see his stress on the unfulfilled potential of Jesus's ministry in *Die Lehre Jesu* as consonant with some of the ideas animating the emergent church movement.

But as tantalizing as these possible connections are, one desideratum for transposing Brentano's philosophy into other areas must be a better grasp of his commitment to the unremittingly historical flow of ideas. Brentano was always reflecting on his philosophy in conjunction with broader changes in culture and history. He was convinced that his work, and in particular his restoration of a scientific philosophy, was an event of historical significance, a harbinger of better things to come. Brentano approached thought as a process, and while he was extremely critical of certain trends in philosophy, one of the things his four phases theory (see Brentano 1895b/1998) makes clear is that he saw these trends as inherently linked with basic human impulses (e.g., the desire to apply philosophy and the impulse toward skepticism).[4] This commitment to understanding philosophy as historical likewise saturated his understanding of religion, and he was equally convinced that religion manifested clear lines of development. In his letters to Hermann Schell, for example, especially those written in the 1890s, Brentano declared that Christianity was being supplanted by modern ideas in the same way that Judaism had been supplanted by Christianity. At the same time, Brentano explicitly contrasts the "old Christianity" with "his new Christianity" and cites two prayers he wrote reflecting this new faith (Hasenfuss 1978: 63). A serious engagement with Brentano's philosophy of religion will therefore resist the tendency to simply mine his work for specific bits of wisdom, and ask how his various statements on philosophy, religion, and culture mutually inform each other.

NOTES

1. Brentano privileges Christianity over Judaism, whose ancient form he considers to be still tainted with polytheism, and over Islam, which he dismisses as a deviation from Christianity.
2. The story is well known. When Brentano decided to leave the priesthood, he also left his post at the University in Würzburg, since his position involved training future priests, and he felt he could no longer do this in good conscience. He left Würzburg for the university in Vienna, where he assumed the position of professor *ordinarius* in 1874. However, when he married in 1877, he inadvertently ran afoul of a law that forbade former priests from marrying. In order to marry, Brentano gave up his professorship and became a citizen of Saxony, having been given reassurances from Austrian officials that he would be able to resume his professorship in the near future. This turned out to be a false promise, however, and Brentano lived out the rest of his career at Vienna as a *Privatdozent*, though not without protesting vigorously the justice of his case.
3. Brentano's most comprehensive summary of his philosophy of religion appears in "The Train of Thought in the Proof of God's Existence" (Brentano 1929a/1987b). For a good analysis of Brentano's thought in the piece, see Krantz Gabriel 2004.
4. According to Brentano, the history of philosophy followed a four phase pattern driven by broadly psychological impulses: in phase one, philosophy is pursued according to purely theoretical interests; in phase two, efforts are made to apply philosophy according to practical interests; in phase three, philosophy turns skeptical; and in phase four, it turns mystical.

II

The Brentano School

25

The Rise of the Brentano School

Arnaud Dewalque

Franz Brentano's works are not just full of deep and innovative insights into mind, world, and values. His views also turned out to be highly influential upon several generations of students, who made them the basis of their own philosophical investigations, giving rise to what is known as the *Brentano School* (Albertazzi et al. 1996; Fisette and Fréchette 2007). In this chapter, I give a bird's eye view of the Brentano School from a rather historical perspective. My leading hypothesis is that one crucial factor explaining the rise of the school is Brentano's unique strategy, within the academic context of the time, to promote the revival of philosophy as a rigorous science. After a brief introduction, I reconstruct the three main phases in the school's development, namely Brentano's teaching in Würzburg (1866–73), his teaching in Vienna (1874–95), and Anton Marty's teaching in Prague (1880–1913).

1 INTRODUCTION

On a merely factual understanding, the "Brentano School" encompasses all the philosophers who, at a certain stage of their academic path, were Brentano's students or students' students. There is evidence that the notion of "school" was used by Brentano and his students in a self-referential fashion at least from 1873 onward. In his correspondence with Carl Stumpf, Brentano occasionally refers to what he calls "our overall philosophical orientation" or "our school" (Brentano 1989: 44, 128). It is not rare for his students themselves to talk about the "Brentano School," be it to express their debt to Brentano's teaching or to distance themselves from what they take to be sheer Brentanian orthodoxy.[1]

The question as to whether the phrase "Brentano School" may be understood in a stronger sense, to name a group of authors whose "philosophical orientation" was roughly the same, is disputable and is better left unanswered at the outset. My own contention is that most of the members of the school *do* share some key assumptions about what philosophy is and how it should be carried out (see Chapter 26). The rise of the school, however, can hardly be traced back to a common doctrinal content that would be endorsed without exception by all its representatives. There are many reasons for that.

First of all, Brentano's views mostly spread through his courses, his correspondence, and his personal discussions with his students. This makes his influence difficult to pin down by drawing solely on his publications, all the more so because the picture of Brentano that emerges from the rather occasional works he had published during his life doesn't exactly fit with the picture that emerges from the unpublished materials (Eisenmeier 1918: 473; Kraus 1919a: 1–3; Utitz 1954: 74). Since we still don't have, to date, a critically accurate edition of Brentano's works, including his course notes and letters, the access to the primary sources is not without difficulties.[2]

Next, the views endorsed by Brentano in his main book, the *Psychology from an Empirical Standpoint*, have been subject to more or less substantial revisions or supplementations during the subsequent years. To be sure, Brentano never renounced his theory of inner consciousness (see Chapter 5) or his classification of mental phenomena (see Chapter 9), for which he even provided new arguments in the second edition of his *Psychology* (Brentano 1911a). However, he did come to develop a number of new theories. One of the most notable changes is his so-called "reist" turn, according to which only *realia* or particulars may be the direct objects of a presentation (see Chapter 13). But a more comprehensive list of Brentano's mature views should include at least his theory of double judgment, his theory of modes of presentation (*direct* vs. *oblique* presentations), his theory of individuation, and his theory of continua—to name but a few (see, e.g., Kraus 1919a: 22 *sq.*).

Furthermore, Brentano's students developed some of his views in various, more or less diverging directions, thereby creating a number of highly diversified ramifications within the school. Importantly, some of these ramifications became schools on their own: This is the case of the school of object theory founded by Alexius Meinong in Graz (see Albertazzi *et al.* 2001), the phenomenological movement initiated by Edmund Husserl in Göttingen (see Spiegelberg 1994), or the school of polish philosophy initiated by Kazimierz Twardowski in Lviv (see Coniglione *at al.* 1993).[3] This situation created an ambiguity as to what should be considered as the external borders of the Brentano School. To remove the ambiguity, it has been customary to distinguish between the "broad" school, which includes the above-mentioned ramifications *plus* Carl Stumpf, and the "narrow" school, which centers around Brentano himself and Anton Marty (Kraus 1919a: 17). I will briefly address the Prague "orthodox" branch of the school in §3. For now, the most promising way to reconstruct the rise of the school is to start with Brentano's teaching activities in Würzburg.

2 BRENTANO IN WÜRZBURG 1866–1873

The story of the school begins somehow with Brentano's fourth habilitation thesis, which reads: "the true method of philosophy is none other than that of the natural sciences" (Brentano 1968: 136). We know that the 18-year-old Carl Stumpf met Brentano at the public defense of the latter's habilitation theses at Würzburg on July 14, 1866, and decided to attend his courses the next semester. He was joined by Anton Marty, who came to

Würzburg after having read Brentano's doctoral dissertation (Brentano 1862). Both Stumpf and Marty felt most attracted by the conception of philosophy that underpinned the fourth thesis (Brentano 1968: 30; Kraus 1919a: 19; Utitz 1954: 73). They gave converging statements to the effect that Brentano's position was suggestive of "a new, incomparably more deep and serious way of conceiving philosophy" (Stumpf 1919: 88). As Marty put it in his personal diary: "A new world opened up to me" (Kraus 1916: 4).

To understand what was "new" in Brentano's conception of philosophy, it might be helpful to recall that one fundamental challenge, at the time Brentano began his teaching activities, was to overcome the so-called "identity crisis of philosophy" (Schnädelbach 1984: 5; Beiser 2014: 188–92). The crisis began soon after Hegel's death in 1831 and is usually regarded as the result of a clash between two opposite trends: on the one hand, the speculative approach to the world which was illustrated by the representatives of German idealism; on the other, the appeal to observation and experimentation made by the natural sciences. The clash, of course, was to the disadvantage of the idealist systems, which came to be regarded as mere speculations beyond any empirical justification and, therefore, devoid of any scientific value (see Freuler 1997). In the 1860s, several strategies began to rise in order to restore the lost confidence in philosophy and rehabilitate the latter as a scientific discipline. There is strong evidence that Brentano's fourth habilitation thesis may precisely be seen as containing the outlines of a rehabilitation strategy of his own.[4]

If philosophy has to be scientific, Brentano thinks, it has to take the path the natural sciences have taken in their own area. This means, first, that philosophy has to be based on observation or, at least, on experience. As Brentano puts it later on in his inaugural lecture in Vienna: "In the philosophical things, too, there can be no other teacher than experience" (Brentano 1968: 85).[5] This also means that philosophy, like the specialized sciences, has to tackle each philosophical issue one by one, rather than trying to grasp the overall structure of reality by means of unwarranted "intuition," as in the speculative systems. In sum, the philosopher, like the natural scientist, should (i) proceed to his investigations from an empirical standpoint and (ii) endorse the "divide and rule" method. In his habilitation book, dedicated to Aristotle's theory of the *noûs poietikos*, Brentano added another important claim that is obviously part of the conception of philosophy he worked with. He maintained that (iii) logic—along with all the other departments of philosophy—has to be "rooted" in "the soil of psychology," which is bound to provide the philosophical sciences with the "food" they need to grow up (Brentano 1867: 1).[6] Claims (i)–(iii) arguably display the core of the rehabilitation strategy launched by Brentano in order to overcome the "identity crisis of philosophy."

Let us now turn to Brentano's teaching activities at Würzburg. Stumpf reports that, between 1866 and 1873, Brentano mostly taught history of philosophy and metaphysics, along with a course on Comte's positivism and another on deductive and inductive logic (Stumpf 1919: 97–107; 131–7). Stumpf and Marty both attended Brentano's courses from 1867 up to 1870. Neither was able to attend Brentano's first course dedicated to psychology, which took place during the summer semester of 1871. Still, we know Brentano provided them with up-to-date information and, sometimes, made his course notes available to them. In any case, both Stumpf and Marty were well-informed about the content of Brentano's courses and adopted his "philosophical orientation" in their own writings.

On Brentano's advice, Carl Stumpf wrote his doctoral dissertation under the supervision of Hermann Lotze in Göttingen, where he graduated in 1868 before going back to Würzburg. He taught in Prague, Halle, Munich, and Berlin, where he founded a psychological laboratory. In his book *On the Psychological Origin of the Presentation of Space* (Stumpf 1873), he argues against Kant's claim that space is an "*a priori* form of intuition," maintaining instead that the status of space is that of a "partial presentation" (*Teilvorstellung*), that is, a presentation that is necessarily experienced as part of a broader presentation. A similar line of thought was adopted in his important article "Psychology and Theory of Knowledge," where he maintains that psychological analysis is central to philosophical and epistemological investigations (Stumpf 1892). That said, Stumpf is best known for having introduced the notion of "state of affairs" (*Sachverhalte*) in his logic courses in Halle (see Stumpf 1924: 36) and, above all, for being the father of the *Psychology of the Sound*. The two-volume book he published under this title (Stumpf 1883, 1890) offers a comprehensive analysis of our judgments related to acoustic sensations and contains numerous references to Brentano's *Psychology from an Empirical Standpoint*. However, Stumpf disagreed with Brentano on several points—the most important disagreement being probably about Stumpf's interpretation of pain and pleasure as "affective sensations" (see Stumpf 2015b; also Chapter 28).

Anton Marty, in turn, is best known for his works in the philosophy of language. After his dissertation on *The Origin of Language* under Lotze's supervision (Marty 1875), he made his habilitation in Vienna on *The Historical Development of the Sense of Color* (Marty 1879) and eventually obtained a position at the University of Prague (1880). He then published, between 1884 and 1895, two important series of articles in which he mainly addresses the relation between grammar, logic, and psychology. His major book, the *Investigations for the Foundation of a General Grammar and Philosophy of Language*, is dedicated to Brentano for his 70th birthday and contains extensive discussions of views held by Brentano and other Brentanians. Marty distinguishes between autosemantical and synsemantical expressions. One of his main claims is that the classes of autosemantical expressions—names, sentences, and "expressions which arouse interest"—are in line with Brentano's three classes of mental phenomena (Marty 1908: 224–79; see Chapter 27). Even though Marty counted among Brentano's most faithful followers, he disagreed, for example, with Brentano's reist turn.

Other significant works by former students of Brentano at Würzburg include Georg von Hertling's book on Aristotle (Von Hertling 1871), Hermann Schell's doctoral dissertation on the unity of mental life (Schell 1873), Jakob Mohr's *On the Foundations of Empirical Psychology* (Mohr 1882), and Johannes Wolff's *Consciousness and its Object* (Wolff 1889). Despite the fact that Brentano was not in a position to supervise dissertations before his appointment as extraordinarius in May 1872, his influence can be detected in all these works. For reasons tied to his withdrawal from priesthood, he nevertheless renounced the status of extraordinarius in 1873 and designed the project to be appointed at the University of Vienna, where a full-professor position had been vacant since April 1872. Whereas his Würzburg colleagues were rather hostile toward his philosophical orientation (see Stumpf 1919: 120), he nevertheless succeeded in having Stumpf as his successor in Würzburg and was appointed ordinarius at the University of Vienna on January 22, 1874.

3 BRENTANO IN VIENNA 1874–1895

When he arrived in Vienna, Brentano had already written the *Psychology from an Empirical Standpoint*, published the same year. He arrived "at a time one was clearly aware of the emptiness of doctrinal systems filled with gas like balloons, but where the seeds of genuine philosophy were almost completely missing" (Brentano 1895a: 10). Facing this situation, Brentano considered that his own mission was to initiate the rise of scientific philosophy in Austria (*ibid.*; see also Husserl 1919: 161).

In his inaugural lecture on "The Reasons of the Discouragement in the Field of Philosophy" (April 22, 1874), he offered his own diagnosis of the identity crisis of philosophy. Drawing on Auguste Comte's idea of a "natural order" among the sciences, he maintains that the only reason philosophy had not yet reached the stage of scientific maturity is that it requires *psychological* investigations, which in turn are dependent upon *physiology*. Since physiology and psychology are emerging as full-blown scientific disciplines, Brentano writes in 1874, all the conditions are now created to enable the rise of scientific philosophy. This diagnosis gave Brentano the occasion to reiterate his confidence that philosophy can and must be scientific, on the condition that it follows the method of the natural sciences. Here is the description he gives of the attitude adopted by the natural scientist:

> [The researcher in the natural sciences] never starts from the principle that he has to penetrate the genuine essence of things. He never demands that the inner How and Why of a causal connection would be grounded. He observes the natural phenomena and their succession, seeks to establish similarities between the various cases and wants thereby to discover general and unchanging relations between the phenomena, that is, laws of their connection.
>
> (Brentano 1968: 89)[7]

Again, thus, one crucial idea behind Brentano's position at the beginning of his teaching activity in Vienna is that philosophical issues are best tackled by adopting the empirical and inductive method of the natural sciences.[8] In his correspondence, Brentano reports how the audience, which was rather hostile at first sight, eventually met his inaugural lecture with great enthusiasm.[9]

During his first years in Vienna, Brentano taught history of Greek philosophy, psychology, logic, practical philosophy, and metaphysics.[10] The "first wave" of students (1874–1880) included Thomas Masaryk, Alexius Meinong, Alois Höfler, and Christian Ehrenfels—to name just the most prominent figures.

Thomas Masaryk, who later became the first president of Czechoslovakia, attended Brentano's courses from 1874 to 1876. He did his doctoral dissertation (*The Essence of the Soul in Plato. A Critical Study from the Empirical Standpoint*) in 1876 under Brentano's supervision (Capek and Masaryk 1995: 7, 80), and obtained a position as ordinarius at the Czech University of Prague in 1882. His main contribution to the scientific production of the Brentano School certainly is his *Essay of Concrete Logic*, in which he argues against Comte's classification of sciences (Masaryk 1885). Whereas the title of Masaryk's dissertation clearly is reminiscent of the empirical orientation of Brentano's philosophy, Masaryk distanced himself from the Brentanian views (see Haller 1992: 13).

Alexius Meinong attended Brentano's courses from 1875 to 1878. In 1878, he presented his habilitation on Hume (Meinong 1877) and obtained a position as lecturer at the University of Vienna. During the subsequent period, he published a number of papers on psychological, epistemological, and axiological issues. In his major book, *On Assumptions* (Meinong 1910), first published in 1902, he challenges Brentano's classification of mental phenomena, claiming that assumptions form an intermediary group of phenomena that is neither reducible to the class of presentations nor to that of judgments (see Chapter 29). He also argued against Brentano's view that self-evidence (*Evidenz*) doesn't admit of degrees, by maintaining that one can recollect something, for instance, in a way which is more or less evident (see Meinong 1915). Both the assumption theory and the theory of evident presumptions were rejected by Brentano (1969: 55; 1995a: 284–5) and Marty (1906; 1908: 242–71). In 1882, Meinong was appointed extraordinarius at the University of Graz, where he founded the first psychological laboratory of Austria in 1894 and laid down the foundations of the so-called object theory. His students in Graz included Rudolf Ameseder, Vittorio Benussi, Ernst Mally, Eduard Martinak, and Stefan Witasek.

During their studies at the University of Vienna, Alois Höfler and Christian Ehrenfels attended both Brentano's and Meinong's courses. While they acknowledged their debt to Brentano, the philosophical positions they adopted in their writings were closer to Meinong's, under the supervision of whom they both graduated in Graz in 1885.[11] In 1887, Ehrenfels presented his habilitation *On Feeling and Volition* at the University of Vienna, where he was appointed lecturer the next year. He later moved to Prague. One central goal of his habilitation was to argue, against Brentano's classification, that feelings and volitions are distinct phenomena that cannot be put in one and the same class (Ehrenfels 1887; see Chapter 30). Alois Höfler also habilitated at the University of Vienna. He obtained a position as professor of pedagogy at the University of Prague (1903–07) and then at the University of Vienna (1907–22).[12] Among other things, he authored a huge handbook of *Logic* (1890, dedicated to his "master and friend Alexius Meinong") and another one of *Psychology* (1894), which are full of Brentanian and Meinongian views. Höfler's *Logic* is arguably the source of the distinction between content and object of presentation (see Höfler 1922: 33)—a distinction that will be the basis of Kazimierz Twardowski's habilitation in 1894 (see Chapter 32).

In 1880, Brentano married Ida Lieben and consequently renounced his position as ordinarius (see Brentano 1895b). This was the beginning of a new period (1880–1895), during which Brentano was not allowed to supervise dissertations and sent his students to Stumpf or Marty. At the same time, several changes occurred in Brentano's philosophical views. First of all, he introduced the distinction between descriptive and genetic psychology, which form the two branches of scientific, empirical psychology. While genetic psychology seeks to explain mental phenomena, descriptive psychology just aims at describing them by identifying their distinctive features (see Brentano 1995b; see Chapter 3). Furthermore, in his courses on practical philosophy, Brentano came to transpose the distinction between blind and evident judgments onto the emotional domain, thus distinguishing evidently correct emotions from blind emotions (Stumpf 1919: 137). He presented his theory of the correctness of emotions and preference in 1889 in his famous lecture on *The Origin of our Knowledge of Right and Wrong* (Brentano 1969; see Chapter 20).

These views were not without resonance in the "second wave" of Brentano's students, among whom the leading figures were Franz Hillebrand, Edmund Husserl, and Kazimierz Twardowski. (Other students of Brentano at that time included Alfred Berger, Benno Kerry, Josef Kreibig, Hans Schmidkunz, and Norbert Schwaiger.)

Franz Hillebrand attended Brentano's courses in the early 1880s and graduated in Prague under Marty's supervision in 1887. In 1891, back in Vienna, he presented his habilitation on *The New Theories of Categorical Reasonings*, a book that elaborates Brentano's "idiogenetic" theory of judgment and tries to show its implications for the reform of traditional logic (Hillebrand 1891). In the second edition of his *Psychology*, Brentano mentions Hillebrand's book as a reference on that score (Brentano 1995a: 230, 232). In 1896, Hillebrand was designated extraordinarius at Innsbruck, were he founded a psychological laboratory (see Göller 1989). Under the influence of Ernst Mach and Ewald Hering, who had been his teachers alongside Marty in Prague, he conducted several investigations in the field of the psychology of the senses (e.g., Hillebrand 1918; 1929). In 1905, he was joined by another Marty student, Emil Arleth, who also obtained a position at the same university—an event that is usually seen as a "consolidation" of the Brentanian orientation at Innsbruck.

Edmund Husserl was Brentano's student from 1884 to 1886 and presented his habilitation *On the Concept of Number* in Halle under Stumpf's supervision. His project of a *Raumbuch* bears the marks of both Brentano and Stumpf (see Husserl 1983). His major book, *Logical Investigations*, is dedicated to Stumpf and contains, among other things, a critique of Brentano's distinction between inner and outer perception (Husserl 1901: 335–48; see Bergmann 1908; Katkov 1937a). While Husserl, in the first edition, still conceived his own phenomenology as a "descriptive psychology" in Brentano's sense, he later advocated a strong distinction between the two, maintaining that his "pure" phenomenology had nothing to do with the empirical recording of individual facts (see Chapter 31). Brentano didn't really read Husserl's books and restricted himself to answer the charge of psychologism that had been raised in the *Logical Investigations* (see Brentano 1995a: 306–7).

Kazimierz Twardowski arrived in Vienna in 1885. He attended Brentano's courses and those of Robert Zimmermann, through whom he became acquainted with Bolzano's *Theory of Science*. His dissertation, *Idea and Perception* (Twardowski 1892), was devoted to Descartes. His major work is his habilitation, *On the Content and Object of Presentations. A Psychological Investigation*, which he presented in Vienna in 1894 (Twardowski 1894/1977) before being appointed at the University of Lemberg (today "Lviv"). Twardowski's habilitation was a major source for Husserl's theory of intentionality and Meinong's theory of objects (see Meinong 1904b).

4 MARTY AND THE PRAGUE CIRCLE

Despite promises from the ministry of education, Brentano never regained his full professorship (see Brentano 1895b). In 1895, he eventually resolved to leave Vienna and move to Italy. Before leaving Austria, he published his book on the *Four Phases of Philosophy*, in which he offered a still broader diagnosis for the "identity crisis" of philosophy. On his view, Kant and German idealists are the representatives of the extreme phase of decadent philosophy. By contrast, "ascending" philosophical investigations are to be conducted according to "a purely theoretical" interest and a method "fitting the nature of things" (*naturgemäße*) (Brentano 1895a: 8). This idea, again, is reminiscent of the fourth habilitation thesis. Actually, it is probably not unfair to see the publication of the *Four Phases* as an attempt to secure the proposed rehabilitation strategy and strengthen the view that philosophers may escape both skepticism and speculation on the condition that they follow in the natural scientists' footsteps.

One remarkable change that occurred after Brentano's departure from Vienna was that Prague, where Marty was teaching from 1880 onward, became somehow the "center of the school" (Ehrenfels 1922: 95; Kastil 1951: 20; see Chapter 33). Not only did Marty, in his correspondence with Brentano, generate critical discussions on a number of issues in the field of descriptive psychology, but he also played a major role in the dissemination of Brentanian thought among the second generation of students (the so-called *Enkelschülern*). We know that he gave in particular a series of courses on genetic and descriptive psychology in which he drew on Brentano's classification of mental phenomena (see Marty 2011).

Marty's students in Prague include Oskar Kraus, Alfred Kastil, Emil Arleth, Emil Utitz, Josef Eisenmeier, Hugo Bergman, and Otto Funke.[13] They used to meet at the Café Louvre and became known as the *Louvre Circle*. Brentano himself sometimes refers to the existence of the Prague "philosophical club" made up of Marty's students (Bergman and Brentano 1946: 109).

Among the members of the Prague circle, Kraus probably deserves a particular place. He first became acquainted with Marty during the winter semester of 1890–91, when he was 19 years old. He describes his encounter with him as a "metamorphosis": Marty, Kraus writes, "freed me from my earlier materialist and pessimistic positions" (Kraus 1929: 5). Kraus is best known for his work in philosophy of law and philosophy of values (see, e.g., Kraus 1937). He was Marty's successor in Prague and edited Marty's complete works alongside Eisenmeier and Kastil. In 1931, he also founded, with Masaryk's financial support, the *Prague Brentano Society*, the main aim of which was to preserve Brentano's manuscripts and to promote Brentanian studies.[14]

Kraus and Kastil regarded it as their own task to preserve Brentano's views from the "distortions" introduced by his students (Utitz 1954: 79). For that reason, they have sometimes been charged with disseminating a Brentanian "propaganda" through their own writings (*ibid.*: 74). This attitude was at the origin of a divide within the school, between the "secessionists" of the Graz school and the supporters of Brentanian "orthodoxy." The main point at issue was the content–object distinction systematized by Twardowski, Meinong, and Husserl, along with the autonomy of the so-called intentional object (see Kastil 1909). On Brentano's mature view, indeed, the proponents of the object theory tend to reify universals and go back to a kind of "Platonism," which had been eschewed by psychological analysis (see Brentano 1995a: 367–8; Utitz 1954: 87, 89).[15]

Kraus taught in turn several students who became active members of the Brentano School. Among them, probably the most important is Georg Katkov. Katkov graduated in 1929 with a thesis on the analysis of consciousness, in which he maintained, against Husserl and Meinong, that the notions of "relation," "intentional object," and "state of affairs" are not required to account for the acts of consciousness and, consequently, should be eliminated from the psychological description thereof (Katkov 1930). Katkov worked at the Brentano Archives until the Nazi occupation of Prague in 1939, when he and Kraus fled to London with Brentano's manuscripts.

CONCLUSION

The Brentano School had a significant place in the philosophical landscape at the beginning of the 20th century. As a matter of fact, most of the philosophical chairs in Austrian universities at that time were occupied by Brentano's students or students' students (Höfler 1917b: 325; Kraft 1952: 1).[16] Another general observation that may be made on the basis of the foregoing sketch is that the literary production of the members of the school covers virtually all the fields of philosophy, from the psychology of the senses (see, e.g., Stumpf 1883, 1890; Eisenmeier 1918; Hillebrand 1918; 1929) to ethics and value theory (Ehrenfels 1887; Meinong 1894; Kraus 1937), logic and theory of science (Hillebrand 1891; Masaryk 1885), philosophy of language (Marty 1908; Martinak 1898; 1901), theory of knowledge (Bergmann 1908; Stumpf 1939–40), aesthetics (Utitz 1908; 1914–20), and history of philosophy (Arleth 1896).

I have suggested that the post-idealism "identity crisis" context illuminates the attractiveness of Brentano's philosophical program, as expressed for the first time in his fourth habilitation thesis. Stumpf's inaugural lecture at the University of Berlin on the "Renaissance of Philosophy" offers further support for this reading. Stumpf indeed suggests that all the tentative rehabilitations of philosophy that took place at the end of the 19th century may be divided into two trends, namely that of the "*a priori* philosophy," which is illustrated by the proponents of the Back-to-Kant movement, and that of the "experience-based philosophy," which obviously corresponds to Brentano's (Stumpf 1907b: 169). Interestingly, Stumpf establishes a sharp contrast between the two, presenting them as two rival strategies.

Again, the key to understanding what makes the two strategies so different lies in the way philosophy is connected to the natural sciences and, more pointedly, to psychology. Proponents of the Back-to-Kant movement initiated by Otto Liebmann (Liebmann 1865) tried to rehabilitate philosophy as a rigorous science by conceiving it, at least in its most fundamental part, as a *higher-order* science, a science of the sciences. This overall strategy results in disconnecting philosophy from the other, first-order sciences and from the empirical method that had proved so successful for them. In contrast, the proponents of the "experience-based philosophy" maintain that philosophy should use the same method as the natural sciences and be kept connected with them, rather than claiming a higher-level position. This holds especially for the philosophy–psychology relationship: "Psychology," Stumpf writes, "is one the fundaments on which the new philosophy must be built" (Stumpf 1907b: 185). This last claim is, arguably, one of the leading principles for the philosophical investigations conducted within the Brentano School (see Chapter 26).

NOTES

1. The latter holds not only for Alexius Meinong and his followers (Meinong 1910; Höfler 1921: 15; Ehrenfels 1922: 95), who form the dissident branch of the school, but for Edmund Husserl as well, who declares about Brentano: "I couldn't stay a member of his school" (Husserl 1919: 164).

2. In their posthumous editions of Brentano's works, Oskar Kraus, Alfred Kastil, and Franziska Mayer-Hillebrand followed the will of Brentano, who wished his manuscripts to be handled the way Étienne Dumont handled those of Jeremy Bentham (letter to Kraus of January 13, 1916; cf. Mayer-Hillebrand 1963a: 150). It is known that Bentham gave Dumont his half-finished manuscripts, on the basis of which the latter wrote the *Traités de législation civilé et pénale* by freely compiling Bentham's notes from various periods, filling in the gaps, developing some ideas, and omitting others. Kraus, Kastil, and Mayer-Hillebrand did the same in compiling and re-writing Brentano's texts.
3. Given the historical significance of such ramifications, it has sometimes been suggested that a table of Brentano's students and student's students would "come close to embracing all of the most important philosophical movements of the twentieth century on the continent of Europe" (Smith 1994a: 21).
4. This reading is not only supported by Brentano's inaugural lecture at the University of Vienna, in which he explicitly addresses the identity crisis of philosophy—or, as he puts it, the "discouragement" in the field of philosophy—and presents the idea underpinning the fourth thesis as a way out of the crisis (Brentano 1968: 85–100). As we will see, the proposed understanding of the fourth thesis is also in line with the overall picture Carl Stumpf offered, later on, in his inaugural lecture at the University of Berlin (Stumpf 1907b).
5. "Experience alone is my teacher," Brentano writes in the preface of his *Psychology* (Brentano 1995a: xxvii).
6. This idea contrasts with the claim that logic should be raised to the level of a philosophical science by being connected not to psychology but to the "theory of knowledge"—a claim that had been made by Eduard Zeller in his inaugural lecture at the University of Heidelberg (Zeller 1862) and which will be at the foundation of the neo-Kantian rehabilitation strategy.
7. The claim that the scientist is not interested in the "hidden essence" of things, but only in the connections between the phenomena, is in line with Auguste Comte's conception of "positive science." See Brentano 1869: 19, 23–4, 27–8.
8. This idea can be traced back to Mill's *System of Logic* (Book III, i, 1). On Mill's View, "all discovery of truths not self-evident, consists of inductions, and the interpretation of inductions" (Mill 1843: 375).
9. See Brentano's letter to Schell of December 22, 1885 (Hasenfuss 1978: 44).
10. An exhaustive list of Brentano's courses is given in Werle 1989: 155–62.
11. Höfler's habilitation was titled *Some Laws of Incompatibility between Judgments* (a revised version was published as Höfler 1917b), and Ehrenfel's *Size-Relations and Numbers. A Psychological Study*.
12. From 1916 onward, he worked as professor of "pedagogy and philosophy."
13. Arleth and Kastil succeeded Franz Hillebrand at the University of Innsbruck. Emil Arleth is a historian of philosophy (see, e.g., Arleth 1896) who studied with Marty and Stumpf in Prague and with Brentano in Vienna. Kastil edited some posthumous works by Brentano and wrote an overall presentation of Brentano's philosophy (Kastil 1951). Emil Utitz was the successor of Ehrenfels in Prague and wrote mainly about aesthetics (Utitz 1908; 1914–20).
14. Members of the Prague Brentano Society include Walter Engel, Oscar Engländer, Alfred Kastil, Georg Katkov, John Kozak, Oskar Kraus, Thomas Masaryk, Kazimierz Twardowski, Emil Utitz, and Eduard Winter. The Society dissolved in 1955.
15. Kraus talks about a "Copernican turn" in Brentano's late philosophy (Kraus 1934a: 62–76).
16. The members of the school also occupied important positions within the "Philosophical Society of the University of Vienna," which arguably has a place in the prehistory of the Vienna Circle (see Blackmore 1988; Fisette 2014). Alois Höfler, in particular, appears to be an important connection between the Brentano School and the Vienna Circle.

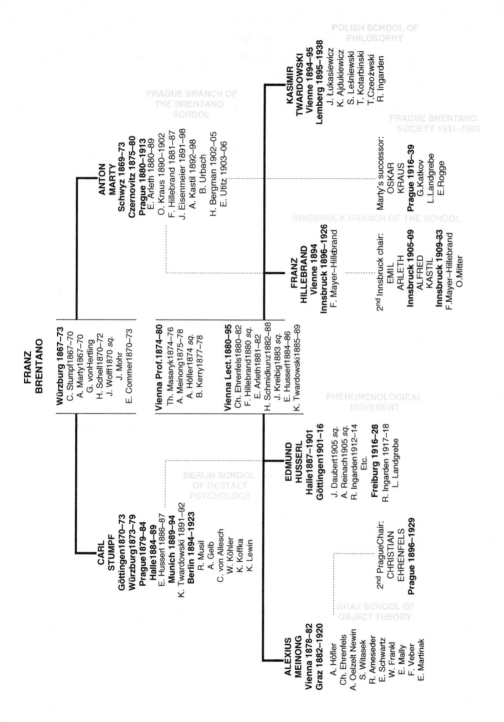

26

The Unity of the Brentano School

Arnaud Dewalque

What, if any, makes the unity and cohesion of the Brentano School? Is there a distinctive mark of what may be called the Brentanian philosophical orientation—or *Brentanism* for short? In this chapter, I argue that those questions are best answered in terms of *metaphilosophical claims*, claims about what philosophy is and how it should be best carried out—descriptive and normative claims. The proposal I wish to make, in sum, is the following: (i) all the members of the Brentano School share a specific conception of philosophy, and (ii) only they share this conception. To begin, I briefly contrast this approach with those seeking the criterion of Brentanism in doctrinal or merely methodological claims. I then identify a cluster of nine metaphilosophical and epistemological claims arguably endorsed by all the members of the school. I do not intend to deny that other, non-Brentanian philosophers have held some of those claims separately. My suggestion, however, is that the *combination* of those nine claims may be considered a plausible mark of what it is to be a Brentanist.

1 IN SEARCH OF A DISTINCTIVE MARK

Unlike the representatives of the Vienna Circle, the members of the Brentano School never wrote down their views in a co-authored manifesto. This fact is not surprising. It is common knowledge that a number of philosophical disagreements divided Brentano and his students, not to mention discrepancies among the students themselves: Brentano disagreed with Stumpf on the nature of emotional states (Stumpf 1907a, 1928; Brentano 1907: 236–40; see Fisette 2015d: 480–6), with Marty on the existence of *entia rationis* (Marty 1908; Brentano 1966a, 1995a: 321–68; Mayer-Hillebrand 1955a), with Husserl on the bearings of antipsychologism (Brentano 1995a: 306–7; see Kastil 1958; Huemer 2004), and most notably with Meinong and Höfler, who were charged with propagating "deviations from the correct doctrine" in advocating the object theory (Kraus 1919a: 15; Höfler 1921: 15).

This situation makes it difficult to find out a single *doctrinal* content that would display a necessary and sufficient criterion of what it is to be a Brentanist. To be sure, intentionality sometimes is regarded as a plausible candidate, and rightly so. The claim that the mental is intentional—or, as Brentano puts it, that every mental phenomenon involves "the reference to something as an object" (Brentano 1995a: 97)—certainly performed a unifying function among Brentano's heirs. In this sense, it is fair to say that exploring the "complex unity of mind and object" was central to so-called Austrian phenomenology (Rollinger 2008: 12). However, difficulties arise as soon as one gives a closer thought to the alleged "intentionalism" of the Brentanists.

First, Brentano's students are far from understanding intentionality all in exactly the same way, and not all of them agree that *every* mental phenomenon is intentional: sensations and some feelings, Husserl argues, are nonintentional (Husserl 2001: 106–12). Next, there is no question that the subsequent elaborations of the intentionality theory outside the Brentano School have very little in common with the spirit of Brentano's analyses.[1] If one makes a distinction between the *intentionality thesis* in the strictest sense ("All and only mental phenomena are intentional") and the *intentional approach* to the mind ("At least a significant group of mental phenomena are intentional"), one could say that endorsing the intentionality thesis is not a necessary condition for being a Brentanist, while supporting the intentional approach may hardly be considered a sufficient condition. For these reasons, appealing to intentionality alone doesn't really settle the question of what it is to be a Brentanist, even though this is certainly part of the story.[2]

Given the difficulty in singling out a doctrinal criterion of Brentanism, one natural move consists in seeking instead a *methodological*, nondoctrinal criterion. Accordingly, being a Brentanist would be a matter of embracing a certain method. It would be a certain way of doing philosophy. It has been suggested, for instance, that the demand of conceptual clarity was central to the Brentano School (see, e.g., Mulligan 1986; Smith 1994a). Still, for obvious reasons, such general considerations provide us with too loose a sense of what makes the unity of the school. Besides, it might be held that the Brentanian way of doing philosophy duplicates, for the most part, the classical Aristotelian method consisting in carefully describing the data of experience, listing the available theoretical options, formulating them as far as possible in exact terms, and refuting those that do not match the described data (Albertazzi *et al.* 1996: 9).

However sketchy these initial observations might be, it seems that, all in all, there are few chances of getting a satisfying answer to our opening questions by examining further the doctrinal content or methodological dimension of Brentano's philosophical investigations. As suggested above, it is my contention that a more promising way to go is to turn our attention, instead, to the Brentanian conception of what philosophy is and how it should be best carried out. To be sure, the methodological aspects I just touched upon *are* part of Brentano's conception of philosophy. Yet, there is more to Brentano's metaphilosophical views than just a demand of description, exactness, and conceptual clarity. At stake is a full-blown conception of the nature of philosophical investigations and the connection thereof with other sciences, starting with psychology. In the remainder of this chapter, I identify three sets of metaphilosophical and epistemological claims that delineate something like a specifically Brentanian view of philosophy. Claims 1–3 concern the relationship of philosophy to *experience*, claims 4–6 concern its relationship to *psychology*, and claims 7–9 determine the kind of psychological investigation that is relevant for the philosophical sciences, namely, the *analytic description* of mental phenomena.

2 EXPERIENCE

Among the 25 habilitation theses Brentano argued for in 1867, the first four clearly are metaphilosophical claims: claims about what philosophy is and how it should be carried out. The first thesis reads: "philosophy must deny that the sciences have to be divided into speculative and exact, and this denial is the right of its very existence" (Brentano 1968: 136). Theses two and three assert the autonomy of philosophy with respect to theology (I won't say more about this), and thesis four famously reads: "the true method of philosophy is none other than that of the natural sciences" (*ibid.*). Importantly, it is precisely those theses that have been responsible for Brentano's philosophical attractiveness to his first students (see Chapter 25). It is therefore reasonable to think that an investigation into what it is to be a Brentanist should start with an examination of the metaphilosophical claims encapsulated in them.

The first thesis suggests that philosophy is a science in the plain or literal sense of the term—not a "speculative" one. The expression "speculative science," Brentano writes, is "a gross misuse of the term science" (Brentano 1995b: 5). One way of understanding this claim is in terms of *determining* versus *modifying* adjectives (see, e.g., Brentano 1995a: 219–20). The term "speculative," it may be argued, does not add any positive determination to the concept of "science" and rather works as a modifying adjective, in the sense that a speculative science is not a science at all ("speculative" has a modifying function here, like "fake" in the phrase "fake diamond"). If one buys this view, it sounds absurd to maintain that sciences are to be divided into exact and speculative ones (compare the claim that diamonds are to be divided into actual diamonds and fake diamonds).[3] Putting such subtleties aside, one of the main claims encapsulated in the first habilitation thesis can probably be paraphrased in a simple and straightforward way as follows:

C1 Philosophy is a science.

The crucial claim encapsulated in thesis four, in turn, may be rendered as:

C2 There is one and only one scientific method, namely, that implemented in the natural sciences.

Let me briefly comment on those claims. C1 states that, despite all the skeptical and speculative tendencies that periodically come to the fore in the history of philosophy (see Brentano 1895a), philosophy *is* scientific and should be considered so. This means that philosophy is not a species, say, of the genus *art*, nor something *sui generis* that cannot be compared to any other human activity (as Heidegger, for example, will argue), but is rather a species of the genus *science*. On a minimal understanding, a human activity is scientific when it aims at achieving a certain form of knowledge. Given the classical notion of knowledge more or less endorsed by Brentano and his students, this amounts to saying that every science purports to produce *justified true judgments* about its specific subject matter. If those remarks are right, then, C1 simply states that philosophy has the same *goal* as any other science: It purports to be a set of justified true judgments.[4]

Now, C2 suggests there is only *one way* to reach this goal, namely, adopting the method that enabled the natural sciences to achieve such successful results. On Brentano's view, this method is "quite modest" (Brentano 1968: 89). It roughly consists in collecting phenomena, reviewing their similarities and differences, and formulating general laws (*ibid.*) by means of either induction or self-evident intuition.[5] Note that this reference to the notion of phenomenon has nothing to do with Kant's distinction between phenomenon and thing-in-itself: "To be a phenomenon, something must exist in itself. It is wrong to set phenomena in opposition to what exists in itself" (Brentano 1995b: 137). 'Phenomenon' rather is to be understood in Auguste Comte's sense as synonymous with positive or empirical fact. Something is a phenomenon in this sense when it manifests itself in experience, when it is *experienced*.[6] Accordingly, a more explicit version of C2 would be:

C2* All sciences must reach their goal by conducting investigations into phenomena (empirical facts), reviewing them and dividing them into groups or classes according to their similarities.[7]

Taken separately, C1 and C2* certainly are not distinctive of Brentanism only. For instance, it is probably fair to say that a series of neo-Kantian philosophers endorsed C1 (but not C2*), while the members of the Vienna Circle endorsed C2 (but not C1). That said, combining C1 and C2 leads to a further, *normative* claim, which considerably narrows the options relative to how philosophy is supposed to be carried out:

C3 Philosophy, like all other sciences, must reach its goal by conducting investigations into phenomena (empirical facts).

I take this claim to be central to Brentanism. On a Brentanian view, thus, philosophy should be performed "from an empirical standpoint": "In the philosophical things, too, there can be no other teacher than experience" (Brentano 1968: 85). Yet, to be sure, this is only a part of the story. The picture that emerges has now to be supplemented by means of a second set of claims regarding the philosophy–psychology relationship.

3 PSYCHOLOGY

As Brentano noted in his Würzburg lectures, C1 is likely to be—and has actually been—challenged for several reasons. Especially, it may be objected that philosophy is not a science for (i) it has been defined in many, sometimes contradictory ways all along its history; (ii) it has been completely discredited with the rise and fall of speculative systems; and (iii) philosophical judgments do not form a single unitary group of judgments. In Brentano's view, objections (i) and (ii) are unessential, since they rest upon historical accidents and lack any actual argumentative force. Objection (iii), however, is a "serious" one (Brentano 1987a: 9). One of the main challenges for the supporters of C1, then, is to settle the following questions: Is it possible to exhibit a commonality between the judgments that belong to the field of philosophy? And if so, what do they have in common? At stake is to demonstrate that the judgments that are taken to be 'philosophical'; form a *unitary* group of judgments, and that philosophy therefore is rightly regarded as a single science.

Brentano's way of tackling this issue may be described as a two-step strategy. First, he concedes, philosophy cannot be said to be unitary "in the narrow sense," for a quick glance at philosophical judgments suffices to show that they are not all about one and the same subject matter: philosophers are traditionally concerned with things as different as the layout of reality, the nature of truth and knowledge, the ascription of ethical properties to human behaviors (e.g., "this action is right/wrong"), that of aesthetic properties to artifacts or parts of nature ("this statue/landscape is beautiful/ugly"), and so on. With respect to its subject matter, thus, it is reasonable to say that philosophy is not the name of *a* science but rather of a *group* of sciences. Indeed, on the basis of the traditional subject matters I just have touched upon, it is customary to distinguish at least between metaphysics, logic, theory of knowledge, ethics, aesthetics, and so on. Accordingly, C1 should be modified as follows:

C1* 'Philosophy' is the name of a group of sciences, the so-called philosophical sciences.[8]

That said, the question remains: Is there nevertheless, *at a more general level*, any commonality between the judgments that are to be found in the philosophical sciences? To be sure, on the face of it, philosophical sciences have very little in common (Marty 1916a: 75). For example, one may doubt there is any commonality between logical and ethical issues (Eisenmeier 1914: 23). Is there any reason, then, why we should regard philosophical sciences as forming a distinctive *group* of disciplines? Is there anything, beside deeply rooted habits, that justifies gathering those disciplines under the heading of 'philosophy'? Brentano and his students think this question must be answered affirmatively: *yes*, appearance to the contrary notwithstanding, there *is* a commonality between all the philosophical sciences. This is the second step of Brentano's strategy: Whereas philosophy is not a single science "in the narrow sense," it is nevertheless unified "in the general sense of the term" (Brentano 1987a: 10). That which philosophical judgments have in common is best captured by saying that philosophical sciences are concerned with a specific class of phenomena or empirical facts, namely, *mental phenomena* or facts given in *inner perception*. More pointedly:

C4 The philosophical sciences cannot achieve their goals without relying upon investigations into mental phenomena.

Since the study of mental phenomena is the task of psychology, C4 suggests that there is a special and unbreakable connection between philosophy and psychology: the philosophical sciences just cannot achieve their goals without relying upon psychological investigations. Far from being independent disciplines, as the neo-Kantian philosophers maintain, philosophy and psychology are, on the contrary, *inseparable*.[9]

To my mind, C4 is a crucial ingredient in an adequate understanding of Brentanism. Its endorsement by Brentano and the Brentanists is, by the way, confirmed by plenty of textual evidences. In the *Psychology from an Empirical Standpoint*, for example, Brentano justifies the significance of psychology in maintaining that it contains the "roots" of aesthetics, logic, ethics, and politics (Brentano 1995a: 21). The unifying function of psychological investigations is clearly put forward in Brentano's inaugural lecture in Vienna, where he says that the connection with psychology is the only reason why the philosophical sciences form a single unitary group of sciences (Brentano 1968: 94). On this view, then, there undoubtedly is a dependence of philosophy upon psychology: "Dissociated from psychology, every philosophical science would shrivel like a branch separated from its stump" (Brentano 1895b: 39). Interestingly, Brentano's pupils also advocate C4. In his rectoral address, Marty defines philosophy as "the field of knowledge which encompasses psychology and all the disciplines that are connected in the most intimate way to psychological investigation according to the principle of division of labor" (Marty 1916c: 82–3). Even Meinong once endorsed C4, insisting that psychology is not the whole of philosophy but rather the binding element that unifies all the philosophical sciences:

> Philosophy is not psychology, for the name 'philosophy', on a closer look, doesn't refer to a single science, but rather to a whole group of sciences. Yet, what gathers them together is their common belonging to the field of mental phenomena.
> (Meinong 1885: 5)[10]

There is no question, thus, that C4 is among the best candidates when it comes to identifying metaphilosophical claims shared by all the members of the Brentano School. The name 'philosophy' refers to a cluster of psychology-based sciences including metaphysics, logic, theory of knowledge, and so on (see also Eisenmeier 1914: 33–4; Hillebrand 1913: 8; Husserl 1983: 302; Kastil 1951: 28; Marty 1916e: 162; Stumpf 1891, 1907b; Twardowski 1999: 59–60).

The idea that metaphysics or logic are psychology-based disciplines may strike the reader as odd, to say the least. Yet, before having a look at the main motivation behind C4, it might be good to address a claim tacitly assumed in it, namely, the assumption that there *are* mental phenomena at all. To make this assumption clear, consider the furniture of your phenomenal world: Which kinds of things manifest themselves to you in your daily experience? To be sure, your phenomenal world involves sensory phenomena like colors, sounds, smells, flavors, and textures. All those things are phenomenally given to you through your senses. But is that all? Obviously not. Right now, while you read those lines, there undoubtedly is more to your phenomenal world than just sensory phenomena. Suppose you feel joyful, or you suddenly remember that you've got an appointment tonight, or you think of another philosophical text you have read on the notion of phenomenon. There is a sense in which feeling joyful, remembering an appointment, or thinking of a philosophical concept are mental episodes that are no less phenomenally manifest to you than the black-and-white letters on this page (even though, of course, they certainly are not manifest in exactly the same sense, being not perceptible through the senses). This suggests that your phenomenal world is not exhausted by phenomena given in sense perception: It involves mental, "inner-perceptible" phenomena as well. One fundamental assumption of the Brentanian approach to the experience, thus, is that our feelings, cognitive states, emotions, and so on are phenomenally manifest and form a specific series of phenomena, thereby justifying the use of the label *phenomenal dualism* (Höfler 1897/1930: 2/9; Dewalque and Seron 2015).

Now, taking for granted that our phenomenal world involves mental phenomena, why should those phenomena be relevant for philosophical investigations, as asserted in C4? The answer is given by a definition of philosophy Brentano was already using in his Würzburg lectures:

> Among the inductive sciences [...], philosophy is that which deals with what is *insofar as it falls under concepts which are given through inner experience*, be it through inner experience alone or through inner and outer experience at the same time.
>
> (Brentano 1987a: 10–1, my emphasis; see also Rollinger 2012: 262; Schmidkunz 1918: 495)

This definition suggests that the concepts philosophers use to describe the world are utterly empirical and have their source in inner perception, that is, in the consciousness of one's own mental states.[11] This is probably Brentano's most substantial—and most striking—metaphilosophical claim:

C5 Philosophy uses empirical concepts, which have their source in inner perception.

Suppose you endorse a common metaphysical view according to which reality is best described as a set of material and mental things that causally interact. If you are asked to make your conceptual scheme explicit, you will probably refer to the metaphysical concept of causation. Now, causation, Brentano claims, is experienced in inner perception, for instance when you are conscious of believing a proposition q because you believe that if p then q, and you believe that p. To be sure, the connection between the *premises* (if p then q; p) and the *conclusion* (q), when the argument is valid, is a relation of logical consequence. This is a relation that obtains between the relevant propositions. Still, the relation between the believing of the premises and the believing of the conclusion is causal: this is a relation that obtains between mental states. The concept of causation, Brentano concludes, arguably comes from inner experience and is likely to be *transposed* from there to the outer world (Brentano 1925/1970: 33–5). This suggests that, far from being a priori, metaphysical concepts are rooted in inner experience. Of course, showing that this holds true for each and every metaphysical concept cannot be settled a priori and is a matter of case-by-case investigations. Nevertheless, Brentano and some Brentanists maintain that inner perception is a fundamental source for the metaphysical concepts of causation, substance, reality, necessity, existence, number, and the like (see Brentano 1995a: 368, 1925/1970: 40; Marty 1916c: 80–1; Stumpf 1924/2012: 31–3/259–61, 1939–40: 9–123).[12]

On Brentano's view, C5 also holds true for logical, ethical, and aesthetic concepts. For instance, logic needs a clarification of the concepts of presentation and judgment (Husserl 1919: 157; Hillebrand 1891), aesthetics needs a clarification of the concept of imagination (Brentano 1959: 36), and ethics needs a clarification of the "ethical, respectively non-ethical behaviors" (Eisenmeier 1914: 55). In short, it may be argued that every philosophical science needs to engage in a process of conceptual clarification by relating concepts to corresponding experiences, which turn out to be instances of inner experiences in Brentano's sense. The metaphilosophical picture we arrive at is summarized by Stumpf as follows:

Philosophy is in the first instance the most general form of science or metaphysics, to which epistemology forms the entry point. That philosophers since ancient times mostly regarded psychology as belonging to their field of study is objectively explained by the fact that *the mental realm has been significantly more important than the physical in forming basic metaphysical concepts*. It is therefore expedient to define philosophy principally as a science according to the most general laws of the mind and of the actual (or vice versa). Only in this way can we justify classifying logic, ethics, aesthetics, philosophy of law, pedagogy, and other branches under the umbrella of the philosophical sciences. *The connecting link is always essentially psychology.*

(Stumpf 1924/2012: 28/254–5; my emphasis)

This passage confirms that C5 is one of the main motivations behind C4. Now, C4 and C5 lead to a further, normative claim:

C6 Philosophy must rely upon psychology.

On C6, thus, psychology takes the place of metaphysics as *prima philosophia*. It is the "fundamental philosophical science" (Twardowski 1999: 31), the foundation of philosophy, while metaphysics is its completion (*ibid.*: 58, 64). The most detailed elaboration of C6 is to be found in Eisenmeier 1914, which maybe comes closest to something like a Brentanian manifesto.[13] Eisenmeier speaks of a "strict dependence" of philosophy on psychology, to the effect that "every philosophical progress is conditioned by the development of psychological knowledge" (Eisenmeier 1914: 35, 16). Logic, aesthetics, and ethics are nothing but "applications" of psychological investigations (Arleth 1896: 242). Twardowski concludes:

If we did not have inner experience, and consequently had no knowledge of the manifestations of mental life, then not only could psychology not exist, but there would also be no logic, no ethics, no aesthetics, no theory of knowledge, not even metaphysics!

(Twardowski 1999: 59)

Again, the main motivation for C6 comes from the endorsement of C5. Yet, there is more to it than just conceptual clarification. Indeed, it is the conviction of Brentano and most of the Brentanists that psychological analysis, by providing philosophers with the required conceptual clarification, may help them to get rid of a number of pseudo-problems.

For the sake of illustration, consider the traditional liar's paradox. From a psychological point of view, the sentence "I'm lying" seems to be tantamount to "I affirm that the opposite of my affirmation is true." This sentence, in turn, is likely to be analyzed in two ways depending on the relationship between the two judgmental acts denoted by "I affirm" (J_1) and "my affirmation" (J_2). Either the phrase "my affirmation" refers to the very same judgment as the one denoted by "I affirm" ($J_2 = J_1$), or it refers to another, unspecified judgment ($J_2 \neq J_1$). If it refers to another judgment, no matter which one, no paradox arises. On this reading, J_1 just is the expression of my taking stance toward the correctness of another judgment, which is just left undetermined. In case J_1 is correct, then J_2 is not—and conversely. There is no paradox, but only *indeterminacy* surrounding J_2. If, however, J_2 is identical to J_1, then the situation is quite different, for the sentence means something like "I judge that this very act of judging denoted by 'I judge' is false." The apparent paradox comes from the fact that, if J_1 is correct, then it is incorrect—and conversely. Now, this is precisely the point at which psychological analysis offers a way out of the dilemma, for psychological analysis teaches that the primary object of a mental act cannot possibly be the act itself: The only way a mental act can be (and, on Brentano's view, actually *is*) directed at itself is as a *secondary* object (Urbach 1927: 168).[14] According to this view, the sentence "I judge that this very act of judging denoted by 'I judge' is false" cannot be the expression of an actually realized intentional state (nor, *a fortiori*, of an actually accomplished judgmental act), for it violates the above-mentioned criterion. And since it is not the expression of a judgment, it makes no sense to inquire about its correctness, for, Brentano maintains, only judgmental acts have correctness conditions in the relevant sense of the term. In sum, the sentence "I'm lying" is neither a correct judgment nor an incorrect judgment, for it simply is not a judgment at all. It is "a linguistic formulation which is absolutely not realizable from a psychological point of view" (Urbach 1927: 170). Thus, providing us with a clarified concept of judgment, psychological analysis enables us to get rid of the pseudo-problem created by the liar's paradox (without appealing to Tarski's hierarchy of languages or other logical solutions).[15]

4 DESCRIPTION AND ANALYSIS

There is no doubt that C6 marks a crucial departure from logical empiricism, whose supporters "neglect the help of psychology and believe that purely *mathematical* methods will do the trick" (Kraus 1934a: 67). By contrast, C6 confers on Brentanian metaphilosophy the character of *psycho-empiricism*. Still, endorsing C6 is necessary but not sufficient to make you a Brentanian philosopher. As a matter of fact, again, non-Brentanian philosophers supported C6 and conceived of psychology as the irreplaceable basis of philosophical investigations (see, e.g., Beneke 1832: 88; Lipps 1912: 3–4; Wundt 1913). To single out the specificity of Brentanism, thus, it is necessary to specify further the character of relevant psychological investigations. This is, basically, the business of Brentano's distinction between descriptive and genetic psychology (see Brentano 1995b).

Since this distinction has already been made explicit elsewhere (Chapter 3), I will confine myself to highlighting three additional claims, which I take to be of particular significance for an adequate understanding of Brentanism. The first is:

C7 Psychological description is prior to psychological explanation.

In a slogan: "Description first, and then explanation" (Schmidkunz 1892: 3). As far as I know, C7 may be motivated by three arguments. The first is the *argument from simplicity*. Like Aristotle and Descartes, Brentano holds that simpler issues are to be solved before addressing the more complex ones (Brentano 1995b: 8). This is why, Marty wrote, Brentano thinks it better to "start with the first issue [i.e., the description of mental states], which is the first one according to the nature of things and is *easier to solve*" (Marty 1916d: 98; my emphasis). The second argument for C7 is that description is a prerequisite for explanation, in the sense that it is necessary to identify the target of the explanation before explaining it (*argument from identification*).¹⁶ Finally, a third argument to be found in the *Psychology from an Empirical Standpoint* is the *argument from extension*. The idea is that many psychological laws don't hold for all mental phenomena but only for a definite sub-class thereof. For instance, not all mental phenomena may be said to be correct or incorrect: this pair of properties (being correct/incorrect), Brentano claims, doesn't hold true for presentations. It is therefore hopeless to try to formulate laws for a specific group of mental phenomena without having first distinguished between the main groups of phenomena under investigation.¹⁷

These arguments certainly speak for the priority of description over explanation. Yet, this priority claim is not the only striking feature of descriptive psychology. Another feature is its relative autonomy from (neuro)physiology.¹⁸ It is, therefore, "purely psychological":

C8 Psychological description is relatively autonomous from (neuro)physiology.

To be sure, there are no mental phenomena without (neuro)physiological support. Mental phenomena are *ontologically dependent* upon (neuro)physiological states. Still, acknowledging this ontological dependence is one thing, asserting that the *description* of the mental phenomena depends upon their physiological support is another. C8 doesn't mean that mental phenomena may exist without physiological support, which would be absurd. It means, rather, that the nature of the physiological support is simply not relevant for the description of mental phenomena. As Twardowski puts it, any attempt to deal with the mental phenomena as a species of (neuro)physiological phenomena is "flawed," for it neglects the fact that "we apprehend the two kinds of phenomena in entirely different ways" (Twardowski 1999: 43–4). The distinction, again, is a phenomenal one, which means that, to assert it, "there is no need to appeal to metaphysical mind/body theories" (*ibid.*). For instance, on C8, considerations about the nature of our sensory organs shouldn't play any role when it comes to describing and classifying sensations as visual, auditory, tactile, and so on. If a visual sensation cannot be set in the same class as an auditory sensation, this is because they are dissimilar "in themselves," not because they are produced by different organs. In other words, when it comes to phenomenological description, the nature of the targeted phenomena as they are given in inner perception is the only thing that matters.

Now, my contention is that the Brentanists do not only share C7 and C8 (see, e.g., Brentano 1895b: 34; Marty 1908: 52–3; Höfler 1897: 4–7, 1930: 50–72; Stumpf 1906b: 35, 1928: 55, among others). I believe they also have in common a strong view of what describing is. As Brentano writes (1995b: 1), the main goal of descriptive psychology is to provide us with knowledge of the main "elements" that manifest themselves in our inner experience and the various connections thereof. Describing first and foremost consists in identifying the aspects of one's mental phenomena and distinguishing them from one another. In a word, it consists in *analyzing* the mental phenomena. To be sure, the notion of analysis can be understood in various senses (see Beaney 2007). For present purposes, suffice it to say that Brentano's conception of mental analysis is roughly to turn inner perception, which is often obscure and confused, to a clear and distinct perception. Mental analysis therefore aims at making one *notice* what previously had gone unnoticed although perceived. This is what Brentano calls "clearly and distinctly perceiving" the aspects of a phenomenon, and Stumpf calls the "noticing of a plurality" (Stumpf 1883: 96). The corresponding claim, thus, may be formulated as follows:

C9 For every mental phenomenon P, describing P is tantamount to analyzing P, where "analyzing P" means "clearly and distinctly perceiving (noticing) all the aspects of P."

This analytic character of phenomenological description has been explicitly acknowledged by a number of Brentanists. Stout, for instance, developed a Brentano-like psychology he called "analytic psychology," claiming that "it is impossible merely to describe without in some measure defining and distinguishing" (Stout 1896: 54). Höfler advocated a similar view:

> Regarding the *compound* mental phenomena, psychological *description* turns into psychological *analysis*. To the extent that there are simple mental phenomena, it is not possible to offer an analysis thereof or to *describe* (or even *define*) them.
> (Höfler 1897: 4–5)

Again, a good indicator that C9 is a plausible candidate when it comes to identifying the main commonalities among the members of the Brentano School is that C9 is endorsed by Brentanists as different as Marty, Meinong, and Stumpf (see Marty 1892: 309; Meinong 1969: 318; Stumpf 1906b: 17). This certainly is an important difference with the later conceptions of description in the phenomenological movement, which arguably tended to dissociate description and analysis.

5 CONCLUSION

Let's take stock. In this chapter, I have identified three sets of metaphilosophical and epistemological claims I take to be distinctive of Brentanism.

Set one. Philosophy and experience

C1* "Philosophy" is the name of a group of sciences, the so-called philosophical sciences.
C2* All sciences must reach their goal by conducting investigations into phenomena (empirical facts), reviewing them and dividing them into "natural classes."
C3 [Therefore] the philosophical sciences, like all other sciences, must reach their goal by conducting investigations into phenomena (empirical facts).

Set two. Philosophy and psychology

C4 Philosophical sciences cannot achieve their goal without relying upon investigations into mental phenomena.
C5 [The reason it is so is that] philosophy uses empirical concepts, which have their source in inner perception.
C6 [Therefore] philosophy must rely upon psychology.

Set three. Description and analysis

C7 Psychological description is prior to psychological explanation.
C8 Psychological description is relatively autonomous from (neuro)physiology.
C9 For every mental phenomenon P, describing P is tantamount to analyzing P, where "analyzing P" means "clearly and distinctly perceiving (noticing) all the aspects of P."

This last set of claims does not concern philosophy as such but psychological description. It has, however, significant bearings on the Brentanian view of philosophy, since it specifies what is meant by 'psychology' in C6.

It is probably fair to say that those claims converge into a specific conception of philosophical inquiry. On this conception, 'philosophy' is the name of a cluster of scientific disciplines that are based upon one's consciousness of mental phenomena and the descriptive, nonphysiological analysis thereof. In the course of this chapter, I have gathered some evidence suggesting that all the members of the Brentano School have actually endorsed, in a way that is more or less explicit, most of those claims. Showing that it is so for each of them would require considerably more space than available in this chapter. Still, I think the metaphilosophical view just outlined gives us a plausible and serviceable sense of what it is to be a Brentanist.[19]

NOTES

1. In Heidegger and Sartre, for instance, intentionality is no longer regarded as a property of *mental* states, but rather as something distinctive of *Dasein* or human being.
2. According to the above-quoted phrase by Rollinger, the subject matter of Brentano's phenomenological investigations is "the complex unity of mind and object." In my opinion, what is informative and relevant in this way of putting things is something else than just the intentional character of the mental: It is the *analytic* character of phenomenological description, that is, the fact that describing is analyzing complex unities or wholes (see §4 below).
3. This doesn't mean that there is no distinction to be made between exact and inexact sciences. Brentano simply holds that this distinction doesn't coincide with that between exact and speculative sciences. See, for example, Brentano 1995b: 5.
4. This view calls for a number of additional remarks. One obvious source of justification is self-evidence: a judgment is justified, in this rather demanding sense, when it is self-evident, as opposed to "blind" (see, e.g., Eisenmeier 1914: 23). Yet, since self-evidence is restricted to a priori judgments or to inner perception, it is obvious that a less demanding notion of justification is required if one has to account for the justifying procedures in empirical sciences. Brentano himself certainly didn't regard self-evidence as the most common—let alone the only—kind of justification available. On his view, probability (*Wahrscheinlichkeit*) also works as an acceptable source of warrant for scientific judgments (see Brentano 1925/1970). Accordingly, the probability theory, along with the self-evidence theory, should certainly be considered a central piece of the theory of knowledge that developed in the Brentano School (see, e.g., Meinong 1915; Stumpf 1938). For a Brentanian account of what science is, see the illuminating critique of Wilhelm Dilthey's definition of 'science' in Hillebrand 1884. As Mulligan reports, echoing investigations made by Chisholm, this text published by Hillebrand might actually be from Brentano's hand (Mulligan 1991: 119–20).
5. In the manuscript H 45, Brentano contrasts the method of the natural sciences with (1) the merely *intuitive* method, (2) the *mathematical-deductive* method, (3) the method of *rhetorical argumentation*, (4) the method of *poetical acquisition*, and (5) *faith testimony*. When it comes to philosophy, he adds, methods 3–5 must be rejected for they do not gave rise to knowledge (self-evidence), method 1 is not possible for every philosophical judgment, and method 2 doesn't preclude errors depending upon the lack of self-evidence of

the axioms. He concludes: "We are left with the method of the natural sciences. This doesn't mean that every philosophy relies upon the basis of the natural sciences. [There] only [is] a *proportional* investigation in the philosophical field, just as the various branches of the natural sciences lead their investigations in a proportional way. [The method is that of] observation and experimentation" (Brentano 1987a: 305–6).

6. This use of the term 'phenomenon' focuses on its "positive component" (Höfler 1930: 3).
7. This claim might seem excessively restrictive, for it seems that it hardly holds for an abstract science like, say, mathematics. However, C2* may be saved if we consider extending the notion of "experience" and "phenomena" to "inner experience" and "mental phenomena" (see §3). Even concepts and concept-based intuitions may be taken as something which manifests itself in experience, in the sense that I experience or "feel," so to speak, the self-evidence of true mathematical judgments ("There is no triangle that hasn't three corners"). As a mental act, an "intuition" is no less manifest than any other mental phenomenon.
8. There is evidence that C1* actually is in line with Brentano's metaphilosophy and has been explicitly endorsed by some Brentanists (see, e.g., Marty 1916c; Meinong 1885: 5; Twardowski 1999: 60).
9. The point at issue is the inseparability of philosophy from psychology. There is no need here to address the question as to whether this inseparability is bilateral or merely unilateral. Suffice it to say that some people (e.g., Wundt, Külpe, etc.) think that psychology eventually took its departure from philosophy and should be considered an autonomous science (for a critical discussion, see Twardowski 1999: 55 sq.).
10. For a critical discussion of this definition of 'philosophy' as "the cluster of psychological sciences," see Höfler 1920: 21–3, 1922: 4–14. It may be argued that, later on, C4 became a main point of contention in the Brentano–Meinong dispute. On Meinong's view, the object theory should be considered a completely autonomous discipline, interested in the "object as such" (not in the object as distinctional part of a mental phenomenon). At the same time, it is probably fair to say that the unifying function performed by psychology has been transferred to the object theory (I owe this suggestion to Riccardo Martinelli).
11. The fact that philosophical concepts may be given "through inner and outer experience at the same time" somehow illuminates if one remembers that, on Brentano's view, the experience of the outer world always is encapsulated in the experience of my own mental states: the portion of the world I am presently seeing, for example, is a "distinctional part" ("content") of my act of seeing. On this view, the examination of the so-called (outer-)perceptual content also falls within the jurisdiction of descriptive psychology.
12. Marty (1916c: 81) notices that the dependence of metaphysics upon psychological investigations had already been emphasized in Brentano's Würzburg lectures.
13. Eisenmeier's book takes place within the context of a huge dispute about the relationship between philosophy and psychology (see also Hillebrand 1913; Wundt 1913). The dispute exploded with the petition against the occupation of philosophical chairs by experimental psychologists. Husserl and Utitz supported the petition, while Meinong refused to sign (Dölling 2001: 157).
14. Suppose, for instance, that you are perceiving a tree. It seems you cannot be aware of (the act of) perceiving without being aware of the perceived tree; this is why, in Brentano's terminology, the tree is best referred to as *primary* object, while the act of perceiving only is conscious "on the side," as a secondary object.
15. As Urbach (1927: 265 sq.) suggests, one could adopt a similar approach to Russell's paradox. Before introducing the notion of a "class" or speaking about "concepts," Brentano argues, psychological analysis is required: "All this should be first and foremost analyzed from a psychological point of view" (Bergmann 1946: 122).
16. The issue at stake is summarized by Kastil in these terms: "To explain the facts of consciousness in a causal way, one has first and foremost to know what they are, one has to know and to conceive *that* which is to be explained, and this is precisely the task of psychognosy, of the descriptive, fundamental part of the theory of the mind" (Kastil 1951: 30).
17. Here again, the analogy with the natural sciences must make the point clear: "Until this [determination of the fundamental classes of mental phenomena] is accomplished, it will be impossible to make further progress in the investigation of psychological laws, inasmuch as these laws apply for the most part only to one or another kind of phenomena. What would be the outcome of the researches of the physicist experimenting upon heat, light and sound if these phenomena were not divided into natural groups for him by a patently obvious classification?" (Brentano 1995a: 44).
18. The autonomy of descriptive psychology is said to be "relative," for the description of mental phenomena requires experimental variation, which is made easier by the application of genetic or explanatory laws (see Brentano 1995b: 8–9).
19. I am grateful to Uriah Kriegel for his comments on a previous version of this chapter.

2.1
Brentano's Students

27

Marty and Brentano

Laurent Cesalli and Kevin Mulligan

The Swiss philosopher Anton Marty (Schwyz, 1847–Prague, 1914) belongs, with Carl Stumpf, to the first circle of Brentano's pupils. Within Brentano's school (and, to some extent, in the secondary literature), Marty has often been considered (in particular by Meinong) a kind of would-be epigone of his master (Fisette and Fréchette 2007: 61–2). There is no doubt that Brentano's doctrine often provides Marty with his philosophical starting points. But Marty often arrives at original conclusions that are diametrically opposed to Brentano's views. This is true of his views about space and time and about judgement, emotions and intentionality. In the latter case, for example, Marty develops Brentano's view and its implications in great detail (Mulligan 1989; Rollinger 2004) but uses them to formulate a very un-Brentanian account of intentionality as a relation of ideal assimilation (Chrudzimski 2001b; Cesalli and Taieb 2013). Marty's philosophy of language, on the other hand, is one of the first worthy of the name.

In what follows, we contrast briefly their accounts of (i) judgement and states of affairs and of (ii) emotings and value (two topics of foremost significance, for Brentano and Marty's theoretical and practical philosophies respectively) (§1); and their philosophies of language (§2). Brentano's view of language is based on his philosophy of mind. Marty takes over the latter and turns a couple of claims by Brentano about language into a sophisticated philosophy of language of a kind made familiar much later by Grice. Marty's philosophy of states of affairs and value and of the mind's relations to these also takes off from views sketched by the early Brentano, views forcefully rejected by the later Brentano.

1 CORRECTNESS, STATES OF AFFAIRS AND VALUES

Two categories prominent in twentieth-century philosophy are *states of affairs* and *value*. The prominence of these categories in subsequent philosophical discussion owes much to Brentano. His philosophy of what he called *judgement contents*, and which his students Stumpf and Husserl successfully baptised *Sachverhalte*, or states of affairs, and his philosophy of value, went through three phases. He initially toyed with what might be called a naively realist view of states of affairs and values: judgings are directed toward judgement contents and are correct only if these obtain or exist; emotings are directed toward value and are correct only if value is exemplified.[1] But predication of value, he then came to think, should be understood in terms of correct emoting and knowledge thereof (see Chapter 20). And the distinction between correct and incorrect judging, he argued, should be understood without any reference to judgement contents or states of affairs (see Chapter 10). These two analogous developments received further support from a final turn in his thinking about ontology. As he came to think that there are only things (i.e. real entities, *res*), a view sometimes called *reism*, he had further reasons to reject such non-things as states of affairs and values and value-properties, as well as judgings and emotings, reasons that are independent of his views about correct judging and emoting, or rather, correct judgers and emoters. In what follows, we shall pay no attention to Brentano's reism (see Chapter 13 for discussion).

The three greatest philosophers formed by Brentano—Husserl, Meinong and Marty—all came to reject his turn away from naive realism about states of affairs and values and never endorsed his reism. They all developed versions of Brentano's early naive realism and employed Brentano's distinctions between correct and incorrect judging and emotings. The idea that not only beliefs but also non-intellectual mental states and acts, such as desire and choice, are correct or incorrect goes back at least to Plato and Aristotle (see for example Kraus 1937: 7–34). But it surfaces only sporadically in the history of subsequent philosophy, for example in Anselm of Canterbury's *De veritate*, with the notion of *rectitudo*, and later in Aquinas, until Brentano puts it at the heart of his philosophy and so at the heart of the philosophies of his students. Naively realist views about the relations between correct judging and states of affairs were published by Husserl and Meinong at the beginning of the twentieth century. But it is Marty who published the first unified naively realist account of the relation between (in)correct judging, emoting and preferring, on the one hand and states of affairs, values and comparative values, on the other hand.[2]

In what follows, we first outline Brentano's early view about (in)correct judging and emotion, judgement contents and value; then Marty's 1908 development of this view; and only then Brentano's mature view.

1.1 Early Brentano

In a note appended to his 1889 lecture *Vom Ursprung sittlicher Erkenntnis*, Brentano writes that truth has often been said to be an agreement of judgement and its object. He dismisses one way of understanding this dictum: "as a sort of identity between something contained in the judgement or the presentation on which the judgement is based and something which lies outside the mind". But the dictum is "in a certain sense correct" provided we bear in mind that "agreement" here means "fit" (*passen*), "correspond" or "be in harmony with" (*in Einklang stehen, harmonieren*):

> The concepts of existence and non-existence are the correlates of the concepts of the truth of (*einheitlicher*) affirmative and negative judgements. Just as what is judged belongs to the judgement … so there belongs to the correctness of the affirmative judgement the existence of what is affirmatively judged, to the correctness of the

negative judgement the non-existence of what is judged negatively, and whether I say that a negative judgement is true or that its object is non-existent, in both cases I say the same thing.

(Brentano 1889: 75–7, n. 25)

It is difficult to know how Brentano thought he could reconcile the claim that the concepts of existence and of true judgement are correlatives, and the claim that to say that a negative judgement is true and that its object does not exist is to say the same thing. But that is not our concern here.

What is it that is judged? In his 1875 logic lectures, Brentano refers to contents of judgements (*Urteilsinhalte*). He also says that what one states is the content of the judgement corresponding to the statement and that this is the meaning (*Bedeutung*) of the statement (EL 80, 13.143[3]). In 1907, Stumpf asserts that, three decades earlier, Brentano had sharply emphasised in his logic lectures that "to a judgement there corresponds a specific judgement content, which is to be distinguished from the content of presentation (the presentation's matter) and is expressed in that-clauses or nominalised infinitives" (1907d: 29). Stumpf also says that he himself employs for this specific judgement content the expression "*Sachverhalt*", or "state of affairs", and had introduced this expression in 1888 in his own logic lectures. Stumpf says that Bolzano had employed the term "*Satz an sich*" for what Brentano called a judgement content (Stumpf 1907d: 29–30). But a *Satz an sich* consists only of concepts. Did Stumpf really want to attribute to Brentano the view that judgement contents consist only of concepts?[3]

Brentano's early views about the mind and value resemble his early views about mind and judgement contents. In 1866, Brentano asserted that

> the concepts of the good and the beautiful differ in that we call something good in so far as it is worthy of being desired (*begehrenswert*), and beautiful in so far as its appearing is worthy of being desired.
>
> (Brentano 1968: 141)

In 1889, desire-worthiness is replaced by love-worthiness and correct love, where "love" comprehends all pro-emoting, desiring and willing:

> We call something good, if love of it is correct. What is to be loved with correct love, what is worthy of love, is the good in the widest sense.
>
> (Brentano 1889: 17, §23)

And Brentano asserts that every loving, hating, being pleased by and being displeased by is either correct or incorrect (Brentano 1889: 17, §22). In the same year, he also asserts that every loving and every hating is either fitting (*passend*) or unfitting and that

> accordingly, whatever is thinkable falls into two classes, one of which contains everything for which love is fitting and the other everything for which hate is fitting. We call what belongs to the first class good and what belongs to the second bad. Thus we may say, a loving and hating is correct or incorrect according to whether it is a loving of what is good or a hating of what is bad or, conversely,

according to whether it is a loving of what is bad and a hating of what is good. We may also say that in cases where our behaviour (*Verhalten*) is correct *our emotion corresponds to the object, is in harmony with its value*, and that, on the other hand, in cases where behaviour is wrong (*verkehrt*) it is opposed (*widerspreche*) to its object, is in a relation of disharmony with its value.

(Brentano 1930: 25, §53)

In *Vom Ursprung sittlicher Erkenntnis*, Brentano is also tempted by a view of preferring and betterness very different from the view he will subsequently adopt. He there contrasts two views about correct preferences. According to the first view, certain acts of preferring are "characterised as correct", as are certain acts of liking something; our knowledge that one thing is better than another has its origin in preferrings that are characterised as correct. This view is the one he will develop later. According to the second view, preferrings "are characterised as correct because they allow themselves to be guided by an already apprehended betterness". According to this second view, preferrings are not the source of our knowledge of betterness, and the apprehension of betterness involves knowledge of analytic judgements. Brentano says that someone who accepts the second rather than the first view "perhaps has more right on his side" but does not endorse either view (Brentano 1889: 24, §31).

The harmonies between correct emoting and the exemplification of value and between correct judging and existence or truth to which Brentano refers in these passages are just that. Neither side of the harmony enjoys any priority. Brentano does not say, as a certain sort of realist does, that loving love is correct *because* love is valuable.

1.2 Marty

Judging, choosing, desiring, acting, inferring, emoting, preferring and even sympathy, Marty thinks, are correct or incorrect. He argues, like the early Brentano, that judging and emoting are correct iff the world is a certain way. In this context, he talks of the relations of correspondence, fitting, adequation and ideal similarity between the mind and the way the world is. Unlike the early Brentano and like Husserl, Marty argues that if emoting or judging is correct, it is correct *because* of the way the world is. Just as judgement contents make judgings correct or incorrect, so too, the exemplification of value of different types—"objective value situations (*Wertverhalt*) … value, disvalue, lesser value" (Marty 1908: 427)—makes emoting correct or incorrect. There can only be analogues of the correctness and incorrectness of judging in the realm of interest, he argues,

> if there is something which is independent of the subjective phenomenon of loving and hating and which is in this sense objective, which grounds (*begründet*) this correctness of mental behaviour, just as the being of the object provides the foundation for the correctness of acceptance of this object.
>
> (Marty 1908: 370)[4]

> By judgement content … is to be understood that by which the correctness of the judgement is objectively grounded, and so what, if the uttered judgement is correct, is intimated in the proper sense of the term by the statement.
>
> (Marty 1908: 369–70)

The "valuable is something objective, which stands in a relation to loving which is analogous to the relation between the true and what is (*das Seiende*)" (Marty 1908: 428). Thus:

> Just like certain judgements, so too, certain acts of interest are distinguished by the fact that they announce themselves as correct and thereby characterise what they love as truly valuable.
>
> (Marty 1908: 370)

Marty, then, is precisely the sort of realist Brentano is not.

1.3 Brentano's Mature View

Brentano's suspicions about the naive-realist view of value emerge clearly in a note (footnote 28) to *Vom Ursprung sittlicher Erkenntnis*. Aristotle, he says, seems to have given in to the "understandable temptation" to think "we recognize the good as good, independently of the stimulation of affective activity" (Brentano 1889: 89).[5] This, he suggests, is connected with Aristotle's claim

> that the good and the bad are in things, unlike the true and the false[6] ... that although predicates such as "true God", "false friend" are attributed to things only in relation to certain mental acts, namely, true and false judgements, the predicates "good" and "bad" hold of things in a dissimilar way, that is, not merely in relation to a certain class of mental activities.
>
> (Brentano 1889: 89)

But "all this", he says, is "incorrect". Indeed Hume, the *Gefühlsmoralist*, has the advantage over Aristotle "when he stresses: how should one recognize that something is to be loved without the experience of love?" (Brentano 1889: 90, n.28).[7] The temptation to which Aristotle has succumbed is understandable:

> It is due to the fact that together with the experience of an emotion (*Gemütstätigkeit*) characterised as correct knowledge of the goodness of the object is always simultaneously given. It then easily happens that one gets the relation the wrong way round and believes that one loves here as a result of (*in Folge*) the knowledge and apprehends the love as correct through (*an*) its agreement with this, its standard (*Regel*).
>
> (Brentano 1889: 90)

The relation that those who think goodness and badness are in things get the wrong way round seems to be a relation of causal explanation. The naive realist thinks that one comes to know that an object is good and then, on this basis, comes to love the object and then comes to grasp that this love of an object that is good is correct. Knowledge of goodness is prior to knowledge of correct emotion.

Brentano's diagnosis of what he takes to be Aristotle's mistakes about goodness suggests that Brentano thought that Aristotle was wrong to treat truth and goodness in different ways, and that Aristotle's account of truth was closer to the truth than his account of goodness. We see here one of the roots of Brentano's later philosophy of truth, existence and value. According to this philosophy, it is important to distinguish between two types of predicate: on the one hand, predicates such as "red", "round", "warm", "thinking"; on the other hand, predicates such as "good" and "existing", "non-existing". The first group of predicates Brentano calls "*sachlich*", material or objective, predicates. Brentano's distinction between material or objective predicates and nonobjective predicates is related to the medieval distinction between intrinsic and extrinsic denominations and also to Husserl's distinction between formal and material concepts. Brentano employs his distinction as follows:

> If we call (*nennen*) an object good ... we do not thereby want to add a further determination (*Bestimmung*) to the determinations of the thing in question ... If we call certain objects good, and others bad, we say no more than that whoever loves this, hates that, is correct to do so (*verhalte sich richtig*).
> (Brentano 1952: 144)

Similarly, to say of something that it exists is just to say that whoever accepts it judges truly or correctly (*ibid.*).[8] Here and in other places, Brentano does not say that if something is good, it is good *because* love of it is correct; the latter claim is one he makes very rarely. Nor is he a non-cognitivist about value-claims. He thinks that axiological and ethical claims have truth-values.[9] Even before his rejection of properties (his reist turn), he denies that being valuable is a determination of things in the sense in which redness is. There are interesting questions about the exact content of his view that to *say* or *mean* that something is valuable is just to say or mean that love of it is correct. But it is not necessary to answer these questions in order to measure the difference between Brentano's mature view and Marty.

1.4 Marty's Last Word

In 1916, a year before Brentano's death, Marty's final verdict on Brentano's views was published posthumously:

> According to Brentano, the ... correctness of a judgement does not consist in its adequation to a content or state of affairs. In reality there is no such thing as contents of judgements and of relations of interest (states of affairs and values), but only differences between correct and incorrect ... psychological modes of being related....
> [I]f there is no such thing as the "contents" of these relations, then what we have taken to be ... the concepts of which these contents are the objects are not truly concepts of non-real determinations of being nor of real determinations of being.
> (Marty 1916g: 155)

Brentano's "attempt to give an account of the objectivity of judgement and interest without any appeal to what we have called 'contents' seems to me", says Marty, "to be unsatisfactory and untenable":

> The only possible explanation (*Erklärung*) of [such] objectivity or correctness ... is that it consists in an ideal (*ideellen*) adequation to something (which is not

merely mental and subjective, but objective, that is, independent of what is given in consciousness). In the case of judgement this is the state of affairs, in the case of interest, the value or disvalue of the object to which the judgement or interest relates.

(Marty 1916g: 155–6)

Marty also, like Husserl (1988a: 344), rejects Brentano's account of self-evidence (*Evidenz*): "the concept of correctness is not to be clarified by appealing to *Evidenz*, it is *Evidenz* which … is a manifestation (*kundgeben*) of correctness" (Marty 1916g: 157).[10]

2 BRENTANO AND MARTY ON LANGUAGE

2.1 Brentano

Brentano's writings contain no detailed philosophy of language and meaning.[11] But the topic is by no means absent from his work, as one would expect given the prominence there of the reform of logic and his conviction that philosophers are often misled by ordinary language. The best and most reliable source for his views on language and meaning are his logic lectures from the late 1880s (manuscript EL 80).[12]

2.1.1 Language and Thought

In very general terms, Brentano characterises language as being "essentially a sign of thinking" (*Zeichen des Denkens*) (EL 80, 12.978[9]). This is not to say, however, that linguistic expressions faithfully reflect thoughts. As Brentano insists in *Sprechen und Denken*:

> Language should express what we think. In such a case, the utterance corresponds to the thought. Some think therefore that in the case of truthfulness, expressions and thoughts correspond completely, and therefore also part by part. This is in no way the case.
>
> (Brentano 1965b: 117)[13]

This suspicion about the ability of linguistic expressions to reflect the way the mind works and Brentano's further suspicion about the ability of language to represent the way the world is are at the heart of Brentano's *Sprachkritik*, the opening shots of the Austrian critique of language to which Marty, Mauthner, Oskar Kraus, Karl Kraus and Wittgenstein will all contribute.

Brentano points out that the immediate aim of language, as a sign of thinking, is the communication of thoughts (12.986[4]). Language also influences thinking, both positively and negatively. It contributes to a more fine-grained distinction of ideas, compensates for the shortcomings of memory, and allows for the simple expression of complex contents (sentences are useful for the logicians as symbols and written numbers are useful for the mathematician, see EL 80 12.978[7]). On the other hand, language disturbs and perturbs thinking by making equivocation and synonymy possible, thereby facilitating paralogisms and other mistakes (EL 80 12.990[2]–12.997[2]).[14]

2.1.2 The Nature of Linguistic Meaning

At several points in the first part of his logic lectures, Brentano tackles the question of what linguistic expressions mean, focusing, as one would expect, on names and statements. As it turns out, both cases are similar, with an important difference:

> [W]hat do *names* designate (*bezeichnen*)? The name designates in a certain way a presentation's *content* as such, [*i.e.*] the immanent object. In a certain way, [names designate] that which is presented by the content of a presentation. The former is the meaning (*Bedeutung*) of the name. The latter is that which the name names. Of it we say that it has the name (*kommt ihm zu*). It is that which, when it exists, is the external object of the presentation. One names through the mediation of meaning.
> (EL 80:13.016[1]–13.018[5]; see also EL 80:13.001[3]–13.002[7])

> What do [statements] designate (*bezeichnen*)? 1. When we raised that question for names, we distinguished between what they mean (*bedeuten*) and what they name (*nennen*). Here, as well, we make a distinction, but not the same one. They [*i.e.* the statements] mean (*bedeuten*), but they do not name. 2. Like names, they have a twofold relation, *a*, to the *content* of a mental phenomenon as such, and *b*, to possible external objects. The former is the meaning (*Bedeutung*). 3. In such a case, however, the phenomenon at stake is not a presentation, but a judgement. The judged (*das Geurteilte*) as such is the meaning (*Bedeutung*).
> (EL 80:13.020[1]–13.020[5])

Names and statements are linguistic signs and, as such, have a meaning. Both mean the *content* (or immanent object) of the mental phenomenon they express: the content of a presentation for names, that of a judgement for statements.[15] The very nature of contents thus understood provides them with a mediating function: the content of a presentation is itself said to *present* the external object.

The difference between the semantics of names and statements consists in the fact that names stand in a twofold semantic relation—meaning and naming—to something else, whereas statements mean judgement contents (i.e., the immanent objects of judgings), but are not semantically related to the object of the presentation on which the expressed judgement is (necessarily) based.[16]

It is, of course, one thing to specify what different types of linguistic expressions *mean*, quite another to identify the very nature of linguistic meaning *as such*. Unlike Marty, Brentano does not pay much attention to this crucial distinction. In one passage, however, he seems to suggest that what is meant by a statement possesses a *normative* feature, something that may motivate a hearer to form a judgement similar to the one expressed by the statement:

> the linguistic expression of the judgement obviously indicates in a twofold manner: 1) the judgement whose expression it is, 2) by means of the judgement, that the object is to be judged in a certain manner, to be accepted or rejected, in a word: the content of the judgement.
> (EL 80:13.132)

Brentano's claim that among the things indicated by the expression of a judgement is a norm—"the object is to be judged in a certain manner"—is at the heart of Marty's philosophy of language. In the passage quoted, Brentano does not see that this norm is the content not of a judgement but of an intention of the speaker. The statement that Socrates is wise expresses the judgement that Socrates is wise, and its content, [Socrates is wise], differs from the content [Socrates is to be judged as wise]. The latter is not the content of a *judgement* but of an *intention*, the content of which is normative; in the language of Brentano's psychology, an intention is a phenomenon of interest. The recognition of this point, a point Brentano does not make, is the fundamental idea of Marty's intentionalist semantics. The passage quoted may well have been the starting point for Marty's original theory. If so, it is a hint Marty was to transform into a subtle philosophy of language.

2.2 Marty

Brentano's only Swiss pupil developed a sophisticated philosophy of language (or descriptive theory of meaning) based on the psychology of his master.[17] The theory contains three core ideas. We take them up in turn.

2.2.1 The Empirico-Teleological Nature of Language

As Marty showed in his first monograph—*On the Origin of Language* (1875: 64)—the most plausible way to account for the development of language is to suppose that it progressively emerged from human interactions guided by the need to communicate (a view explicitly directed against the nativists Lazarus, Steinthal and Wundt). The resulting view is the so-called "empirico-teleological" account of language, according to which language is a vocal communication tool developed intentionally (*absichtlich*) but without any plan (*planlos*), that is, according to the principle of trial and error and thus something akin to Darwinian natural selection (see Marty 1916b, GS I.2: 157, see also Marty 1908: 89).[18]

Although language is directly dependent on thought,[19] there is nothing like a parallelism between the two (Marty 1879; 1893; 1916a):

> Language is certainly not logical in the sense that it is simply the expression of our thinking, something like its immediate and necessary emanation (*Ausfluss*) ... [L]anguage does not display any strict and trustworthy parallelism with thoughts.
> (Marty 1893: 99–100)

One of the most striking examples of this absence of a strict correspondence between thought and language is the discrepancy between the logical (i.e. psychological) and the grammatical (i.e. the linguistic) form of the judgement: whereas the *linguistic* expression of judgement is propositional, the mental act of judging is nonpropositional (i.e. it is the mere acceptance or rejection of a presented object—Marty 1920b).[20]

2.2.2 The Central Role of Intention and Action in the Account of Meaning

Marty distinguishes three classes of linguistic tools (or means), corresponding to Brentano's threefold division of mental phenomena into presentations, judgements and emotions: names (*Vorstellungssuggestive*), statements (*Aussagen*) and expressions of interest (*Emotive*, see Marty 1908: 224–7). Linguistic meaning is a functional property of certain sounds used as communication tools. It is to be explained primarily in terms of *intentions*. In that sense, Marty's theory can be labelled an intentionalist or intention-based theory of meaning (Mulligan 2012: 101–24; Cesalli 2013). In that context, Marty likes to refer to the medieval principle: *"voces significant res mediantibus conceptibus"* ("words signify things by means of concepts"—see, for example, Marty 1908: 436, n.1).

The fact that a linguistic tool is a sign (i.e. its *Zeichensein*) is analyzed in terms of a twofold intention: the speaker's immediate, but secondary, intention to intimate or express (*kundgeben*) her inner life; the speaker's mediate, but primary, intention to guide (or influence) the inner life of an interlocutor. The content of the primary intention possesses a *normative* dimension. As Marty says, what a speaker primarily intends is "that the hearer should form a mental phenomenon similar to the one expressed by the uttered expression" (cf., e.g., Marty 1908: 288). This *Bedeutung* is always mediated by intimation or expression, and the primary intention aims at triggering in an interlocutor a mental phenomenon analogous to the one intimated by the speaker:

> in the case of voluntary speech, and thus in the case of statements as well, we always have to do with a twofold way of meaning (*Bezeichnen*): something which is primarily, and something which is secondarily intended, and correspondingly, something which is mediately intended, and something which is immediately intended. And just as we use the term "to express" (*Ausdrücken*) or "to intimate" (*Äussern*) for the latter, so, we want (as a rule) to use the term "to mean" (*Bedeuten*) and "meaning" (*Bedeutung*) in order to designate mediately and primarily intended sign-giving (*Zeichengebung*]).
>
> (Marty 1908: 286)

"Voluntary speech", says Marty, "is a special kind of action whose ultimate aim is to trigger certain mental phenomena in other beings" (Marty 1908: 284) and involves the two semantic functions of intimating and meaning.

One class of linguistic tools—names or, more generally, *Vorstellungssuggestive*—possesses a further semantic function, that of naming (*Nennung*). Just like meaning (*Bedeutung*), naming is a mediated function:

> However, through the intermediary of the functions of intimating (*Kundgabe*) and of meaning (*Bedeutung*), names also acquire that which we call [the property of] naming (*Nennen*). We speak of naming in relation to the objects which possibly do correspond in reality to the presentations produced by the names, or at least can correspond (without contradiction) to them. These <objects of the presentations> are that which is named (*das Genannte*).
>
> (Marty 1908: 436)

What is named by a name is the *object* of the presentation it intimates and triggers. In that sense, what is named—*das Genannte*—can be qualified as the "objectual moment" of a name's meaning, or, as Marty himself puts it, as its meaning "in the narrow sense" (whereas a name's meaning "in the broad sense" is its *Bedeutung*—Marty 1908: 495–6).

The same distinction applies for statements: in the broad sense, statements mean "that a hearer should form a judgement such that …", whereas in the narrow sense, they only mean the content of the judgement intimated and triggered:

> We said that in a broad sense, statements mean as a rule that the hearer should perform an act of judging whose matter and quality are identical to the ones of the act of judging which, by the utterance, is indicated as taking place in the speaker. In a narrower sense, however, … one also calls something else the meaning of the statement …: the statement indicates the content of the judging and, in this sense, means it.
> (Marty 1908: 291–2)

2.2.3 The Hylomorphic Account of Language and Meaning

The correlates *matter* and *form* play a crucial role in Marty's philosophy of language and, it seems, no role in Brentano's account of language. "Form" is understood in the precise sense of container (*Gefäß*), and "matter" (*Stoff*) as being what the container contains (Marty 1908: 101–20, see also Majolino 2003). This is what allows Marty to say that meaning is the matter of language. As for the form of language, one has to distinguish external (i.e. externally perceivable) and inner (i.e. only internally perceivable) linguistic form (Marty 1893: 68–75; Marty 1908: 121–50).[21]

From a descriptive point of view,[22] inner linguistic form is constituted by auxiliary presentations that are required by (but do not constitute) meaning. They facilitate the association of the heard sound with the intended meaning. For example, the auxiliary presentation (the image) of a body in an unstable position facilitates the grasping of what is meant by a speaker using an expression such as "unstable in judgement" (*schwankend im Urteil*), although a body and its physical instability cannot possibly be meant by the expression at stake.

The recognition of the existence, uses, misuses and effects of inner linguistic form by Marty goes well beyond Brentano's *Sprachkritik* in numerous directions and to great effect. In particular, Marty argues that numerous views in the philosophy of mind and metaphysics are based on misleading pictures. Thus the view that mental acts have immanent objects, a view endorsed by the early Brentano, is, Marty argues, a result of a failure to understand the role of inner linguistic form.[23]

CONCLUSION

In what precedes, we have given an overview of the relationship between Brentano and the philosopher Meinong once called, in a slightly ironic and exasperated remark, Brentano's "prophet" (Fisette and Fréchette 2007: 61n). In §1, we considered the issue on which Brentano and Marty came to disagree most seriously: the account of what it means for a judgement, and an emotion, to be *correct*. At the end of the day, the main point of disagreement is an ontological one: if one accepts an ontology of *judgement contents*, one can describe correctness as a correlation holding between a mental phenomenon and a certain entity. Brentano held this view early in his career, and Marty maintained this realist line—although he always was and remained a nominalist with respect to universals—against the *Evidenz*-based new theory of later Brentano. In §2, we turned to Marty's acknowledged field of expertise—philosophy of language—in order to distinguish his Brentanian heritage from Marty's own, distinctive contribution. The result, *pace* Meinong, shows that Marty made an essential move, a move certainly *based* on Brentano (and actually more on Brentano's psychology than on what he has to say on language and meaning), but clearly *absent* from the master's works, namely, the conception of linguistic meaning as fundamentally *intentional*, that is, dependent on what language users *intend to do* whenever they speak.[24]

NOTES

1. On the phase during which Brentano was prepared to allow that judgings and emotings may correspond to something, cf. Kraus 1937: 194, 182.
2. Some of Husserl's views about correct emotions and values were published in 1914 by one of his students, cf. Lessing 1914. They are now to be found in Husserl 1988a.
3. Outside the Brentanian tradition, Julius Bergmann employs the term *Sachverhalt* (Bergmann 1879: 2, 4) in the same year in which Frege, in his *Begriffsschrift*, refers to circumstances (*Umstände*).
4. One may wonder what Marty took to be the relation between grounding the correctness of judging and being a necessary condition thereof. At one point he writes, "a judgement content is what objectively grounds the correctness of our judging, or *to put things more exactly*, is that without which that behaviour could not be correct or adequate" (Marty 1908: 295—our emphasis).
5. Brentano refers to Aristotle *Metaphysics* XII.7, 1072a29 and to *De Anima* III.9–10.
6. Brentano here refers to Aristotle *Metaphysics* VI.4, 1027b25.
7. Brentano gives no reference here to Hume's writings.
8. For Brentano's rejection of judgement contents, cf. Brentano 1956: 38–40.
9. Brentano thinks that there are true ethical principles. And God, he thinks, has axiological knowledge (Brentano 1929a: 477). See Chapter 20.
10. Thanks to Guillaume Fréchette for his helpful comments on the first part of this paper.
11. This fact is reflected in the literature. See, however, Srzednicki 1965 (which contains as appendix A a transcription and translation of EL 66, *Sprechen und Denken*), Albertazzi 1989, as well as Rollinger 2009 and 2014.
12. Robin Rollinger provided a preliminary edition of EL 80, which, for a while, was accessible on the web. Another thematically relevant text, which should be treated with extreme caution from an editorial point of view, is *Die Lehre vom richtigen Urteil* (Brentano 1956).
13. See also EL 80 12.998[1]–12.999[2], where Brentano (in the context of his discussion of the possibility and plausibility of a universal language) criticises the idea that there is something *common* to all languages *and expressible* in speech in spite of the diversity of the different languages.
14. In later works, Brentano will point to a more harmful influence of language with respect to thinking, namely the fact that some expressions behave grammatically like referring expressions, but are not—see Brentano 1956.
15. For the presentation [Socrates], Socrates is the external object, and presented-Socrates is the immanent object.
16. Brentano, EL 80:13.127[4]: "The names name (*nennen*), while the statements state (*sagen aus*): It therefore does not follow that, because the names mean (*bedeuten*) the objects of the mental phenomenon of which they are the expression, the same is also true of statements: that these must therefore mean (*bedeuten*) the objects of the relevant judgements".
17. On Marty's philosophy of language, see Raynaud 1982, Mulligan 1990a, 1990b, Spinicci 1991 and, more recently, Rollinger 2010 and Cesalli and Friedrich 2014. The two most important developments of this philosophy are Ahlman 1926 and Landgrebe 1934. On the relations between the analyses of language of Marty, Ahlman, Bühler and Wittgenstein, see Mulligan 2012: 111–5, 125–52.

18. Brentano and his pupils, like their Scottish predecessors and Austrian contemporaries such as Carl Menger, compared the planless development of social institutions (including the legal system and economic phenomena) to that of language. See, for example, the comparison of the emergence of the Roman legal system to that of natural language in Brentano 1893a: 58. On this, see Mulligan 2004: 77–8.
19. Marty defines language as "the intentional indication (*Kundgabe*) of [one's] mental life by means of sounds, in particular by sounds which are not understandable by themselves, but only in virtue of convention and habit" (Marty 1940: 81).
20. See the series of seven articles *Über subjektlose Sätze* (Marty 1920b, see also Miklosich 1883, and Brentano 1889: 116–39 as well as Brentano 1911a, appendix). Subjectless sentences (impersonal sentences like "it is raining"), far from being anomalies, reveal the authentic form of judgements: the postulation of the existence of the subject–predicate couple at the mental level is a fiction of inner linguistic form (the image at work here is that of the inherence of a quality in a substance)—see below, §2.3.
21. Meaning can itself be analysed in terms of matter and form: meaning's matter is constituted by the semantic value of "autosemantic" linguistic means; meaning's form by the semantic value of "synsemantic" linguistic means. A linguistic means is "autosemantic" iff it is by itself able to express a complete mental phenomenon. If a linguistic means is not "autosemantic," it is "synsemantic" (see Marty 1908: 205–6).
22. Unlike the *genetic* approach, the *descriptive* approach to a given phenomenon ignores the chain of its causal history and considers only the elements and principles at work in its present state. This fundamental methodological distinction is genuinely Brentanian (see e.g. Brentano 1889: 3; see also Chapter 3). Inner linguistic form also plays a central role in the *genetic* perspective: it is the main principle at work in the development of the vocabulary and syntax of conventional linguistic means (Funke 1924: 45–72). On the distinction between the description of the structure of some phenomenon and hypotheses about the genesis of the phenomenon in the Brentanian tradition and Wittgenstein, cf. Mulligan 2012: 11–48.
23. Marty also thinks that the view that judging is propositional (see above, §2.1, and note 12) is due to a failure to understand the workings of inner linguistic form (see Marty 1908: 415–6; Marty 1920b: 256–7). On the relation between misleading pictures in Marty and Wittgenstein, cf. Mulligan 2012: 39–42.
24. Work on this paper was made possible by the Swiss FNS project n°100012_152921 (2014–2017), *Signification et intentionnalité chez Anton Marty. Aux confins de la philosophie du langage et de l'esprit*.

28

Stumpf and Brentano

Denis Fisette

Carl Friedrich Stumpf (1848–1936) met Franz Brentano for the first time on July 14, 1866, during Brentano's defense of his habilitation thesis at the University of Würzburg. The deep impression that Brentano's *disputatio* left on the young Stumpf encouraged him to attend Brentano's lectures in the next semester and then to undertake studies in philosophy. Brentano and Hermann Lotze, who supervised Stumpf's doctoral dissertation on Plato (Stumpf 1869) and his habilitation thesis on mathematical axioms (Stumpf 2008), are the two main sources of Stumpf's philosophy (see Fisette 2015a, 2015b, 2015c).

1 CARL STUMPF'S PHILOSOPHICAL PROGRAM

Stumpf's work is very diversified and reflects the interdisciplinary nature of his research. However, Stumpf's research was guided by a unitary philosophical program, as evidenced by his classification of the sciences (Stumpf 1906a). The starting point of this classification is Brentano's cardinal distinction between physical and mental phenomena, or what Stumpf calls *phenomena* and *psychical functions*. Following Aristotle, Stumpf distinguishes two main classes of functions, *intellectual* and *emotional*. All functions that fall under one of these two classes entertain a hierarchical relationship, ranging from the simplest to the most complex functions, in such a way that the functions of the second class presuppose and are based on the lower-order functions of the first class. The class of intellectual functions subsumes several species of mental states: sensory perception, which gives access to first-order (physical) phenomena; presentations, which are linked to second-order (mental) phenomena; and the functions of abstraction and judgment. Stumpf further distinguishes the affective functions from the class of intellectual functions, the former being as varied as the latter in that it includes emotion, desire, and will. It rests on the distinction between *passive* sentiments, to which emotions belong; and the subclass of *active* sentiments, under which fall desire and will. An emotion is considered a state of a passive sentiment and rests on the subclass of intellectual functions (Stumpf 1928).

The psychical functions have a specific structure that is characterized by the distinction between the content of a function and its relation to an object. This relationship is characterized by the notion of *specific content*, which Stumpf calls a product (*Gebilde*), and by the *quality* and *matter* of an act. In a judgment, for example, the quality is an affirmation or a negation, and it is characterized linguistically by the copula *is* or its negation. The matter of a judgment is what remains when one disregards the affirmation and negation, that is, the mere complex of presentations. In addition to its quality and matter, the judgment conveys a specific formation or product that Stumpf sometimes calls a *state of affairs*. Products are "correlates" of thought and distinguish themselves from individual acts, of which they are the specific content, through their objective character. All other functions, from the simplest to the most complex, have their specific content (Stumpf 1906b).

The domain of psychical functions belongs to descriptive psychology, which constitutes the foundation of one of the two branches of Stumpf's classification of sciences, namely human sciences (*Geisteswissenschaften*). The other branch is that of natural sciences and is based on physics. Stumpf advocates a deterministic and mechanical conception of nature; he considers that physics takes as its starting point the phenomena of external perception, and that its task is to explain the regularity of phenomena through the laws of physics. But Stumpf is not a phenomenalist, because he believes that phenomenalism amounts to reducing physical objects and subjectivity to functional relations between sensations (or elements) and it inevitably leads, according to Stumpf, to idealism and solipsism. Stumpf advocates instead a form of critical realism according to which "the existence of the outside world is a truth and also knowledge that is however not immediate but mediate" (Stumpf 2015a: 450).

Descriptive psychology, understood as the science of elementary functions, is the foundation of human sciences. The human sciences are closely related to descriptive psychology's main classes of elementary functions, because a human science like ethics, for example, is based on the class of affective functions. That is why human sciences are defined as sciences of complex functions (Stumpf 1906a: 21). From these two main classes, Stumpf distinguishes within his classification three neutral sciences whose task is to study the structure of the contents of psychical functions and of sensory phenomena in general. The first neutral science is phenomenology, which studies the properties of sensory phenomena; the second is the theory of relations, whose field of study includes, among other things, the relations and laws of structures underlying sensory contents; and eidology, which is responsible for the study of psychical products (*Gebilde*). They are characterized as "neutral" sciences in order to mark both the distinctive character of these three domains of study with regard to that of the traditional sciences, and because their respective domain of study extends to all other sciences (they are "topic-neutral"). They serve as "propaedeutic" sciences, because the study of their respective domains is a prerequisite and an essential step for both natural and human sciences (Stumpf 1906a).

Stumpf sometimes associates this field of research with his theory of knowledge, which occupies a central place in his philosophy. One of the central questions of the theory of knowledge is psychologism, which is the main subject of his 1891 paper "Psychology and the Theory of Knowledge." Stumpf distinguishes the theory of knowledge from psychology on the basis of the distinction between the domain of concepts and that of propositions and necessary truths. The research on the origin of concepts is a task specific to psychology, whereas the theory of knowledge is limited to the research and justification of "the most general and immediately evident truths" (Stumpf 1891: 501). Stumpf opposes two schools of thought on the question of the relationship between the two: Kantian criticism, which dissociates the theory of knowledge from psychology; and psychologism, which Stumpf defines as "the reduction of all philosophical investigation, and especially all epistemological investigations, to psychology" (1891: 468). The argument in favor of psychologism boils down to the idea that "knowledge is itself a mental process and accordingly the study of its conditions would be a psychological investigation" (*ibid.*). Antipsychologists, on the other hand, argue that a psychological investigation can never lead to "knowledge of general and necessary truths" (Stumpf 1891: 469). The position advocated by Stumpf in this debate consists in conceding to criticism that necessary truths are irreducible to facts while admitting, with psychologists, that psychology is essential to the theory of knowledge.

Now, within this architectonic of sciences, philosophy is meant to be the ultimate science responsible for issues that are common to natural and human sciences but are not specifically handled by any *per se*. That is why philosophy is considered the most general science of all and is defined "as the science of the most general laws of the mental and of those of reality in general" (Stumpf 1906a: 91; 1924: 414–5). Philosophy thus understood is first philosophy, and its main task is to investigate the laws that ensure the cohesion and unity between mind and nature. It is closely related to metaphysics, which, for Stumpf, is based on experience insofar as it is continuous with the empirical sciences and it proceeds inductively (Stumpf 2015a). Following Brentano, Stumpf distinguished four main branches of metaphysics: transcendental philosophy, which focuses on the justification of our knowledge of the external world; ontology, whose domain includes, in addition to the categories, the topic of psychophysical relations and that of causality, among other things; theology, which is concerned with the evidence of the existence of a foundation of the world; and, finally, cosmology, which deals with issues related to the actual infinite (Stumpf 2015a).

Stumpf's empirical works take on their full philosophical significance in light of this architectonic of sciences. Indeed, regarding first the field of psychical functions, Stumpf distinguishes genetic or physiological psychology from descriptive psychology and emphasizes "the impossibility of separating psychology from the corpus (*Organismus*) of the philosophical sciences" (Stumpf 1906a: 91). He argues that descriptive psychology has a methodological priority over experimental psychology in that it provides it with its *explanandum* (Stumpf 1906a: 31; see also Chapter 3).

Stumpf's scientific contribution to psychology is very diversified as well, in that it bears on several subdisciplines of psychology, including psychology of sound, Gestalt psychology, animal psychology, developmental psychology, and so on. Stumpf's most important contribution to the field of psychology, understood in the narrow sense of science of psychical functions, is his *Psychology of Sound* (Stumpf 1883, 1890). In the field of experimental psychology, Stumpf was also known for the famous case of Clever Hans, a horse who seemed to have acquired capacities for arithmetical calculations. This case aroused great interest in the early twentieth century and represents a significant step in the development of experimental psychology (Stumpf 1907e). In the general field of musicology, we owe to Stumpf numerous studies on acoustics, which for the most part have been collected in his *Beiträge zur Akustik und Musikwissenschaft* and his book *Sprachlaute*. Stumpf's contributions to ethnomusicology have been published in his *Sammelbände für vergleichende Musikwissenschaft*, and we also owe to Stumpf several studies on the history of music (Stumpf 1885, 1897a, 1897b, 2012). Worth mentioning is Stumpf's classic work *The Origins of Music*, which constitutes the culmination of more than 25 years of empirical and theoretical research in musicology (Stumpf 2012).

2 STUMPF'S RELATION TO BRENTANO

Stumpf's relationship with Brentano is extensively documented in his writings. One of the most important sources is the rich and abundant correspondence that both philosophers exchange until Brentano's death in 1917 (Brentano and Stumpf 2014). This correspondence not only demonstrates the close relationship between the two but also shows that, on several issues, they were deeply divided. This is confirmed by Stumpf in a manuscript recently published under the title "*Einleitung zu Brentanos Briefen an mich*," which was intended to serve as an introduction to an edition of his correspondence with Brentano (Stumpf 2015b). This document contains important information regarding Stumpf's personal and scientific relationship with Brentano and completes the information contained in the second part of his autobiography (1924), where Stumpf briefly describes his own work until 1924 and emphasizes his debt to Brentano. Stumpf has also published three studies on the life and work of Brentano. The first and most substantial is "Reminiscences of Franz Brentano" (Stumpf 1919), which focuses on the life, teaching, and publications of Brentano during the Würzburg period. The second is "Franz Brentano, Philosopher," in which Stumpf presents an overview of Brentano's philosophy and a description of his major works (Stumpf 1920). In the third, Stumpf complements his description of Brentano's philosophical program and stresses Brentano's influence on the history of philosophy in Austria and the contribution of his students to his program (Stumpf 1922).

In his autobiography, Stumpf stresses that his work in philosophy reflects "the initial inspiration received from Brentano" (Stumpf 1924: 413), and a passage from his "Reminiscences of Franz Brentano" testifies unequivocally to Stumpf's debt to the philosophy of Brentano:

> My whole understanding of philosophy and the correct and mistaken methods of philosophizing, essential basic doctrines in logic, theory of knowledge, psychology, ethics, and metaphysics that I still maintain today, are his doctrines.
>
> (Stumpf 1919: 43)

One could add to Stumpf's list his philosophy of history, which is based on Brentano's four-phase theory (Stumpf 1924: 28–9; see Brentano 1895a/1998), his work on the relation between logic and the theory of probabilities (Stumpf 1892), and his early work on space perception (Stumpf 1873, 1939–40: 183). His last book, *The Theory of Knowledge*, which is dedicated to Brentano, clearly testifies that Stumpf advocated Brentano's philosophical program throughout his entire career (Stumpf 1939–40).

However, Stumpf disagrees with Brentano on several crucial issues, and, like many of Brentano's students, he has slightly deviated from the master's teaching. In this respect, Stumpf's attitude toward Brentano is not different from that of Husserl and several other Brentano students:

> My deviations from Brentano's theories were the result of an internal, constant mental development. The pupils of Brentano naturally have many things in common in consequence of the same starting point; many others, however, because of the necessity of changes, additions, and continuations simultaneously felt by those who proceed in the same direction.
>
> (Stumpf 1924: 28)

Stumpf's introduction to his correspondence with Brentano provides useful information regarding his main deviations from Brentano's theories. It was meant to protect himself against the objections that could possibly be raised on the basis of the information contained in this correspondence. Stumpf seeks to clarify several events in his personal relationship with Brentano and to explain the main philosophical discussions that he had with his mentor.

The first event relates to Stumpf's resignation from his chair in Prague. After 5 years in Prague, Stumpf was appointed in Halle in August 1884. Brentano reacted vigorously to Stumpf's decision to definitively leave Austria, and this event marks the beginning of a personal rupture between the two philosophers. For Brentano never took seriously the reasons given by Stumpf for not considering a call in Vienna, and he saw in Stumpf's decision a sign of ingratitude toward Austria, from which he received a preferential treatment in Prague. This is confirmed by a long letter from Brentano to Stumpf in which he harshly criticizes Stumpf for not taking into account the devastating consequences of his decision on Brentano's plans for Austria (Stumpf 2015b: 493).

The second point concerns both Brentano's reaction to Stumpf's decision to accept a position in Berlin and the initiatives taken by Brentano to fill Stumpf's vacant chair in Munich. Brentano's reaction was similar to that he had when Stumpf decided to accept a position in Halle, and it is also based on his opinions regarding the Prussian policy and his doubts concerning Stumpf's chances to develop in the Prussian capital. Brentano's doubts were unfounded, however, if we judge by Stumpf's many accomplishments in Berlin and the distinguished career he had in the capital of music until his retirement in 1921. As for Brentano's candidacy in Munich, we know that because of the many unfulfilled promises of the Austrian Ministry to rehabilitate Brentano to his chair in Vienna, Brentano decided to definitively leave Austria (Brentano 1895b: 15 ff.), and it is in this context that he undertook several actions to fill Stumpf's chair in Munich. Stumpf had to justify himself against Brentano's accusations that he had not done everything in his power to assure the hiring of Brentano in Munich. However, several sources indicate that the main obstacle to Brentano's hiring in Munich was his cousin Georg von Hertling, who, mainly for religious reasons, used all his political influence to prevent Brentano's candidacy.

Stumpf mentions a third event relating to his attitude toward Brentano during the third International Congress of Psychology held in Munich in 1896, which Stumpf chaired with Lipps. Brentano gave a talk entitled "On the Theory of Sensations" (Brentano 1897), which raised much interest from the audience. But Brentano had to stop mid-way through his presentation and was once again so angered that he abruptly decided to leave Munich without informing Stumpf. Stumpf's presidential address in this congress (Stumpf 1903), in which he criticized the doctrine of psychophysical parallelism and defended a form of interactionism, did not please Brentano, who suspected him of defending a form of materialistic monism.

The fourth episode of this dispute pertains to their long discussion on emotions, which lasted until Brentano's death in 1917. The starting point of this polemic is the publication in 1899 of Stumpf's paper "On the Concept of Emotion" and a letter from Brentano in which he accuses Stumpf of departing from the initial doctrine and suggests that Stumpf was a "renegade" (Stumpf 2015b: 495). This discussion is paradigmatic of Brentano's attitude toward the work of his own students, and, as Stumpf explains (Stumpf 1919: 44), Brentano was particularly sensitive to the deviations of his students with respect to his own doctrines, including his positions not available in printed form:

> It is very awkward to have to refer to lectures or even conversations in order to explain to the reader the assumptions one uses as a starting point; it is even more awkward to attack viewpoints which came from your teacher and which you can no longer share, if these viewpoints are not available in printed form ... I admit that this was one of my motives for devoting a considerable amount of time to the area of the psychology of sound and acoustical observation. There I could hope to achieve something useful without taking a position of agreement or dissent with regard to a great number of unpublished views of the teacher. It was the same with Marty in philosophy of language and Kraus in philosophy of law.
>
> (Stumpf 1919: 43–4)

The last episode occurred in 1903 and pertains to three letters from Brentano to Stumpf that can be considered as a general settlement of accounts with Stumpf on the main events that marked their personal relationship after Stumpf's departure from Austria in 1884. Stumpf nevertheless claims that the main accusation that Brentano raised against him in these letters was his ingratitude, both personally and scientifically, toward Brentano. In his response to Brentano, Stumpf claimed that he had always acknowledged his debt to him and his loyalty had never been in question. Stumpf evokes the academic career he had since his teaching in Göttingen and his contributions to science and philosophy, which can be considered a testimony of how he succeeded to fructify the master's teaching.

Philosophically, the controversy caused by the publication of Stumpf's 1899 paper "On the Concept of Emotion" is the most instructive with regard to the divergences between the two philosophers. In fact, this discussion goes well beyond the issue of emotions, since it involves many aspects of Brentano's descriptive psychology. The starting point of this controversy rests on Stumpf's distinction in his 1899 paper between emotions (*Gemüthsbewegung*) from what he calls sense feelings (*Gefühlsempfindungen*) (Stumpf 1928: 68). The main difference between sense feelings and emotion is the intentional nature of the latter. To put it in a nutshell, in Stumpf's conception of intentional states in 1899, an emotion is "a state of a passive sentiment which refers to a judged state of affairs" (Stumpf 1899: 10) and is therefore a state that belongs to the class of emotions (and to a subclass of passive sentiments), which, as in Brentano, presupposes an act of judgment and the corresponding state of affairs. In contrast, sense feelings are not, strictly speaking, sentiments, contrary to what the term suggests, nor functions or intentional states, but rather sensory phenomena, such as color and sound. This is the thesis in dispute.

According to Brentano, Stumpf's position in this article departs in several respects from the positions he advocated in his *Psychology*. Brentano first points out that one does not find in this article the *Psychology*'s classification criterion in terms of intentional inexistence (see Chapter 9). Brentano also deplores the abandonment of his tripartite classification in favor of a classification based on the two main classes of intellectual and emotional functions. Hence the question of what justifies subsuming presentations and judgments under a single class. Brentano further questions the validity of the distinction, in the second class, between passive sentiments, to which emotions belong, and the subclass of active sentiments to which belong desire and will. But Brentano criticized Stumpf above all for not taking into account his doctrine of emotions. According to Brentano, one may only call *affect* or *emotion* the complex states of mind that can only be found in "humans [who show] higher-order mental activities based on general presentations" (Brentano and Stumpf 2014: 344).

Seven years later, Stumpf informed Brentano of the forthcoming publication of a lecture delivered in Würzburg on the topic of sense feelings, and claimed to advocate Brentano's position according to which sense feelings fall under a class of sensations corresponding to that which sensualists such as his friend William James combine with the affective coloring of higher-order senses. In this lecture "On Affective Sensations," Stumpf claims that he then agrees with Brentano's position on the basis of a conversation that he had with him at the time. But this is not Brentano's position as confirmed by the correspondence and a long footnote to Brentano's article "Of the Psychological Analysis of Sound Qualities in Their First Proper Elements" (Brentano 1907). Brentano summarized the main points of his dispute with Stumpf over sense feelings and reiterated his main arguments that he raised against Stumpf in the correspondence.

Stumpf took a decade to reply to Brentano's objections. He published, in 1916, an article entitled "Apology of Affective Sensations," in which he addressed the objections of several psychologists and philosophers including Ribot, Titchener, Ziehen, and Brentano. Stumpf responded point by point to Brentano's objections in his contribution to the Congress of Rome (see Fisette 2013).

Finally, in 1928, Stumpf collected his three main articles on emotions (Stumpf 1899, 1907a, 1916) in a book entitled *Emotion and Sense Feelings* (Stumpf 1928), for which he wrote a substantial introduction in which he proposed his own classification of psychical functions. Here again, Stumpf's main interlocutor is Brentano, and one can see in this introduction an attempt by Stumpf to demarcate his own position from that of Brentano on several issues, including the classification of acts into two classes; the principle of this classification (intentionality); the class of intellectual functions versus Brentano's two classes of presentation and judgment; the class of emotions and the distinction between passive and active sentiments; external perception and the evidence of internal perception; the doctrine of primary and secondary objects and Brentano's conception of consciousness; Brentano's concomitant sensations; and, finally, aesthetic enjoyment.

Most of Stumpf's deviations may be reduced to the question of the relationship between affective sensations, which Stumpf understands as sensory phenomena, and sentiments (and emotions) as a class of higher-order functions. This raises two distinct issues: first, that of the relationship between the field of sensory phenomena and that of psychical functions, which Brentano conceives of in a representationalist perspective, secondly, the hierarchical relationship between elementary and complex functions. Brentano's solution to that problem rests on the principle according to which any mental state is either a presentation or is based on a presentation. Stumpf agrees with Brentano that there is a link between lower-order founding acts and higher-order founded acts such as the will, but he unequivocally rejects Brentano's attribution of the status of founding acts to the class of presentation. For, according to Stumpf, this status is only attributable to sensory perception. In his 1907 paper on affective sensations, Stumpf points out that the revision he proposed to Brentano's initial classification (which he himself adopted until 1899) was primarily motivated by his research on sensory perception (Stumpf 1928: 95). On the one hand, sensory perception is considered the most basic mode of consciousness, which gives direct access to the field of sensory phenomena (the contents of perception); on the other hand, the rehabilitation of sensory perception brings about a major revision of the status of presentation and judgment in Brentano's classification, and it is this revision that motivated Stumpf to subsume them under the class of intellectual functions. Stumpf does not dispute the fundamental role of judgment for the class of sentiments, but he does not recognize the force of Brentano's arguments to raise it to the rank of *Hauptgattung* (principal genus), to the extent that these arguments are not drawn from psychology as such but rather from the theory of knowledge (see Chapter 12) and from logic.

29

Meinong and Brentano

Johann Christian Marek

Alexius Meinong, Ritter von Handschuchsheim (1853–1920), was an Austrian philosopher and psychologist who became renowned for his "theory of objects," a kind of extensive ontology that also includes nonexistent objects. Furthermore, he made original contributions to philosophical psychology, to value theory, and to epistemology; and he initiated experimental psychology in Austria as he founded the first psychological laboratory in Austria–Hungary in 1894. Meinong was professor of philosophy at the University of Graz from 1882 until his death. He was the head of the Graz School, a group of theorists in experimental and philosophical psychology, gestalt theory, and theory of objects, and was the teacher of Anton von Oelzelt-Newin, Christian von Ehrenfels, Alois Höfler, Eduard Martinak, Stephan Witasek, Ernst Mally, Vittorio Benussi, Joseph Marx, Franz Weber, and Fritz Heider, for example.

Meinong studied history (and not philosophy) as his major at the University of Vienna, where he finished his studies with the doctoral dissertation *On the History of Arnold of Brescia* in 1874. Nonetheless, he had also to pass the "Philosophicum," a final mandatory doctoral examination in philosophy, for which Franz Brentano was one of his examiners. His minor was German philology, and already shortly before 1874 he started attending lectures on economics by Carl Menger ("and this, no doubt, must have been of help to my later work in the theory of value," Meinong 1921a: 93; Grossmann 1974: 231). He decided to turn to philosophy before the winter semester of 1874–75 and asked Brentano for his guidance. Brentano, who came to Vienna in 1874 and had just published his *Psychology from an Empirical Standpoint*, fulfilled this request. Meinong attended courses by Brentano for four semesters, and his habilitation thesis *Hume-Studies I. On the History and Criticism of Modern Nominalism* (1877) was supervised by Brentano.

Brentano formed Meinong's philosophical development, mainly with respect to British Empiricism, epistemology, and psychology. There are several affinities between

Brentano and his disciple. Both Meinong and Brentano adhere to the ideal of a scientific philosophy and agree that the correct method of philosophy does not diverge from that of natural, empirical sciences. Although getting more and more opposed to psychologism, Meinong recognizes Brentano's conception of the fundamental role of psychology for philosophy (Meinong 1885: 4–7) and develops something like Brentano's "descriptive psychology," which has the notion of intentionality as its basis. Meinong acknowledges Brentano's idea of self-evidence as a basis for doing epistemology, and even in value theory, Meinong's later transition to an objectivistic point of view shows in some respect similarities to Brentano's ethics and aesthetics. Brentano and Meinong seem to have been on friendly terms with each other until about 1886. The relationship deteriorated primarily not because of intellectual but emotional, personal differences. Meinong had not shown the respect Brentano thought he deserved.[1] Brentano saw in Meinong an example of "insolence and ingratitude"[2] without any particular talent and merit and considered his philosophy as a degenerated deviation.[3] Meinong, on the other hand, saw his "intellectual freedom of conscience" endangered by Brentano (Meinong 1921b: 234, 1921a: 4) and felt the missing appreciation of his teacher. Despite these personal differences, Meinong's philosophical work can be regarded as a continuation of Brentano's teachings, though he decisively revised them.

Meinong's international reputation is largely due to Bertrand Russell's initial appreciation and later depreciation of Meinong. Russell's rejection of Meinong's philosophical psychology (*inter alia*, the thesis that consciousness is a relation to objects via mental contents; see Russell 1914), and, especially, of Meinong's object theory (with its conception of nonbeing objects), made Meinong notorious (see Russell 1905a, 1905b, 1907). On the other hand, the discussion of the consistency and efficiency of Meinong's object-theoretical semantics shows that a Meinongian object theory is not naïve but tenable and fruitful (cf. Simons 1992, Reicher 2015, Nelson 2012). Very important for the resumption and dissemination of Meinong's thoughts in Anglo-Saxon countries was John Findlay's doctoral dissertation, which was submitted to Ernst Mally in 1933 and published in the same year (Findlay 1933). Intrigued by Meinong, Roderick Chisholm endeavored to defend the theory of objects against Russell. Chisholm also applied Brentanian and Meinongian theories in his own work and co-translated and co-edited Brentano's and Meinong's writings (see Chapter 38).

In the following sections, the central views of Meinong's philosophy shall be delineated, with a special focus on those aspects where Meinong deviates from Brentano. The main divergences comprise, *inter alia*, Meinong's view on the pure ("Meinongian") object, especially his introduction of beingless and nonreal objects (see §1 and §3.2); his special interpretation of the distinction between act, content, and object of a mental phenomenon (see §2); his dividing up the class of emotions into the classes of feelings and desires (see §3.1); his denial of Brentano's thesis that we can be intentionally directed to one and the same object in different ways and his arguments in favor of proper, nonreal (ideal) objects corresponding to judging, feeling, and desiring (see §3.2); his distinction between serious and fantasy experiences (the latter include what he called "assumptions," see §3.3); his notion of self-presentation as alternative to Brentano's inner consciousness (see §4); and his different interpretation of Brentano's notion of self-evidence, especially his postulation of a direct conjectural self-evidence (often also called *immediate* or *direct evidence* of surmise or presumption, see §5).[4]

1 BRENTANO'S "INTENTIONAL IN-EXISTENCE" VERSUS MEINONG'S "HAVING AN OBJECT"

It was Brentano's theory of intentionality that shaped Meinong's philosophy thoroughly. Meinong makes use of Brentano's conception when he, for example, says that "it is essential of everything psychic to have an object" (1899: 185 [140])[5] or "no one fails to recognize that psychological events so very commonly have this distinctive 'character of being directed to something' as to suggest very strongly (at least) that we should take it to be a characteristic aspect of the psychological as opposed to the non-psychological" (1904b: 2 [77]). However, Meinong did not suitably cite his teacher and did not use at all the scholastic term "intentional (in-existence)" that Brentano re-introduced in his philosophical psychology. One reason for this might have been that Meinong was persuaded that his views on intentionality were essentially different from Brentano's. As a matter of fact, Meinong's and Brentano's views differ in some important respects.

Meinong agrees with Brentano that the expression "object" (*Gegenstand*) is a "relation term" in the sense that "you shall not speak of an object without considering a mental activity" (1888–1903: 47). Meinong does not see an ontological but only a conceptual dependence expressed by the term "object," and he does not determine an object intentionally as something that is grasped but only as something that *can* be grasped by experiences (it *can* be represented, judged, etc.). He is neither a constructivist nor a subjective idealist as he admits that the experiences are not already to be thought of as something that construct, create an object. Meinong sees the following connection between "(every) thing" and "object": Everything is an object, but everything is logically prior to its apprehending and pre-given (*vorgegeben*) to the mind (1904b: §4, 1921a: 20).

The object as such, the pure object, is "beyond being and non-being"; it has the (ontological) status of *indifference to being* (or outside-being, in German *Außersein*) (1904b: 12 [86]). According to Meinong's distinction between judgments that state that something is so and so (*Soseinsurteile*) and judgments about the mode of being of an object (*Seinsurteile*), the most general determination of so-being is *being an object*, and the most general determination of being is *outside-being*. It is not possible to define the term "object" in terms of a qualified genus and differentia and it does not have a negative counterpart, and likewise for outside-being (cf. 1921a: Sect. B). Meinong struggles with the question of whether outside-being is an additional mode of being or just a lack of being. He finally interprets outside-being as a borderline case of a particular kind of being (1904b: §4, 1910: §12, 1917: §2, 1913: 153–4, 261, 358–9, 377, 1921a: 19). Accordingly, Meinong states that everything is an object, and every object has outside-being. Some of them have being, some do not, for example nonexistent objects like the golden mountain or even impossible objects like the round square. Some objects that have being, such as abstract objects (e.g., facts), merely subsist; others both subsist and exist, for example concrete particulars like Mount Everest (for details, see Marek 2013: §4.3).

Meinong clears up the apparently paradoxical sentence "There are objects of which it is true that there are no such objects" (1904b: §3) by introducing two meanings of "there are": first as *outside-being* (pre-givenness), second as *being*. He states that we are always directed to objects, which are all intrinsically indifferent to being at least as "both being and non-being are equally external to an object" (1904b: §4). The mind can be directed to something that does not have being at all or is not determined with respect to being.

The mind can have even impossible and paradoxical ("defective") things as object. In other words, Meinong tries to resolve the paradox by referring to two closely related principles (1904b: §3–4). These are (1) the principle of the independence of so-being from being (*Prinzip der Unabhängigkeit des Soseins vom Sein*), which comes from Ernst Mally and means that an object's having properties is independent of whether it has being or not; and (2) the principle of the indifference of the pure object to being (*Satz vom Außersein des reinen Gegenstandes*, also called "the principle of the outside-being of the pure object"), which says, "the object is by nature indifferent to being, although in any case one of the object's two objectives of being, its being or its non-being, subsists" (1904b: §4). Meinong's remarks regarding these principles show that several claims can be associated with them, for example the "characterization postulate," which postulates that any object has those properties that it is characterized as having ("The *AB* is *A* and *B*, respectively"); and the denial of the ontological assumption, which says an object has properties presupposes that it has being (cf. Routley 1980: 21–52).

Like Meinong, Brentano also claims that "object" expresses a relation of something to a mental activity, when he says, for example, "every thinking is directed in some manner to something as an object" and "when someone thinks, he is the thinking subject and has something, perhaps also several things, as an object."[6] However, Brentano does not share at all Meinong's view that there is always some thing the mental act is directed to, even though the object under consideration does not exist, and he thinks that using "object" with the meaning of the nonrelational expression "thing" is already a case of a "degenerated linguistic usage." Answering Anton Marty's letter from December 30, 1906 (Nachlass – Houghton Library, BrL 2530), Brentano condemns Meinong's object theory in claiming, on the one hand, that "object" as a relational term presupposes actually a thinking person; and, on the other, that the ontological thesis that only existent entities have properties is to be upheld, and talking about beingless objects is inconsistent:

> The Meinongian name "Theory of Objects" seems particularly outrageous (*abgeschmackt*) to me, as it is impossible to speak of objects without relating them to someone who has the object. Teaching objects means to teach that there are objects, but it seems that the theory of objects teaches no objects.

Brentano and Meinong agree that the object of a mental act is usually (that is, apart from inner experience) neither an entity existing in the mind (consciousness) nor an entity that has a diminished, merely "mental," existence. Brentano emphasized that his theory of intentional in-existence of the object had never supposed that the object of a thought (a stone, for example) was an immanent, mental object (a "thought-of-object") (cf. Brentano 1995a: 251, Brentano 1930: 87f). In Brentano's pre-reistic period, the immanent object was something that inhabited the mind, but later on he saw therein only an intentional correlate, an *ens rationis* with no ontological import. When something is affirmed as being thought-of, its being is affirmed only in an improper sense, but "nevertheless there is also something affirmed in the strict and proper sense, namely the person thinking of it" (Brentano 1995a: 261). In the case of thinking of a unicorn, there is the thinking person that has a unicorn as object, but the intentional object does not exist, and speaking of the thought-of-unicorn is only correlative to saying "a thinking person has a unicorn as object."[7] Meinong deviates from these views at least in two respects. In having something as object, (1) there is always a mental content that is immanent to the mind and (2) there is always an object—even if it does not have being—pre-given to the mind.

2 MEINONG'S DISTINCTION BETWEEN PSYCHOLOGICAL (MENTAL) AND LOGICAL (CONCEPTUAL) CONTENT

According to Meinong, in an experience "there are three elements: act, content and object."[8] The first component, the *object*, is (usually) extrinsic to the mental; the other two, the *act* and the *psychological (mental) content*, are intrinsically mental. Although, of course, the distinction between act and object is also to be found in Brentano, he does not have something exactly like Meinong's mental content. What comes close to it is Brentano's concept of an immanent object, which, however, Brentano adopted only in an early period and abandoned, later on, in favor of the intentional correlate.

Like Kazimierz Twardowski (1894), Meinong admits nonexisting objects, although, in contrast to him, he takes the (psychological) content as something purely mental and concrete and not just as something abstract or conceptual. Meinong's mental content is a real part of the whole experience; it is a kind of *quale*, that is, something that feels a certain way. In contrast, Twardowski claims that "while the act of having a presentation is something real, the content of the presentation always lacks reality" (Twardowski 1894: 31/1977: 29).

Meinong explains how experiences are able to present different objects by pointing out that any variation in object is correlated to a variation in mental content: if you have two different representations, one of black and another of a square, for example, the difference between the objects corresponds to a genuinely mental difference, namely the difference between the mental black-content and the mental square-content. The psychological content exists; it is real, present, and also mental of course, even if the object represented through the content is nonexistent, nonreal, nonpresent, and nonmental—as it is, for example in the case when you think of the round square (1899: §2).

Meinong tries to explain the representative function of mental content by supposing an *ideal* correlation between content and its corresponding object; he calls it "adequation" (*Adäquatheit*) (1910: §§43–4).[9] But this relation is mainly negatively determined. Because it is an ideal rather than real relation, it cannot be understood as a special kind of causal relation, nor as similarity or even identity. Meinong uses "fitting" (*Passen*) in its figurative sense as illustration of adequation: the content and its object must be *fitted* to each other. However, the question still arises, "What makes it the case that the experience is directed to its corresponding object?," and Meinong has to concede that he cannot give a definitive answer to this question (1910: §43).

Because Meinong accepts the ideal character of adequation, he cannot be counted as naturalist or psychologist. Psychologism is the "inappropriate use of psychological method" in philosophy, says Meinong (1904b, §8: 23 [95]). This incongruous use is made if one does not sufficiently distinguish between (mental) content and object of an experience. Meinong argues, against psychologism, that logical, conceptual, and epistemological matters cannot be treated "as if there were only a psychological side of cognition" (*ibid.*; see also 1907: §26).

The Meinongian psychological (= mental) content should not be confused with the *logical (= conceptual) content* he mentions in his later work, where he stresses the point that the so-called "logical content" is not mental content but object or, more exactly, it is the proximate object a mental content is related to (1915: 163n). The mental black-content, for example, has the object *black* as its immediate counterpart. When an external object is presented to you (your pen, for example, whether in perception, imagination, or conceptual consideration), not all determinations of the presented object are present to you, because you see or contemplate only a few characteristics of it: something black, with a golden nib, lying on your desk, and so on. According to Meinong, all the characteristics you consider are objects mediated by the corresponding mental contents. The objects under consideration—pen, something black, golden, nib, and so on; and complexes of them, such as pen with a golden nib, respectively—are themselves not completely determined with respect to properties an object may have or not have. Your thought leaves it open whether your pen is a small one or not, whether it is 14-carat gold or not, and so on. These incompletely determined or, for short, *incomplete* (*unvollständige*) *objects* you are thinking of may serve as "auxiliary objects" (*Hilfsgegenstände*) to give access to the objects you are aiming at, that is, the so-called "target objects" (*Zielgegenstände*), which are usually completely determined objects.[10] In order to apprehend such a complete object (your black pen with a golden nib lying on your desk ...), incomplete auxiliary objects like "something black lying on my desk" are required. This auxiliary object has an "implexive" being in the complete object, as it is in a way embedded, "implected" (*implektiert*) in it. An incomplete object *I* can roughly be said to be *implected* in a complete object *C* if and only if object *C* has all the determinations *I* has (cf. 1915: §§27, 29). According to Meinong, auxiliary objects can be seen as the conceptual content or intension of a concept, in contrast to the denoted target objects, or, more generally, to the collective of the corresponding target objects (1917–18: 400).[11] In contrast, Brentano considers such contents as *entia rationis* and, therefore, as fictions and not as objects of mental activities as things can be. He regards Meinong's object theory as a view that "revived the error of Plato and the ultra-realists like William of Champeaux with certain modifications, by ascribing a being to universals as universals" (Brentano 1995a: 287).

3 SOME REMARKABLE DEVIATIONS FROM BRENTANO'S CLASSIFICATION OF BASIC MENTAL ACTIVITIES

Meinong deviates from Brentano's tripartite division into presentations, judgments, and phenomena of love and hate (or emotions [*Gemütsbewegungen*]) (see Chapter 9) in several ways.

(1) One deviation consists *in dividing up the class of Brentano's emotions* and, therefore, in introducing four classes of mental elementary experiences (*psychische Elementarerlebnisse*), which are either of intellectual or emotional nature. Representations (*Vorstellungen*)[12] and thoughts (*Gedanken*) belong to the former sphere, feelings (*Gefühle*) and desires (*Begehrungen*) to the latter.

(2) To some extent, Meinong approves of Brentano's view that one and the same object may be the object of different mental acts and that representations are the essential bases of the other mental acts, as both judgments and emotions include representations as their constituents. According to Brentano (1995a: 156), the object is grasped (*aufgenommen*) "in consciousness in a twofold way, first as an object of presentation [*vorgestellt*], then as

an object held to be true or denied, just as when someone desires an object, the object is immanent both as presented and as desired at the same time." To judge that a thing exists, therefore, is *to present* (*vorstellen*) the thing and then *to affirm* it. The judgment is not directed to a further object, something like a proposition, that is, to the existence or nonexistence of the presented object you affirm or deny. Judgments and emotions do not reveal new kinds of objects; what is new is a novel type of reference to the object.

Meinong differs from this approach mainly in two respects. First, objects can be presented (*präsentiert*) to the mind without representations; this happens in cases of self-presentation (see §4). Second, even if it is granted that representations may "deliver" the objects that the judgments, feelings, or desires, respectively, are about, there are further, genuine objects of the judgments, feelings, or desires. There is a difference between *what* you think (e.g., that your pen is black) and *what* you think *about* (e.g., your pen). Representations are not "complete" (*fertige*) experiences, as they do not occur in isolation; they always come to mind in a further, more complex mental act that includes this very representation as a psychological presupposition. In Meinong's own words:

> Though proper objects (*Eigengegenstände*) of representations are also appropriated objects (*angeeignete Gegenstände*) of judging, feeling, and desiring at the same time, it is quite clear that the object of representation bears different relations to the different elementary classes. This [is] surely the legitimate point in Brentano's position on the diversity of intentional relations. The essential difference of the present drawing up [is] that every class of experience has in addition its peculiar object as well, what becomes particularly conspicuous in the case of judgments with regard to the objective.
>
> (Meinong 1978, Vol. 3: 747)

Meinong, then, states that to each basic class of experiences, there is a corresponding category of objects (1921a: Sect. B). As there are the intellectual objects of representing and thinking, there are objects of emotions and conations. Representations are directed to *objecta* (*Objekte*, e.g., my pen), thoughts to *objectives* (*Objektive*, e.g., that my pen is black), emotions to *dignitatives* (*Dignitative*, e.g., the beauty of my pen), and desires to *desideratives* (*Desiderative*, e.g., that my pen should be treated with care). Objectives are similar to propositions and states of affairs; dignitatives and desideratives are the objects of value judgments and normative judgments, respectively. However, Brentano (1995a: 228) condemns these objects as "mere fictions," which do not have being in the proper sense of the word. All facts—empirical, logical, moral, or aesthetic—are not existing objects in the world; they are mere correlates of correctly judging and correctly loving and hating. A judgment's or emotion's commitment to truth, goodness, beauty, or something like that is not part of what is represented by the act; it is rather an aspect of the way (i.e., the correctness) the act is directed to its object of presentation (see Chapter 2).

The introduction of dignitatives and desideratives is important for Meinong's change from value subjectivism to value objectivism. Brentano's ethics and aesthetics are objectivistic, whereas Meinong's early value theory (1894, 1895) is affected by Carl Menger's subjectivist interpretation of values in economics. For the time being, Meinong claims there are values because of our value attitudes, and not that we value things because they have value. Later on, Meinong (1912, 1917, 1923) develops an objectivistic account of values and norms. When impersonal dignitatives and desideratives subsist (have being), they are evaluative or normative facts and are to be called *dignities* and *desiderata*, respectively. Emotions have a presenting function of their own ("emotional presentation") and are a means of apprehending values analogous to sensations in perception. As sense experiences alone are not complete perceptions of objects yet—they have to be completed by judgment—emotions do not make up the complete apprehension of subsisting impersonal values and have to be completed by judgment too. In order to get knowledge of such values, the emotions have to be "justified" emotions (1917: §12). Meinong sees here an affinity to Brentano's "correct love" (*richtige Liebe*), but he thinks that the self-evidence (*Evidenz*) of judgments itself—rather than its analogue in the sphere of emotions, as Brentano (1969: §27, 1973b: §42) held—makes such a justification possible. "A self-evidence-analogue for feelings and desires is therefore not required," Meinong (1917: 131 [115]) notes.

(3) Another important divergence consists in the distinction between *serious* (*ernstartige*) and *fantasy* (*phantasieartige*) experiences. This distinction is a generalization of Meinong's division of thoughts into assumptions (*Annahmen*) and judgments (*Urteile*), which he introduces in *On Assumptions* (1902). Meinong considers assumptions as a subclass of thoughts and places them "between representations and judgments," as they are, like judgments, affirmative or negative, and, like representations, without belief (1910: §§1, 59). There are not only explicit assumptions (when I utter, "I assume that ...") but also inexplicit ones. When I judge "not-p" or "if p then q," I judge neither "p" nor "q"; I only assume them. Meinong argues that the notion of assumption is indispensable for the understanding of numerous situations, like reasoning, asking questions, playing, and practicing art.

Serious and fantasy cases can also be found in the other mental realms. A perceptual representation is of a serious nature, whereas reproductive representations (*Einbildungsvorstellungen*), that is, recollective and imaginative ones, are fantasy experiences. Empathic experiences and reception of art provide us with paradigmatic cases of fantasy feelings and fantasy desires. They are neither merely representations of emotions nor serious emotions but something intermediate between representations and serious emotions (1910: §§54f.). In watching a movie, for example, it may happen that you get so immersed into the story that you really feel "serious" hatred, but usually the feelings you experience in the cinema are modified, are fantasy feelings.

4 MEINONG'S NOTION OF SELF-PRESENTATION AS ALTERNATIVE TO BRENTANO'S INNER CONSCIOUSNESS

Brentano holds that if a subject S is in a conscious state, S is also conscious of being in this state. This concomitant self-consciousness is to be interpreted as inner perception but neither as a separate higher-order perception nor a supplementary self-observation. The act of my hearing a sound, for example, has the sound as its primary object and, *incidentally*, it has itself as secondary object (cf. Brentano 1995a, Book Two, Chap. II: §§8–9, 1982: 22–5; see Chapter 5).

Meinong's notion of self-presentation (*Selbstpräsentation*) is entirely different from Brentano's conception of the accompanying inner consciousness. It should also be set apart from self-observation and higher-order thinking and from self-evidence in the sense of infallibility, as well as from the presentation of the self or the ego, which was an issue neither for Meinong nor for Brentano. Nevertheless, the self-presentation in the Meinongian sense can be regarded as a mark of consciousness since only experiences, that is, conscious mental occurrences (and parts of them), are able to present themselves to a self.

Usually, the objects of experiences are something mind-independent and not immanent to consciousness. In such cases of "other-presentation" (*Fremdpräsentation*) the experiences are transparent as they are "turned outwards" (*auswärts gewendet*). In hearing a sound, you represent the sound by means of the mental sound content, which serves as a kind of mental sign of the sound. The mental content (as well as the act component) of an experience is something immanent to the mind, but it is usually *not* an immanent object in the sense that it *is part and object* of the experience as well. As the mental content is rather a medium for external presentation, it becomes such an immanent object only if it is the object of a so-called *self-presentation*, that is to say, if the content, the act-feature, or the whole experience presents itself to the mind. In such cases the experiences are, so to speak, "turned inwards"(*einwärts gewendet*) (cf. Meinong 1906: §§11, 13, 1910: §43, 1917: §1).

Meinong does not put forward a concomitant inner perception, but he claims that you do not need an additional psychological content that would serve as a sign of the experience you are reflecting on and, further on, that you can have an additional reflective act that is directed to your experience in question. This experience has the capacity to offer itself to your mind: it is the object of your reflecting act and functions so to speak ("quasi") as a psychological content of this act. Because of this, Meinong calls the self-presenting experiences or parts of them *quasi-contents* (*Quasiinhalte*), and he thinks that all experiences and all parts of them (namely the act and the content component) are able to be apprehended through self-presentation. When you hate something, it may also happen that you are ashamed of your hatred. Your hatred, then, presents itself to your feeling without any supplementary interfering content.

Meinong's use of the term "self-presentation" seems to have two readings: (1) as an *ability-based term*, when you say that the self-presentation of an experience consists in its *ability* to be apprehended directly, that is, without any supplementary psychological content; (2) as a *nondispositional term that expresses a manifest self-presentation* in the sense that the experience is actually self-presented.[13] The whole manifest mental life is self-presenting (understood as "self-present*able*," as an ability-based term); that is, all experiences of a subject are in this sense self-presenting to the experiencing subject.

5 MEINONG ON TRUTH, SELF-EVIDENCE, AND DIRECT CONJECTURAL SELF-EVIDENCE

Like Brentano, Meinong stood up for a concept of self-evidence as a basis for the theory of knowledge. But he deviated severely from some of Brentano's views. Brentano rejected the correspondence theory of truth, on the grounds that (among other things) he did not see anything in reality that would correspond to true negative judgments such as "there are no unicorns." According to Brentano (1966b: 82), truth should be defined by self-evidence: "[truth] pertains to the judgement of one who asserts what the person whose judgements are evident would also assert." Meinong, by contrast, though initially sharing Brentano's truth theory, eventually gave up Brentano's theory of self-evidence and adopted a kind of identity theory of truth, which can be seen as a borderline case of a correspondence theory as well (Meinong 1915: §7, 1910: §13). According to Meinong, the true negative judgment "there are no unicorns" has a subsistent objective as its object (the fact of the nonbeing of unicorns). If the objective in question does not subsist (has nonbeing), the judgment is false. However, though Meinong (1915) does not use the notion of self-evidence for a definition of truth, he holds it still relevant for the understanding of the normative epistemological term "justification" (*Berechtigung*) and for a truth criterion, because self-evidence makes truth accessible to us.

Meinong accepted Brentano's distinctions between a priori and a posteriori and between indirect and direct self-evidence. Direct self-evidence is given in inner perception (which is also an a posteriori self-evidence) and in knowledge of axiomatic truths (which is an a priori self-evidence). If a judgment is concluded from directly evident judgments, it is indirectly evident. Meinong realized, however, that we trust in memory, outer perception, and induction not blindly and by chance, although our trust in these abilities is not conferred from any self-evidence. This confidence, Meinong (1886) concluded, can be counted as a further source of knowledge because it itself manifests direct self-evidence, but self-evidence for something that may be erroneous, not certain; therefore, he called it "direct conjectural self-evidence" (*unmittelbare Vermutungsevidenz*). Brentano, who only accepted "self-evidence for certainty," strongly disapproved Meinong's conception. He considered Meinong's introduction of a new special mode of cognition a cutting of the Gordian knot (Kindinger 1965: 22f.). Actually, this disagreement was the beginning of the estrangement between them.

Further developments in epistemology have shown Meinong's relevance for this matter. Some of Chisholm's (1966: 38–55) rules of evidence, for example, are a kind of application of Meinong's conception of direct self-evidence for conjecture. In connection with this, it is also worth mentioning that Meinong (1915: §54) linked the "principle of the self-validity of all knowing" (*Selbstgültigkeitsprinzip*), a kind of *prima facie* justification principle, with the fallibilistic methodological-epistemological "principle of the critical openness of all knowing" (*Unabgeschlossenheitsprinzip*), which says that critical examination is always possible, since there is always an unverified judgment left at the end of a justification process.[14]

NOTES

1. The correspondence between Meinong and Brentano seems to have ended with a letter by Brentano from February 15, 1886 (in Kindinger 1965: 22f.). In a letter from November 29, 1886 to Stumpf, Brentano (1989: 87) complains: "And how easily it happens that somebody produces someone else's work like its own and old stuff like new one that I have experienced often … also in Meinong."
2. "*Insolenz und Undank*," in Marty's own words, in the letter to Brentano from February 15, 1890 (Nachlass – Houghton Library, BrL 2284).
3. See Brentano's enclosure in the letter to Marty from November 22, 1913. This enclosure contains a letter to Dr. Oesterreich (dated Nov. 21, 1913), where Brentano dismisses the reproach that he would persecute Meinong as an heretic (Nachlass – Houghton Library, BrL 1449).

4. For further investigations regarding the affinities and divergences between both philosophers, see Rollinger 2005.
5. Here and in the remainder of the chapter, I refer to the English translation in brackets.
6. The citations are from "*Von den Objekten*," in Brentano 1966a: 341–6 (Brentano uses "*Objekt*," which is quite synonymous with "*Gegenstand*"). By the way, on the suggestion of Ameseder 1904, Meinong uses "*Objekt*" (translated: "objectum") for a subclass of "*Gegenstand*." Objecta are the prototypical objects of representations.
7. For a thorough presentation of Brentano's distinction between intentional object and correlate, see Antonelli 2015 and Sauer 2006.
8. Russell (1959: Chapter 12) ascribed this view to Brentano—a view Russell had originally accepted but had given up in about 1918.
9. According to Meinong, ideal relations, in contrast to real relations, subsist necessarily between the terms of the relation. If one color, say red, is different from another, say green, then they *must be* different. If you compare colors located somewhere, the relation between a color spot and its location is called *real* because the color, say red, could be located elsewhere, or another color could be in the place of the red color spot.
10. Only "usually" because Meinong (1915: 197) mentions that we are sometimes directed to incompletely determined target objects; referring to fictitious objects or to things *in abstracto* such as the triangle *in abstracto* are examples of it.
11. In the distinction between auxiliary and target objects, Meinong makes out analogies to James Mill's opposition between "notion" and "connotation"—and also to John Stuart Mill, who used his father's terms rather the other way around (1915, §28: 206).
12. Notice: Meinong's term *vorstellen* is rendered as "represent and his *präsentieren* as "present."
13. There are interesting affinities to Nelson Goodman's notion of "exemplification" and Keith Lehrer's "exemplarization"; see Marek 2012.
14. I would like to thank Maria E. Reicher and Uriah Kriegel for helpful comments.

30

Ehrenfels and Brentano

Maria E. Reicher

1 CHRISTIAN VON EHRENFELS' PHILOSOPHICAL WORKS

Christian Freiherr von Ehrenfels (1859–1932) was born in Rodaun, near Vienna. He began his studies in philosophy in Vienna with Franz Brentano and Alexius Meinong. In 1885, he followed Meinong, who was his dissertation supervisor, to the University of Graz. From 1896 to 1929, he was professor of philosophy at the University of Prague.[1]

Ehrenfels was an opalescent figure, whose interests as well as authorial work comprise a broad range of fields and topics, including religion, art (especially music and drama), sexual ethics and population policy. He published some 20 plays and was a declared Wagner enthusiast and a fervent fighter for the abolition of monogamy (though for men only). His philosophical works comprise writings on metaphysics, philosophy of mathematics, ethics and aesthetics. His most important contributions, however, are to philosophical psychology and the theory of value.[2]

Philosophical Psychology

Ehrenfels develops his philosophical psychology in *Über Fühlen und Wollen* (*On Feeling and Willing*) and in his seminal paper "Über 'Gestaltqualitäten'" ("On 'Gestalt qualities'").

In *On Feeling and Willing*, Ehrenfels investigates the nature of desires (*Begehrungen*) and their relation to emotions (*Gefühle*). In the final analysis, he reduces desires to a particular combination of presentations (*Vorstellungen*) and emotions. He distinguishes *demanding desire* (*verlangendes Begehren*) from *detesting desire* (*verabscheuendes Begehren*). According to him, a demanding desire for an x occurs if the presentation of x's existence provides more pleasure than either (i) the presentation of x's nonexistence or (ii) a "plain" presentation (*schlechthinnige Vorstellung*) of x, that is, a presentation of x disregarding the question of x's existence or nonexistence. In other words, a demanding desire for x occurs if the presentation of x's existence provides a "relative advancement of happiness" (*relative Glücksförderung*). Analogously, a detesting desire occurs if the presentation of *x*'s nonexistence provides a relative advancement of happiness (Ehrenfels 1988b, §18).

Ehrenfels' most influential work is his "On 'Gestalt Qualities'" (Ehrenfels 1988c; 1988f).[3] His concept of *Gestalt quality* became the starting point of the psychological movement of Gestalt psychology. As he explains, a Gestalt quality is

> a positive content of presentation bound up in consciousness with the presence of complexes of mutually separable (i.e. independently presentable) elements. That complex of presentations which is necessary for the existence of a given Gestalt quality we call the *foundation* [*Grundlage*] of that quality.
>
> (Ehrenfels 1988f: 93)

Ehrenfels' favourite example of a Gestalt is a *melody*. The foundation of a melody is the totality of the single notes it consists of. A Gestalt is ontologically dependent on but not reducible to its foundation. A melody cannot exist without the single notes, but the former is not reducible to the latter. Thus, one might say that the gist of Gestalt theory is the slogan "The whole is more than the sum of its parts".

The most important argument against the reducibility of a Gestalt quality to its foundation is as follows: if a melody is transposed from one key into another, we easily recognize it as the same, although its foundation is altogether different (Ehrenfels 1988f: 90).

In order to perceive a Gestalt quality, it is necessary to have presentations of all those objects that are the Gestalt's foundation. Originally, Ehrenfels thought that the perception of the foundation is not only necessary but also sufficient for the perception of the Gestalt: we perceive the Gestalt immediately when we perceive its foundation, without any further activity of the consciousness (Ehrenfels 1988f: 110–2). Later, however, Ehrenfels conceded that in some (though not all) cases, over and above the perception of the foundation, the consciousness must produce the presentation of the Gestalt through an act of its own (Ehrenfels 1988c: 156).

Theory of Value: I. Value and Desire

As Ehrenfels himself notes, one of the origins of his theory of value is the theory of marginal utility of the Austrian school of economics (Ehrenfels 1982b: 23). The theory of marginal utility tackles the problem of the relation between a good's (economic) value and the good's utility: One should expect that a good's value is proportional to its utility. As a matter of fact, however, this principle is not universally valid; the utility of iron, for instance, is much bigger than that of gold, yet the economic value of gold far exceeds the economic value of iron. The theory of marginal utility is supposed to explain facts like this and at the same time do justice to the intuition that a good's utility is *in some way* relevant for its economic value.

Thereby, it is an essential observation that a good's economic value crucially depends on the good's *availability*. If there is plenty of it, so that all the needs for it can easily be met, then the good's economic value decreases; if, however, the supply of the good does not suffice anymore to fulfil all the needs, the economic value increases (Ehrenfels 1982b: 23–5f.).

Ehrenfels applies this idea to ethical values. He sets out to rebut the common utilitarian conception of the ethical value of character traits, which says that our appreciation of a character trait is proportional to the trait's utility. Ehrenfels objects to this that there are extremely useful character traits that do not receive any moral appreciation, notably human instincts of self-preservation. Their utility, he remarks, far exceeds the utility of such highly morally appreciated traits as "general philanthropy". Further, the appreciation of a character trait depends on its value, and a trait's value, in turn, does not depend directly on its utility but on its *relative sparsity*. That a trait is relatively sparse means that it occurs not as often as would be desirable from the point of view of general welfare. Obviously, there is no shortage of human instincts of self-preservation; on the other hand, there is not as much general philanthropy as would be desirable. According to Ehrenfels, general philanthropy is ethically valuable because the need for it exceeds the supply; since this does not hold for instincts of self-preservation, the latter lack ethical value (Ehrenfels 1982e: 192–4; Ehrenfels 1982f).

From this it follows that in a morally highly developed society, a character trait such as altruism would have no ethical value anymore. Some of his contemporaries found this consequence counterintuitive, but Ehrenfels accepted it and argued that it does not rule out that we, from our less developed point of view, nevertheless may appreciate altruism (Ehrenfels 1982f: 199f.).

On the face of it, Ehrenfels defends a robust and thoroughgoing value subjectivism and relativism. He observes that, in our everyday value judgements, we express an intuitive conception of value as an objectively subsisting property of (external) objects but describes this conception as a "prejudice" (Ehrenfels 1982c: 218f.). He explicitly denies that value is "something independent, attached to the things in themselves" (Ehrenfels 1982b: 29f.) and declares that the concept of value is thoroughly relative. Value concepts are supposed to express "nothing else than a thing's relation to the emotional functions of human psyche" (*ibid.*: 31). The emotional function on which value depends is, according to Ehrenfels, not the feeling, but the *desire*: "This thing is valuable to me means: this thing is an object of my desire. Value is the thing's relation to a human desire that is directed to it, where this relation is erroneously objectified by language" (*ibid.*).[4]

Ehrenfels turns on its head, as it were, what he takes to be the traditional view of the matter: "It is not that we desire things because we recognize in them this mystical, unfathomable essence 'value', but rather that we ascribe 'value' to things because we desire them" (Ehrenfels 1982c: 219).

In grounding value in desire, Ehrenfels sets his theory of value apart from Meinong's. In contrast to Ehrenfels, for Meinong acts of valuation involve feelings, not desires. Thus, Meinong raised the following objection against Ehrenfels' view: if I am convinced that a certain object exists, I cannot desire this object anymore (for one can only desire something if one believes that it does not exist or if one doubts, at least, its existence).[5] Nevertheless, of course, an object may have value for me, although I am convinced of its existence. As a result of Ehrenfels' exchange with Meinong on this matter, however, the two philosophers reached, as Ehrenfels himself puts it, "a considerable *rapprochement* of our views on the basis of mutual concessions, if not a complete agreement" (Ehrenfels 1982d: 182). On the one hand, Meinong conceded that "one might understand value as the capacity of an object to maintain itself as an object of desire in the struggle of motives" (*ibid.*). On the other hand, Ehrenfels revised his central thesis as follows: an object has value for a person if either the person actually desires it or has the disposition to desire it under appropriate circumstances, where the appropriate circumstances include that the person is not convinced of the object's existence:

> *Value is a relation between an object and a subject which expresses that the subject either actually desires the object or at least would desire it if it were not convinced of its existence—or that a maximally colourful, vivid, and complete presentation of the respective object's existence causes in the subject a state that ranges higher on the displeasure-pleasure scale than a similar presentation of the object's nonexistence. The value's magnitude is proportional to the desire's strength and to the distance between the two feelings characterized above.*
> (Ehrenfels 1982c: 261; italics are original)

Theory of Value: II. Intrinsic vs. Instrumental Value

Ehrenfels emphasizes the distinction between *intrinsic value* (*Eigenwert*) and *instrumental value* (*Wirkungswert*): "Those things that we desire for their own sake we shall call *intrinsic values*, those which we desire for the sake of others, for the sake of the effects which we expect from them, we shall call *instrumental values*" (Ehrenfels 1982b: 32).

The question which things are intrinsically valuable is answered as follows: "Each object (in the widest sense of the word, which includes states as well as events) whose imagined realization provides a relative advancement of the state of happiness is desired and is thus an intrinsic value for the individual in question" (Ehrenfels 1982b: 34).

Ehrenfels uses the distinction between intrinsic and instrumental values to explain the widespread intuition that—contrary to his relativist doctrine—it makes sense to distinguish between "true" values on the one hand and only pretended or "illusory" values on the other. He states that the distinction between true and illusory values can be applied to *instrumental values* only. It makes sense to say that an object has "true instrumental value" if our appreciation of the object is based on a true judgement and that an object's instrumental value is illusory if our appreciation of the object is based on a false judgement. This conception of true and false values, however, cannot be applied to intrinsic values, for intrinsic values are not based on judgements at all: The intellect cannot point us to the true final aims of life. Only in a completely different sense can one possibly talk about false intrinsic values, namely if a person erroneously believes herself to appreciate something as an intrinsic value which in fact she either does not appreciate at all or appreciates as an instrumental value only. Ehrenfels explains that an instrumental value can easily be mistaken for an intrinsic value, since means and ends are often imagined together (Ehrenfels 1982b: 38f.; 1982c: 286–8).

However, Ehrenfels is interested not only in the nature of value in an atemporal sense but also, and eminently, in the phenomenon of *value change*. This is, as he notes, to be understood as a change of *valuations*, not as a change of objects of valuations, and it is analysed basically as a (permanent) change of *emotional dispositions*. More exactly, the change of *intrinsic* values is exclusively a matter of the (permanent) change of dispositions, whereas the change of instrumental values depends on various factors (Ehrenfels 1982c, § 34).

As he sees it, there is a "struggle for existence" between values, which he models after Darwin's theory of evolution (Ehrenfels 1982b: 72; Ehrenfels 1982c, Part Two,

Chapter IV). Values are displaced by other values. There are no values which couldn't, in principle, fall prey to such a process of displacement (Ehrenfels 1982b: 76–8).

Since each valuation consumes vital force and each human being has only a limited quantity of vital force, a valuation displaces other valuations by its sheer occurrence alone. Nevertheless, there are interconnections between valuations which bring it about that valuations might mutually foster each other (Ehrenfels 1982c: 319f.). A particularly important process within the struggle of valuations is the "dying off" of instrumental values as a result of the decay of those intrinsic values on which they depend (*ibid.*: 320–3).

Although Ehrenfels is a staunch defender of relativism and subjectivism with respect to *ethical* values, when it comes to *aesthetic* values, it is less clear whether he is to be categorised as a subjectivist or as an objectivist. According to him, aesthetic values are attached to the aesthetic objects themselves, that is, to the intentional objects of aesthetic appreciation. At first sight, this seems to be in sharp contrast to his overall value subjectivism. However, the contrast is at least alleviated by another feature of his aesthetics: according to him, the proper objects of aesthetic appreciation are not objects in the external world (paintings, flowers, human bodies, etc.) but rather "complexes of presentations" (*Vorstellungsgebilde*) thereof, which are produced by the recipients' consciousness (Ehrenfels 1982b: 127–9; 1986b; 1986c). In other words, aesthetic value properties are objective values of aesthetic objects; aesthetic objects, though, are immanent objects within the recipients' minds.

2 BRENTANO IN EHRENFELS' PHILOSOPHY

Surely, Ehrenfels was deeply influenced by Brentano's descriptive psychology. Yet, he does not belong to those of Brentano's students who uncritically adopted Brentano's doctrines and stuck to them for the rest of their lives, willing to defend them against heretics at all costs. On the contrary, when he explicitly mentions Brentano in his writings, usually he strives to set himself apart from the views of his former teacher. This concerns his psychology as well as his theory of values.

Ehrenfels on Brentano's Theory of Love and Hate

Ehrenfels adopts Brentano's division of mental phenomena in presentations (*Vorstellungen*), judgements (*Urteile*) and a third class (called *Gemütsbewegungen*), which includes emotions as well as desires and will (see Chapter 9). It is this third class of mental phenomena where he departs from Brentano. According to Brentano, there is no principled difference between emotions on the one hand and phenomena of desire and will on the other (see Chapter 11). As he sees it, all those phenomena are to be characterised as varieties of love and hate, and it is impossible to draw a sharp line between emotions on the one hand and desires on the other. To support the latter thesis, he presents the following list of mental phenomena: "sadness—yearning for the absent good—hope that it will be ours—the desire to bring it about—the courage to make the attempt—the decision to act" (Brentano 1973a: 236).

Ehrenfels does not deny that emotions and desires belong to the same fundamental class of mental phenomena. (In this regard, he departs from Meinong.) However, in contrast to Brentano, he is convinced that, within this fundamental class, one can strictly distinguish between emotions and desires. He draws the line between the first and the second element of Brentano's series of examples: sadness is an emotion, while yearning, hope, desire and decision of will all belong to the subclass of desires (Ehrenfels 1988b: 36). The phenomenon of courage, which also figures in Brentano's series, is, according to Ehrenfels, "not a desire at all, but a cheerful confidence in a dangerous endeavour's success, which either precedes or goes along with the respective endeavour, that is, a complex consisting of a judgement and an emotion, which presupposes a desire, though" (*ibid.*).

In addition, Ehrenfels rejects Brentano's characterization of both emotions and desires as forms of love and hate. He blames Brentano for using the locutions "love" and "hate" in an unusual meaning. Firstly, Ehrenfels claims (convincingly) that these locutions usually denote only *dispositions* to manifest mental phenomena, not manifest mental phenomena themselves. Secondly, he claims (less convincingly) that "love" and "hate" denote, *if* they denote manifest mental phenomena at all, phenomena of desire: "Those who love or hate wish either the well-being, the presence, the possession, or the harm and the absence of either living or dead objects" (Ehrenfels 1988b: 34).

In favour of the latter claim, Ehrenfels argues roughly as follows: If love and hate were emotions, they would have to be either pleasure or displeasure. It suggests itself to consider love as a kind of pleasure and hate as a kind of displeasure. This would not do, however, because neither is love always pleasant (think of lovesickness!) nor is hate always unpleasant (think of "sweet revenge" and schadenfreude!). Therefore, love and hate cannot be kinds of emotions (Ehrenfels 1988b: 34).

This reasoning, however, is unconvincing. Granted, lovesickness is unpleasant, but it is not the love itself that is experienced as unpleasant by the lovesick person but rather the fact that the love is not returned by the beloved object. As for cases of schadenfreude and revenge, it is the fulfilment of a desire (that someone should be harmed), not the hate itself, that is experienced as pleasant.

Ehrenfels on Brentano's Theory of Intensity

Another target of Ehrenfels' criticism is Brentano's theory of the *intensity of mental phenomena*. The foundation of this view is a theory of the intensity of *sense qualities* (colour, sound, smell etc.), which, roughly, runs as follows: We have to think of the "subjective space of sensation" (*subjektiver Sinnesraum*) as partitioned into small fields, as in a fine grid pattern. If all these fields are filled with the sense quality in question, the sense quality has maximal intensity; if some of these fields are empty, the sense quality has less intensity. Of course, we do not sense the empty fields as such; rather, we perceive the space of sensation as continuously filled: the empty fields are experienced just as a lack of the sense quality's intensity. In a further step, Brentano claims that the intensity of all mental phenomena that are directed to sense qualities is proportional to the intensity of the sense qualities themselves. Thus, the intensity of a sensation of smell, for instance, depends directly and solely on the intensity of the sensed odour. Mental acts which are not directed at sense qualities, however, do not have any intensity, according to Brentano (Brentano 1897; cf. Ehrenfels 1988d: 98–100).[6]

Ehrenfels accepts Brentano's theory of the intensity of sense qualities but rejects its transposition to mental acts. He argues that this doctrine has a number of absurd consequences and thus ought to be rejected.

One of the consequences of Brentano's theory is that some judgements have intensity, namely those judgements (and only those) that are directed to an object that is presented to the mind through sense perception. Ehrenfels points out: According to Brentano, if I close my eyes and judge (nonsensorily, merely conceptually) that there is a cup on the table in front of me, then this judgement does not have any intensity at all. If, however, I open my eyes, perceive the cup und judge again that there is a cup on the table (only this time on the basis of sense perception), then

> this judgement has intensity, even the highest conceivable degree of intensity—since the colour appearance fills out the space of sensation all-over!—If I hear, on the other hand, a swelling sound, which I affirm at the same time, then, together with the sound also my judging is swelling!—To me it seems that these consequences suffice to be permitted to consider Brentano's theory of the mental intensities as disproved.
>
> (Ehrenfels 1988d: 102)

A further consequence of Brentano's theory is that the intensity of an emotion that is directed toward something presented through sense perception is proportional to the intensity of the respective sensation. Ehrenfels argues that this doctrine contradicts empirical evidence. Imagine you spend your holidays in a holiday home that is situated directly at a rustling beck. At the beginning, the rustling may be felt as pleasurable; after a while, the feeling of pleasure may become attenuated and even be reversed into displeasure; still later, it may be that the sense quality does not raise any feelings anymore, because of habituation. Furthermore, Ehrenfels asks the reader to compare the emotions related to various unpleasant smells. He argues that a faint smell of rotten fish (i.e., a sense quality with very low intensity) may be object of a more intense feeling of displeasure than an intense smell of fresh tar (Ehrenfels 1988d: 102).

A third consequence of Brentano's theory is that emotions that are directed at mere conceptual (nonsensory) contents lack any intensity. This too, Ehrenfels argues, contradicts empirical evidence:

> For this we shall hardly allow to be disputed that the grief over the death of a close relative is, in the most genuine and proper sense, stronger than the light emotional wave that may be raised when, for instance, we tread down, inadvertently, a beautiful beetle.
>
> (Ehrenfels 1988d: 105)

Ehrenfels believes that presentations and judgements in general lack intensity (no matter whether they are sensory or merely conceptual). On the other hand, Ehrenfels cannot bring himself to deny intensity to emotions. By this, together with two further assumptions, Ehrenfels finds himself led into a dilemma. The two further assumptions are, first, that Brentano's theory of intensity of *sense qualities* is correct, and, second, that all phenomena of intensity must be explained in an analogous way. That is, as Ehrenfels sees it, the explication of the intensity of mental phenomena cannot be fundamentally different from the explication of the intensity of sense qualities. Therefore, Ehrenfels sees himself confronted with—in his lights—two equally unpalatable consequences: Either Brentano's theory of intensity is erroneous *tout court* (i.e., not only for mental acts but also for sense qualities) or emotions lack intensity.

Ehrenfels discusses a radical third option, namely to consider emotions no longer as mental but as *physical* phenomena. Although he is aware that this is quite an unorthodox view, he takes this option seriously. In the final resort, however, he cannot bring himself to adopt it. The dilemma remains unresolved (Ehrenfels 1988d: 108–11).

Ehrenfels on Brentano's Theory of Preferring and Adequate Emotions

Ehrenfels continues his criticism of Brentano's theory of the intensity of mental phenomena in a fragmentary and only posthumously published writing entitled "Fragen und Einwände an die Adresse der Anhänger von Franz Brentanos Ethik" ("Questions and objections addressed to the adherents of Franz Brentano's ethics"). He points out that Brentano's doctrine that emotions that are not directed at sensory objects lack intensity entails difficulties relevant also for ethical concerns: In folk psychology, it seems natural to say that we love or hate *A* more than *B*. It suggests itself to interpret phenomena of this kind as cases of bigger intensity of the respective love or hate. But this is not open to Brentano, since he considers nonsensory emotions as void of intensity. To fill this gap, Brentano introduces a further kind of mental phenomenon, namely the act of *preferring* (*Vorziehen*): for a person *S* to love *A* more than *B* means that *S* prefers *A* to *B*, where preferring itself is supposed to be an act of love of a certain kind (Brentano 1889, §§ 29–31, see Chapter 20; Ehrenfels 1988e: 208).

To this, Ehrenfels raises several objections. First, he observes that sometimes one prefers a lesser evil to a bigger one. In such cases, evidently no love at all is involved. As a remedy to this, Ehrenfels proposes to assume an additional act, which is contrary to the act of preferring, namely, the act of "subordinating" (*Nachsetzen*). Thus, if I have to choose between *A* and *B*, where I hate both of them, and I choose *A*, then I would not prefer *A* to *B* but rather subordinate *B* to *A*, where subordinating is a kind of hate (Ehrenfels 1988e: 211).

Second, Ehrenfels points out that there are cases where one chooses between two alternatives, where one of them is emotionally indifferent, that is, is neither loved nor hated. It may be, for instance, that I hate *A* but that I am indifferent to *B*. In this case, I surely would prefer *B*, although I do not love *B*. This case, too, could be explained as a case of subordinating (Ehrenfels 1988e: 211).

So far, Ehrenfels has proposed just slight modifications of and additions to Brentano's doctrine, which seem to fit nicely with Brentano's basic tenets. However, Ehrenfels claims to have a more fundamental objection up his sleeve. He wants to show that

> even the assumption of those phenomena of preferring (and perhaps also subordinating) does not release one of the necessity to explain the result of a choice between two "loved" (or "hated") objects from the *bigger strength* of the "love" or the "hate" to an object, in contrast to the other—only that, if one refuses to relate this bigger strength to the manifest act of "love" or "hate", one has to stick with the *disposition* to those acts, which are (as manifest acts) considered as void of intensity.
>
> (Ehrenfels 1988e: 211f.)

Roughly, one might sum up Ehrenfels' reasoning as follows. If I have to choose between two objects A and B (which I both love), and I pick A, it would suggest itself to explain my choice by saying that I love A more than B. Brentano (who denies that love and hate come in degrees) offers an alternative explanation: I choose A just because I have the *disposition to prefer A to B*. Naturally, according to Brentano, this disposition cannot be based on the disposition to love A more than B; the disposition to prefer A to B is not further analysable. But if this disposition is not further analysable, it becomes a miracle why there are systematic relations between our preferences, such as: if one has the disposition to prefer A to B and the disposition to prefer B to C, then one has also the disposition to prefer A to C. These systematic relations between preferences call for an explanation, and, as Ehrenfels sees it, the only explanation available is that my disposition to desire A is stronger than my disposition to desire B. The upshot of the argument is that Brentano and his followers have to accept, if not degrees of intensity of manifest acts, at least degrees of intensity of *dispositions* of emotions or desires (Ehrenfels 1988e: 212f.). Even if one hesitates to follow Ehrenfels through all the steps of the argument, he seems right to point out that the doctrine of the unanalysability of preferring raises an explanatory gap.

Ehrenfels also attacks Brentano's notorious doctrine of "love (hate) with the character of correctness" (*als richtig charakterisierte Liebe/als richtig charakterisierter Hass*). To have the character of correctness is, according to Brentano, an *intrinsic* feature of emotional acts; it is analogous to the feature of *evidence* in the domain of judgements (Brentano 1889, §27). This doctrine is the foundation of Brentano's objectivist theory of values:

> This feature is, according to Brentano, the psychological substratum for the construction of the absolute value concept. Valuable or good in itself is thus that which can be loved with a love which exhibits the character of correctness, bad in itself that which can be hated with a hate which exhibits the character of correctness, the better of two objects is the one which can be preferred to the other with an act of preferring which exhibits the character of correctness.
>
> (Ehrenfels 1988e: 213)

Ehrenfels expresses doubts about the feature of having the character of correctness (Ehrenfels 1988e: 214). Moreover, in a marginal note, Ehrenfels raises an epistemic problem for Brentano's doctrine: If a person does not have a particular feeling (e.g., compassion), how could she come to know that it would be right to have it?

> Are we able to recognize the "having of the character of correctness" of an emotional phenomenon from its mere presentation, or is it necessary, to this end, to experience it in reality?—How comes a man who does not have charity to realise that it would have the character of correctness if he had it?
>
> (Ehrenfels 1988e: 216)

After having delineated Ehrenfels' most important contributions to philosophy (which belong to the fields of philosophical psychology and theory of value), I have presented those passages within Ehrenfels' work in which he explicitly deals with Brentano. Ehrenfels' stance toward Brentano is appropriately respectful but at the same time articulately critical throughout. Brentano's influence on Ehrenfels is most obvious in his philosophical psychology; here, the divergences between the two philosophers are relatively minor, concerning details rather than basic tenets. In the field of value theory, however, there is deep disagreement: Ehrenfels' value theory is irreconcilable with Brentano's ethical objectivism.[7]

NOTES

1. For detailed biographical information on Ehrenfels, see Fabian 1986. For an introduction to Ehrenfels' sexual ethics, philosophy of mathematics and metaphysics, see Rollinger and Ierna 2015. The latter source contains also hints to online resources of works by Ehrenfels.
2. For a complete list of Ehrenfels' publications, see Ehrenfels 1990.
3. It appeared first in 1890 and was reprinted in 1922. The version from 1922 contains an additional section, "Continuing remarks" (*Weiterführende Bemerkungen*). The version from 1890 has been translated into English. In what follows, I shall refer to the English version (Ehrenfels 1988f) as far as it goes. References to the "continuing remarks" are, perforce, to the German version (Ehrenfels 1988c).
4. This and all other translations that follow are by M. E. R.
5. At first sight, this claim seems obviously wrong, for surely one may desire a thing if one is convinced of its existence—as long as one does not *possess* it. However, this objection would be based on a misunderstanding of Meinong's position, because, for Meinong, if one desires to possess a thing x, the object of desire is not x but the *possession of x*. This seems to be right: if I firmly believe that I possess x, I cannot desire anymore to possess x.
6. However, in the *Psychology*, Brentano advocated a different view on this matter. See Brentano 1973a, Book Two, Chap. VII. (I owe this hint to Uriah Kriegel.)
7. For many helpful comments to previous versions of this paper I owe thanks to Uriah Kriegel, Johann Christian Marek, Nicola Mößner and Rochus Sowa.

31

Husserl and Brentano

Dermot Moran

1 INTRODUCTION: BRENTANO AS MENTOR TO HUSSERL

In this chapter, I discuss Franz Brentano's influence on the Moravian-born philosopher Edmund Husserl (1859–1938), founder of phenomenology and mentor of Martin Heidegger, among other notable twentieth-century philosophers (Moran 2005). The main areas of Brentano's influence on Husserl include: the ideal of exact scientific philosophy leading to essential definitions and a priori laws (Husserl's *strenge Wissenschaft*); the adoption of a mereological compositional analysis in the dissection of philosophical problems; the project for "descriptive psychology" (also called by both "phenomenology") of the essences of conscious acts (perception, imagination, memory, etc.) and their interdependency (i.e., relations of founding); and problems concerning the nature of time-consciousness, especially the nature of the awareness of past experiences.

Husserl's relationship with Brentano was complex and many-sided. It extended over a long period—from 1884 (when Husserl first began to attend Brentano's lectures in Vienna) up until shortly before Brentano's death in March 1917, as evidenced by the correspondence between them (Husserl 1994b, I: 3–59). In his Vienna years, Husserl even accompanied Brentano on his vacations. Later, they would occasionally meet up, until their last encounter in 1908. According to the reminiscences of his doctoral student Maria Brück, Husserl had declared in 1932: "without Brentano I could not have written a word of philosophy" (Brück 1933: 3; quoted in Varga 2015: 96). At their 1908 meeting, however, Husserl reported that he had the sense that they no longer understood each other (Hill 1998: 164).

Husserl's correspondence with Brentano is both scientific and respectful and courteous in tone, with Husserl always honoring his master and Brentano asserting (e.g., in a letter of 1904) that the role of the teacher is to be a father figure (Husserl 1994b, I: 23). They discussed not just logic and psychology and technical issues in mathematics and geometry, such as the nature of the continuum (Brentano 1976/1988b), but also professional and family matters, for example the birth of Husserl's children, his long years as *Privatdozent*, and his promotion to full professor in 1905.

Brentano would send Husserl his publications, for example *Über die Zukunft der Philosophie* (*On the Future of Philosophy*, Brentano 1893a), sent in 1892; and, in return, Husserl sent Brentano his publications, notably *Philosophy of Arithmetic* (sent in 1891) and *Logical Investigations* (sent in 1900). In his last extant letter to Husserl (dated April 30, 1916), Brentano sent his condolences, from Geneva, on the death of Husserl's son, killed in the Great War, and he also wished Husserl well on his new professorship in Freiburg (Husserl 1994b, I: 56). Interestingly, the one topic they do *not* address in their correspondence is *intentionality*, although later Husserl would credit Brentano with the rediscovery of this concept, while conceding that Brentano never grasped its true significance nor possessed the method to investigate it properly.

Even after he left Brentano and Vienna in 1886, Husserl diligently collected the transcripts of Brentano's lectures, such as his *Descriptive Psychology* lectures of 1887–91 (Brentano 1982/1995b) and his investigation of the senses, as well as his studies of fantasy, memory, and judgment, which Husserl discussed in his *Phantasy, Image Consciousness and Memory* (1898–1925) lectures (Husserl 1980/2005). Brentano's analysis of time-consciousness, including his peculiar view that recollection of the past must be construed as a kind of fantasy, is also discussed critically by Husserl, in his 1905 lectures *On the Phenomenology of the Consciousness of Internal Time* (Husserl 1966/1990). Husserl sharply distinguishes acts of memory from any kind of fantasy representation.

Almost from the very beginning (c. 1890), however, Husserl was explicitly critical of many aspects of Brentano's philosophical outlook, including Brentano's conception of logic as an art of reasoning (*Kunstlehre*) and his attempt to explain all forms of number in terms of authentic and inauthentic presentations. Furthermore, Husserl's discovery of the phenomenological reduction and his explicit embrace of transcendental philosophy after 1907 meant that he thenceforth characterized Brentano as a naturalist whose project could never be realized because it missed the very essence of consciousness (Hill 1998). In his transcendental philosophy, Husserl also restored the transcendental ego to a central place in his phenomenological psychology, whereas Brentano remained a Humean in disregarding the ego as an item in consciousness and preferred to speak only of the "unity of consciousness."

In fact, despite his criticisms, it took Husserl many years to extract himself from under the shadow of Brentano. As he wrote in a very late letter to his American student Marvin Farber on June 18, 1937 (he died the following April):

> Even though I began in my youth as an enthusiastic admirer [*als begeisterter Verehrer*] of Brentano, I must admit that I deluded myself, for too long, and in a way hard to understand now, into believing that I was a co-worker [*Mitarbeiter*] on his philosophy, especially his psychology. But in truth, my way of thinking was a totally different one [*eine total andere*] from that of Brentano, already in my first work, namely the *Habilitation* work of 1887.
>
> (Husserl 1994b, IV: 82; Cho 1990: 36)

Husserl's intellectual stance toward the whole Brentano School was one of steadfast independence (e.g., Husserl and Meinong were somewhat testy rivals, Rollinger 1999:

124–60). Nevertheless, it has been suggested that Husserl was perhaps over-assiduous in his praise for his former teacher, to the point of having exaggerated his influence on him.

2 HUSSERL'S STUDIES IN VIENNA WITH BRENTANO (1884–1886)

Husserl originally studied mathematics at the University of Berlin under Karl Weierstrass (1815–1897), who was renowned for his success in arithmetizing analysis. According to his wife Malvine's recollection, Husserl claimed Weierstrass instilled in him the "ethos for scientific striving" (M. Husserl 1988: 122). Weierstrass' lectures on the theory of functions awoke Husserl's interest in the foundations of mathematics such that he would later write in 1929 that he hoped to do for philosophy what Weierstrass had done for arithmetic, that is, set it on a single foundation (Schuhmann 1977: 344–5). In deference to his father, who believed that an Austrian degree might improve his son's chances of employment (Schuhmann 1977: 9)—as his wife Malvine confirmed in her reminiscences (M. Husserl 1988: 112)—Husserl transferred to the University of Vienna to study mathematics in 1881, and there he completed his doctoral degree in 1882 with a dissertation on differential calculus, *Beiträge zur Theorie der Variationsrechnung* [*Contributions to the Theory of the Calculus of Variations*, unpublished], supervised by the mathematician Leopold Königsberger (1837–1921), a disciple of Weierstrass'. Until that time, Husserl had little exposure to philosophy during his university years (the philosophy courses he did attend did not make a lasting impact), until his friend Tomas Masaryk (1850–1937), then a *Privatdozent* in philosophy in Vienna, persuaded him to attend Franz Brentano's lectures in Vienna, which were making a stir at the time.

Husserl arrived in Vienna having completed his military service there and went on to spend two years (1884–1886) there, attending Brentano's lectures in particular (but see Varga 2015, who emphasizes Robert Zimmermann). Masaryk and Husserl attended Brentano's seminar on Hume's *Essay on Human Understanding* (Schuhmann 1977: 14). Husserl was particularly drawn to Brentano's efforts to reform classical Aristotelian logic in his 1884–85 lecture course *Die elementare Logik und die in ihr nötigen Reformen* [*Elementary Logic and its Necessary Reform*]. As Husserl wrote: "Brentano's pre-eminent and admirable strength was in logical theory" (McCormick and Elliston 1981: 345; Husserl 1986: 309). Late in life, Husserl was still crediting Brentano, for instance in his *Crisis of European Sciences* §68, "for the fact that he [Brentano] began his attempt to reform psychology with an investigation of the peculiar characteristics of the mental (in contrast to the physical) and showed intentionality to be one of these characteristics; the science of 'mental phenomena' then has to do everywhere with conscious experiences" (Husserl 1954: 236/1970a: 233–4).

Husserl would discuss, in his own lectures on ethics and value theory (*Vorlesungen über Ethik und Wertlehre*, Husserl 1988a), delivered between 1908 and 1914, Brentano's conception of value theory based on Brentano's lectures on "Practical Philosophy" (*Praktische Philosophie*, winter semester 1884) that he had audited in Vienna (and which rejected Kant's categorical imperative as a foundation for morality and replaced it with "do the best one can") (Husserl 1988a: 90, 221). Brentano drew a structural parallel between acts of judgment and acts of feeling and willing in terms of their object-directedness. But Husserl departed from Brentano in thinking (with Kant) that the moral good is produced by the good will. Subsequently, in *Ideas* I (Husserl 1977: 323 n.1/2014: 278 n.13), Husserl will cite Brentano's *Vom Ursprung sittlicher Erkenntnis* (Brentano 1889/1969). Husserl and Brentano both agreed on the need for a formal axiology. Husserl also attended Brentano's 1885–86 course "Selected Questions from Psychology and Aesthetics" (*Ausgewählte Fragen aus Psychologie und Ästhetik*) and later in a letter to Brentano of March 27, 1905, recalled that these lectures helped him to reflect on the relation between perception and fantasy. Husserl will resist Brentano's view that memory of the past is actually a kind of fantasy.

As Husserl later recorded in his "Recollections of Franz Brentano," written in 1917 (McCormick and Elliston 1981; Husserl 1986), it was Brentano's commitment to rigorous descriptive philosophy that inspired Husserl to abandon mathematics for a career as a philosopher. He wrote:

> Brentano's lectures gave me for the first time the conviction that encouraged me to choose philosophy as my life's work, the conviction that philosophy too was a serious discipline which also could be and must be dealt with in the spirit of the strictest science.
> (McCormick and Elliston 1981: 343; Husserl 1986: 305)

Husserl embraced Brentano's passion for exact philosophical analysis, which he equated with the analytical rigor of Weierstrass. Both were interested in foundational issues in mathematics. Husserl also initially adopted Brentano's conception of the stages of evolution of philosophy (from exact philosophy to its decline into skepticism and mysticism) as explicated in his *Die vier Phasen der Philosophie* ("The Four Stages of Philosophy," Brentano 1895a/1998). All great periods of growth in philosophy (Aristotle, Aquinas, Descartes) are characterized by the presence of the *purely theoretical interest*, before practical interests emerge (e.g., Stoics); thirdly, there is an age of skepticism; and finally, the emergence of mysticism (e.g., Schelling, Hegel). Thus Husserl inherited from Brentano—and from Masaryk—a general suspicion of German Idealism (including Kant) and a strong appreciation of British empiricism (especially Berkeley and Hume, both of whom are discussed in Husserl's Second Logical Investigation; Husserl, however, was more critical of John Stuart Mill, whom Brentano admired).

Husserl was particularly taken with Brentano's project for a descriptive analysis of the essential features of consciousness as given in his *Psychology from an Empirical Standpoint*. In his *Amsterdam Lectures* of 1928, commenting on the situation at the beginning of the twentieth century, he writes of the efforts of scientists like Ernst Mach to offer a theory-free description of phenomena:

> Parallel to this we find in certain psychologists, and first in Brentano, a systematic effort to create a rigorously scientific psychology on the basis of pure internal experience and the rigorous description of its data ("*Psychognosia*").
> (Husserl 1977: 212–3)

Clearly, Husserl's conception of descriptive psychology came directly from Brentano, and he possessed a manuscript of Brentano's lectures on *Descriptive Psychology* (1887–91). "Psychognosy" was one of Brentano's terms, along with "descriptive phenomenology" for descriptive psychology (see Brentano 1982: 128–9/1995b: 137).

3 HUSSERL'S *PHILOSOPHY OF ARITHMETIC*: A BRENTANIAN ANALYSIS OF GENUINE AND NONGENUINE PRESENTATIONS OF NUMBER

Because of his precarious position as a *Privatdozent* at the University of Vienna (Brentano was a laicized priest but his subsequent marriage violated the Church–State concordat, so he had to resign his chair in 1880 and was demoted to *Privatdozent* and never reinstated), Brentano was unable to take on Husserl for his *Habilitation* studies. Instead, in 1886, he recommended Husserl to his friend and former student Carl Stumpf (1848–1936) (Schuhmann 1977: 17)—and, *nota bene*, not to the only other professor of philosophy at Vienna, Robert Zimmerman—at the University of Halle. There, Husserl attended Stumpf's lectures on "Psychology" (winter semester 1886–87), where Stumpf discussed the relations between perception and fantasy.

Husserl seems initially to have accepted from Brentano that mathematics and hence logic could somehow be founded on or grounded in psychology (Husserl 1975: xvii–xxi). In the autumn of 1887, Husserl published (it was printed but never circulated) his *Habilitation On the Concept of Number* (Ierna 2005). Four years later, he published *Philosophy of Arithmetic. Logical and Psychological Investigations* (Husserl 1970b/2003), which contained the *Habilitation* thesis, and aimed, following Brentano, at the clarification of arithmetical concepts by elucidating their "psychological origin." In both works, Husserl applied Brentanian descriptive psychology to arithmetic by identifying the essential mental acts involved in the formation of the concept of number. His basic principle, which was also Brentano's, was that "no concept can be thought without a foundation [*Fundierung*] in a concrete intuition" (Husserl 1970b: 79/2003: 83), a view he would maintain throughout his life (e.g., see Husserl 1985: 46–7). He was seeking the "origin" (*Ursprung*) or *source* (*Quelle*) of "mathematical presentations [*Vorstellungen*]," as he later put it in the foreword to his *Logical Investigations*, based on the testimony of "inner experience" (*innere Erfahrung*, Husserl 1970b: 66/2003: 69), for instance, in regard to the manner certain kinds of relations are intuitively apprehended. According to Husserl, the concept of number is derived from the concept of "collective combination" (*kollektive Verbindung*, Husserl 1970b: 20/2003: 21), which is a fundamental relation of a new kind, which he will call—following Brentano—a "mental" relation. Husserl is invoking a modified version of Brentano's distinction between the "physical" and the "mental" (1970b: 68/2003: 70 n.1). As he puts it, his descriptive psychology seeks to gain insight from the experienced phenomena themselves (1970b: 22/2003: 23) and makes careful distinctions, for instance, between a presentation of a *temporal series* and a *temporal presentation* of a series (1970b: 27/2003: 28). Similarly, Husserl claims that a representation of a multiplicity involves the recognition that the elements of the multiple are distinct from one another but that the *differences themselves* need not be explicitly noticed. Many years later, in his *Formale und transzendentale Logik* (*Formal and Transcendental Logic*, 1929), Husserl described his early efforts in the *Philosophy of Arithmetic* as follows:

> presented an initial attempt to go back to the spontaneous activities of collecting and counting, in which collections ("sums," "sets") and cardinal numbers are given in the manner characteristic of something that is being generated *originaliter*, and thereby to gain clarity [*Klarheit*] respecting the proper, the authentic, sense of the

concepts fundamental to the theory of sets and of cardinal numbers. It was therefore, in my later terminology, a phenomenologico-constitutional investigation.
(Husserl 1974: 90–1/1969: 86–7)

Brentano had distinguished generally between what he termed "genuine" or "authentic" (*eigentlich*) presentations, where the object is directly given; and nongenuine, "inauthentic," or "symbolic" (*uneigentlich, symbolisch*) presentations, where the object is referred to in some kind of indirect, empty, or symbolic manner. According to Brentano, large numbers and irrational numbers as well as concepts like God are given in such inauthentic presentations. Husserl took over this distinction in his *Philosophy of Arithmetic*, which is divided into two parts: Part One, "The Genuine Concepts of Unity, Plurality, and Number"; Part Two, the *symbolic* or *inauthentic* intuitions of higher numbers. Authentic or genuine presentations present the object as it appears directly in the intuition (Husserl's example is the house I actually see before me), in the flesh, as it were, whereas I have a merely symbolic or inauthentic intuition of a house described to me as the house on the corner of such and such a street (Husserl 1970b: 193/2003: 205).

For Husserl, it is a matter of fact that humans apprehend groups or collections of objects. The question is, how does the apprehension of a definite multiplicity get converted into the apprehension of a number, for example three? Perceived objects must be treated as "items" (all other characteristics are ignored) and then colligated in an ordered way. His second problem was how the mathematician can proceed from numbers given in full intuition (very small numbers such as one can count on one's fingers) to knowledge of higher numbers (e.g., millions) that cannot be given intuitively. Only a small set of numbers can be intuitively apprehended in a genuine manner. Indeed, in his 1887 *Habilitation* defense, Husserl lists as one of the theses he will defend in his oral examination or *rigorosum*: "One can hardly count beyond three in the authentic sense" (1970b: 339/2003: 357).

Almost as soon as *Philosophy of Arithmetic* was published, Husserl had abandoned his attempt to found arithmetic on the notions of authentic presentations and inauthentic presentations. As he acknowledges in a recently discovered 1889 letter to Brentano, he could not make sense of all of arithmetic with the concept of inauthentic presentations:

> I had great difficulties with the full understanding of the logical character of the system of signs of the *arithmetica universalis*, with its negative and imaginary, rational and irrational numbers. The matter is not so simple that everything could be completely settled with the concept of amount and the theory of improper presenting.
> (Ierna 2015: 67)

Over the next 10 years, at Halle, Husserl turned toward the descriptive psychological investigation of the foundations of logic, culminating in his next major publication, *Logical Investigations* (Husserl 1975, 1984/2001).

4 HUSSERL'S 1900 *PROLEGOMENA*: IS BRENTANO THE TARGET OF HIS CRITIQUE OF PSYCHOLOGISM?

Ten years after the *Philosophy of Arithmetic*, Husserl published his *Logical Investigations*, the first volume of which, entitled *Prolegomena to a Pure Logic* (1900) (Husserl

1975/2001), was devoted to an extensive refutation of psychologism—the view that logical concepts and operations can be explained fully in terms of psychological concepts and operations. In particular, Husserl criticizes a prevailing conception of logic as a "technique" or "art" of reasoning, a *Kunstlehre* (a view espoused by Brentano), and instead advocates a conception of logic as a pure and formal discipline entirely independent of psychology (Husserl emphasizes this point in his letter to Brentano of January 3, 1905, Husserl 1994b, I: 27). Husserl mentions here that he is inspired in particular by Bolzano. It is clear from Brentano's 1905 letters to Husserl (as well as Brentano's ongoing discussions with his other students) that he felt this attack on psychologism was personally directed at him. Brentano insists that what Husserl calls psychologism is really the ancient relativism of Protagoras, which Brentano has always opposed (see his letter to Husserl of January 9, 1905, Husserl 1994b, I: 34). Although, in his letter of March 27, 1905, Husserl reassures Brentano that his *Prolegomena* was "not directed against you and your students" (Husserl 1994b, I: 39), this seems somewhat duplicitous, as he had earlier indicated in a letter of January 21, 1897, to Paul Natorp that, in the book he was writing, he was targeting "the subjective-psychologizing tendency of the logic of our time (and also against the standpoint that I, as one of Brentano's students, earlier held" (Husserl 1994b, V: 43). Nevertheless, Husserl reassures Brentano that he has always felt and called himself his student (1994b, I: 39). Somewhat later, in 1907, Husserl's student Johannes Daubert tried to reconcile them (Rollinger 1999: 17 n.1). Husserl himself states in the foreword to the first edition:

> The course of my development has led to my drawing apart, as regards basic logical convictions, from men and writings to whom I owe most of my philosophical education.
>
> (Husserl 1975: 7/2001, I: 2)

He goes on to quote Goethe to the effect that one opposes most strongly the errors one has just abandoned (Husserl 1975: 7/2001, I: 3). This surely was aimed at Brentano, although Brentano is mentioned only once in the *Prolegomena*, in a list of logicians that includes Sigwart, Schuppe, and Überweg (Husserl 1975: 48/2001, I: 31). Subsequently, in his 1911 *Von der Klassification der psychischen Phänomene* (*On the Classification of Psychic Phenomena*), Brentano protested against "the charge of psychologism" that certain of his students were making against him and mentions his friendly relations with Husserl (Brentano 1995a: 306). Brentano is insistent that not only was he never psychologistic but that he always fought against such "absurd subjectivism" (Brentano 1995a: 306).

5 HUSSERL'S *LOGICAL INVESTIGATIONS*: THE CRITIQUE OF BRENTANIAN DESCRIPTIVE PSYCHOLOGY

The second volume (1901) of the *Logical Investigations* is devoted to descriptive psychological or phenomenological investigations that are heavily influenced by Brentano and Stumpf (especially the Third Investigation on parts and wholes, which develops from Brentano's distinction between separable and distinguishable parts). In the Introduction, Husserl explicitly mentions that Brentano's "attempted reform of formal logic" exaggerated the connection between grammar and logic by excluding many logical concepts as merely grammatical (Husserl 1984: 19/2001, I: 173) and in the First Investigation §3, he acknowledges taking over Brentano's language of "motivation" but distinguishes it from "causation" (1984: 35/2001, I: 186).

An extended critique of Brentano's classification of physical and mental phenomena is found Husserl's Fifth Logical Investigation, and subsequently there is an analysis of judgment in the Sixth Investigation that is a total rejection of the Brentanian account (where judgment is an affirmation or negation of a presentation) (Jacquette 2004: 45–65). Finally, Husserl adds a long appendix to the Sixth Investigation, in which he engages in a detailed critique of Brentano's distinction between inner and outer perception.

In *Logical Investigations*, then, Husserl grappled directly and critically with Brentano's descriptive psychology, his distinction between outer and inner perception, his distinction between physical and mental "acts," his division of the three fundamental classes of psychic acts (presentations, judgments, phenomena of love and hate), and just about every aspect of Brentano's contribution and nomenclature. Husserl is deliberately and emphatically marking his difference from Brentano in terms of all the latter's key conceptions, including his analysis of the nature of presentations, of the intentional relation, and of intentional contents and objects. Indeed, so radical is Husserl's critique that it is difficult to see how anything remains of Brentanian descriptive psychology, especially after 1903, when Husserl rejected the very notion that phenomenology was descriptive psychology; and even more so after 1907, when he discovered the phenomenological reduction.

In the Fifth Investigation §9, Husserl himself refers to his "deviations" from Brentano (1984: 378n/2001, II: 353 n.1), his "departures" (*Abweichungen*) from his master's "convictions" (*Überzeugungen*) and technical "vocabulary" (Fifth Investigation §11). In the Sixth Investigation, moreover, Husserl says he wants to distinguish "what is indubitably significant in Brentano's thought-motivation from what is erroneous in its elaboration" (1984: 760/2001, II: 340). Husserl refines Brentano's account of mental acts and the inner structure of intentional experiences both by questioning its consistency and conceptual sense and especially through a recourse to what he claims is evidence given immediately in intuition (something on which he puts greater stress in the 1913 second edition or "B-Edition," e.g., in the paragraphs added to Fifth Investigation §27).

Husserl wants to challenge Brentano's fundamental notion that "presentations" (*Vorstellungen*) are a distinct class of psychic acts that are found nested or embedded in all other acts. Instead, he wants to argue that each class of "objectivating acts" has its own kind of objectual intending, leading to a completely different construal of intentionality and of the essential relations between intentional acts.

Husserl's focus is on the *inner essential structure* of intentional acts, their contents and objects, independent of all reference to real mental episodes with their causal structure and interconnections and focused solely on their ideal, a priori conceptual interconnections. He criticizes Brentano's account of the intentional relation; it is not a relation between two "real" (*reale*) things, that is, a consciousness and a thing. Nor is it a psycho–physical relation, nor are we dealing with an act and its content, a sort of "box-within-a-box" view (*wie eine Ineinanderschachtelung*, Husserl 1984: 371/2001, II: 98). Intentionality is neither a real relation nor a psychological relation (as he will repeat in *Ideas* I §36). It is a relation *sui generis*, a claim that continues to puzzle commentators.

Perhaps most famously, in the Fifth Investigation, Husserl rejects the Brentanian conception of the "intentional inexistence of the object" and especially its supposed immanence in the mental act. Husserl maintained that Brentano's true discovery was that intentionality had the specific character of "relating beyond itself." In the Second Investigation (1984: 168–9/2001, I: 384–5), he had already introduced the idea that the central feature of consciousness was its *intending* (*Vermeinen, Intention*) character and had already stated there that objects are not in consciousness as in a box (an image that is repeated over and over by Husserl; see, for example, *Formal and Transcendental Logic* §94).

According to Husserl, if we were to dissect the mental act of thinking the God Jupiter, the God Jupiter would not be found inside that thought in any real sense:

> The "immanent," "mental object" is not therefore part of the descriptive or real make-up [*Bestand*] of the experience, it is in truth not really immanent or mental. But it also does not exist extramentally, it does not exist at all.
> (Husserl 1984: 373/2001, II: 99)

Husserl also wants to distinguish sensations from the objects of intentional acts. Sensations are felt, but they are part of the phenomenality of the intentional act itself. One does not directly apprehend sensations as objects of intentions. Husserl says: "I see a thing, e.g., this box, but I do not see my sensations" (1984: 396/2001, II: 104). He goes on to explain that sensations are taken up and arranged through some kind of act of apprehension (*Auffassung*). One perceives objects; one experiences or undergoes sensations. Husserl had thereby clarified the domain of "presentations" that Brentano left in a confused state.

In the appendix to the Sixth Investigation, Husserl is critical of Brentano's conception of inner experience as an area of apodictic certainty (Moran 2000b). For Husserl, contra Brentano, not every perception of a mental episode is given with "self-evidence" (*Evidenz*). Some bodily experiences, for instance, can present with bodily locations (e.g., a toothache or a pain in the stomach), which can be mistaken (Husserl 1984: 240/2001, II: 346).

6 HUSSERL'S MOVE FROM BRENTANIAN DESCRIPTIVE PSYCHOLOGY TO TRANSCENDENTAL PHENOMENOLOGY

Soon after *Logical Investigations* appeared, Husserl began to revise his conception of descriptive psychology in a way that moved him further from Brentano, whom he increasingly believed remained caught up in empirical psychology. He now proposes to distinguish between his phenomenology as a "pure theory of essences" (*reine Wesenslehre*) and descriptive psychology. Most notably, in his *Bericht über deutsche Schriften zur Logik in den Jahren 1895–1899* ("A Report on German Writings in Logic From the Years 1895–1899"), he repudiates his initial characterization of the work as a set of investigations in "descriptive psychology" and proclaims that phenomenology "views that which, in the strongest sense, is given: lived experience, just as it is in itself" (Husserl 1979: 207/1994a: 251).

After 1907, Husserl's thought took a transcendental turn, and he introduced the *epoché* and phenomenological reduction as necessary steps to uncover the essence of the life of consciousness, thus putting himself permanently at a distance from Brentanian descriptive psychology. Husserl now describes intentionality in terms of *noesis* and *noema*, as became evident in *Ideas* I (1913) (Moran 2015).

Alongside *Ideas* I, Husserl also publishes a partially revised second edition of the *Logical Investigations* in 1913, in which he highlights the central discovery of *phenomenology* as an eidetic science that brackets actuality. Thus, invoking his 1903 essay (Husserl 1975: 13), Husserl claims that the chief error of the 1901 edition was to call phenomenology a "descriptive psychology," whereas in fact, phenomenology knows nothing of personal experiences, of a self, or of others; similarly, it neither sets itself questions, nor answers them, nor makes hypotheses. In 1903, he had claimed that this purely immanent phenomenology was to be free of all suppositions about the nature of the psychological and, furthermore, it would actually provide a critique of knowledge that might then be used as a basis for empirical psychology or other sciences. But, in itself, phenomenology is not identical with descriptive psychology (Husserl 1979: 206–7/1994a: 251). This phenomenological approach rather brings to evidence the general essences of the concepts and laws of logic. While both descriptive psychology and phenomenology are a priori disciplines, phenomenology cuts all its ties with individual minds and real mental processes, even those understood in the most exemplary manner (Husserl 1984: 14/2001, I: 170, added in the second edition). The revisions of the second edition constantly underscore the pure a priori, eidetic character of phenomenology. In keeping with his new transcendental orientation, Husserl has more appreciation in the second edition of "the pure ego" (*das reine Ich*) of the Neo-Kantians (especially Paul Natorp), which he had originally dismissed as an unnecessary postulate for the unification of consciousness (Husserl 1984: 374/2001, II: 92).

Ideas I offers a new account of intentionality that moves decisively away from Brentano by rejecting the language of mental acts, contents, and objects in favor of the noetic–noematic structure of intentional consciousness. Husserl still writes that Brentano's distinction between physical and mental phenomena was the starting point of his own analyses of intentionality:

> [A]lthough Brentano himself still remained quite far from the phenomenological terrain, and although, in the course of making this division, Brentano did not attain what he genuinely sought, namely, the division of the domains of experience [*Erfahrung*] of physical natural sciences and of psychology.... Brentano, to be sure, had not yet uncovered the concept of the inherent material aspect [*stoffliches Moment*]—and the reason he did not is that he did not account for the intrinsic division between "psychic phenomena" as inherent material aspects (data of sensation) and "physical phenomena" as inherent objective aspects (a thing's color, a thing's shape, and the like), appearing in the noetic grasp of the data of sensation. Nonetheless, he did manage to characterize the concept of "psychic phenomena" through the distinctiveness of intentionality.
> (Husserl 1977: 195/2014: 167)

Husserl offers (following on from *Logical Investigations*) a new distinction between the quality and matter of the act and tries to distinguish carefully between the sensuous content (hyletic data) in the act itself and the corresponding sensuous characteristics of the intended object. But the key difference from Brentano is that Husserl's new eidetic inquiry into the essence of intentional consciousness (and the a priori correlation between *noesis* and *noema*) is conducted under the phenomenological *epoché* and the concept of "bracketing" or "parenthesis" (*Einklammerung, Ideas* I §88, §94). Thus, Husserl writes:

> Not to be overlooked thereby is the phenomenological reduction [*die phänomenologische Reduktion*] that requires us "to bracket" ["*einzuklammern*"] [the actual process of] making the judgment, insofar we want to obtain just the pure noema of the experience of judgment.
>
> (Husserl 1977: 217/2014: 187)

Husserl now stresses that phenomenological description must be purified of everything empirical by the application of the phenomenological–transcendental *epoché*. All reference to actual existence must be bracketed, and the essential nature of conscious experiences and their objects must be examined in their phenomenological purity, uncontaminated by assumptions imported from the positive sciences. This leads the mature Husserl in *Ideas* I, and thereafter in *Formal and Transcendental Logic* (1929) and *Crisis of the European Sciences*, to reject what he regarded as Brentano's "naturalism." Husserl's mature transcendental phenomenology joined with contemporary Neo-Kantianism (represented by Heinrich Rickert) in being vigorously anti-naturalistic, regarding the project of the "naturalization of consciousness"—a phrase he himself presciently used—as at best a conceptual confusion and at worst a contradiction in terms. With regard to the assessment of Brentano as a naturalist, in his *Crisis of European Sciences*, Husserl wrote:

> Unfortunately, in the most essential matters he [Brentano] remained bound to the prejudices of the naturalistic tradition [*in den Vorurteilen der naturalistischen Tradition*].
>
> (Husserl 1954: 236/1970a: 234)

Similarly, in his 1928 *Amsterdam Lectures*, Husserl remarks that the "distinctive meaning and method needed for a pure analysis of consciousness remained hidden" from Brentano (Husserl 1968: 309/1994a: 219), again because of the prevailing "naturalization of the mental" that has pervaded twentieth-century philosophy and psychology.

Finally, Husserl widened the scope of intentionality in a radical new way. Already in the *Logical Investigations*, he had noted that in perception of a physical thing in space, one "profile" of the object was given directly and "in the flesh," surrounded by a "fringe" or "halo" of other possible profiles that were not so given. One sees the house from the front but is aware, in what Husserl calls and "empty intending," of the other sides of the house that are not immediately present. Every perceived object is given as having more sides than the one currently apprehended. This led Husserl to think of intentionality as including an awareness of "co-intended" horizons of the object. Indeed, Husserl believed he had made a great breakthrough—pushing decisively beyond Brentano—with his conception of horizon intentionality, which receives its first expression in *Ideas* §44. Thus Husserl remarks in his 1929 *Formal and Transcendental Logic*:

> Brentano's discovery of intentionality never led to seeing in it a complex of performances, which are included as sedimented history in the currently constituted

intentional unity and its current manners of givenness—a history that one can always uncover following a strict method.

(Husserl 1974: 251/1969: 245)

CONCLUSION

In conclusion, it is worth attempting to summarize Brentano's influence on Husserl. There is no doubt that Husserl promoted himself as someone who began philosophy inspired by the methodological vision and inspirational mentorship of Brentano. Brentano's focus on exact, descriptive analysis and the identification of general laws, including the practice of examining structures in terms of part–whole composition and in terms of relations of founding, remained a permanent inspiration to Husserl. However, Husserl himself went on to promote a form of transcendental phenomenology divorced from empirical psychology that was very remote from Brentano's intention. Although he always credited Brentano with making him realize the importance of intentionality for understanding the life of consciousness, he thought that Brentano lacked the conceptual tools (chiefly the reduction) to make proper use of it (Husserl 1939). Husserl felt that Brentano remained immersed in a naturalistic, empirical psychology and could not make the breakthrough to the phenomenological realm of pure essences. Moreover, in many other areas of influence—for example, in his conception of logic, or the nature of judgment, or the structure of time-consciousness, or the relation between memory and fantasy—Husserl quite explicitly opposed Brentano's position. Finally, Husserl included Brentano within the "naturalizing tendency" in philosophy that he himself saw as beginning with Locke but continuing in twentieth-century psychology and philosophy (e.g., Wilhelm Wundt) and to which he as a transcendental philosopher was vehemently opposed.

32

Twardowski and Brentano

Arianna Betti

1 INTRODUCTION

A student of Franz Brentano's in 1886–1895, Kazimierz Twardowski (1866–1938) was born in Vienna to a Polish family. His Polish roots and Brentano's teaching determined Twardowski's plans and future career virtually in full. When in 1895 Twardowski took up a position in Lvov—now Lviv, Ukraine, then a Polish-speaking university city in the Habsburg empire—he "felt a calling" to export Brentano's teaching onto Polish soil (Twardowski 1991: 26). Indeed, notwithstanding the value of Twardowski's original contribution as a philosopher (Betti and Raspa 2016: x), his most impressive achievement is uncontroversially considered to be his legacy as an organizer and educator in Poland, the establishment of the Lvov-Warsaw School (see Chapter 35).

At present, Twardowski's ideas and Brentano's influence upon them are undergoing a reassessment in the light of new translations and editions of works by both (Brentano EL 80, Twardowski 1894/95a, Twardowski, 1894/95b, Twardowski 2014). This newly available material shows that despite the important and disruptive changes Twardowski brought to Brentano's doctrines, some of which were of substantial influence upon other Brentanians, such as Meinong (Findlay 1963) and Husserl (Cavallin 1997), his intellectual debts to Brentano remain enormous. Moreover, it has been argued, some of Twardowski's main innovations, including the famous content/object distinction, were geared toward solving pressing difficulties arising from within Brentano's own framework (Betti 2013).

In this chapter, I highlight Twardowski's intellectual debts to Brentano's ideas in terms of his (dis)agreements with the latter. An important thing to keep in mind is that whenever I refer, in this chapter, to "Brentano" and "Brentano's ideas", I am talking about Brentano and his ideas in the 1880s–1890s—those ideas that Twardowski absorbed in his Vienna years.[1]

2 THE AGREEMENTS WITH BRENTANO

Throughout his life, Twardowski mostly shared Brentano's framework, that is, the range of problems, methods, fundamental assumptions and conceptual parameters set by Brentano before 1904. Four general elements of this framework are briefly discussed in this section. There are additional general traits that Brentano and Twardowski have in common, such as realism, respect for a broadly construed Aristotelian metaphysics,[2] and a preference for scientifically oriented philosophy (clear, precise, rationalistic, antispeculative in its method) over German idealism. However, these traits should rather be attributed to a shared intellectual *milieu*: they are often seen as characteristic marks of nineteenth-century Austrian, Catholic academic philosophy and opposed to nineteenth-century German Protestant, post-Kantian academic philosophy (Huemer and Landerer 2010: 92 n. 21; Smith 1994b: 127–8; Tassone 2012: 39 and ff.). This opposition is arguably a little unsophisticated (see Smith *ibid.*), but it will serve me well enough here, for all I want to stress is that the three elements mentioned are by no means particularly distinctive of Brentano's own position; they are also common to that of, for example, Bernard Bolzano, another influential Austrian thinker, upon Twardowski (Twardowski 1991: 24).

A fourth trait common to both Brentano and Twardowski is the correspondence theory of truth—trivially so, for practically no alternative was on the market at that time. That makes the circumstance that both philosophers defended correspondentism rather uninteresting. What is interesting, however, is that Twardowski, as a direct consequence of his tweaking of Brentano's intentionality theory, inaugurated a distinctively modern variant of correspondentism involving states of affairs (cf. TW4 in §3).

(Agr.i) (*Descriptive*) *psychology is the fundamental science*. As known, Brentano distinguishes between descriptive psychology ("psychognosy" or pure psychology) and genetic psychology; whereas the latter is a science based on experiments and inductive generalisations, the former is a pure a priori, apodictic science that is to serve as a basis for a *characteristica universalis* (Brentano 1895b: 34; Schaar 2015: 19; Chapter 3). One way to understand Brentano's talk of *characteristica universalis* is the following. For Brentano, descriptive psychology plays a foundational role with respect to other sciences, including all philosophical ones (among which metaphysics and logic), and it does so by providing all these sciences with a stock of basic concepts—such as *mental phenomenon, intentionality, presentation, judgement, inner perception*, and so on—and fundamental relations among them (Mulligan and Smith 1985: §1.1). Twardowski followed Brentano closely in taking psychology to be foundational in this sense (for logic in particular, see Betti and Raspa 2016: ix), although as we shall see in later phases of his thought the way he saw the relationship between logic and psychology was to change.

(Agr.ii) *Descriptive analysis is the method of descriptive psychology*. Brentano holds that the way we come to the basic concepts of (descriptive) psychology—and thus to the ontology of basic, essential components of our mental life that these concepts capture—is by descriptive analysis, a method resting on Brentano's technical concept of *inner perception*. "Descriptive" here is opposed to "normative" and refers to describing (mental) phenomena as they are actually given in consciousness; "analysis" is strictly linked to the idea of such (mental) phenomena as wholes to be decomposed into parts. Brentano's descriptive analysis is a non-inductive mental process consisting in the introspective application of formal, part–whole principles and patterns of reasoning to one's own complex mental phenomena given in inner perception. The aim of descriptive analysis is to distil from a single albeit complex (i.e. not mereologically simple) mental phenomenon given in consciousness the (essential, universal, necessary) simple (i.e. basic, partless) building blocks of our mental life and their relations (see e.g. Mulligan and Smith *ibid.*) by some kind of intuition or "*ideale Anschauung*" (Brentano 1874: xv, quoted in Bell 1990), and ultimately in order to come to general, universal truths such as "every mental phenomenon is either a presentation or is based on a presentation" (cf. BR1 below). An example of this method is the application of mereological concepts such as, say, *two-sided separability (of parts in a whole)* to phenomena of seeing and hearing in Brentano 1982. Twardowski's adherence to the method of descriptive analysis can be seen from numerous examples of its applications in Twardowski's work (see e.g. Twardowski 1903).

(Agr.iii) *Descriptive psychology is primary with respect to genetic or experimental psychology*. Notwithstanding Brentano's appreciation of experimental psychology and laboratory work (Huemer and Landerer 2010: 85; Brentano 1895b: 36), descriptive psychology was for him primary (Brentano 1895b: 35), while experimental psychology was to be considered auxiliary and in fact to be conducted by philosophers or trained descriptive psychologists (Huemer and Landerer 2010: 86; Brentano 1895b: 35). Twardowski's attitude tended to remain quite similar to Brentano's (cf. Rzepa 2015: 240-4; Schaar 2015: 22).

(Agr.iv) *Ethics has cognitive content based on emotional experience*. Twardowski followed Brentano in seeing moral judgements as having non-reducible cognitive content based on emotional experience (Brożek 2015: 163 n. 10; Chapter 20). To be sure, there is a deviation as to the third kind of acts, those of love and hate, that are fundamental to ethics, insofar as Twardowski rejected Brentano's identification of volitions and emotions (though not accepting a *fourth* kind of mental phenomena instead of three, *pace* Schaar 2015: 90, siding here with von Ehrenfels 1887: 18-9, see Twardowski 1903/04: 32). For Twardowski, phenomena of love and hate are *parts* of acts of desire or volition (Twardowski 1903/04: 29).

3 THE DISAGREEMENTS WITH BRENTANO

(Dis.i) *Nonexisting objects*. The fundamentals of Brentano's intentionality-based psychology can be fixed as follows:

BR1: Every mental phenomenon has a content or object toward which it is directed (Brentano 1874: Ch. 1 §5, 124 and ff.).

BR2: Mental acts are presentations or have presentations at their basis (Brentano 1874: Book II, Ch. 1, §3, 112).

BR3: A judgement is not a combination of presentations but a *sui generis* mental act that accepts or rejects an object (Hillebrand 1891: 26-7).

BR4: All judgements can be aptly expressed in the existential form "*A* is" (positive judgement) or "*A* is not" (negative judgement) (alternatively, "*A* exists" or "*A* does not exist"). In both cases, the judgement has a so-called "immanent" object, given by the presentation, which is simply A. A judgement "A exists" is true iff A exists (Brentano 1874: Book II, Ch. 7, §5, 49).

BR5: Not every mental act has an outer object corresponding to its immanent object (Rollinger 2009: 7; Brentano, EL 80/13016).

BR1 is famously ambiguous. In conjunction with BR2–BR5, its ambiguity was the source of animated discussions from 1888–9 onwards that opposed Brentano himself and orthodox Brentanians like Marty and Hillebrand, on the one side, and Kantians such as Sigwart and Windelband, on the other side (Betti 2013). Chrudzimski (2001a) suggests on the basis of Brentano EL 80 that Brentano's intended disambiguation of BR1 was this:

BR1*: Every mental phenomenon has a content and an object and is directed toward its content, not toward its object.

It can be shown that, if intentionality is interpreted as a genuine relation, namely as an entity (or even a quasi-entity) having objects as genuine relata, the conjunction of BR1*–BR4 raises serious difficulties.[3] A major difficulty is accounting for (true) negative existentials, that is, judgements such as "the aether does not exist". Twardowski addressed the difficulty by rejecting BR5 and BR1*, and tweaking BR1 as follows:

TW1: Every mental phenomenon has a content and an object, and it is directed toward its object, not toward its content (Twardowski 1894: 4, 9).

The cluster TW1 + BR2 + BR3 + BR4 can account for negative existentials by assuming nonexistents, including contradictory objects, to be the *objects* that are rejected (through a *content*) in such judgements. Although Brentano was never tempted by this option, TW1 can be shown to be the only consistent alternative open to someone who wished to change as little as possible of Brentano's original framework.

(Dis. ii) *Form, and object of judgements*. Difficulties are also posed by true predications about nonexistents such as "the round square is round". In 1894/95a, Twardowski accounted for such judgements by tweaking BR4 as follows (Betti and Raspa 2016: xxxi):

TW4: All judgements can be aptly expressed either in the existential form "A is" or in the relational form "A has b" (for positive judgements; "A is not"/"A does not have b" for negative judgements). The object of an existential judgement is (a simple or complex) A, and such judgements are true iff A exists; the object of a relational judgement is the relationship (*Verhältnis*) of having (quality) b by A, and such judgements are true iff the relationship in question subsists.

Despite the fact that Twardowski sometimes presents TW4 as being fundamentally in the spirit of BR4, Twardowski's relationships are special objects that have been straightforwardly identified with a state of affairs (Betti and Raspa 2016), and that subsist even though their objects may all be nonexisting (such as the having roundness by a round square). Brentano would never have accepted such objects (see Chapter 13), nor would he have accepted two kinds of being (existing/subsisting).

(Dis. iii) Brentano took truth-bearers to be judgement-*types* and truth to be time-dependent (Brentano 1930 Ch.1). By contrast, Twardowski took truth-bearers to be judgement-*tokens* and truth to be absolute (Betti 2006b: 378–9, especially n. 20).

To these points of divergence, the following should also be added. While Twardowski's ideas seem to have been rather stable on Agr. iii (see §1), those on Agr. i–ii underwent development. In 1894, Twardowski agrees with Brentano in describing logic as dependent on psychology and classified as a *practical* doctrine or theory (*Lehre*), not as a science (Twardowski 1894–95a: 12; cf. Brentano EL 80: 12.960[12], 12.962[1]); in 1899, he describes logic—like ethics or aesthetics—as a *theoretical–practical* science (*nauka*) (Twardowski 1899, sh. 1). In a text from 1908, however, Twardowski classifies logic as the "*theoretical* study of the veracity of judgements" (Twardowski 1993: 134, my emphasis), and he deems the view that logic is based on psychology ("psychologism") "untenable" (Twardowski 1993: 134). Along this line, in 1910 Twardowski clarifies that *both* logic and psychology are the basic branches of philosophy, representing two methods of philosophy, *a priori* and *empirical* (Twardowski, 1910a: 55; see also Twardowski 1910b: 64). Finally, in 1911, Twardowski publishes his new theory of actions and products, which is said to have "already contributed enormously to liberating logic from psychological accretions" (Twardowski 1911: 132). Twardowski defends his new "anti-psychologistic" position with the following arguments: (A) logic emerged and developed independently from psychology (Twardowski 1993: 134); (B) the laws of psychology are *a posteriori* generalizations of experiential data and thus are only probable, whereas the laws of logic, like those of mathematics, are a priori and certain (Twardowski 1993: 135); (C) psychology and logic have different objects of inquiry, namely (real) mental functions and (abstract) products of thinking insofar as they are true or false (similarly, physiology studies sweating while chemistry studies sweat, Twardowski 1993: 135). While (C) anticipated Twardowski 1911, (B) has debts to both Łukasiewicz and the first volume of Husserl's *Logische Untersuchungen* (cf. Betti 2006a).

CONCLUSION

Much of Twardowski's contribution is still in manuscript form; something similar can be said of Brentano. What I have reported so far suggests that new editions and translations are bound to further our understanding of the ideas of both philosophers and our knowledge of a crucial period of development of logic and psychology in their relationship with philosophy. Such advances will likely reveal a more original and interesting thinker in Twardowski than ever suspected; however, it is no less likely that such undertakings will confirm Twardowski to be a rather loyal Brentanian, despite any deviation from the thought of the master we might happen to find.

NOTES

1. On this period of Twardowski's life, see Brożek 2012. A more extensive introduction to Twardowski's thought is Betti 2016.
2. As to metaphysics—long-standing methodological use of mereological conceptualizations since antiquity aside—one typical theme at the time was the immortality of the soul, on which both lectured.

Both Brentano and Twardowski deny that the soul is just a sum of mental phenomena (see Chapter 14). Thus, Twardowski writes: "I am, I exist, not as a group of mental phenomena, but as a subject from which those phenomena arise" (Twardowski 1895: 202 n. 1); compare: "Soul refers to the substantial bearer of presentations (*Vorstellungen*), only perceivable through inner perception" (Brentano 1874: 4).

3. For most of (Dis. i), I follow Betti 2013.

2.2
Students' Students and Further Influences

33

The Prague School

Hynek Janoušek and Robin Rollinger

The name the "Prague School of Brentano" refers to three generations of thinkers who temporarily or permanently lived in Prague, bound together by teacher/student relationships, and who accepted the main views of Franz Brentano's philosophy.

In 1879, Carl Stumpf (see Chapter 28) arrived in Prague to take up a professorship of philosophy at the Charles-Ferdinand University. In 1880, Stumpf's close friend and also a student of Brentano, Anton Marty (see Chapter 27), became a professor in the same department. This marks the beginning of the Prague School. The presence of Stumpf and Marty was in fact a dramatic shift in orientation first and foremost in the domain of psychology, for Prague had previously been an enclave of Herbartian psychology, which Brentano had criticized in various respects throughout his *Psychology from an Empirical Standpoint* (Brentano 1874). In a certain sense, their presence even harked back to an earlier time in Prague, when Bernard Bolzano was developing a theory of science very much in opposition to the Kantianism of his time. Though Brentano's philosophy was very different from Bolzano's in many respects, it was no less anti-Kantian. This was very important at that time, for neo-Kantianism was on the rise in the German-speaking world and even beyond, whereas Stumpf and Marty made efforts to combat this kind of philosophy.

Though Stumpf's sojourn in Prague was considerably shorter, lived than Marty's, Stumpf published the first volume of his *Tone Psychology* (Stumpf 1883) during that time. This work drew not only on the general psychological framework that Brentano had developed but also used experimentation as a source of knowledge. Stumpf thereby initiated a competition with other orientations in this domain, most notably with that of Wilhelm Wundt's psychological laboratory in Leipzig. When Stumpf decided to leave Prague in 1884 in order to accept a professorship in Halle, Brentano was very displeased (see the quotation from a letter from Brentano to Marty, July–August 1884, as quoted in Fisette 2015d: 476 n.). As he was advancing his psychology and philosophy in Vienna, Brentano thought that the influence of his teachings would be considerably enhanced in the Habsburg Empire by Stumpf and Marty in Prague.

Nonetheless, Marty continued to live in Prague until his death in 1914. He too was very much concerned with issues in psychology, but with a distinctive concentration on the philosophy of language. While Stumpf had helped to advance Brentanian psychology in opposition to other currents, Marty distinguished himself by describing and analyzing language in competition with other orientations that prevailed at the time in study of language. Moreover, the critique of language remained an enduring aspect of the intellectual climate in Prague, as later exhibited by the Prague linguistic circle.

By the early 20th century, Marty had become a very impressive and effective mentor for students who formed a group around him. These students represent the second generation of the Prague School. Most notable among them were Emil Arleth, Emil Utitz, Oskar Kraus, Alfred Kastil, Franz Hillebrand, Hugo Bergman, Josef Eisenmayer, Otto Funke, and Oskar Engländer (see Chapters 34 and 36). Marty put most of them in contact with Brentano, whom they visited for philosophical conversations and with whom they regularly exchanged philosophical letters.[1]

When in 1916 Oskar Kraus became a professor of philosophy in Prague, his students, as well as students visiting Prague to study under his guidance, constituted the third generation of the Prague School. At least three of them should be mentioned—Georg Katkov, Walter Engel, and Eberhard Rogge. Roughly around 1916, Brentano's reism (see Chapter 13) became the official teaching of the more orthodox members of the Prague Brentano School. The development and application of reism in different areas of descriptive psychology became the main working project of this orthodox group (for a similar development in Innsbruck, see Chapter 36).[2]

Besides Marty and his students, other students and *Enkelschülern* of Brentano's came to Prague as well. After the Charles-Ferdinand University split into the German and the Czech parts in 1882, a former student of Brentano's, Thomas Garrigue Masaryk, attained a professorship in philosophy and sociology at the Czech philosophical faculty. Two students of Meinong's, Christian von Ehrenfels and Alois Höfler (see Chapters 30, 36), became professors in Prague as well (Ehrenfels in 1896 and Höfler in 1903). However, the relationship of Marty and his pupils to Ehrenfels and Höfler was often tense and unfriendly, for they diverged considerably from Brentanian orthodoxy in various respects.

Masaryk became a leading intellectual figure in Bohemia, and his political activities came to fruition when the republic of Czechoslovakia was established in 1918 and he became its first president. In 1930, when he was celebrating his 80th birthday, Masaryk was awarded 20 million crowns by the state for his role in the creation of Czechoslovakia. Masaryk, who had been supporting work done by Kraus on the new editions of Brentano's books since 1925, granted a part of the award to Kraus and other Brentano students to establish the Brentano Society in Prague and the Brentano Archives, with an official goal of publishing Brentano's work and of spreading knowledge of his philosophy (Bayerová 1990). From 1931 to 1939, the Prague members of the society, especially Kraus and Katkov, developed international contacts with England[3] and Poland[4] as well as other interested philosophers abroad. The society published four philosophical volumes of texts of its members and continued editing and transcribing Brentano's work for publication.

Sixty years of the philosophical work done in Prague in the name of Franz Brentano came to an end in 1939 when Kraus followed his student Katkov into exile in England to save his life after the German occupation of Czechoslovakia. Most of the archives were moved to Bodleian Library in Oxford. The society remained in existence, but it was taken over by German authorities. In 1942, Kraus died of cancer in Oxford. Utitz survived the concentration camp in Terezín.[5] Rogge was shot at the eastern front. Engel never wrote on philosophy again. Katkov could not find a proper position in philosophy and switched his research field to the modern history of Russia. At the end of the war, the Prague property of the society was raided by Russian troops. After the communist revolution in 1948, the society remained inactive until 1955, when it was finally dissolved.[6]

Since many of the other chapters in the Handbook deal with the life and work of the members of the Prague school individually or describe it in some way, here the philosophical topics of the Prague school will be discussed mainly with respect to the so-called orthodox school of Brentano—that is, to the work of Kraus and Kraus' students.

1 THE REISTIC TURN WITHIN THE PRAGUE SCHOOL

Initially, all Marty's students—for example, Eisenmeier, Bergman, Kraus, and Kastil—supported and defended Marty's view of intentionality. This meant accepting Marty's version of states of affairs and states of values (*Wertverhalte*) required by his adequation theory of truth and value. Marty viewed these entities as special nonreal contents of judgments and emotions (respectively) and as existing in the present time but devoid of any causal power (see Chapter 27). According to Marty, these contents cannot be reduced to real things, for there are also truths (and values) concerning nonexisting objects. Nor can they be reduced to immanent objects of our acts on Marty's view, for this would make the whole relation of adequacy between correct acts and contents purely subjective (Marty 1908: 295). In the case of judgments, the content is a being or nonbeing or possibility or necessity of presented objects (for further details, see Smith 1994a: 92–115). In the domain of emotions, the contents are either positive or negative values or their betterness or worseness.

A closely related doctrine that Marty taught is that of *nonreal* hypothetical predicates or relative determinations. According to Marty, in affirming, for example, that Barack Obama is bigger than Napoleon, I have affirmed a counterfactual determination of Obama—if Napoleon were here, Obama would be bigger. This property is not real, but it is nevertheless a property that Obama really has (see Marty 1908: 437).

Such determinations were used in Marty's theory of intentional relations. According to Marty, every mental phenomenon is either ideally conformal to its content or, in the case where the content of consciousness does not exist, the conformity of the mental phenomenon is its relative determination (Marty 1908: 423–6). Conformity of an incorrect mental phenomenon to a content is a relative determination as well.

Brentano rejected Marty's nonreal objects and determinations in his correspondence with Marty (see, e.g., Brentano 1930: 87–96/1966b: 52–9). Marty nevertheless kept his view, and all his Prague students initially followed suit. Kastil defended Marty's views in his instructive critique of Twardowski's concept of immanent intentional objects (see Kastil 1909: 51–8; 183–90). Kraus held the theory in his 1914 critique of contemporary theories of value (Kraus 1914: 3–4) and in his introduction to the four volumes of Marty's *Gesammelte Schriften* (Kraus 1916). Similar defense of Marty's views can be found, for example, in Eisenmeier (Eisenmeier 1923: 9–12) and Bergman (Bergman 1908: 8–10).

After Marty's death, Brentano managed to persuade most of Marty's former students to abandon the views of their teacher in favor of his own reism (for Brentano's arguments against nonreal entities, see Brentano 1930: 87–118/1966b: 52–71).

From now on, descriptive psychology was to be done hand in hand with the reistic critique of language, for whenever we believe that we relate ourselves to something nonreal, we are misled by a linguistic fiction. This critique for Brentano was actually his attempt to solve the problem of the many different meanings of "what is" as it was found in the Aristotelian metaphysics. Only a thing, on this view, is (or exists) in the strict and proper sense (*im eigentlichen Sinn*), whereas other alleged objects can be said to be only in an improper sense. The linguistic fictions that result from an improper speech are the result of using so-called synsemantic expressions as if they were autosemantic ones. (In Marty's terminology, these expressions are suggested by the inner grammatical form. See Chapter 27, Kraus 1942: 102–3.) Such "false friends" are, for example, names of properties (form-words) such as "redness"—for according to this view, there is no redness, there are only red objects—or the so-called reflexive words whose meanings have to be decoded by reflexive analysis of intentional mental phenomena. "Existence," "nonexistence," "value," "fiction," "preference" are examples of such reflexive words. Therefore, a proper reistic reformulation of the statements containing hidden synsemantic expressions has to be given such that the real meaning of these expressions becomes visible (Kraus 1942: 116). Since Brentano left the project of reism in its programmatic stage, Kraus, Kastil, and their students tried to offer their own answers to concrete philosophical problems.

2 SELECTED PROBLEMS OF THE REISTIC THEORY OF INTENTIONAL CONSCIOUSNESS

2.1 Reistic Reinterpretation of Hypothetical Determinations

While Marty formulated his theory of nonreal contents and relative determinations to describe intentional relations, Brentano replaced his theory of intentional relations with a view that they are in fact merely relation-like (see Chapter 4). For they do not require (but do not exclude) the existence of both members of the relation. Instead, only the existence of the fundament of the relation is necessary if the relation exists (for other cases of what is relation-like, see Kraus 1942, Kastil 1951: 132–5). Now, Marty used his theory of relative determinations to explain certain cases comparative relations, for example "The population of the world is less than 18 billion." Hence, reistic interpretation of these comparative relations had to be given. Kraus (1924: xxxviii) offered one in his introduction to the *Psychology from an Empirical Standpoint*. Kraus' strategy is based on how we *think* or *present* relatives. Whenever a relative is presented, its fundament is presented directly (in *modo recto*), and the terminus, that is, that to which the fundament stands in relation, is presented indirectly (in *modo obliquo*). In this way, for example, our inner perception as a moment of any mental acts presents intentionality. The inner perception, which is inherent to all mental phenomena, has as its object the mental phenomenon in *modo recto* in relation to its intentional object, which is co-presented in *modo obliquo*. If a relative is affirmed (as is always the case with inner perception), the only thing affirmed is the fundament, while, according to Kraus, the terminus is that through which the affirmed fundament is determined in its presentation. Therefore, in expressions such as "The population of the world is less than 18 billion" we only have in mind what is associated with the term "18 billion" so that we can present a general idea of size to specify the population which really is affirmed. However, Katkov (1930: 83) pointed out that Marty had serious objections to this approach, which echo objections made by Brentano himself (see Taieb 2015: 194–5). For example:

> Relations have often been characterized as forms of thought, as something that would be established or produced by our conception of things. If this is understood in the strict sense, it obviously means that they do not lie in the things themselves, but are rather put into them by our act of presenting. However, someone who regards the relation as something objective, as belonging to the objects, must forego seeing them as a matter of forms of thought in the sense of subjective modes of presentation. If, however, someone wanted to call them a matter of objective modes of our act of presenting—wherein could this objectivity consist but in the fact that what is given therein is something belonging to the objects, hence a differentia of objects … ?
>
> (Marty 1910: 67)

If the affirmation of the comparative relation is *true*, then the relation must be something *objective* and not *just* a part of our subjective presenting of the fundament. Katkov (1930: 486–7) therefore suggested a different reistic solution of the problem. His solution consists in the reduction of Marty's hypothetical predicates into apodictic rejections of complexes of which both fundament and terminus are parts. For example, the judger[7] in the above example apodictically rejects someone evidently affirming a group of 18 billion people that does not include the number of living people as its part. In the judgment "White is a lighter color than pure black" the judger apodictically rejects someone evidently affirming an instance of pure black that has the same or greater lightness than white and without having to worry that perception of pure black is factually impossible (see Katkov 1930: 485–6).

These reistic interpretations presuppose reistic understanding of sentences referring to possibility and impossibility. These were usually treated by the late Prague school of Brentano as judgments pertaining to modes (evident/blind, apodictic/assertoric, affirmative/negative) of judgments made by a judger as such (*als solcher*) of objects presented *in obliquo*. The following elucidations roughly state the reistic strategy (Katkov 1930: 530–1, Rogge 1935: 28–32) in relation to modalities. If I say

1. "*A* is possible" then I apodictically reject a judger as such who is apodictically rejecting *A* with self-evidence.
2. "*A* is impossible" then I apodictically reject a judger as such who is apodictically affirming *A* with self-evidence.

If one leaves out the apodicticity from the affirmation in point 1 or the negation in point 2, one gets an interpretation of "*A* is existing" (point 1) or *A* is not existing (point 2). A similar kind of answer would have to be given to the analysis of "*A* is necessary" (such an attempt was made by Rogge 1935: 32–40).

2.2 Katkov's Reduction of Intentional Contents of Presentations, Judgments

When Twardowski distinguished between the intentional content and the intentional object of presentations (see Chapter 32), his distinction caught on among Brentano's students, as both Meinong and Husserl began employing their own versions of it. However, according to the late Brentano, to call an object "intentional" is only to linguistically fix an intentional activity of which the object is an object and turn it into an external attribute of the object at the risk of creating a fictional class of special "intentional" objects. The horse I see is a "seen horse," the object I want is a "wanted object," but there are not two horses or two objects of desire present. The intentional objects (in both senses distinguished by Twardowski) as special entities have to be rejected. However, Brentano's reism once again had to face the problem of nonexisting objects. Presenting "this" (e.g., a chair) and not "that" (e.g., a person) is a real attribute of intentionality. But if the object of intention does not exist and there are no intentional contents, how can intentionality be differentiated with respect to objects? Once again, the answer of the late Prague school is based on the theory of inner perception. Whenever I present an object, I affirm myself in the secondary inner awareness (see Chapter 5) as a "presenter" of this object, which is presented *modo obliquo*. The so-called immanent content is nothing but a primary intentionality (an intentional relative) presented *as* object of its own inner perception. The differences between intentional contents are in reality differences between people who "take themselves to be."

According to Katkov (1930: 493) and Kraus (1934a: 46–7), the whole theory gives us an a priori proof of the self-reflective nature of intentionality, for according to this theory, the primary presentation of X *must* be *grounded* in being conscious of oneself as being conscious of X in an indirect way (Katkov 1930: 507).[8]

Contents of judgments (states of affairs) must be reduced in a similar way to the character of universal validity of judgments (see Kraus' remark in Brentano 1930: 185–6, Katkov 1930: 539–40). Brentano never really specified how the intention of a universal validity (correctness) of judgment (truth claim) is unified with judgment. Since there are judgments that continue even though we know about their falsity (namely, primitive sensory perceptions), Katkov decided to interpret the intention of correctness of a judgment (i.e., that we take the judgment to be true) as a *second-order* apodictic rejection of the self-evidence of the contradictory judgment (or rather of the contradicting evident "judger" as such). From this, it follows that there could be beings, for example some animals, who could judge about something with self-evidence without being aware that the opposite is necessarily false. Traditionally speaking, such beings would not be conscious of the law of contradiction, and yet they would, for example, have evident inner affirmation of their mental acts. This (blind or evident) intention of objective validity is responsible for the fiction of states of affairs in which "the specific moments of judgments are mixed together into one whole with specific moments of things about which we judge" (Katkov 1930: 536).

This theory improves Marty's theory of communication (Katkov 1930: 527–4, 1937b: 13–4), for it is not enough, as Marty claimed, to manifest that I am making a judgment in order to move the listener to consider following the same judgment. I have to make the listener aware that I take my judgment for a correct one.

2.3 The Self-Evidence of Inner Perception

In 1908, Hugo Bergman devoted a whole book to the problem of explaining Brentano's concept of the self-evidence of inner perception (see Chapter 34). The result was a meager one. A detailed defense of a strictly Brentanian view of the self-evidence of inner consciousness limited this self-evidence to simple existential affirmations of mental phenomena (Bergman 1908: 6). Following hints from the *Psychology from an Empirical Standpoint*, Bergman claimed that this affirmation is only *implicit* and simultaneous with the inwardly perceived phenomenon and—although conceptually differentiable from the perceived act—*recognized as identical with it* (1908: 12). However, it was very hard to see how this implicit consciousness could be of any use in descriptive psychology, since psychology presupposes an *explicit* reflexive grasp that makes the acts *primary* objects of investigation in order to conceptualize them for further general psychological insights. Such a shift of attention presupposes memory, but memory does not admit of self-evidence. Furthermore, the disagreement between different psychological descriptions was explained by the occasional lack of distinctiveness (*Undeutlichkeit*) of our inner consciousness.

In looking for answers, Kraus and his students wrongly[9] ascribed to Brentano a theory of apperception that was published as Brentano's official view in Brentano 1928 (which Kraus billed as Vol. III. of the *Psychology from an Empirical Standpoint*). This theory recognizes an evident act of reflexive perception (the so-called apperception) that is still evident even though it is not identical with the perceived act, because we have evidence that it could not have been caused by anything else. Such evidence of causality is called by Brentano the evidence of motivation (see Kastil 1951: 223–9). Brentano writes: "The act of apperception is therefore caused by the act of perception and has at the same time the character of being motivated by the act of perception. Precisely by this being-motivated the act of apperception is evident" (Brentano 1928: 34–5/1981b: 26).

However, not everybody accepted this explanation. For example, Rogge clearly recognized that this could not have been Brentano's position and rejected it.[10]

2.4 Presentations as a Fundamental Class of Mental Phenomena

One of the most permanent features of Brentano's thinking was his view that all intentional acts are either presentations or based on presentations. The question whether this principle should be upheld was raised among the Prague Brentanists, specifically by Kraus' student Walter Engel. The outlines of Engel's theory were presented by Kraus (Kraus 1937: 167). Unfortunately, the war prevented Engel from publishing his view, and the only thing that survived is Kraus' short report of it:

> According to Brentano's theory, the relation of a presentation is the basis of judgement and emotion in a similar way as substance is to the accident. However, it is possible to advocate another version: Every consciousness, as is well known, is something that relates to something; it can vary in three respects: 1. The one who is relating can change in his individuality. 2. He can, as someone who relates, change qualitatively or modally (by being a presenter, a judger or someone conducting himself emotionally). 3. He can change by relating to something else,

so-called "object-differentia". If this view were correct, it should not be said that there is for every consciousness an underlying presenting, but rather that there could not be a consciousness without object-relation any more than one without a certain quality of relation. Dr. Walter Engel (Prague) advocates this view in a work that is not yet published.

Although this variational Husserl-like approach was presented only as a working hypothesis, it reveals an open-minded approach on the part of Kraus and his students to Brentano's teachings.

2.5 The Character and the Existence of the Outside World

According to the late Brentano, our presentation is always general—sensation being the least general kind of it. We therefore do not perceive time, space, and individual substances as they are in themselves. Hence, there is an unbreachable limit to our experience of the external reality. Among the Prague Brentanians, this difference of *for us/in itself* led to a difference in perspectives. While Kraus and Kastil presented this view in a realistic fashion, stressing the fact that in the sciences we can judge about features of transcendent reality even though certain absolute determinations elude us (Kraus 1934a: 131–5, Kastil 1951: 239–40), Eisenmeier (1923) stressed the relational character of our scientific understanding of transcendent reality as something that *excludes* and *confines us* to the narrow limits of our experience. When Bergman refused Brentano's use of the probability calculus in his proof of the external world,[11] he was left with a relational structure of our knowledge that could be interpreted in a Neo-Kantian fashion as well as in a more Russellian style (see Bergman 1920). Furthermore, Rogge (1938: 168–9) not only criticized Brentano's proof of the external world but also pointed out the circularity in Brentano's claim that the natural sciences experimentally prove the nonexistence of sensory qualities in the real world, for in his *Psychology*, Brentano already defines the natural sciences as dealing with a world radically different from what external perception shows us (see Brentano 1874: 138).

3 PREFERENCE AND CRITIQUE OF THE SUM OF THE GREATEST GOOD

Brentano's ethics (as distinct from Brentano's theory of moral valuation) is based on the principle of the best attainable good, that is, we should strive for "the greatest possible spiritual good for all animate beings who fall within our sphere of influence" (Brentano 1952: 222/1973b: 139; see Chapter 21). Since the will is for Brentano an act of practical preference, the general concept of preference and the ethical principle of the greatest possible good were often discussed among the Prague Brentanists. The characteristic feature of these discussions about "the greatest value" was an interest in the theories of economic value and marginal utility, especially in the form developed by the so-called Austrian school of Economics. A critique of the general points of these theories from the Brentanian standpoint was offered by Kraus (1937: 357–86) and by Oskar Engländer (1914, 1931), who was a professor of economics at the Prague German University.

Another feature of these discussions was a critique of the utilitarian principle of the sum of the greatest good, which Brentano himself might not have differentiated clear enough from his own conception. The critique of the sum of the greatest good based on the development of Brentano's remarks in Katkov's interesting book is worth mentioning here (Katkov 1937b: 43–70, see also Chisholm 1986). According to Katkov, an essential difference between correct emotion and correct judgment (besides the fact that correct judgments do not admit of the distinction of better and worse and correct emotions do not fall under the law of the excluded middle) is that, for example, from correctly loving pleasure as such, it does not follow that it is correct to love all cases of pleasure. The love (or hate) of the object as such based in the content of its general content does not imply love (or hate) of all objects constituting its extension. Other considerations suggest that the positive value of a whole is not a simple sum of the positive values of its parts. Thus the principle of *bonum variationis* states that if two goods of different types A and B have the same positive value, then the whole consisting of goods of the type $A + B$ will be more valuable than the whole consisting merely from goods of the type $A + A$ or $B + B$. The principle of *bonum progressionis* states that given that the total value of unordered parts of a development of some entity is the same, a progress or rise of a value of that entity in time is more valuable than the process of its degeneration. The principle of the individual perfection says that the same goods will create a better whole if they belong to the same individuum than if they belong to different individua. "Dostoyevsky's principle" states that an evil done to one individuum cannot be somehow undone by good done to another individuum. The same logic led Katkov to claim that the nonexistence of a whole containing one part unworthy of existence is preferable to its existence. The whole treatise also defends the view that simple multiplication of an individual possessing a positive value would create only more objects with the value but not something more valuable (compare: the multiplication of a golden individual will create more golden things but not a more golden whole). The classic utilitarian principle of the greatest good is for Katkov and for his teacher Kraus a secondary rule derived from the main principle that the existence of something good is itself good and therefore preferable to its nonexistence. However, its grounding is rather different: "It is not for the sake of increasing goods and reducing evils, but rather for the sake of elevating as much as possible the incalculable intrinsic value of the relevant beings, that we seek to make the goods accessible to as many as possible and we strive to reduce the evils as much as possible" (Kraus 1937: 275).

CONCLUSION

The title "The Prague School of Brentano" covers a work of three generations of followers of Brentano. In this chapter, we mostly tried to cover some selected philosophical motives distinctive of its last, reistic phase, to show that the whole movement might not have been as orthodox in relation to its teacher as it looks from the apologetic introductions to Brentano's work written by Kastil and Kraus. This overview hopefully gives the impression of an intellectual movement of great vitality and critical acumen forming contacts abroad in order to expand its horizons. Unfortunately, the promising signs of development of Brentano's thought by Prague "reists" in the 1930s were cut short and subsequently erased from the history of 20th-century philosophy due to the National Socialistic and later Communistic regimes that brought darkness and devastation upon Masaryk's democratic Czechoslovakia.[12]

NOTES

1. The Prague Brentano circle, of which many were German-speaking Jews (e.g., Kraus, Utitz, Bergman), used to meet after Marty's lectures in the Café Louvre to continue philosophical discussions. There they were sometimes joined by other intellectual members of the Prague German Jewish community: Oskar Pollack, Max Brod, and Franz Kafka.
2. Brentano gave Kraus and Kastil free hand to organize and put together the unpublished materials from his literary estate in a way that would correspond to his late reistic views. Reism and the philosophical theories contained in the resulting books (notably Brentano 1930, 1933) are often a result of heavy-handed editing and even rewriting and reformulating of Brentano's texts. While it is sometimes hard to say whether a position expressed in these volumes corresponds to Brentano's views, these books can be safely read as expressing positions of the Prague and Innsbruck reism at the time of their publications.
3. The list of known members of the Prague Brentano Society given by Binder (see Binder 2000: 564) states the following English members: G. E. Moore, H. Eaton, D. Hicks, R. Reeds.
4. The reism of Brentano and his followers and the reism of Tadeusz Kotarbinski were being developed independently until Twardowski and Katkov made Kotarbinski aware of the close proximity of his views and the views of the late Brentano (a short description of this development and a comparison of both reistic views is given in Kraus 1937: 268–71). Kotarbinski was in touch with Kraus and his pupils from 1930. The ties between Prague and Lvov were strengthened in 1937 when, on account of Twardowski's invitation, Kraus gave a series of lectures in Poland. Another Polish philosopher, apart from Twardowski, who had ties to the Prague Brentano circle was Wladislaw Tatarkiewicz. Both Kotarbinski and Tatarkiewicz were on the list of the contributors for the second volume of the *Abhandlungen zum Gedächtnis des 100. Geburtages von Franz Brentano* that was to be published by the Prague Brentano Society in 1939. The volume never saw the light of day due to the outbreak of the war.
5. Utitz wrote a book about the psychology of life in the Terezín concentration camp, which has recently been republished together with his shorter texts from the same camp (see Utitz 2015).
6. The following discussions are necessarily selective, for the output and the range of topics of the orthodox Brentanists was quite large.
7. It would be more proper to say "someone who judges," but this makes the structure of some further statements overly complicated.
8. Since conscious subjects differentiate themselves also as "judger" and "lovers and haters," the argument could be extended to involve all fundamental classes of intentionality. For a more formalized version of the Katkovian perspective, see Chisholm 1990. An a priori argument for the grounding of intentionality in inner perception could be also deduced from Brentano's late conception of time, which claims that to be conscious of time is to be conscious of the time *modes* of presenting acts (see Chapter 7), which presupposes self-consciousness.
9. Kraus confesses that the whole theory comes from what he wrote down after he read and discussed a psychognostic fragment of Brentano during his visit with Brentano in 1901 and that he wasn't able to find this view in Brentano's manuscripts (Kraus in Brentano 1928: 146/1981b: 105). What Brentano discussed with Kraus was most likely inspired by Brentano's reading of Leibniz' *Nouveaux Essais*. In his 1908 letter to Husserl, Brentano writes: "However, I saw that he [Leibniz] in the second book assumes an apperception of one's own acts by acts that occur later. And here you find yourself in agreement with him, but I don't." Kraus could not have known the letter since it was published only in 1994 (Husserl 1994b, Vol. I: 50).
10. "[This theory of apperception] can only be a casual witticism, not a serious expression of belief, for otherwise wherever the origins of the concept of causality are noted [in the works of Brentano] the case of inner apperception would have to be mentioned as well.… [F]or an immediate knowledge of causality very definite conditions must be fulfilled; these conditions are fulfilled only in the case of axiomatic grasping" (Rogge 1938: 172).
11. *Psychology from an Empirical Standpoint* works within the confines of critical realism without providing any serious "metaphysical" proof of the existence of the outside world. Later, Brentano offered a proof of an independent world or real objects standing under causal laws (see Brentano 1925: 118–30, Kastil 1951: 223–9; for critique, see Rogge 1935: 57–67, 77–87).
12. This chapter is an outcome of the project "From Logical Objectivism to Reism: Bolzano and the School of Brentano" P401 15-18149S (Czech Science Foundation), realized at the Institute of Philosophy of the Czech Academy of Sciences.

34

Bergman and Brentano

Guillaume Fréchette

1 BIOGRAPHY

Shmuel Hugo Bergman[1] was born in Prague to a modest family. He started school in 1889 at the Deutsche *Volks- und Bürgerschule*, where he first met Franz Kafka (1883–1924). Together with Kafka, art historian Oskar Pollak (1883–1915), aesthetician and Brentano student Emil Utitz (1883–1956), and Paul Kisch (1883–1944), brother of Egon Erwin Kisch and editor of the *Neue Freie Presse*, Bergman entered the *Altstädter Gymnasium* in Prague in 1893, from which he received his diploma in 1901.

Together with Kafka and Pollak, Bergman enrolled at the German University in Prague, where he studied chemistry in his first university year, changing to philosophy in 1902 under the influence of Marty's lectures on descriptive psychology (1901/02) and selected metaphysical questions (1902).[2] A year later, he joined the *Cercle du Louvre*, a circle of Prague intellectuals meeting at the Café Louvre, which was influenced by Brentanian philosophy and to which Marty's students belonged—Oskar Kraus, Emil Arleth, Emil Utitz, Max Brod, Benno Urbach, Josef Adolf Bondy, Josef Eisenmeier, and Franz Kafka, but also Christian von Ehrenfels.[3] A few years later, under the supervision of Marty, Bergman wrote his PhD dissertation on atomic theory in the 19th century (Bergman 1905). Between 1905 and 1911, he paid at least five visits to Brentano in Schönbühel and Florence.[4] As a Jew, Zionist, and follower of Brentano, Bergman's options for an academic career were practically nonexistent. Of all the Jewish students and "grand-students" of Brentano, only Husserl, Kraus, and Utitz—who all converted to Protestantism very early in their careers—were able to pursue an academic career in philosophy in Germany or Austria. As he had done for Husserl, but with less success, Brentano repeatedly tried to convince Bergman to abandon the Jewish faith, seeing in his Zionism an "exaggerated feeling of Israelite belongingness,"[5] and his faith as a "tough devotion to a legacy from barbaric times."[6] Stumpf accused Bergman of showing two contradictory faces, as a Zionist and German philosopher (Bergman 1985: 49),[7] which made it impossible for

Bergman, in his view, to habilitate in Berlin. Marty saw Zionism as Bergman's mortal sin.[8] He didn't actually see Bergman's Jewish faith as an obstacle to his habilitation in Prague but couldn't promote him "insofar as it would endanger Kraus' future—and with it the future of the School."[9] Without this opportunity, Bergman was forced to take up a career as assistant librarian at the University Library in Prague,[10] but continued to publish extensively in philosophy and engaged in an intense philosophical correspondence with Brentano.[11]

In 1920, Bergman emigrated to Palestine and settled in Jerusalem, where he was appointed the first director of the Jewish National and University Library. Bergman began lecturing at the newly founded National Hebrew University in 1928, just after the creation of the Faculty of Humanities, and was appointed Professor of Philosophy in 1935. On November 11, 1935, he was elected the first rector of the Hebrew University. He retired from the university in 1955.

To some extent, it might be helpful to divide Bergman's philosophical development into a Brentanian and a post-Brentanian phase.[12] This shouldn't, however, be taken to mean that Bergman's later philosophy is completely free of Brentanian influence, since many of the works of the late Bergman engage with Bolzano and the School of Brentano. In the first period (1902–1913), which covers the years between his studies and his repeated attempts to habilitate in Germany and Austria, Bergman endorsed, developed, and discussed many of Brentano's philosophical positions: his philosophy of history (Bergman 1905), his theory of inner perception (Bergman 1908), his conception of intentionality (Bergman 1909), and the rejection of *irrealia* (Bergman 1908; 1910a).

The second period (1913–1975) is characterized primarily by Bergman's dominant interest in the history and philosophy of science, already obvious in Bergman 1905 but more critically developed around 1912–1913, and which remained constant until the end of his life. More decisively, however, Bergman's growing sympathies for Kantian philosophy and his rejection of empiricism in the philosophy of mathematics in Bergman 1913 mark the change between the Brentanian and post-Brentanian phases.[13] Although he continued to engage with issues in Brentanian philosophy during this second period, he also became interested in advances in philosophical and mathematical logic (Bergman 1950), in logical positivism, and in the works of Carnap (Bergman 1948) and Quine, like some other students of Brentano in the 1930s in Prague and later on in Innsbruck.[14]

Bergman's career as a professor of philosophy in Jerusalem after 1935, and more generally his works on Judaism, Kantian philosophy, idealism, and his pioneering role in the development of logic and epistemology soon after the birth of the State of Israel, would each need a treatment of their own.[15] They will be dealt with here only to the extent that they are directly relevant to Bergman's position in the Brentano School. However, a larger picture of Bergman's achievements as a philosopher might be helpful. As a Prague Jew at the turn of the 20th century, as a philosopher formed at the School of Brentano, and also someone who fought in World War I as an Austrian citizen in the Imperial and Royal Army,[16] Bergman's worldview was aptly described by his friend Brod as that of "Generation nevertheless" (*Generation des Trotzdem*):

> It is incorrect ... to characterize the generation that received its decisive impulses in the sufferings of the First World War a "lost generation," as happened in England

and America. On the contrary, this generation, which has been sorely tried, is a courageous generation, with a strong propensity in attempting to let the Good become reality: I would like to call it a "Generation of 'nevertheless'".... Ehrenfels' *Cosmogony* was a document of this generation, which for the first time embodied a mood of impending doom, tough without vanishing into fear.

(1960: 340)

... it was a generation of unafraid humanists.

(1960: 371)[17]

As a "particularly impressive representative" of this generation (Brod 1960: 371), Bergman was convinced from early on, even in his early articles on Zionism (Bergman 1903a; 1903b; 1904a; 1904b), of the necessity of a binational solution in Palestine, which would bring equal good to both nations, much along the lines of the Habsburger multinational state. In his years as a student of Brentano, he was also convinced by the intrinsic value of all acts of thought—the idea that every act of thought is something good in itself (see Brentano 1889: 22–3/1969: 12; also Chapter 21)—a conviction stemming from Brentanian practical philosophy that didn't fade in his later years, despite his growing affinity for Kant (see, e.g., Bergman 1938, 1966). Years later, and in a similar way, in proclaiming the need for a courageous philosophy (Bergman 1960), Bergman showed himself to be part of this "Generation nevertheless," characteristic of many important figures from the Prague branch of the School of Brentano.

2 PHILOSOPHY

2.1 Ontology and Logic

In Bergman 1909a, the first monograph devoted exclusively to the philosophy of Bolzano, Bergman discusses the main theses of Bolzano's ontology and logic. His standpoint is largely Brentanian: Bolzano's realist thesis that there are propositions (*Sätze an sich*) (and notions [*Vorstellungen an sich*]) in themselves, independently of their being thought of, is interpreted by Bergman in terms of the mental contents of actual or possible judgers (Bergman 1909a: 14f.); he thereby rejects propositions as *entia rationis* in a Brentanian fashion (see Brentano 1930: 139/1966b: 122). His reading of Bolzano also makes use of a distinction inspired by Marty: in his discussion of Bolzano's claim that there are objectless notions, Bergman insists on a distinction between having an object and being directed toward an object—a distinction that Bolzano only sketches *en passant* in the *Wissenschaftslehre*—seeing in it a forerunner of Marty's distinction between real and possible correlation (Bergman 1909a: 35).[18] According to Bergman, Bolzano's claim that there are objectless notions—like the notion of a golden mountain—simply means that there is no real correlation between the notion and the object, but only an ideal correlation: there *would* be a correlation *if* there were a golden mountain. This idea is at the basis of Marty's correspondence account of truth, which presupposes the acceptance of *irrealia*, namely of the states of affairs that are the truth-makers of true propositions, for example the nonexistence of a golden mountain.[19]

Bergman never pursued this early attempt to reconcile Brentano's reism with Marty's realism toward subsisting states of affairs—as an interpretation of Bolzano—and it remained as such unsuccessful.[20] Many years later, he developed a different account of the opposition between Brentano and Marty. In a lecture presented at Harvard's Philosophy Club in 1937, Bergman clarified his position, attributing to Marty's judgment-contents just the same Platonic properties as Bolzano's propositions in themselves, and isolating Brentano's account of truth in terms of self-evidence from Marty's and Bolzano's.[21] At this point, however, Bergman was dissatisfied with both the Brentanian and the Martian theories:

> The proposition P is true when it is possible that somebody will evidently judge ["]P is true["]. But what is the meaning of the words ["]It is possible that somebody will evidently judge["]? The existence of the possibility is only the existence of the proposition in itself, and this proposition can [only] be explained in the way [that the] truth of P was explained. ["]It is possible that …["] means ["]It is possible that somebody will evidently judge: 'It is possible that …'["].
> (Bergman 1937: 12)

Here, Bergman obviously agrees with Husserl's account of possibilities as ideal objects (in the *Logical Investigations*). If the truth of *P* is to be explained by "the possible being of what is real, [it] must obviously suffer shipwreck on the fact that possibilities themselves are ideal objects" (Husserl 1901: 115). In Bergman's account of the late Brentano's analysis of the concept of truth for non-evident propositions, this shipwreck is the infinite regress of the truth of non-evident propositions. It stops only when one actually states an evident proposition, which brings Brentano's account of truth too close to subjectivism, according to Bergman. As for Marty, Bergman affirms that his account of objective judgment-contents as truth-makers has the inconvenient consequence, mentioned earlier, of accepting entities like *the nonexistence of A* as the truth-maker of the true proposition "A is not," that is, of explaining the truth of a proposition by the existence of nonexistence. More problematically, it is unable to account for the truth of first-person propositions such as "I exist," whose truth involves the actual thinking of the utterer of the proposition.

In his later works on logic, Bergman developed a strong interest for the logic of Solomon Maimon,[22] and more particularly for his principle of determinability. According to Maimon, the standard for synthetic a priori judgments is a relation between a determinable (the subject) and a determinate (the predicate). Subject-concepts and predicate-concepts belong together organically and are essentially ordered in series of degrees of determinateness: for example, space-figure-triangle, or color-yellow. In logical or a priori truths, a subject-concept is determined by the predicate-concept that belongs to the same series, and not to another. This explains why judgments like "a triangle is yellow" are not logical judgments in Maimon's view. Following the principle of determinability, the determinable may be determined in different ways (the concept of figure may be determined by the concept of triangle, rectangle, etc.) and may be thought independently of the determinate, while the determinate can only be thought with its determinable. Maimon's principle of determinability, which Bergman also connects with Marty's critique of Meinong's theory of objects and with Brentano's mereological principle (Bergman 1967: 120), also plays an important role in Bergman 1967 and in Bergman 1953, the first work on logic to appear in Hebrew in modern times,[23] where the contributions to symbolic logic by Maimon, Bolzano, and Brentano are developed in detail.[24]

Bergman comes back to Brentano's existential theory of judgment (see Chapter 10) in Bergman 1950, where he argues against the conception of existence defended, for instance, in Frege's logic, where existence is considered a second-order property, using Brentano's reduction of predicative judgments to existential judgments as a reference point: "the connection of the concept of existence with a predicate and the corresponding statement function is certainly right in many cases, but it doesn't exhaust the essence of the concept of existence" (Bergman 1950: 33). Existence in mathematical logic is a property of classes of individuals, while existence in the usual, or Brentanian, sense of acknowledgement is the acknowledgement of what the presentation the acknowledgement is based on presents. He therefore argues for a *logical* distinction between being and existence but refuses to see an *ontological* distinction:

> [F]rom the standpoint of logic, it suffices to distinguish between the concept of being and the concept of existence ... and to hold the view that a judgment of being is not a predicative judgment and that being is not a property nor dependent upon a property. However, the question of which objects to attribute being or reality in the strict sense is not a question of logic. [Logic] has only to establish a framework for all sciences, including ontology.
>
> (Bergman 1950: 35)

This attempt to coordinate Brentanian and Fregean logic into a general logic understood as a framework for all sciences was received very critically, however, and it is indeed not clear what kind of ontology would be at play here.[25] Here again, as in some of his later reviews of Brentano's editions (see Bergman 1936; 1952; 1965), Bergman remains doubtful about the late Brentano's reistic enterprise (see Chapter 13), as championed by his epigones Kastil, Kraus, and Mayer-Hillebrand. According to him, it is not at all clear where to draw the line between the late Brentano (or its reconstruction by the epigones) and Nominalism (Bergman 1966: 366). In Bergman's view, Brentano defended an ontological conception of truth before his reistic phase, and this conception, which is developed further in Marty 1908, should be given priority. Bergman's reading of Brentano's theory of judgment (Bergman 1950) also gives an interesting perspective on the Prague school of Brentano: in his view, Brentano was misled in his interpretation of "*A* is" as the acknowledgement of *A*. Rather, he should have said that it was the acceptance of a state of affairs (1950: 25).

2.2 Philosophy of Mind

Bergman's early views on philosophy of mind can be found in Bergman 1908, where he attempts to defend the Brentanian view that inner perception should be understood in terms of elementary simple judgment, in "the simple acceptance of the intuited object" (1908: 6). In this work, Bergman advocates the view that in inner perception, act, and object are *identical*, although conceptually distinct (see, e.g., pp. 12 and 83, but also elsewhere).[26] He also defends the Brentanian view that inner perception is simultaneous with the acts perceived through it. For this reason, he argues against Ehrenfels and Meinong that there can't be a perception of temporally extended objects.

Bergman (1908: 56ff.) also follows Brentano and Marty (against Husserl) in their conception of improper presentations. In his view, intending (*meinen*) a content that isn't intuitively present (like thinking of a chiliagon) is always based on an intuitive presentation of something else (e.g., a presentation of the square instantiated by the surface of a table) and on a presentation of the relation (e.g., the relation of having 250 times more sides than the square). Strictly speaking, there is no perception of improperly presented objects: "authentic perception is always a simple judgment (*eingliedriges Urteil*), an intuitive, simple act. It doesn't have anything to do with naming (*Benennung*), interpreting, or classifying" (Bergman 1908: 58). Bergman therefore rejects Husserl's account, according to which there is a change in the mode of consciousness depending on whether you perceive something or intend it in a particular way; and he also rejects Meinong's conception of *Meinen* as the act through which one grasps objects (Bergman 1910b).

2.3 Metaphysics, Epistemology, and Philosophy of Science

Bergman's philosophical dissertation (Bergman 1905) is concerned with atomic theory in physics and was written under the supervision of Marty, with Alois Höfler as a second evaluator. In his thesis, Bergman applies Brentano's theory of the four phases of philosophy to the atomic theory of the 19th century, with John Dalton's theory of atoms representing the first and ascendant phase, while Ostwald's natural philosophy and Mach's theory of elements, rejecting atoms as fictions, represent the phase of utmost decline.[27]

Albert Einstein's stay in Prague in 1911–1912 made an impression on the young Bergman, who was able to further develop his interest in the history and philosophy of science and in the theory of relativity thanks to his participation in Einstein's seminar and numerous discussions (Bergman 1974b). Many years later, Einstein prefaced Bergman's book on the theory of relativity (Bergman 1929/1974a), which is dedicated to Marty.

Interestingly, in this book, Bergman rejects Brentanian epistemology and the idea that the law of causality could be proven thanks to the probability calculus, an idea that he was keen to defend in Bergman 1906. In his later view, published in his 1929 with a foreword by Einstein, the theory of relativity showed that causality could not be proven and was a mere hypothesis, pointing to a new path in the philosophy of science (see also Bergman 1944). In this sense, Bergman clearly positioned himself against Kraus' attacks on the theory of relativity as a mistake in "taking fictions for reality" and "introducing a metaphysics which overshadows in paradoxes everything that has been done in philosophy until today" (Kraus 1919b: 152).[28] Discussing the accounts of causality proposed by Einstein, Weyl, Schlick, Reichenbach, Planck, and other philosophers of science, Bergman argues for an understanding of the law of causality based on the practical necessity of the hypothesis of causality, seeing in it—as did his fellow Brentano student Benno Kerry many years before him—an "earthly creation of our thought which we should mould daily as we use it" (Bergman 1929: 73/1974: 458 and Kerry [Kohn] 1881: 127). This change of view follows from Bergman's observation that the development of the theory of relativity and quantum mechanics showed the failure of empiricism and positivism, that is, of the views that we read off the physical laws from our experience.

2.4 Philosophy of Mathematics

Bergman's early works on the philosophy of mathematics were conducted in a Brentanian spirit. In Bergman 1909b and 1910a, he offers a defense of the Brentanian thesis of the analyticity of mathematics against the Kantian conception of mathematical propositions as synthetic a priori. In Bergman 1913, however, his position undergoes significant changes: he describes mathematics as "freed from any existential considerations whatsoever in the empirical sense" (Bergman 1913: 1), as "moving purely in the domain of the a priori" (*ibid.*: 2). Mathematics "doesn't need something real to be counted in the exposition of its theorems" (*ibid.*: 5). In this work, he follows Cantor and Bolzano in acknowledging the existence of infinite sets, classes, and pluralities (1913: 19). In Bergman's view, a number (in the sense of quantity: *Anzahl*) answers the question "how many?" (Bergman 1913: 13, 19) and is countable, while infinite sets are, by definition, not countable. Following this distinction, Bergman refuses to identify the cardinality (of infinite sets) with the concept of counting (*Anzahlbegriff*).

The views on numbers and sets advocated in Bergman 1913 were totally unacceptable for Brentano: the rejection of empiricism, the distinction between mathematics and the sciences of realities, and the criticism of Gutberlet's (and Brentano's) position against the actual infinite in Cantor were clear signs, in Brentano's view, that Bergman no longer belonged to the school (see Bergman 1946: 138f.).

2.5 History of Philosophy

While in his early years, thanks to the influence of his teacher Marty, Bergman was a truly orthodox defender of Brentano's philosophy, this orthodoxy was more questionable in his later years. Concerning the history of philosophy, this becomes clear in Bergman 1965, where he calls Brentano's four-phase law of development of the history of philosophy into question:

> [T]his law seems to me now … neither important nor right. It seems to me that this alleged law had devastating consequences for Brentano's School. The thinkers of the alleged periods of decline … remained for his disciples a closed book.
> (Bergman 1965: 95)

Bergman also published extensively on the history of philosophy. His four volumes on the History of Philosophy from Cusanus to post-Kantian philosophy (Bergman 1970; 1973; 1977; 1979) are probably the best example of his erudition and are still the main reference in Israel in this field. The last volume contains a detailed overview of Brentano's thought (Bergman 1979: 145–71).

3 EPILOGUE

Bergman taught at the University of Jerusalem from 1928 to 1955 and continued to lecture there many years after his retirement. He held lectures and seminars on the most varied topics, ranging from Cusanus to Kant, Fichte, Schelling, Maimon, Brentano, Husserl, Heidegger, Carnap, Reichenbach, Wittgenstein, and Quine, among others. Among the many students he introduced to and guided in philosophy was Beno Rothenberg, who would later become an important figure in Israeli archaeology and who in 1937 wrote an M.A. thesis comparing Brentano's logic with modern mathematical logic, which he expanded into a PhD dissertation written in Hebrew in 1940. Both works were written under the supervision of Bergman.[29] The same year, Edward Poznanski—not a student of Bergman but a close collaborator—from the Lwow-Warsaw school settled down in Jerusalem, where he lectured in philosophy and took part in the lecture and research groups supervised by Bergman. These groups were also attended by another student of Bergman's, Yehoshua Bar-Hillel, best known for his work in formal linguistics and set theory and his later collaborations with Carnap and Chomsky. Bar-Hillel was introduced by Bergman to the works of Bolzano, Husserl, Carnap, and Reichenbach and defended his PhD thesis in 1949,[30] one year after Nathan Rotenstreich, best known for his works on Jewish philosophy and German idealism, who was a close student of Bergman's. Among Bergman's students, it is worth mentioning Jacob Fleischmann, well known for his work in German philosophy, and philosopher of science Joseph Agassi. Finally, it is worth mentioning that Bergman also had Arab students, among them Wasfi Ahmad Hijab (1919–2004), who later pursued his studies in Cambridge under the supervision of Wittgenstein.[31]

After the Nazi book burnings of spring 1933, the journal *Cahiers juifs* invited many Jewish intellectuals to reflect on the contribution of German Jews to German culture, including, among others, Siegfried Kracauer (published anonymously), Joseph Roth, and Hugo Bergman. After going into detail on the contribution from Mendelssohn to Husserl, with an important section on the School of Brentano and Husserl's phenomenology, Bergman makes it clear that it would be mistaken to speak of a German–Jewish philosophy, and by extension, one may add, of a Jewish branch of the school of Brentano:

> Let us admit frankly that the philosophy of the scholars mentioned above is not a Jewish philosophy, neither by its language, nor by its sources or by the audience to which it is addressed.... While we were bringing here so many brilliant gifts, our own spiritual existence remained poor, narrow, and anaemic. The great problem of the fifty years to come is to know whether we are able to make room for great philosophical talents in our lives.
>
> (Bergman 1933: 187)

Sadly enough, Bergman's own philosophy, both in his Brentanian and post-Brentanian phases, has been largely ignored, as much by Brentanians as by historians of Jewish philosophy.[32] We should certainly make room for this great philosophical talent.[33]

NOTES

1. After his settlement in Jerusalem in the early 1920s, Bergman changed the presentation of his name in publications from Hugo Bergmann to Shmuel Hugo Bergman. For the sake of unity, the latter spelling is preserved here for all publications, both pre- and post-1920s.
2. A reference to these lectures and to the impression that the school of Brentano left on Kafka is given in Bergman 1972.
3. On the Café Louvre and these Brentanians, see Neesen 1972, Utitz 1954, Brod 1960, and Chapter 33.

4. These meetings are described in Bergman 1985. See also Sambursky 1981.
5. From a letter from Brentano to Marty, dated October 3, 1911.
6. Letter from Brentano to Bergman from December 23, 1911, reproduced in Bergman 1985: 42. In the same letter, Brentano makes it clear that only a conversion would give him access to a university career: "you are certainly gaining more and more the knowledge of how important it would be if an obstacle of completely external nature [=Bergman's confession, GF], which threatens your university career, could be eliminated." Here as in all other places, all translations from German and French into English are my own.
7. In a letter from Marty to Brentano, dated January 12, 1911, Marty reports from a discussion with Stumpf that "he [Stumpf] … would give his approval to Bergmann's habilitation if he weren't a Jew, since they are so richly blessed with this race in Berlin." Quoted in Gimpl 2001: 366.
8. See in particular Marty's letter to Brentano from January 9, 1912, also quoted in Gimpl 2001: 330f.
9. Letter from Marty to Brentano, April 8, 1912, also quoted in Gimpl 2001: 332. Marty retired in 1913, a year before his death. Kraus took over Marty's chair in 1916.
10. During these years, Bergman was also very active in the Jewish intellectual circle led by his mother-in-law Berta Fanta (1866–1918), who also attended Marty's lectures. See Gimpl 2001 and Reuveni 1993. As Bergman recalls in Bergman 1974a, Albert Einstein also took part in these meetings during his Prague years in 1911–12. According to another member of the circle, mathematician Gerhard Kowalewski (Kowalewski 1950: 249ff), Ehrenfels and Philipp Frank attended regularly.
11. See Bergman 1946 for a selection of these letters. According to Marvin Farber, editor of *Philosophy and Phenomenological Research* at the time when Bergman published these letters, Brentano's son John Brentano, following the advice of Kraus, insisted on "omitting" certain letters. Bergman agreed, since eight letters from Brentano to Bergman that are still preserved in the Bergman Archives in Jerusalem are not published in Bergman 1946. See Bergman, ARC 1502-01-858, which also contains Farber's letter to Bergman from August 27, 1941.
12. Slightly different characterizations have been proposed by Rotenstreich (1985), who sees the line falling between the Prague School period and his later interest in the natural sciences; and by Zvie Bar-On (1985), who sees the settlement in Jerusalem in 1920 as the intersection between the early and the late Bergman.
13. More on this in the next section. Bergman sent a copy of Bergman 1913 to Brentano in the autumn of 1913. From that point on, Brentano stopped addressing Bergman in his letters as "Dear Friend" and switched to "Esteemed Herr Doktor." The tone of the correspondence between Brentano and Bergman changed drastically after this event and ceased shortly after (see Bergman 1946). On Bergman's sympathies with idealism and transcendental phenomenology, see, for instance, Bergman 1927; 1955; 1964; 1967.
14. This was not only the case for Oskar Kraus, but also for Georg Katkov, Walter Del-Negro, Ernst Foradori, and many other "grand-students" of Brentano and Meinong in Graz and Innsbruck (see Chapter 36).
15. On Bergman's general contribution to philosophy, see the collections published in Zvi Bar-On 1985 and in the special issue of *Iyyun* (Melzer 1975). For a study of Bergman's Judaism in English, see Kluback 1992. An exhaustive bibliography of the works of Bergman published before 1967 has been published in Shohetman and Shunami 1968.
16. Bergman fought as a lieutenant and later on as a captain until the end of the war.
17. According to Johnston (1972: 306), Bergman held similar views on Ehrenfels 1916/1948.
18. For the relevant passages from Bolzano's *Wissenschaftslehre*, see Bolzano (1837/2014), I:316/I:228. For a discussion of Bergman's interpretation, see Fréchette 2010: 124ff.
19. Like other irrealia (e.g., values, relations, collectives), the existence of Marty's states of affairs (*Urteilsinhalte*, "judgment-contents") stands and fails with the existence of the objects (the realia) on which they are based. They are however ontologically independent of the act of judging. See Marty 1908: 294, and Chapter 27.
20. Bergman admitted later that his Brentanian interpretation of Bolzano in Bergman 1909a didn't fully do justice to the work of the Bohemian philosopher (according to his private correspondence with Edgar Morscher).
21. "[W]e must consider Bolzano and Lotze as its [Marty's theory] fathers, although the pedigree of this theory is much older and its foundation is Plato's theory of ideas" (Bergman 1937: 5).

22. See also Bergman 1931; 1938; 1967. Bergman (1938) proposes the first reconstruction of the symbolism of Maimon's logical calculus, as exposed in Maimon 1794.
23. See Bar-Hillel (1954: 149). For a more critical view of Bergman 1953, see Bar-Hillel 1955.
24. In Bergman 1953, he still defends the Brentanian view that logic concerns the laws of thought. On Maimon's principle of determinability, see also Bergman 1931; 1938.
25. The ideas of Bergman 1950 are developed further in Bergman 1953. Bar-Hillel (1955) is a very incisive critic of the latter work, although, according to Poznanski, it was the result of tremendous pressure put on him to attenuate its hostility (private communication from Joseph Agassi).
26. The same idea is repeated in Bergman 1910b: 112, where he endorses Marty's account of the reference to nonexistence of objects in terms of a possible correlation between consciousness and its objects.
27. The dissertation also deals with the opposition between Boltzmann and Mach on the reality of atoms. Bergman relied to an important extent on the expositions of Stallo (1901), a friend of Mach and Brentano in Florence. The topic was of central interest at that time, especially since Elster and Geitel's experiments on Crooke's spinthariscope from 1903 was taken by some to be an empirical proof of the existence of atoms. Following the report of an assistant of Boltzmann, Stefan Meyer, even Mach accepted the proof after looking at the spinthariscope: "Now I believe in the existence of atoms." On Mach and Elster and Geitel's experiment, see the report in Meyer 1992.
28. Reichenbach (1921/1978) provides a systematic dismantling of the arguments of Kraus 1919.
29. According to a letter from the secretary of the Brentano Society, Georg Katkov, to Bergman from February 17, 1938, Rothenberg sent a version of his M.A. thesis written in German to Oskar Kraus, most likely hoping to get it published by the Brentano Society. Katkov judged the work to be insufficiently informed about Brentano's logic. The copy sent by Rothenberg (Rothenberg 1937) is still in Kraus' archives in Prague. In his later years, Rothenberg validated a German version of this PhD dissertation in his hometown of Frankfurt, probably the only work on Brentano or on mathematical logic supervised jointly by Theodor Adorno and Max Horkheimer. See Rothenberg 1962. On Adorno's and Horkheimer's appreciation of Rothenberg and his dissertation, see Angermann 2015.
30. See also his articles on Bolzano and analyticity (Bar-Hillel 1950; 1952) and on Husserl's purely logical grammar (1957).
31. Hijab was secretary at the meeting of the Moral Sciences Club when the poker affair between Wittgenstein and Popper occurred. He left Cambridge in 1948 and later became professor of Mathematics at the American University of Beirut. He reported to Bergman on his stay in Cambridge in a letter from January 26, 1947.
32. For example, the name of Bergman is not mentioned once in the nearly 1000 pages on the history of Jewish philosophy by Frank and Leaman (1997). Kavka, Braiterman, and Novak 2012, focusing only on Jewish philosophy from the modern era, do slightly better: Bergman is mentioned in five footnotes distributed over 900 pages.
33. I would like to thank the National and University Library of Jerusalem for giving me access to Hugo Bergman's archives, in particular Gil Weissblei and Oded Fluss for their support. Many thanks also to Joseph Agassi, Johannes Brandl, Denis Fisette, Uriah Kriegel, Enrico Lucca, Edgar Morscher, Kevin Mulligan, and Hamid Taieb for helpful comments. This paper has been written as part of the project "Signification et intentionnalité chez Anton Marty" directed by Kevin Mulligan and Laurent Cesalli and funded by the Swiss National Science Foundation (SNF), project number 152921.

ARCHIVAL MATERIALS

Bergman, S. H. (1937) "What is truth?" lecture presented in Harvard, 1937. Archives of the National and University Library of Jerusalem, ARC. 4* 1502 03 70b.

Rothenberg, B. (1937) Work without title [Bez označení titulu—práce z odborné logiky. Strojopis, 74 s.], Archiv akademie věd České Republiky Praha, Osobní fond Oskara Krause, IIIa-Č-15-17. [Authorship attributed by the author of this paper, GF]

Letter from Brentano to Marty, October 3, 1911. Archives of the Houghton Library, Harvard University, Cambridge (MA).

Letter from Marty to Brentano, January 12, 1912. Archives of the Houghton Library, Harvard University, Cambridge (MA).

Letter from Marty to Brentano, April 8, 1912. Archives of the Houghton Library, Harvard University, Cambridge (MA).

Letter from Marvin Farber to Hugo Bergman, August 27, 1941. Archives of the National and University Library of Jerusalem, ARC. 4* 1502 01 858.

Letter from Georg Katkov to Hugo Bergman, February 17, 1938. Archives of the National and University Library of Jerusalem, ARC. 4* 1502 01 1415.

Letter from Wasfi Hamad Hijab to Hugo Bergman, January 26, 1947. Archives of the National and University Library of Jerusalem, ARC. 4* 1502 01 1421.

35

Brentano and the Lvov-Warsaw school

Arianna Betti

1 INTRODUCTION

The Lvov-Warsaw School was one of the (two, in fact) most important movements in twentieth-century scientifically oriented philosophy. Its foundation can be uncontroversially identified with the appointment in 1895 to the Chair of Philosophy in Lvov (currently Lviv, Ukraine) of Kazimierz Twardowski (1866–1938), who had been a student and follower of Franz Brentano in Vienna in 1886–1895.[1] One can safely say that both the Lvov-Warsaw School's existence and its flourishing were mostly due to Twardowski's strenuous organizational and didactic activity—so much that "member of the Lvov-Warsaw School" appears synonymous with "direct or indirect pupil of Twardowski".[2] Also beyond doubt is that Brentano's influence on Twardowski was profound, that Twardowski arrived in Lvov with the intention of spreading Brentano's ideas on Polish soil and that he emphatically put that intention into practice (Twardowski 1991: 26; cf. Betti 2006a: 55). Far from being conclusively established, by contrast, is the extent of Brentano's influence on the Lvov-Warsaw School. Shortly put, and in some anticipation of what follows, in certain aspects that influence was all-pervading, in other aspects quite limited. Jerzy Giedymin captured the situation like this:

> The Brentano–Twardowski philosophy did not appeal much to most of Twardowski's students. He influenced them not so much through any specific philosophical doctrine as through his teaching activities and the ideals of clarity, precision and rationality which he preached.
>
> (Giedymin 1986: 190)

Giedymin makes two points. The first regards issues of metaphilosophical kind (of great influence), the second "Brentano–Twardowski"-specific philosophical doctrines (of little influence).

The first point is ubiquitously echoed in the scholarly literature. There was a set of ideas regarding the nature of philosophical inquiry and the methodology of philosophy that simply *defined* the kind of philosophy done in the Lvov-Warsaw School. Philosophy should be clear, precise, antispeculative (i.e. rationality driven) and consisting of justified statements; as Brentano's fourth *Habilitation* thesis stated, the true method of philosophy is the same as that of the natural sciences. As a corollary, German idealistic metaphysics was to be opposed (Woleński 2014: 174; see also Twardowski 2014: 49). To get an idea of the kind of philosophical work done and appreciated by the School, one might consider Kotarbińska 1932, where Janina Kotarbińska (Dina Sztejnbarg-Kamińska, 1901–1997) distinguished a full 26 different meanings of the term "chance".

Giedymin's second point is rarely echoed. Quite the contrary, in fact: there have been several attempts to establish that "Brentano–Twardowski"-specific philosophical doctrines *did* exert considerable influence upon the Lvov-Warsaw School. Most influential among these attempts is probably Woleński and Simons' (1989) seminal article on the influence of Brentano's ideas on truth in the Lvov-Warsaw School up to Tarski. The paper clearly focused on one theme, truth—but perhaps because truth is such an important and iconic theme, given its association with Tarski and his Polish background, a general picture somehow emerged according to which Tarski was Brentano's philosophical great-grandson.[3]

An alternative line of research has recently brought renewed support for Giedymin's stance. If specific "Brentano–Twardowski" doctrines are present, it is argued, they are present only in (some phases of the thought of) some exponents of the Lvov-Warsaw School. Even general philosophical stances such as the respect for Aristotle-style metaphysics in the sense of a (formal) theory of objects, including mereology,[4] it is argued, are due to an intellectual mix stemming from the philosophical tradition in general, including a substantial share of ideas coming from Bernard Bolzano (Betti 2006a, 2006b, forthcoming). If so, similar considerations, one might argue, presumably hold for traits strongly connected to traditional metaphysics, namely realism and the correspondence theory of truth.[5] In this paper, I will provide some additional focus to this alternative, back-to-Giedymin line.

2 THE "BRENTANO–TWARDOWSKI" DOCTRINES

Importantly, Twardowski did not belong to Brentanian orthodoxy (unlike Marty, Kraus and Kastil; see Haller 1986: 17–18); he deviated instead in substantial aspects from Brentano's own stances (like Meinong and Husserl; *ibid.*). Giedymin aptly speaks of "Brentano–Twardowski philosophy", for Brentano's doctrines came to Poland thus variously altered. In this light, a good way to proceed is to first distinguish the specific themes on which Twardowski agreed with Brentano (the "Brentano–Twardowski" philosophy) from the specific themes on which he disagreed with him, and then to investigate which (dis)agreements were actually taken up by Twardowski's pupils. In this and the following section, I will offer some remarks on both points and conclude with a general suggestion for further research.

The "Brentano–Twardowski" doctrines that are sensible for us to consider here— Twardowski's agreements with Brentano—are the following. (Agr.i) Twardowski took descriptive psychology to be foundational for the whole of philosophy, including logic (Betti and Raspa 2016: ix; see also this volume, Chapter 4). Twardowski's general apparatus of key philosophical concepts revolved around *intentionality* as mark of the mental, that is, concepts such as *presentation, judgement, inner perception*, etc., played a fundamental role in philosophy and thus in logic (*ibid.*); (Agr.ii) Twardowski adhered to the method of descriptive analysis or analytic description, rather than championing the formal methods of logic (Woleński 2014: 173–4). Moreover, (Agr.iii) descriptive psychology had to keep its primacy (Schaar 2015: 22) and was to be preferred to experimental psychology, especially as far as the role and value of introspection was concerned (Rzepa 2015: 240, 244), notwithstanding the fact that, according to Twardowski, descriptive psychology needed to be supplemented by experimental psychology to overcome certain shortcomings (Rzepa 2015: 243); an example of the latter is Wundt's experiments, which had the advantage of being repeatable and also accessible to others, not only to the agent who has the perceptions (Schaar 2015: 22). Finally, (Agr.iv) Twardowski saw ethics as having cognitive content, with a basis in emotional experience (Brożek 2015: 163 n. 10).

All four points just highlighted are related in an important manner: in particular, (Agr. ii) and (Agr.iii) concern the method of (Agr.i), and (Agr.iv) derives directly from (Agr.i).

As to Twardowski's deviations from Brentano, those that might be sensible for us to consider here are the following. (Dev.i) Twardowski took *truth* to be absolute instead of time-dependent, a move that went hand in hand with his choosing judgement-tokens as truth-bearers instead of judgement-types like Brentano (Betti 2006b: 378–9, especially n. 20).[6] (Dev.ii) Twardowski took *truth-bearers* to come in two forms, existential and relational (instead of accepting only the existential form like Brentano—see Chapter 10); those of relational form had S-P form, to wit the Bolzanian form of propositions "*A* has *b*" (Betti and van der Schaar 2004: 8, Betti and Raspa 2016: xxxi). (Dev.iii) Twardowski took the (non-simple) *object* of truth-bearers to be of two kinds, complexes and relationships (instead of one kind, complexes, as Brentano did), taking relationships to be Bolzano-like relationships of *having* between an object *A* and quality *b*. Twardowski's relationships as objects of judgements are special objects that have been likened to (Betti and van der Schaar 2004), or straightforwardly identified with (Betti and Raspa 2016) a state of affairs. (Dev.iv) Twardowski accepted *nonexisting objects* in his ontology, a consequence of his specific grafting of the content–object distinction onto Brentano's theory of intentionality (Betti 2013: §2, §5); in this way, Twardowski legitimated Aristotle-style metaphysics (whether or not broadened with nonexistents) as a respectable field of inquiry. Lastly, (Dev.v) by contrast with Brentano's theism (see Chapter 24), Twardowski had a rather complicated relationship with religion (Brożek 2012: ch. 7, §2).[7]

* * *

Let's now ask: to what extent did the Lvov-Warsaw School follow the elements above, in particular the agreements, the "Brentano–Twardowski" doctrines? Given the sheer scope of such an investigation—Woleński (1989: 15, 352–3) offers an incomplete list of *80* exponents of the Lvov-Warsaw School—nothing remotely near to an exhaustive answer is going to follow in the next couple of pages, nor is it in fact as yet available. At any rate, a credible conjecture should at least take the following into account.

Even if the School's most renowned exponents were formal logicians (notably Łukasiewicz, Leśniewski, and Tarski), Twardowski trained philosophers also in many other fields: epistemology, ethics, aesthetics and, importantly for us, psychology. Indeed, as it was common in his time, and in keeping with (Agr.i), Twardowski saw psychology as one of the "philosophical sciences".[8] Now, as I show elsewhere (Betti 2006a, forthcoming), it was the logicians that were *least* influenced, when not outright critical of, the first two "Brentano–Twardowski" doctrines (the foundational role of psychology in logic, and the primacy of descriptive analysis over formal logic). By contrast, the psychologists (and some of the ethicists, arguably) seem to have built upon all four doctrines (Agr.i-iv)—while also taking up some of the deviating elements, notably Twardowski's absolutist position on truth (Dev.i). This is ratified by Kotarbiński's 1933 overview of what was going on in Polish philosophy at the time. After mentioning absolutism as a common trait of the School (notably the sole non-metaphilosophical trait he mentions), Kotarbiński writes:

> The group of the psychologists [has] come far less further from the original direction of the School than the logicians. I am thinking of Władysław Witwicki … Stefan Baley … Stefan Błachowski … and Mieczysław Kreutz.
>
> (Kotarbiński 1933: 220)[9]

> The main role is, however, played since a while by the Warsaw School, headed by three exponents of the logicistic direction: Prof. J. Łukasiewicz, Prof. S. Leśniewski and lecturer A. Tarski.
>
> (Kotarbiński 1933: 222)

In light of the above, a promising general reconstruction of the influence of (the early) Brentano upon the Lvov-Warsaw School should centre around local and (inter)national developments in those philosophical fields that were soon to become separate scientific disciplines, to wit: psychology and logic. For a first sample, let's now take a brief look to a small selection of first-generation Lvov–Warsaw exponents.

3 THE "BRENTANO–TWARDOWSKI" DOCTRINES IN THE LVOV-WARSAW SCHOOL

3.1 (Mostly) Agreements: Primacy of Psychology and Descriptive Analysis

Tadeusz Czeżowski (1889–1981) is considered the most Brentanian among Twardowski's students (Brożek 2012: ch. 10, §2.2.).[10] He followed Brentano's idiogenetic theory of judgement (Czeżowski 1925) and—at least after 1938 (Łukasiewicz 2006: 204 ff.)—a Brentano-like "existential" reading of judgements (though modified as in (Dev.iii) above). He also clearly endorsed the method of analytic description (Agr.ii)—"the most certain method of philosophy" (Czeżowski 2000: 51)—which, as mentioned, is key to Brentano's descriptive psychology as a science yielding self-evident, certain statements, and fundamental to its foundational role with respect to other sciences. The method consists in inferring general and apodictic statements from an analysis by a certain form of intuition of a single example taken to represent a totality, for instance "*every* mental phenomenon has its object" or "in *every* conviction the existence of its object is asserted or negated"

(Czeżowski 2000: 44). Among examples of works in psychology that apply the method of analytic description, Czeżowski mentions Witwicki's psychological analysis of the concept of ambition (Witwicki 1900, the first PhD dissertation that Twardowski supervised).

Władysław Witwicki (1878–1948) was one of Twardowski's closest pupils. Though active in several other fields, including ethics, aesthetics and philosophy of culture, he is most known for his work in psychology. He authored the first handbook of psychology in Poland (Witwicki 1925), a work reflecting introspection-based psychology à la Brentano. In keeping with (Agr.iii) above, in 1902, Witwicki visited both the Brentanian Alois Höfler in Vienna (see Chapter 36) and Wundt's famous laboratory in Leipzig (Jadczak 1997: 30). Witwicki developed *cratism*, a theory including a concept similar to that of inferiority complex developed later by Alfred Adler, the main difference being Witwicki's positive evaluation of ambition (Nowicki 1982: 63). Particularly interesting for (Dev.v) is Witwicki's work in psychology of religion, which was very critical of religion as meaningless (Grzymała-Moszczyńska 2008: 580). Worth mentioning in this connection is *La foi des éclairés* ("The Faith of the Enlightened"), written in 1935 but published in French four years later (Witwicki 1939) after editorial difficulties in Poland (Nowicki 1982: 8). In Witwicki 1939, he anticipated the idea of *cognitive dissonance* to explain religious belief among educated people—the *éclairés* of the title, today's individuals with an MA degree, say (Grzymała-Moszczyńska 2008: 581), by drawing upon conceptualisations resting on Alexius Meinong's concept of assumption (see Chapter 29).

3.2 (Mostly) Disagreements: Antipsychologism in Logic and Formal Methods

Singularly scarce are discussions of Brentano's ideas in the *oeuvre* of Kazimierz Ajdukiewicz (1890–1963). As Brożek (2012: ch. 10, §2.2.) also notices, there is, tellingly, no mention of Brentano in *Main Trends in Philosophy* (Ajdukiewicz 1923), a famous philosophical anthology in Poland. Although we find one mention of Brentano's existential reading of the traditional S-P syllogistic forms in Ajdukiewicz 1937, Ajdukiewicz calls such reading "without existential import"—something that goes right against Brentano's view. Finally, Ajdukiewicz 1937, a popularising overview article on trends and currents in present-day philosophy, in which Ajdukiewicz quotes about 100 other philosophers in six pages, devotes as much space to Brentano as to, for example, Mach, Avenarius or Heidegger.

Likewise, despite the (dis)similarities between the reism of Tadeusz Kotarbiński (1886–1981) and Brentano's post-1904 position (see Chapter 13), Kotarbiński's *oeuvre* contains little acknowledgment of Brentano, except for a few cursory niceties,[11] and for Kotarbiński 1966. The latter, together with Kotarbiński 1970, is particularly telling for us. Kotarbiński 1966 explains that the reason for his lack of consideration for Brentano's ideas as a young philosopher was his antipsychologistic interest in formal logic; Kotarbiński 1970 mentions in a critical tone Brentano's view that psychology was "even the main part of philosophy".

This brings us to two towering figures of Polish logic, Jan Łukasiewicz (1878–1956) and Stanisław Leśniewski (1886–1939), most famously associated, respectively, with many-valued logics and with a nominalistic system of the foundations of mathematics and a formal mereology (roughly, classical extensional mereology). Both Łukasiewicz and Leśniewski had early traditional beginnings in logic (up to around 1915), during which they adhered to (Dev.i-iii) together with Kotarbiński, sometimes in an even stronger version. For instance, as regards the form of truth-bearers (Dev.ii), Łukasiewicz and Leśniewski departed completely from Brentano in taking *all* truth-bearers to have S-P form (Betti forthcoming, §2);[12] as regards (Dev.iii), they all took relations of inherence (as opposed to Brentano's complex objects) as objects of their truth-bearers of choice (*ibid.*).

No matter how strongly one might desire to find some element of general Brentanian continuity even in the Brentano-deviant traits I have mentioned, Leśniewski and Łukasiewicz forcefully recanted those traits as poor traditional "philosophico-grammatical" beginnings. One might want to insist that Łukasiewicz's and Leśniewski's early beginnings still were influenced, respectively, by Marty, Mill and Husserl, and by Meinong, but in doing so, one should not forget that those juvenile flirtations were soon over; as soon as Russell's *Principia* and Frege's *Grundgesetze* arrived in Poland, what was kept of those beginnings were only those parts that could be recast into deductive theories using formal methods. In little-known sources, Łukasiewicz appears as the most virulent anti-Brentanian of Twardowski's pupils.[13] By contrast with (Agr.ii), he radicalized as it were the scientific approach to philosophy into what Twardowski was to define as "symbolomania", that is, the acceptance of formal methods as the only method of philosophy (cf. Brożek 2012: ch. 10, §2.2.).[14] According to Łukasiewicz, Twardowski's worst mistake, next to psychologism, was the (strongly related) fact that he did not keep up with the newest developments in mathematical logic—or, as it was called then, *logistics*.

> I had been disliking the psychologism cultivated by Twardowski already for long time…. The apparatus of ideas and problems that Twardowski brought with him from Vienna to Lvov was incredibly poor and sterile. Whether a conviction was a mental phenomenon of a separate kind or a connection of concepts was incessantly under discussion, intuitions, presentations, concepts, their content and object were incessantly under discussion, and no one knew whether the analyses carried out … belonged to psychology, logic or grammar.
> (from Łukasiewicz's 1949–54 diary, quoted in Betti 2006a: 64)

Łukasiewicz's points, minus the contempt, resonate in every published piece by Kotarbiński in which the heritage of the "Brentano–Twardowski" doctrines is discussed in the context of the developments of the relationship between logic and psychology with respect to philosophy ("From today's perspective, the times of psychologism, when formal logic considered itself as a part of psychology, appear prehistorical", Kotarbiński 1933: 221). Łukasiewicz's points are also indirectly confirmed—from the opposite point of view, this time—in letters to Twardowski from those pupils who instead remained closer to the master's original doctrines.[15]

CONCLUSION

The influence of Brentano on the Lvov-Warsaw School was all-pervading as far as metaphilosophical ideals such as rationality and scientifically oriented precision and clarity of style were concerned. As far as specific doctrines were concerned, however, things stand otherwise. The considerations in this paper suggest that it might be sensible to investigate the issue further from the perspective of the general historical development, in and outside Poland, of those disciplines that, at the time, were about to become independent sciences: logic and psychology, and including, importantly, their relationship to philosophy. For the more an exponent of the Lvov-Warsaw School was involved in the development of formal *logic* as a discipline, or *logistics*, it seems, the further away s(he) was from what I have marked as "Brentano–Twardowski" doctrines, whereas the closer s(he) was to *psychology* as a discipline, the closer s(he) stayed to those doctrines. To test this claim adequately, a more extensive investigation, preferably aided by quantitative analysis, of the works of the exponents of the Lvov-Warsaw School (ideally, all 80!) would be desirable.

NOTES

1. On this period of Twardowski's life, see Brożek 2012.
2. For a problematisation, cf. Zamecki 1977: 33 ff. A good place to start for information on the Lvov-Warsaw School is (Woleński 2015).
3. Along this line, Rojszczak (2006), followed by Schaar (2015), maintains that Brentano's choice of *judgements* as primary truth-bearers was influential on the choice of *meaningful sentences* as truth-bearers in the majority of Twardowski's students (and up to Tarski).
4. This was an important element of difference between the Poles and the Vienna Circle (see Łukasiewicz 1936 §II).
5. Here I thus dissent from Albertazzi 1993: 28.
6. Note that we cannot ascribe, for example, (Dev.i) in full to the later Twardowski (1911), because according to the latter, the truths of logic aren't token-judgements (cf. Betti, 2006b: 15).
7. I disregard here a possible (Dev.vi), that is, the fact that Twardowski accepted four kinds of mental phenomena instead of three (Schaar 2015: 90).
8. See Brożek 2015: 158 and the references to Twardowski's writings there.
9. This and all other translations in this paper are my own.
10. For an extensive introduction to Czeżowski, see Coniglione 1997.
11. Kotarbiński (1929), arguably his *opus majus*, contains exactly *one* insignificant footnote mentioning Brentano. It is appended to a discussion of psychology characterised in a non-Brentanian way as a *natural* science next to physics and biology.
12. Kotarbiński, and according to Łukasiewicz (2006: 202 ff.), Czeżowski at least at some point, endorsed (Dev.ii).
13. The last three claims find their support in Betti 2006a: esp. 64–6, 69.
14. *Pace* Woleński's (1989: 45 ff.), Twardowski's target seem to have indeed been Łukasiewicz (and arguably Leśniewski). In a letter of January 11, 1920, from Witwicki to Twardowski, we read: "I don't know which tooth actually aches me when next to me Łukasiewicz talks to Lesniewski about 'sentences', as if it were only about the grammar of words and about expressions, and not about things, objects, and, facts, statements, rejections, cognitions and about the objective world, and knowing subjects and their mutual relations" (quoted from Jadczak 1997: 32). See also Halpern's letter to Twardowski from May 2, 1921, on http://segr-did2.fmag.unict.it/~polphil/PolPhil////Lesnie/LesnieDoc.html#IH1921
15. "He [Leśniewski] says that while sciences were confused and not worth a damn, they were grouped under the name of 'philosophy'—and as soon as one of them improved, a special science was suddenly made of it, to indicate just physics, which came from philosophy. They say the same about logic, which now abjures its great link with philosophy; the same applies to psychology, which has ceased philosophizing and only measures response times". Witwicki to Twardowski, December 3, 1920, see http://segr-did2.fmag.unict.it/~polphil/PolPhil//Lesnie/LesnieDoc.html#Witwicki (see also the previous note).

36

The Innsbruck School

Wilhelm Baumgartner

The roots of the Innsbruck School of philosophy and psychology—with its representatives, especially Franz Hillebrand, Emil Arleth, Alfred Kastil, and Franziska Mayer-Hillebrand—lay in Prague and, further back, in Vienna. There, Franz Brentano was a most influential teacher, but after losing his chair in 1880, he had to send his most promising students to his former students Carl Stumpf and Anton Marty. Both Stumpf and Marty held positions at Prague's Charles University at the same time (1880–1884). Stumpf then followed calls elsewhere (see Chapter 28). Marty stayed in Prague and formed a franchise, so to speak, of Brentano's Vienna School (see Chapter 27).

Marty's early work focusses on investigations on "color sense" (Marty 1879). He rejects (a) the "physiological" hypothesis that the development of color sensation originated by way of the development of physiology. Instead, he tries to show that the "development" of color sensation can be explained by the attempt to get "more distinct impressions of the manifold [color] qualities," that is, by developing a capacity for better noticing their differences, which enables one to judge about them in the whole spectrum of the visual field (Marty 1916a: 227 f.). Marty also rejects (b) a contemporary hypothesis suggesting (on the basis of interpretation of literary sources) that our ancestors suffered from color blindness. This historical or rather philological "quasi-argument" (*Scheinargument*) shows, claims Marty, ignorance of "laws of psychology of language" (*ibid.*: 197–229). Therefore, the issue of color sensation should be treated neither in a "historical" nor in a pure "physiological" way (as in Hering's doctrine of the light sense) but first of all in a philosophical–psychological manner—especially so long as physiology is not fully developed as a science. Marty instead takes a descriptive psychology approach to color sensation, suggesting the hypothesis that it is our interest in color qualities and their brightness that had grown (Marty 1879: 119 ff.).[1]

In May 1887, Marty requested the installment of a "psychological cabinet" in Prague. To Brentano he writes: "I visited Hering and Mach and talked to both about the psychological cabinet. Both reacted most positively to the idea and assured their assistance, especially Hering." (MB 11.01.1887) Carl Stumpf was involved in this initiative, as well as Franz Hillebrand. "Meanwhile," Brentano replies, "Hillebrand has written to you my opinion regarding the petition for the cabinet.... It is good that Hering and Mach are giving you good advice." (BM 27.01.1887) Marty's request was successful, and eventually he was able to furnish his cabinet with "a small collection of apparatus for purposes of illustration" (Antonelli 2011: LXXVII).

Marty was on good terms with his Prague colleagues Hering and Mach. Marty's increasing descriptive approach, Hering's more physiological approach, and Mach's more physicalistic one not only competed with, but also complemented, each other.

1 FRANZ HILLEBRAND

Such was the situation when Brentano sent his student Hillebrand from Vienna to Prague. Under Marty, Hillebrand wrote his dissertation on "Synechology" (Hillebrand 1887). He investigated the role of continua ("synechonta") and their relations. In the relation of connections there are the relations (i) of part to part, (ii) of part and whole, or of part and continuum. The latter comes in two varieties. First, there are (a) the "homousious" part–whole relation, where part and whole share the same essence (*ousia*) as in the relation of a genus (e.g., color) and its *differentia specifica* (e.g., red). Brentano in his metaphysics lectures had called this the relation logical parthood. Hillebrand had attended Brentano's lectures and now was making use of them. Secondly, there are also (b) the "allousious" part–whole relations, where part and whole are connected but have different essences, like color qualities (e.g., red) and their spatial determinations (e.g., location). These essentially different parts are united *in* the whole phenomenon *color*; they mutually *determine* the whole and *individuate* a physical phenomenon. It is impossible for there to be a quality (of a thing) without *some* place it "takes up," nor for there to be a place not "filled" with some quality (see Chapter 15). There is, in reality, no empty space or place per se, nor nonlocated quality or quality per se. The location of a thing is its substantial part. If it disappears, its quality (which is its accidental part) also disappears. The quality may change, that is, be replaced by another one, but the location must persist. The result of synechology is an example of how to think of the relation of substance and accident, thereby solving an old metaphysical problem.

Back in Vienna, Hillebrand wrote his *Habilitationsschrift* (Hillebrand 1891), an explanation and development of Brentano's logic, the lectures on which he had attended. Hillebrand defends the following claims. (a) Judgment is not a mere connection of the content of presentations but a mental act in its own right (this is Brentano's "idiogenetic" theory of judgment—see Chapter 10). (b) "The essence of a judgment consists in a specific intentional relation towards the immanent object" (1891: 25 f.). (c) A judgment is evident if it is correct and known as correct (characterized as correct), so that it is neither capable of proof nor in need of proof; it is evident when and only when it refers to axioms based on immediate perception (*ibid*.: 6). (d) Brentano's reduction of categorical judgments to existential ones is the most adequate expression of judgments. "Just as the existential proposition 'S is (exists)' expresses nothing but the simple acknowledgment of S, the so-called categorical proposition 'S is P' expresses the simple acknowledgment of SP" (*ibid*.: 28). Therefore, "fundamental reforms of the syllogistics" are needed (*ibid*.: 2;

cf. Brentano 1874 Bk. II, Chapter. 8.). In 1872–3, Brentano had already tried to convince John Stuart Mill of his "new ideas on the mental operation of judgment," yet not with complete success (see Mill 1972: 1927–9).

Meinong harshly criticized Hillebrand's book and ridiculed him for his repeated function as Brentano's "substitute speaker" (cf. Meinong 1892: 200; Goller 1989: 89–91). Yet, Meinong's statement seems rather unjust, as Hillebrand's role as a genuine Brentano interpreter is by far not his entire story. He was also a student of Hering and a collaborator in his physiological laboratory, and he also studied Mach (Mach 1886) and approved of his theory of hypotheses (Hillebrand 1896a). He dropped Mill's theory according to which hypotheses cannot be verified if they lack a *"vera causa."* Following Mach, he recommends as the goal of scientific hypotheses not an instruction of the "true nature" of external procedures but "just an utmost comprehensive and at the same time parsimonious description of phenomena which are immediately accessible to our experience" (1896a: 61). This sort of description, Brentano protests, neglects the "principle of the higher probability of the simpler hypothesis" (Brentano 1982: 71).

Mach in his turn applauded Hillebrand for his criticism of Mill for, among other things, his investigation on "binary vision" (Hillebrand 1902), in which he described his experiments with long parallel strings (*Fadenexperimente*), which seem to converge in the distance with the result that the geometrical properties of the visual field differ from those in the real field. This coincided not only with Mach's distinction between physiological and metrical areas and with Hering's distinction between real space and physiological space but also with Brentano's distinction between physical appearances and real physical objects (see Chapter 18). In a series of papers, Hillebrand (1893, 1894, 1898) confirmed Hering 1878. In the investigation on "colour brightness" (Hillebrand 1889; cf. Hillebrand 1918: 19 ff.), he approved of Hering's opponent-processing theory of colour. He concluded that (a) to each colour sensation there corresponds a different colour quality, independently of its intensity; (b) colours as such have brightness; (c) the brightness diminishes by the change of the colours from white to yellow, to green, to blue, to black, in this order; (d) the colour grey, or colourless sensation, gets brighter if mixed up with colours of specific brightness. Hillebrand also went along with Hering's theory of "mixed colours."

Brentano opposes (a) the opponent-processing theory, according to which green is one of the simple saturated colours like red, blue, and yellow:

> Green in the proper sense of an exclusive object of our visual experience (but not in reality), e.g. a green body which reflects these rays, is a composition of blue and yellow parts. Hering and others just failed to see the yellow and blue elements in the colour green and then quickly drew the conclusion of the nonexistence of these elements.
>
> (Brentano 2009: 95)

Brentano also opposes (b) the mixed colour theory. He insists on a "law of impenetrability" according to which:

> colours like bodies in reality exclude each other [and] cannot take up the same part of the visual field … It is known that very small phenomenal parts for themselves

are unnoticeable. If we think of the visual field as mutually being filled by two colors in unnoticeable small parts, e.g. red and blue, neither will be noticeable for itself, yet the whole visual field will be noticed, and its color without a clear distinction of the different allotments will appear as a union of red and blue. The color must be what we now call purple.

(*Ibid.*: 103)

Properly speaking, "there takes place a supplanting (*Verdrängung*), not a mixture" (*ibid.*: 106). The so-called mixture is but an "improper description of facts" (*ibid.*: 114).

Brentano, in his critique of Hering's theory, implicitly criticizes Hillebrand's too. The *Privatdozent* Hillebrand had become in 1892 a Viennese colleague of Brentano's. But instead of giving regular lectures, Hillebrand undertook in summer 1893 research in Hering's laboratory (Schweinhammer 1995: 53) and visited psychological institutes abroad in summer 1894. Brentano finds Hillebrand's behavior "strange": "I am informed by students that Hille[brand] all of a sudden finished his lectures … He does not say a word about this to me, he does not even set a foot on my doorstep" (BM, 12.05.1894).

Soon thereafter, Brentano said farewell to Austria (see Brentano 1895b). Hillebrand became "substitute of the chair for philosophy under special consideration of experimental psychology," and a psychological laboratory was to be installed for this purpose. Ultimately, Hillebrand did deliver lectures on philosophy but not on psychophysics, because the faculty could provide neither financing nor available rooms for a laboratory (Schweinhammer 1995: 54–8). For Hillebrand, this problem was solved when he was appointed as ordinarius for philosophy with respect to experimental psychology at Innsbruck University in 1896, with a laboratory to be installed.

His initial Innsbruck lecture expounds his programme (Hillebrand 1896b). He first recollects Brentano's thoughts diagnosing the breakdown of philosophical systems and describing the difficult way of contemporary philosophy (see Brentano 1893a, 1895a). He then reflects on the development of modern systematic experimental psychology. Methodologically, relevant phenomena "first are to be described correctly" in order to be readied for their genetic studies (Hillebrand 1896b: 10; see Hillebrand 1929: 1, 10, 88, Brentano 1982: 1ff., 129 ff.; also Chapter 3). Corresponding to the growing duties of psychology, he recommends collaboration of well-trained physicians, physiologists, and psychologists.

The university at Innsbruck could not provide rooms for a laboratory either, however, except for a provisional room in the old city hospital that turned out to be unsuitable for housing instruments and for work in. Hillebrand had to postpone the realization of his programme until 1904, when a new university edifice was built. (cf. Goller 1989: 50, 83, 85 f., 96; Schweinhammer 1995: 94 ff.). Hans Rupp, Hillebrand's Innsbruck student (later Stumpf's assistant in Berlin), was probably the first of very few who could do experimental work in Innsbruck (Rupp 1904; cf. Labenbacher 1982: 7).

On the issue of whether chairs of (pure) philosophy could be filled by (experimental) psychologists, Hillebrand justified his call for the chair of philosophy *and* experimental psychology: He sharply argued *against* the separation of the two disciplines, the one-sided specialization on both sides, the claim that chairs of philosophy should be reserved exclusively for philosophers while separate chairs are installed in psychology; and *for* the strengthening of the philosophical education of psychologists and the mutual fruitful collaboration between the two groups of researchers (Hillebrand 1913: 1, 4f., 12 f., 19).

Hillebrand could put into practice this notion of scientific collaboration when both the philosopher Emil Arleth and the physiologist Hofmann, a Hering student, followed calls from Prague to take up positions in Innsbruck in 1905.

2 EMIL ARLETH

Arleth studied philosophy in Prague and Vienna under Stumpf, Marty, and indeed Brentano (whose lectures he followed in Vienna in 1881–82), as well as physiology under Hering and Brücke. His interests centered around Aristotle's ethics, however (Arleth 1884, 1888, 1889, 1903). In the latter area he attempted, analogously to Brentano (1862), an interpretation of Aristotelian ethics in light of the categories: "There are as many highest genera of the good," he wrote, as there are "highest categories of real beings" (Arleth 1903: 12). His 1884 dissertation, under Marty's supervision, concerned Aristotle's doctrine of *eudaimonia*. In 1903, Arleth was appointed professor extraordinarius in Prague, and in 1905 ordinarius in Innsbruck. Hillebrand had voted in favor of Arleth as the only thoroughly qualified domestic candidate.

By then, the "Innsbruck School" could rightly be seen as a direct follower of the Prague constellation, the Hering School, and the Marty–Brentano School. As Arleth had to teach history of philosophy, Hillebrand could now more and more devote his research and teaching to psychology. Due to his growing reputation and broad scientific contacts in the field, Hillebrand was elected president and organizer of the 4th congress for experimental psychology held in 1910 in Innsbruck.

Arleth died early, in 1909. According to Alfred Kastil's report to Brentano (KB, 29.03.1909), Hillebrand in his "Necrology for Arleth" had uttered his "fear of reproach of in-breeding." He concluded that rather than an Austrian philosopher, a German one ("*Reichsdeutscher*") should be Arleth's successor. Nonetheless, the Austrian Kastil got the call. The latter writes to Brentano: "As far as the method of his lectures is concerned, Hille[brand] seems to strive after you, like Marty ... I am pleased to stay in good relation to him" (KB, 03.01.1912). And two months later: "Hille[brand]'s proposal regarding my appointment as ordinarius was accepted unanimously, retroactive to the summer term" (KB, 15.03.1912).

3 ALFRED KASTIL

Kastil began his philosophical studies in Prague under Marty and Arleth. Like Arleth's, Kastil's early work focused on Aristotelian ethics (Kastil 1901, 1902). His research on the theory of knowledge (Kastil 1909), *inter alia*, tried to address the contemporary dispute between empiricists and nativists (regarding the existence of innate ideas). Hillebrand emphasized the importance of this dispute for clarifying problems such as the role of axioms and how far they involve "empirical" and/or "hardwired" elements. According to Hillebrand, Kastil first "made clear that Descartes was the first to see that an external stimulus is but a conditional cause which only gives opportunity to the sense organ to react the way inborn to it. This paves the way to ... Kant"; and further clarifies "Descartes' theory of evident judgments and the uncertain concept of the a priori that ... had created confusion over centuries" (in Goller 1989: 126). Brentano expresses his hope that this dissertation "appears just at the very right time for promotion to Innsbruck" (BK, 17.03.1909). Stumpf reckons it would "recommend him for Innsbruck" (KB, 29.03.1909) and tells Hillebrand that "Kastil's Descartes doubtless is an excellent study, a combination of objective and historical investigation which serves a deep understanding" (Oberkofler 1882/83: 151). It worked out: Kastil was appointed in Innsbruck, where he had to give lectures on philosophy and on education.

In a later work on immediate knowledge, Kastil (1912) argues that a recent attempt (by Fries and Nelson) to reform Kant's transcendental philosophy by introducing immediate knowledge as a missing psychological basis fails, for four reasons: (a) it does not reflect on the nature of judgments as a class of its own; (b) it does not appreciate that perceptions are a form of judgments (see Chapter 10); (c) it does not sufficiently consider the self-evident status of immediate knowledge; (d) it does not see that the Kantian categories, the so-called aprioristic forms of understanding, result from inner perception and thus are not aprioristic. Hillebrand is full of praise (Goller 1989: 133 f.) and successfully recommends a full professorship for Kastil.

Kastil's philosophical lectures (see Binder and Höfer 2004, Kastil-*Nachlass* A.1.2.; A.1.5.) are devoted to the interpretation and promulgation of Brentano's philosophy. The doctorates he supervised (*inter alia* of Faradori, Del Negro, and Mayer-Hillebrand) followed the Brentano–Kastil line. In Kastil's *Nachlass*, there are his numerous annotations to Brentano's posthumous writings (*ibid.*: B.1.1.–15.; BK.1.–3.), of which he prepared a "synthesis" (Kastil 1951). In his correspondence (*Nachlass*, K.1.–3.), he tries to develop Brentano's theories and to convince many contemporaries; he also edits many of Brentano's work (Brentano 1922, 1925, 1929a, 1933).[2]

When in 1934 Kastil prematurely resigned from the university for political reasons—he opposed the Nazi system and faced serious trouble as a result—his chair remained vacant. Other members of the School were at least close to the Nazi ideology. Some died in the war. A decline of the original Innsbruck School was to be observed.[3]

4 FRANZISKA MAYER-HILLEBRAND

Kastil, Kraus, and Mayer-Hillebrand emphasized Brentano's role both as midwife to and remedy against Husserl's Phenomenology (cf. Kraus 1924, Mayer-Hillebrand 1955b); the same holds for their attitude for (as far as the *Sprachkritik* is concerned) and against the neopositivistic Vienna Circle. In addition to the descriptive approach and the *Sprachkritik*, the resistance to the antimetaphysical neopositivism now became a mark of the Innsbruck School.

As Kastil could live and work in Brentano's Schönbühel home amidst the *Nachlass*, he was all the more engaged in his editorial life work. Together with Kraus, Kastil had gotten the rights of publications (see Brentano 1966a: 288, 1956: XIII). After Kraus' death, he was the sole responsible editor—with subsidy from Brentano's son, John Brentano. After Kastil died in 1950, Mayer-Hillebrand took over with the approval of John Brentano (whom she visited in the United States) and catalogued the Brentano *Nachlass*.

All three editors followed the policy of publishing Brentano's work not "in its earlier stage of development but in the latest valid" version, which "calls for omission and substitution of parts in favor of later work" in order to better "correspond to Brentano's intention" (Mayer-Hillebrand 1956: XIII).

Mayer-Hillebrand (then Reicher) had studied psychology and philosophy under Kastil and Hillebrand, as well as biology. Kastil was about to introduce her to Franz Brentano, but this attempt failed: "I regret. It is impossible for Baroness Reicher to come over Easter," writes Brentano (BK 21.03.1916). Instead, Kastil gave her relevant instructions and materials for her dissertation on "The unreal as fiction" (Reicher 1918, Mayer-Hillebrand 1966).

Reicher set forth her studies with Kastil and Hillebrand and also tried to enlarge her psychological knowledge by lectures on physiology given by Brücke. When she married Franz Hillebrand in 1920, she had the "opportunity to become acquainted with experimental psychology" as collaborator, as well as with Hillebrand's "logic and theory of knowledge" (Mayer-Hillebrand 1975: 225 f.). After her husband's death, she carried on, not in Erismann's (Hillebrand's successor's) laboratory, however, but in the neurological institute with the help of Brücke. She prepared posthumous editions of Franz Hillebrand (1929). When she married Carl Mayer in 1928, she (now Mayer-Hillebrand) continued her work on visual experiences in the tradition of Franz Hillebrand (Mayer-Hillebrand 1927, 1932). These investigations led, with Kastil's help, to her habilitation in 1932 (Mayer-Hillebrand 1975: 233–6). The results of her lectures on "geometric–optical illusions" (Mayer-Hillebrand 1942) helped her gain professorship in 1943 (a professorship withdrawn after the war and renewed in 1948).

After the war, Mayer-Hillebrand got back in touch with Kastil and told him about her plan to lecture on Brentano's philosophy. John Brentano agreed to Kastil's intention to install Mayer-Hillebrand as his successor as Brentano editor. Her editorship began after Kastil died in 1950. She gave up her work on experimental psychology, edited Kastil's *Brentano's Philosophy* (Kastil 1951), finished and edited Kastil's elaborations of the Brentano *Nachlass* (Brentano 1952, 1954, 1956, 1959, 1963, 1966a), prepared revised re-editions of already published works, and offered remarks on how to interpret correctly Brentano's philosophy (Mayer-Hillebrand 1963a, 1963b).

In her edition of *The Renunciation of the Unreal* (Brentano 1966a), she uses large parts of her dissertation as introduction. She contrasts the "ontological" view she attributes to the young Brentano with his later "reistic" philosophy, in which he (a) more and more excluded the immanent objects of thought as superfluous and dangerous duplications of the real and (b) argued in favor of the "complexity of thinking, though not by multiplying [objects] but rather by multiplying and special modifications of the relations of the thinker toward the real objects" (*ibid.*: 35).

In this division into the early and the late Brentano, with the exclusive accent on the latter as his "mature" views, Brentano himself was not innocent, as he urged his editors to follow this line.

CONCLUSION

In retrospect, it respectfully has to be confirmed that the Innsbruck School, in the sense of Hillebrand's idea of collaboration (Hillebrand 1896b), tried to fulfill its double duty: to pay its (conflicting) contribution to both Brentanian descriptive philosophy and

Hering's emancipating experimental psychology. Franziska Mayer-Hillebrand followed Franz Hillebrand's policy of doing both, working on experimental psychology and on Brentano's philosophy. Kastil, isolated in Brentano's retreat before and during the war, almost exclusively dedicated his work to Brentano. Toward the end of his life, when reading recent volumes of *Mind* provided by Rush Rhees, he came to wonder whether he and his Innsbruck colleague might not "have one-sidedly dealt too much with our own school" (to Rhees, 08.08.1948; *Nachlass* p. 833).[4]

NOTES

1. In order to prove exact impressions of the manifold color qualities and their brightness, he experimented with differently colored glasses and with an "erythroscope" (cf. Marty 1916a: 202 f.).
2. Interestingly, there is a correspondence (1933–36 and 1946–49) between Kastil and Rush Rhees, later Wittgenstein's editor, about the work of Brentano's School. Rhees also paid a visit to Kastil to read and discuss Brentano's papers.
3. To make things worse, post-war restaurative Catholic politics suppressed Brentanian philosophy. Neither the progressive Wolfgang Stegmüller, who was favored by the faculty, nor Reinhard Kamitz were given the chance to set forth their career at Innsbruck (cf. Goller 2005: 838 f.).
4. My thanks to Peter Goller, Innsbruck University library, for providing literature and suggestions.

37

Brentano, Stout and Moore

Maria van der Schaar

G. F. Stout (1860–1944), working as a philosopher in Cambridge in the early 1890s, was engaged in the new science of empirical psychology. His main inspiration for his *Analytic Psychology* (1896) was Brentano's *Psychology from an Empirical Standpoint*. I have argued elsewhere that Stout's theories of intentionality and judgement and his method of analytic psychology have played a role in the transition from Bradley's idealism to early analytic philosophy.[1] Stout's theory is best understood as a reaction to Brentano's innovative account of these notions, and I will argue that Moore was thus acquainted with Brentanian ideas. As there was no direct influence of Brentano on Moore or Russell before 1903 with respect to intentionality, judgement or ethics, Stout's Brentanian ideas may have played a mediating role. Both Russell and Moore read Stout's *Analytic Psychology* carefully, and they must also have become acquainted with Stout's ideas, when they were studying under Stout around 1894. I have focussed on Stout and Russell elsewhere; here I look mainly at Moore. Moore is also of interest, because he saw the agreements of his ethics with Brentano's (see Chapter 20), although he did not notice this before 1903. Of even more interest, there are also some important differences between Brentano and Moore regarding the question of the objectivity of logic and ethics. I will argue that these differences can be explained by Stout's typical reception of Brentano's ideas.

Stout's interest in Brentano and his students also had a more general influence on British philosophy, as Stout was the editor of *Mind* from late 1891 until 1920, that is, until Moore took over. *Mind* published reviews of the writings of the Brentano School on a regular basis, especially from the moment the new series started under Stout in 1892. According to the new editor, the aim of the journal was "to give regularly full notices of the more important articles in foreign periodicals, such as appeared in the early numbers of the old series, but were afterwards discontinued" (*Mind* 1 (n.s.), 1892: 10). There had thus already been an interest in continental psychologists and philosophers in the first volumes of the old series of *Mind*, that is, from 1876 on. The very first volume shows two reviews of Franz Brentano's *Psychologie vom empirischen Standpunkte* (1874): a seven-page notice by R. Flint on his psychology, and a four-page critique of Brentano's logic and his existential account of judgement. The latter was written by the Leyden professor J. P. N. Land, still known for his edition of Spinoza's work. According to Flint, Brentano's "style is clear, direct, and pleasant—very unlike that in which German works on psychology are generally written" (Flint 1876: 116). Although full of enthusiasm about the method, it is of interest to see what must have been new at the time: "the radical separation of conception [*Vorstellung*] and judgment—is almost certain to meet with extremely little commendation" (idem: 122). Twenty years later, the distinction was to play a crucial role in Stout's *Analytic Psychology* (1896).

1 INTENTIONALITY AND JUDGEMENT

Essential to Brentano's psychology is a distinction between act and object. Every mental phenomenon is characterised by the *intentional inexistence* of an object, that is, by its relation to a content, its being directed to an object. Brentano does not distinguish here between the content and the object of the act, but he does make it clear that the object of the act is not a reality existing independently of the act (see Chapter 4). The object of the act may be a colour, a tone, or a chimera; it may be a concept or characteristic (a *Merkmal*), such as *learned man*; or the act may itself have a mental act as its object. Colours, tones, chimeras and concepts do not have an existence independently of the act. Only the objects of inner perception, our mental acts, are known to exist (see Chapter 18).

There are three ways in which we may be related to an object, according to Brentano: we may have a presentation of it, judge it or be emotionally related to it. The essence of judgement is not to be found in a special, propositional object, but in the act of judging. Judging is a unique way in which we are related to the object. Judging is not a kind of presentation, although every judgement is dependent upon an act of presentation. Brentano is opposed to the idea of judgement as a connection of presentations, unified by the act of judgement. A judgemental act may be founded on a simple, incomposite presentation. As for Hume, a propositional account of judgement is anathema to Brentano's philosophy, as he does not want to commit himself to abstract entities such as propositions. Brentano, though, considers Hume's account of belief to be defective: judgement is not a lively idea, nor an idea accompanied by a sentiment or feeling.[2] Although Hume was right that judgement is not to be explained as a synthesis of ideas, he did not understand that the uniqueness of judgement is to be found on the side of the act. For Brentano, the act of judgement is characterised by its being an acknowledgement or rejection of existence (see Chapter 10). Every judgement is thus existential in form. In order to judge that some man is learned, one needs to have a presentation of the concept of learned man, and one acknowledges that there is an (external) object that has the characteristics of being a learned man. If one judges that something red exists, one's presentation has the colour red as content, and one acknowledges the existence of something red out there, independent of the act.

In this nonpropositional account of judgement, the judgement, rather than its object or content, is the primary bearer of truth and falsity. Judgement has thus an essential role to play in the account of the objectivity of logic. The correspondence definition of truth in terms of (non)existence of the object is merely nominal and cannot be used to explain the concept of truth (Brentano 1930, Part 1, Chap. IV, §§57–60). In order to understand any concept, we need to go back to where it is given in intuition (*Anschauung*). The concept of truth becomes clear by comparing an evident judgement with a blind judgement. A certain inner rightness (*Richtigkeit*) distinguishes the one from the other (*idem*, §12). This inner rightness is not to be identified with a feeling. As Brentano puts it in later writings from 1915, a true judgement is the judgement of those who judge as the one would judge who judges with self-evidence, that is, the one who judges rightly (Brentano 1930, Part 4, Chap. III, §3). For Brentano, the objectivity of logic is thus founded on the rightness of the act of judgement.

Stout reacts to Brentano's account of intentionality by disambiguating the notion of content to which the act is directed. For Stout, the act is directed to the object by mediation of a content (Stout 1893: 112). Whereas Brentano is right that the content is dependent upon the act, the object is not so, according to Stout. The perceptual contents by means of which we perceive the same tree differ from act to act. Content and object have to be distinguished, for (1) object and content may vary independently (Stout 1896, I: 44); (2) as a dependent part of the act, the content may exist even though no corresponding object exists and (3) the object may have properties, such as being absurd, which cannot be attributed to the existing content (*idem*: 45). As all acts have both a content and an object, which may be existing or nonexisting (*idem*: 46), we see a general theory of objects in the making. With this account of intentionality belongs a semantics in which the content plays no role, as the latter is understood to be dependent upon the mental act. The signification of a word is, for Stout, whatever we refer by means of the word, and this varies from one context to another. Although Stout does acknowledge a general meaning of a word as a condition for the different applications of the term, the general meaning is merely the result of abstraction.

Once the distinction between act and object is made, Stout agrees with Brentano that the uniqueness of judgement is to be found on the side of the act, the mode of being conscious. With reference to Brentano, Stout argues that "believing and merely thinking of something are radically distinct modes of conscious reference to an object" (*idem*: 99). Judgement or belief is a special mode of being conscious. According to Stout it is

> the Yes–No consciousness; under it I include every mode and degree of affirmation and denial—everything in the nature of an acknowledgement explicit or implicit of objective existence.
>
> (*idem*: 97)

As affirmation and denial, *yes–no consciousness* includes acts of judgement; as degrees of belief, it includes conviction. Like Brentano and Hume, Stout thus uses the term "judgement" to cover both *the act of judging*, which is an all-or-nothing affair, and *the state of conviction* (what we call today *credence*), which allows for degrees (*idem*: 97). Just as for Brentano, for Stout, judgement supervenes on an apprehension of the object (*idem*: 99). It also seems that there are two modes of judging for Stout: affirming and denying. The difference between the two modes is merely a psychological distinction, though, Stout adds. From a logical point of view, "to disbelieve a proposition is to believe its contradictory" (*idem*: 99). For Brentano, the psychological distinction *is* a logical distinction, as we know from his logic.

Another point on which Stout agrees only partly with Brentano is the idea that judgement is an acknowledgement of existence. For Brentano, if *red* is affirmed, a red object is acknowledged to exist, whereas for Stout, what is acknowledged to exist is an "objective state of things" (*idem*: 98). This objective state of things, which is a complex whole, may or may not exist. The object of judgement is thus a complex, with characteristics of a state of affairs. States of affairs may or may not exist, and their parts, which are objects of presentations, may likewise exist or not, independently of the question whether the state of affairs exists. The fact that this bird is in a state of flying is a complex whole consisting of this bird and the state of flying, a dependent part of the bird, referred to as "flying" (Stout 1896, II: 20–01). States of affairs are also called *alternatives* by Stout, as they need not be actual (*idem*, I: 101). The alternative that this bird is sitting on his nest equally includes the bird as well as a possible, nonactual state of sitting. States of affairs, alternatives, are typically expressed by (linguistic) propositions. They are capable of being affirmed or denied, but need not be so (*idem*: 111); one may merely apprehend a state of affairs. In contrast to Brentano, Stout thus defends a propositional account of judgement. This does not mean, though, that Stout in the early nineties already presents already a form of logical realism, in which states of affairs are understood as beyond space and time. *Analytic Psychology* is not meant to give an account of the objectivity of either logic or ethics. Stout's claim that the object of the act is independent of the act is not to be understood as a metaphysical thesis. For analytic psychology deals with those questions that precede any metaphysics.

In 1898, Moore presents an account of the objectivity of thought, knowledge, semantics, and logic, by means of a critique of Bradley's account of ideas and judgement. For Bradley, a logical idea is an ideal content, not having any independent existence. Brentano's idea of intentionality, in which a mental act is directed to an object, is modified already by Stout insofar as the object of the act is understood to be independent of the act. It is thus that Bradley's account can be criticised. For Moore and Russell, as for Stout, the content is dependent upon the act, and is therefore not to play any semantic role. A subjective notion like the act's content cannot be used to account for the objectivity of semantics. As the object of the act is understood to be independent of the act, a foundation for the objectivity of semantics and thought is to be given in terms of the act's object. As Moore puts it a few years later, "the *object* of a belief or idea is [to be distinguished from] the attribute or content of such belief or idea" (Moore 1901b: 717).

Bradley's account of judging is sometimes characterised as existential. The logical subject of each judgement is Reality as a whole. In the act of judgement, we refer an ideal content to a Reality beyond the act. There is no doubt that his account of judgement is nonpropositional, as Bradley is as much opposed to the abstract, Platonic notion of proposition as Brentano is. In this sense, both differ from Moore in his account of judgement in 1898, where the term "proposition" is given an objective sense, as being independent of consciousness (Moore 1898: 161–2). Distinguishing between the act and the object of judgement, Moore gives an account of judgement and truth in terms of a judgement's object rather than in terms of the act, as it is the object of judgement that is the bearer of truth and falsity, according to Moore. Truth and falsity are independent of consciousness (Moore 1898: 148, 152). These notions are not to be explained in terms of correspondence, as truth is an indefinable notion. The possible objects of thought are, for Moore, Platonic concepts, immutable and timeless, with a being independent of their being thought of. This form of Platonism is also to play an important role in Moore's account of the nature of the *good*, as we will see in §2 (cf. Moore 1897: 14). Propositions are those complex concepts that are true or false. Propositions may be composed of tables and chairs, but these tables and chairs are nothing but complex concepts themselves, having a special relation to the concept of existence.

From Bradley's account of judgement to Moore's logical realism in 1898 is a great step. On the one hand, Moore's education in classics and his knowledge of Plato may have influenced him to consider the object of thought to be a Platonic concept. This may give a background to his logical realism. On the other hand, his propositional account of judgement may have been stimulated by Stout's account of judgement, in which the object is understood as a state of affairs, a complex of objects, independent of the act of judgement. Stout's stance on Brentano's notion of intentionality may have influenced Moore in his thesis that the objectivity of logic is not to be founded on the act of judgement or on the act's content but on the *object* of the act, that is, on what is independent of the act of judgement. Stout's reaction to Brentano may thus have played a role in the development of Moore's new theory of intentionality and judgement.

2 WHOLES, PARTS AND THE OBJECTIVITY OF ETHICS

For Bradley, considering a part without the whole to which it belongs distorts the part; whole–part analysis is not a fruitful method for Bradley. For Moore, "A thing becomes intelligible first when it is analysed into its constituent concepts" (Moore 1898: 168; 1899: 182). Concepts are, for Moore, the substances of the world. They are possible objects of thought, but need not be thought of. Because things and propositions are nothing but complex concepts, understanding a thing or a proposition means analysing it into its substantial parts. Philosophical analysis is thus for Moore whole–part analysis, where each part can be understood independently of the whole. Soon, Moore was to change the idea that the world consists of nothing but Platonic concepts. For how can a proposition or a thing form a unity if all its parts have an independent existence? How can we account for relations, if both relations and their terms have an independent existence? Moore's idea that an individual is nothing but a complex of concepts is modified into the thesis that an individual thing is nothing but a complex of particular instances of universals. These particular qualities form the parts of individuals, and they are also needed to account for the relating aspect of relations (Moore 1901a: 406–7). Particular qualities are dependent parts; they would not be what they are if they were part of another individual. Philosophical analysis can stay whole–part analysis, although both independent and dependent parts are now acknowledged by Moore.

Already in 1898, in his second dissertation, Moore was in need of a nonatomistic account of wholes and parts as far as his ethics is concerned. Parts may change, they may increase their value, insofar as they become part of a whole:

> two things, which would separately be comparatively worthless, may by a special conjunction become highly valuable as parts of that whole which they combine to

form. Organisms do not appear to me to be at all good examples of such wholes; but such wholes there certainly are.

(Moore 1898: 228)

This precursor of what Moore later called *the principle of organic unities* seems to be close to Bradley's account of wholes and parts, but there is one important difference. Moore assumes that the parts have an existence independently of such a whole, which means that philosophical analysis is still a valuable method. It is rather that there are now restrictions to Moore's atomism.

One might argue that the method of whole–part analysis, at least the atomistic variant in which only independent parts are acknowledged, was already a part of the empiricist tradition, but it also plays an important role in Stout's nonatomistic analytic psychology. Directly opposing both association psychology as well as Bradley's critique of analysis, Stout claims that analysis is a central part of psychology and is needed to account for the fact that the mind is a unity (Stout 1896, I: 1). The aim of analytic psychology is

to discover the ultimate and irreducible constituents of consciousness in general. The only modern writer who appears to have fully realised the importance of this preliminary inquiry is Brentano.

(idem: 36)

"Analytic psychology" is meant as a translation of Brentano's term *deskriptive Psychologie*. For Brentano, as for Stout, mental phenomena are not atomic elements of the mental but parts of a unity of consciousness (Brentano 1874, I: 232). According to Brentano, psychological analysis reveals parts that can be separated from the whole, as well as parts with a dependent existence (see Chapter 3). In the Brentano tradition, there are two concepts of *Gestalt* to be distinguished: we may speak of a *Gestalt quality*, and of *being a Gestalt*. The former notion is introduced by Brentano's student Christian von Ehrenfels (cf. Ehrenfels 1890) (see Chapter 30). When we hear a melody, we hear more than an aggregate. We hear the melody as a separate quality of a whole of different elements, which have a relatively independent existence. This structuring quality is as much given to us in experience as the elements are; no intellectual act of the mind is needed to bring the elements together. Stout agrees in this respect with Ehrenfels, calling the *Gestalt* quality a *form of unity* (Stout 1896, I, ch. III). As qualities are for him, as for Ehrenfels, particulars, the form of unity is dependent upon the whole. When we hear the same melody in a different key, or played on a different instrument, we perceive an exactly similar form of unity. Brentano's distinction between independent and dependent parts has paved the way for Ehrenfels' notion of *Gestalt* as a dependent part of a complex whole, although Brentano himself was critical of Ehrenfels' notion. We may also find in Brentano a precursor of the idea that wholes may *be* a *Gestalt*, where all the parts are dependent upon such a whole: Brentano calls them *unities*. The question of the unity of consciousness is an important one for Brentano. How can we know that consciousness forms a unity without presupposing that there is a soul, or substance, underlying the different mental phenomena? Through inner perception, we perceive those mental acts that are simultaneous within us as part of a unified reality (*einheitliche Realität*, Brentano 1874: 214). The mind is not a simple thing but a plurality and unity at once. We may say that it is a *Gestalt* whose parts have a dependent existence, but it is important to note that the unity would be nothing without the partial phenomena.

When Moore needs to explain in his *Principia Ethica* (1903) that consciousness of beauty has more intrinsic value than the sum of the value of consciousness and of the object's beauty, he is in need of the principle of organic unities: "The value of a whole must not be assumed to be the same as the sum of the values of its parts" (Moore 1903b: 28). The whole has thus a property that cannot be reduced to a property of its parts, although the parts may have a relative independence of the whole: the object of beauty need not be related to any consciousness. Without using either Ehrenfels' or Stout's terminology, Moore thus introduces the idea of a *Gestalt* quality. From 1901, Moore would also agree that such a quality is a dependent particular. One might think that Bradley has had an influence on Moore's principle of organic unities, but it is to be noted that for Moore, the parts of a whole have a relative independence, whereas for Bradley all parts are dependent upon the whole. As Moore was acquainted with Stout's *Analytic Psychology* at an early date, Stout's ideas on wholes and parts, and especially his notion of form of unity, may have had some influence on Moore in this respect.

As Moore himself already noted in the introduction to the *Principia Ethica*, the agreements between Brentano's and Moore's ethics are striking. In both, an objective foundation is given for a nonnaturalist ethics. In order to attain this, the central ethical notion should not be explained in naturalist terms such as pleasure; ethics is in need of a primitive, nonnatural notion. Furthermore, ethics needs to make a distinction between intrinsic and instrumental value; and, there is a plurality of goods.

The differences between Brentano's and Moore's ethics are not to be neglected, though.[3] Whereas for Moore the primitive ethical notion is the Platonic notion of the Good, for Brentano it is the rightness of the emotional act that is to give a foundation to ethics. Brentano is opposed to any form of Platonism, as we have seen in the first section. Whereas Moore simply states that we can have direct cognitive access to Platonic goodness, Brentano would argue that such a transcendent notion is not accessible to our minds. Both philosophers give a parallel solution to the question of the objectivity of ethics and that of logic, but here the agreement ends. For Moore, both truth and goodness are primitive notions. For Brentano, truth and goodness are to be explained in terms of the rightness of the act, respectively the rightness of the act of judgement, its self-evidence, as we have seen in section 1, and the rightness of the act of loving or hating (Brentano 1889, §23). Moore rightly addresses the question whether the notion of rightness is the same for both kinds of act (Moore 1903a: 117). When Brentano speaks of an analogy between the self-evidence of a judgement and the clarity of an act of loving, he seems to deny the identity of the two notions of rightness (Brentano 1889: 22). What is precisely the relation between the two notions? For Moore, knowledge of the good is based upon a direct, a priori intuition, comparable to the way a sense-datum is given (Moore 1898: 176–7). The point that we can have access to independently existing, substantial concepts and to the Good in itself is not explained but taken for granted. For Brentano, our knowledge of right and wrong is founded on the inner perception of right acts of loving or hating. Our knowledge that something is good has its origin in our experiences of a love that is characterised as right (Brentano 1889: 23–4). For Moore, the question of the origin of our concepts is merely a psychological question and irrelevant to logic and ethics (Moore 1898: 176–7). For Brentano, such questions of descriptive psychology lead us to the essence of logic and ethics (Brentano 1889, §14). Just as the notion of truth finds its origin in the intuitive presentation of a judgemental act characterised by clarity, so the notion of goodness finds its origin in the intuitive presentation of an act of loving or hating that is right and experienced as such (see Chapter 20).

Moore's most important critique of Brentano's ethics concerns precisely this point: although we may experience a right act, we can never infallibly experience it as right. We cannot experience the *rightness* of the act (Moore 1903a: 118). Moore is right; we never know whether what we experience as right is in fact right, but in answer to Moore we should say: it is all we have access to. In order to prevent relativism, Brentano is in need of a distinction between the notion of rightness as experienced by us and the rightness of the judgement of an ideal judger. Brentano is thus in need of a transcendent notion of rightness, in order to be able to give an objective foundation both to logic and to ethics. As the later Brentano acknowledges this point (Brentano 1930, Part 4, Chap. III, §3), he is, eventually, not the empiricist philosopher that Moore took him to be in this respect.

CONCLUSION

There is no evidence that Moore had read Brentano before 1903, and the differences between them are so striking that there is no reason to think that Moore had read Brentano's nonethical works. At the same time, there are enough agreements between the two philosophers on a more general level. Brentano's student Meinong is often understood as a mediating figure between Brentano and early analytic philosophy. Meinong's theory of objects was published in 1899, and his theory of judgement and "the objective" in 1902 (see Chapter 29). This theory was thus published too late to have had any influence on Moore's development toward the logical realism presented in his second dissertation from 1898 and in "The Nature of Judgment" (Moore 1899).

As far as intentionality, judgement and the theory of wholes and parts are concerned, we have seen that Stout may have played a mediating role in this respect. In *Analytic Psychology*, Stout also deals with Brentano's account of loving and hating but only in a psychological context (Stout 1896, I: 110). The idea that an objective foundation for logic and ethics can be given only in nonnaturalist terms cannot be found in Stout. Stout's account of intentionality made it possible, though, for Moore, to understand that the objectivity of logic and ethics is not to be found in the act itself or the act's content but in the *object* of the act, which is understood as being independent of the act. It is precisely this modification of Brentano's notion of intentionality that made it possible for Moore to break more radically with the empiricist tradition and to move toward a logical or Platonic realism as far as the question of the objectivity of judgement is concerned; and toward an analogous position, a Platonic realism, in ethics.

NOTES

1. Cf. Schaar 2013. The role of Brentano is also dealt with in this book and in Schaar 2016.
2. As Hume's account of belief does not involve relations of ideas, it may be argued that Hume's account of belief is a precursor of Brentano's existential account of judgement. For Hume, judgements may contain

only one idea. In the judgement *God is, existence* is not a distinct idea. Cf. Hume's *Treatise of Human Nature*, book I, part 3, §7, note 20.

3. I do not acknowledge as many points of agreement between Moore and Brentano as Bell has claimed there are (Bell 1999: 206–7). In opposition to Bell, it can be argued that (1) Platonism cannot be found in Brentano; (2) the primitive notion is for Brentano not that of intrinsic value or goodness: goodness is explained in terms of rightness of the emotional act; (3) there is not an agreement concerning the notion of judgement, as Brentano defends a nonpropositional account of judgement. Sometimes, there is more agreement than Bell has noticed: already in 1898, Moore defended a version of the principle of organic unities; notwithstanding the fact that Moore is a logical atomist, he is not an atomist as far as ethics is concerned.

38

Chisholm and Brentano

Dale Jacquette

1 CHISHOLM'S NEO-BRENTANISM

Among the most prominent recent neo-Brentanian analytic philosophers, Roderick M. Chisholm (1916–1999) has made significant contributions not only to Brentano scholarship but also to the furtherance of Brentano's ideas deemed relevant to contemporary philosophical concerns. Chisholm recounts the events, during graduate school days at Harvard University, by which he came to his appreciation of Brentano and Brentano's student Alexius Meinong. Chisholm's essay "My Philosophical Development" (1997) explains that C. I. Lewis recommended he enroll with the unfortunately named lecturer Edwin G. Boring. "In this course," Chisholm states, "I first learned something about Franz Brentano. (But I was not to read Brentano until a few years later when I had seen Russell's discussion of Brentano and Meinong in *The Analysis of Mind*.)" Then he adds, significantly, connecting his native interests in philosophical psychology to Brentanian phenomenology or *deskriptive Psychologie*: "The seminar with Boring prepared me to serve with Reinhard Fabian, some years later, as co-editor of the second edition of Brentano's *Untersuchungen zur Sinnespsychologie*, a work which is important primarily as a contribution to what Brentano called 'descriptive psychology,' or '*beschreibende Phänomenologie*'." (Chisholm 1997: 7–8)

Chisholm did not confine his historical studies to Brentano and Brentano's school, but extended it to the writings also of more analytical authors, including Frege, Russell, Moore, Wittgenstein, Ryle, the Vienna Circle of Logical Positivists, and certainly the prominent thinkers of the day, especially Quine, Gettier (all three pages), Armstrong, Davidson, and David Lewis, among numerous others, as he advanced along with the profession in these halcyon days of analytic philosophy. Chisholm takes interest with many elements of Brentano's philosophy, with which he is not always in full philosophical agreement. It is, with appropriate qualifications, the often unseen ballast that lends depth and dimension to Chisholm's otherwise purely analytic definition-building conceptual systematizations.

Chisholm is rightly designated an American Brentanian, at a time when it was a more unpopular categorization than it has since become. Brentano's increasing presence in contemporary analytic philosophy has largely been brought about through Chisholm's example and his subtle efforts to introduce Brentano's ideas into critical analytic discussions. There is not one of Chisholm's seven main books that does not mention and refer to, cite as authority, or take an idea from Brentano as a starting place for philosophical inquiry. A survey of his journal-length articles and book chapters discloses much the same. For analytic philosophers reading and admiring Chisholm's clear, plain-spoken philosophical prose and meticulous reconstruction of conceptual connections against a historically informed background to be scratching their heads on seeing repeated references to whoever this Brentano was, was in a sense precisely the point. The opening sentence of Chisholm's *Brentano and Meinong Studies* says without embellishment or further rationale: "I present these papers on Brentano and Meinong in the hope that they will lead the reader back to the original sources" (Chisholm 1982: 1). The next two sentences state: "Some of the papers are expositions and commentaries. Others are developments of certain suggestions first made by Brentano or by Meinong" (*ibid*.). It is in the "developments" of Brentano's philosophical ideas that Chisholm's Brentanism is most profound and, predictably, also where it is most difficult to excavate.[1]

2 DUAL PHILOSOPHICAL PERSONAE

Philosophically, Chisholm led at least two apparently unrelated lives. As an American philosopher established as one of the premier analytic thinkers of his generation, Chisholm is often associated with philosophical analysis presented as series of definitions of philosophically salient or problematic concepts. Like Frege, Chisholm strives to make his assumptions transparent and then builds toward interesting concepts from the ground up, once it is secured, definition by definition. Chisholm's three editions of *Theory of Knowledge* and his contributions to foundational epistemology in a modernized Cartesian vein come naturally to mind in this context, painstakingly building systems of definitions to avoid Gettier problems in a reformulation of Plato's understanding of knowledge as some relation of appropriately qualified justified true belief. The interesting twist is that Chisholm, whatever his religious beliefs, does not rely on God as does Descartes in securing knowledge against the possibility of doubt, but rather invokes Brentano's category of self-presenting properties (Chisholm 1989: 18–20, 62).

The other Chisholm was a well-respected scholar of the history of philosophical psychology and in particular of early Austrian phenomenology. Chisholm had a detailed knowledge of many branches, when distinctions can be drawn, of philosophical and scientific psychology, from the nineteenth century onward. He investigated in original sources a wide network of students of Brentano, and Brentano's seminal methodological revolution in all major branches of philosophy. Chisholm seems to have invested more interest in the Graz school's object theory (*Gegenstandstheorie*), which Brentano himself disowned, than in phenomenology as branded by the later Edmund Husserl. One expects from experience in other cases that a philosopher's scholarly familiarity with historical source materials is likely to direct and have an impact on his or her own philosophical reflections. Close scholarly historical study of a thinker of the past is nevertheless a two-way street. The reason a philosopher becomes interested in specific figures in the history of philosophy often reflects either an affinity of philosophical outlook or a sense that the relevant thinker may serve as an antipode that can sharpen ideas and their expression in productive dialectical exchange.

Chisholm may have been motivated by a complex combination of factors in his intellectual involvement with the philosophy of the Brentano school. Some may try to dismiss Chisholm's Brentanism as a hobby in history of philosophy or an early infatuation, like Wittgenstein's for Schopenhauer or Russell's and Dewey's for Hegel. Counting references in the second and third editions of Chisholm 1966, his most widely discussed book in analytic circles after Chisholm 1957, Chisholm credits Brentano only incidentally for concepts and terminology. The ahistorical analytic philosophical community that equally embraces Chisholm might call attention to the fact that Chisholm cites Brentano incidentally on nine pages of the second edition (1977), for example, and on only four pages of the third edition (1989). Whether this bean-counting reflects Chisholm's later disaffection for neo-Brentanism, or whether he merely wanted to concentrate on other topics in the third edition of a book specifically on analytic epistemology and intended for that readership, remains open to interpretation.

3 BRENTANO SCHOLARSHIP: TRANSLATIONS AND COMMENTARIES

Even allowing that Chisholm's interest in Brentano may have been a history of philosophy hobby, Chisholm makes such substantial contributions to the field that it would be hard to explain the energy he expended if Brentano's thought did not also have deeper philosophical meaning in his own constructive philosophical efforts. Chisholm, unfortunately, as a rule, does not take the opportunity in his scholarly efforts to explain or elaborate at any length about why he is involved in Brentano research. He first heard the name from Boring. Then he read Brentano after becoming intrigued by Russell 1921 as part of his general interest in philosophical psychology. Then one thing led to another with invitations and opportunities to study or later teach in Graz, after spending time at Oxford where Chisholm met Meinong scholar J. N. Findlay—all detailed in Chisholm 1997. Chisholm's attitude seems to be that Brentano is an important figure in the history of a philosophical tradition that deserves more attention than it has generally received. This proposition, if true, would be perfectly compatible with the historical hobby hypothesis.

Chisholm, in editorial and translation teams typically including native German speakers, presents especially Brentano's lesser-known monographs, unpublished writings, lecture notes, and correspondence. The Brentano bibliography at the end of the present volume features translations by Chisholm of Brentano 1889, 1930, and 1933. Chisholm generally explains Brentano by his own philosophical lights (Chisholm 1982, 1986) but otherwise allows Brentano's attractions to speak for themselves. He never proselytizes for Brentano, or at most and on rare occasions only lightly so, while by the same token he leaves unanswered questions as to why he finds Brentano interesting and important. Chisholm on Brentano, except by the most tenuous inferences, always tells us more about Brentano on the subject addressed than about Chisholm. What we have to work with in understanding the influence of Brentano on Chisholm are scattered remarks that seem to endorse Brentano's ideas as exploration-worthy, plus the fact that many of these Brentanian theses are ultimately upheld afterward by Chisholm on independent philosophical grounds.

4 CHISHOLM'S PHILOSOPHICAL INSPIRATIONS IN BRENTANO

Philosophy, even more so than other creative enterprises, often self-consciously builds on its past, with which it is frequently in dialogue. Problems, unsolved tasks, concepts, distinctions, principles, analogies, and much else besides are assimilated selectively or ignored, and the chosen strands woven together according to new lights in each generation of thinkers. Philosophers often cast about in the history of the discipline for likeminded theorists with whose tradition to associate, or to serve as an antipodal point of departure for their very different points of view.

That Chisholm should have done so in his philosophical development is therefore no surprise. For him to have chosen Brentano in particular to play this role in the development of his philosophy is the unexpected penchant, judging only from Chisholm's philosophical background (see Chisholm 1997). Undoubtedly, Chisholm must have heard at Brown and Harvard many new-to-him names dropped and had thumbnail sketches of many thinkers tossed off by his professors. Why did Boring's mention of Brentano in historical context resonate so powerfully with Chisholm as a student? What can we learn about Chisholm's philosophical predispositions from the fact that he eventually gravitated so decisively toward Brentano's philosophy?

Brentano's influence on Chisholm's philosophical psychology and concept of person, sympathy to phenomenology, Brentano's revival of Aristotle's *De Anima* doctrine of an inner sense (*noûs poetikos*) in Brentano's (1867a) *Habilitationsschrift*, his empirical methodology in epistemology and reference to self-presenting properties, his metaphysics of categories, and value theory are all central to Chisholm's thought, which they complement but do not exhaust. These factors, important as they are, take second place to Chisholm's predominant interest in Brentano's concept of intentionality, which Chisholm (rather than Brentano) eventually designates as "the mark of the mental." Psychological phenomena are intentional, *about* or *directed upon* intended objects, whereas extrapsychological, purely physical phenomena are not. My belief that it is raining is about a particular state of affairs. The rain itself, should it turn out to be raining, is not about anything. It is not an entirely original idea in Brentano, but one that becomes the common thread defining the entire Brentano school, object theory (see Chapter 29), and Husserlian phenomenology (Chapter 31), in a family of related philosophical traditions.

The impact of Brentano's intentionality thesis is already self-evident in Chisholm's (1957) first, highly acclaimed book *Perceiving*, the final chapter of which concludes with a discussion of "Intentional Inexistence." Chisholm's strategic purpose in the chapter is to consider his adverbial theory of perception ("I am being appeared to redly" rather than "I see something red") as satisfying Brentano's intentionality thesis. Brentano's (1874) original intentional inexistence or immanent intentionality thesis would indeed seem straightforwardly to apply to the explicit internalism of Chisholm's adverbial interpretation of perception, without need of argument. Chisholm nevertheless defends the categorization, defending Brentano's thesis against five imagined objections, thereby offering positive unequivocal endorsement of Brentanian intentionality.

Unfortunately, Chisholm misinterprets Brentano's thesis of intentional inexistence. He makes the common mistake of confusing intentional inexistence with nonexistence, thereby casting Brentano's philosophical psychology in Meinongian terms that Brentano's Aristotelian realism and later reism cannot tolerate. Meinong and Husserl, among others alike, broke with the Brentano party line in different ways. Brentano, who maintained consistently throughout his career that only concrete individuals (and no universals) exist, was even less tolerant of Meinong's nonexistent objects. Despite Meinong belonging historically to the Brentano school, Brentano did not accept the application of his intentionality principle in Meinong's extraontic theory of reference and predication. Meinong infers from the Brentanian thesis that all psychological states intend objects of thought that some thoughts must be directed upon nonexistent objects. The very concept was repellent to Brentano's Aristotelianism, although it takes enormous ingenuity on Brentano's part to paraphrase his way out of precisely the kinds of psychological occurrences that Meinong believed must point toward beingless intended objects. Fiction and false science and history are good places to start testing a philosophy's ontic–semantic adaptability beyond starter cases involving existent objects with perceptible properties.

Chisholm at first makes a promising beginning in the book's final chapter, when he writes: "The phenomena most clearly illustrating the concept of 'intentional inexistence' are what are sometimes called psychological attitudes; for example, desiring, hoping, wishing, seeking, believing, and assuming" (Chisholm 1957: 169). Chisholm then radically steps away from Brentano's intentionality thesis, adding immediately thereafter: "When Brentano said that these attitudes 'intentionally contain an object in themselves,' he was referring to the fact that they can be truly said to 'have objects' even though the objects which they can be said to have do not in fact exist" (*ibid.*) This is not recognizably Brentano's intentionality thesis, which states instead, to the dismay of most of Brentano's students, that the intended objects of thoughts, by which psychological properties are distinguished from purely physical properties, literally belong to or exist in the mental acts by which the objects are intended (see Chapter 4). As Linda McAlister (1976b) remarks, the "inexistence" part of Brentano's phrase "intentional inexistence" is *locative* rather than *ontic*.[2]

What is significant for present purposes, in understanding Brentano's influence on Chisholm's philosophy, is that Chisholm professes an early indebtedness to a thesis in Brentano that runs through Chisholm's systematic philosophical writings from beginning to end, but that Chisholm at the outset misunderstands. That all thought should be intentional is something that almost all the Brentano school, including Meinong, wholeheartedly accepts. That the intentionality of thought should consist in intended objects belonging to and residing immanently in the thoughts by which the intended objects are intended is quite another thing. Chisholm reaches for an analysis that avoids the unwanted consequences of intentional inexistence as Brentano expected the concept to be understood. Chisholm breaks his first lance in support of Brentano's intentionality thesis, understood in Meinongian terms that Brentano himself strenuously repudiated from the moment he learned of Meinong's nonrealist anti-Aristotelian tangent.[3]

5 UNDERSTANDING BRENTANO'S SIGNIFICANCE FOR CHISHOLM'S PHILOSOPHY

The challenge in explaining Brentano's influence on Chisholm's philosophy is that although Chisholm was active in translating and promoting Brentano's writings, he goes almost no distance toward illuminating the motivations governing his interests, why he gravitated toward Brentano in the first place, and exactly how Brentano's ideas fit into his evolving philosophical psychology, metaphysics, epistemology, and value theory.

The key to understanding Brentano's significance for Chisholm's philosophy is found in Chisholm's characterization of his contributions to the field as a *continuation* of Brentano's philosophical model: "I hope that these essays will be thought of as carrying out the tradition of the Brentano school" (Chisholm 1982: 2). Terse but vital, Chisholm in these few words aligns this part of his own work explicitly with Brentano's. He regards his systematic philosophy as moving forward within the general framework of "the Brentano school tradition." What this neo-Brentanian structure involves, previous essays in the present volume will have explained. Chisholm understands at least a major fragment of his philosophical work as a continuation of Brentano's philosophy and as part of his extended school. Some of Brentano's students and followers, like Meinong, Twardowski, Marty, and others, had known Brentano personally as their teacher. Others, like Chisholm, were later students of Brentano's only through his living tradition in the medium of the written word.[4]

NOTES

1. Remarkably, Chisholm does not take advantage of the opportunity to explain the relation of his Brentanism to the more purely analytic definition-building systematizations undertaken in Chisholm 1966, 1976d, 1981, or 1996, all of which were published before his "My Philosophical Development." Chisholm begins with an account of his Brentano scholarship, suggesting some kind of prioritization, and only halfway through begins explaining his systematic work in perception theory, foundationalist epistemology, and other more ahistorical analytic philosophical studies, which he does not relate to his scholarly research on Brentano. This division and absence of an explicit bridge in Chisholm's own explanation of his philosophical background increases some of the mystique surrounding his Brentanism.
2. McAlister cites Chisholm 1952 and 1957 as misrepresenting Brentano's intentionality thesis. McAlister's essay is preceded in the relevant volume by Chisholm 1976c. See Jacquette 2004a.
3. See Jacquette 2015, esp. Ch.2 ("Origins of *Gegenstandstheorie*: Immanent and Trancendent Objects in Brentano, Twardowski, and Meinong"), revised from Jacquette (1990–1991). The extensive literature on the interpretation of Brentano's intentional inexistence or immanent intentionality thesis is partly catalogued there.
4. There is no survey essay on Brentano's influence on Chisholm in Hahn 1997. The only essay in that volume to deal at length with Brentano's influence on Chisholm is Sanford 1997. Sanford does not investigate historical questions connected with Chisholm's acceptance of Brentano's intentionality thesis but takes it instead as a point of departure for ahistorical conceptual and modal studies of related topics in philosophical psychology.

Notes on Contributors

Wilhelm Baumgartner is Professor of Philosophy at the University of Wurzburg and head of the Institute for Franz Brentano Research there. He founded the journal *Brentano-Studien* in 1988 and co-founded the International Franz Brentano Society in 1998.

Arianna Betti holds the Chair of Philosophy of Language at the University of Amsterdam and is the author, most recently, of *Against Facts* (MIT Press, 2015).

Thomas Binder heads the Franz Brentano Archive at the University of Graz and has published a number of articles on Brentano and his literary estate.

Johannes L. Brandl is Professor of Philosophy at the University of Salzburg and has published a number of articles on Brentano, especially his theories of consciousness and judgment.

Laurent Cesalli holds the Chair for Medieval Philosophy at the University of Geneva and has published a dozen articles on Marty's philosophy.

Tim Crane is Professor of Philosophy at Central European University and the author, most recently, of *Aspects of Psychologism* (Harvard University Press, 2014).

Barry Dainton is Professor of Philosophy at the University of Liverpool and the author, most recently, of *Self* (Penguin, 2014).

Arnaud Dewalque is Senior Lecturer at the University of Liège. He has published a number of articles on Brentano and his school in English and French and has translated a number of Brentano's work into French.

Denis Fisette is Professor of Philosophy at the Université du Québec à Montréal and is the co-editor, most recently, of *Philosophy from an Empirical Standpoint: Essays on Carl Stumpf* (Rodopi, 2015).

Guillaume Fréchette is the co-editor in chief of *Brentano-Studien* and an FWF project director at the University of Salzburg. He has edited a number of collections and has published over a dozen articles on Brentano and his school.

Susan Krantz Gabriel is Professor of Philosophy at Anselm College. She edited and translated into English Brentano's *On the Existence of God*.

Wolfgang Huemer is Professor of Philosophy at the University of Parma and the author of *The Constitution of Consciousness: A Study in Analytic Phenomenology* (Routledge, 2005).

Dale Jacquette was Professor of Theoretical Philosophy at the University of Bern and the editor, among other things, of the *Cambridge Companion to Brentano* (Cambridge University Press, 2004).

Hynek Janoušek is Researcher at the Czech Academy of Science's Institute of Philosophy and has published a number of articles on Brentano and his students.

Uriah Kriegel is a CNRS senior researcher. His book *Mind and Reality in Brentano's Philosophical System* is forthcoming from Oxford University Press.

Johann Christian Marek is Professor of Philosophy at the University of Graz, where he is also member of the Alexius Meinong Institute. He has edited a number of works on Austrian philosophy and has published about a dozen articles on Meinong in English and German.

Olivier Massin is Lecturer at the University of Geneva and has published a number of articles on Brentano, focusing on his theories of sensation and pleasure.

Michelle Montague is Associate Professor of Philosophy at the University of Texas—Austin and the author, most recently, of *The Given: Experience and Its Content*.

Dermot Moran is Professor of Philosophy at University College Dublin and is co-author, most recently, of *The Husserl Dictionary* (Continuum, 2012).

Kevin Mulligan held the Chair of Analytic Philosophy at the University of Geneva from 1986 to 2016 and is the author, most recently, of *Wittgenstein et la philosophie austro-allemande* (Vrin, 2012).

Jonas Olson is Professor of Practical Philosophy at Stockholm University and co-editor of the *Oxford Handbook of Value Theory*. He has published on Brentano's value theory in such journals as *Mind* and *The Monist*.

Lynn Pasquerella is the President of Mount Holyoke College. Her 1985 PhD dissertation, written under Roderick Chisholm, was on Brentano's theory of intrinsic value.

Maria E. Reicher is Professor of Philosophy at the University of Aachen and is the author, most recently, of *Referenz, Quantifikation und ontologische Festlegung*.

Robin Rollinger is Researcher at the Czech Academy of Science's Institute of Philosophy. His book *Franz Brentano's Early Logic: A Study Based on Manuscripts* is forthcoming from Rodopi.

Alessandro Salice is Lecturer at University College Cork and author, most recently, of *Intentionality* (Philosophia, 2012).

Werner Sauer is Professor of Philosophy at the University of Graz and the author of a number of articles on Brentano, in particular his metaphysics and theory of intentionality.

Maria van der Schaar is Lecturer at Leiden University and the author, most recently, of *Kazimiers Twardowski: A Grammar for Philosophy* (Brill, 2015) and *G. F. Stout and the Psychological Origins of Analytic Philosophy* (Palgrave Macmillan, 2013).

Richard Schaefer is Associate Professor of History at SUNY—Plattsburgh and the author of a number of articles on Brentano and his relevance to religious studies.

Denis Seron is Senior Lecturer at the University of Liège as well as a FNRS researcher, and he has published a dozen articles on Brentano's philosophical psychology.

Gianfranco Soldati holds the Chair of Modern and Contemporary Philosophy at the University of Fribourg and has published a number of articles on Brentano's approach to self-knowledge.

Hamid Taieb is a Postdoctoral Fellow at the University of Geneva and has published a number of articles on Brentano's theory of intentionality.

Ion Tănăsescu is Senior Researcher at the Romanian Academy's Institute of Philosophy. He is the author of two monographs on Brentano in Romanian and three dozen articles on Brentano in Romanian, German, English, and French.

Mark Textor is Professor of Philosophy at Kings College London. His book *'Perceiving Perceiving': Brentano on Consciousness and Intentionality* is forthcoming from Oxford UP.

Wojciech Żełaniec is Associate Professor of Philosophy at the University of Gdańsk and the author of a number of articles in English, German, and French on Brentano's metaphysics and epistemology.

Brentano Bibliography

IN GERMAN

Brentano, Franz (1862). *Von der mannigfachen Bedeutung des Seienden nach Aristoteles.* Freiburg: Herder.
Brentano, Franz (1866). *Ad Disputationem Qua Theses Gratiosi Philosophorum Ordinis Consensu Et Auctoritate Pro Impetranda Venia Docendi in Alma Universitate Julio-Maximiliana Defendet.* Aschaffenburg: Schipner.
Brentano, Franz (1867). *Die Psychologie des Aristoteles.* Mainz: Kirchheim.
Brentano, Franz (1869). "Auguste Comte und die positive Philosophie." *Chilianeum* 2: 15–37.
Brentano, Franz (1873). "Der Atheismus und die Wissenschaft." *Historisch-Politische Blätter für das Katholische Deutschland* 72: 916–929.
Brentano, Franz (1874). *Psychologie vom empirischen Standpunkte.* Berlin: Duncker & Humblot. All references are to the 1924 edition.
Brentano, Franz (1875). "Herr Horwicz als Rezensent. Ein Beitrag zur Orientierung über unsere wissenschaftlichen Kulturzustände." *Philosophische Monatshefte* 4: 180–187.
Brentano, Franz (1876). *Was für ein Philosoph manchmal Epoche macht.* Leipzig: Hartleben.
Brentano, Franz (1879). *Neue Rätsel von Änigmatias.* Wien: C. Gerolds Sohn.
Brentano, Franz (1882). "Über der Kreationismus des Aristoteles." *Sitzungsberichte der kaiserlichen Akademie der Wissenschaften* 100: 95–126.
Brentano, Franz (1883). *Offener Brief an Herrn Professor Dr. Eduard Zeller aus Anlass seiner Schrift über die Lehre des Aristoteles von der Ewigkeit des Geistes.* Leipzig: Duncker.
Brentano, Franz (1889). *Vom Ursprung sittlicher Erkenntnis.* Berlin: Duncker & Humblot.
Brentano, Franz (1892a). *Das Genie.* Berlin: Duncker & Humblot.
Brentano, Franz (1892b). *Das Schlechte als Gegenstand dichterischer Darstellung.* Berlin: Duncker & Humblot.
Brentano, Franz (1892c). "Über ein optisches Paradoxon." *Zeitschrift für Psychologie und Physiologie der Sinnesorgane* 3: 349–358.
Brentano, Franz (1893a). *Über die Zukunft der Philosophie.* Wien: Alfred Hölder.
Brentano, Franz (1893b). "Über ein optisches Paradoxon (Zweiter Artikel)." *Zeitschrift für Psychologie und Physiologie der Sinnesorgane* 5: 61–82.
Brentano, Franz (1894). "Zur Lehre von den optischen Täuschungen." *Zeitschrift für Psychologie und Physiologie der Sinnesorgane* 6: 1–7.
Brentano, Franz (1895a). *Die vier Phasen der Philosophie und ihr augenblicklicher Stand.* Stuttgart: Cotta.
Brentano, Franz (1895b). *Meine letzten Wünsche für Österreich.* Stuttgart: Cotta.

Brentano, Franz (1896). *Zur eherentlichen Frage in Österreich*. Berlin: Guttentag.
Brentano, Franz (1897). "Zur Lehre von der Empfindung." In *Dritter internationaler Kongreß für Psychologie in München*. München: Lehmann.
Brentano, Franz (1899). "Dichtung und Weisheit." In August Ströbel (ed.), *Goethe-Festschrift zum 150*. Prag: Lese- und Redehalle.
Brentano, Franz (1907). *Untersuchungen zur Sinnespsychologie*. Berlin: Duncker & Humblot.
Brentano, Franz (1909). *Änigmatias: Neue Rätsel*. München: Beck.
Brentano, Franz (1911a). *Von der Klassifikation der psychischen Phänomene*. Berlin: Duncker & Humblot. All references are to the 1924 edition.
Brentano, Franz (1911b). *Aristoteles Lehre vom Ursprung des menschlichen Geistes*. Leipzig: Velt & Comp.
Brentano, Franz (1911c). *Aristoteles und seine Weltanschauung*. Leipzig: Quelle & Meyer.
Brentano, Franz (1920). "Zur Lehre vom Raum und Zeit." *Kant Studien* 25: 1–23.
Brentano, Franz (1922). *Die Lehre Jesu und ihre bleibende Bedeutung*. Leipzig: Felix Meiner.
Brentano, Franz (1924). *Psychologie vom empirischen Standpunkte* (2 Vol.). Leipzig: Meiner.
Brentano, Franz (1924a). "Vom Ens Rationis," in Brentano 1924.
Brentano, Franz (1924b). "Über das Sein im uneigentlichen Sinne, abstrakte Namen und Verstandesdinge," in Brentano 1924.
Brentano, Franz (1924c). "Von den Gegenständen des Denkens," in Brentano 1924.
Brentano, Franz (1925). *Versuch über die Erkenntnis*. Leipzig: Felix Meiner.
Brentano, Franz (1926a). "Zur Klassifikation der Künste." *Hochschulwissen* 3: 57–62.
Brentano, Franz (1926b). "Über Prophetie." *Jahrbuch der Charakterologie* 2: 259–264.
Brentano, Franz (1928). *Vom sinnlichen und noetischen Bewusstsein*. Leipzig: Felix Meiner.
Brentano, Franz (1929a). *Vom Dasein Gottes*. Leipzig: Felix Meiner.
Brentano, Franz (1929b). "Die 25 Habilitationsthesen," in Brentano, *Über die Zukunft der Philosophie, nebst den Vorträgen Über die Gründe der Entmutigung auf philosophischen Gebiet, Über Schellings System, sowie 25 Habilitationsthesen*. Hamburg: Meiner.
Brentano, Franz (1930). *Wahrheit und Evidenz*. Leipzig: Felix Meiner.
Brentano, Franz (1933). *Kategorienlehre*. Leipzig: Felix Meiner.
Brentano, Franz (1952). *Grundlegung und Aufbau der Ethik*. Bern: Francke.
Brentano, Franz (1954). *Religion und Philosophie*. Bern: Francke.
Brentano, Franz (1956). *Die Lehre vom richtigen Urteil*. Bern: Francke.
Brentano, Franz (1959). *Grundzüge der Ästhetik*. Bern: Francke.
Brentano, Franz (1963). *Geschichte der griechischen Philosophie*. Bern: Francke.
Brentano, Franz (1964). "Zwei Briefe an E. Mach," in K. P. Heller (ed.), *Ernst Mach: Wegbereiter der modernen Physik*. Dordrecht: Springer.
Brentano, Franz (1965a). "Sechs Briefe an A. Meinong," in R. Kindinger (ed.), *Philosophenbriefe: Aus der Wissenschaftlichen Korrespondenz von A. Meinong*. Graz: Akademische Druck- und Verlagsanstalt.
Brentano, Franz (1965b). "Sprechen und Denken," in J. Srzednicki (ed.), *Franz Brentano's Analysis of Truth*. The Hague: Martinus Nijhoff.
Brentano, Franz (1966a). *Die Abkehr vom Nichtrealen*. Bern: Francke.
Brentano, Franz (1968). "Die 25 Habilitationsthesen," in 1968 edition of Brentano 1893a.
Brentano, Franz (1975b). "Was an Reid zu Loben: Über die Philosophie von Thomas Reid." *Grazer Philosophische Studien* 1: 1–18.
Brentano, Franz (1976). *Philosophische Untersuchungen zu Raum, Zeit und Kontinuum*. Leipzig: Felix Meiner.
Brentano, Franz (1977b). "Aristoteles Lehre vom Guten." *Perspektiven der Philosophie* 3: 135–147.
Brentano, Franz (1980). *Geschichte der mittelalterlichen Philosophie im christlichen Abendland*. Hamburg: Felix Meiner.
Brentano, Franz (1982). *Deskriptive Psychologie*. Hamburg: Felix Meiner.
Brentano, Franz (1986). *Über Aristoteles*. Hamburg: Felix Meiner.
Brentano, Franz (1987a). *Geschichte der Philosophie der Neuzeit*. Hamburg: Felix Meiner.
Brentano, Franz (1987c). "Von der Natur der Vorstellung." *Conceptus* 21: 25–31.
Brentano, Franz (1988a). *Über Ernst Machs "Erkenntnis und Irrtum."* Amsterdam: Rodopi.
Brentano, Franz (1989). *Briefe an Carl Stumpf 1867–1917*. Graz: Akademische Druck–und Verlagsanstalt.

Brentano, Franz (1992). "Ein Brief Franz Brentanos an Carl Stumpf vom 10.02.1876." *Acta Analytica* 8: 33–42.
Brentano, Franz (1992–3). "Zur Kategorienlehre." *Brentano Studien* 4: 251–270.
Brentano, Franz (1993). "Von der Substanz." *Axiomathes* 4: 2–40.
Brentano, Franz (1994a). "Grundlegung der Tonpsychologie." *Brentano Studien* 5: 219–233.
Brentano, Franz (1994b). "Diktate über die Zeit (1907 und 1915)." *Axiomathes* 5: 325–344.
Brentano, Franz (2009). *Schriften zur Sinnespsychologie*. Frankfurt: Ontos Verlag.
Brentano, Franz (2013a). "Abstraktion und Relation," in Denis Fisette and Guillaume Fréchette (eds.), *Themes from Brentano*. Amsterdam: Rodopi.
Brentano, Franz (2013b). "Ausgewahlte Briefe an Marty," in Denis Fisette and Guillaume Fréchette (eds.), *Themes from Brentano*. Amsterdam: Rodopi.
Brentano, Franz (forthcoming-1). *Metaphysik. Vorlesung 1867*. Edited by W. Baumgartner *et al.*
Brentano, Franz (forthcoming-2). *Deskriptive Psychologie (1887–88), beschreibende Phänomenologie (1888–89), Psychognosie (1890–91)*, 3 Vols. Edited by G. Fréchette *et al.* (with English translation).

IN ENGLISH

Brentano, Franz (1960). "Genuine and Fictitious Objects." Trans. R. M. Chisholm. In Roderick M. Chisholm (ed.), *Realism and the Background of Phenomenology*. Atascadero, CA: Ridgeview.
Brentano, Franz (1966b). *The True and the Evident*. Trans. R. M. Chisholm, I. Politzer, and K. R. Fischer. London: Routledge.
Brentano, Franz (1969). *The Origins of Our Knowledge of Right and Wrong*. Trans. R. M. Chisholm and E. H. Schneewind. London: Routledge.
Brentano, Franz (1973a). *Psychology from an Empirical Standpoint*. Trans. A. C. Rancurello, D. B. Terrell, and L. L. McAlister. London: Routledge.
Brentano, Franz (1973b). *The Foundation and Construction of Ethics*. Trans. E. H. Schneewind. London: Routledge.
Brentano, Franz (1975a). *On the Several Senses of Being in Aristotle*. Trans. R. George. Berkeley: University of California Press.
Brentano, Franz (1977a). *The Psychology of Aristotle*. Trans. R. George. Berkeley: University of California Press.
Brentano, Franz (1978). *Aristotle and His World View*. Trans. R. George and R. M. Chisholm. University of California Press.
Brentano, Franz (1981a). *The Theory of Categories*. Trans. R. M. Chisholm and N. Guterman. The Hague: Martinus Nijhoff.
Brentano, Franz (1981b). *Sensory and Noetic Consciousness*. Trans. M. Schättle and L. L. McAlister. London: Routledge.
Brentano, Franz (1987b). *On the Existence of God*. Trans. S. Krantz. The Hague: Martinus Nijhoff.
Brentano, Franz (1988b). *Philosophical Investigations on Space, Time, and the Continuum*. Trans. B. Smith. London: Routledge and Kegan Paul.
Brentano, Franz (1995a). *Psychology from an Empirical Standpoint*. Trans. A. C. Rancurello, D. B. Terrell, and L. L. McAlister. London: Routledge.
Brentano, Franz (1995b). *Descriptive Psychology*. Trans. B. Müller. London: Routledge.
Brentano, Franz (1998). "The Four Phases of Philosophy and Its Current State." Trans. B. M. Mezei and B. Smith. In Balázs M. Mezei and Barry Smith (eds.), *The Four Phases of Philosophy*. Amsterdam: Rodopi.
Brentano, Franz (2013c). "Abstraction and Relation." Trans. R. Rollinger. In Denis Fisette and Guillaume Fréchette (eds.), *Themes from Brentano*. Amsterdam: Rodopi.
Brentano, Franz (2013d). "Selected Letters to Marty." Trans. R. Rollinger. In Denis Fisette and Guillaume Fréchette (eds.), *Themes from Brentano*. Amsterdam: Rodopi.

Brentano Bibliography—Archival Material

Brentano, F. C. EL 74: *Psychognosie. 2-stündig* [1890–91], Franz Clemens Brentano Compositions (MS Ger 230), Houghton Library, Harvard University.
Brentano, F. C. EL 80: "Logik." Ed. R. Rollinger. gams.uni graz.at/archive/objects/context:bag/methods/sdef:Context/get?mode=logic
Brentano, F. C. M 70: "Der Name Seiendes im eigentlichen und uneigentlichen Sinne." Franz Clemens Brentano Compositions (MS Ger 230), Houghton Library, Harvard University.
Brentano, F. C. M 96: "Ontologie (Metaphysik)." Franz Clemens Brentano Compositions (MS Ger 230), Houghton Library, Harvard University.
Brentano, F. C. N7: "Zur Lorentz-Einsteinfrage." Franz Clemens Brentano Compositions (MS Ger 230), Houghton Library, Harvard University.
Brentano, F. C. Ps 62: *Psychologie 1872/73*, Franz Clemens Brentano Compositions (MS Ger 230), Houghton Library, Harvard University.
Brentano, F. C. Ps 53: *Drittes Buch: Von den Vorstellungen* (s.d.), Franz Clemens Brentano Compositions (MS Ger 230), Houghton Library, Harvard University.
Brentano, F. C. BrL 1449: Letter to Dr Oesterreich, 22 November 1913. Franz Clemens Brentano Compositions (MS Ger 230), Houghton Library, Harvard University.

BK = *Briefe Franz Brentanos an Alfred Kastil*. Transkript: Franz Brentano-Forschung, Würzburg.
BM = *Briefe Franz Brentanos an Anton Marty*. Transkript: Franz Brentano-Forschung, Würzburg.
KB = *Briefe von Alfred Kastil an Franz Brentano*. Transkript: Franz Brentano Forschung, Würzburg.
MB = *Briefe von Anton Marty an Franz Brentano*. Transkript: Franz Brentano Forschung, Würzburg.

References

Ahlman, E. (1926). *Das normative Moment im Bedeutungsbegriff*. Helsingfors: Suomalaisen Tiedeakatemian Toimituksia.
Ajdukiewicz, K. (1923). *Główne kierunki filozofii w wyjątkach z dzieł ich klasycznych przedstawicieli (Teoria poznania, logika, metafizyka)*. Lwów: K. S. Jakubowski.
Ajdukiewicz, K. (1937). "Kierunki i prądy filozofii współczesnej." *Kalendarz IKC*. Kraków, 78–84.
Albertazzi, L. (1989). "Brentano's and Mauthner's *Sprachkritik*." *Brentano Studien* 2: 145–157.
Albertazzi, L. (1990/91). "Brentano, Meinong and Husserl on Internal Time." *Brentano Studien* 3: 89–109.
Albertazzi, L. (1993). "Brentano, Twardowski, and Polish Scientific Philosophy," in F. Coniglione, R. Poli and J. Wolenski (eds.), *Polish Scientific Philosophy: The Lvov-Warsaw School*. Amsterdam: Rodopi, 11–40.
Albertazzi, L. (2006). *Immanent Realism. An Introduction to Brentano*. Dordrecht: Springer.
Albertazzi, L. (2014). "De la psychologie descriptive à l'analyse objective du psychique: Florence et Padoue au début du 20ème siècle," in Charles-Édouard Niveleau (ed.), *Vers une philosophie scientifique. Le programme de Brentano*. Paris: Demopolis.
Albertazzi, L., M. Libardi, and R. Poli (1996). *The School of Franz Brentano*. The Hague: Springer.
Albertazzi, L., D. Jacquette, and R. Poli (eds.) (2001). *The School of Alexius Meinong*. Aldershot: Ashgate.
Allesch, C. G. (1987). *Geschichte der psychologischen Ästhetik. Untersuchungen zur historischen Entwicklung eines psychologischen Verständnisses ästhetischer Phänomene*. Göttingen: Verlag für Psychologie.
Allesch, C. G. (1989). "Das Schöne als Gegenstand seelischer Intentionalität: Zu Brentanos deskriptiver Ästhetik und ihren problemgeschichtlichen Hintergründen." *Brentano Studien* 2: 131–137.
Ameseder, R. (1904). "Beiträge zur Grundlegung der Gegenstandstheorie," in Meinong 1904a: 51–120.
Angermann, A. (ed.) (2015). *Theodor W. Adorno, Gershom Scholem. Briefwechsel 1939–1969*. Frankfurt: Suhrkamp.
Anscombe, E. (1978). "Will and Emotion." *Grazer Philosophische Studien* 5: 139–148.
Antonelli, M. (2000). "Franz Brentano und die Wiederentdeckung der Intentionalität: Richtigstellung herkömmlicher Missverständnisse und Missdeutungen." *Grazer Philosophische Studien* 58/59.
Antonelli, M. (2011). "Die deskriptive Psychologie von Anton Marty. Wege und Abwege eines Brentano-Schülers," in Marty 2011: XI–LXXVIII.
Antonelli, M. (2012). "Franz Brentano's Intentionality Thesis," in A. Salice (ed.) *Intentionality. Historical and Systematic Perspectives*. Munich: Philosophia, 109–144.

Antonelli, M. (2015). "Franz Brentano's Intentionality Thesis. A New Objection to the 'Nonsense that was Dreamt up and Attributed to him.'" *Brentano Studien* 13: 23–53.
Aquinas, T. 1265ff. *Summa Theologica*. http://dhspriory.org/thomas/summa/
Arleth, E. (1884). *Die Aristotelische Eudämonie*. Dissertation Universität Prag.
Arleth, E. (1888). "Bios Teleios in der aristotelischen Ethik." *Archiv für Geschichte der Philosophie* 2: 13–21.
Arleth, E. (1889). *System der Aristotelischen Ethik*. Habilitationsschrift Universität Prag.
Arleth, E. (1894). "Die Lehre des Anaxagoras vom Geist und der Seele." *Archiv für Geschichte der Philosophie* 8: 59–85, 8: 190–205.
Arleth, E. (1896). "Die Philosophie und ihre Geschichte." *Österreichische Mittelschule* 10: 235–253.
Arleth, E. (1903). *Die metaphysischen Grundlagen der Aristotelischen Ethik*. Prag: Calve.
Armstrong, D. M. (1978). *Universals and Scientific Realism*, Vol. 1–2. Cambridge: Cambridge University Press.
Bardon, A. and H. Dyke (eds.) (2015). *A Companion to the Philosophy of Time*. Maldon: Wiley-Blackwell.
Bar-Hillel, Y. (1950). "Bolzano's Definition of Analytic Propositions." *Theoria* 16: 91–117.
Bar-Hillel, Y. (1952). "Bolzano's Propositional Logic." *Archiv für mathematische Logik und Grundlagenforschung* 1: 65–98.
Bar-Hillel, Y. (1954). "Bergmann Shmuel Hugo. M'vo l'torat ha-higayon (Introduction to logic)." *The Journal of Symbolic Logic* 19(2): 149.
Bar-Hillel, Y. (1955). "מבוא לתורת ההיגיון: השגות על הספר 'מבוא תלתור ההיגיון' פרופלסור ש.ה. ברגמן" [Some objections to 'An Introduction to Logic' by S. H. Bergman]. *Iyyun* 5: 25–37.
Bar-Hillel, Y. (1957). "Husserl's Conception of a Purely Logical Grammar." *Philosophy and Phenomenological Research* 17: 362–369.
Baumann, R., F. Loebe, and H. Herre (2014). "Axiomatic Theories of the Ontology of Time in GFO." *Applied Ontology* 9: 171–201.
Baumgartner, W. (2013). "Franz Brentano's Mereology," in D. Fisette and G. Fréchette (eds.), *Themes from Brentano*. Amsterdam: Rodopi.
Baumgartner, W. and L. Pasquerella (2004). "Brentano's Value Theory: Beauty, Goodness, and the Concept of Correct Emotion," in D. Jacquette (ed.), *The Cambridge Companion to Brentano*. Cambridge: Cambridge University Press, 220–237.
Baumgartner, W. and P. Simons (1992–3). "Brentanos Mereologie." *Brentano Studien* 4: 53–77.
Baumgartner, W. and P. Simons (1994). "Brentano's Mereology." *Axiomathes* 1: 55–76.
Bayerová, M. (1990). "Brentanova společnost v Praze." *Filosofický časopis* 38: 859–864.
Bealer, G. (1992). "The Incoherence of Empiricism." *Proceedings of the Aristotelian Society*, supp., 66.
Beaney, M. (ed.) (2007). *The Analytic Turn: Analysis in Early Analytic Philosophy and Phenomenology*. London: Routledge.
Beiser, F. C. (2014). *The Genesis of Neo-Kantianism 1796–1880*. Oxford: Oxford University Press.
Bell, C. (2006). "Paradigms Behind (and Before) the Study of Religion." *History and Theory* 45: 1–20.
Bell, D. A. (1990). *Husserl*. London: Routledge.
Bell, D. A. (1999). "The Revolution of Moore and Russell: A Very British Coup?" in A. O'Hear (ed.), *German Philosophy since Kant*. Cambridge: Cambridge University Press, 193–208.
Bell, J. L. (2005). *The Continuous and the Infinitesimal in Mathematics and Philosophy*. Monza—Milano: Polimetrica s.a.s.
Bellah, R. (2011). *Religion in Human Evolution*. Cambridge MA: Harvard University Press.
Beneke, F. E. (1832). *Kant und die philosophische Aufgabe unserer Zeit*. Berlin: Mittler.
Bergman, H. (1920). "Bertrand Russells 'Erkenntnis der Außenwelt.'" *Kant-Studien* 25: 50–56.
Bergman, S. H. (1903a). "Jüdische Schulfragen." *Revue der israelitischen Kultusgemeinden in Böhmen*, Oktober 1903, S. 3ff.
Bergman, S. H. (1903b). *Die Judenfrage und ihre Lösungsversuche*. Prag: Verlag des Vereines "Bar Kochba" in Prag.
Bergman, S. H. (1904a). "Über die Bedeutung des Hebräischen für die jüdischen Studenten." *Unsere Hoffnung* 1: 85–88.
Bergman, S. H. (1904b). "Einiges über das Jüdische ('Jargon')." *Unsere Hoffnung* 1: 292–296.
Bergman, S. H. (1905). *Die Atomtheorie im 19. Jahrhundert. Ein Beitrag für die Problemgeschichte der Philosophie*. [unpublished dissertation, Prague, Charles University]

Bergman, S. H. (1906). "Das philosophische Bedürfnis in der modernen Physik." *Philosophische Wochenschrift und Literaturzeitung* 1: 332–338.
Bergman, S. H. (1909a). *Das philosophische Werk Bernard Bolzanos*. Halle: Niemeyer.
Bergman, S. H. (1909b). "Über den analytischen Charakter des Existenztheorems in der reinen Mathematik." *Annalen der Naturphilosophie* 8: 495–502.
Bergman, S. H. (1910a). "Zur Frage des Nachweises synthetischer Urteile a priori in der Mathematik." *Archiv für systematische Philosophie* 14: 254–273.
Bergman, S. H. (1910b). "Review of Alexius Meinong, *Über Annahme*." *Zeitschrift für Philosophie und philosophische Kritik* 143: 111–117.
Bergman, S. H. (1911). "Alfred Brunswig: Das Vergleichen und die Relationserkenntnis." *Deutsche Literaturzeitung* 45: 2844–6.
Bergman, S. H. (1913). *Das Unendliche und die Zahl*. Halle: Niemeyer.
Bergman, S. H. (1927). *Ha-filosofyah Shel Immanuel Kant* [*The Philosophy of Immanuel Kant*]. Jerusalem: Magnes Press.
Bergman, S. H. (1929). *Der Kampf um das Kausalgesetz in der jüngsten Physik*. Braunschweig: Vieweg & Sohn.
Bergman, S. H. (1931). "Salomon Maimons Philosophie der Mathematik." *Isis* 16: 220–232.
Bergman, S. H. (1933). "De Kant à Husserl." *Cahiers Juifs* 2: 180–187.
Bergman, S. H. (1936). "Book reviews of Franz Brentano, *Wahrheit und Evidenz, Vom Ursprung sittlicher Erkenntnis, Kategorienlehre*." *Scripta Mathematica* 4: 161–165.
Bergman, S. H. (1937). "What is Truth?", lecture presented at Harvard Philosophical Society. Archives of the National and University Library of Jerusalem, ARC. 4* 1502 03 70b.
Bergman, S. H. (1938). "Maimons logischer Kalkül." *Philosophia* 3: 252–265.
Bergman, S. H. (1944). "Brentano's Theory of Induction." *Philosophy and Phenomenological Research* 5: 281–292.
Bergman, S. H. (1948). "Physicalism." *The Philosophical Quarterly (Calcutta, Indian Institute of Philosophy)*, 21: 57–81.
Bergman, S. H. (1950). "Probleme des Existenzbegriffes." *Theoria* 16: 21–35.
Bergman, S. H. (1952). "Review of *Die Philosophie Franz Brentanos* (Alfred Kastil)." *Philosophy and Phenomenological Research* 13: 267–268.
Bergman, S. H. (1953). *M'vo l'torat ha-higayon* [*Introduction to Logic*]. Jerusalem: Bialik Institute.
Bergman, S. H. (1955). "Metaphysical Implications of Husserl's Phenomenology." *Scripta Hierosolymitana* 2: 220–230.
Bergman, S. H. (1960). "The Need of a Courageous Philosophy." *Scripta Hierosolymitana* 6: 104–119.
Bergman, S. H. (1964). "Schelling on the Source of Eternal Truth." *Proceedings of the Israel Academy of Sciences and Humanities* 2: 17–28.
Bergman, S. H. (1965). "Brentano on the History of Greek Philosophy." *Philosophy and Phenomenological Research* 26: 94–99.
Bergman, S. H. (1966). "Franz Brentano." *Revue internationale de philosophie* 20: 349–372.
Bergman, S. H. (1967). *The Philosophy of Solomon Maimon*. Trans. N. J. Jacobs, Jerusalem: Magnes Press.
Bergman, S. H. (1970). *Toldot ha-filosofyah ha-ḥadashah: me-Niḳolaus Ḳuzanus 'ad teḳufat ha-haśkalah* [*A History of Philosophy: From Nicolaus Cusanus to the Age of the Enlightment*]. Jerusalem: Bialik.
Bergman, S. H. (1972). "Erinnerungen an Franz Kafka." *Universitas* 27: 739–750.
Bergman, S. H. (1973). *Toldot ha-filosofyah ha-ḥadashah: mi-teḳufat ha-haśkalah 'ad 'Imanu'el Ḳanṭ* [*A History of Philosophy: From the Age of the Enlightenment to Immanuel Kant*]. Jerusalem: Bialik.
Bergman, S. H. (1974a). "The Controversy Concerning the Law of Causality in Contemporary Physics," in R. Cohen and M. Wartofsky (eds.), *Logical and Epistemological Studies in Contemporary Physics*. Dordrecht: Reidel, 395–462.
Bergman, S. H. (1974b). "Personal Remembrances of Albert Einstein," in R. Cohen and M. Wartofsky (eds.), *Logical and Epistemological Studies in Contemporary Physics*. Dordrecht: Reidel, 388–394.
Bergman, S. H. (1977). *Toldot ha-filosofyah ha-hadashah: Ya'akobi, Fikhte, Sheling* [*A History of Philosophy: Jakobi, Fichte, Schelling*]. Jerusalem: Bialik.
Bergman, S. H. (1979). *Toldot ha-filosofyah ha-hadashah: Shitoth ba-filosofyah shele'akhar Kant* [*A History of Philosophy : Systems of Post-Kantian Philosophy*]. Jerusalem: Bialik.
Bergman, S. H. (1985). *Tagebücher und Briefe I. 1901–1948*. Königstein: Athenäum.

Bergmann, H. (1908). *Untersuchungen zum Problem der Evidenz der inneren Wahrnehmung*. Halle: Niemeyer.
Bergmann, H. (1946). "Briefe Franz Brentanos an Hugo Bergmann." *Philosophy and Phenomenological Research* 7: 83–158.
Bergmann, J. (1879). *Allgemeine Logik. Erster Teil, Reine Logik*. Berlin: Mittler.
Bernet, R., I. Kern, and E. Marbach (1993). *An Introduction to Husserlian Phenomenology*. Evanston: Northwestern University Press.
Betti, A. (2006a). "The Strange Case of Savonarola and the Painted Fish. On the Bolzanization of Polish Thought," in A. Chrudzimski and D. Łukasiewicz (eds.), *Actions, Products and Things: Brentano and Polish Philosophy*. Frankfurt am Main: Ontos Verlag, 55–81.
Betti, A. (2006b). "Sempiternal Truth. The Bolzano-Leśniewski-Twardowski Axis," in J. J. Jadacki and J. Pasniczek (eds.), *Lvov-Warsaw School: The New Generation*. Amsterdam and New York: Rodopi, 371–399.
Betti, A. (2013). "We owe it to Sigwart! A New Look at the Content/Object Distinction in Early Phenomenological Theories of Judgment from Brentano to Twardowski," in M. Textor (ed.), *Judgement and Truth in Early Analytic Philosophy and Phenomenology*. Basingstoke: Palgrave Macmillan, 74–96.
Betti, A. (2016). "Kazimierz Twardowski," in E. N. Zalta (ed.), *The Stanford Encyclopedia of Philosophy* (Summer 2016 Edition). http://plato.stanford.edu/archives/sum2016/entries/twardowski/
Betti, A. (Forthcoming). "A Note on Early Polish Semantics, Bolzano and the Woleński Thesis," in J. Hartman and J. Rebus (eds.), *Essays for Jan Woleński*. Amsterdam/New York, NY: Brill/Rodopi.
Betti, A. and V. Raspa (2016). "Einleitung zur Logik 1894/5," in Twardowski 2016.
Betti, A. and M. van der Schaar (2004). "The Road from Vienna to Lvov. Twardowski's Theory of Judgement between 1894 and 1897." *Grazer Philosophische Studien* 67: 1–20.
Bigelow, J. (1998). "Particulars," in E. Craig (ed.), *The Routledge Encyclopedia of Philosophy*. Vol. VII. London: Routledge, 235–38.
Binder, T. (2000). "Die Brentano-Gesellschaft und das Brentano-Archiv in Prag." *Grazer philosophische Studien* 58: 533–565.
Binder, T. (2013). "There and Back Again. An Updated History of Franz Brentano's Unpublished Papers," in D. Fisette and G. Fréchette (eds.), *Themes from Brentano*. Amsterdam/New York: Rodopi, 369–418.
Binder, T. and U. Höfer (2004). *Gesamtverzeichnis des Nachlasses von Alfred Kastil (1874–1950) im Schönbüheler Brentano-Haus*. Graz: Forschungsstelle und Dokumentationszentrum für Österreichische Philosophie.
Black, M. (1952). "The Identity of Indiscernibles." *Mind* 61: 153–164.
Blackmore, J. (1998). "Franz Brentano and the University of Vienna Philosophical Society," in R. Poli (ed.), *The Brentano Puzzle*. Aldershot: Ashgate, 73–92.
Boghossian, P. and C. Peacocke (2000). *New Essays on the A Priori*. Oxford: Clarendon Press.
Bolzano, B. (1837). *Wissenschaftslehre*, 4 Vols., Sulzbach: Seidel'sche Buchhandlung.
Bolzano, B. (2014). *Theory of Science*, 4 Vols., trans. Paul Rusnock and Rolf George. Oxford: Oxford University Press.
BonJour, L. (1998). *In Defense of Pure Reason: A Rationalist Account of A Priori Justification*. Cambridge: Cambridge University Press.
Borsato, A. (2009). *Innere Wahrnehmung und innere Vergegenwärtigung*. Würzburg: Königshausen und Neumann.
Brandl, J. (2013). "What is Pre-Reflective Self-Awareness? Brentano's Theory of Inner Consciousness Revisited," in D. Fisette and G. Fréchette (eds.), *Themes from Brentano*. Amsterdam/New York: Rodopi, 41–67.
Brandl, J. (2014). "Brentano's Theory of Judgment," in *Stanford Encyclopedia of Philosophy (Summer 2014 Edition)*, edited by Edward N. Zalta. https://plato.stanford.edu/entries/brentano-judgement/
Brandl, J. (2017). "Was Brentano an Early Deflationist about Truth?" *The Monist* 100.
Brentano, F. and C. Stumpf (2014). *Briefwechsel 1867–1917*. T. Binder and M. Kaiser-el-Saffi (eds.), Frankfurt am Main: Peter Lang.
Brod, M. (1960). *Streitbares Leben. Autobiographie*. Munich: Kindler.
Brożek, A. (2012). *Kazimierz Twardowski: die Wiener Jahre*. Vienna: Springer.
Brożek, A. (2015). "Kazimierz Twardowski on Philosophy and Science," in A. Brożek, A. Chybińska, J. Woleński and J. J. Jadacki (eds.), *Tradition of the Lvov-Warsaw School: Ideas and Continuations*. Leiden/Boston: Brill, 153–176.

Brück, M. (1933). *Über das Verhältnis Edmund Husserls zu Franz Brentano, vornehmlich mit Rücksicht auf Brentanos Psychologie*. Würzburg: Triltsch.
Callender, C. (ed.) (2011). *The Oxford Handbook of Philosophy of Time*. Oxford: Oxford University Press.
Campbell, K. (1981). "The Metaphysic of Abstract Particulars." *Midwest Studies in Philosophy* 6: 477–488.
Campbell, K. (1990). *Abstract Particulars*. Oxford: Basil Blackwell.
Capek, K. and T. G. Masaryk (1995). *Talks with T. G. Masaryk*. Trans. by M. Henry Heim. North Haven, CT: Catbird Press.
Carnap, R. (1967). *The Logical Structure of the World*, trans. Rolf A. George. Berkeley and Los Angeles: University of California Press.
Carritt, E. F. (1947). *Ethical and Political Thinking*. Oxford: Clarendon Press.
Caston, V. (2002). "Aristotle on Consciousness." *Mind* 111: 751–815.
Cavallin, J. (1997). *Content and Object—Husserl, Twardowski, and Psychologism*. Dordrecht: Kluwer.
Cesalli, L. (2013). "Anton Marty's Intentionalist Theory of Meaning," in D. Fisette and G. Fréchette (eds.), *Themes from Brentano*. Amsterdam: Rodopi, 139–163.
Cesalli, L. and J. Friedrich (eds.) (2014). *Anton Marty and Karl Bühler. Between Mind and Language*. Basel: Schwabe.
Cesalli, L. and H. Taieb (2013). "The Road to *ideelle Verähnlichung*. Anton Marty's Conception of Intentionality in the Light of its Brentanian Background." *Quaestio* 12: 25–86.
Chisholm, R. M. (1952). "Intentionality and the Theory of Signs." *Philosophical Studies* 3: 56–63.
Chisholm, R. M. (1955-6). "Sentences about Believing." *Proceedings of the Aristotelian Society* 56: 125–148.
Chisholm, R. M. (1957). *Perceiving: A Philosophical Study*. Ithaca: Cornell University Press.
Chisholm, R. M. (1966). *Theory of Knowledge*. Englewood Cliffs: Prentice-Hall.
Chisholm R. M. (1967). "Intentionality," in P. Edwards (ed.), *Encyclopedia of Philosophy* IV. New York: MacMillan.
Chisholm, R. M. (1976a). "Brentano's Nonpropositional Theory of Judgment." *Midwest Studies in Philosophy of Mind* 1: 91–95.
Chisholm, R. M. (1976b). "Brentano's Theory of Correct and Incorrect Emotion," in McAlister 1976a.
Chisholm, R. M. (1976c). "Intentional Inexistence," in McAlister 1976a.
Chisholm, R. M. (1976d). *Person and Object: A Metaphysical Study*. LaSalle: Open Court Publishing Company.
Chisholm, R. M. (1977). *Perceiving: A Philosophical Study*. Second edition. Ithaca: Cornell University Press.
Chisholm, R. M. (1981). "Brentano's Analysis of the Consciousness of Time." *Midwest Studies in Philosophy* 6: 3–16.
Chisholm, R. M. (1982). *Brentano and Meinong Studies*. Atlantic Highlands: Humanities Press.
Chisholm, R. M. (1986). *Brentano and Intrinsic Value*. Cambridge: Cambridge University Press.
Chisholm, R. M. (1987). "Brentano's Theory of Pleasure and Pain." *Topoi* 6: 59–64.
Chisholm, R. M. (1989). *Perceiving: A Philosophical Study*. Third edition. Ithaca: Cornell University Press.
Chisholm, R. M. (1990). "Brentano and Marty on Content: A Synthesis Suggested by Brentano," in K. Mulligan (ed.), *Mind, Meaning and Metaphysics*. Dordrecht: Kluwer, 1–11.
Chisholm, R. M. (1996). *A Realistic Theory of Categories: An Essay on Ontology*. Cambridge: Cambridge University Press.
Chisholm, R. M. (1997). "My Philosophical Development," in L. E. Hahn (ed.), *The Philosophy of Roderick M. Chisholm*. Peru, IL: Open Court Publishing.
Cho, K. K. (1990). "Phenomenology as Cooperative Task: Husserl-Farber Correspondence during 1936-37." *Philosophy and Phenomenological Research* 50 (Supplement): 36–43.
Chrudzimski, A. (1998/99). "Die Theorie des Zeitbewußtseins Franz Brentanos aufgrund der unpublizierten Manuskripte." *Brentano Studien* 8: 149–161.
Chrudzimski, A. (2001a). *Intentionalitätstheorie beim frühen Brentano*. Dordrecht: Kluwer.
Chrudzimski, A. (2001b). "Die Intentionalitätstheorie Anton Martys." *Grazer Philosophische Studien* 62: 175–214.
Chrudzimski, A. (2004). *Die Ontologie Franz Brentanos*. Dordrecht: Kluwer.
Chrudzimski, A. (2005). *Intentionalität, Zeitbewußtsein und Intersubjektivität. Studien zur Phänomenologie von Brentano bis Ingarden*. Frankfurt: Ontos Verlag.
Chrudzimski, A. and D. Łukasiewicz (eds.) (2006). *Actions, Products and Things. Brentano and Polish Philosophy*. Frankfurt am Main: Ontos Verlag.

Chrudzimski, A. and B. Smith (2004). "Brentano's Ontology: From Conceptualism to Reism," in D. Jacquette (ed.), *The Cambridge Companion to Franz Brentano*. Cambridge: Cambridge University Press.
Clark, A. (1993). *Sensory Qualities*. New York: Oxford University Press.
Coniglione, F. (1997). "Logica, scienza e filosofia in Tadeusz Czeżowski." *Axiomathes* 8: 191–250.
Coniglione, F., R. Poli, and J. Wolenski (eds.) (1993). *Polish Scientific Philosophy. The Lvov-Warsaw School*. Amsterdam: Rodopi.
Crane, T. (2001). *Elements of Mind*. Oxford: Oxford University Press.
Crane, T. (2006). "Brentano's concept of intentional inexistence," in M. Textor (ed.), *The Austrian Contribution to Analytic Philosophy*. New York: Routledge, 20–35.
Czeżowski, T. (1925)."Teoria pojęć Kazimierza Twardowskiego." *Przegląd Filozoficzny* 28: 106–110.
Czeżowski, T. (2000). *Knowledge, Science, and Values: A Program for Scientific Philosophy*. Trans. L. Gumanski. Amsterdam/Atlanta: Rodopi.
Czyż, J. (1994). *Paradoxes of Measures and Dimensions Originating in Felix Hausdorff's Ideas*. Singapore/New Jersey/London/Hong Kong: World Scientific.
Dainton, B. (2000). *Stream of Consciousness: Unity and Continuity on Conscious Experience*. London: Routledge.
Danielsson, S. and J. Olson (2007). "Brentano and the Buck-Passers." *Mind* 116: 511–522.
Davidson, D. (1980). "Mental Events," in *His essays on Actions and Events*. Oxford: Oxford University Press, 79–101.
Deigh, J. (1994). "Cognitivism in the Theory of Emotions." *Ethics* 104: 824–854.
De Libera, A. (2011). "Le direct et l'oblique: Sur quelques aspects antiques et médiévaux de la théorie brentanienne des relatifs," in A. Reboul (ed.), *Philosophical Papers dedicated to Kevin Mulligan*. Geneva: University of Geneva.
Deonna, J. and F. Teroni (2012). *The Emotions: A Philosophical Introduction*. New York, NY: Routledge.
Derrida, J. (1967). *La voix et le phénomène*. Paris: Presses Universitaires de France.
Derrida, J. (1973). *Speech and Phenomena: And other Essays on Husserl's Theory of Signs*, Trans. D. B. Allison. Evanston: Northwestern University Press.
Derrida, J. (1990). *Le problème de la genèse dans la philosophie de Husserl*. Paris: Presses Universitaires de France.
Derrida, J. (2003). *The Problem of Genesis in Husserl's Philosophy*, Trans. M. Hobson. Chicago: University of Chicago Press.
Descartes, R. (1641/1985). "Meditations" and "Objections and Replies," in *The Philosophical Writings of Descartes*, Vol. 2, Trans. J. Cottingham *et al.* Cambridge: Cambridge University Press.
Dewalque, A. (2013). "Brentano and the Parts of the Mental: A Mereological Approach to Phenomenal Intentionality." *Phenomenology and the Cognitive Sciences* 12: 447–464.
Dewalque, A. (2014). "Intentionnalité et représentations *in obliquo*." *Bulletin d'analyse phénoménologique* 10 (6): 40–84.
Dewalque, A. and D. Seron (2015). "Existe-t-il des phénomènes mentaux?" *Philosophie* 124: 105–126.
De Warren, N. (2009). *Husserl and the Promise of Time. Subjectivity in Transcendental Phenomenology*. Cambridge: Cambridge University Press.
Dilthey, W. (1991). *Introduction to the Human Sciences*. Trans. M. Neville *et al.* Princeton: Princeton University Press.
Dölling, E. (2001). "Alexius Meinong. Von der philosophischen Societät zum philosophischen Seminar," in T. Binder. *et al.* (eds.), *Bausteine zu einer Geschichte der Philosophie an der Universität Graz*. Amsterdam: Rodopi, 149–172.
Driver, J. (2004). *Uneasy Virtue*. Cambridge: Cambridge University Press.
Ehrenfels, C. (1887). "Über Fühlen und Wollen. Eine psychologische Studie." *Sitzungsberichte der Kaiserlichen Akademie der Wissenschaften* (Wien), Philosophisch-historische Klasse 114: 523–636. Reprinted as Ehrenfels 1988b.
Ehrenfels, C. (1890). "Über 'Gestaltqualitäten.'" *Vierteljahrsschrift für wissenschaftliche Philosophie* 14: 249–292. Reprinted as Ehrenfels 1988c.
Ehrenfels, C. (1916). *Kosmogonie*. Jena: Dietrichs.

Ehrenfels, C. (1922). *Das Primzahlengesetz: Entwickelt und dargestellt auf grund der Gestalttheorie.* Leipzig: Reisland.

Ehrenfels, C. (1948). *Cosmogony.* Trans. M. Focht. New York: The Comet Press.

Ehrenfels, C. (1982a). *Werttheorie. Philosophische Schriften. Band 1.* Ed. by Reinhard Fabian. München: Philosophia.

Ehrenfels, C. (1982b). "Werttheorie und Ethik," in Ehrenfels 1982a: 23–166. [First published in *Vierteljahresschrift für wissenschaftliche Philosophie* 17 (1893): 76–110, 200–66, 321–363 and 18 (1894): 77–97.]

Ehrenfels, C. (1982c). *System der Werttheorie. I. Band. Allgemeine Werttheorie, Psychologie des Begehrens.* In Ehrenfels 1982a: 201–405. [Originally published 1897, Leipzig: Reisland.]

Ehrenfels, C. (1982d). "The Ethical Theory of Value," in Ehrenfels 1982a: 181–191. [Originally published in *International Journal of Ethics* 6, 1896: 371–384.]

Ehrenfels, C. (1982e). "Über ethische Wertgefühle," in Ehrenfels 1982a: 192–197. [Only posthumously published manuscript.]

Ehrenfels, C. (1982f). "Über ethische Wertgefühle," in Ehrenfels 1982a: 198–200. [Originally published in *Dritter Internationaler Congress für Psychologie in München.* München: Lehmann, 1897: 231–234.]

Ehrenfels, C. (1986a). *Ästhetik. Philosophische Schriften. Band 2.* Ed. by Reinhard Fabian. München: Philosophia.

Ehrenfels, C. (1986b). "Was ist Schönheit?" in Ehrenfels 1986a: 155–171.

Ehrenfels, C. (1986c). "Über das ästhetische Urteil," in Ehrenfels 1986a: 201–260.

Ehrenfels, C. (1988a). *Psychologie. Ethik. Erkenntnistheorie. Philosophische Schriften. Band 3.* Ed. by Reinhard Fabian. München: Philosophia.

Ehrenfels, C. (1988b). "Über Fühlen und Wollen. Eine psychologische Studie," in Ehrenfels 1988a: 16–97. [First published in *Sitzungsberichte der Kaiserlichen Akademie der Wissenschaften* (Wien), phil.-hist. Klasse, Bd. 14 (1887): 523–636.]

Ehrenfels, C. (1988c). "Über 'Gestaltqualitäten,'" in Ehrenfels 1988a: 128–167. [This is an augmented reprint of the original "Über 'Gestaltqualitäten'" from 1890, which Ehrenfels included into his monograph *Das Primzahlengesetz, entwickelt und dargestellt auf Grund der Gestalttheorie* (Leipzig: Reisland, 1922). Here Ehrenfels added to his original essay a further section, "Continuing remarks." The English translation of "Über 'Gestaltqualitäten'" in Smith 1988 does not contain this further section.]

Ehrenfels, C. (1988d). "Die Intensität der Gefühle. Eine Entgegnung auf Franz Brentanos neue Intensitätslehre," in Ehrenfels 1988a: 98–112. [Originally published in *Zeitschrift für Psychologie und Physiologie der Sinnesorgane* 16 (1898): 49–70.]

Ehrenfels, C. (1988e). "Fragen und Einwände an die Adresse der Anhänger von Franz Brentanos Ethik," in Ehrenfels 1988a: 206–219. [Only posthumously published fragment.]

Ehrenfels, C. (1988f). "On 'Gestalt Qualities,'" in B. Smith (ed.), *Foundations of Gestalt Theory.* München: Philosophia, 82–117.

Ehrenfels, C. (1990). *Metaphysik. Philosophische Schriften. Band 4.* Ed. by Reinhard Fabian. München: Philosophia.

Eisenmeier, J. (1914). *Die Psychologie und ihre zentrale Stellung in der Philosophie.* Halle: Niemeyer.

Eisenmeier, J. (1918). "Brentanos Lehre von der Empfindung." *Monatshefte für pädagogische Reform* 68: 473–493.

Eisenmeier, J. (1923). *Hranice našeho poznání.* Praha: B. Kočí.

Engländer, O. (1914). "Die Erkenntnise des Sittlich Richtigen und die Nationalökonomie." *Schmollers Jahrbuch für Gesetzgebung, Verwaltung und Volkswirtschaft* 3: 397–453 (part 1), 4: 33–90 (part 2).

Engländer, O. (1931). "Wertlehre," in H. Mayer, F. A. Fetter and R. Reisch (eds.), *Die Wirtschaftstheorie der Gegenwart.* Wien: Springer, 1–26.

Erismann, Ch. (2011). *L'homme commun. La genèse du réalisme ontologique durant le haut Moyen Âge.* Paris: Vrin.

Evans, G. (1982). *The Varieties of Reference.* Oxford: Oxford University Press.

Fabian, R. (1986). *Christian von Ehrenfels: Leben und Werk.* Amsterdam: Rodopi.

Farkas, K. (2013). "Constructing a World for the Senses," in U. Kriegel (ed.), *Phenomenal Intentionality.* Oxford: Oxford University Press, 99–115.

Fechner, G. T. (1860). *Elemente der Psychophysik.* Leipzig: Breitkopf und Härtel.

Feest, U. (2014). "The Continuing Relevance of Nineteenth-Century Philosophy of Psychology: Brentano and the Autonomy of Psychological Methods," in M. C. Galavotti, D. Dieks, W. J. Gonzalez, S. Hartmann, T. Uebel and M. Weber (eds.), *New Directions in the Philosophy of Science*. London: Springer.
Feldman, F. (1997). *Utilitarianism, Hedonism, and Desert*. Cambridge: Cambridge University Press.
Findlay, J. N. (1933). *Meinong's Theory of Objects*. London: Oxford University Press.
Findlay, J. N. (1963). *Meinong's Theory of Objects and Values*. Oxford: Clarendon Press.
Fine, K. (2000). "Neutral Relations." *Philosophical Review* 109: 1–33.
Fisette, D. (2013). "Mixed feelings. Carl Stumpf's Criticism of James and Brentano on Emotions," in D. Fisette and G. Fréchette (eds.), *Themes from Brentano*. Amsterdam: Rodopi, 281–305.
Fisette, D. (2014). "Austrian Philosophy and Its Institutions: Remarks on the Philosophical Society of the University of Vienna (1888–1938)," in A. Reboul (ed.), *Mind, Values, and Metaphysics: Philosophical Essays in Honnor of Kevin Mulligan*. Dordrecht: Springer, 349–374.
Fisette, D. (2015a). "The Reception and Actuality of Carl Stumpf," in D. Fisette and R. Martinelli (eds.), *Philosophy from an Empirical Standpoint. Essays on Carl Stumpf*. Amsterdam: Rodopi, 11–44.
Fisette, D. (2015b). "Bibliography of Carl Stumpf's Publications," in D. Fisette and R. Martinelli (eds.), *Philosophy from an Empirical Standpoint. Essays on Carl Stumpf*. Amsterdam: Rodopi, 529–542.
Fisette, D. (2015c). "Carl Stumpf." *Stanford Encyclopedia of Philosophy*. https://plato.stanford.edu/entries/stumpf/
Fisette, D. (2015d). "Introduction to Carl Stumpf's Correspondence with Franz Brentano," in D. Fisette and R. Martinelli (eds.), *Philosophy from an Empirical Standpoint. Essays on Carl Stumpf*. Leiden: Brill, 473–489.
Fisette, D. and G. Fréchette (eds.) (2007). *À l'école de Brentano. De Würzbourg à Vienne*. Paris: Vrin.
Fisette D. and G. Fréchette (eds.) (2013). *Themes from Brentano*. Amsterdam: Rodopi.
Fisette, D. and R. Martinelli (eds.) (2015). *Philosophy from an Empirical Standpoint: Essays on Carl Stumpf*. Leiden: Brill.
Flint, R. (1876). "'Critical Notice' of Brentano's *Psychologie vom Empirischen Standpunkte*." *Mind* 1 (o.s.): 116–122.
Frank, D. H. and O. Leaman (eds.) (1997). *History of Jewish Philosophy*. London: Routledge.
Frank, M. (2012). *Ansichten der Subjektivität*. Frankfurt am Main: Suhrkamp.
Fréchette, G. (2010). *Gegenstandslose Vorstellungen. Bolzano und seine Kritiker*. St-Augustin: Academia Verlag.
Fréchette. G. (2013). "Brentano's Thesis (Revisited)," in D. Fisette and G. Fréchette (eds.), *Themes from Brentano*. Amsterdam: Rodopi, 91–119.
Fréchette, G. (2014). "Austrian Logical Realism? Brentano on States of Affairs," in G. Bonino, J. Cumpa, and G. Jesson (eds.), *Defending Realism: Ontological and Epistemological Investigation*. Berlin: De Gruyter.
Frege, G. (1920). "The Thought," trans. A. and M. Quinton. *Mind* 65 (1956): 289–311.
Freudenberger, T. (1969). *Die Universität Würzburg und das erste vatikanische Konzil. Ein Beitrag zur Kirchen- und Geistesgeschichte des 19. Jahrhunderts. 1. Teil: Würzburger Professoren und Dozenten als Mitarbeiter und Gutachter vor Beginn des Konzils. Mit einem Anhang von Gutachten, Briefen und ergänzenden Aktenstücken*. Neustadt an der Aisch: Degener & Co.
Freuler, L. (1997). *La Crise de la philosophie au XIXe siècle*. Paris: Vrin.
Fugali, E. (2004). *Die Zeit des Selbst und die Zeit des Seienden*. Würzburg: Königshausen und Neumann.
Funke, O. (1924). *Innere Sprachform. Eine Einführung in Anton Martys Sprachphilosophie*. Reichenberg: F. Kraus.
Gabriel, S. K. (2004). "Brentano on Religion and Natural Theology," in D. Jacquette (ed.), *Cambridge Companion to Brentano*. Cambridge: Cambridge University Press, 237–254.
Gabriel, S. K. (2013). "Brentano at the Intersection of Psychology, Ontology, and the Good," in D. Fisette and G. Fréchette (eds.), *Themes from Brentano*. Amsterdam: Rodopi.
Gertler, B. (2011). *Self-Knowledge*. London: Routledge.
Gibbard, A. (2012). *Meaning and Normativity*. Oxford: Oxford University Press.
Giedymin, J. (1986). "Polish Philosophy in the Inter-War Period and Ludwik Fleck's Theory of Thought-Styles and Thought Collectives," in R. S. Cohen and T. Schnelle (eds.), *Cognition and Fact: Materials on Ludwik Fleck*. Dordrecht: Springer, 179–215.
Gilson, L. (1955). *La psychologie descriptive de Franz Brentano*. Paris: Vrin.

Gimpl, G. (2001). *Weil der Boden selbst hier brennt. Aus dem Prager Salon der Berta Fanta (1865–1918)*. Prague: Vitalis.
Giustina, A. (Forthcoming). "Conscious Unity from the Top Down: A Brentanian Approach." *The Monist*. http://philpapers.org/archive/GIUCUF.pdf
Goetz, S. and C. Taliaferro (2011). *A Brief History of the Soul*. Oxford: Wiley-Blackwell.
Goller, P. (1989). "Die Lehrkanzeln für Philosophie an der Philosophischen Fakultät der Universität Innsbruck 1848–1945." *Forschungen zur Innsbrucker Universitätgeschichte, 14*. Innsbruck: Universitätsverlag.
Goller, P. (2005). "Innsbrucker Universitätphilosophie im 20. Jahrhundert: Zwischen rational-humanistischer Brentano-Tradition, faschischtischem Irrationalismus und Analytischer Philosophie," *Verdrängter Humanismus—verzögerte Aufklärung. V. Im Schatten der Totalitarismen. Vom philosophischen Empirismus zur kritischen Anthropologie. Philosophie in Österreich 1920–1951*. Wien: WUF, 835–841.
Goodman, N. (1977). *The Structure of Appearance*, 3rd ed. Boston: Reidel.
Gordon, R. (1987). *The Structure of Emotions*. Cambridge: Cambridge University Press.
Greenspan, P. (1988). *Emotions and Reasons*. London: Routledge and Kegan Paul.
Grossmann, R. (1969). "Non-Existent Objects: Recent Work on Brentano and Meinong." *American Philosophical Quarterly* 6: 17–32.
Grossmann, R. (1974). *Meinong*. London and Boston: Routledge and Kegan Paul.
Grzymała-Moszczyńska, H. (2008). "The 'Faith of the Enlightened' by Władysław Witwicki: An Example of the Conflict between Academic Research and Political Correctness," in H. Junginger (ed.), *The Study of Religion under the Impact of Fascism*. Leiden/Boston: Brill, 577–589.
Hahn, L. E. (ed.) (1997). *The Philosophy of Roderick M. Chisholm*. Peru, IL: Open Court Publishing.
Haller, R. (ed.) (1972). *Jenseits von Sein und Nichtsein. Beiträge zur Meinong-Forschung*. Graz: Akademische Druck- u. Verlagsanstalt.
Haller, R. (1986). "The Philosophy of Hugo Bergman and the Brentano School." *Grazer Philosophische Studien* 24: 15–28.
Haller, R. (1989). "Franz Brentano, ein Philosoph des Empirismus." *Brentano Studien* 1: 19–30.
Haller, R. (1992). "Brentanos Spuren in Werk Masaryks," in J. Zumr and T. Binder (eds.), *T. G. Masaryk und die Brentano Schule*. Praha-Graz: Filozoficky ustav Ceskoslovenske akademie ved/Forschungstelle und Dokumentationszentrum für österreichischen Philosophie, 10–20.
Haller, R. (1994). "Bemerkungen zu Brentanos Ästhetik." *Brentano Studien* 5: 177–186.
Haller, R. (ed.) (1995). *Meinong and the Theory of Objects*. Amsterdam: Rodopi.
Hamilton, W. (1859). *Lectures on Metaphysics and Logic*, Vol. 1: *Metaphysics*. Boston: Gould & Lincoln.
Hamilton, W. (1882). *Lectures on Metaphysics and Logic*, Vol. 2: *Logic*. Edinburgh: William Blackwood and Sons.
Hamlyn, D. W. (1968). *Aristotle's De Anima, Books II and III*. Oxford: Oxford University Press.
Hart, D. B. (2013). *The Experience of God: Being, Consciousness, Bliss*. New Haven: Yale University Press.
Hasenfuss, J. (1978). *Hermann Schell als Wegbereiter zum II. Vatikanischen Konzil*. Paderborn: Schöningh.
Henninger, M. (1989). *Relations: Medieval Theories 1250–1325*. Oxford: Clarendon Press.
Hering, E. (1878). *Zur Lehre vom Lichtsinne*. Wien: Gerold.
Hering, E. (1911). *Grundzüge der Lehre vom Lichtsinn*. Berlin: Julius Springer.
Hering, E. (1929). *Lehre von den Gesichtsempfindungen*. Wien: Julius Springer.
Hertling, G. (1871). *Materie und Form und die Definition der Seele bei Aristoteles*. Bonn: Weber.
Hill, C. O. (1998). "From Empirical Psychology to Phenomenology: Edmund Husserl and the 'Brentano Puzzle,'" in R. Poli (ed.), *The Brentano Puzzle*. Aldershot: Ashgate, 151–167.
Hillebrand, F. (1884). "Über einen neuen Versuch zur Grundlegung der Geisteswissenschaften." *Zeitschrift für das Privat- und öffentliche Recht der Gegenwart* 11: 632–642.
Hillebrand, F. (1887). *Synechologische Probleme in der Scholastik*. Dissertation, Universität Prag.
Hillebrand, F. (1889). "Über die spezifische Helligkeit der Farben." *Sitzungsberichte der Kaiserlichen Akademie der Wissenschaften in Wien. Mathematisch-naturwissenschaftlichen Classe, 48*. Wien: Gerold.
Hillebrand, F. (1891). *Die neuen Theorien der kategorischen Schlüsse*. Wien: Hölder.
Hillebrand, F. (1893). "Die Stabilität der Raumwerte auf der Netzhaut." *Zeitschrift für Psychologie und Physiologie der Sinnesorgane* 5: 1–60.

Hillebrand, F. (1894). "Das Verhältnis von Akkomodation und Konvergenz zur Tiefenlokalisation." *Zeitschrift für Psychologie und Physiologie der Sinnesorgane* 7: 97–151.
Hillebrand, F. (1896a). "Zur Lehre von der Hypothesenbildung." *Sitzungsberichte der philosophisch-historischen Klasse der Kaiserlichen Akademie der Wissenschaften, 134.* Wien: Gerold.
Hillebrand, F. (1896b). "Die experimentelle Psychologie, ihre Entstehung und ihre Aufgaben." *Personalakte Franz Hillebrand*, Universität Innsbruck.
Hillebrand, F. (1898). "In Sachen der optischen Tiefenlokalisation." *Zeitschrift für Psychologie und Physiologie der Sinnesorgane* 16: 71–151.
Hillebrand, F. (1902). "Theorie der scheinbaren Größe beim binokularen Sehen." *Denkschrift der Kaiserlichen Akademie der Wissenschaften, mathematisch-naturwissenschaftliche Klasse, 72.* Wien: Gerold.
Hillebrand, F. (1909). "Zu Kastil 30.06.1909." *Personalakte Franz Hillebrand*, Universität Innsbruck.
Hillebrand, F. (1910). "Die Heterophorie und das Gesetz der identischen Sehrichtung." *Zeitschrift für Psychologie und Physiologie der Sinnesorgane* 54: 1–55.
Hillebrand, F. (1913). *Die Aussperrung der Psychologen: Ein Wort zur Klärung.* Leipzig: Barth.
Hillebrand, F. (1918). *Ewald Hering. Ein Gedenkwort der Psychophysik.* Berlin: Julius Springer.
Hillebrand, F. (1929). *Lehre von den Gesichtsempfindungen.* Wien: Julius Springer.
Höfler, A. (1890). *Philosophische Propädeutik. I. Theil: Logik.* Wien: Tempsky.
Höfler, A. (1897). *Psychologie.* Bd. I. Wien: Tempsky. 2nd supplemented ed. 1930.
Höfler, A. (1917a). *Abhängigkeitsbeziehungen zwischen Abhägigkeitsbeziehungen. Beiträge zur Relations- und zur Gegenstandstheorie.* Vienna: Hölder.
Höfler, A. (1917b). "Franz Brentano in Wien." *Süddeutsche Monatshefte.* Special issue: Österreich von Innen.
Höfler, A. (1920). *Naturwissenschaft und Philosophie. Vier Studien zum Gestaltungsgesetz.* Vienna: Hölder.
Höfler, A. (1921). "Die Philosophie des Alois Höfler" [= *Selbstdarstellung*]. In R. Schmidt (ed.), *Die deutsche Philosophie der Gegenwart in Sebstdarstellungen.* Bd. 2. Leipzig: Meiner, 117–160.
Höfler, A. (1922). *Logik.* Bd. I. 2nd ed. Vienna: Hölder.
Höfler, A. (1930). *Psychologie.* 2nd ed. Vienna: Tempsky.
Hood, P. M. (2004). *Aristotle on the Category of Relation.* Lanham, Maryland: University Press of America.
Horwich, P. (2010). *Truth, Meaning, Reality.* Oxford and New York: Oxford University Press.
Huemer, W. (2002/03). "Die Entwicklung von Brentano Theorie des Zeitbewußtseins." *Brentano Studien* 10: 193–220.
Huemer, W. (2004). "Husserl's Critique of Psychologism and his Relation to the Brentano School," in A. Chrudzimski and W. Huemer (eds.), *Phenomenology and Analysis. Essays on Central European Philosophy*, Frankfurt: Ontos, 199–214.
Huemer, W. (2009). "Experiencing Art: Austrian Aesthetics between Psychology and Psychologism," in B. Centi and W. Huemer (eds.), *Values and Ontology*, Frankfurt: Ontos, 267–288.
Huemer, W. and C. Landerer (2010). "Mathematics, Experience and Laboratories: Herbart's and Brentano's Role in the Rise of Scientific Psychology." *History of the Human Sciences* 23: 72–94.
Hume, D. (1740). *Treatise of Human Nature.* Oxford: Oxford University Press, 1978.
Husserl, E. (1901). *Logical Investigations* II. Trans. J. N. Findlay. London: Routledge, 2001.
Husserl, E. (1913a). *Logische Untersuchungen II/2. Untersuchungen zur Phänomenologie und Theorie der Erkenntnis.* 2nd ed. Tübingen: Niemeyer 1980.
Husserl, E. (1913b). "Äussere und innere Wahrnehmung. Physische and Psychische Phänomene." Appendix to his *Logische Untersuchungen II/2. Elemente einer phänomenologischen Auklärung der Erkenntnis.* 2nd ed. Tübingen: Niemeyer, 1980.
Husserl, E. (1919). "Erinnerungen an Franz Brentano," in Kraus 1919a: 151–167.
Husserl, E. (1928). *Vorlesungen zur Phänomenologie des Zeitbewußtseins.* Halle: Max Niemeyer.
Husserl, E. (1939). "Entwurf einer 'Vorrede' zu den *Logischen Untersuchungen* (1913)." *Tijdschrift voor Filosofie* 1: 107–133, 319–339.
Husserl, E. (1954). *Die Krisis der europäischen Wissenschaften und die transzendentale Phänomenologie: Eine Einleitung in die phänomenologische Philosophie.* The Hague: Nijhoff.
Husserl, E. (1966). *Zur Phänomenologie des inneren Zeitbewusstseins (1893-1917).* The Hague: Nijhoff.
Husserl, E. (1968). *Phänomenologische Psychologie. Vorlesungen Sommersemester 1925.* The Hague: Nijhoff.

Husserl, E. (1969). *Formal and Transcendental Logic*. Trans. D. Cairns. The Hague: Nijhoff.
Husserl, E. (1970a). *The Crisis of European Sciences and Transcendental Phenomenology: An Introduction to Phenomenological Philosophy*. Trans. D. Carr. Evanston, Ill.: Northwestern University Press.
Husserl, E. (1970b). *Philosophie der Arithmetik*. Dordrecht: Kluwer.
Husserl, E. (1974). *Formale und transzendentale Logik*. The Hague: Nijhoff.
Husserl, E. (1975). *Logische Untersuchungen*. Erster Band: *Prolegomena zur reinen Logik*. Dordrecht: Kluwer.
Husserl, E. (1977). *Ideen zu einer reinen Phänomenologie und phänomenologischen Philosophie*. The Hague: Nijhoff.
Husserl, E. (1979). *Aufsätze und Rezensionen (1890–1910)*. The Hague: Nijhoff.
Husserl, E. (1980). *Phantasie, Bildbewusstsein, Erinnerung. Zur Phänomenologie der anschaulichen Vergegenwärtigungen. Texte aus dem Nachlaß (1898–1925)*. Dordrecht: Kluwer.
Husserl, E. (1983). *Studien zur Arithmetik und Geometrie*. The Hague: Nijhoff.
Husserl, E. (1984). *Logische Untersuchungen*. Zweiter Band: *Untersuchungen zur Phänomenologie und Theorie der Erkenntnis*. Dordrecht: Kluwer.
Husserl, E. (1985). *Einleitung in die Logik und Erkenntnistheorie. Vorlesungen 1906/07*. Dordrecht: Kluwer.
Husserl, E. (1986). *Aufsätze und Vorträge 1911–1921*. Dordrecht: Kluwer.
Husserl, E. (1988a). *Vorlesungen über Ethik und Wertlehre (1908–1914)*. Dordrecht: Kluwer.
Husserl, E. (1988b). *Analysen zur passiven Synthesis. Aus Vorlesungs- und Forschungsmanuskripten (1918–1926)*. Dordrecht: Kluwer.
Husserl, E. (1990). *On the Phenomenology of the Consciousness of Internal Time*. Trans. J. B. Brough. Dordrecht: Kluwer.
Husserl, E. (1994a). *Early Writings in the Philosophy of Logic and Mathematics*. Trans. D. Willard. Dordrecht: Kluwer.
Husserl, E. (1994b). *Briefwechsel*, 10 Vol. In E. Schuhmann and K. Schuhmann (eds.), Dordrecht: Kluwer.
Husserl, E. (2001). *Logical Investigations*, 2 Vols. Trans. J. Findlay. London and New York: Routledge.
Husserl, E. (2003). *Philosophy of Arithmetic*. Trans. D. Willard. Dordrecht: Kluwer.
Husserl, E. (2005). *Phantasy, Image Consciousness and Memory (1895–1925)*. Trans. J. Brough. Dordrecht: Springer.
Husserl, E. (2009). *Untersuchungen zur Urteilstheorie*. Dordrecht: Springer.
Husserl, E. (2014). *Ideas for a Pure Phenomenology and Phenomenological Philosophy. First Book: General Introduction to Pure Phenomenology*. Trans. D. O. Dahlstrom. Indianapolis: Hackett Publishing Company.
Husserl, M. (1988). "Skizze eines Lebensbildes von Edmund Husserl." *Husserl Studies* 5: 105–25.
Ierna, C. (2005). "The Beginnings of Husserl's Philosophy, Part 1: From *Über den Begriff der Zahl* to *Philosophie der Arithmetik*." *The New Yearbook for Phenomenology and Phenomenological Philosophy* 5: 1–56.
Ierna, C. (2012). "Brentano and Mathematics," in I. Tănăsescu (ed.), *Franz Brentano's Metaphysics and Psychology*. Bucharest: Zeta Books.
Ierna, C. (2014). "Making the Humanities Scientific: Brentano's Project of Philosophy as Science," in R. Bod, J. Maat and T. Weststeijn (eds.), *The Making of the Humanities*, Vol. 3: *The Modern Humanities*. Amsterdam: Amsterdam University Press.
Ierna, C. (2015). "A Letter from Edmund Husserl to Franz Brentano from 29 XII 1889." *Husserl Studies* 31: 65–72.
Jacquette, D. (1990–91). "Origins of Gegenstandstheorie: Immanent and Trancendent Objects in Brentano, Twardowski, and Meinong." *Brentano Studien* 3: 277–302.
Jacquette, D. (ed.) (2004). *The Cambridge Companion to Brentano*. Cambridge: Cambridge University Press.
Jacquette, D. (2004a). "Brentano's Concept of Intentionality," in Jacquette 2004.
Jacquette, D. (2015). *Alexius Meinong: The Shepherd of Non-Being*. Berlin: Springer.
Jadczak, R. (1997). *Mistrz i jego uczniowie*. Warszawa: Wydawnictwo Scholar.
James, W. (1884). "What is emotion?" *Mind* 9: 188–205.
James, W. (1909). *A Pluralistic Universe*. Cambridge MA: Harvard University Press, 1977.
Johnston, W. (1972). *The Austrian Mind*. Berkeley: University of California Press.
Kamitz, R. (1983). "Franz Brentano: Wahrheit und Evidenz," in *Grundprobleme der Großen Philosophen. Philosophie der Neuzeit III*, 160–97. Göttingen: Vandenhoeck & Ruprecht.
Kant, I. (1998). *Critique of Pure Reason*. Trans. Paul Guyer and Allen Wood. Cambridge: Cambridge University Press.

Kant, I. (2000). *Critique of the Power of Judgment*. Trans. P. Guyer and E. Matthews. Cambridge: Cambridge University Press.
Kastil, A. (1901). "Die Frage nach der Erkenntnis des Guten bei Aristoteles und Thomas v. Aquin." *Sitzungsberichte der Kaiserlichen Akademie der Wissenschaften in Wien, philosophisch-historische Klasse*, 142, Vienna: Gerold.
Kastil, A. (1902). *Zur Lehre von der Willensfreiheit in der Nikomachischen Ethik*. Prag: Habilitationsschrift.
Kastil, A. (1909). *Studien zur neueren Erkenntnistheorie*. Halle: Niemeyer.
Kastil, A. (1912). *Jakob Friedrich Fries Lehre von der unmittelbaren Erkenntnis*. Göttingen: Vandenhoeck & Ruprecht.
Kastil, A. (1932). "Gutachten über die Arbeiten von Franziska Mayer-Hillebrand vom 10.6.1932." *Habilitationsakt Mayer-Hillebrand*. Universität Innsbruck.
Kastil, A. (1933). "Anmerkungen des Herausgebers," in Brentano 1933. Trans. R. M. Chisholm and N. Guterman. In Brentano 1981a.
Kastil, A. (1934). "Ontologischer und gnoseologischer Wahrheitsbegriff," in *Zur Philosophie der Gegenwart*, 23–34: Brentano Gesellschaft.
Kastil, A. (1949). "Franz Brentano und der Positivismus." *Wissenschaft und Weltbild* 2: 272–282.
Kastil, A. (1951). *Die Philosophie Franz Brentanos: eine Einführung in seine Lehre*. Bern: Lehnen.
Kastil, A. (1958). "Brentano und der Psychologismus." *Zeitschrift für philosophische Forschung* 12: 351–359.
Katkov, G. (1930). "Bewusstsein, Gegenstand, Sachverhalt. Eine Brentano-Studie." *Archiv für die gesamte Psychologie* 75: 459–544.
Katkov, G. (1937a). "Descartes und Brentano. Eine erkenntnistheoretische Gegenüberstellung." *Archiv für Rechts- und Sozialphilosophie* 30: 116–151.
Katkov, G. (1937b). *Untersuchungen zur Werttheorie und Theodizee*, Brün/Wien/Leipzig: Rohrer.
Kavanaugh, L. (2008). "Brentano on Space." *Footprint* 3: 39–50.
Kavka, M., Z. Braiterman, and D. Novak (eds.) (2012). *The Cambridge History of Jewish Philosophy: The Modern Era*. Cambridge: Cambridge University Press.
Kerry, B. (1881). *Untersuchungen über das Causalproblem auf dem Boden einer Kritik der einschlägigen Lehren J. St. Mills*. Vienna: Carl Gerold's son.
Kindinger, R. (ed.) (1965). *Philosophenbriefe. Aus der wissenschaftlichen Korrespondenz von Alexius Meinong*. Graz: Akademische Druck- u. Verlagsanstalt.
Kluback, W. (1992). *Courageous Universality: The Work of Schmuel Hugo Bergman*. Atlanta: Scholars Press.
Körner, S. and R. Chisholm (1988). "Editors' Introduction to the English Edition," in Brentano 1988: vii–xxiii.
Kotarbiński, T. (1929). *Elementy teorji poznania: logiki formalnej i metodologji nauk*. Lwów: Ossolińskich.
Kotarbińska, J. (1932). "Z zagadnień indeterminizmu na terenie fizyki." *Przegląd Filozoficzny* 25: 34–69.
Kotarbiński, T. (1933). "Grundlinien und Tendenzen der Philosophie in Polen." *Slawische Rundschau* 5: 218–229.
Kotarbiński, T. (1966). "Franz Brentano comme reiste." *Revue Internationale de Philosophie* 20: 459–476.
Kotarbiński, T. (1970). "Logika jako szkolny przedmiot pomocniczy." *Studia Logica* 26: 99–105.
Kowalewski, G. (1950). *Bestand und Wandel. Meine Lebenserinnerungen. Zugleich ein Beitrag zur neueren Geschichte der Mathematik*. Munich: Oldenburg.
Kraft, V. (1952). "Franz Brentano. Rede anläßlich der Enthüllung seines Denkmales in den Arkaden der Universität." *Wiener Zeitschrift für Philosophie, Psychologie und Pädagogik*, Bd. IV/1.
Krantz, S. (1990/91). "Brentano's Revision of the Correspondence Theory." *Brentano Studien* 3: 79–87.
Kraus, O. (1914). "Die Grundlagen der Werttheorie." *Philosophische Jarbücher* 2: 1–48.
Kraus, O. (1916). *Anton Marty. Sein Leben und seine Werke*. Halle: Niemeyer.
Kraus, O. (1919a). *Franz Brentano. Zur Kenntnis seines Lebens und seiner Lehre*. Munich: Beck.
Kraus, O. (1919b). "Über die Deutung der Relativitätstheorie Einsteins." *Lotos* 67: 146–152.
Kraus, O. (1924). "Einleitung," in Brentano 1924.
Kraus, O. (1928): "Einleitung (Auch ein Wort zur Krise in der Psychologie)," in Brentano 1928: xvii–xlviii.
Kraus, O. (1929). *Selbstdarstellung*. Leipzig: Meiner.
Kraus, O. (1930). "Zur Phänomenognosie des Zeitbewußtseins: Aus dem Briefwechsel Franz Brentanos mit Anton Marty, nebst einem Vorlesungsbruchstück über Brentanos Zeitlehre aus dem Jahre 1895, nebst Einleitung und Anmerkungen veröffentlicht von Oskar Kraus." *Archiv für die gesamte Psychologie* 75: 1–22.
Kraus, O. (1934a). *Wege und Abwege der Philosophie*. Calve'sche: Universitäts-Buchhandlung.

Kraus, O. (1934b). "Rundfunk-Epilog zum Philosophenkongress," in O. Engländer (ed.), *Zur Philosophie der Gegenwart. Vorträge und Reden anlässlich des 8. internationalen Philosophenkongresses in Prag*. Prag: Brentano-Gesellschaft.

Kraus, O. (1937). *Die Werttheorien. Geschichte und Kritik*. Brünn, Vienna, and Leipzig: Rorher.

Kraus, O. (1942). "On Categories, Relations and Fictions." *Proceedings of the Aristotelian Society* 42: 101–116.

Kraus, O. (1966). "Introduction," in Brentano 1966b: xi–xxix. London: Routledge.

Kraus, O. (1976). "Toward a Phenomenognosy of Time-Consciousness," in L. McAlister (ed.), 1976a: 224–239.

Kriegel, U. (2003). "Consciousness and Intransitive Self-Consciousness." *Canadian Journal of Philosophy* 33: 103–132.

Kriegel, U. (2007). "Intentional Inexistence and Phenomenal Intentionality." *Philosophical Perspectives* 21: 307–340.

Kriegel, U. (2013). "Brentano's Most Striking Thesis: No Representation Without Self-Representation," in D. Fisette and G. Fréchette (eds.), *Themes from Brentano*. Amsterdam/New York: Rodopi, 23–41.

Kriegel U. (2015). "Thought and Things: Brentano's Reism as Truthmaker Nominalism." *Philosophy and Phenomenological Research* 91: 153–180.

Kriegel U. (2016). "Brentano's Latter-day Monism." *Brentano Studien* 14: 69–77.

Kriegel, U. (Forthcoming). "Belief-that and Belief-in," in A. Gzrankowski and M. Montague (eds.), *Non-Propositional Intentionality*. Oxford and New York: Oxford University Press.

Künne, W. (2003). *Conceptions of Truth*. Oxford: Oxford University Press.

Labenbacher, G. (1982). "Dissertations-Verzeichnis der UniversitätInnsbruck. Band I: Philosophische Fakultät," in *Tiroler Bibliographien, IX*. Innsbruck and Vienna: Tyrolia-Verlag.

Lange, C. G. (1887). *Über Gemütsbewegungen*. Leipzig: T. Thomas.

Lange, F. A. (1865). *The History of Materialism*. Trans. E. Chester. New York: Humanities Press.

Landgrebe, L. (1934). *Nennfunktion und Wortbedeutung. Eine Studie über Martys Sprachphilosophie*. Halle: Akademischer Verlag.

Lessing, T. (1914). *Studien zur Wertaxiomatik*. Leipzig: Meiner.

Levine, J. (2006). "Conscious Awareness and (Self-)representation," in U. Kriegel and K. Williford (eds.), *Self-Representational Approaches to Consciousness*. Cambridge, Mass.: MIT Press, 173–199.

Libardi, M. (1996). "Franz Brentano (1838–1917). 17. The Continuum," in Albertazzi, Libardi, and Poli 1996.

Liebmann, O. (1865). *Kant und die Epigonen. Eine kritische Abhandlung*. Stuttgart: Schober.

Lipps, T. (1912). *Grundtatsachen des Seelenlebens*. Bonn: Cohen.

Locke, J. (1689). *An Essay Concerning Human Understanding*. Oxford: Oxford University Press, 1975.

Locke, J. (1690). *An Enquiry Concerning Human Understanding*. Cambridge: Cambridge University Press, 2007.

Lockwood, M. (1989). *Mind, Brain and the Quantum*. Oxford: Blackwell.

Lotze, H. (1852). *Medizinische Psychologie oder Physiologie der Seele*. Leipzig: Weidmann'sche Buchhandlung.

Łukasiewicz, D. (2006). "Brentanian Philosophy and Czeżowski's Conception of Existence," in Chrudzimski and Łukasiewicz 2006: 185–216.

Łukasiewicz, J. (1936). Logistyka a filozofia. *Przegląd filozoficzny* 39: 115–131.

Lyons, W. (1980). *Emotion*. Cambridge: Cambridge University Press.

McAlister, L. L. (ed.) (1976a). *The Philosophy of Brentano*. London: Duckworth.

McAlister, L. L. (1976b). "Chisholm and Brentano on Intentionality," in McAlister 1976a.

McCormick, P. and F. Elliston (eds.) (1981). *Husserl: Shorter Works*. South Bend: University of Notre Dame Press.

Mach, E. (1886). *Die Analyse der Empfindungen und das Verhältnis des Physischen zum Psychischen*. Jena: G. Fischer.

Maimon, S. (1794). *Versuch einer neuen Logik oder Theorie des Denkens*. Berlin: Ernst Felisch.

Majolino, C. (2003). "Remarques sur le couple forme/matière. Entre ontologie et grammaire chez Anton Marty." *Les Études Philosophiques* 1: 65–81.

Marek, J. C. (2001). "Meinong on Psychological Content," in Albertazzi, Jacquette, and Poli 2001: 261–86.

Marek, J. C. (2012). "Exemplarization and Self-presentation: Lehrer and Meinong on Consciousness." *Philosophical Studies* 161: 119–129.

Marek, J. C. (2013). "Alexius Meinong," in E. N. Zalta (ed.), *The Stanford Encyclopedia of Philosophy* (Fall 2013 edition). http://plato.stanford.edu/archives/fall2013/entries/meinong/
Martinak, E. (1898). *Zur Psychologie des Sprachlebens.* Vienna: C. Gerold's Sohn.
Martinak, E. (1901). *Psychologische Untersuchungen zur Bedeutungslehre.* Leipzig: Barth.
Marty, A. (1875). *Über den Ursprung der Sprache.* Würzburg: Stuber.
Marty, A. (1879). *Die Frage nach der geschichtlichen Entwicklung des Farbensinnes.* Vienna: C. Gerold.
Marty, A. (1892). "William James, *The Principles of Psychology.*" *Zeitschrift für Psychologie und Physiologie der Sinnesorgane* 3: 297–333. (Reprinted in *Id., Gesammelte Schriften.* Niemeyer, 105–156.)
Marty, A. (1893). "Über das Verhältnis von Grammatik und Logik," in Marty (1920a), 57–99.
Marty, A. (1906). "Über Annahmen (Ein kritischer Beitrag zur Psychologie, namentlich der descriptiven)." *Zeitschrift für Psychologie und Physiologie der Sinnesorgane* 40: 1–54.
Marty, A. (1908). *Untersuchungen zur Grundlegung der allgemeinen Grammatik und Sprachphilosophie.* Erster Band. Halle: Niemeyer.
Marty, A. (1910). *Die logische, lokalistische und andere Kasustheorien.* Halle: Niemeyer.
Marty, A. (1916a). *Gesammelte Schriften* I.1 (*GS* I.1). Halle: Niemeyer.
Marty, A. (1916b). *Gesammelte Schriften* I.2 (*GS* I.2). Halle: M. Niemeyer.
Marty, A. (1916c). "Was ist Philosophie?" in *Id., Gesammelte Schriften*, Bd. I/1. Tübingen: Niemeyer, 69–93.
Marty, A. (1916d). "Franz Brentano. Eine biographische Skizze," in *Id., Gesammelte Schriften*, Bd. I/1. Tübingen: Niemeyer, 95–104.
Marty, A. (1916e). "Zwei akademische Reden von Karl Stumpf," in *Id., Gesammelte Schriften*, Bd. I/1. Tübingen: Niemeyer, 157–167.
Marty, A. (1916f). "Über Sprachreflex, Nativismus und absichtliche Sprachbildung," in Marty (1916b), 1–304.
Marty, A. (1916g). *Raum und Zeit.* Halle: Niemeyer.
Marty, A. (1918). *Gesammelte Schriften* II.1 (*GS* II.1). Halle: M. Niemeyer.
Marty, A. (1920a). *Gesammelte Schriften* II.2 (*GS* II.2). Halle: M. Niemeyer.
Marty, A. (1920b). "Über subjectlose Sätze und das Verhältnis der Grammatik zu Logik und Psychologie," in Marty (1920a), 3–307.
Marty, A. (1940). *Psyche und Sprachstruktur. Nachgelassene Schriften I.* Bern: Franke.
Marty, A. (2011). *Deskriptive Psychologie.* Würzburg: Königshausen & Neumann.
Marty, A. Br 7/1: *F. Brentano, Logik Kollegien* [*Deduktive und inductive Logik*] [Logic Lectures of Franz Brentano: Summer Semester 1869–70 and 1870–71 (Deductive and Inductive Logic), abridged as *Logic Lectures 1869/70*]. Archives of Anton Marty, Franz-Brentano Archiv, Graz.
Marty, A. BrL 2284: Letter to Franz Brentano, 15 February 1890. Franz Clemens Brentano Compositions (MS Ger 230), Houghton Library, Harvard University.
Marty, A. BrL 2530: Letter to Franz Brentano, 30 December 1906. Franz Clemens Brentano Compositions (MS Ger 230), Houghton Library, Harvard University.
Marty, A. IIIg č 46: *Deskriptive Psychologie.* in *Lesefrüchte.* Název O. Krause, výpisy z různých autorů, Rukopis, 1. složka, s.d in Archiv akademie věd České Republiky Praha, Osobní fond Antona Marty.
Masaryk, T. G. (1885). *Základové konkretné logiky.* German trans. *Versuch einer concreten Logik.* Vienna: Konegan, 1887.
Massin O. (2009). "The Metaphysics of Forces." *Dialectica* 63: 555–589.
Massin, O. (2013). "The Intentionality of Pleasures and Other Feelings," in D. Fisette and G. Fréchette (eds.), *Themes from Brentano.* Amsterdam: Rodopi.
Maurin A.-S. (2002). *If Tropes.* Dordrecht: Kluwer Academic Publishers.
Maurin A.-S. (2014). "Tropes," in E. N. Zalta (ed.), *The Stanford Encyclopedia of Philosophy.* http://plato.stanford.edu/archives/fall2014/entries/tropes/
Mayer-Hillebrand, F. (1927). "Über die scheinbare Streckenverkürzung im indirekten Sehen." *Zeitschrift für Sinnesphysiologie* 57: 174–196.
Mayer-Hillebrand, F. (1932). "Über die scheinbare Größe der Sehdinge." *Zeitschrift für Sinnesphysiologie* 61: 268–324.
Mayer-Hillebrand, F. (1942). "Die geometrisch-optischen Täuschungen als Auswirkungen allgemein geltender Wahrnehmungsgesetze." *Zeitschrift für Psychologie* 152: 126–210, 292–331.

Mayer-Hillebrand, F. (1955a). "Franz Brentanos Lehre von der Fiktionen der Sprache." *Innsbrucker Beiträge zur Kulturwissenschaft* 3: 13–18.
Mayer-Hillebrand, F. (1955b). "Franz Brentanos ursprüngliche und spätere Seinslehre und ihre Beziehungen zu Husserls Phänomenologie." *Zeitschrift für philosophische Forschung* 13: 313–339.
Mayer-Hillebrand, F. (1956). "Einlatung." In Brentano 1956.
Mayer-Hillebrand, F. (1963a). "Rückblick auf die bisherigen Bestrebungen zur Erhaltung und Verbreitung von Franz Brentanos philosophische Lehren und kurze Darstellung dieser Lehren." *Zeitschrift für philosophische Forschung* 17: 146–169.
Mayer-Hillebrand, F. (1963b). "Remarks Concerning the Interpretation of Franz Brentano: A reply to Dr. Srzednicki." *Philosophy and Phenomenological Research* 23: 438–444.
Mayer-Hillebrand, F. (1966). "Einlatung." In Brentano 1966a.
Mayer-Hillebrand, F. (1975). "Selbstdarstellung." *Philosophie in Selbstdarstellungen, II*. Hamburg: Felix Meiner, 224–269.
Meinong, A. (1877). "Hume-Studien I. Zur Geschichte und Kritik des modernen Nominalismus," in *Sitzungsberichte der philosophisch-historischen Klasse der Kaiserlichen Akademie der Wissenschaften in Wien* 87: 185–260. In Meinong 1978, Vol. I: 1–76.
Meinong, A. (1885). "Über philosophische Wissenschaft und ihre Propädeutik." Wien: Hölder. In Meinong 1978, Vol. V: 1–196.
Meinong, A. (1886). "Zur erkenntnistheoretischen Würdigung des Gedächtnisses." *Vierteljahresschrift für wissenschaftliche Philosophie* 10: 7–33. In Meinong 1978, Vol. II: 185–213.
Meinong, A. (1888–1903). "Sach-Index zur Logik und Erkenntnistheorie." Ms in Meinong-*Nachlass*, No. X/a-b. In Meinong 1978, Vol. VIII: 25–128.
Meinong, A. (1892). "Rezension von Franz Hillebrands 'Die neuen Theorien kategorischer Schlüsse,'" in Meinong 1978, Vol. VII: 197–222.
Meinong, A. (1894). *Psychologisch-ethische Untersuchungen zur Werth-Theorie*. Graz: Leuschner & Lubensky. In Meinong 1978, Vol. III: 1–244.
Meinong, A. (1895). "Über Werthaltung und Wert." *Archiv für systematische Philosophie* 1: 327–346. In Meinong 1978, Vol. III: 245–266.
Meinong, A. (1899). "Über Gegenstände höherer Ordnung und deren Verhältnis zur inneren Wahrnehmung." *Zeitschrift für Psychologie und Physiologie der Sinnesorgane* 21: 182–272. In Meinong 1978, Vol. II: 377–480.
Meinong, A. (1902). *Ueber Annahmen*, Leipzig: J. A. Barth. Erg.-Bd. II of *Zeitschrift für Psychologie und Physiologie der Sinnesorgane*.
Meinong, A. (ed.) (1904a). *Untersuchungen zur Gegenstandstheorie und Psychologie*. Leipzig: J. A. Barth.
Meinong, A. (1904b). "Über Gegenstandstheorie," in Meinong 1904a: 1–51. In Meinong 1978, Vol. II: 481–535.
Meinong, A. (1906). "Über die Erfahrungsgrundlagen unseres Wissens." *Abhandlungen zur Didaktik und Philosophie der Naturwissenschaften* 1: 1–113, Berlin: J. Springer. In Meinong 1978, Vol. V: 367–481.
Meinong, A. (1907). *Über die Stellung der Gegenstandstheorie im System der Wissenschaften*. Leipzig: R. Voigtländer. In Meinong 1978, Vol. V: 197–365.
Meinong, A. (1910). *Über Annahmen*. 2nd ed. Leipzig: J. A. Barth. In Meinong 1978, Vol. IV: xv–xxv, 1–384.
Meinong, A. (1912). "Für die Psychologie und gegen den Psychologismus in der allgemeinen Werttheorie." *Logos* 3: 1–14. In Meinong 1978, Vol. III: 267–282.
Meinong, A. (1913). "Zweites Kolleg über gegenstandstheoretische Logik." Lecture notebook in Meinong *Nachlass*, No. IV/a. In Meinong 1978: 237–272.
Meinong, A. (1915). *Über Möglichkeit und Wahrscheinlichkeit. Beiträge zur Gegenstandstheorie und Erkenntnistheorie*. Leipzig: J. A. Barth. In Meinong 1978, Vol. VI: XIII–XXII, 1–728.
Meinong, A. (1917). "Über emotionale Präsentation." *Sitzungsberichte der Kaiserlichen Akademie der Wissenschaften in Wien. Philosophisch-historische Klasse*, 183: 1–183. In Meinong 1978, Vol. III: 283–467.
Meinong, A. (1917–18). "Viertes Kolleg über Erkenntnistheorie." Lecture notebook in Meinong *Nachlass*, No. X/f. In Meinong 1978: 337–401.
Meinong, A. (1921a). "A. Meinong (Selbstdarstellung)," in R. Schmidt (ed.), *Die deutsche Philosophie der Gegenwart in Selbstdarstellungen*. Vol. I. Leipzig: F. Meiner, 91–150. In Meinong 1978, Vol. VII: 1–62.

Meinong, A. (1921b). Autobiographical notes, dated from November 1906 (instead of a necrology), in *Almanach der Akademie der Wissenschaften in Wien*, Jahrgang 71: 232–241.
Meinong, A. (1923). *Zur Grundlegung der allgemeinen Werttheorie*. Graz: Leuschner & Lubensky. In Meinong 1978, Vol. III: 469–656.
Meinong, A. (1968). *Abhandlungen zur Werttheorie*, in Meinong 1978.
Meinong, A. (1969). "Beiträge zur Theorie der psychischen Analyse." In Meinong 1978, Vol. I: 307–395.
Meinong, A. (1971). *Abhandlungen zur Erkenntnistheorie und Gegenstandstheorie*, in Meinong 1978.
Meinong, A. (1973). *Über philosophische Wissenschaft und ihre Propädeutik*, in Meinong 1978.
Meinong, A. (1978). *Ergänzungsband zur Gesamtausgabe*. Graz: Akademische Druck- u. Verlagsanstalt.
Meinong, A. (1983). *On Assumptions*. Trans J. Heanue. Berkeley: University of California Press.
Melzer, Y. (ed.) (1975). *Shmuel Hugo Bergman*, Special Issue of *Iyyun. A Hebrew Philosophical Quarterly* 26 (4).
Merlan, P. (1945). "Brentano and Freud." *Journal of the History of Ideas* 6: 375–377.
Meyer, S. (1903). "Die Vorgeschichte der Gründung und das erste Jahrzehnt des Institutes für Radiumforschung." *Sitzungsberichte der Österreichischen Akademie der Wissenschaften* 159: 1–26.
Meyer, S. (1992). "Mach looks through a spinthariscope," in J. Blackmore (ed.), *Ernst Mach—A Deeper Look*, Dordrecht: Kluwer, 151–152.
Miklosich, F. (1883). *Subjectlose Sätze*. Wien: Braumüller.
Mill, J. S. (1843). *System of Logic, Ratiocinative and Inductive, Being a Connected View of the Principles of Evidence, and the Methods of Scientific Investigation*, Vol. 2. London: John W. Parker.
Mill, J. S. (1972). *Collected Works of John Stuart Mill, Vol. XVII: Later Letters 1849–1873*. London: Routledge and Kegan Paul.
Mohr, J. (1882). *Grundlage der empirischen Psychologie*. Leipzig: Mutze.
Moore, G. E. (1897). "*The 1897 dissertation*: The Metaphysical Basis of Ethics," in T. Baldwin and C. Preti (eds.), *G. E. Moore: Early Philosophical Writings*. Cambridge: Cambridge University Press, 1–94.
Moore, G. E. (1898). "*The 1898 dissertation*: The Metaphysical Basis of Ethics," in T. Baldwin and C. Preti (eds.), *G. E. Moore: Early Philosophical Writings*. Cambridge: Cambridge University Press, 115–242.
Moore, G. E. (1899). "The Nature of Judgement." *Mind* 8: 176–93.
Moore, G. E. (1901a). "Quality," in J. M. Baldwin (ed.), *Dictionary of Philosophy and Psychology*. New York, London: Macmillan, 1901–1902, Vol. II: 406–408.
Moore, G. E. (1901b). "Truth and Falsity," in J. M. Baldwin (ed.), *Dictionary of Philosophy and Psychology*. New York, London: Macmillan, 1901–1902, Vol. II: 716–719.
Moore, G. E. (1903a). "Review of *The Origin of Our Knowledge of Right and Wrong*." *International Journal of Ethics* 14: 115–123.
Moore, G. E. (1903b). *Principia Ethica*, rev. ed. Cambridge: Cambridge University Press, 1993.
Moran, Dermot (1996). "The Inaugural Address: Brentano's Thesis." *Proceedings of the Aristotelian Society* (Supplementary Volume) 70: 1–27.
Moran, D. (2000a). *Introduction to Phenomenology*. London, New York: Routledge.
Moran, D. (2000b). "Husserl's Critique of Brentano in the *Logical Investigations*." *Manuscrito* 23: 163–205.
Moran, D. (2005). *Edmund Husserl: Founder of Phenomenology*. Cambridge: Polity Press.
Moran, D. (2015). "Noetic Moments, Noematic Correlates, and the Stratified Whole that is the *Erlebnis*," in A. Staiti (ed.), *Husserl's Ideas: A Commentary*. Berlin: DeGruyter, 195–224.
Moreland J. P. (2001). *Universals*. Chesham: Acumen Publishing.
Mulligan, K. (1986). "Exactness, Description and Variation: How Austrian Analytical Philosophy Was Done," in J.-C. Nyiri, (ed.), *From Bolzano to Wittgenstein*. Vienna: Hölder-Pichler-Tempsky, 86–97.
Mulligan, K. (1989). "Judgings: Their Parts and Counterparts." 6: 117–148.
Mulligan, K. (ed.) (1990a). *Mind, Meaning and Metaphysics. The Philosophy and Theory of Language of Anton Marty*. Dordrecht: Kluwer.
Mulligan, K. (1990b). "Marty's philosophical grammar," in Mulligan 1990a: 11–27.
Mulligan, K. (1991). "On the history of continental philosophy." *Topoi* 10 (2): 115–120.
Mulligan, K. (2004). "Brentano on the mind," in D. Jacquette (ed.), *The Cambridge Companion to Brentano*. Cambridge: Cambridge University Press, 66–97.

Mulligan, K. (2012). *Wittgenstein et la philosophie austro-allemande*. Paris: Vrin.
Mulligan, K. and B. Smith (1985). "Franz Brentano on the Ontology of Mind." *Philosophy and Phenomenological Research*, 45: 627–644.
Neale, S. (1990). *Descriptions*. Cambridge, MA: MIT Press.
Neesen, P. (1972). *Vom Louvrezirkel zum Prozess. Franz Kafka und die Psychologie Franz Brentanos*. Göppingen: Alfred Kümmerle.
Nelson, M. (2012). "Existence," in E. N. Zalta (ed.), *The Stanford Encyclopedia of Philosophy* (Winter 2012 edition). http://plato.stanford.edu/archives/win2012/entries/existence/
Nowicki, A. (1982). *Witwicki, Wiedza Powszechna*. Warszawa: PWN.
Nussbaum, M. (2001). *Upheavals of Thought: The Intelligence of Emotions*. Cambridge: Cambridge University Press.
Oakley, J. (1992). *Morality and the Emotions*. London: Routledge and Kegan Paul.
Oberkofler, G. (1882/83). "Carl Stumpf an Franz Hillebrand. Briefe 1894–1926." *Tiroler Heimat*, 46/47.
Oddie, G. (2005). *Value, Reality, and Desire*. New York: Oxford University Press.
Pacherie, E. (1993). *Naturaliser l'intentionnalité: Essai de philosophie de la psychologie*. Paris: PUF.
Parfit, D. (1984). *Reasons and Persons*. Oxford: Clarendon Press.
Parsons, C. (2004). "Brentano on Judgment and Truth," in D. Jacquette (ed.), *The Cambridge Companion to Brentano*. Cambridge: Cambridge University Press.
Pasquerella, L. (1993). "Brentano and Aesthetic Intentions." *Brentano Studien* 4: 235–249.
Peano, G. (1887). *Applicazione geometriche del calcolo infinitesimale*. Turin: Fratelli Bocca.
Poli, R. (2012). "Modes and Boundaries," in I. Tănăsescu (ed.), *Franz Brentano's Metaphysics and Psychology*. Bucharest: Zeta Books.
Potrč, M. (1997). "Haller and Brentano's Empiricism," in K. Lehrer and J. C. Marek (eds.), *Austrian Philosophy Past and Present: Essays in Honor of Rudolf Haller*. Dordrecht: Springer.
Potrč, M. (2013). "Phenomenology of Intentionality," in D. Fisette and G. Fréchette (eds.), *Themes from Brentano*. Amsterdam: Rodopi.
Prinz, J. (2004). *Gut Reactions: A Perceptual Theory of Emotion*. New York: Oxford University Press.
Prior, A. N. (1971). *Objects of Thought*. Oxford: Clarendon.
Quine, W. V. O. (1951). "Two Dogmas of Empiricism." *Philosophical Review* 60: 20–43.
Quine, W. V. O. (1956). "Quantifiers and Propositional Attitudes." *The Journal of Philosophy* 53: 177–187.
Quine, W. V. O. (1960). *Word and Object*. Cambridge, MA: MIT Press.
Rabinowicz, W. and T. Ronnow-Rasmussen (2004). "The Strike of the Demon: On Fitting Pro-Attitudes and Value." *Ethics* 114: 391–423.
Rawls, J. (1971). *A Theory of Justice*. Cambridge, MA: Harvard University Press.
Raynaud, S. (1982). *Anton Marty, filosofo del linguaggio: uno strutturalismo presaussuriano*. Roma: La goliardica editrice.
Reichenbach, H. (1921). "Der gegenwärtige Stand der Relativitätsdiskussion." *Logos* 10: 316–378.
Reichenbach, H. (1978). "The Present State of the Discussion on Relativity," trans. M. Reichenbach, in *H. Reichenbach, Selected Writings, 1909–1953, Vol. II*. Dordrecht: Reidel, 3–48.
Reicher, F. (1918). *Das Nichtreale als Fiktion. (Franz Brentanos ursprüngliche Lehre vom Nichtrealen, ihr Ausbau durch andere und ihr Abbau durch ihn selbst)*. Dissertation, Universität Innsbruck.
Reicher, M. (2015). "Nonexistent Objects," in E. N. Zalta (ed.), *The Stanford Encyclopedia of Philosophy* (Winter 2015 edition). http://plato.stanford.edu/archives/win2015/entries/nonexistent-objects/
Reinach, A. (1911/1982). "On the Theory of the Negative Judgment," in B. Smith (ed.), *Parts and Moments. Studies in Logic and Formal Ontology*. Munich: Philosophia Verlag, 315–346, 351–377.
Reuveni, A. (1993). "Berta Fanta zu ihrem 75. Todestag." *Das Goethanum: Wochenschrift für Anthroposophie*, 50: 515–517.
Ricoeur, P. (1985). *Temps et récit. Volume 3: le temps raconté*. Paris: Seuil.
Ricoeur, P. (1988). *Time and Narrative, Vol. 3*, Trans. K. Blamey and D. Pellauer. Chicago: University of Chicago Press.
Rogge, E. (1935). *Das Kausalproblem bei Franz Brentano*. Stuttgart: Kohlhammer.
Rogge, E. (1938). "Traum, Wirklichkeit, Gott," in *Brentano-Gesellschaft in Prag, Naturwissenschaft und Methaphysik*. Brünn-Leipzig: Rohrer.

Rojszcak, A. (2005). *From the Act of Judging to the Sentence: The Problem of Truth Bearers from Bolzano to Tarski.* Dordrecht: Springer.
Rollinger, R. D. (1999). *Husserl's Position in the School of Brentano.* Dordrecht: Springer.
Rollinger, R. D. (2004). "Austrian Theories of Judgment: Bolzano, Brentano, Meinong, and Husserl," in A. Chrudzimski and W. Huemer (eds.), *Phenomenology and Analysis: Essays on Central European Philosophy.* Frankfurt: Ontos, 257–284.
Rollinger, R. D. (2005). "Meinong and Brentano." *Meinong Studies* 1: 159–198.
Rollinger, R. D. (2008). *Austrian Phenomenology. Brentano, Husserl, Meinong and Others on Mind and Object.* Frankfurt: Ontos.
Rollinger, R. D. (2009). "Brentano's Logic and Marty's Early Philosophy of Language." *Brentano Studien* 12: 77–98.
Rollinger, R. D. (2010). *Philosophy of Language and Other Matters in the Work of Anton Marty. Analysis and Translations.* Amsterdam: Rodopi.
Rollinger, R. D. (2011). "Editor's Preface," in Brentano, EL 80: "Logik."
Rollinger, R. D. (2012). "Brentano's *Psychology from an Empirical Standpoint*: Its Background and Conception," in I. Tănăsescu (ed.), *Franz Brentano's Metaphysics and Psychology.* Bucharest: Zeta Books.
Rollinger, R. D. (2014). "Brentano and Marty on Logical Names and Linguistic Fictions: A Parting of Ways in the Philosophy of Language," in Laurent Cesalli and Janette Friedrich (eds.), *Anton Marty & Karl Bühler. Between Mind and Language.* Basel: Schwabe, 167–200.
Rollinger, R. and C. Ierna (2015). "Christian von Ehrenfels," in E. N. Zalta (ed.), *The Stanford Encyclopedia of Philosophy* (Summer 2015 edition), http://plato.stanford.edu/archives/sum2015/entries/ehrenfels/
Ross, W. D. (1930). *The Right and the Good.* Oxford: Clarendon Press.
Rotenstreich, N. (1985). "Between Construction and Evidence." *Grazer Philosophische Studien* 24: 3–14.
Rothenberg, B. (1937). Work without title [Bez označení titulu – práce z odborné logiky. Strojopis, 74 s.], Archiv akademie věd České Republiky Praha, Osobní fond Oskara Krause, IIIa Č 15–17.
Rothenberg, B. (1962). *Studien zur Logik Franz Brentanos,* Ph.D. Dissertation, University of Frankfurt.
Routley, R. (1980). *Exploring Meinong's Jungle and Beyond. An Investigation of Noneism and the Theory of Items.* Canberra: Research School of Social Sciences, Australian National University.
Rupp, H. (1904). *Schnelligkeit der Lokalisation von Tastreizen auf die Hände bei verschiedenen Stellungen derselben.* Dissertation, Universität Innsbruck.
Russell B. (1903). *The Principles of Mathematics.* Cambridge: Cambridge University Press.
Russell, B. (1904). "Meinong's Theory of Complexes and Assumptions." *Mind* 13: 509–524.
Russell, B. (1905a). "On Denoting." *Mind* 14: 479–493.
Russell, B. (1905b.) "Review of A. Meinong, *Untersuchungen zur Gegenstandstheorie und Psychologie.*" *Mind* 14: 530–538.
Russell, B. (1906). "*Ueber die Erfahrungsgrundlagen unseres Wissens.* By Dr. A. Meinong." *Mind* 15: 412–415.
Russell, B. (1907). "*Über die Stellung der Gegenstandstheorie im System der Wissenschaften.* Von A. Meinong." *Mind* 16: 436–439.
Russell, B. (1914). "On the Nature of Acquaintance. III. Analysis of Experience." *The Monist* 24: 435–453.
Russell, B. (1921). *The Analysis of Mind.* London: Allen and Unwin.
Russell, B. (1959). *My Philosophical Development.* London: Allen and Unwin.
Ryle, G. (1976). "Disgusted Grandfather of Phenomenology." *Times Higher Education Supplement,* September 10, 1976, 15.
Rzepa, T. (2015). "The Humanistic Traits of Psychology at the Lvov-Warsaw School," in A. Brożek, A. Chybińska, J. Woleński and J. J. Jadacki (eds.), *Tradition of the Lvov-Warsaw School: Ideas and Continuations.* Leiden/Boston: Brill, 153–176.
Sambursky, M. (1981). "Zionist und Philosoph. Das Habilitierungsproblem des jungen Hugo Bergmann." *Bulletin des Leo Baeck Instituts* 58: 17–39.
Sanford, D. H. (1997). "Chisholm on Brentano's Thesis," in L. E. Hahn (ed.), *The Philosophy of Roderick M. Chisholm.* Peru, IL: Open Court Publishing.
Sauer W. (2006). "Die Einheit der Intentionalitätskonzeption bei Brentano." *Grazer Philosophische Studien* 73: 1–26.
Sauer, W. (2013). "Being as the True. From Aristotle to Brentano," in D. Fisette and G. Fréchette (eds.), *Themes from Brentano.* Amsterdam: Rodopi, 193–225.

Scanlon, T. (1998). *What We Owe to Each Other*. Cambridge MA: MIT Press.
Schaar, M. van der (1997). "Judgment and Negation," in L. E. Hahn (ed.), *The Philosophy of Roderick M. Chisholm*. The Library of Living Philosophers XXV, Chicago and La Salle: Open Court, 291–318.
Schaar, M. van der (1999). "Evidence and the Law of Excluded Middle: Brentano on Truth," in T. Childers (ed.), *The Logica Yearbook 1998*. Prague: Filosofia.
Schaar, M. van der (2003). "Brentano on Logic, Truth and Evidence", *Brentano Studien* 10: 119–50.
Schaar, M. van der (2013). *G. F. Stout and the Psychological Origins of Analytic Philosophy*. Basingstoke: Palgrave Macmillan.
Schaar, M. van der (2015). *Kazimierz Twardowski: A Grammar for Philosophy*. Leiden: Brill.
Schaar, M. van der (2016). "Brentano, Twardowski and Stout: From Psychology to Ontology," in M. Beaney (ed.), *The Oxford Handbook of the History of Analytic Philosophy*. Oxford: Oxford University Press, supplemented online edition.
Schaffer, J. (2009). "Spacetime the One Substance." *Philosophical Studies* 145: 131–148.
Schell, H. (1873). *Die Einheit des Seelenlebens aus den Prinzipien der Aristotelischen Psychologie*. Freiburg: Scheuberl.
Schmidkunz, H. (1892). *Psychologie der Suggestion*. Stuttgart: Enke.
Schmidkunz, H. (1918). "Brentanos Logik und ihre pädagogischen Folgen." *Monatshefte für pädagogische Reform* 68: 494–506.
Schnädelbach, H. (1984). *Philosophy in Germany 1831–1933*. Cambridge: Cambridge University Press.
Schroeder, M. (2008). *Being For: Evaluating the Semantic Program of Expressivism*. Oxford: Oxford University Press.
Schubert Kalsi, M.-L. (1978). *Alexius Meinong on Objects of Higher Order and Husserl's Phenomenology*. The Hague: Martinus Nijhoff.
Schultess, D. (1999). "L'individuation selon Brentano." *Philosophiques* 26 (2): 219–230.
Schuhmann, K. (1977). *Husserl-Chronik (Denk- und Lebensweg Edmund Husserls)*. Den Haag: Martinus Nijhoff.
Schweinhammer, S. (1995). *Die Geschichte des Instituts für Experimentelle Psychologie an der Universität Innsbruck*. Diplomarbeit, Universität Wien.
Searle, J. R. (1983). *Intentionality*. Cambridge: Cambridge University Press.
Seron, D. (2008). "Sur l'analogie entre théorie et pratique chez Brentano." *Bulletin d'analyse phénoménologique* 4: 23–51.
Seron, D. (2012). "The Fechner-Brentano Controversy on the Measurement of Sensation," in I. Tănăsescu (ed.), *Franz Brentano's Metaphysics and Psychology*. Bucharest: Zeta Books, 342–365.
Seron, D. (2014). "Brentano's "Descriptive" Realism." *Bulletin d'analyse phénoménologique* 10: 1–14.
Seron, D. (2015). "Problèmes de l'auto-représentationalisme," in L.-J. Lestocart (ed.), *Esthétique et complexité II, neurosciences, évolution, épistémologie et philosophie*. Paris: CNRS Editions.
Seron, D. (forthcoming). "Intentionalisme et phénoménologie de l'intentionnalité." *Études phénoménologiques–Phenomenological Studies*.
Shoemaker, Sydney (1968). "Self-Reference and Self-Awareness." *Journal of Philosophy* 65: 555–567.
Shohetman, B. and S. Shunami (1968). *The Writings of Hugo Bergman. A Bibliography. 1903–1967*. Jerusalem: The Magnes Press.
Simons, P. M. (1984). "A Brentanian Basis for a Leśniewskian Logic." *Logique et Analyse* 27: 279–307.
Simons, P. M. (1987). "Brentano's Reform of Logic." *Topoi* 6: 25–38.
Simons, P. M. (1988). "Brentano's Theory of Categories: A Critical Appraisal." *Brentano Studien* 1: 47–61.
Simons, P. M. (1992). "On What There Isn't: The Meinong—Russell Dispute," in P. Simons (ed.), *Philosophy and Logic in Central Europe from Bolzano to Tarski*. Dordrecht: Kluwer, 159–191.
Simons, P. M. (1995). "Introduction," in Brentano 1995a.
Simons, P. M. (2006). "Things and Truths: Brentano and Leśniewski, Ontology and Logic," in A. Chrudzimski and D. Łukasiewicz (eds.), *Action, Products, and Things. Brentano and Polish Philosophy*. Frankfurt am Main: Ontos, 83–105.
Smith, B. (1987). "The Substance of Brentano's Ontology." *Topoi*, 6: 39–49.
Smith, B. (1988). "The Soul and Its Parts: A Study in Aristotle and Brentano." *Brentano Studien* 1: 75–88.

Smith, B. (1989). "The Primacy of Place: An Investigation in Brentanian Ontology." *Topoi*, 8: 43–51.
Smith, B. (1992–3). "The Soul and Its Parts II: Varieties of Inexistence." *Brentano Studien* 4: 35–51.
Smith, B. (1994a). *Austrian Philosophy*. LaSalle, Il. and Chicago: Open Court.
Smith, B. (1994b). "The Philosophy of Austrian Economics." *The Review of Austrian Economics* 7: 127–132.
Smith, D. W. (1986). "The Structure of (Self-)Consciousness." *Topoi* 5: 149–156.
Smith, W. C. (1991). *The Meaning and End of Religion*. Minneapolis: Fortress.
Solomon, R. C. (1976). *The Passions*. Garden City, New York: Doubleday.
Sorabji, R. (1971). "Aristotle on Demarcating the Five Senses." *The Philosophical Review* 80: 55–79.
de Sousa, R. (1987). *The Rationality of Emotion*. Cambridge: MIT Press.
Spiegelberg, H. (1978). "On the Significance of the Correspondence Between Franz Brentano and Edmund Husserl," in R. M. Chisholm and R. Haller (eds.), *Die Philosophie Franz Brentanos*. Amsterdam: Rodopi, 95–116.
Spiegelberg, H. (ed.) (1994). *The Phenomenological Movement. A Historical Introduction*. Dordrecht: Springer.
Spinicci, P. (1991). *Il significato e la forma linguistica. Pensiero, esperienza e linguaggio nella filosofia di Anton Marty*. Milano: Franco Angeli.
Stallo, J. B. (1901). *Die Begriffe und Theorien der modernen Physik*, German trans. from the 3rd English edition by Hans Kleinpeter, with a foreword by E. Mach. Leipzig: Barth.
Stampe, D. (1986). "Defining Desire," in J. Marks (ed.), *The Ways of Desire*. Chicago: Precedent.
Stegmüller, W. (1969). *Main Currents in Contemporary German, British, and American Philosophy*, Vol. 31. Bloomington: Indiana University Press.
Stout, G. F. (1893). "The Philosophy of Mr. Shadworth Hodgson." *Proceedings of the Aristotelian Society* 2: 107–120.
Stout, G. F. (1896). *Analytic Psychology*. London: Sonnenschein.
Strawson, G. (1994). *Mental Reality*. Cambridge, MA: MIT Press.
Stumpf, C. (1869). *Verhältnis des platonischen Gottes zur Idee des Guten*. Halle: C.E.M. Pfeffer.
Stumpf, C. (1873). *Über den psychologischen Ursprung der Raumvorstellung*. Leipzig: S. Hirzel.
Stumpf, C. (1883). *Tonpsychologie*, Vol. 1. Leipzig: Hirzel.
Stumpf, C. (1885). "Musikpsychologie in England." *Vierteljahrsschrift für Musikwissenschaft* 1: 261–349.
Stumpf, C. (1890). *Tonpsychologie*, Vol. 2. Leipzig: Hirzel.
Stumpf, C. (1891). "Psychologie und Erkenntnistheorie." *Abhandlungen der Königlich Bayerischen Akademie der Wissenschaften* 19, zweite Abteilung. München: Franz, 465–516.
Stumpf, C. (1892). "Über den Begriff der mathematischen Wahrscheinlichkeit." *Sitzungsberichte der philosophisch-philologischen und historischen Classe der Königlich Bayerischen Akademie der Wissenschaften* 20. München: Franz, 37–120.
Stumpf, C. (1897a). "Geschichte des Consonanzbegriffs. Erster Teil. Die Definition der Consonanz in Altertum." *Abhandlungen der Königlich bayerischen Akademie der Wissenschaften*, 1. Classe 21, 1. Abteilung. München: Franz, 1–78.
Stumpf, C. (1897b). "Die Pseudo-aristotelischen Probleme über Musik." *Abhandlungen der Königlich-Preußischen Akademie der Wissenschaften*, Philosophisch-historische Abhandlungen. Berlin: Reimer, 1–85.
Stumpf, C. (1898–1924). *Beiträge zur Akustik und Musikwissenschaft*. Vol. 1–9. Leipzig: J. A. Barth.
Stumpf, C. (1899). "Über den Begriff der Gemüthsbewegung." *Zeitschrift für Psychologie und Physiologie der Sinnesorgane* 21: 47–99.
Stumpf, C. (1903). *Leib und Seele. Der Entwicklungsgedanke in der gegenwärtigen Philosophie. Zwei Reden*. Leipzig: Barth.
Stumpf, C. (1906a). "Zur Einteilung der Wissenschaften." *Abhandlungen der Königlich-Preußischen Akademie der Wissenschaften, Philosophish-historische Classe*. Berlin: V. der Königliche Akademie der Wissenschaften, 1–94.
Stumpf, C. (1906b). "Erscheinungen und psychische Funktionen." *Abhandlungen der Königlich-Preußischen Akademie der Wissenschaften, Philosophish-historische Classe*. Berlin: V. der Königliche Akademie der Wissenschaften, 3–40.
Stumpf, C. (1907a). "Über Gefühlsempfindungen." *Zeitschrift für Psychologie und Physiologie der Sinnesorgane* 44: 1–49.

Stumpf, C. (1907b). *Die Wiedergeburt der Philosophie*. Francke. Reprinted in *Id., Philosophische Reden und Vorträge*. Leipzig: Barth, 1910, 161–196.
Stumpf, C. (1907c). *Zur Einteilung der Wissenschaften*. Berlin: Verlag der königlichen Akademie der Wissenschaften.
Stumpf, C. (1907d). "Erscheinungen und psychische Funktionen." *Abhandlungen der preussischen Akademie der Wissenschaften*, 3–39.
Stumpf, C. (1907e). "Einleitung," in O. Pfungst, *Das Pferd des Herrn von Osten. Der Kluge Hans*. Leipzig: Barth, 7–15.
Stumpf, C. (1916). "Apologie der Gefühlsempfindungen." *Zeitschrift für Psychologie und Physiologie der Sinnesorgane* 75: 330–350.
Stumpf, C. (1919). "Erinnerungen an Franz Brentano," in O. Kraus (ed.), *Franz Brentano. Zur Kenntnis seines Lebens und seiner Lehre*. Munich: Beck, 87–149.
Stumpf, C. (1920). "Franz Brentano, Philosoph." *Deutsches biographisches Jahrbuch* 2: 54–61.
Stumpf, C. (1922). "Franz Brentano, Professor der Philosophie, 1838–1917," in A. Chroust (ed.), *Lebensläufe aus Franken* II. Würzburg: Kabitzsch & Mönnich, 67–85.
Stumpf, C. (1924). "Carl Stumpf," In R. Schmidt, (ed.), *Die Philosophie der Gegenwart in Selbsdarstellung*. Bd. V. Leipzig: Meiner, 1–57.
Stumpf, C. (1926). *Die Sprachlaute: experimentell-phonetische Untersuchungen (nebst einem Anhang über Instrumentalklänge)*. Berlin: Springer.
Stumpf, C. (1928). *Gefühl und Gefühlsempfindung*. Leipzig: Barth.
Stumpf, C. (1938). *Studien zur Wahrscheinlichkeitsrechnung*. Berlin: De Gruyter.
Stumpf, C. (1939–40). *Erkenntnislehre*. 2 Vol. Leipzig: Barth.
Stumpf, C. (1976). "Reminiscences of Franz Brentano," in L. McAlister 1976a: 10–46.
Stumpf, C. (2008). *Über die Grundsätze der Mathematik*. Würzburg: Königshausen & Neumann.
Stumpf, C. (2012). *The Origins of Music*. Trans. D. Tippett. Oxford: Oxford University Press.
Stumpf, C. (2015a). "Metaphysic. Vorlesung," in D. Fisette and R. Martinelli (eds.), *Philosophy from an Empirical Standpoint. Essays on Carl Stumpf*. Amsterdam: Rodopi, 443–472.
Stumpf, C. (2015b). "Einleitung zu Brentanos Briefen an mich," followed by selected letters from Brentano and Stumpf, in D. Fisette and R. Martinelli (eds.), *Philosophy from an Empirical Standpoint. Essays on Carl Stumpf*. Amsterdam: Rodopi, 491–528.
Stumpf, C. and E. M. von Hornbostel (eds.) (1922–1923). *Sammelbände für vergleichende Musikwissenschaft* (4 Vols.). München: Drei Masken.
Szrednicki, J. (1965). *Franz Brentano's Analysis of Truth*. The Hague: Martinus Nijhoff.
Taieb H. (2015). "Relations and Intentionality in Brentano's Last Texts." *Brentano Studien* 13: 183–210.
Tănăsescu, I. (2011). "Le concept psychologique de la représentation de la fantaisie chez Brentano et sa réception chez Husserl." *Studia Phaenomenologica* 10: 45–75.
Tassone, B. G. (2012). *From Psychology to Phenomenology: Franz Brentano's Psychology from an Empirical Standpoint and Contemporary Philosophy of Mind*. Basingstoke: Palgrave Macmillan.
Taves, T. (2009). *Religious Experience Reconsidered*. Princeton: Princeton University Press.
Terrell, D. B. (1976). "Franz Brentano's Logical Innovations." *Midwest Studies in Philosophy of Mind* 1: 81–91.
Textor, M. (2006). "Brentano (and some Neo-Brentanians) on Inner Consciousness." *Dialectica* 60: 411–432.
Textor, M. (2007). "Seeing Something and Believing IN It," in M. M. McCabe and M. Textor (eds.), *Perspectives on Perception*. Frankfurt: Ontos.
Textor, M. (2015). "'Inner Perception can never become Inner Observation': Brentano on Awareness and Observation." *Philosophers' Imprint* 15.
Thomasson, A. (2000). "After Brentano: A One-Level Theory of Consciousness." *European Journal of Philosophy* 8: 190–209.
Tolman, C. W. (1987). "Intentionality, Meaning, and Evolution," in W. J. Baker, M. E. Hyland, H. Van Rappard, and A. W. Staats (eds.), *Current Issues in Theoretical Psychology*. Amsterdam: Elsevier (North-Holland), 365–377.
Twardowski, K. (1892). *Idee und Perception. Eine erkenntnis-theoretische Untersuchung aus Descartes*. Vienna: Hölder.

Twardowski, K. (1894). *Zur Lehre vom Inhalt und Gegenstand der Vorstellungen. Eine Psychologische Untersuchung*. Vienna: Hölder.
Twardowski, K. (1894/95a). "Logik," in Twardowski 2016.
Twardowski, K. (1894/95b). "Die Unsterblichkeitsfrage." Now edited in id., *Die Unsterblichkeitsfrage*, Wydawnictwo WFiS UW, Warszawa Twardowski Archives, Biblioteka IFiS PAN, Warsaw, 2009.
Twardowski, K. (1895). "Metafizyka duszy." *Przełom* 1: 467–480.
Twardowski, K. (1899). "Etyka." Ms. AKT P14, 1. Now edited in id., *Etyka*. Warszawa: PWN (1996).
Twardowski, K. (1903). "Über begriffliche Vorstellungen," in *Wissenschaftliche Beilage Zum 16. Jahresberichte Der Philosophischen Gesellschaft an Der Universität Zu Wien*. Leipzig: Barth, 1–28.
Twardowski, K. (1903/04). "Psychologia pożądań i woli." Lato 1903/4. Ms. AKT P12, 3. Now edited in id., *Wybór pism psychologicznych i pedagogicznych*, Warszawa, Wydawnictwo Szkolne i Pedagogiczne (1992): 203–248; and in TEI/XML at http://www.elv-akt.net/ressources/archives.php?id_archive=52
Twardowski, K. (1910a). "Jak studiować filozofię?" *Widnokręgi* 1: 1–4.
Twardowski, K. (1910b). "O metodzie psychologii: przyczynek do metodologii porównawczej badań naukowych," in *Prace I Zjazd Neurologów, Psychiatrów i Psychologów Polskich* (1909). Warszawa: Wende i S-ka, 5–16.
Twardowski, K. (1911). *O czynnościach i wytworach. Kilka uwag z pogranicza psychologii, gramatyki i logiki*. Krakow: Skład główny w Księgarni Gubrynowicza i Syna we Lwowie.
Twardowski, K. (1977). *On the Content and Object of Presentations*. Trans. R. Grossmann. The Hague: M. Nijhoff.
Twardowski, K. (1991). "Kazimierz Twardowski: Selbstdarstellung." *Grazer Philosophische Studien* 39: 1–26.
Twardowski, K. (1993). "Psychologia myślenia." *Filozofia Nauki* 1: 127–149.
Twardowski, K. (1999). *On Actions, Products and Other Topics in Philosophy*. Amsterdam: Rodopi.
Twardowski, K. (2014). *On Prejudices, Judgments and Other Topics in Philosophy*. Amsterdam and New York: Brill.
Twardowski, K. (2016). *Logik. Wiener Logikkolleg 1894/95*. Berlin: De Gruyter.
Tye, M. (2007). "The Problem of Common Sensibles." *Erkenntnis* 66: 287–303.
Urbach, B. (1927). "Das logische Paradoxon." *Annalen der Philosophie und philosophischen Kritik* 6: 161–176, 265–273.
Utitz, E. (1908). *Grundzüge der ästhetischen Farbenlehre*. Stuttgart: Enke.
Utitz, E. (1914–20). *Grundlegung der allgemeinen Kunstwissenschaft*. 2 Bde. Stuttgart: Enke.
Utitz, E. (1954). "Erinnerungen an Franz Brentano." *Wissenschaftliche Zeitschrift der Martin-Luther Universität Halle-Wittenberg* 4: 73–90.
Utitz, E. (2015). *Ethik nach Theresienstadt: Späte Texte des Prager Philosophen Emil Utitz (1883–1956)*. Würzburg: Königshausen u. Neumann.
Varga, P. A. (2015). "Was hat Husserl in Wien außerhalb von Brentanos Philosophie gelernt? Über die Einflüsse auf den frühen Husserl jenseits von Brentano und Bolzano." *Husserl Studies* 31: 95–121.
Volpi, F. (1989). "The Experience of Temporal Objects and the Constitution of Time-consciousness by Brentano," in *The Object and its Identity: Supplements of Topoi 4*. Dordrecht, Boston, London: Kluwer, 127–140.
Werle, J. (1989). *Franz Brentano und die Zukunft der Philosophie*. Amsterdam: Rodopi.
Wigley, S. (2012). "Justiciced Consequentialism: Prioritizing the Right or the Good?" *Journal of Value Inquiry* 46: 467–497.
Williamson, T. (1985). "Converse Relations." *Philosophical Review* 94: 249–262.
Williford, K. (2006). "Zahavi versus Brentano: A Rejoinder." *Psyche* 12: 2.
Wittgenstein, Ludwig (1958). *The Blue and the Brown Book*. Oxford: Oxford University Press.
Witwicki, W. (1900). "Analiza psychologiczna ambicji." *Przegląd Filozoficzny* 3: 26–49.
Witwicki, W. (1925). *Psychologja: dla użytku słuchaczów wyższych zakładów naukowych*. Lwów: Ossolińskich.
Witwicki, W. (1939). *La foi des éclairés*. Paris: F. Alcan.
Woleński, J. (1989). *Logic and Philosophy in the Lvov-Warsaw School*. Dordrecht: Kluwer.
Woleński, J. (2012). "Reism," in E. N. Zalta (ed.), *The Stanford Encyclopedia of Philosophy* (Summer 2012 edition). https://plato.stanford.edu/archives/sum2012/entries/reism/

Woleński, J. (2014). "Kazimierz Twardowski and the Development of Philosophy of Science in Poland," in M. C. Galavotti, E. Nemeth, and F. Stadler (eds.), *European Philosophy of Science—Philosophy of Science in Europe and the Viennese Heritage*. Dordrecht: Springer, 173–182.

Woleński, J. (2015). "Lvov-Warsaw School," in E. N. Zalta (ed.), *The Stanford Encyclopedia of Philosophy* (Winter 2015 Edition). https://plato.stanford.edu/archives/win2015/entries/lvov-warsaw/

Woleński, J. and P. Simons (1989). "De Veritate: Austro-Polish Contributions to the Theory of Truth from Brentano to Tarski," in A. Szaniawski (ed.), *The Vienna Circle and the Lvov-Warsaw School*. Dordrecht: Springer, 391–442.

Wolff, J. (1889). *Das Bewusstsein und sein Object*. Berlin: Mayer & Müller.

Wundt, W. (1874). *Grundzüge der physiologischen Psychologie*. Leipzig: Engelmann.

Wundt, W. (1913). *Die Psychologie im Kampf ums Dasein*. Leipzig: Kröner.

Zahavi, D. (2004). "Back to Brentano?" *Journal of Consciousness Studies* 11: 66–87.

Zahavi, D. (2006). "Two Takes on a One-Level Theory of Consciousness." *Psyche* 12: 2.

Zamecki, S. (1977). *Koncepcja nauki w Szkole Lwowsko-Warszawskiej*. Lvov: Ossolińskich.

Żełaniec, W. (1996). "Franz Brentano and the Principle of Individuation." *Brentano Studien* 6: 145–164.

Żełaniec, W. (1997). "Disentangling Brentano: Why Did He Get Individuation Wrong?" *Brentano Studien* 7: 455–463.

Żełaniec, W. (2013). "A Solution of the Problem of A 'Principle Of Individuation.'" *Filo-Sofija* 23: 19–56.

Zeller, E. (1862). *Über Bedeutung und Aufgabe der Erkenntniss-Theorie. Ein akademischer Vortrag*. Heidelberg: Groos.

Zimmerman, D. W. (1996). "Indivisible Parts and Extended Objects: Some Philosophical Episodes from Topology's Prehistory." *The Monist* 79: 148–180.

Zvie Bar-on, A. (1985). "From Prague to Jerusalem." *Grazer Philosophische Studien* 24: 29–46.

INDEX

aboutness 176; *see also* intentionality
accident *see* substance and accident
aesthetics 202–8; Brentano's writings on 202–3; empirical approach to 206–7; impact of Brentano's 208; and psychology 203–4
Albertazzi, Liliana 29, 219
algedonic qualities 3, 94–6
Ameseder, Rudolf 230
Anscombe, Elizabeth 114
antirealism *see* realism
appearance and reality 169–76
apperception 319
Aquinas, Thomas 44, 52, 79, 133, 144, 149, 252
Aristotle 65, 134–5, 140, 144–6, 211–12, 335–6; Brentano's work on 15–16, 49, 156, 178, 227, 255, 361; on consciousness 53–6; on desire 113, 252; ethics of 255, 345; on God 216, 219; logic of 104, 295; on method 237, 244; on relations 159; on the senses 51–3, 92; on truth 166–7
Arleth, Emil 8, 10–11, 231–2, 314, 323, 341, 345
Austrian Economics 284, 320
axiology 200–1, 230, 256, 296; *see also* value theory

Baader, Franz von 16
Baumgartner, Wilhelm 11, 341
beauty 2, 7, 21, 27–31, 197, 202–7, 211–12, 253, 278, 355
Benussi, Vittorio 230, 272
Bergman, Hugo 10–11, 232, 314–15, 319–20, 323–30
Betti, Arianna 10, 305, 334

Binder, Thomas 1–2, 15, 217
Black, M. 154
Bolzano, Bernard 231, 253, 299, 306, 313, 324–7, 335–6
Bondy, Josef Adolf 323
Brandl, Johannes 6, 128, 163
British Empiricism 16, 272, 296; *see also* empiricism
Brod, Max 323

Caston, Victor 52
Catholic Church 16, 216; *see also* Vatican Council
Catholicism 1, 15–16, 216–18
causal efficacy 6, 157
causation/causality 119, 160–1, 191, 242, 300, 319
Cesalli, Laurent 8, 251
Chisholm, Roderick 11–12, 47–8, 118, 122, 137, 198, 273, 281, 358–63
Chrudzimski, Arakadiusz 157, 308
Clarke, Samuel 192
cognition (*Erkenntnis*) 124, 192, 218
colors 43–5, 51–4, 66, 88–96, 102, 175, 228, 288–9, 341–4
Comte, Auguste 16, 216, 227, 229
consciousness 49–60; Cartesian dualism about 61; inner sense view of 54–7; objectification objection to 58–60; same-order view of 57; unity of 61–74
consequentialism 7, 9, 200–1
content 43–5, 172, 179, 230–2, 251, 256–61, 265, 273, 276–7, 280, 305, 315, 318, 350–3; *see also* intentionality

continuum 5, 76–84, 150–3, 293, 342
correct attitudes 7, 24–30, 118–22, 188, 191–4; see also correctness
correctness 7, 24–9, 116–22, 163, 188–94, 204, 251–4, 261, 291, 318
Crane, Tim 2, 41, 173
Czeżowski, Tadeusz 11, 337–8

Dainton, Barry 3, 61
Darwinism 219
Davidson, Donald 48, 358
Descartes, R. 61, 63, 67, 110, 125, 145, 147, 154, 231, 345–6
descriptive psychology 35–40; and "analytic psychology" 11, 246, 336–8, 349–6; a priori psychological laws in 39–40; role of induction in 38; role of introspection in 36–7; as "science of mental phenomena" 35
desire 4, 9, 25, 44–5, 113–16, 252–3, 270, 277–9, 283–8, 307; see also will, the
Dewalque, Arnaud 8, 225, 236
Dilthey, W. 212
distinctional parts see divisives/divisiva
divisives/divisiva 3, 38, 65–71, 73, 90, 95–6, 126
dualism 5, 61; see also materialism

Ehrenfels, Christian von 8–9, 18, 82, 229–30, 283–92, 272, 314, 323, 325, 354–5
Einstein, Albert 150, 328
Eisenmayer, Josef 10, 314
Eisenmeier, Josef 10, 232–3, 243, 314–15, 320, 323
emotions: cognitivist theories of 111; correct 2, 7, 21, 25–7, 116–22, 189–94, 197; as intentional phenomena 100, 111–12; James-Lange theory of 112; as pro or anti attitudes 112; united with will into a fundamental class 98, 112–16
empiricism 16, 36, 167, 169, 244, 329
Engel, Walter 10, 314–15, 319–20
Engländer, Oskar 10, 314, 320
entia rationis 80, 105, 133, 236, 277, 325
ethics see metaethics; normative ethics
eudaimonia 345; see also Aristotle, ethics of
evidence (Evidenz) see self-evidence
existence 23–7, 83, 107, 180, 242, 252–3, 327; see also judgment
experience, inner see inner perception

fantasy 7, 80, 212–14, 273, 279, 294–7
Feldman, Fred 7, 200
first philosophy 30
Fisette, Denis 9, 264
fitting attitudes 7, 24, 122; see also correct attitudes
Fréchette, Guillaume 3, 10, 75, 323
Frege, Gottlob 44–5, 327
Funke, Otto 232, 314

Gabriel, Susan Krantz 5, 12, 144, 217
genetic psychology 2, 10, 36, 39, 42, 230, 244, 266, 306–7
genius 7, 207, 210–15
German Idealism 208, 227, 296, 306, 330
Gestalt psychology 266, 272
Gestalt qualities 9, 82, 283–4, 354–5
Gibbard, Allan 193
Giedymin, Jerzy 334–5
Giustina, Anna 70–1
God 7–8, 107, 147–8, 153, 216–20; see also religion, philosophy of
Goetz, Stewart 149
goodness 2, 24–8, 98, 116–17, 122, 188–94, 198–200, 255–6, 355–6
Graz school 208, 232, 272
greatest good, sum of 320–21
Grossmann, R. 161

Hamilton, William 37
Hegel, G. W. 169, 227, 296, 360; see also German Idealism
Heidegger, Martin 75, 293, 329
Heider, Fritz 272
Helmholz, Hermann von 39–40, 90–3
Hertling, Georg von 228, 268
Herzen, Alexander 18
Hillebrand, Franz 10–11, 108–9, 231, 308, 314, 342–8
history of philosophy, Brentano on 16, 221, 227, 229, 329
Höfler, Alois 18, 229–30, 272, 314, 328, 338
Hofmann, Franz 16
Horwich, Paul 167
Huemer, Wolfgang 7, 202
Husserl, Edmund 1, 8–10, 18–9, 46–9, 58–60, 75, 175, 203, 214, 231–2, 237, 252, 256–7, 293–305, 323, 328–30, 339

immanent object 31, 43–6, 99, 161, 181, 258, 261, 275–6, 280, 287, 301, 307–8, 315, 347
individual accident 5, 140, 158–9; see also tropes
inner perception 53–5, 59, 62–74, 97, 118–19, 124–8, 145–8, 151, 165, 172, 189, 206–7, 240–2, 245–7, 279–81, 306–7, 316–19, 324, 327, 346, 350, 354–5
Innsbruck School 8, 11, 231, 324, 341–8
intensity 3, 88–92, 205–6, 288–91, 343
intentional inexistence 6, 31, 41–6, 172, 274–5, 301, 350, 361–2; see also intentionality
intentionality 1–2, 12, 31, 41–8, 99–100, 108, 111–12, 169–75, 251, 274, 300, 303–4, 308, 318, 349–53, 361–2; adverbial theory of 175; as mark of the mental 43–4, 47–8, 99, 111, 336, 361; modes of 4, 22, 31, 100–1; secondary 2–3; thesis 37, 237
interest see phenomena of love and hate

Jacquette, Dale 11, 358
James, William 42, 270
"James-Lange" theory 112
Janoušek, Hynek 10, 313
judgment 2, 4, 88–9, 98–109; apodictic 100–1, 119, 189, 194, 317–18; categorical 104; double 181, 226; existential 23, 45, 103–7, 327, 337, 350; hypothetical 104; "idiogenetic" theory of 179, 231, 337, 342; moral 187–94; negative 106, 181, 253, 280–1; as objectual attitude 23, 107–9, 259, 352; and truth 6, 21–2, 29, 111, 118, 163–8, 175–83, 254–6, 280–1, 308, 351
judgment-contents 251–5, 258, 261, 318, 326; *see also* states of affairs

Kafka, Franz 323
Kant, I. 39–42, 99, 107, 125, 151, 167, 211–13, 231, 295–6, 329, 345–6
Kantian 11, 125–7, 313, 324; *see also* neo-Kantian
Kastil, Alfred 10–11, 19, 146–7, 153, 232, 314–16, 345–8
Katkov, Georg 10, 232, 314–18, 321
Kerry, Benno 231, 328
Ketteler, Wilhelm Emmanuel von 16
Kisch, Paul 323
Körner, Stephan 150–2
Kotarbińska, Janina 335
Kotarbiński, Tadeusz 11, 337–9
Kraus, Oskar 10, 19, 41, 78, 164, 232–3, 257, 314–24, 328
Kriegel, Uriah 1, 21, 97, 103, 128

Lange, F. A. 43, 62–4
language, Brentano and Marty on 257–61; Brentano's philosophy of 134, 251, 257–9; Marty's philosophy of 9, 228, 259–61, 314
Levine, Joseph 57
liar's paradox 243
Lieben, Ida 17, 230
Locke, J. 49–50, 169, 304
logic 11, 16, 104, 108, 138, 202–3, 227, 230–1, 241–3, 257, 267, 293–4, 297–300, 309, 326–7, 330, 336–40, 342, 350–3
Louvre Circle 232, 323
love and hate, phenomena of 4, 24–6, 94, 98–102, 112–13, 187–8, 277, 287–8, 300, 307; *see also* emotion; interest
Lvov-Warsaw School 11, 305, 334–40

Maimon, Solomon 326
Mally, Ernst 230, 272–5
Marek, Johann 9, 272
Martinak, Eduard 230, 272
Marty, Anton 8–11, 55, 178, 225–33, 241, 251–62, 313–18, 323–29, 339–42, 345
Marx, Joseph 272

Masaryk, Tomas 10, 17, 229, 295–6, 314
Massin, Olivier 3, 87
materialism 144, 147, 219, 269; *see also* dualism
Mayer-Hillebrand, Franziska 11, 346–8
McAlister, Linda L. 12, 41, 362–3
Meinong, Alexius 8–9, 47, 178, 226, 229–32, 236, 241, 252, 272–81, 328, 339, 343, 358–9, 362; classification of mental phenomena in 277–9, 338; ethics of 285; on nonexistent objects 274–7; relationship with Brentano 272–3; relationship with Ehrenfels 283; on self-evidence 9, 82, 279–81
Mereology 38, 180, 307, 38; *see also* divisives/divisiva; part–whole relations
metaethics 6–7, 187–94; cognitivism vs. non-cognitivism 192–3; correct emotions in 189–90; internalism vs. externalism 194; naturalism vs. non-naturalism 194; rationalism vs. sentimentalism 192; realism vs. anti-realism 193; "wrong kind of reason problem" in 191
Mill, John Stuart 16, 38, 179, 197–9, 296, 339, 343
modality *see* necessity and impossibility
Mohr, Jakob 228
Montague, Michelle 4, 110
Moore, G. E. 11, 45, 194, 197–8, 349, 352–6
Moran, Dermot 10, 293
Mulligan, Kevin 8–9, 251

naturalism 7–8, 11, 194, 294, 303–4, 355
Nazi invasion/occupation 10, 19, 233, 330, 346
necessity and impossibility 189, 242, 315, 317, 325; *see also* judgment, apodictic
neo-Kantian 11, 163, 239–40, 302–3, 313, 320
nominalism 10, 262, 272, 327, 338; *see also* reism
nonexistence 4, 9–10, 43, 46–7, 178–83, 252–3, 272, 283, 308, 318, 326, 336, 362; *see also* Meinong
Nussbaum, M. 112

objectivity 45, 110–11, 116–17, 169–70, 187, 198, 256, 287, 349, 351–6
object theory 47, 230–2, 237, 272–7, 326, 335, 359–61
Ockham's Razor 149
Oelzelt-Newin, Anton von 272
Olson, Jonas 7, 187
organic unities 64, 198, 354–5
original association 77, 80
outer/external/sensory perception 38, 44, 49–52, 59, 91, 98, 103, 151, 231, 265, 271, 289, 300, 303, 361; *see also* sensation

Parfit, Derek 200
Parsons, Charles 163, 166–7
part–whole relations 37, 65–6, 70–1, 76, 89, 126, 135, 140, 145–6, 156–9, 198, 284, 304, 307, 321, 342, 352–5; *see also* divisives/divisiva; mereology

Pasquerella, Lynn 7, 12, 196
Peano, G. 151
Perception *see* inner perception; outer/external/ sensory perception
phenomena of love and hate *see* love and hate, phenomena of
phenomenology 9, 35, 39, 47, 75, 226, 231, 237, 246, 265, 293–4, 300–4, 346, 359, 361; *see also* descriptive psychology; Husserl
Platonism 232, 353, 355
pleasure 3–4, 7, 27, 88, 93–8, 188–91, 197–202, 205–7, 288–9
Pollak, Oskar 323
possibility *see* necessity and impossibility
Prague School 10, 225–6, 231–3, 313–27, 345
presentation 4, 27, 44–5, 79, 98–102, 112, 179–80, 204–5, 210, 213–14, 258, 278–80, 294, 298–301, 319, 328
presentism 76, 153
Price, Richard 192
Priority monism 70
properties 5–6, 156–60
proteraesthesis 78, 81–2, 152; *see also* time-consciousness
psychology, experimental 36, 266, 272, 307, 336, 344, 347–8
psychology *see* descriptive psychology; genetic psychology; psychology, experimental

Quine, W. V. O. 11, 45, 47

Rancurello, Antos C. 41
rationalism 7, 169, 192
Rawls, John 199
Realism 43–5, 96, 193, 219, 252, 265, 335, 362
Reicher, Maria 9, 283
reism 5–6, 133–41, 156, 159–61, 226, 252, 314–18, 326–7, 338, 362; *see also* nominalism
relations 6, 156–61
religion 7, 216–21, 283, 338
Rogge, Eberhard 10, 314–20
Rollinger, Robin 10, 313
Ross, W. D. 199–200
Rotenstreich, Nathan 330
Russell, Bertrand 11, 45, 48, 116, 273, 339, 349, 358

Salice, Alessandro 6, 178
Sauer, Werner 5, 133
Schaar, Maria van der 11, 349
Schaefer, Richard 7, 216
Schell, Hermann 18, 228
self-evidence (*Evidenz*) 6, 9, 24, 26, 119–21, 127–8, 163–8, 182, 189–90, 230, 257, 279–81, 291, 301, 317–19, 326, 337
self-knowledge 4, 124–8

sensation 3, 37, 49–54, 80, 87–96, 245, 270–1, 288–9, 301–2, 341; *see also* outer/external/ sensory perception
Seron, Denis 2, 6, 35, 169
Simons, Peter 46, 135, 137, 335
Smith, Barry 43–4, 157
Smith, David Woodruff 55
Socrates 180, 259
Soldati, Gianfranco 4, 124
Solomon, Robert 112
soul 5, 35, 41–3, 65, 125–6, 135, 144–9, 216, 354
space 5, 76, 91–2, 150–4, 167, 342–3
states of affairs 5, 9, 105, 164, 182–3, 251–2, 265, 278, 315, 318, 326, 352
Stein, Edith 75
Stout, George F. 11, 246, 349–56
Stumpf, Carl 8–9, 16, 93, 225–8, 231, 242, 253, 264–71, 297, 299, 313–14, 323, 341–6
substance and accident 5, 76, 91, 134–6, 139–41, 158–9
supplementation, principle of 135–6, 139
synsemantic expressions 134, 139, 228, 316
system, philosophical 29–31, 202, 208, 239, 344, 363

Taieb, Hamid 5, 156
Taliaferro, Charles 149
Tănăsescu, Ion 7, 210
Taves, Ann 220
Terrell, D. B. 41
Textor, Mark 2–3, 49
time 5, 150–4
time-consciousness 3, 75–84
transcendental philosophy 10, 266, 294, 346
Trendelenburg, Friedrich Adolf 15
tropes 5, 90, 139, 157–8; *see also* individual accidents
truth 6, 21–6, 163–8, 255–6, 280–1, 325–7, 355; concept of 117, 164–6, 281, 351; correspondence theory of 79, 118, 280, 306, 325, 335, 351–3; deflationary/minimalist theory of 166–8; moral 187–9, 192–3; *see also* judgment; self-evidence
Twardowski, Kazimierz 10–11, 18, 226, 230–1, 243, 276, 305–9, 318, 334–40

unconscious, the 57–8, 62, 210–13
unity of consciousness *see* consciousness, unity of
universals 5, 44, 140, 165, 232, 262, 277
Urbach, Benno 244, 323
utilitarianism 197–200, 285, 320–1; *see also* consequentialism
Utitz, Emil 10, 232–3, 314–15, 323

value, aesthetic 27–8, 205–7, 287; *see also* beauty
value, intrinsic 12, 188, 196–201, 204, 286–7, 325, 355
value theory 4, 6–10, 18, 196, 233, 272–3, 283–4, 291–2, 295, 361; *see also* axiology

Vatican Council (1870) 16
Vienna Circle 236, 239, 346, 358
volition 110, 113–14, 230, 307; *see also* will, the

Weber, Franz 272
Weierstrass, Karl 295
Wigley, Simon 201
will, the 9, 24–5, 45, 112–16, 198, 253, 270–1, 287–8; *see also* volition; desire

Witasek, Stefan 230, 272
Wittgenstein, Ludwig 125, 257, 358
Witwicki, Władysław 11, 338
Wolff, Johannes 228

Żełaniec, Wojciech 5, 150
Zimmerman, Dean 12
Zimmerman, Robert 10, 18, 231, 295, 297
Zionism 10, 323–4